Rock Hudson
Erotic Fire

What is Blood Moon Productions?

"Blood Moon, in case you don't know, is a small publishing house on Staten Island that cranks out Hollywood gossip books, about two or three a year, usually of five-, six-, or 700-page length, chocked with stories and pictures about people who used to consume the imaginations of the American public, back when we actually had a public imagination. That is, when people were really interested in each other, rather than in Apple 'devices.' In other words, back when we had vices, not devices."

—The Huffington Post

Biographies that Focus on the Ironies of Fame

www.BloodMoonProductions.com

Award-Winning Entertainment About
How America Interprets Its Celebrities

Rock Hudson

Erotic Fire

Darwin Porter & Danforth Prince

Rock Hudson Erotic Fire

Darwin Porter and Danforth Prince

Manufactured in the United States of America

ISBN 978-1-936003-55-6

Cover Designs by Danforth Prince
Distributed worldwide through National Book Network
(www.NBNBooks.com)

national book network

PREVIOUS WORKS BY DARWIN PORTER
PRODUCED IN COLLABORATION WITH BLOOD MOON

BIOGRAPHIES

Lana Turner, Hearts & Diamonds Take All

Donald Trump, The Man Who Would Be King

James Dean, Tomorrow Never Comes

Bill and Hillary, So This Is That Thing Called Love

Peter O'Toole, Hellraiser, Sexual Outlaw, Irish Rebel

Love Triangle, Ronald Reagan, Jane Wyman, & Nancy Davis

Jacqueline Kennedy Onassis, A Life Beyond Her Wildest Dreams

Pink Triangle, The Feuds and Private Lives of Tennessee Williams, Gore Vidal, Truman Capote, and Famous Members of their Entourages.

Those Glamorous Gabors, Bombshells from Budapest

Inside Linda Lovelace's Deep Throat, Degradation, Porno Chic, and the Rise of Feminism

Elizabeth Taylor, There is Nothing Like a Dame

Marilyn at Rainbow's End, Sex, Lies, Murder, and the Great Cover-up

J. Edgar Hoover and Clyde Tolson
Investigating the Sexual Secrets of America's Most Famous Men and Women

Frank Sinatra, The Boudoir Singer. All the Gossip Unfit to Print

The Kennedys, All the Gossip Unfit to Print

Humphrey Bogart, The Making of a Legend (2010) , and

The Secret Life of Humphrey Bogart (2003)

Howard Hughes, Hell's Angel

Steve McQueen, King of Cool, Tales of a Lurid Life

Paul Newman, The Man Behind the Baby Blues

Merv Griffin, A Life in the Closet

Brando Unzipped

Katharine the Great, Hepburn, Secrets of a Lifetime Revealed

Jacko, His Rise and Fall, The Social and Sexual History of Michael Jackson

Damn You, Scarlett O'Hara, The Private Lives of Vivien Leigh and Laurence Olivier (co-authored with Roy Moseley)

FILM CRITICISM
Blood Moon's 2005 Guide to the Glitter Awards
Blood Moon's 2006 Guide to Film
Blood Moon's 2007 Guide to Film, and
50 Years of Queer Cinema, 500 of the Best GLBTQ Films Ever Made

NON-FICTION
Hollywood Babylon, It's Back! and Hollywood Babylon Strikes Again!

NOVELS
Blood Moon,
Hollywood's Silent Closet,
Rhinestone Country,
Razzle Dazzle
Midnight in Savannah

OTHER PUBLICATIONS BY DARWIN PORTER
NOT DIRECTLY ASSOCIATED WITH BLOOD MOON

NOVELS

The Delinquent Heart
The Taste of Steak Tartare
Butterflies in Heat
Marika (a roman à clef based on the life of Marlene Dietrich)
Venus (a roman à clef based on the life of Anaïs Nin)
Bitter Orange
Sister Rose

TRAVEL GUIDES

Many Editions and Many Variations of *The Frommer Guides*,
The American Express Guides, and/or TWA Guides, et alia to:

Andalusia, Andorra, Anguilla, Aruba, Atlanta, Austria, the Azores, The Bahamas, Barbados, the Bavarian Alps, Berlin, Bermuda, Bonaire and Curaçao, Boston, the British Virgin Islands, Budapest, Bulgaria, California, the Canary Islands, the Caribbean and its "Ports of Call," the Cayman Islands, Ceuta, the Channel Islands (UK), Charleston (SC), Corsica, Costa del Sol (Spain), Denmark, Dominica, the Dominican Republic, Edinburgh, England, Estonia, Europe, "Europe by Rail," the Faroe Islands, Finland, Florence, France, Frankfurt, the French Riviera, Geneva, Georgia (USA), Germany, Gibraltar, Glasgow, Granada (Spain), Great Britain, Greenland, Grenada (West Indies), Haiti, Hungary, Iceland, Ireland, Isle of Man, Italy, Jamaica, Key West & the Florida Keys, Las Vegas, Liechtenstein, Lisbon, London, Los Angeles, Madrid, Maine, Malta, Martinique & Guadeloupe, Massachusetts, Melilla, Morocco, Munich, New England, New Orleans, North Carolina, Norway, Paris, Poland, Portugal, Provence, Puerto Rico, Romania, Rome, Salzburg, San Diego, San Francisco, San Marino, Sardinia, Savannah, Scandinavia, Scotland, Seville, the Shetland Islands, Sicily, St. Martin & Sint Maarten, St. Vincent & the Grenadines, South Carolina, Spain, St. Kitts & Nevis, Sweden, Switzerland, the Turks & Caicos, the U.S.A., the U.S. Virgin Islands, Venice, Vienna and the Danube, Wales, and Zurich.

With Acknowledgments to a Cast of Thousands,
We extend special thanks and dedicate this book
to four men who were crucial to our
understanding of Rock Hudson

George Nader

Mark Miller

Tom Clark

Henry Willson

ROCK

Contents

COMES "THE LOVE OF MY LIFE"
Making screen love to Claudia Cardinale & Leslie Caron. More Doris! More Gina! Tired of romantic comedies, he films *Blindfold* and *Seconds,* disappointing thrillers which threaten his reign as Box Office Champion. He and George Peppard find solace together.

A Word About Phraseologies:

Since we at Blood Moon weren't privy to long-ago conversations as they were unfolding, we have relied on the memories of our sources for the conversational tone and phraseologies of what we've recorded within the pages of this book.

This writing technique, as it applies to modern biography, has been defined as "conversational storytelling" by *The New York Times*, which labeled it as an acceptable literary device for "engaging reading."

Blood Moon is not alone in replicating "as remembered" dialogues from dead sources. Truman Capote and Norman Mailer were pioneers of direct quotes, and today, they appear in countless other memoirs, ranging from those of Eddie Fisher to those of the long-time mistress (Verita Thompson) of Humphrey Bogart.

Some people have expressed displeasure in the fact that direct quotes and "as remembered" dialogue have become a standard—some would say "mandatory"—fixture in pop culture biographies today.

If that is the case with anyone who's reading this now, they should perhaps turn to other, more traditional and self-consciously "scholastic" works instead.

Best wishes to all of you, with thanks for your interest in our work.

Danforth Prince
President and Founder
Blood Moon Productions

PROLOGUE

As the 20th Century reached its midpoint, there was no leading man as popular as Rock Hudson in both comedy and drama. For seven consecutive years (1957-1964), he was one of the Top Ten Stars of the year.

He repeatedly beat out all "the bubblegum boys," such as blonde Tab Hunter or blonder Troy Donahue, at the box office, not just in the United States, but around the world.

For raw masculinity, he was a walking mass of testosterone. He fitted into that leading man category occupied by Clark Gable, Burt Lancaster, and Robert Mitchum. Women by the millions wanted him, and men wanted to be like him. Other men just wanted him.

Just released from the Navy, the muscled, 6'4" hunk, then known as Roy Fitzgerald, arrived in Hollywood with a clear understanding of what he wanted: "I don't want to be an actor...I want to be a movie star! And I don't give a damn how many casting couches I have to lie on!"

To that end, between gigs as a truck driver, he donned very tight, faded jeans and seductively stationed himself near the entrances to Warners and Universal. Eventually, he was "discovered."

Almost from the moment he set foot in Tinseltown, young Rock set off an "erotic fire" that blazed all the way to the Hollywood Hills. He was given such appellations as "Hollywood's Sexiest Man" and "The Reincarnation of Apollo." Columnist James Bacon said, "If Hollywood ever makes a film called *Adonis,* it should star Rock Hudson."

Always after the new boy in town, Joan Crawford was the first diva to lure him into her boudoir, later pronouncing him "a cross between Gary Cooper and Robert Taylor." Others followed, including a drunken Judy Garland and a very young Marilyn Monroe. His affair with Elizabeth Taylor, his co-star in *Giant* (1956), developed into a life-long friendship.

Also during the production of *Giant,* his affair with James Dean turned sour. While making two soap opera dramas with Rock, Jane Wyman, the ex-Mrs. Ronald Reagan, wanted to marry Rock. His most bizarre seductions ranged from Tallulah Bankhead to Liberace.

The matinee idols of yesterday also wanted him—Tyrone Power, Errol Flynn, Robert Taylor, Jeff Chandler, Tony Curtis. Rock also seduced many

1

of the emerging young stars of the 1950s: Marlon Brando, Monty Clift, Jeffrey Hunter, Troy Donahue, Steve McQueen, and Tony Perkins.

Early in his career, he was assigned roles in a string of B-pictures, playing handsome Apaches, easy-on-the-eyes sea captains, and "Ordinary Joes" whose charm moviegoers remembered way beyond the limited scale of his roles. Meanwhile, power players in Hollywood clamored for him up close and personal, too.

Stardom finally arrived based on a performance opposite Jane Wyman in that tear-jerking melodrama, *Magnificent Obsession* (1954).

Three eventful years later, his status as one of the most popular (and most consistently profitable) actors in Hollywood was reinforced, based on his co-starring performance opposite Doris Day in the spectacularly successful *Pillow Talk* (1959). Together, as a captivating duo, they went on to appear together in other "artfully campy" battles of the sexes.

Compiled as a memorial for the 30th anniversary of his death, *Rock Hudson Erotic Fire* is based on dozens of face-to-face interviews with Rock Hudson's friends, co-conspirators, and enemies. Researched over a period of a half century, it reveals the secretive actor's complete, never-before-told story within a context of scandal-soaked and historic ironies, many of which have never been fully explored—until now.

Although maligned by the media because of the stigmas associated with his AIDS-related death, Rock showed inner courage and manly grace as he lay dying. "This is my shining hour," he told his closest friends, as the media rushed to "Out" him as a "celebrity bisexual" who'd been stricken by the then-stigmatizing scourge.

Today, beloved by hordes of cultish fans and film buffs around the world, Rock Hudson is the often misunderstood (until now) Golden Icon of a glamourous bygone era.

Chapter One

Roy Fitzgerald Grows Up in Illinois As a Depression-Era Kid

Sexually Experimental, He Joins the U.S. Navy. Stationed in the War-Torn Pacific, He Becomes "The Love Machine"

Roy Fitzgerald, movie-star handsome and almost ready to Rock!

It was a cold, windy, and rainy pre-dawn of November 17, 1925 in Winnetka, Illinois, when Roy Harold Scherer, Jr. came into the world.

He was a healthy baby boy born to Katherine Wood, a descendant of

Irish and English parents, and a Swiss-German, Roy Harold Scherer, Sr., an auto mechanic.

The town of Winnetka was a suburb of Chicago, fifteen minutes to its north. It was where Roy would grow up during a turbulent boyhood that left scars that never healed.

His birth had been difficult for Katherine (nicknamed "Kay"). The boy infant emerging from her womb measured twenty-seven inches, although weighing less than six pounds. When she was allowed to examine him, she told the nurses, "I bet he'll grow up to be the skinniest kid on the block."

Roy Fitzgerald at three

Not so. In time, he became "The Baron of Beefcake."

For a few years, Roy experienced a fairly normal boyhood, with a strong-willed but loving mother and a father who was reasonably supportive, though a bit distant.

All that family life was imperiled when the Wall Street Crash descended in 1929, and a long, deep-rooted Depression fell over on the land.

The effect was felt immediately as Roy Sr. lost his job as a mechanic, and could find no other work. "No jobs anywhere," he said, after going day after day into Chicago, seeking some opening, but often standing in bread lines for his lunch.

When their very limited money ran out, Katherine and her husband faced a decision. They had to go live with their parents. It is not known why the impoverished couple and their young son didn't move in with the Scherer family, who lived on a 600-acre farm in Olney, Illinois. There they had extensive fields to plant every summer, and livestock to raise. Roy Sr. had eight brothers and sisters who came and went from their farm, most of them living elsewhere.

As it happened, Kay had never felt that much at home with her in-laws, and she took Roy Sr. and Jr. to move in with her own parents, James and Mary Ellen Wood. Their little house had only one upstairs bedroom. The grandparents had already surrendered that room to Kay's brother, John, and his wife, Hedwig, along with their four children.

The grandparents placed a bed for themselves out on the sunporch which, more or less, had been winterized.

When the two Roys and Kay arrived, they were given the upstairs bedroom, and her brother and his family moved into a converted attic. The house was very cramped, and sometimes tempers flared.

Roy's maternal grandfather worked for the Winnetka Coal & Lumber Company. After dinner, the entire family sat in the living room listening to their favorite radio programs.

Grandma Wood quickly adopted Roy Jr. as her own, causing the other children to be envious. Kay's sister, Pearl, a nurse, had been in attendance at the birth of Roy Jr. She said "To mother, Roy could do no wrong. Regardless of what devilment he got into, she was always the forever forgiving grandma."

Roy Scherer, Sr. with Roy Scherer, Jr. (later, Roy Fitzgerald).

As Roy Jr. came of school age, Kay rebelled against sending him to a Catholic school like the other children in the household. She insisted he be enrolled in a public school. Kay and Roy Jr. were the only members of the household who did not attend church on Sunday.

Back at the house, Grandma Wood "ruled the roost with an iron fist," in the words of Pearl.

"When my mother said 'jump,' you asked her, 'How high?'" Kay said. "Money was scarce, but she set a full table served promptly at 5:30PM. "Beef liver was a staple because it was so cheap," Kay said. "We had the usual Depression fare: A big cabbage cooked in salt pork, a heaping bowl of mashed potatoes, corn on the cob, plenty of gravy, and a soup made from the stock of whatever bones were left over from the night before."

Eventually, Roy's father grew tired of trying to find a job. He returned home at night defeated and disappointed that he could no longer support his family.

In 1931, when Roy Jr. was seven, his father decided to pack his one suitcase and head west, without them, to California, hoping to find a job in Los Angeles. He did not leave a note.

It was summertime and Roy Jr. was spending it at the farm of his paternal grandparents.

Kay almost experienced a nervous breakdown when her husband left her, but she bravely carried on. She decided not to tell Roy that his father had deserted them until she went to retrieve him at the Scherer family farm at the end of the summer, before the beginning of his school term that September.

When he heard the news, her son burst into tears. "It's my fault," he sobbed. "I must have done something wrong."

She assured him that he had not, and, as the weeks went by, she kept reassuring him that his father would send for them as soon as he found a good job and a home for them.

Eight months went by before a letter from him arrived. He did not make any proposal to send for them. Nor did he say he had a job. Many more months would go by before he sent another letter.

Although Kay's parents provided food and a place to stay, they did not have any money left over to pay for clothing or other basics. To support herself and her son, she found a temporary job as a waitress in a diner catering to truckers. When that fell through, she became a "wash woman" at two of the mansions of the rich families who lived nearby. One of Roy's earliest memories involved sitting in a kitchen watching his mother washing and ironing clothes.

In spite of the dire forecast, Kay never gave up hope of getting her husband back. When a second letter arrived, it had an address written in the upper left-hand corner. She'd managed to scrape together enough money to buy one-way tickets for herself and Roy on a Greyhound bus to Los Angeles.

With hope in her heart, and bolstered by Roy's bubbling enthusiasm, mother and son rode across the rolling plains of America into what they hoped would be a bright new future.

Arriving almost broke in Los Angeles, Kay and Roy headed for that street address. It turned out to be a seedy motel that seemed to rent rooms by the hour. Increasingly obvious was the prospect they'd come all this way for nothing. Roy Sr. wasn't there. However, the night manager told them he'd left a forwarding address in case mail came in for him.

His new address was ten blocks away. Carrying one suitcase, with Roy tagging along, mother and son walked to a dilapidated apartment house that turned out to be filled with prostitutes and drunks.

One of the tenants directed Kay to an apartment in the rear. As she knocked on the door, she heard loud music inside. Kay recognized her husband's voice when he shouted, "You'll get your god damn rent tomorrow!"

When she kept knocking, he threw open the door. He was unshaven and in his underwear. In this dingy, unkempt apartment was a bosomy girlfriend who had bleached blonde hair and looked as if she'd never see forty again.

"Mamie," he shouted at her. "Get the hell out of here and into the bedroom."

The woman, clad in her slip, jumped up and rushed out of the living room and into the bedroom, slamming the door behind her. It turned out that she had been a stripper at a joint called "Pink's," until she was fired—"too old."

Scherer picked up his young son and tossed him into the air. "My god, kid, how you've grown!" When Roy Jr. moved to kiss him, he averted his face.

Even though Kay pleaded with him to return to Illinois with her, Scherer refused. "I'm flat broke. Not enough money to pay the rent. I work three hours in the morning hawking doughnuts at this roadside stand."

When he learned that they didn't have enough money for the fare back to Chicago, he borrowed enough from Mamie for their ticket on the Greyhound bus. He also gave his wife and son five dollars for their food *en route* back to Illinois.

At the bus station, he just said, "Good bye and good luck."

Then he turned and walked away without hugs or kisses.

Watching him go, Kay said, "The bastard!"

"The bus ride back to Chicago was the most desolate and miserable of my life," Roy recalled. "I remember stopping at this awful little bus stop café. Kay ordered a bowl of watery soup which we shared. It tasted like dishwater. When we got off the bus we must have looked like refugees from the *Grapes of Wrath*, heading East instead of toward the Promised Land in the West. But I vowed not to give up," he said. "Perhaps years from now, I would go back to the West to the Promised Land where fame and riches awaited me. I felt that all the way to my toenails."

Within a year of her return to Illinois, Kay divorced her husband. She had met a handsome ex-Marine, Wallace ("Wally") Fitzgerald. He not only wanted to marry her, but promised to adopt Roy, changing his name to "Roy Fitzgerald."

Wally Fitzgerald already had a reputation for being a womanizer and heavy drinker given to barroom brawls, which he invariably won. He had powerful fists and had once done some boxing.

She wed Wally in February of 1934, a marriage that would drag on for one miserable year after another. He had a job shoveling coal at the "Water Works," the town's water and electric plant. He came home covered in coal dust, and forced Roy to assist him like a bath attendant, soaping and rinsing off his back, even drying parts of his body with a towel. He was heavily muscled and well-endowed.

Roy admitted later that it was while viewing his stepfather's body that he first realized he was a homosexual. "Even though he was a brute, I was turned on by him. He beat me severely at times and for no particular reason. I could endure those. What broke my heart was when he beat Kay, too. I wanted to grab a knife and slash him, but I held back. I hated myself for thinking of this brute every time I jacked off."

Two years into her marriage, Kay lost her mother. She was inconsolable for several weeks. "I feel I've lost my pillar, my guiding light."

It was at this time that Roy grew very close to his mother, a relationship that would endure for the rest of his life. "She was my mother, my mom, my dad, and even my older sister. To her, I was more than a son. More like an older brother."

One night, Wally spotted Roy kissing Kay good night. He came over to his stepson and knocked him down so hard he fell on the floor, hitting his head on the leg of a table. "If I catch you doing that again, boy, I'll beat you half to death. I'm not going to have some momma's boy for a son."

The next morning, when Wally left for work, Roy complained to his mother about his stepfather's violence. "I hate him the moment he comes through the door."

"He's your father and you must learn to respect him," she said.

"He's not my father. My father lives in Los Angeles."

One night, Wally asked Roy what he wanted to be when he grew up. "A policeman, a fireman, or a U.S. Marine?"

"None of that," Roy answered. "I want to be an actor."

The news prompted Wally to sock him in the face, bloodying his nose. As Roy cowered in his presence, whimpering in pain, Wally said, "actors are faggots. I'm not going to have a son of mine grow up to be a girlie man. I'll beat that dumb actor shit out of your head right now."

He then proceeded to give me the

Roy's High School
Yearbook Photo

beating of my life," Roy recalled. "I thought he was going to kill me. I vowed never to bring up the subject with him again."

As the months went by, Roy became very stoic, passively accepting whatever came down. At least that's how he appeared to people. "But my insides were churning with anguish," he recalled. "I felt unloved, abused, and unwanted. At one point, I heard Wally suggesting to my mother that she should get some family to adopt me. When I was old enough, I vowed I'd run away and join the Navy. Certainly not the Marines. Wally wanted that for me. NO WAY!"

Many of the kids at school were given allowances, but Roy was told that if he needed spending money, including for school supplies, he had to earn it himself.

As he grew older, he proved adept at finding part-time work. For a while, he had a paper route for the *Chicago Daily News.* He had other odd jobs, working once for an awning company. He was also employed as a "chicken plucker," a window washer, and a "bag boy" at a grocery store. For a few weeks, he worked in a local dive, frying hamburgers as a short order cook.

His favorite job was as a caddy for the Winnetka Golf Club. Part of his duties was to be the towel boy in the dressing room. The men would emerge nude and dripping wet, and he'd give them a fresh towel or two, and even volunteer to dry their backs. He didn't like to touch the older men, especially those with big bellies, but he was drawn to the young businessmen and salesmen, many of whom were married. He was fascinated by the different sizes and shapes of their cocks.

He soon became adept at giving massages, and was often awarded with a five-dollar tip. Although he was careful not to touch any golfer's genitals, he figured out ways to induce an erection by massaging close to erotically sensitive areas. He felt that some of them got excited and wanted him to go farther, but he was too shy and afraid.

He had been in love with the movies ever since 1929, when his mother had gotten a job playing the piano at the local Bijou, providing music for the silent films. He'd sit there with her, endlessly watching John Gilbert make love to Greta Garbo on the screen, or else the antics of Charlie Chaplin.

She eventually lost that job with the advent of the Talkies.

With the tips he earned at the golf course, he went to the movies at least three times a week. Myrna Loy, William Powell, Jean Arthur, Clark Gable, Cary Grant, Bette Davis, and Joan Crawford were among his favorites.

But one film, as he later claimed, "changed my life." At the age of twelve, he'd gone to see the 1937 film, *Hurricane*, starring Dorothy Lamour and Jon Hall. Perhaps he was exaggerating, but he claimed that he saw the movie more than a dozen times. He was mesmerized by Hall, the sarong-wearing body beautiful, especially his athletic dives into the water from a high perch.

JON HALL
THE SCREEN'S *NEWEST* ROMANTIC STAR!

Young Roy's role model and lust object: Jon Hall

As author Robert Hofler wrote: "Gazing up from his popcorn, Roy Fitzgerald took one look at the near naked Jon Hall and knew he had to see himself on the big screen. It would be Henry Willson, the gay talent agent, who would take this star-struck homosexual boy and turn him into Rock Hudson."

There was a certain irony here. When he moved to Hollywood, he and Hall would have a torrid love affair.

One Christmas in 1937, Kay had saved enough money for months to buy her son a Flexible Flyer sled, so he could have fun in the snow with the other children. He found the sled, tied with a red ribbon, under the Christmas tree.

Within the hour, he'd taken the sled up a hill. Racing down that hill on his belly, he crashed the sled into a tree. He ended up with cuts and bruises—no serious injury—but the sled was demolished.

When he got home and reported that, his stepfather was there. "He beat me severely and called me a son of a bitch,"

Kay stood by helplessly, watching the beating and hearing herself referred to as a bitch.

***

The time came for him to enter New Trier High School, the *alma mater* for many future stars. Ralph Bellamy, the movie star known for playing second leads, had graduated from the school. Two future movie stars also attended the school with Roy—Hugh O'Brian, who was in his class; and Charlton Heston, in a class above Roy.

10

Roy was the tallest boy in his class, towering over the other students at six feet, four inches. "But I weighed only about 150 pounds. I was so damn skinny, I looked like a lead pencil."

At the school's glee club, he sang soprano in the choir glee club. (His voice hadn't yet deepened.)

He tried out for the role of Brutus in Shakespeare's *Julius Caesar* but didn't get the part. The drama teacher, Sylvia Clark, said, "Roy had no talent, and I later got the shock of my life when he became a bigtime movie star. I gave the role of Brutus to Hugh (O'Brian), with Charlton (Heston) cast as Julius Caesar."

Not to be deterred, Roy joined the Winnetka Drama Club. He found that Heston, a fellow member, was just as shy in private as he was. "I'm too scared to ask a girl out on a date," Heston said to Roy.

"But you act so well," Roy said. "You're the best in the class."

"That's because when I'm on stage, I can assume the personality of someone else—Romeo, the great lover, or a Eugene O'Neill character. I can hide behind beards and fake noses."

[Quite by chance, Roy ran into Heston several years later. Heston at the time was twenty-two and living in Manhattan after having spent time in Chicago at Northwestern University. "I'm still knocking on the doors of casting agents," Heston answered, "still trying to make a living acting. I've got a girl now. Name's Lydia. I make a living posing as a nude model for art studies."

"Obviously, you've gotten over your shyness," Roy said.]

O'Brian became Roy's friend in high school. When Roy met him, he was known as Hugh Charles Krampe. He'd had a vagabond existence, moving from town to town with his parents. O'Brian's father, a former Marine, was defined by his son as "the toughest man I ever knew."

"That couldn't be true," Roy responded. "My stepfather is the world's toughest piece of shit."

[It was ironic that when both Rock Hudson and Hugh O'Brian became movie stars, they would be compared to each other as actors. O'Brian's greatest fame came when he played quick-on-the-draw Wyatt Earp in the hit TV series of the 1950s.

O'Brian and Rock would co-star in three movies, beginning with The Lawless Breed *(1952),* Seminole *(1953), and* Back to God's Country *(also 1953).*

Young Charlton Heston

While making The Lawless Breed, *O'Brian confided to director Raoul Walsh that Rock was a closeted homosexual.*

"I didn't know that when we were in high school together. He'd seen They Won't Forget *(1937), and talked a lot about the bouncing tits of Lana Turner. One afternoon, he invited me to the back of this old barn, where he showed me some hot French postcards he'd found in his stepfather's bedroom. He lured me into a jack-off fest."*

"I know now that Rock got hot looking at me whack off instead of at those damn pictures. He never touched me, but he must have enjoyed the sight of me. God, I was dumb back then."

Young Hugh O'Brian

For years, Rock would tell the press, "I think of Lana Turner, and I can't go to sleep."

O'Brian also had a link to Lana. After high school, he told Roy Fitzgerald goodbye and enrolled in the Kemper Military School in Boonville, Missouri. His roommate was Johnny Stompanato, who in 1958 would be fatally stabbed by either daughter Cheryl Crane or else by Lana herself. (Take your pick.)

When co-starring with Lana in Love Has Many Faces *(1965), O'Brian would seduce the blonde goddess.]*

***

In addition to O'Brian in high school, Roy formed even closer bonds with Patrick McGuire and James Matteoni. "We hung out together and went everywhere together," Matteoni said. "They called us 'The Three Musketeers.' We were avid movie fans, and we often went to films, sometimes driving with fake drivers' licenses to neighboring towns to see some movie that wasn't playing locally."

Roy had not given up his ambition to become an actor, and he got his two buddies to join the Threshold Players, a struggling theater group in Winnetka.

None of members of that trio ever got to play a lead role: As McGuire remembered it, the starring role always went to Charlton Heston, an upperclassman.

"We sold theater tickets to housewives, going door to door," Matteoni said. "We worked with the props, the costumes, any shit job that had to be done. For a while, Roy wanted to learn how to apply makeup on the actors. I was more interested in the music—in fact, I became a music teacher after I left college."

McGuire was less dedicated, always asking, "When are you guys going to finish here so we can chase gals?"

Music also played a role in Roy's life after his mother had taught him to play the piano. He specialized in boogie-woogie, and the Andrew Sisters were his favorite singers.

"Roy played the piano at our high school parties," said Sally Cunningham. "I had a crush on him, even though he was too skinny. He did a mean jitterbug with me. We attended beach parties on Lake Michigan in summer. It was sleigh rides in winter, kid stuff like that."

"No one knew at the time that Roy was a homosexual," she said. "He didn't act effeminate at all. Back then, we thought all queers were effeminate. What we now know is that gays are also bodybuilders and football players. Frankly, I think Roy turned homosexual in the Navy. He probably got mixed up with a lot of perverted sailors. But I'm not sure."

Roy's school chums recalled that he dated two different girls in high school, Susan Ford and Nancy Gillogly. On most occasions, "The Three Musketeers" went out on triple dates together, often ending up in a car parked beside Lake Michigan where they indulged in what they called "heavy petting but no commando stuff."

"We thought Roy was a gay blade," McGuire said. "Of course, gay blade meant something different back in those days."

***

The summer Roy turned fourteen, he went to stay at the Scherer family's farm. There, he was introduced to a 35-year-old drifter, who had been employed by Roy's grandparents as a hired hand to look after the livestock and work in the fields.

Rock Hudson later told his lovers, including Marc Christian, that Don Reynolds immediately attracted him with "his muscular build—he was usually shirtless—and his smouldering good looks."

"He wasn't traditionally handsome, but a real turn-on," Rock said. "We showered together when we came in from the fields and slept in the nude. He insisted on that. One thing led to another. By the third night, in a bed with him in a small room above the garage, I woke up to find him going down on me."

"It was thrilling, the greatest sensation I'd ever known. When I exploded, he demanded I return the favor. At first, I was reluctant and not very good. But with some practice, I really took to it. I wouldn't have traded Don for a dozen pretty boys."

By the end of August, the siren call of the road was heard by Reynolds. "I'm going to stick out my thumb all the way to Montana, where I plan to lasso some cowboys," was his farewell comment to Roy.

When he returned home to his mother Kay, he found her living in a two-room apartment above Walgreen's Drug Store, where she worked as a clerk. Wally Fitzgerald had gone, and she would divorce him in 1941.

Roy was supposed to graduate with the rest of his class in 1943, but his grades were so bad he remained behind. He didn't get his high school diploma until June of 1944.

For a few weeks, he worked as a mail carrier, earning $1.25 an hour.

America was still at war in 1944 when he joined the U.S. Navy, heading for the South Pacific, in his words, "to fight those Japs."

A new life and new adventures awaited him unlike anything he'd ever known.

***

Growing up, Roy had never liked regimentation, but that had been important to his stepfather, Wally Fitzgerald. He'd insisted that his stepson join the Boy Scouts. "Boys need to learn how to wear a uniform early in life. It'll help to learn to march in step with a troupe. It'll make life easier for you when you're drafted into the Army."

Forced to join the Boy Scouts, Roy detested it and hated his uniform. But fearing another severe beating from his stepfather, he endured it. He later recalled, "The only thing I liked about the Scouts was when we'd go camping in the woods."

He'd left high school while the war was still raging in 1944, with a lot of bloody battles to come. He read the newspapers daily, following the ongoing saga of the war on both the continent of Europe against the Nazis and in the Pacific against the Japanese. He'd been heartened to read in June of 1944 that Allied forces had arrived on the beaches of Normandy to reclaim France from the Nazis.

"I don't know if Roy really wanted to go into the Army," his mother, Kay, said. "Actually, he didn't want to be a soldier or a Marine. That's what my former husband, Wally, wanted for him. If Wally wanted it, Roy didn't. Every week, he lived in fear of getting drafted. His friends were going into service. Fearing he'd get his notice every day from the draft board, he decided to enlist in the Navy."

"I like black and white uniforms better than a drab soldier's uniform," he told his mother. I'm going to be a sailor."

"When I went into the service, I was still reed-thin, rather shy, and definitely not an athlete. In school, I avoided all sports except swimming. I could swim but I was no Esther Williams."

Boot camp was at the Great Lakes Naval Training Station, which was only a 30-minute drive from Winnetka. Kay drove there every weekend to see him, bringing him a special treat, home-baked cake. "Roy would eat the whole thing. He needed to put on some extra pounds."

When he took his first communal showers, as he later claimed to friends, "I was about the skinniest guy in boot camp. I guess even straight guys check to see how another guy is hung. I may not have had the most developed body, but I sure had those guys beat in one department."

Kay managed to get a job as a telephone operator on the naval base as a means of being near her son. She got to see a lot of him except when he was on special duty, such as watch or else driving an officer into Chicago.

"Boot camp was living hell," he recalled. "My superiors were like Mr. Hyde versions of my stepfather. I saw in the Charles Atlas ads that skinny kids get picked on by brutes. Such was my case. Part of my not performing in step with the other guys was that I was rather gangly and didn't do everything in group cohesion. I sure got hell for it."

His two closest friends, James Matteoni and Patrick McGuire, were also in the service. When he got his first pass, he hooked up with them.

"The Three Musketeers" went on the town in St. Louis. At around 11PM, on the first night, Roy picked up this good-looking redhead in a bar. He learned that her husband was in the Army, stationed in England.

"I guess the bitch decided to play around while he was away," said McGuire. "At any rate, Roy took her back to his hotel room and had us wait downstairs while he did the dirty deed. We were bunking together. After the whore left, we came up to the room where we found him bubbling over with bragging rights."

"We fucked like crazy," Roy said. "Her husband is one lucky man. She does everything."

"You mean...even *that?*" McGuire

"Yes, even *that.*"

***

What happened to Roy in the Navy has never been told in any of the sketchy biographies published about him. However, a dossier of his private life was pieced together with stories he told his three most trusted Hollywood friends, Tom Clark, George Nader, and Mark Miller. After telling a story, he'd order his secretary, Miller, to write it down for "The Book." That was a reference to his authorized biography, to be published only after his death.

Regrettably, that book was never written, but his friends shared many of these stories and memories of their dear friend, Rock Hudson, after his death.

"He was taking such a beating in the press because of the AIDS thing," Nader claimed. "We wanted to show his human side, flaws and all, scandal or whatever, but a portrait of Rock the

Hello, Sailor, in this case, the future Rock Hudson

Man, a loving, kind soul always looking for the love he never found."

***

Before setting out for the South Pacific, he endured a course as an apprentice aircraft repairman. He admitted, "I was no good at it. I was never a mechanic. My father was, or so I was told, but not his kid."

Before he left the States, someone took a picture of Roy in his sailor's uniform. It would later be widely published after he became a star. Except for a jagged eye tooth [sometimes known as a "canine tooth," in Roy's case, in the upper jaw] which he had capped later in Hollywood, there's nothing in it that detracts from his handsome good looks.

***

Only a few of his fellow sailors recognized Spangler Arlington Brugh after he joined the U.S. Navy on February 9, 1943. At this time in his life, he sported an uncharacteristic buzz haircut, and he had shaved off his familiar mustache.

Brugh was better known at the time as the world-famous matinee idol, Robert Taylor. The bisexual actor was married to Barbara Stanwyck, who, that year, was the highest-paid woman in America. Thousands of besotten female fans wanted Taylor to take them in their arms, as he had Greta Garbo in *Camille* (1936); Janet Gaynor in *Small Town Girl* (1936); Jean Harlow in *Personal Property* (1936); Vivien Leigh in *Waterloo Bridge* (1940); and Lana Turner in *Johnny Eager* (1942). During his filming of *Small Town Girl*, he'd taken the virginity of Thelma ("Pat") Ryan, who later became better known as Mrs. Richard Nixon.

Unknown to his fans, he'd also had affairs with Howard Hughes, Tyrone Power, Errol Flynn, and even John Gilbert, who had once made love to Garbo.

Megastar Robert Taylor being sworn into the U.S. Navy at the Hollywood Recruiting Station. He would become Rock's flight instructor and sex partner.

Taylor was also known as a faithful patron of a brothel run by MGM to service its male stars. Before joining the Navy, this ardent anti-communist had been forced, by studio mandate, to star in *Song of Russia* (1943), a film with a pro-Soviet theme. For years after, especially as the Cold War intensified after World War II, Taylor regretted his appearance in that film.

In the Navy, he was commissioned as a lieutenant, junior grade. Basic training was in Corpus Christi, Texas, but he was later transferred to the Naval Air Station in New Orleans for more instructor training.

After that, the Navy brass decided that Taylor could best be used as an instructor and also as a Navy spokesman who could star in propaganda films for the U.S. military. *[He would have preferred, he later stated, to pilot planes, as he had, after strenuous effort, earned his wings, graduating fifth in his class in January of 1944.]*

At one point, he was transferred to Glenview, Illinois, to train a class of twenty-five young men in the art and science of flying an airplane. One of his students was a bit gangly and rather shy, and didn't look quite eighteen. Taylor was introduced to Roy Scherer Fitzgerald, hardly realizing that one day he would be the biggest box office draw in America.

Roy had been assigned to the Aviation Repair and Overhaul Unit with the understanding that he'd eventually be shipped to the war-torn Philippines for his tour of duty.

In the meantime, he needed to learn how to pilot a plane, and Taylor was there to teach him. As Rock later confessed to his friends, Taylor was one of only a few top movie actors who thrilled him on the screen. He wanted to emulate them, even make love to them, as impossible as it seemed at the time.

As Roy claimed, "When I first shook Taylor's hand, I got the feeling he was checking me out. Maybe it was just a stupid thought, but it occurred to me. As it turned out, I was flattered that he sent out a signal."

"During my first class with him, I felt him constantly looking in my direction, but very discreetly, before his eyes darted elsewhere."

After four training sessions, Roy approached his instructor after class. "I'm gonna ask you a big favor, and I hope I'm not out of line."

"What is it, young man?" Taylor asked.

Rock recalled that if he had been the slightest bit hostile, "I would have hurried out, but he was warm and friendly. He seemed genuinely interested in what I had to say."

He blurted out that he was "scared to death of going up in an airplane, especially of piloting one. I don't want to make a fool out of myself, but I was hoping, as a real personal favor to me, that you could take me up once or twice this weekend so at least I could get the feel of what it's like up there in the Wild Blue Yonder."

Taylor reminded him that it was totally against the rules, "But god damn it, I'll do it." Roy was warned that it had to be kept as a secret between just the two of them. He was told to meet his instructor the next morning at 5AM at Hangar 3 on the nearby airfield.

Rock had a hard time falling asleep that night, contemplating what was about to happen. He prayed he had not misread the signals.

He revealed that in a small plane, they'd flown together to an airfield near a lake, where they went by taxi to a remote little inn in the backwoods. Taylor wore sunglasses and a cap that covered most of his face, and he had Roy check in for them. "He really didn't want to be seen with me."

As Rock recalled years later in Hollywood, "It was an incredible experience making love to a world famous movie star. He really went for my equipment. It was so much bigger than his own, and he took delight in it. He wanted it, and I wanted to give it to him. I figured that if I was really good, he'd want me again and again."

"I did things with Bob I've never done before. The room was hot, and I licked the sweat off his chest, paying special attention to that patch of hair."

[In 1937, that patch of hair had been written up, and to some degree, celebrated, in the press. When the Queen Mary docked in New York in December of that year, a reporter had asked Taylor if he thought he was pretty. In response, and heatedly, Taylor had said, "I'm a red-blooded American, and I resent people calling me beautiful. I've got hair on my chest."

Taylor later posed for publicity pictures showing off that patch of hair.]

18

"I licked the guy's nipples, stuff like that, and did some other things I'm not quite up to talking about," Rock confessed.

"When we checked out to fly back to Glenview, I think I'd satisfied him in every way possible. It was thrilling for me, too. Of course, he was far more experienced than I was. He taught me a few tricks I would carry with me the rest of my life."

That Monday afternoon in class, Taylor ignored Roy, not even looking in his direction. At first, Roy was disappointed, interpreting it as a rejection. But that changed when Taylor asked him to stay after class to go over a paper.

Once the room was empty, he whispered to Roy, "I have this place where we can go. Here's the address." He handed him a slip of paper. "Meet me there at eight tonight. I haven't begun to get enough of you."

Roy was thrilled at the invitation and the subsequent ones that followed.

When it came time for Roy to head off to war, and for Taylor to return to California, they promised to meet again, "Somewhere, sometime."

"He even invited me to Hollywood, but he wasn't very specific about how we would hook up once I was there. But I figured that hundreds of homosexuals were throwing themselves at him, and I'd never hear from him again. How wrong I was."

***

Among the many untold stories about Roy Fitzgerald before he became Rock Hudson is an interlude he had in the Navy when he was allowed to go back to Winnetka on leave before shipping out.

A sexual tryst he had there is referenced briefly in a memoir by Tom Clark, his longtime companion.

Before heading home, Roy told his Navy buddies, "I'm going back to see dear ol' Mom, but I want to break free of all this regimentation, all these commands, and have some fun. Read that to mean 'getting laid.'"

Originally, he hated wearing a uniform, but when he returned to Illinois, he found that he was admired in it. "Everybody was friendlier. I was offered a free meal when I went to a diner, even a cold beer at the bar. I felt I really belonged for the first time in my life. No longer alienated."

"I also came to realize just how dull my hometown was. The world was at war, but everybody seemed to be going quietly about their business. It was good seeing my mother again, but I soon got bored and wanted some action."

"I'd found out that both of the girls I'd dated were no longer available—one had gotten married and had a kid, another was working in a defense plant in Chicago."

"I thought I was going to have a wild time on leave," he said. "All my fellow sailors had talked about going home and getting laid. What wild times they were going to have. I was disappointed. It was sexier hanging out with those guys in boot camp, with them running around naked. I had to break loose. One night, when Kay went to bed early, I headed out to this local tavern and dance bar. It was packed—the joint was jumping."

"I met this girl I'd known slightly in high school, Pat Blair. She wasn't the prettiest thing, but she was okay. She remembered me, and we did some wild jitterbugging. I drank a few beers, and she stuck to coke."

"I agreed to walk her home and asked if I could come in, but she turned me down, saying that her mother would be arriving any minute. She worked as a waitress until midnight at a diner. Her husband (Pat's father) had deserted them, something we shared in common."

"I was a bit pissed at her, since I was seeking a certain kind of 'nightcap.' I stood out in front of her house, looking back. I saw the light go on upstairs in her bedroom, but it wasn't on for long. She must have been really tired. In hardly enough time to brush her teeth, the light was turned off."

"Just as I was leaving, a taxi pulled up, and this woman in a waitress uniform got out of the back seat. This was obviously the mother."

"She asked who I was, and I told her I was just returning from a date with her daughter. 'She's exhausted from all that jitterbugging.'"

"She told me her name was Martha Blair, and we seemed to be sizing each other up. She didn't look a day over thirty-five, and she was better-looking than her daughter. She must have had Pat when she was a teenager."

"I was a bit surprised when she invited me in for a beer, warning me to keep quiet, because she didn't want to wake her daughter. One thing led to another. I didn't even finish my Bud before she invited me into her bedroom at the rear for some action."

"She was hot to trot. I screwed her without a rubber, but I was too far gone to pull out. She didn't seem concerned about it, so I wasn't, either."

After giving her a goodbye kiss, I headed out the door, tiptoeing. No sound from Pat upstairs."

"The next day I returned to base to learn we were being sent to San Francisco."

"I never saw this mother-daughter act ever again, but Martha came back into my life in an unexpected way."

[*During his early days in Hollywood, when Rock Hudson was making low-budget movies for Universal, he began to receive quite a bit of fan mail.*

Kay had also moved to California, and Rock asked his mother to open the fan mail and answer it, signing his name to the responses she crafted.

As she later related to Tom Clark, a letter arrived from Winnetka, which she opened, thinking it was a fan letter from one of the people they knew.

It was from a woman, Martha Blair. She claimed that Roy (now Rock) had seduced her one night when he was on leave from the Navy. She even gave the correct date.

"I became pregnant after Roy's visit," she claimed. "When I found out I was pregnant with Roy's child, I got married right away to a Marine. I told my husband that he was the father. My husband is named Larry Poston. My son is Richard Poston."

Kay feared that the woman's letter was a prelude to blackmail. She phoned Martha and threatened her.

As Kay later told Clark, "I knew this lady's reputation and it was pretty bad. I told her that if she persisted with her claim, I'd let everybody in Winnetka know she was a whore, including the man she'd tricked into marrying her. My threat was valid, because she was known for sleeping with half the men in the town. I bet her Marine husband didn't know that. He might not have married her if he did."

In her letter, Martha had written, "My boy is the spitting image of Roy, now movie star Rock Hudson. I've seen him in two pictures. The name's changed, but I know it was Roy Fitzgerald."

Clark later told Rock about the letter that had come in from Martha Blair. (Kay had chosen not to show it to him.)

"He had mixed feelings about it," Clark said. "He loved kids and always said he'd wanted to have a son. He was dying to meet the kid, but he didn't think it would be wise to return to Winnetka and expose the woman."

"I might open a keg of worms that would turn into a bed of rattlesnakes," he said. "It could wreck her life, maybe the kid's, too. But I can't help but wonder."

Shortly after her marriage to the Marine, he went to war. Back home, Martha had claimed that the birth of her infant son was premature.

In 1954, as Rock Hudson had begun to morph into a major-league movie star, a reporter from Chicago, Roger Denton, heard a rumor that he had a son living in Winnetka. The reporter drove over there to meet Martha and her son.

He arrived unannounced at the Poston bungalow. When he identified himself, Martha would not let him in or speak to him. However, the son, Richard, by now an early teenager ran out to his car and agreed to meet the reporter later at a diner.

"When the kid entered the diner, I saw that he did look like Rock, at least his

younger brother," Denton said. *"Over a beer I asked him if he felt that Rock Hudson was his real father."*

"Everybody in town says I look just like Roy Fitzgerald used to." He said. "Without letting my mother know, I wrote Rock Hudson three letters at Universal, enclosing a photograph of myself. The bastard never answered them. I asked him if he'd send me a bus ticket to Los Angeles to spend a weekend with him, his very own son. You'd think he'd want to see what his own boy was like. But not Mr. Hudson, the Movie Star."

"Isn't there some kind of blood test to determine if I'm his boy?" he asked the reporter. "There must be. But when the fuck didn't even have the courtesy to answer my letters, I decided not to pursue him any more. Actually, I did want something from him. I wanted him to give me the money to go to college. I guess I never will now. We can't afford it."

The city editor in Chicago rejected the story about Rock's son, claiming, "Not enough evidence."

***

Early in 1985, Tom Clark recalled speaking to Rock as "AIDS was eating away at his body."

"I should have gone back home and looked up my son," Rock said. "Maybe brought him here to live with me at the Castle. I always wanted to have a son, someone to carry on my legacy. He might be that part of me that will live on into the 21st Century. Alas, the saddest words in the English language is the expression, 'What might have been…'"

***

The time had come for Roy to head to the theater of war.

In San Francisco Harbor, he boarded the Liberty ship, the SS *Lew Wallace*. With tears in his eyes, he remembered that a record was playing by Doris Day singing "Sentimental Journey."

It would seem inconceivable to him at the time that before the end of the 1950s, he would be co-starring with her in a big hit comedy.

Along with his fellow sailors, he landed on the sandy island of Samar in the Philippines. It had been liberated by U.S. forces on land, at sea, and in the air. Part of the Visaya Archipelago, in the Central Philippines, Samar is the third largest land mass in the country. To the south is Leyte Gulf, site of one of the decisive naval battles of World War II.

On Samar, Roy's first job involved the unloading of damaged aircraft carriers attacked by Japanese pilots waging kamikaze attacks and fearing

22

an imminent invasion of their homeland.

Aboard various U.S. carriers, Roy faced an armada of American-made dive bombers, torpedo bombers, and fighters, all of which, though damaged, were capable of being repaired and re-entered into combat.

He was eventually assigned to work in the mechanics' division of Aviation Repair and Overhaul, mending Corsairs and TBF Avengers, each a state-of-the-art fighter aircraft later credited with helping win World War II.

In part because of his good humor and his role as a prankster, Roy became popular with his fellow sailors, who nicknamed him "Fitz." In the mechanics' unit, he was surrounded by at least a dozen Navy men. Because of the brutally hot tropical climate, the men tended to take off their shirts.

He recalled, "At least eight of them had bodies that would qualify them as male models. Perfectly sculpted, more like swimmer's build than a muscleman, I got to observe a very sexy group of guys. I noticed some of the sailors checking me out. I knew they could be had."

Yet despite his popularity, Roy, as a G.I. and aircraft mechanic, made many technical and mechanical errors and received stern lectures from his commander, who eventually reassigned him to the base's laundry detail for the remainder of his time abroad.

Although initially humiliating, there was a new perk to this job that brought him better food, more money, and love (perhaps).

Years later in Hollywood, Rock Hudson told gossip columnist Hedda Hopper that "the cooks came to us with their dirty whites to be washed every day. We told these guys to get us better food...or else! They did. Soon we were eating the same chow as the officers."

The officers would come in with their dirty uniforms, and Roy found many of them attractive. "I went through their pockets and found they'd left money there. In just one week, I could pick up forty to fifty dollars."

He stayed in touch with his friends back home, writing to Patrick McGuire, who was stationed at Chanute Field in Rantoul, about 130 miles south of Chicago, in his home state of Illinois. "You sissy boys back home have it easy," Roy wrote. "We in the Philippines get air raids worse than Pearl Harbor."

Of course, that was pure exaggeration. The Japanese were no long attacking his base.

Roy also wrote, "I'll have to wait to get back home to tell you about all the good ass. These Filipino girls are really hot! They tell me that American dicks are bigger than those of the Japs who fucked them when they controlled the island."

That, too, was a misstatement. He was having an active sex life, but not with girls.

He had never led a life as a homosexual until he served in Samar. Cut off from sex back home, and having only each other to turn to for relief, many of the enlisted men indulged in sexual liaisons, although in secret.

Each sailor feared he'd get caught. "I was amazed at how many guys would be open to a come-on," Roy said. "In fact, I invented the question, 'What's the difference between a straight sailor and a gay one?' The answer? 'A six-pack.'"

There were no great romances going on except in a few cases when two sailors would have sex together and decide to live together when they returned home. "Many of them planned to settle in San Francisco when they were discharged, never returning to that farm in Iowa."

"Mostly, it was some heavy tongue-kissing and a quick blow-job in some secluded spot," Roy said. "We lived in constant fear of being discovered and turned in as homosexuals. Most of the guys weren't homosexual at all. You can't throw a lot of horny young guys, many of them eighteen or nineteen years old, in close quarters day and night, and not expect some hot action."

It was on Samar that Roy was introduced to the seamier side of homosexual life. He'd gone to this rowdy bar catering to sailors, where he ordered a few beers. Eventually, he had to go to the toilet. A waiter pointed the way at the back of an alley.

As he neared the "piss hole," he heard noises coming from the inside.

As he later told his friends, "I walked in on a cesspool of randy butt-fucking. A Filipino drag queen was in one of the stalls getting gang banged—and loving it. At least six sailors were lined up to take their turns at porking. One of them motioned for me to get in line."

"I didn't want to look like some sissy, and I stood in line for a while, fascinated by what was going on in that open-door stall. It was like a five-car crash on a highway. You didn't want to see the carnage but you looked at it anyway."

"Sounds of grunts and groans came from the stall, with a lot of raspy breathing. After a few minutes, I decided it was not my scene. I fled from the smelly joint."

***

Back in Hollywood years later, Rock Hudson revealed that his life changed one afternoon when Ludwig (nicknamed "Luddy") Wünsche walked into the laundry room with his dirty clothes. "I thought he was a heartthrob, a blonde-haired stud with broad shoulders, a narrow waist,

24

and height almost as tall as me. He had dreamy blue eyes. He was very sexy in spite of those wire-framed eyeglasses. He looked at me and flashed an award-winning smile—and that was it."

He asked me to drop off his clean clothes in his quarters. Before going, he turned to me, 'Oh, another thing. Take special care of my underwear. It's not regulation Navy underwear. I buy it special."

"Yes, sir!" Roy answered. "I was in love. While I talked to him, I couldn't help checking out his crotch. He caught me doing that, too."

"I later learned that his parents had been born in Warsaw. Both father and mother were Polish, and they had emigrated to America together before the war started. Luddy had been born in New York and had grown up on its tough streets. He had two brothers, each of them in the service, both in the Army. One was a pilot. He also had two older sisters, each of them married and living in Brooklyn. I also learned that his favorite vegetable was cabbage. Can you imagine that? Stinking old boiled cabbage!"

When Roy delivered Luddy's clothing, he found him lying on his bunk clad only with a towel around his waist. He'd freshly emerged from the shower. Roy delivered his laundry. He noticed that Luddy discreetly let the towel edge upward.

In a low voice, he said, "We've both got a weekend pass. Enlisted men are not supposed to fraternize with officers. But we'll meet outside the gates way down the road tomorrow at 9AM. I have this place we can go. It's a safe haven."

"I'll count the hours," Roy promised him.

When Saturday morning came, Roy was waiting beside the road when Luddy drove up in a Jeep. "Hop in. Let's get the hell out of here."

He drove him to a modest home outside of town where he was introduced to an older Filipino man and his wife. They rented a "love nest" in their garden to Luddy. He gave them some American dollars, and told them he and his friend wanted them to buy meals to bring to the shack out back.

As Rock Hudson later confessed, "That was a turning point for me. Luddy taught me every form of gay sex. I mean, erotic zones I didn't know I had, from 'the rosebud' (as he called it) to the pits. He not only fucked me, I fucked him. What a terrific sensation. To muffle my first cry of pain at penetration, if felt my ass was on fire. But he muffled my anguish by pressing his mouth hard down on mine. When he said 'I love you,' that was it! I could endure anything. Suddenly pain turned into the greatest sexual pleasure I had ever known."

"After that weekend, I would do anything for Luddy. We slipped around all the time. He was good at getting me assigned to go with him on 'missions' to other parts of the island, the more secluded places. If we didn't have a place to go, we had that love shack with the Filipino family."

Roy remembered that after sex, they often would lie quietly in each other's arms talking about their future. Roy proposed that when they both got back to San Francisco, they should take an apartment, find jobs, and settle in there. He pointed out that many other sailors who met on Samar were planning to do that. "He didn't agree to it," Roy said. "On the other hand, he didn't say no."

One day, Roy learned that Luddy was going to be shipped home six weeks before him on another carrier. "I wanted a commitment from him, and he'd stalled long enough. I pointedly asked him, 'Are we going to make a future together as lovers?'"

He thought about it for a minute before reaching for his wallet. He removed a picture of a beautiful young woman with two blonde-haired children, a boy and a girl.

"That's my wife. I love her very much. Those are my kids. I love them with all my heart, and I'm going home to them. We're moving to Sacramento where her father has offered me a job in his real estate firm. I'm sorry!"

As Roy remembered it, "There is a thing called first love. There is also a thing called heartbreak. I'm told you never quite get over your first heartbreak and will remember it for the rest of your life. More heartbreaks would follow in my future, but it wouldn't be the same. As I sailed back to San Francisco, I decided that from now on, I would be the heartbreaker—not the victim with the broken heart. I owe Luddy for that."

***

[Another sailor, Hal Halbert, who served with "Fitz" on Samar, was shocked in 1985 when Rock was exposed as a homosexual suffering from AIDS.

"I just couldn't believe it. Not old Fitz. I stood naked in the shower next to him. He never even looked down, or so I thought. He never cruised me, and I used to be considered good looking."

"We were close buddies." Halbert said. "I even slept in the bunk next to him. I think Hollywood ruined him, Tinseltown and its casting couches. All those faggots out there turned Fitz gay, I just know it."

"Let's face it: Acting is a sissy's profession. Guys putting on makeup. Even Gary Cooper wore lipstick in those early movies. It was about dressing up in costumes and play-acting. Come on!"]

***

Rock Hudson would remember that foggy early dawn when his ship sailed into San Francisco Harbor after its transit across the Pacific. As he passed beneath the Golden Gate Bridge, he thought of the day he'd gone to sea, listening to Doris Day singing "Sentimental Journey."

"I shed tears then, and now I was shedding tears once again. But this time, they were tears of joy. A boat arrived to deliver frosted cokes in that famous green hourglass bottle. Instead of champagne, we toasted our homecoming with coke. Fireboats sprayed water to welcome us back home. As we passed Angel Island, a huge red-lettered banner greeted us— WELCOME HOME, GUYS. GREAT JOB!"

It was not Luddy waiting at the pier, but his anxious mother, Kay. She showered him with kisses and hugs. Over breakfast, she was amazed at how "My gawky little kid is now a strapping young man who fills out his sailor suit."

She asked him if he'd return home with her to Winnetka when he was discharged in May of 1946.

"I'd not going to do that," he answered. "Perhaps I'll go to college in Southern California. Everybody tells me how good looking I am and that I should be in pictures."

"In Hollywood, I may be discovered. I'll find some way to make those jerks sit up and take notice of Roy Fitzgerald. You'll be proud of me when I'm glistening on the silver screen. Just you wait and see!"

Indeed, Rock's wish for movie stardom came true. Photo above shows him looking luscious with the equally luscious Elizabeth Taylor.

The *Führer* had been dead for months when Japan surrendered after two atomic bombs were dropped on their land. Americans went wild, celebrating as exemplified by these two drunken sailors sleeping it off.

Rock returned to his native shores uncertain about what role he'd play in the post-war recovery period. He had a dream, and that was to go to Hollywood and become "a god damn movie star."

Chapter Two

A Truck Driver and Navy Veteran Emerges as the Future Mega-Celebrity, Rock Hudson

"I don't want to be an actor... I wanna be a movie star."

This photo of Rock immersed in the Sunday morning papers turned heads across America, as thousands of fans wondered what he might have been up to the night before.

Still bitten with the acting bug, Roy Fitzgerald de-
layed moving to Southern California. Instead, he returned home to Winnetka to plot his future.

Kay was still employed as a telephone operator, and for the first two weeks of his renewed residency in her home, she spoiled him, cooking all his favorite dishes. She'd also saved some money during his time in the Philippines, and she purchased a new wardrobe for him.

For his spending money, he was drawing twenty dollars a week from the government as veteran's pay, with the clear understanding that that wouldn't last forever.

Before the war, one in a series of temporary jobs, he'd been a mail carrier, and he applied once again to his former boss, the local postmaster, Arthur Klepter, who gladly rehired him. It was a boring job, and he soon grew restless.

His two best friends, Patrick McGuire and James Matteoni, were also out of the service. Roy began to hang out with them, even going out on a few triple dates, as he'd done in high school. But service in the Navy had changed him. He grew tired of upholding his macho image, faking stories about all the "hot Filipino pussy" he'd had as a Navy man.

He began making excursions into Chicago in his mother's car. In the big city, he discovered a network of homosexual bars, although they were subjected to raids.

His favorite joint was The Tattoo, which was filled with a wide assortment of young men, many, like himself, just released from the military. There was also an array of bikers, truckers, musclemen, *faux* urban "cowboys," salesclerks, hairdressers, and short order cooks. A few of the more daring patrons appeared in drag on Saturday night, when shows were staged with bawdy humor and "gay insider" jokes.

As he'd later tell George Nader in Hollywood, "I had my pick of conquests. A lot of guys came on to me. Since I'd been in the Navy, I was called 'seafood.' I was always hauled back to someone's room or apartment."

"One balding, middle-aged, and out-of-shape salesman from St. Louis offered me a hundred dollars, but I found him too repulsive. I really didn't know what a hustler was back then, but the bar was filled with what were later called 'gay for pay' boys."

Without letting Kay know—he didn't want to upset her—he began to write letters to his father, Roy Scherer. By then, he was living in Long Beach, south of Los Angeles, running a small appliance store.

Roy shared his ambition of moving to Los Angeles and enrolling in college under the massively popular GI Bill. At this point, he didn't dare tell his father that he wanted to be an

Versatile, photogenic, rough-edged, charismatic, and hip to the undercover motivations of Hollywood.

actor, although he didn't expect a response as violent as when he'd shared that dream with his stepfather, the long-departed Wally Fitzgerald. "He left me nothing but his name when he split," Roy said.

Back home in Winnetka, Roy looked forward to receiving the latest issue of *Photoplay*, devouring the articles and reading about June Allyson, Elizabeth Taylor, Van Johnson, and Errol Flynn.

Roy also read of former stars who had returned from service and were reactivating their careers, Clark Gable and Tyrone Power among them. Roy had gone to see Jon Hall in *Sudan* (1945), and that handsome actor remained a special favorite, although he dreamed one day of meeting Tyrone Power, whom he considered the most beautiful male animal in the movies. But it seemed that his favorite female star, Lana Turner, had already snared him.

One day, a letter arrived from Scherer in Long Beach, inviting him to come and stay with him in his modest home in Long Beach. "There's a small room in back I can fix up for you. At least you can stay here temporarily until you get started. I can give you a job working for my appliance store. It doesn't carry a salary, but you can make money on commissions."

Roy wrote back that he was on his way. He dreaded telling Kay, but finally got up the courage, even though she urged him to go to one of the many colleges in Illinois. "I fear that in Los Angeles, you'll fall in with the wrong company," she warned. "I heard what people are like out there."

His last act was to resign from his job as a mail carrier. Klepfer got angry when he heard the news. "You're the best postman I have. I don't want to lose you. You'll never get a job in the postal service again."

[That turned out to be true. However, since then, the Winnetka Post Office has declared Roy's birthday, November 17, as a yearly event, Rock Hudson Day.]

***

The day of his reunion in California with his father, Roy was driven by him to the little appliance store where he worked. His new job wasn't at all what he had hoped it would be. He'd have to go door to door, attempting to sell vacuum cleaners. He'd arrive on a doorstep with a rubber hose around his neck, almost like a giant necklace, and then *segué* into a sales pitch.

He was still shy, and he greeted mostly housewives with an awkward sales pitch: "You don't want to buy a vacuum cleaner, do you?"

The answer was invariably no.

Some women invited him into their homes for a demonstration, but it

31

turned out that they just wanted to get their floor cleaned, with the intention of eventually rejecting his offer. Two women invited him in for coffee, but with something else in mind.

***

Life in Southern California had begun for Roy, albeit with a rough start. Roy Scherer, Sr. had welcomed the former Roy Scherer, Jr. to his modest bungalow home with a handshake.

After a brief chat, he directed him to his bedroom in back, which looked like it had been originally conceived as a utility room. It contained only a bed and a dresser. For use of a bathroom, Roy had to walk up the steps to the family bathroom, located off the upstairs hall, with bedrooms on either side.

Coming in through the front door carrying groceries were his new stepmother and her daughter, whom Scherer had adopted. Neither of them seemed particularly welcoming. They called dinner "supper," and it was modest fare. Scherer's second wife could not cook anywhere near as well as his first one.

His attempt to enroll in the University of Southern California didn't work out. The admissions office was already flooded with applications from returning veterans. To control the overflow, the Dean of Admissions ordered that only students with a B-plus grade average in high school would be accepted. Roy's dismal record in Winnetka was only C-minus— sometimes a D.

One night in a tavern, drinking a beer with his father, Scherer asked his son, "What do you want to be?"

"An actor," he blurted out.

His father's reaction was totally negative, but not violent, like the one his stepfather had demonstrated. "That's a good way to starve," Scherer said. "Do you know that for every role in Hollywood, there are at least a thousand wannabes vying for the part—at least that's what I heard. Besides, all actors are emotionally unstable. It's in their nature."

Roy needed a steady, income-generating job, and soon. Scherer had a friend Wilfred Rollins, who hired truck drivers to make deliveries for Budget Pack, a transporter of pre-ordered food, mostly dry items like pastas and beans in plastic bags. Their trucks were equipped with refrigerators for frozen foods, mainly peas and carrots.

Rollins met him and decided to give him a job. With Roy's first paycheck, he decided to move out of his father's home and share an apartment with three other truckers, Steve Barrett, Howard Cooke, and Darryl Morton.

Roy later described these muscular young men as "Tom of Finland" types." He quickly surmised that they were homosexuals, especially when they introduced him to a string of gay bars along Long Beach's Ocean Boulevard.

The three men, with Roy in the back seat, drove over to the bars on Friday and Saturday nights, leaving their Westlake Park apartment at around 9PM. "The action doesn't begin until later," Morton said.

Roy thought the men were talking about picking up sexual partners for the night. But his roommates had another motive. Each of them dressed provocatively in the briefest of clothing, tight-fitting shorts and T-shirts. "They were advertising their wares, especially their thick crotches, and selling it to the highest bidder," Roy said. "They told me that on some weekends, they averaged at least two hundred dollars, and every now and then, they hit a rich "john," who might give them five-hundred dollars for a weekend tryst in Palm Springs.

"Even though at the time I didn't have the build of these guys, they urged me to 'sell my meat' (their words) since many homos like young, thin guys," Roy said. "But I just couldn't bring myself to do that—it just wasn't in my nature, I mean, let's face it. They were urging me to be a male whore. Not my thing at all."

"Sometimes, on nights we stayed at home, I more or less suggested to these guys, especially that Steve fellow, that I might be interested in a little (private, one-on-one) action."

"He turned me down, telling me that he had to save it for the paying customers. I never approached another one of them, even though they paraded around jaybird naked most of the time."

Instead of being a prostitute, Roy decided he had to break into movies, and he shared his goal with his "roomies."

They didn't find the idea preposterous like his father and stepfather had. "But you've got to get discovered," Morton advised.

Barrett had an idea about how that could happen.

"After you've made your deliver-

Rock...hot, young, sexually adventurous, and on the make

33

ies, drive your truck over to the gates of either Universal or Warners. Park in front and get out and just stand there looking as sexy as possible. A lot of directors and producers, even successful actors, are queer, and they might go for you. Your body needs to be built up, but you're very good looking."

Cooke had another suggestion: "Before you get there, take off those baggy clothes. You've got to have an outfit like we have when we head to Ocean Boulevard."

The trio agreed that Roy should buy a pair of blue jeans two sizes too small. "So small you can barely fit into them." Cooke said. "Real tight, enough to show everything off. But in case someone doesn't have good vision, make it very obvious. Bleach the crotch area. You've got a big dick. Advertise it. Let some director know you're willing to lie on the casting couch."

After buying those tight jeans and bleaching the crotch, he drove his truck over every afternoon—first to Universal, then to Warners. Although men and women emerged from the studio gates, no one paid him any attention. He would stand there, posing seductively, smoking cigarette after cigarette.

He did attract unwanted attention from members of the crew, especially grips and makeup men. But no producer or director ever approached him. He began to fear that this was a stupid way to get cast into the movies. He told Cooke, "There must be a better way."

It became rather obvious that the really important producers and directors emerged through the gates of their respective studios not as pedestrians, but within private cars.

Then Barrett came up with another idea. He'd heard that a new men-only bar had opened in Hollywood, provocatively named "The Hard of Texas." It was said to be frequented by some of the cream of the Hollywood colony, even off-the-record male movie stars along with homosexual directors and producers such as George Cukor and Ross Hunter.

Dressed only in an undershirt and those tight, crotch-bleached jeans, Roy hit the bar at around ten at night. It was packed. There were some obvious hustlers, but most of the patrons were dressed in suits and ties, and many of them were middle-aged.

An hour went by and no one had propositioned him, even with the familiar refrain, "You should be in pictures."

At the head of the bar, an older man seemed to have been eyeing him for some time. Roy had furtively checked him out without actually staring.

His roomies had never made it clear if he should be the one who approached a prospect, or whether he should remain there waiting to be propositioned.

The well-dressed man answered that question for him. He'd seen that Roy had earlier ordered a Budweiser, so he asked the bartender for two mugs of the same beer.

With both drinks in hand, he headed toward Roy. "Hi, handsome," the man said. "You look like you could use a beer."

Then he handed Roy the mug and he accepted. "Thanks," he managed to say, even though he felt nervous and even a bit silly in his "hustler drag" standing with such an immaculately groomed man.

"Where have you been hiding all my life?" the stranger asked.

"It's my first visit here," Roy stammered, feeling more and more awkward by the minute.

"Kid, I don't know if anyone has ever told you this, but you should be in pictures." These well-seasoned words, previously employed as a pickup line thousands of times before and since, were being uttered now in front of Roy, a desperately ambitious wannabe.

"Are you telling me that you're the man to do that for me?"

"You've got that right, kid. I'm Ken Hodge. This is your lucky night."

***

Kenneth G. Hodge eventually evolved into Roy's temporary Svengali during the interim before he met his more powerful and more effective Svengali, Henry Willson.

After picking Roy up in the "Hard of Texas," Hodge invited him into the front seat of his Cadillac, where he drove him to the Château Marmont, the Hollywood hotel of choice for many stars.

He explained that the hotel was owned by his "Aunt Bernadette."

Along the way, Roy learned who Hodge was. At the age of thirty-two, as opposed to Roy's twenty-one years, Hodge was a tall, blonde-haired, blue-eyed man who was remarkably trim. He'd been born in Rialto, California, in San Bernardino County. His first job in Hollywood had been in public relations, but he had moved up the ladder, becoming an assistant producer on the popular Lux Radio Theater, which Roy had listened to faithfully every week.

Hodge had worked for the Lux Theater when it was broadcast on CBS Radio from 1935 to 1954, hosted by director Cecil B. DeMille. Hodge had signed on in 1942, and he got to work with and know some of the biggest stars in the industry, including John Wayne, Katharine Hepburn, Spencer Tracy, Cary Grant, Humphrey Bogart, Judy Garland, Bette Davis, and Joan Crawford.

"He knew all of them, and invited many of them to his parties," Roy said. "At one gala evening, I met Hedy Lamarr, James Stewart, and Robert Mitchum, along with Edward G. Robinson and Ginger Rogers."

At one party, Roy was introduced to Mickey Rooney. The pint-sized bundle of manic talent later said, "He propositioned me. I was really surprised. I thought he knew I went only for girls. Everybody knew that!"

Every weekend, Hodge drove to Long Beach to stay at the Villa Riviera, where he maintained a luxurious apartment, across from the gay cruising grounds on the sands.

After Hodge's weekend of love-making with Roy, he invited the young man to move in with him. Roy would later tell George Nader, "Ken fell head over heels for me. I mean, he couldn't get enough of me. Around the world, all that shit, no crevice left unexplored. Actually, I enjoyed being worshipped, though I suspected he had cannibal instincts, but restrained himself."

"By Monday morning, he was besotten. Only trouble is, I didn't love him. He was a lot of fun. A lot of johns make idle promises to young pick-ups, then drop them before Monday morning. Not so, Ken."

He promised Roy that he'd become an agent again and morph him into a star. He was already hard at work at the task before 10AM, when Roy drove the green Cadillac south with Hodge in his car's passenger seat.

Their first stop was at the trucking firm where Roy, on the spot, resigned from his job. The next stop was at the apartment he shared with the other truckers. Since his roommates were gone, he left them a farewell note, in which he claimed, "I'm going to be a god damn movie star."

The next day, back in Hollywood, Hodge took Roy to Beverly Hills to an exclusive tailor, where he ordered him fitted for three suits. Until then, he'd had only one suit in which the pant legs stopped above his ankles. Next, he went to an exclusive men's store for all the accessories, shoes, socks, shirts, and belts. Hodge admitted he had fun selecting the underwear and bathing suits.

That afternoon, he enrolled Roy in a gym to build up his chest. In a relatively short time, he would increase his weight to 220 pounds of hard muscle. It was only then that Hodge commissioned a series of publicity photos of him, preferring to send out a very handsome one with Roy depicted shirtless. Not only that, but Hodge hired an acting coach for Roy and also an older woman who taught him diction. "I want you to rid Roy of that Midwestern drawl," were Hodge's instructions.

Hodge even signed him up to take fencing lessons, even ballet training. After two weeks, his ballet instructor told him, "The legend of Nijinski need not fear from you. I think you'd be more successful playing a lumberjack in a movie instead of a ballet dancer. Forget it!"

Only when Hodge had taken Roy to the dentist's office did he learn what was about to happen to him. "He's going to cap your teeth."

When not remaking Roy, Hodge introduced him to the elite of Hollywood—the producer seemingly knew everyone. He hosted as many as three parties a week at the Château Marmont, some of these were filled with mixed company; others had a guest list of men only. As a first for Roy, he noticed that many of the male guests were couples, living together like man and wife, or, more accurately, as husband and husband.

At the first party Roy attended, he spotted an old woman with a wide-brimmed hat sitting in a distant corner all by herself. She seemed shy, not wanting to mix with the other guests. He felt the same way himself, although Hodge had told him to mingle.

He approached the woman, who had little to say to him at first. She was of a certain age; he wasn't sure just how old she was. She spoke to him briefly when he gave his name. "I'm Harriet Brown," she said.

As they spoke, he told her he wanted to be an actor. "Acting is so silly," she said. She did confess that she was homesick and wanted to return to her native Sweden as soon as she could. "I'm here to make a picture… *maybe.*" She sounded very hesitant.

After fifteen minutes, she rose to her feet and left. Later, when he reconnected with Hodge, his friend said, "So you've just arrived in Hollywood, and you've gotten to talk to Greta Garbo."

"I've heard of her," Roy answered, "but they never showed any of her pictures in my hometown."

"She retired from the movies in 1941," he said.

"Maybe she's coming back," Roy said. "She told me she's going to make a picture."

[Garbo's comeback picture was never made.]

After Roy had been living together with Hodge for a few weeks, a man who was to change his life walked through the door to the penthouse. Spotting Roy, he came over to him. "And who are you?" he asked.

"I'm Roy Fitzgerald. And who are you?"

"I'm Henry Willson, a talent scout."

"You can scout me," Roy said. "I want to be in the movies, not just attend them."

"You've come to the right place," Willson said. "Only I'll have to change your name."

***

37

Before Kenneth Hodge and Henry Willson entered the life of Roy Fitzgerald, he had tried, on his own, to break into the movies. A friend had taken some very unprofessional publicity pictures of him before he'd gotten his teeth fixed and put on more muscle at the gym. While still a truck driver, he'd made the rounds of studio casting offices, dropping off these portraits.

His friend, Tom Clark, later wrote about this period in Roy's life. "He was bandied about, forced to wait in outer offices for auditions that were superficial, his ego trampled, and his self-confidence—at that point in his life practically nonexistent—dragged through a lot of considerable mire."

Clark called Willson "the diabolical agent."

Willson specialized in promoting the "pretty boy movie stars" of the 1950s, but didn't possess good looks himself—far from it. His personality was bitchy, his pear-shaped body was flabby, and he had frizzy hair and a pudgy chin. He was a known sexual predator, with a voracious sexual appetite, preying upon well-built young men who were willing to exchange sex in the hope that he could help them break into movies.

For reasons known only to herself, Margaret Truman, daughter of President Harry S Truman, dated Willson for several months, despite her father's harsh protests.

The agent had become well known for renaming young actors, evaluating their original names as "not worthy of a marquee." Thus, Arthur Gellen became Tab Hunter; Robert Moseley, Guy Madison; Francis Durgin, Rory Calhoun; Carmen Orrico, John Saxon; Nicholas Adamschock, Nick Adams; Merle Johnson, Troy Donahue; and perhaps the most laughable of all, Elmore Rual Torn became Rip Torn.

Right from the beginning, Willson had warned Roy that he needed a name change. There are many versions of how he came up with the name Rock Hudson. Roy feared that the name might be too close to that of the B-starlet, Rochelle Hudson, but Willson insisted.

Whether true or not, he told the press that he got "Rock" from the Rock of Gibraltar, and Hudson from the name of the river that flowed along the west side of Manhattan.

Roy was impressed that Willson had once represented Lana Turner during her early days in Hollywood. What he didn't tell him was that she had fired him and signed with Johnny Hyde, who in time became more famous as Marilyn Monroe's agent.

When Roy met Willson, he was still working for David O. Selznick, who had produced *Gone With the Wind*. In theory, Willson's new stated job description involved finding new talent for Selznick Studio, but his real purpose was to pimp for Selznick, rounding up starlets for him to seduce.

However, when Selznick fell in love with Jennifer Jones, the wife of the young actor, Robert Walker, Willson spent part of the time serving as a "beard," covering up the Selznick/Jones affair until her divorce came through.

But Selznick Studio was being phased out, and Willson eventually found himself out of a job. That's when he decided to form his own agency, signing the newly christened Rock Hudson as a client.

On most weekends, Roy had accompanied Hodge to Long Beach, where they'd sun themselves on the gay beach and patronize the bars along Ocean Boulevard. But one weekend, Roy decided not to join him. When Hodge returned home on Monday morning, he found that Roy had packed his luggage, including the new wardrobe Hodge had purchased for him, and gone. He didn't leave a forwarding address, only a note. It read simply, "Time to move on. Thanks for everything."

With his vast network of spies in the industry, Hodge soon learned that Roy was living with Willson. To Clifton Webb and others, he admitted, "I have fallen in love with Roy, as stupid as that is. His leaving has left me heartbroken. It's too much to take. I will never speak to that slob, Henry Willson, as long as I live. He came to my party and enticed Roy away from me."

***

Willson was determined to make Rock a star, and he took him on a round of studios trying to get him cast. He even persuaded five separate studios to each craft a screen test of him. The one that Rock made for 20th Century was shown for many years to the studio's emerging actors as an example of "how not to act unless the role calls for a wooden Indian."

Rock later described to his friend, Mark Miller, what happened on his first date with Willson. "He took me to dinner at Frascati's. Before the first course was served, I felt his hand on my knee. When I didn't object, that hand began its northern trek until he hit the mother lode. When he got his first feel, he knew he'd struck gold."

"Even though I found him physically repulsive, his fingers were very talented. He found out I was just what he wanted. I think he named me Rock as in 'rock hard.'"

That night in bed with him, I encountered the most voracious mouth ever invented. Thank god he didn't take off his pants, only his shirt. And thank somebody I didn't have to do anything but just lie there while he feasted on me."

The next day, Willson drove Rock over to his office and asked him to read for him. As he later said, "It was a disaster. He was impossible. But there was something there I knew I could mold. Only twice in my life had I asked two of my clients to read for me: Lana Turner and Rock. Both were hopeless. But in a few short months, Lana would be Queen of MGM. So I had high hopes for Rock, too. I mean, since it was Hollywood, he might one day be nominated for an Oscar. Stranger things have happened."

Henry Willson with Rock Hudson

At MGM, Willson and Rock couldn't get past Lucille Ryman Carroll, the gatekeeper to the office of Louis B. Mayer. But when Willson learned that the mogul was getting a shave and a haircut, he took Rock over to the MGM barbershop.

Mayer knew Willson and, for the most part, held him in contempt, dismissing him as a "cocksucker."

He introduced Mayer to Rock, who did not extend his hand. At that point, the barber slapped a hot towel onto his face. Mayer called out, "Take this giant anywhere else but MGM."

Willson was on good terms with Walter Wanger, so he set up an appointment for the producer to see Rock, instructing him to define his age as twenty-four.

Wanger later commented on that very short interview: "I might have seen a diamond in the rough there. But in all honesty, I didn't. No jewel at all, much less a diamond. The kid looked awkward, nervous, and frustrated. When I asked him how old he was, he turned to Willson: 'How old did you tell me to be?' That was it for me. 'Out, out, boy!'"

In the aftermath of their interview, both Willson and Rock were filled with despair. But one afternoon, the agent came up with an idea. "I'm taking you over to meet Raoul Walsh."

***

Henry Willson had known director Raoul Walsh for many years. They were not friends, but each man respected the other. "Willson's a god damn cocksucker, but he has a certain eye for talent," Walsh said. "Personally, I detest him. I detest most of the shitheads in Hollywood, yet I still work with them."

Before their meeting in Walsh's office, Willson dressed Rock in blue jeans, a plaid shirt, and "shit-kickin' boots," as he called them. "Walsh always wears boots, even if he's wearing a tux," Willson said.

The agent topped off Rock's wardrobe with a large leather belt with a big silver buckle.

He had already warned Rock not to get a haircut. "Walsh might cast you in a western. After all, he discovered John Wayne."

[In 1930, Walsh had spotted a prop man, Marion Morrison, and thought he might be ideal to star in The Big Trail. *"I had to change his name to John Wayne. I didn't know it at the time, but I had just discovered the world's greatest box office star."]*

Before being introduced to Walsh, Willson filled Rock in on who he was, as Rock had never heard of him.

"He's a tough-talking son of a bitch. He was the quintessential Hollywood rebel, having gained fame as an actor when he played the assassin, John Wilkes Booth, in D.W. Griffith's *The Birth of a Nation* (1915).

He'd been Gloria Swanson's boyfriend in the silent film, *Sadie Thompson* (1928), which he also directed. While driving through the desert, a jackrabbit had jumped through his windshield. The shattering glass cost Walsh his right eye, and forever after, he wore an eyepatch. He never acted again.

Rock was intimidated when he learned of all the legendary stars Walsh had directed: Not just John Wayne, but Errol Flynn, George Raft, Humphrey Bogart, Ida Lupino, Edward G. Robinson, James Cagney, Marlene Dietrich. In time, he would also helm Clark Gable in three of his movies.

Jesse Lasky, Jr., son of the famous Hollywood pioneer, was one of Walsh's best friends. He said, "Raoul is hot for the solar plexus rather than the cerebellum. Let Marlon Brando or Montgomery Clift worry about the psychic probing into a character."

After sizing Rock up in his office, Walsh turned to Willson. "This big lug's got something. He looks like he can make women cream in

Raoul Walsh

their panties. I don't want to give him a typical screen test. I'll actually cast him in an uncredited bit part in my next movie, *Fighter Squadron* (1948). That will be his screen test."

At the end of the meeting, he shook Rock's hand. "Welcome to the movies, kid. Expect a hell of a ride."

***

Fighter Squadron, whose script was by Seton I. Miller, a veteran screen-writer, was an update of two previous films, *The Dawn Patrol* (1930), with Richard Barthelmess and Douglas Fairbanks, Jr., and another movie with the same title from 1938, co-starring Errol Flynn and David Niven.

A Warner Brothers reboot, *Fighter Squadron* (1948) marked Rock's film debut. Although a work of fiction, the movie was based on the exploits of fighter pilots in England before the Normandy landings in 1944.

The lead was played by Edmond O'Brien, who never had the looks of a traditional leading man, and always had to battle a weight problem. He was more at home as a character heavy or as a sidekick. He always seemed to have a troubled squint, and a voice that was adept at delivering bad news. In *Fighter Squadron,* he played a maverick World War II fighter pilot. Robert Stack was cast in the film's secondary lead, as a rebellious pilot.

Other than some minor appearances on screen, Rock had only one major line: "Pretty soon, we're going to have to get a bigger blackboard."

Walsh's patience had worn thin. He yelled at him, "You big dumb bastard! Don't just get in the center of the camera and stand there like a tree! Move your fucking ass!"

When Walsh saw the final cut, he said, "Rock is a terrible actor, but he sure photographs great. He may go far...or perhaps not."

Even with all the abuse heaped on him, Rock was delighted to draw his first paycheck of $125. "I felt rich," he said. Before that, he'd been earning sixty dollars a week as a truck driver.

When Jack Warner heard of Rock's repeated "fuck-ups," he barked out

Rock (second from left) in *Fighter Squadron,* with Robert Stack (center), and Edmond O'Brien (right).

an order: "Fire the hick!"

Walsh did not obey and signed Rock to a personal contract, although he didn't use him again until years later, when they made two more movies, *Sea Devils* (1953) and *Gun Fury* (also 1953).

Along the way, Walsh gave him some advice on acting. "Don't let the audience catch you acting. You've got to be natural, or else it'll show up on the screen, which magnifies a human face at least forty times or more. You've got to underplay, not stand around looking like a dumb but handsome shit."

Devoted to her son, Kay moved to Hollywood to be near him, and almost immediately got hired as a telephone operator in Pasadena.

One night, he invited her to go to the movies with him. He took her to see *Fighter Squadron*, without telling her it was his first movie role.

She sat patiently through it—it wasn't to her taste—but practically jumped up in her seat when she saw him on the screen.

"That's you!" she said, so loudly that the patrons near her turned and stared. "You're a movie star!"

"Not quite," he said, "but I'm getting there."

***

On the set of *Fighter Squadron*, Henry Willson showed up with his new discovery, Arthur Gellen, soon to become the movie star, Tab Hunter.

Willson pulled up at Warner Brothers in his "boat-sized Chrysler" to show Hunter how movies were made. First, he introduced Hunter to Raoul Walsh, whom the wannabe actor found "a salty old character with an eye-patch, a director who commanded his set like a sergeant herding his troops."

Hunter painfully watched as Rock—Willson's big new discovery—blew "many takes, *dozens*, and things got so tense you could hear a pin drop on the sound stage. Walsh was patient, though."

Between failed shots, Willson signaled Rock over to meet Hunter.

Rock shook hands with him, perhaps sizing the handsome, blonde-haired newcomer as competition. As he later told Willson, "Are you setting me up with this guy? You know I'm famished for handsome, blonde cuties."

Hunter, in a memoir, admitted, "I snickered to myself about his name: Rock. Henry obviously planned to mold this rangy, handsome guy into another Guy Madison or Rory Calhoun. I remember thinking, 'thank goodness I've already got a good, short, strong name: Art.'"

Hunter later recalled that long-ago day on the Warners set. "Rock and

I could never imagine what lay in store for us. There was certainly no hint that in a few short years, Rock Hudson would go from a bumbling bit player to being voted 'Most Male' Movie Star of the 1950s. Or that I'd return to the same soundstage to work with Raoul Walsh myself and for a while become Warner Brothers' biggest box office attraction."

Tab Hunter...was he to become Rock's main rival?

***

On the set of *Fighter Squadron*, the picture's leading man, Robert Stack, also cast as a doomed pilot, began a life-long friendship with Rock. "Before I met Rock, I thought I was the best-looking guy in Hollywood. No more!"

The two men came from completely different backgrounds and educations. "I found Rock charming and possessed of a certain masculine charisma. I thought he had a big chance for stardom if he could get over his terrible shyness. I invited him to share my dressing room to change into his pilot's uniform."

Reared in wealth by Hollywood royalty, Stack was the son of an advertising executive who created the famous slogan: "The beer that made Milwaukee famous."

Stack was an outstanding athlete, having been a polo player and skeet-shooting champion, winning the national championship at the age of seventeen.

That was the year he became a close friend and temporary roommate of a visitor from Massachusetts, John F. Kennedy, the son of ambassador Joseph P. Kennedy. "I've known many of the great stars of Hollywood, from Clark Gable on down, but Jack held more attention from women than any of them did, even Errol Flynn. A close friend of mine, Errol, by the way, was always inviting him to bisexual orgies."

"When Jack lived with me, we seduced an extraordinary number of starlets and, on a few occasions, Oscar winners. I won't name them."

Years later, Stack admitted, "I knew from the first night that Rock was a homosexual and was attracted to me. But he was not a predator—in fact, we both set out to prove that a straight man can have a close relationship with a gay one, without it being a torrid affair. We had a different sexual preference, but there was much that bonded us. We often slept in the same bed without me humping him. I had that kind of relationship with JFK—and I didn't hump him, either."

"We went out together to clubs and to restaurants." [*Today, the relationship would be called a "bromance."*]

Robert Stack...slow to reveal his hidden desires.

***

Three years older than Rock, Rory Calhoun had some things in common with him. Both men had been abandoned by their fathers and had taken the surnames of their stepfathers. In Hollywood, both of the actor wannabes became the "prize studs" in the stable of their gay agent, Henry Willson, who helped create their careers.

Willson had gotten Rock his small role in *Fighter Squadron*. But weeks earlier, he had promoted Calhoun for the second lead that eventually went to Robert Stack. Willson viewed Calhoun as a star after his appearance with Ronald Reagan and Shirley Temple in *That Hagen Girl* (1947). But Walsh wanted "a more clean-cut type" than Calhoun.

Rock first met Calhoun at one of Willson's notorious all-male pool parties one Sunday afternoon at his home. "The first thing we did after shaking hands was to strip bare-assed and get into these skimpy bathing suits Henry had bought for us. When wet, the damn material became almost transparent. Henry's motto was always, 'If you've got it, flaunt it.'"

After having "sized" each other up in the dressing room, Rock later whispered a "midnight" invitation for Calhoun to visit him at his home. Calhoun accepted, but instead of saying "It will be my pleasure," his exact words were "It will be *your* pleasure."

Rock and Calhoun did not want Willson to know they were sexually involved with each other, because at the time, he was seducing both of the young actors.

Rock talked very little about his fling with Calhoun except for a brief confession much later to George Nader. "Rory was the most sexually compatible partner I ever had. Our plumbing was in harmony. He had only one demand, a first for me. When he's in the saddle, he insists that his pits be licked."

Rock's affair with Calhoun became so intense during their first month together that Rock asked him to move in with him. The actor turned him down, but suggested that he'd be available for an occasional one-night or a possible three-way (with either a man or woman) in the future.

"I'll take you up on that, cowboy," Rock said. Calhoun told him he wanted to enjoy a lot of lovers and to screw many female stars too. He was also continuing an intense affair with Guy Madison, another of Willson's favorite *protégés*.

Rory Calhoun...a secret tryst with Rock.

As time went by, Rock learned more about Calhoun's notorious past.

He had skipped high school for the Federal penitentiary, based on a charge of grand auto theft. Among the prisons in which he was incarcerated was San Quentin, known as "The Big House."

Willson immediately began to promote Calhoun's career. At a Hollywood party, he introduced him to the gossip maven, Louella Parsons, defining him as "the next Clark Gable."

Even though Calhoun and Rock were passionate for each other for only a short time, they would meet in the future, occasionally having drinks or dinner together.

"In addition, to servicing men, Rory was a notorious womanizer, seducing everyone from Betty Grable to Susan Hayward," Rock said. "He also fucked Marilyn Monroe when they made *How to Marry a Millionaire* (1953) and *River of No Return* (1954)."

Although they started out as friends, Rory became very jealous of Rock by the late 50s. Rock was enjoying the box office triumphs that Willson had promised Rory.

***

After *Fighter Squadron*, Raoul Walsh decided he had no more film work for Rock, and a year would go by before he got another movie role. Since he was under contract to Walsh, the director got his money's worth out of the budding star by configuring him into a handyman and chauffeur. Rock painted his house, washed his windows, shopped for his groceries, and picked up his dry cleaning, or else mailed scripts for him, many of them containing a rejection for a screenwriting hopeful.

Walsh finally sold Rock's contract to Universal for $9,000. At the time, Universal was one of the oldest and most famous of Hollywood studios, billing itself as "The Entertainment Capital of L.A." Around this time, it was merging with International, reorganizing itself into a new entity named Universal International Studio.

The head of the studio was William Goetz, married to Edith Mayer, the daughter of Louis B. Mayer. She was known as the premier hostess in Hollywood, and Rock wanted to get invited to one of their lavish parties as a means of meeting the Hollywood elite. But no invitations were forthcoming, at least not in his early days.

Goetz was launching his "Stars of Tomorrow" program, based on a perception that the matinee idols and love goddesses of the late 1930s and '40s were beyond their "expiration dates."

To replace them, he'd signed a talented list of young wannabe stars who included, in addition to Rock, Tony Curtis (then billed as Anthony), Piper Laurie, Jeff Chandler, Rod McKuen, Julie Adams, Richard Long, Mamie Van Doren, Barbara Rush, and Hugh O'Brian.

According to the terms of his contract, Rock would be paid $150 a week, which he considered "a hell of a lot of money."

Roger Jones, a Universal publicist, said, "Of all the young hopefuls, I thought Jeff Chandler and Rock Hudson had the most star potential among the men. I didn't think Tony Curtis could go anywhere unless he lost that Bronx accent. As for the girls, Piper Laurie had promise, but Universal would waste her talent in the years ahead, and it would also take Rock a hell of a lot of bad films to make it big."

Back in the Golden Days of the Hollywood studio system, MGM and Universal, among others, put their stars of tomorrow into a rigid training program. The studio wanted to prepare them for roles in the coming years. Rock was taught fencing lessons in case he was cast in a swashbuckling movie of the kind associated with Errol Flynn.

He already knew how to ride a horse, but took more training for possible Western movies. "It was fun watching that Bronx kid, Tony Curtis, try to ride a horse," he said.

Of course, he was given lessons in acting, as well as for diction, even ballet and singing.

He became particularly close to his drama coach, Sophie Rosenstein, who taught him to be "less wooden." She evolved into something like a surrogate mother to him, and he learned much from her.

At the time, he had a passable singing voice, but spoke in a register that recorded as too high. One day he phoned his vocal coach, Lester

Luther, and told him he'd come down with a sore throat and a head cold. Luther demanded that he come over anyway.

Once in the studio, he ordered Rock to shout louder, as loud as he could, and he commanded that he do so time and time again. The object involved breaking down his vocal chords. Amazingly, when his throat healed, he spoke in a lower register than before. After that, his voice became known as "one of the sexiest on the screen."

Universal's wardrobe department was commissioned to make a replica of his body for use as a "stunt double" that could get shot at or mangled in a fight. Rock remembered one of its designers, a man, "spending a lot of time measuring all parts of my body. He was obviously enjoying himself, particularly when he ordered me to strip naked. He told me, 'I want to make sure all my measurements are precise.' I knew what he wanted to measure."

No longer would he wear trousers that ended above his ankles. In his new clothes, he was taught how to create "the look"—that is, how to enter a restaurant, or how to emerge from a limousine to greet waiting photographers. He worked out at a gym, continuing to build up his chest for publicity pictures. His trainer told him, "When a director sees that build on you, he's going to insist that you do at least two or three scenes shirtless."

An electrician, Ralph Martine, who, at MGM, had illuminated Greta Garbo and Joan Crawford during some of their scenes, taught Rock where and how to position himself, with the goal of benefitting from the best angles.

Unlike the occasionally rebellious or uncooperative Piper Laurie and Robert Stack, Rock was always the studio's obedient servant, doing whatever was assigned to him without complaint.

"He wasn't demanding better roles, he was asking for just one role," Henry Willson said.

"During my time at Universal, I never turned down a role," Rock said. "Who did I think I was? Marlon Brando? No way! I took the part, even that of an Indian, and did my best."

He learned about "studio dating." Even Universal's homosexual actors were assigned dates, keeping their boyfriends at home. Rock was asked to attend premieres and night clubs where photographers would take pictures of him and his date which would end up in the fan magazines flourishing at the time.

Rock went out with Piper Laurie on a number of occasions, but most often visited her home at dinner time. "He could really eat," she said. "When Rock came to dinner, my mother could rest assured that there would be no leftovers."

She remembered him as a sort of overgrown kid from a small town, a bit naïve at the time. "Instead of being my lover, he was more like a brother to me."

Although many people thought that they were entwined in a passionate romance, they were not.

**

When he became known around the Universal lot, Rock's expertise in male flesh became more prevalent and more obvious. Word was passed around, especially among the grips, cameramen, and prop men. His preference was for men who were "big, blonde-haired, blue-eyed, and hunky." He didn't mind—in fact, preferred—if they were mainly straight but liked, on occasion, to indulge, "for variety's sake," in a same-sex encounter with a gay man. As the 1950s moved on, after he became a big star, he demanded that a director or producer arrange and afternoon break from filming for a "TBF," the initials representing a "Token Blonde Fuck."

"It was amazing how many young men volunteered to service him, later going home to their wives or girlfriends," said Ross Hunter, the producer.

That was only part of the behind-the-scenes story of this complicated young man. In their American Legends series, the editors at Charles River Publishers presented another side of Rock: "During the seven years he was under contract to Universal, publicists made sure he was photographed with women, many of whom he slept with. In fact, he slept with a lot of women, something that was hard for the men in his life to come to terms with. This habit helped him to keep his sexuality a secret for decades. Every time a tabloid would accuse him of being gay, two or three women would easily step forward and say that they had been involved in romantic relationships with him. The other way in which Hudson stayed in the closet was by only taking male lovers who themselves were in the closet and thought to be straight."

**

At long last, Universal cast Rock in a movie, *Undertow* (1948), and gave him his first screen credit, playing an unnamed detective in this mystery. The stars included Scott Brady, John Russell, Dorothy Hart, Peggy Dow, and Bruce Bennett.

The producer and director, William Castle, dropped out of high school at the age of fifteen to work in the theater and in film. In movies, he had one goal in mind: "To scare the pants off the audience." His most important screen credit lay far in his future when he produced *Rosemary's Baby* (1968), starring Mia Farrow, Rock's future co-star.

Undertow was the drama of an ex-con, a former Chicago mobster, Tony Reagan, played by Scott Brady, who is wrongly accused of the murder of a high-ranking Chicago boss.

In the second lead, John Russell played Danny Morgan, an old friend and former colleague of Reagan who ultimately betrays him.

As the plot unfolds, it's made clear that he's engaged to Sally Lee (Dorothy Hart). Together, they murder her uncle and frame Reagan for the crime.

Peggy Dow...who was going to win Scott Brady?

Undertow, whose ad slogans included EVERY BULLET IN CHICAGO HAD HIS NAME ON IT, did routine business at the box office.

***

Rock was immediately attracted to the handsome, macho leading man in *Undertow,* Scott Brady. Both the Brooklyn-born Brady and Rock were breaking into films at the same time.

After graduating from high school, where he had excelled as an athlete, Brady had joined the U.S. Navy. Upon his discharge, he worked as a lumberjack and prize fighter before drifting into Hollywood.

He had this dream of breaking into movies, a goal he achieved with some help from his older brother, Laurence Tierney, who had become an established star after he'd scored a hit portraying the Depression-era gangster in the movie *Dillinger* (1945).

Brady had already made four films in 1948, and would also star in Rock's next movie, *I Was a Shoplifter* (1950).

The day that Rock and Brady first shook hands on the set of *Undertow,* they seemed to size each other up and liked what they saw.

"There was a raw, animal sexuality to Brady," Rock told George Nader. "His motto was 'all cats are grey at night.' He also had another saying: 'A hole is a hole.'"

As Rock later boasted, "I beat Joan Crawford to Scott."

He was referencing Brady's appearance with her, when he co-starred as the Dancin' Kid in their campy classic, *Johnny Guitar* (1954).

As Rock later confessed to Nader, "Scott and I had one problem. Before we hopped into bed, we argued over which of us was going to be 'The Man' that night."

"Both Scott and I talked a lot about our futures, and I knew we were not going to be screen rivals," Rock said. "He wanted to specialize in tough guy roles and perhaps do a lot of Westerns. I, on the other hand, had hopes of becoming a leading romantic man."

On some nights, Brady and Rock were joined by his older brother, Lawrence Tierney, who had one of the worst reputations in Hollywood, having endured several arrests for drunkenness and disturbing the peace.

"Larry was a god damn hellraiser," Rock said. "But I liked him in a funny sort of way. He told me that women liked to get beaten up by a real man, claiming 'It turns on the bitches.' At

Scott Brady's self-appraisal—
"a prize hunk of beef."

times, he was Dr. Jekyll, but after a few drinks, he became Mr. Hyde."

"Scott and I had an on-again, off-again affair that lasted for several months," Rock said. "In the 1950s, we often shared a cozy cubicle at this notorious bath house. There was never any mushy talk about love or shit like that. Our relationship was based entirely on unadulterated, dirty sex. He'd issue a warning before bedtime, claiming, 'I do everything, and I expect you to do the same.'"

***

Joan Crawford was always on the prowl for "the next new kid on the block." When she saw the first publicity photos of a shirtless Rock released by Universal, she told director George Cukor, "Honey, buy me some of that!"

"Forget it!" he warned her. "He likes men, or so I've heard."

"So did my first three husbands *[Douglas Fairbanks, Jr., Franchot Tone, and Phillip Terry]*. I'm sure a man who looks as manly as this Rock Hudson kid is at least bi-…*at least.*"

Crawford called a contact at Universal, who gave her Rock's private phone number. She placed a call to him, and at first, he thought some friend of his was playing a prank on him, imitating the inimitable voice of Joan Crawford.

"I'm the real thing, baby, and I want you to come to my house for drinks tonight. Later we'll dine out, my treat, and go dancing."

To sweeten the deal, she also said that they were likely to be photographed and that his picture would appear in the papers the next day. "A young actor struggling to get ahead in Hollywood needs all the publicity he can get. That trick worked for me."

Dressed in a suit that Universal's wardrobe department had tailor-made for him, Rock arrived at her Brentwood home at 6PM. At that time, she still had her beauty and hadn't yet dressed for dinner, arriving at her door in a pair of shorts. She invited him for cocktails beside her pool after telling him, "You're better looking than your picture."

Since their dining reservation wasn't until 9PM, she sat with him drinking by her pool. She amused him with "wicked stories" about Jean Harlow, Spencer Tracy, Clark Gable and her nemesis, Norma Shearer.

At one point, she suggested he go swimming, since it was such a hot California night. "There's a new pair of swimming trunks in my dressing room over there. You can change into them and have a few laps."

As she downed her vodka, she did not join him in the pool, but sat taking in his magnificent, athletic body as he swam a few laps.

When he emerged from her pool dripping wet, she was waiting there with the largest pink bath towel he'd ever seen.

"Why don't you take a quick shower and then get dressed." He agreed to do that, but didn't feel that it was really necessary for him to shower.

After he'd been in her shower for only two minutes, all the lights went dark. He saw a shadowy figure moving toward him.

"*Shhh*, baby," she whispered in his ear as she stood on her tiptoes. "Close your eyes and pretend I'm Clark Gable."

Joan Crawford..."I beat out all the other Hollywood hussies to audition the newly arrived."

Chapter Three

Joining Willson's Stable of Studs, Moving in a Male Lover, & Seducing Judy Garland

Some Like It Hot:
Stag Night at the Finlandia Baths

Mating Games of Divas Three: Judy Garland, the Rock, and Joan Crawford

Ever on the lookout for new ways to publicize his emerging client, Rock Hudson, Henry Willson conceived his most brilliant idea yet. He'd hook him up with Vera-Ellen, who always cooperated with him for publicity purposes, and paint their bodies with gold paint. He'd then send them to the October, 1949, Photographer's Ball as "Mr. and Mrs. Oscar," the walking, talking manifestation of golden statuettes.

Rock had seen Vera-Ellen as "Miss Turnstiles" in the hit musical, *On the Town* (1949), in which Gene Kelly as a sailor had pursued her.

The Ohio-born dancer, five years older than Rock, would sustain a career that lasted only a decade. She was sweet, agile, and petite on the screen, but off screen, she had a bit of an acid tongue. A former Rockette at Radio City Music Hall, she'd broken into motion pictures in *Wonder Man* (1945), dancing with the gay actor, Danny Kaye.

Both the already-established star and Rock, in separate rooms, agreed to strip down and let Willson paint their bodies in gold. Rock was given a skull cap and bathing trunks to wear, and Vera-Ellen was attired in a bikini. Each of them carried matching gold swords.

Arriving at Ciro's that evening to attend the ball, Vera-Ellen, with Rock, emerged from a studio limousine onto the red carpet. Immediately, the photographers went wild, frantically snapping their pictures.

Before their spectacular arrival, other stars had captured the attention of both the press and the cameramen: Roddy McDowall as a walking mail-bag; Betty Hutton as a bearded cowpoke; Red Skelton as a Confederate soldier, and Ann Blyth, of all things, as a rotating helicopter.

Although he was a bit tongue-tied, Rock became the subject of his first radio interview with the gossip maven, Louella Parsons. Vera-Ellen, also part of the interview, had to do most of the talking. As the gold dust twins departed, Parsons announced to her mass radio audience, "Is that the sound of wedding bells I hear?"

Under the glare of klieg lights, Rock and Vera-Ellen had staged a publicity coup. By the following morning, anyone left in the film industry who didn't know who Rock Hudson was found out. Nearly all the newspapers, including the *Los Angeles Examiner,* carried pictures of them.

Frank Liberman, the personal publicist for Bob Hope and other stars, could only look on in envy. "I knew Henry Willson was behind this. I heard that Rock was a homo, but all his publicity the next morning portrayed him as a heterosexual stud with a great body."

Rock was not in any condition to enjoy the biggest publicity break of his fledgling career. He was in bed sick. That Goldfinger-like paint, obsessively slathered on by Willson (he'd even covered his penis and testicles) had temporarily poisoned him.

[After the night of the ball, Willson learned his lesson. No more gold paint for his prize star. For the 1950 ball, he used blackface paint on a stripped down Rock, who went as "The Wild Man of Borneo."]

Gold-plated starlets outfitted as Oscars: Vera-Ellen with Rock Hudson

To capitalize on the publicity they'd generated, Willson sent Vera-Ellen and Rock out on a series of widely publicized dates. One headline read: "VERA-ELLEN AND ROCK HUDSON IN LOVE." Parsons had been the first to predict an upcoming marriage, and other reporters echoed her "scoop."

Privately, the dancer had a different story to tell her friends, who asked for wedding invitations. "Rock would take me out somewhere. We'd be photographed. As soon as he could, he'd drop me off at my house, then head out to be with his *male du jour*. To put this diplomatically, he is so *queeeeeeeer.*"

***

One of the least-known secrets of Rock's love life was his long-enduring affair with matinee idol Tyrone Power. It was a romance that had begun on the night when Rock, dressed as "Mr. Oscar," escorted Vera-Ellen to the Photographer's Ball at Ciro's.

For years, Rock had been thrilled by Power's presence on the screen, especially in his swashbuckler roles such as *The Mark of Zorro* (1940) and as a bullfighter in *Blood and Sand* (1941). He was known for his striking good looks. As one publicist said, "Ty is as good looking as Robert Taylor thinks he is."

When Rock first met Power, he had emerged from a divorce from his first wife, the French actress Annabella. In the later months of that marriage, he'd engaged in a torrid affair with Lana Turner, in which she'd proclaimed, "He is the love of my life."

But he'd dumped the blonde goddess to marry Linda Christian in January of 1949, a turbulent union that would be characterized by many extramarital affairs on both of their parts.

Months before Rock met Power, Willson had told him that "The handsome mother fucker is the best known bisexual in Hollywood. He dates from the A-list." The agent then cited a list of lovers who ranged from Errol Flynn to Robert Taylor, from Judy Garland to Joan Crawford, from Betty Grable to Rita Hayworth, from Noël Coward to songwriter Lorenz Hart.

As for his many seductions, Power once

Ambisexual and adroit:
Tyrone Power

said: "Why frustrate people? If I'm feeling horny at the time, and I like them, I'll oblige them."

For years, he'd been "serviced" by his close friend and fellow actor, Cesar Romero. The Latin Lover would later provide details of Power's sex life following the death of his beloved. Howard Hughes had been among the first to chase after Power when he had newly arrived in Hollywood.

Although it was a tacky setting, Power's first meeting with Rock occurred in the men's room at Ciro's at the height of the Photographer's Ball.

Both men found themselves standing side by side at urinals at the same time. Perhaps Power had followed Rock there. By his side, Power watched as Rock pulled down his golden trunks to urinate. Power leaned over, pretending to inspect the gold paint job.

"Henry Willson didn't overlook any parts of my body with that god damn gold paint."

"I know," Power answered. "I doubt very seriously if he overlooked *that*."

At the sink, as the two actors washed their hands, Power suggested that they get together—"Just the two of us"—for a get-acquainted session.

"I'd like that, Mr. Power," Rock answered.

"Regardless of what happens, before the morning comes, you'll no longer be calling me 'Mr. Power.'"

On the way out the door, he winked at Rock "From what I've seen so far, I have no doubt why Henry named you Mr. Oscar. I'm sure you and Oscar have something in common."

"You've got that right," Rock said, affectionately squeezing Power's arm.

***

On the Hollywood party circuit, Rock met Jon Hall, the handsome, sarong-clad "body beautiful" who'd made such an impression on him when, as a boy, he'd gone to see him perform in *The Hurricane* (1937) with Dorothy Lamour. "After watching you, I decided I wanted to grow up to be a movie star myself."

"I'm delighted to hear I made an impression on someone," Hall said. "The 'special effects' of that staged hurricane stole the picture from Dorothy and me."

Although Hall was married at the time to the diminutive, blonde-haired singer, Frances Langford, he'd arrived at the party alone.

After seeing him in *The Hurricane*, Rock had followed his career as he appeared in one kitschy flick after another: *Arabian Nights* (1942), *Ali Baba and the Forty Thieves* (1944), and *Cobra Woman* (1944) with Maria Montez. He'd play an invisible man in two pictures for Universal—*Invisible Agent* (1941) and *The Invisible Man's Revenge* (1944).

Dorothy Lamour with Jon Hall in *The Hurricane* (1937)

"If Universal does to you what it did to me, you're in for trouble," Hall claimed. "I went from one silly picture to one even sillier."

Ten years older than Rock, Hall was still looking good and still had the physique of an athlete. The two actors spent most of the party talking to each other on the terrace. When it came time to leave, Hall told Rock that his wife was far away in New York. "I'm facing a lonely weekend, which you could prevent me from having by coming home with me—at least until Monday morning."

"I'm game," Rock said, almost not believing he'd been invited to spend the night with his boyhood idol.

As he later told his friends, "I knew by then he was bisexual. But isn't every actor in Hollywood? I was looking forward to a hell of a weekend. I'd get to see what that sarong was hiding."

Once in Hall's home, the actor went into his kitchen and came back with a bottle of champagne and a fruit plate that the maid had prepared earlier. He handed Rock a corkscrew and the bottle of champagne. "Would you do the honor?"

As Rock began to uncork the bubbly, Hall's hand reached out for him. Before he could open the champagne, he felt Hall's mouth pressed hard against his own, his tongue probing his mouth.

He would share the details of this tryst with the voyeuristic Henry Willson. His gay agent always claimed that he had been the one who had discovered Charles Locher, born in Fresno, Califonia, and that he had changed his name to "the sexier Jon Hall."

Although born in the States, Hall grew up in Tahiti and always claimed he was from Tahitian royalty. Actually, his father was the Swiss-born actor, Felix Locher, and his uncle was Norman Hall, the novelist who had co-authored *Mutiny on the Bounty,* published in 1932.

Willson demanded to know the most intimate details about Rock's weekend with Hall.

"Even before I uncorked that bubbly, Hall's hands were unbuttoning my shirt."

"I have a better idea," he told Rock. "Let's go for a swim. I don't have my sarong, so let's go skinny dipping."

"Our clothes were peeled off on the way to the pool, where we jumped in, more for love-making than for swimming," Rock told Willson. "In fact, we stayed bare-assed all the way to Monday morning. It was one of the most memorable weekends of my life. All that hot sex, those massages with musk-scented oil."

Despite the intensely sexual nature of their mating, the two actors never got together again.

Willson related some surprising details about Hall. "At certain small parties, he'll invite men and women to form a circle around him to watch him jerk off."

"No wonder he's a party favorite," Rock said.

Rock found that story amusing, but later was disillusioned when he met stuntman Paul Stader. From him, he learned that it was he who had performed those hair-raising dives in *The Hurricane* that had so impressed the twelve-year-old Rock. "I was hired as Jon Hall's body double," Stader said. "I did all the risky dives while he got to make on-screen love to Dorothy Lamour."

"I should have known," Rock said. "Another fantasy burst. Let's face it: Hollywood is all about illusion."

***

For his first live-in lover, Rock chose another handsome young actor, Robert Preble, whom he'd met at one of Henry Willson's Sunday afternoon pool parties.

After the party, Rock invited Preble—"Call me Bob"—to spend the night at his recently rented home in Sherman Oaks. After he'd cashed his first three paychecks, he decided he wanted a home of his own, even if it belonged to a landlord.

The sleepover with Preble extended for three years. "Bob and I are great in bed together," Rock proclaimed to Willson. "All our plumbing works in harmony."

Willson warned him, "You're being a god damn fool living with a man. Your career's about to take off. Do you want to fuck it up even before it's off the launch pad?"

Preble expanded Rock's horizons since he'd had such a poor education. His new lover was well-read and knew much about art, literature, and music, even fine wines. "After the first week, I knew he was wonderful to have around the house—and not just to throw a good fuck," Rock said.

Soon, the two men were known as a couple in the very closeted gay circles of the early 1950s. Rock was so unknown in 1950 that he could drive Preble in his convertible to the men-only nude beach at Malibu.

According to Rock, "On Sundays, when Bob and I took off our trunks, there was a mad rush of guys who wanted to put their beach blankets near ours. We were a voyeur's delight."

But usually, they didn't like to be in a crowd: Their favorite times were weekends spent in a little log cabin opening onto the shores of Lake Arrowhead.

This photo was less spontaneous than viewers at the time might have thought. Carefully staged, it highlighted the beefcake charms of then-emergent Rock Hudson with another Henry Willson wannabe, Bob Preble.

Theirs wasn't one of those passionate love affairs of the Romeo/Romeo type. Preble was bisexual, perhaps far more so that Rock. The two men never went to mixed parties together, and both of them dated women on the side. In Rock's case, he not only went out with women—several times with Joan Crawford—but also slipped around and seduced a number of young men as well, sometimes a fellow actor.

Preble soon grew bored with hearing about what Willson was going to do to advance his film career. After a few months, he reacted to the gay talent agent as "so offensive" that he broke from him, in noteworthy contrast to Rock, who retained him and cultivated his friendship.

On his own, without benefit of an agent, Preble nabbed a short-term contract at 20th Century Fox, but his dream of becoming a star, or even a minor actor, didn't work out for him. "That's why Hollywood is called the Boulevard of Broken Dreams," he said to Rock.

If Preble and Rock were ever "outed" as a couple, it was when they posed for a magazine spread evocative of the one that those lovers, Cary Grant and Randolph Scott, once gave to a magazine in the 1930s.

The article was entitled "Bachelor's Bedlam." One picture was especially revealing. Rock was photographed in his bed with his bare chest showing. Preble stands beside him with an alarm clock, as Rock seems to have slept through the bell. The caption read, "Rip Van Hudson invariably sleeps through the alarm—which awakens Bob Preble in the next room!"

The only thing untrue within that caption was that there was no next room. The small house they occupied had only one bedroom, and it contained one double bed. In it, the two men slept every night in each other's arms, usually after having sex.

As Rock made six films in 1950, each a minor role, a feature writer wanted to interview him for Ivy Crane Wilson's annual Tinseltown movie album, *The Wonderful City and Its Famous Inhabitants*.

In anticipation of that interview, Rock had established that Preble would exit from the house before breakfast and return for lunch. However, both men had partied the night before. When the doorbell rang, they were still together in bed. After frantically throwing on his clothes, Preble answered the door. He told the reporter, "I'm the plumber. I'll check on Mr. Hudson and see if he's up."

Back in the living room, he told the journalist that Rock would be right out. He then disappeared into the bathroom.

A few minutes later, a sleepy Rock gave his first fan magazine interview, presenting an edited version of his dreams and aspirations, even though his statements had nothing to do with the life he was actually leading.

"My present routine: a drive to the beach, a visit with some friends, or staying at home listening to records or playing the old-fashioned Pianola some pals gave me for my birthday. My ambition is for pictures with a punch, perhaps *Red Dust* (1932), that movie Clark Gable made with Jean Harlow; or *Honky Tonk* (1941), with Gable and Lana Turner. Of course, my greatest dream would be to play Rhett Butler in a remake of *Gone With the Wind* (1939)."

"I'd be hypocritical if I denied that I'm looking to the security that being a successful star brings. Someday I hope to be having a look at the South Seas from the deck of a luxurious liner—not through a Navy porthole. Been there, done that. I'll rate that swimming pool and a specially built convertible, but no matter how swanky the house, there will be room for my prized Pianola. Best of all, maybe I'll have a wife to share the fun. Then all the dreams I had in Winnetka, Illinois, will come true."

In 1949, Rock Hudson was not widely known to movie fans, as he'd only appeared in bit parts. But more and more Hollywood insiders were asking questions about his private life. Although it was only whispered about, by that time, it was no secret among many in the Hollywood film colony that he was gay.

Although Preble and Rock had continued to date other people outside their relationship, their home life was harmonious, with only an occasional squabble. Rock told Willson that at times, he felt Preble resented all the success he was having, even if the pictures that featured him were minor.

"If he had stayed with me, I could have made him a star," Willson claimed. "He fucked up his own career."

Finally, Rock acquiesced to Willson's demands. In the late afternoon, when Preble arrived at Rock's rented house, he saw his two suitcases, each of them packed with his belongings and waiting by the door.

When Preble confronted Rock, he was told, "The heat is on. I hate to do this, but I've got to ask you to leave. I can't risk getting exposed in one of those magazines, especially *Confidential*. I've worked too hard to get this far in my career to throw it all away. Besides, you told me you wanted to get married one day and raise some kids. Maybe that time has come."

It is not known what Preble's reaction was that day, or what he said to Rock, perhaps some recriminations. Rock shared what he'd done with his newly minted friends, George Nader and Mark Miller. They each applauded his decision.

Preble never spoke about it, at least not in 1953.

At one point, *Confidential* found out about it and offered him $10,000 if he'd expose Rock as a homosexual—and that he had been his lover. Still loyal to Rock, and even though the money was tempting, Preble refused the offer.

***

For a 1949 release, Joan Crawford was shooting *Flamingo Road* with Zachory Scott and Sydney Greenstreet. She was having an affair with David Brian, a bleached blonde hunk who was also one of her co-stars. Since he was busy on the night she wanted to go to the Cocoanut Grove, she called Rock and asked him if he'd be her escort.

On that afternoon, he'd read a statement that had appeared in *Variety* after originating in the *Daily Telegraph* in London. In it, the attorney, Greg Bautzer, her longtime lover, who must have been disenchanted with her at the time, had given an interview in which he stated, "Joan Crawford has a tempestuous masculine side. Guess where I got these?" The interviewer declared that Bautzer then pointed to some scars on his face allegedly caused by her blood-red fingernails.

Joan Crawford in *Flamingo Road* (1949), cast as Lane Bellamy, a carnival dancer.

Henry Willson had already advised Rock that Crawford "bores easily and has these unpredictable mood swings. But go out with her: The publicity will be worth it. She's known around town for the sheer number of her conquests. She has men stacked up on the left and right. As new lovers are recruited, she shoves the used ones to the rear of the line."

James M. Cain, who'd written the novel *Mildred Pierce,* published in 1941, on which the 1945 film was based, said, "Love with Joan Crawford might be a strenuous business, perhaps a little difficult at times, but well worth the effort."

That night, when Rock arrived at Crawford's home in Brentwood, exactly on time, the maid directed him to her upstairs bedroom. After he knocked, she called out through the door for him to enter. Confronting her in front of her full-length vanity mirror, he was mildly surprised to find her in a pair of gold-colored panties with a matching brassiere.

"I was just laying out my evening clothes," she said. "I want you to select a gown for me."

Warning her that he knew little about women's clothing, he selected the red one. After that, she also asked him for his help in jewelry selection.

With her wardrobe chosen, she turned to him. "Before I get dressed, we have some business to attend to." Right before him, she unhooked her brassiere and pulled it off, followed by the removal of her panties. "Now, why don't you unburden yourself of your wardrobe?"

Since he'd already performed the sex act with her before, he knew what to expect. As he would later tell his friends, "When it comes to sex, Crawford is the director, telling you all the exact moves to make—or not to make."

***

Van Johnson invited Rock to his first A-list Hollywood party. Unfamiliar with how such parties went, Rock was unaware that the hosts usually hired valet parkers to attend to the cars. He parked two blocks away, where he positioned his car in the first available space, and arrived on foot, much to the surprise of the attendants.

As he entered, he heard the sound of Judy Garland's voice, and just assumed it was a recording. But as soon as he was inside the living room, he spotted Oscar Levant playing the piano and Garland herself performing beside him. She had kicked off her shoes and was

America's Sweetheart, Van Johnson.

going through her repertoire. In the far corner of the room, he spotted Elizabeth Taylor seemingly having a tense moment with her new husband, Nicky Hilton.

Rock looked around the room and didn't know anyone. Johnson caught his eye and beckoned him to join them. When Johnson introduced Rock to his wife Evie, she looked at him a bit skeptically. "What movies might I have seen you in?" she asked.

"Oh, I'm just getting started. I've done *Fighter Squadron* (1948) and *Undertow* (1949), but I wasn't on the screen for very long."

Rock told Johnson, "Judy Garland is my favorite female singer. I can't believe I'm getting to see and hear her in person."

"Judy's having a rough time," Johnson answered. "We're filming a movie called *In the Good Old Summertime,* but nobody is having much fun making it. Judy is unhappy and shows up late for work. And sometimes she doesn't show up at all."

"I'm very sympathetic to her and know the strain she's under," Johnson continued. "She's a real pro. She can read a script and get it right away. Her problem is in the love department—or should I say the lack of love department? Men don't do her right. She's actually the loneliest person I know."

Then Evie said, "Mr. Hudson, I'm glad you like Judy. I just adore her. But she's drunk tonight. Since you arrived stag, I'm going to ask you to take her home. She's all alone."

"I'd like to," he said. "My buddies back in Illinois will never believe this."

"Suddenly, another Hollywood legend, Lana Turner, joined their group. Rock had seen all of her movies, including multiple viewings of *The Postman Always Rings Twice* (1946).

When he was introduced to her by Johnson, who had co-starred with her in *Week-End at the Waldorf* (1945), Rock was shocked. She was not the screen goddess he had envisioned.

As he later told Bob Preble, "Lana can curse like a sailor. From those succulent lips emerge a torrent of vulgar words."

Lana was in a foul mood that night. Ignoring Rock, she let Evie and Johnson know the cause of her troubles. "Look at him over there," she said, pointing to her husband, the tin plate heir, Bob Topping. "The fucker started drinking at ten this morning. By midnight, I'll need to call for an ambulance. I married him for security, but I'm paying the bills. He's going through every penny he's inherited. Just throwing it away on gambling and in bad investments. Shit! Shit! SHIT! I'm going to dump the asshole. Another failed marriage."

"Perhaps you can make it work," Evie said, sympathetically.

"Like hell I can," Lana said. "The son of a bitch is lousy in bed. His dick's not big enough. As you know, I've been fucked by the best of them. Where is Victor Mature now that I need the big lug? I need another drink." Then she rose abruptly from her chair and staggered off.

As Rock watched Lana leave, he saw Garland approaching.

"Here comes another drunk," Evie said. "Welcome to Hollywood, Mr. Hudson. We're the sweetest, dearest people on earth."

When Evie finally got around to introducing Rock to Judy Garland, she stood on her tiptoes and kissed him on the lips. "What a big, strong, handsome man with a kind, loving face," she said. "The type of man I always fail to attract."

"I'm honored to meet you, Miss Garland. "You're my favorite *sinner.*" She laughed at his mistake. "I mean '*singer.*' I've been designated to drive you home tonight."

"We'll see the dawn come up," she answered.

After midnight, he left Garland standing in front of the Johnson home during the time it took to retrieve his car two blocks away. When he returned, he found her laughing and talking to the two valet attendants.

Once he got her into the car, she directed him to Marlene Dietrich's former apartment on Sweetzer Avenue, off Sunset Strip. She explained that she'd recently moved there, leaving her daughter, Liza, with her father, the director Vincente Minnelli, whom she planned to divorce. "He was always more in love with Gene Kelly than with me."

Inside her apartment, she made for the bar, inviting him to get comfortable if he wanted to. "Strip down to your underwear, or whatever. We're very casual around here." Between bouts of drinking, she would disappear into the bathroom, where he suspected she was downing pills.

Although a lot of his manuscript was censored, actor John Carlyle gave us a preview of the burgeoning Garland/Hudson friendship when he published *Under the Rainbow: An Intimate Memoir of Judy Garland, Rock Hudson, and My Life in Old Hollywood* (2006). Many of the passages in his original manuscript were removed by his editor at Carroll & Graf.

Carlyle was one of the young men, who,

Actor John Carlyle...the revelations in his memoirs about "Judy and Rock" were heavily censored by his publisher.

like Rock, had signed with Henry Willson as part of his stable. Carlyle became a companion of Garland and lived with her for a time.

He remembered driving with his lover, actor Craig Hill, and Rock to a weekend cabin near Lake Arrowhead.

There, Rock told the two men about his first night with Judy Garland, which marked the beginning of a long friendship and "an occasional fuck," as Rock so ungallantly phrased it.

"In good humor, Rock was high camp," Carlyle wrote in his memoir, "a laughing lunatic, but he was a glowering bore when he wasn't. He kept his closet door shut, which he said was hell. His towering melancholy and inherent unhappiness could empty a room, and his buck-toothed haw-haw could convulse the same. The lighter side of him usually prevailed."

"In Judy, Rock found a new friend who could lovingly accept both sides of his personality," Carlyle claimed.

On their first night together, in the early dawn of a Wednesday morning, Judy found a kindred spirit in Rock, and they talked for hours. As Rock later said, "We ripped open each other's insides."

Although he'd been a total stranger, she seemed desperate to talk to someone. "She spoke to me with an openness and candor that I'd never known before. I'd always kept things bottled up. She spoke of her failed marriage to Minnelli and her love for her daughter. 'At times, my husband wore more lipstick than I did,' she said."

"Before Vincente, there was a first marriage to the musician, David Rose," Garland said. "Why did that marriage fail? He told me he was repulsed when I demanded that he perform cunnilingus on me. For that, I have to turn to Hollywood's lesbians. Ethel Merman is very good at it, men usually aren't. I hope you don't have an aversion to it."

"I rarely have any aversion to any kind of sex," he confessed.

"When one of my dark spells comes, it follows with uncontrollable weeping," Garland said. "I'm not able to sleep, pacing the floor, drinking, and pill popping. I become so tired it's like climbing Mount Everest to perform the simplest task. Even if I go to bed, I just lie there staring at the ceiling."

"When a depression comes over me, it's because I get tired of living a lie, not being allowed to be myself," he confessed. "Living a life of pretense can be very exhausting, very demoralizing."

Craig Hill...a secret affair

"I can't be myself either," she claimed. "Ever since I was a little girl, I've tried to do what other people wanted me to do. But at times I can't even do that. Something inside me clicks, and I rebel. Even as a kid, I was a born trouper come hell or high water. Today, I'm known for not showing up and leaving cast and crew standing around waiting for me. I don't know how long Louis B. Mayer is going to put up with my shit. But I can't help myself."

"My reputation in Hollywood was destroyed a long time ago," she continued. "Perhaps you spend too much time worrying about your reputation before you've even begun to build one. People will believe anything, good or bad, about movie stars. I should know. You get used to it. Of course, lies still have shock value, and they can still hurt."

When the first streaks of dawn began breaking through the windows, she invited him to come out and enjoy the sunrise. He stood with his arm around her, watching the sun rise in the east.

"I fear every morning when the sun comes up," she said, "and I have to go out in the world and be Judy Garland."

Then she turned to him. "Now take me to the bedroom and fuck hell out of me."

When he woke up the next morning, it was after eleven o'clock. As he stumbled toward the bathroom, he found a note, hastily scribbled, "You're welcome to put your shoes under my bed any night. Love, Judy."

***

The Finlandia Baths opened in the early 1950s and became an immediate success with many of Hollywood's male stars, who—usually in the late afternoon and early evening—made it the hottest homosexual gathering place in Los Angeles.

It was located on the basement level of the Bing Crosby Building, 9023 Sunset Blvd, in West Hollywood, at the western end of the Sunset Strip.

Rock's first appearance in a movie magazine came in the October 1950

stag night at the steam room

Voyeuristic *ooooh-la-la* from the 1950s. On the top row (left to right) Hugh O'Brian, Scott Brady, and Rock.

Bottom row: John Bromfield (left) shares a wooden bench with Tony Curtis. Rock got to know (in the Biblical sense) each of these hunks.

issue of *Modern Screen*. At the Finlandia, the magazine's photographer was allowed inside the steam room. The manager, Sam Amundsen, asked "my boys" to wear towels around their midriffs for the shoot. Otherwise, they went nude in the steam room. Minimally clad and streaming with sweat, Rock was photographed with his high school friend, Hugh O'Brian and also with Tony Curtis, who was currently appearing with Rock in *I Am a Shoplifter*. Scott Brady, Rock's co-star in *Undertow*, was also a frequent visitor.

The photographer also took pictures of Rock shaving while Curtis looked on; Rock getting a massage from "Richard," the attendant; Brady playing gin rummy with Curtis; and Curtis and Brady frolicking together in the shower. The magazine's editor entitled the article "Stag Night at the Steam Room."

As they were open to the public without restrictions, any gay, bisexual or "bi- curious" male who wanted to spend an afternoon at the baths could do so. They could take some steam, cool off under a shower, enjoy a luncheon spread, and see the hunks of Hollywood in various states of dress or undress. If one made eye contact, there was always a private cubicle where men could get better acquainted. It was a voyeur's paradise, and Rock, one of the bath's most regular devotees, didn't mind exhibiting himself in front of some of his adoring fans and fellow actors.

"We were selling our buffed bodies to the movie-going public, and we had to keep in shape," Rock said: "The boys tried to have a physique like mine, but didn't quite measure up. In one department, I was the subject of envy. They didn't have the 'muscle' I had. Okay, I know it's not a muscle. It doesn't get bigger by constant work-outs."

One of the first of the hunks who captured Rock's roving eye in the steam bath was handsome John Bromfield, who in spite of his marriages (to women) was said to have seduced more actors in the baths than any other member, perhaps equaled only by Rock himself.

As he told Rock, "Pussy I can get at home."

[At the time, Bromfield was married to the French actress, Corrine Calvet. During that ill-fated marriage, Bromfield spent "more time with the boys than going ooh-

John Bromfield...Corinne Calvet had to share her husband with Rock.

la-la *over Calvet."]*

"John was a sort of Steve Cochran and Rory Calhoun blended together," said Roddy McDowall. "I'm sure Rock agreed with me. If a gay man wanted sex, John never minded dropping the towel. He was always generous in offering his body—he was very accommodating, with absolutely no hangups."

During his brief film career, Bromfield starred in a number of *films noirs* and Westerns, including fright movies such as *The Revenge of the Creature* (1955). He hit it big in the syndicated western TV series,

Who might Rock be cruising at the Finlandia Baths?

Sheriff of Cochise (1956), which was later retitled *U.S. Marshal.* He told Rock he'd developed his body beautiful by eating shark liver, rich in Vitamin A.

He was rejected by Cecil B. DeMille during the casting of *Samson and Delilah* (1949), the role eventually going to Victor Mature.

Bromfield could still be seen working out every day with the body-building equipment in the gym, showing off his sculpted physique. He often appeared in public in skimpy swim wear, revealing the outlines of his package. "Do you stuff an orange in there?" Burt Lancaster asked. His question was rhetorical. Lancaster was fully aware of what was tucked into that bathing suit.

At the time, the Finlandia attracted some of the biggest names in Hollywood, including Kirk Douglas and Humphrey Bogart. Forrest Tucker was a frequent visitor, and he liked to lie on a massage table and get an alcoholic rubdown while downing a pint of whiskey. He would then lie there drunk throughout most of the afternoon, exhibiting one of the biggest endowments in Tinseltown. Seeing Tucker in the nude became one of the most gossiped-about attractions of the bathhouse.

Perhaps Paul Douglas would drop in, reciting tales of lesbian love between Barbara Stanwyck and Marilyn Monroe during their filming of *Clash by Night* (1952). His other co-star in that film, Keith Andes, arrived with him, and on one afternoon went home with Brady.

Nick Adams, a former hustler who had been best friends of both James

Dean and Elvis Presley, visited at least twice a week. He never bothered to wear a towel. "If you've got it, flaunt it," he said.

John Agar, an ex-Army sergeant who had married Shirley Temple, occasionally turned up "to show the boys what 'Little Miss Lollipop' used to suck" (his words).

Dana Andrews used to show "basket" in many of his films. "At the baths, I could prove that was no sock in my jockey shorts."

The impossibly handsome and muscular Lex Barker, the former screen Tarzan, was married to Lana Turner. He appeared at the baths on occasion, revealing what was under that loincloth. The gay actor, Roddy McDowall, said, "Lex is the sexiest man who ever lived, with or without clothes, preferably without."

He-man Bruce Cabot, a former roommate of Errol Flynn, was the actor who rescued Fay Wray from *King Kong* (1933) atop the Empire State Building. He was quite daring, allowing a photographer to take a full frontal of him in the shower.

In his memoir about Judy Garland and Rock Hudson, actor John Carlyle claimed that Rock often went to the bathhouse to nurse a hangover.

Carlyle wrote that Rock chose his lover, fellow actor Craig Hill, and himself as his confidants when he caught "crabs" (pubic lice), that niggling hazard of promiscuity before the penalties of swapping body fluids became life-threatening.

George Nader...known as "the poor man's Rock Hudson."

According to Carlyle, "We spread newspapers on our living room floor while he used our bathroom to douse himself with Cuprex, the smelly, greasy, stinking ointment used as a cure for crabs. While Craig and I laughed for the twenty minutes required before he could take a shower, Rock just sat there, nude, large and writhing in discomfort upon open pages of *The Los Angeles Times*."

"Later," according to Carlyle, "when I romped with more people than I knew what to do with, oblivious and insatiable on uppers in the 'tubs,' and also before AIDS, Cuprex was obsolete. Now, so are bathhouses. I wonder where everybody goes?"

***

Two young actors, George Nader and Mark Miller, were to have the greatest impact on Rock Hudson's life—in fact, they became his heirs.

The year was 1947 when Nader and Miller met at the Pasadena Playhouse during a production of *Oh, Susannah!* Nader was a chorus boy, and Miller—a singer taking opera lessons at the time—one of the leads. After only three days of working together, the two

Bosom Buddies: Rock Hudson with George Nader

men ended up in bed, a sleeping arrangement that would last for fifty-three years, a true "until-death-do-we-part" pledge. "Our love affair gave our lives a meaning they didn't have before."

These two young men had met another actor-model, Dick Clayton, and a friendship was formed. Nader and Miller invited Clayton to dinner, and he asked if he could bring along a friend he'd picked up in a bar the night before. "He's a terrific guy. His name is "Roc" Hudson. Universal insists he spell it Roc, without the K. He hopes he won't be confused with the actress, Rochelle Hudson."

[Dick Clayton while still an actor, met James Dean when each of them performed bit parts in Sailor Beware *(1951), a movie starring Dean Martin and Jerry Lewis.*

Clayton eventually gave up acting to become an agent, joining the Famous Artist Agency, where he represented not only Dean, but Jane Fonda, Harrison Ford, Nick Nolte, Angie Dickenson, Farah Fawcett, Clint Walker, Chad Everett, Lee Majors, Jon-Michael Vincent, and Richard Chamberlain. In the late 1950s, Clayton built a house in Palm Desert for Tab Hunter and himself. He later became the guiding light and business manager for Burt Reynolds for 22 years, helping make him the number one box office star in the world.]

Arriving at the home of Miller and Nader, Clayton introduced the actors to "Roc" Hudson, who in a few weeks would become Rock Hudson. The hosts were startled by his size and good looks, but a bit put off by his shabby wardrobe. His frayed blue jeans came to an end two inches above his ankles, and he wore loafers with no socks. His red Pendleton woolen shirt looked in dire need of a laundry, and he also had a distinctive bad odor to his body. Years ago, his stepfather had convinced him that only sissies used deodorant.

Rock was a bit gangly and shy, but he seemed to bond with his hosts, and soon he was laughing and joking with them. All four told wicked and scandalous stories about their introduction to the film colony and the gay gossip they'd picked up. Nader claimed that Cary Grant had come on to him, and Clayton revealed that Fred Astaire had once been arrested with a nine-year-old boy, and that MGM publicists had hushed it up.

By midnight, Clayton stood up and took Rock's hand, telling the hosts, "I've got an early call, but I want to get this big lug into bed with me again for another audition."

The following afternoon, Nader picked up the phone to hear Rock's voice on the other end. At first, he thought Rock was calling him to thank them for the previous night.

"What've you got cooking on the stove?" he asked.

"Beef stew."

"My favorite dish," Rock said. "I'm hungry. Mind if I come over?"

"You're most welcome," Nader said. "Both Mark and I enjoyed your company last night."

Without Clayton, the dinner that night went even better than before, as Rock, Nader, and Miller laughed, drank, ate, and gossiped until 2AM, sharing their hopes and dreams for success in Hollywood.

After that, Rock began to drop in at least three nights a week. Some afternoons, he'd call and say, "Let's go out to dinner tonight. But you guys will have to pay. I'm broke."

Rock, accompanied by Miller and Nader, went out so often together that Henry Willson accused them of having a three-way.

Slowly, Rock began to learn just who his new friends were. A son of Pasadena, Nader was four years older than Rock and had served in the U.S. Navy, stationed in the Pacific during World War II.

George Nader...Cary Grant liked what he saw emerging from the Pacific.

Many of Rock's future contacts considered Nader even better-looking than Rock himself.

He wanted to be a movie actor, but readily admitted that he had no special ability except for his rugged good looks, which he hoped would open doors for him. Eventually, he would be awarded with the leads for some B pictures. But at Universal, he always lived in the shadow not only of Rock, but of Tony Curtis and Jeff Chandler.

For his first publicity pictures, he posed in a tight-fitting bathing suit. As Nader confessed, "Studio publicists found my bulge too big and ordered that the picture be retaken of me in trunks. They didn't want to give American men a case of penis envy."

A year younger than Rock, Miller had grown up a corn-fed boy in Iowa until his family moved to Los Angeles, where he was enrolled in high school. All his life, he wanted to be an opera singer and was known for his beautiful voice. His talent had led him to the Pasadena Playhouse, where at the age of 22 he'd met the love of his life.

Miller was known for his witty repertoire, and for a zest for living and adventure that was almost unquenchable. He always kept Rock and Nader entertained during their long evenings together, always coming up with some new amusement for his friend and lover.

Rock found Miller "a great, big, lovable Teddy Bear," who most of the time was attired in battleship gray sweat pants and mukluks. "He was a vision in brown," Rock said. "Brown from the sun, brown eyes, brown hair, and even a brown mustache."

"Right from the beginning, I let Rock and George be the sex symbols in our newly formed family," Miller said.

In contrast, Nader had dark hair and "eyes as blue as the sky" [Miller's words]. "He had the body of a lean, buffed athlete, and he wasn't afraid to exhibit it."

He also revealed that he, along with Nader and Rock—at least before they became well known—often spent Sundays together at the beach, usually at Point Dume in Malibu, where gay men gathered to sunbathe in the nude, body surf, and cruise. Miller noticed that "George and Rock were the hottest and best hung guys at the beach, as a constant parade of other guys must have known since they kept parading back and forth in front of our beach blankets."

Before heading home, they dined at the Trancas Restaurant, where Rock always allowed his friends to pick up the check. Some nights, they'd go over to Rock's house where he was living on Long Ridge in Sherman Oaks. In his back yard was a barbecue grill where Rock would cook the steaks that his friends had brought over, knowing he had a low budget.

"He always cremated them, reminding me of the old Charlie Chaplin movie where he ate shoe leather," Miller said.

Sometimes, they'd go to the movies together to see *Samson & Delilah* (1949), with Victor Mature or *Prince of Foxes* (also 1949) with Tyrone Power. Their two alltime favorites were *Sunset Blvd.* (1950) with Gloria Swanson and *All About Eve* (also 1950) with Bette Davis. Back at home, they'd practice their impressions of Swanson as Norma Desmond and Davis as Margo Channing.

At least once a week, all three men visited Wallick's Music City, where Rock liked to sit in a soundproof booth. He purchased recordings of Patti Page's "Mocking' Bird Hill," and "Tennessee Waltz," which he played endlessly, driving Nader and Miller crazy.

To make a living while waiting for Nader to be discovered, Miller worked as a carhop at Jack's Drive-In. Rock often dropped by for a late night meal. There, Miller introduced him to another carhop, Floyd Johnson. "It was love at first sight," Miller said. "Within two days, Floyd had moved in with Rock. Our threesome became a foursome. Bob Preble had already moved out to live with some gal called Yvonne. He eventually married her."

Nader recalled that Floyd was very good looking "and just Rock's type. By that, I mean he was very blonde, with blue eyes, very tall and very masculine, just like Rock might order on the menu of love. I thought they were a perfect match. Mark and I kept suggesting that Rock should settle down, fearing he might get into trouble...even arrested."

Mark warned Rock, "Just because it wiggles, you don't have to fuck it."

The happy home life of Rock and Johnson ended almost as quickly as it had begun. He was drafted into the U.S. Army and shipped to Korea. Rock received two letters before the stream of communications abruptly ended. Later, he learned that Johnson had been shot and killed by a North Korean soldier.

The 804-page Kinsey report (*Sexual Behavior of the Human Male*) had been published in 1948. All three men eagerly read Kinsey's claims that some 37 percent of American males have a homosexual experience at some time in their lives. "That's the American average," Rock said. "In Hollywood, it would be like 90 percent instead of 37."

The Kinsey revelations didn't change Hollywood's intolerant attitude toward gays.

Rock told them, "If George and I get exposed as homosexuals, our chances of playing romantic leads will go down the tubes with our careers. No movie fan would believe us in a love scene. They might even yell out at the screen."

He had a theory: "Whereas it was all right for the three of them to go out together (we'd be viewed as buddies); if four of us go out together, we'd look like couples."

Miller noted that when he and Nader went out with Rock, he flirted with almost every pretty girl he met. Sometimes, he even picked up a young woman and took her home. "Unlike George and me, I think Rock was 22½ percent bisexual," Miller said. "To my knowledge, George performed stud duties outside our home only one time."

He was referring to the night when Nader, through an arrangement with Rock, escorted Joan Crawford to Ciro's. Early one afternoon, she'd phoned Rock to be her escort. He had a prior commitment and couldn't, based on having invited a number of people to a party at his house that evening. He told Crawford that he could get a good-looking actor friend of his to escort her instead. "He should have been a bullfighter, if you get my meaning," Rock allegedly told her.

"Send him over!" Crawford demanded.

Later, it took some persuading of Nader to accept the offer, because first he had to overcome Miller's objections. But Rock convinced them that the ensuing publicity of getting photographed in a nightclub with Crawford would help him break into the movies.

"I cried all night until George came back home at 6AM," Miller said.

Two nights later, when Rock dined with Miller and Nader, he said, "When Crawford demanded I fuck her, she told me to close my eyes and think of Clark Gable. What image did she ask you to conjure up?"

"None. I just closed my eyes and dreamed of Mark here," he claimed. Then he reached for his lover's hand. "What happened with Crawford will never happen again—and that's a solid promise."

Rock had been right in predicting that the publicity with Crawford would jump-start his film career. When Crawford made a spectacular entrance into Ciro's, there had been speculation. "Who is her gorgeous date?"

Nader was cast into a small part in *Hustlers on Horseback* (1950), and other minor roles followed in rapid succession.

***

Author David Shipman, in his widely respected biography of Judy Garland, wrote:

"Judy never considered any of her homosexual friends as being incomplete people, and always enjoyed the company of gay men such as Van Johnson or

Rock Hudson. She never regarded them as a threat, and there were several of them whom she succeeded in seducing.

Rock was one of those who fell under her charm, in spite of the difficulties she brought to a friendship… An alternative for Judy was homosexuality for herself, and throughout her life, she was to have affairs with women."

Over the Rainbow: Judy Garland

Over time, Rock became Garland's steadfast friend, sharing in tragedy and triumph. In the early years, he'd been attracted to her sexually, but in time, the relationship would evolve into a deep friendship, when she traveled with him on bridges over troubled waters. Each artist maintained the deepest respect for the other.

In the early months of his relationship with her, he helped her face a major screen crisis: On Broadway, that "belter," Ethel Merman had scored a big hit with the Irving Berlin musical, *Annie Get Your Gun.* In 1949, MGM paid its highest price ever for the film rights, with a lavish budget of $3 million earmarked for its production. Garland, at the time, was envisioned as its star. The plot involved sharpshooters, with Garland cast as Annie Oakley and with Howard Keel as Frank Butler. Although their characters meet as rivals and competitors, in time, they fall in love.

But from the beginning, her physical and mental breakdown, along with her on-set feuds, spelled trouble for the musical. Things became so desperate that Dore Schary, who was in charge of the production, concluded that she was a drug addict in dire need of medical attention. He called in Dr. Fred Pobirs, hoping he might end her dependency on drugs.

At the time, as her personal anguish increased, she began swallowing Nembutals and Seconals like candy. She'd already built up a tolerance for huge dosages of amphetamines and barbiturates. Her situation grew so desperate that she'd undergone a series of six electric shock treatments earlier that spring.

Since he had only small roles, often only a walk-on, Rock, in the movies he was filming at the time, had time to visit her on the set of *Annie.* He found her in a wretched condition, not ready to face the camera.

She showed him clumps of her hair. "It's falling out in pieces. I may soon be bald. Howard Keel has a powerful baritone voice and such an imposing presence I fear he'll steal the picture right from under me. The role is a bit broad for me. It requires an Ethel Merman type."

He reassured her, "You'll be terrific. You're a real trouper. Judy Garland always comes through. Let's face it: You've made millions for MGM, and you will again."

She'd spent six grueling days filming just one song, "I'm an Indian Too," and the footage was unusable. As she told Rock, "I was awful trying to prance around like a squaw singing that dreadful number. Not only that, but after another sleepless night, I can't remember my lines."

He had brought her something to eat, but she claimed she was suffering from nausea and couldn't hold anything down.

He didn't hear from her until three weeks later. It was a night in May of 1949 when his phone rang at 2AM. It was Garland calling to tell him, "Those bastards have fired me. Can you believe that? FIRED! After all I've done for them. There's a rumor they're borrowing Betty Hutton from Paramount and replacing me."

"I've got to see you," she continued. "I'm unable to drive, but I'll take a taxi to your place."

He didn't actually invite her, and—with great inconvenience—had to get rid of a male companion before her arrival.

Within thirty minutes, a taxi delivered her to his home in Sherman Oaks. Covering her nudity, and distraught, she was wearing only a raincoat.

"At that point in our relationship, I hadn't seen very much of her, but that night, she was almost out of her mind."

Inside his house, as the evening progressed, she made frequent trips to his bar, at one point demanding, "Hold me real tight. Hold me and protect me from the world that's moving in on me."

He did his best to reassure her and to re-assert her self-confidence, assuring her that she would make a comeback bigger and better than ever. "I don't think she really believed that, but she seemed to want to hear somebody say it."

She broke free of him as a dark, destructive mood descended. "She was out of control, storming around the room and throwing things. I didn't know how to handle her. She was cursing everybody at MGM."

She finally persuaded him to go to bed with her. She remained awake until dawn, just wanting him to hold her and comfort her.

He drove her home the next morning. She sat in the car in silence. He didn't know if she even remembered the night before.

Sometime later, he was relieved to learn that she'd been flown to Boston, where she was registered as a patient in the Peter Brigham Hospital, a part of Harvard Medical School. MGM had agreed to pick up her

$40,000 hospital bill, plus—since she was broke—extend to her a loan of $9,000.

At the hospital, she endured the painful process of withdrawal from her heavy dosage of addictive drugs. On some nights, the nurses reported that she couldn't stop screaming.

Both Frank Sinatra and Rock phoned her every day, hoping to stay abreast of her condition. On some days, neither of them could get through to her, but they usually kept trying.

During one phone call, she lamented, "I fear I'll never sing again. My career is over."

"Honey, when you're eighty, you'll still be belting them out," Rock assured her.

Three nights later, he picked up the receiver to hear her familiar voice singing "Over the Rainbow."

"I found out today that I could still sing," she said, sobbing. "My voice has returned."

"For that, millions of your fans will be grateful, and especially this fan here," Rock said. He was happy with news that she had "retrieved" her voice, because a rumor had circulated around Hollywood that she had developed a malignant brain tumor.

When she returned to Los Angeles from Boston, he picked her up at the airport and drove her home. He took joy in her recovery, though fearing it would be only temporary.

Two weeks after her return from Boston, she arrived after midnight at his house without any advance warning. Fortunately, he was sleeping alone that night. She confessed that only that afternoon, she'd gone to MGM and visited the set where a crew was shooting *Annie Get Your Gun.*

As Rock later relayed to his friends, Garland told him, "When Betty Hutton emerged from a musical number, I confronted her. She greeted me with a cheery smile. But I backed away. 'You son of a bitch!' I said to her before stalking off."

Even though he felt he shouldn't, he asked her if she wanted a drink. "Not tonight," she said. "I'm also not here for words of comfort. What I'm after is a really good fuck."

In the weeks and months ahead, he would learn that there was a price to pay for being Garland's friend. Until her death, his phone might ring at 2AM, even 3AM. It would be Garland calling him during the lonely predawn hours of another day, when she felt isolated from people, even from the world itself.

Throughout the rest of their days, Rock would follow Garland whenever she performed somewhere that he could easily reach. "I saw her gain weight and lose her looks, but she was still Judy with that amazing talent. Privately, I knew she was a time bomb waiting to go off."

***

Rock's next movie was the 1950 *film noir, I Was a Shoplifter*, in which he was cast once again "with my fuck buddy," a reference to Scott Brady, the star of his most recent movie, *Undertow* (1949). In *Shoplifter*, Rock played only a bit part as an unnamed store detective on the alert for thieves.

The female lead was essayed by young Mona Freeman, a Baltimore beauty who had become the first "Miss Subways" of New York City. Eventually, she migrated to Hollywood, where Howard Hughes put her under contract.

Rock's role was so minor that it was almost over before it began. During its filming, he'd head, usually after work in the late afternoon, to the Finlandia Baths with Brady. Often, they were joined by Tony Curtis.

***

During their early days at Universal, before their career really got jump-started, both Rock and Curtis were bisexuals. "Much later on, we went our separate ways and played for different teams," Curtis said. That was his way of saying that one of them became exclusively homosexual, the other heterosexual.

But before that happened, both of them sustained affairs with an unknown starlet, who had changed her name to Marilyn Monroe.

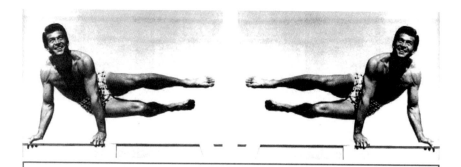

Rock's alter ego and best friend: George Nader. "I got roles only after Rock Hudson, Jeff Chandler, and Tony Curtis rejected them."

Chapter Four

HUNGRY STARLET MARILYN MONROE SWAYS HER SHAPELY HIPS INTO ROCK'S LIFE

Nancy Reagan Merely Flirts, But Matinee Idols Errol Flynn & Tyrone Power Lure Rock Into Bed

With a cigarette dangling from his lips, Rock (right) ponders a question: "Which one will it be tonight? The son of *Ali Baba* (Tony Curtis; left) or Marilyn Monroe?"

Even during the early days of his fledgling career, as he drifted from one small part to another, Rock tended to pick wannabe hopefuls as sexual partners, both men and women. Some of them were destined for stardom; others would drift off into the mass labor force of California—never to be heard from again.

In 1949, a young starlet was seen drifting around the Universal lot.

She'd been dropped by Harry Cohn at Columbia and hadn't yet come into her long-term contract with 20th Century Fox. She'd recently changed her name to Marilyn Monroe.

Rock first met her when he was heading alone to the commissary for lunch. He saw her coming toward him from a distance. She was still practicing what came to be known as "The Walk," which by the time she made *Niagara* in 1953, she would have perfected. As her biographer, Lois Banner, wrote: "She had double-jointed knees that threw her hips off center, so they swayed as she walked. She later used the sway as the basis of her signature walk."

As she got closer, he noticed to his surprise that she was wearing a see-through blouse that showed off her brassiere and her large breasts. She seemed very approachable, very friendly. At this point in his life, he still nursed a desire for women, especially one who seemed as innocent, beautiful, and vulnerable as she was. She stopped in front of him. "Are you an actor signed by Universal?" she asked.

"You've got that right. Roy Fitzgerald here is now Rock Hudson."

She giggled. "I like the sound of it. Hard as a Rock. Do you mind if I make a slight suggestion? Why not Rock Hard?"

Both of them laughed at that.

"Just who are you?" he asked.

"A short time ago, I was called Norma Jeane. Now I'm newly christened as Marilyn Monroe. I hope you've got some money on you. I haven't had anything to eat since this man bought me breakfast yesterday. Times are hard for us struggling actresses."

"I've got a ten-dollar bill burning a hole in my wallet? How about lunch with me?"

"You're on, big boy!"

At table, she meant what she'd said about being hungry. She ordered bacon and eggs and followed it with a big, juicy hamburger and two chocolate milkshakes.

As he talked, he observed her closely. She had the name, but at that time had not yet transformed herself into THE Marilyn Monroe.

Her reddish hair was pulled back into a kind of ponytail, and her summery dress of floral patterns looked like something she'd picked up in a thrift shop. She wore only a thin coating of lipstick and some mascara. Otherwise, her face was quite plain. She had a bump on her nose and a weak chin.

"I don't know if I'm gonna make it or not," she said. "I tried to get a job modeling. This guy, with a weird name, Emmeline Snively, took some pinup pictures of me. He said I had a nigger ass. He also said my hips were too broad, and I didn't have long, slinky legs like Betty Grable. He claimed they were short like Elizabeth Taylor's."

"I think you look just fine—perhaps too sexy to be a high fashion model, but there are other possibilities for you."

"Thanks, Rock Hard," she said. "I need any compliment I can get. I've been put down a lot. I'm thinking of becoming a blonde like Lana Turner. She's my role model."

Long after their food was devoured, they sat talking for two hours in the commissary, sharing their hopes and dreams while nursing two bottles of Coca-Cola.

"I know many gals come here dreaming of stardom, but I'm gonna be one of the chosen few who make it, because I can dream harder than the others."

As they started to get up, she said, "I like you a lot. If you're one of those actors who actually likes girls, why don't you take me to dinner tonight."

"I'd like that," he said. "Give me your phone number."

"It's important for a girl like me to be seen in expensive places where I might meet directors or producers."

"If I can borrow a hundred bucks from my roommate, I'll take you to the Mocambo. I'll call you before seven if you'll tell me where to pick you up."

That night, Rock borrowed money from Bob Preble, who hadn't moved out yet.

That night at Ciro's, not the Mocambo, he showed up in a suit he'd borrowed from the wardrobe department at Universal. She arrived in a gown that had previously belonged to another actress, Shelley Winters, who had become her roommate.

Over drinks, she told him about her film at Columbia, *Ladies of the Chorus* (1949). "I played the daughter of Adele Jergens," she said. "She's only nine years older than me, but she was cast as my mother. We were both burlesque dancers."

"After Jane Wyman dumped him, Ronald Reagan started dating Adele and proposed marriage to her. He gave her a diamond ring. One afternoon, he showed up on the set to pick her up. Unfortunately for her, it was good-bye Adele, hello Marilyn!"

"Reagan's career is going nowhere, so I dropped him and took up with this attorney, Greg Bautzer. He sometimes sees me when he's not with Joan Crawford. He introduced me to Howard Hughes. Right now, I'm seeing Joe Schenck. He's a big deal over at Fox and he promised me a contract."

"I fear you'd be wasting your time with me," Rock said. "I can't advance your career. I can't advance my own."

"You should spend more time on the casting couch," she said. "I'm told it works for men, too. A lot of producers and directors are homosexuals."

"I know that," he said. "My agent has made me all too aware of that."

That night at Ciro's, they made an attractive couple. They talked, flirted, giggled, and bonded, and he genuinely liked her.

"Maybe some producer or director will go for both of us and invite us home for three-way," she said.

"Maybe," he said. "But maybe not."

He drove her home alone. At the entrance to her apartment house, she leaned over and gave him a deep kiss. "You're a real nice guy, Rock Hard."

She waved goodbye, but went only a few steps before rushing back to the car. "It's wrong for me to leave you with blue balls." Then she climbed back into his car and scooted over to his side of the front seat and unzipped his pants. Then she proceeded to give him a blow job that showed a vast experience in one so young.

"Call me again when you get some more money to take me out," she said, exiting from the car. "You sure are big all over. Good night!"

Two nights later, he picked her up again. "This time I told her I had already shot my wad—no pun intended—so funds were low."

He drove her to a hamburger joint in Malibu, where he claimed that many stars hung out when they wanted to go "slumming."

"We didn't see any movie stars there that night, but later, we went for a walk on the sands at Malibu," he confided to George Nader. "It was a moonlit night, and the stars were out. I'd taken a blanket from the car. At a secluded point, I took off my shirt. She got the message, stripping off that summer dress. I unhooked her bra and sampled those luscious breasts, and she slipped off her panties. She wasn't as innocent as she looked. Perhaps Reagan taught her a lot of tricks, although I suspected she'd learned them long before she'd met him."

Rock took her out two more times, on each occasion to a dive. When he asked for a third date, she apologized and bowed out. "We've been acting like high school

Rock from the era of *One Way Street* (1950). "I was a truck driver trying to become a movie star; now I'm in the movies playing a truck driver."

sweethearts, which we aren't. Time to move on with our careers. With you, it's been fun, but right now, I can't spend my nights having fun. I want to be a movie star."

"You're right," he said. "It's been fun. Good luck, Marilyn. Go for it!"

"Someday, when you're a big box office attraction, we'll make a movie together. That's a promise."

***

For his next picture, *One Way Street* (1950), Rock was typecast. He'd been a truck driver when he first arrived in Hollywood, and now he was playing one on the screen. The star of the movie, based on a novel, *Death on a Side Street*, written by Lawrence Kimble, was James Mason.

Producer Leonard Goldstein had liked Rock in *I Was a Shoplifter* and wanted to use him again. "He's got promise," he told his Argentine director, Hugo Fregonese, who didn't quite see it.

Rock's next picture, again for Universal, was *Winchester '73*, a star vehicle for James Stewart, who was no longer the almost femininely diffident character that he'd played in *The Philadelphia Story* (1940). *Winchester '73* was a watershed movie in the aging actor's career as he blazed a trail into the 1950s. By now, he played a much tougher cowboy, filled with an inner ferocity rarely seen from him.

Rock read his part, strictly limited to a single page, and sighed, defining it as "another walk-on—and an Indian at that. ME, an Indian! That's Hollywood! I didn't have to audition for my role, such as it was. You were told what to do, and you went and did it—and that was that. At least you got a paycheck!"

Tony Curtis and Rock, cozy buddies from the Finlandia Baths, found themselves working together again as they had on *I Was a Shoplifter*.

"I'm called Young Bull," Rock told Curtis.

"That's an apt name for you," Curtis said with a wink.

In his first memoirs, published in 1978 while Rock was still alive, Curtis wrote: "In

"I never understood it," Rock complained. "When I first arrived in Hollywood, directors kept casting me as an Indian. I was the least likely actor in Hollywood to play an Indian. Anthony Quinn as an Indian, *sí*, Me as a cowboy, *sí*. Me as an Indian, never. At least in *Winchester'73*, I was aptly named 'Young Bull.'"

83

I Was a Shoplifter, my first picture with Rock, I was a fence who bought stolen goods from the girl who did the shoplifting, and Rock played a house detective trying to catch her. It was not a Grade B movie—rather a Grade Z"

"We started going out to clubs together at night, Curtis confessed. "Even though word was getting around that he was a homosexual. I surmised that because his agent, Henry Willson, was very swishy, with a stable of gay clients. Rock also liked women at the time, and had a good time with them. But eventually, as time went by, he played more for the other team."

Rock, as a house detective, with Charles Drake in *I Was a Shoplifter* (1950).

Curtis left out that he and Rock were often seen at the Finlandia Baths, disappearing together into one of the cubicles for greater privacy.

"Rock and I became best buddies when we met, and that was pure crap in the movie mags that tried to make us out to be rivals," Curtis claimed. "There was never any rivalry or envy because we were never in the same character category. Rock and I had the sweetest relationship and the best times." He also expressed these sentiments in yet another autobiography, this one published in 1993.

What wasn't known to Curtis at the time was that both of them were having brief flings with the emerging starlet, Marilyn Monroe, during her attempt to get Universal to hire her.

[Shortly thereafter, Darryl F. Zanuck took the bait and hired her at Fox.]

In his memoirs, Curtis recalled his brief appearance with Rock in *Winchester '73.* "He played an Indian carrying the gun of the movie's title. He gets shot by Sergeant Wilkes (played by Jay C. Flippen), a tin-horn gambler and gunrunner who sells rifles to the Indians. My job as a cavalry officer was to run up the hill, only to find Rock with the rifle in his hand, stone dead."

Nearly all westerns required some sort of love story, and in *Winchester '73,* Shelley Winters was given the role of a shady lady, a saloon hall girl, Lola Manners, who has a coward for a fiancé, Steve Miller (Charles Drake), who had worked with Rock in *I Was a Shoplifter* (1950).

In reference to the film's plot, Winters said, "Here you've got all these men—James Stewart, Dan Duryea, Rock Hudson, Stephen McNally, Charles Drake, and the rest of them—all running around to get their hands on a goddamn *Winchester '73* instead of going after a beautiful blonde like me. What does that tell you about Hollywood?"

Winchester '73 was not only a big success at the box office, but was credited with launching a renewed interest in the western genre, an interest that thrived in Hollywood throughout the rest of the decade. It did little, however, for Rock's struggling career.

***

A Kentuckian, James Best would appear with Rock in four of his movies, beginning with *One Way Street* (1950) and moving on to *Winchester '73* (1950), *Air Cadet* (1951), *and Seminole* (1953). In the lattermost of those four, Rock had star billing.

A tall, lanky, exceedingly handsome, dark-haired young man, Best exuded a masculine sex appeal, as he demonstrated time and time again, mostly in westerns.

A year younger than Rock, he had begun his seven-decades-long career in 1950, appearing with Audie Murphy in *Kansas Raiders* (1950). Henry Willson told Rock that Best was straight, but not so straight that he wouldn't give in to a gay man's desire on occasion.

He was known to be seeing a lot of Murphy, who had been the most decorated U.S. soldier of World War II, and was rumored to be a secret homosexual.

According to Rock's close friend, Mark Miller, Best represented a turning point in the life of Rock. More than any other star in Hollywood, Rock seemed to have realized that he had an amazing talent for seducing men who did not immediately self-identify as gay. In fact, he pre-

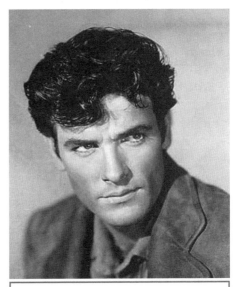

To attract James Best, a basically straight actor, Rock had stiff competition: The most decorated soldier of World War II.

ferred men who were basically straight or at least bisexual, and that became more evident as he rose on the rungs of stardom on the Hollywood ladder.

Presumably, Rock interpreted macho and supposedly "straight" men as sexier than their more flamboyant counterparts. This preference became more obvious as Rock's "star quotient" increased and as news of his sexual exploits became more widely bruited, underground, through the entertainment community.

"On many occasions, he couldn't get men such as Best to return the (seductive) favor, but at least he would get them to unbuckle and unzip," Miller claimed. "Sometimes, Rock would pursue a straight man very aggressively, and would almost never give up. In fact, the more these guys held him off, the greater he'd interpret it as a challenge. I think at times he enjoyed the chase more than the conquest."

Rock had been attracted to Best when he spotted him on the set of *One Way Street,* but when he made *Winchester '73,* "he moved in for the kill" (Miller's words). "I guess Rock figured that if Audie was getting it, why not him?"

One weekend, Best accepted Rock's invitation to spend four days with him in a cabin (rented by Willson) beside Lake Arrowhead.

Rock got to know Best, learning that he had lost his mother when he was three years old. She had died in 1929 of tuberculosis, and he had been sent to an orphanage. He was later adopted, and grew up in Indiana.

During World War II, as a soldier trained in Biloxi, Mississippi, he'd been a gunner aboard a B-17 bomber. At war's end, he was stationed in Germany, trying to help stabilize that war-torn land. He later traveled around Europe, performing in plays and skits for U.S. troops.

After his discharge, he headed for Hollywood, where he was pursued by many of the starlets at Universal. Even though he would marry three times, he was also chased by gay men such as Audie Murphy and Rock.

As Rock told Willson, "Those blue movies you kept at the cabin helped me put Jewel in the mood."

"Why are you calling him Jewel? That sounds like a drag queen."

"That's the name his mom gave him back one hot July morning when he was born in Kentucky."

***

Born Bernard Schwarz in the Bronx the same year as Rock (1925), Anthony (Tony) Curtis was the son of Hungarian Jewish immigrants, Manuel Schwarz, who'd been an actor in Budapest, and his mother, Helen. Tony said she was a "deadringer" for Pola Negri, a reference to the silent screen vamp.

Curtis grew up facing the ravages of the Depression, seeing his family get dispossessed and thrown out on the street, surviving in a condemned tenement building on a diet of goulash without meat.

"I was the prettiest boy who ever arrived in Hollywood," Tony Curtis bragged. "Every man or woman in Tinseltown chased after me, and most of them usually got me."

On the tough streets of New York, he suffered the hard knocks. He later admitted that he developed an interest in sex at the age of ten. "This girl and I went to a movie house, where I masturbated as I held her hand."

The soon-to-be renamed Anthony (Tony) Curtis arrived in Hollywood and got cast in a movie, *Criss Cross* (1949) doing the rumba with Yvonne De Carlo, Rock's future leading lady.

"At Universal, I was a big bag of nothing in my first months," he told Rock. "Held together by spit and glue. I had the looks, black, curly hair, and piercing blue eyes, but I had to get rid of my thick Bronx accent with voice lessons."

"I was hungry for success and money...and for lots and lots of pussy," he told director Charles Lamont on the set of *I Was a Shoplifter* (1950).

"That wasn't the complete story he was telling," Lamont said. "The kid went around with a lump in his pants. But he seemed to get it taken care of by our female lead, Mona Freeman, and also by our newcomer, Rock Hudson. Those two guys headed off to the Finlandia Baths after work."

As Curtis recalled, "That *Shoplifter* movie with Rock and me was rated as a Grade B picture. Don't you believe that. It was shit. But Rock and I really bonded and became great pals. He used to invite me to parties at his house. Actually, they were more like orgies. We'd go out to the clubs."

Ironically at this same time in 1949, both Rock and Curtis were also having brief flings with Marilyn Monroe. Rock would listen patiently as Curtis droned on with stories about his seduction of the emerging superstar. Rock never informed Curtis that he was also seducing Marilyn at the time. According to Rock, "I didn't want to make him jealous."

It would not be until near the end of his life that Curtis confessed to a gay newspaper in London that he'd been a bisexual in Hollywood during his early days there. Rock told Mark Miller, "When I used to stage orgies at my home, I could always count on Tony to be at the bottom of the pile."

When not at the Finlandia Baths, Rock and Curtis made Schwab's Drugstore their hangout. "Our two best pals at the time were John Derek, as handsome as could be, and Jeffrey Hunter, almost equally beautiful, and very cool, and friendly, "Curtis said. "Those guys were supposed to be straight, but John, back when he was known as Derek Harris, was a hustler, and I thought Jeffrey was in love with Robert Wagner."

When Curtis married Janet Leigh, he disingenuously told her, "Rock made out like a bandit with both Derek and Hunter. I loved those guys, but we parted company when they wanted to indulge in homo nights. Even back then, I was a man strictly for the ladies."

[Hollywood husbands were never known for being honest or candid with their wives.]

***

Rock's sixth film, *Peggy* (1950), marked a turning point in his fledgling career. It was a fluffy comedy directed by Frederick de Cordova, starring Diana Lynn, Charles Coburn, and Charlotte Greenwood. Cast as an Ohio State quarterback, Johnny ("Scat") Mitchell, Rock in one scene kisses Lynn, who plays the title role of Peggy Brookfield.

During screenings of *Peggy* in movie theaters across America, teenage girls sighed with infatuation, and gay boys celebrated a new "Beefcake King" for the 1950s. Fan letters for Rock from teenage girls, plus a lot of boys, too, poured into the mail room at Universal. The excitement caused studio executives to take notice, many of them looking at Rock for the first time. A suggestion was floated that he might be groomed for future lead roles.

"If only he could act," said one executive. "Let's cast him in a few more Bs and see what happens. At least he's someone to watch."

"In *Peggy* (1950), I played a football jock named Johnny Higgins. Universal was deluged with fan mail from high school girls."

Rock later told Henry Willson, "I've tackled many a man, but never on the football field."

Rock performed and blended so well with his director, Frederick de Cordova, that he also cast him in a small role in an upcoming film. During conversations with De Cordova, Rock found him very candid. "My parents were con artists," he admitted. "When my dad ran up too many bills, we skipped town."

As an adult, De Cordova worked on Broadway as an actor, stage manager, dialogue director, and ultimately as a director of feature films, helming such stars as Errol Flynn, Audie Murphy, Yvonne De Carlo, Bob Hope, Humphrey Bogart, and Elvis Presley. For his next picture, he had cast Diana Lynn once again as the female lead.

[In one of Lynn's future films, Bedtime for Bonzo *(1951), her co-stars would include both Ronald Reagan and a chimpanzee which, in the 1980s, would subject the future President of the United States to ridicule.]*

In *Peggy*, character actor and white supremacist Charles Coburn gets a smooch from Diana Lynn (left) as Barbara Lawrence looks on.

Coburn later said, "Diana had the hots for Ronald Reagan. At the time, I was chasing Nancy Davis (later, Reagan) around the room to pinch her ass."

In the 1970s, De Cordova would become better known as the producer of *The Tonight Show Starring Johnny Carson.* The producer described his job as "chief traffic cop, talent scout, and Johnny's number one fan and critic—all rolled into one."

The plot of *Peggy* was flimsy: Professor "Brooks" Brookfield (played by veteran actor Charles Coburn) moves to Pasadena with his two pretty daughters, Peggy (Diana Lynn) and Susan (Barbara Lawrence). Their neighbor, Mrs. Fielding (Charlotte Greenwood), urges the two beautiful girls to enter the annual Rose Bowl Beauty Pageant. Her son, Tom (Charles Drake), makes eyes at Peggy, not knowing that her heart belongs to Rock, the football star.

A musical prodigy at the age of twelve, Lynn had played with the Los Angeles Junior Symphony. Rock had recently seen her in *My Friend Irma* (1949). She told him that she was looking forward to working with Reagan. "Before that movie is wrapped, I plan to become engaged to him. I'll make him forget all about Jane Wyman."

"I thought you already have a husband," Rock said.

"Darling, all Hollywood husbands carry an expiration date," she said.

Born in 1877, Charles Coburn, a son of Georgia, had made his Broadway debut in 1901. Rock had admired several of his screen performances, but not his politics. He was a staunch member of the White Citizens' Council, a group opposed to integration.

From among the players on the set of *Peggy*, it wasn't Diana Lynn who'd end up in Rock's bed. Rather, it was James Best, cast once again in a minor role with Rock.

As Rock confessed to George Nader, "For about a week or two, we hung out together. I pressed sex onto him, and he kept complaining that he was not into it. But I wouldn't take no for an answer, and I kept the handsome lug drained. He suggested that the two of us should just be friends. But I reminded him that there are all sorts of friends, including one who says he's not into it, yet crawls into bed for a fantastic blast-off. He liked it so much he sometimes wakes me up at 3AM, urging me to do it again."

***

As an assistant and a kind of talent scout for producer David O. Selznick, Henry Willson was always searching "for the next pretty boy," whom he could—after a name change and a few bouts on his casting couch—launch into a movie career.

That led him to the discovery of Derek Sullivan Harris, a strikingly handsome young man with dark, wavy hair and a perfectly sculpted physique. He was the son of Lawson Harris, a writer-director, and a minor actress, Dolores Johnson, who had worked for Hal Roach and Cecil B. De-Mille.

Drafted in 1944, Derek saw action in the Philippines during the closing months of World War II.

Back home, he decided he wanted to be an actor, but couldn't find work. Money was so tight that for a brief time, he worked as a hustler. As he'd later tell Willson, "Guys were always propositioning me, so I decided to make the fuckers pay for it."

Willson was delighted with the bedtime performance of the young man, and changed his name to "Dare Harris." The actor made only two pictures under that name: *Since You Went Away* (1944), followed by *I'll Be Seeing You* (1945) with Ginger Rogers. Bosley Crowther in *The New York Times* wrote that he was "plainly an idol for the girls."

After that, the actor himself changed his name to John Derek.

In gratitude for Rock's cooperation and for his recent successes, Willson decided to present Derek to him as a party favor. The agent told Rock, "The boy is a real winner, baby, hot to trot. If a contest were held in Hollywood for the most beautiful penis, he would win."

He arranged for the two actors to spend three days together at a villa

90

in Palm Springs "where you guys can get better acquainted."

After his first night in the desert with Derek, Rock phoned Willson: "He's the kind of boy I could really go for. Do you think I could get him to bleach his hair blonde? If so, he'd be perfect."

"Listen to me. You let the kid keep his hair the way it is. Rory Calhoun's doing all right with dark hair."

During their long weekend together, Rock got to know more about his new and impressive lover. He claimed that Elizabeth Taylor, though years younger than he was, had developed a crush on him in school. He also confessed that Willson had arranged a weekend for him in this same villa with Lana Turner. "She couldn't get enough of me."

Rock appraised his nude body. "I wonder why."

After their first night together, although Rock was physically attracted to Derek, he evaluated him as "a real bullshitter." As he told Willson, "He swears he's the son of Greta Garbo."

More accurately, Derek went on to inform Rock that Selznick had insisted he go out on dates with his co-star, Shirley Temple, who at the time was trying to make a transition into adult roles.

In her memoir, *Child Star,* she presented an unflattering portrait of Derek: "I found him a self-important young man who had pleasant features, perhaps a little too sensitive for my taste."

She also reported on his psychological problems, stating that on some occasions, he would perform irrational acts such as "stabbing the air with a big kitchen knife."

That Sunday afternoon in Palm Springs, Derek told Rock he was a painter, and asked him to pose for him in the nude.

"Okay," Rock agreed, "but when you go to pick up your artist's supplies, make sure the canvas is big enough to depict me."

"Braggart!" Derek said.

That afternoon, after Rock had posed for three hours in the nude beside the pool, he grew bored. Then he checked out the unfinished

Depicted above, John Derek in *The Leather Saint* (1956).

"He is a beauty, and I posed for him, a nude portrait," Rock said. "But at midnight, Derek goes crazy. I nicknamed him 'The Slasher.'"

portrait. "You certainly captured my manly glory—in fact, you made it the focal point of the painting. I fear it won't hang in any museum. Perhaps in a queen's bathroom."

Derek seemed insulted by that remark, but that night over dinner, many other thoughts seemed to trouble him. He had been drinking heavily and attacking everyone who had come into his life, including Willson, Temple, and Selznick. He claimed that "as a pretty boy, I was held down and raped by four soldiers in the Philippines." He also bitterly resented being "used and abused" by clients when he earned desperately needed cash as a hustler.

"The more liquor he drank, the most hostile he became," Rock confessed in a phone call to Willson the next day. "Hatred was just bubbling out of him."

By midnight, Rock went to bed, but Derek stayed up and continued drinking. At around 2AM, he heard cursing and shouting out by the pool and went to investigate. To his shock, he saw Derek slashing the unfinished portrait of him with a kitchen knife. "This knife-wielding crazy then seemed to stab the air, like he was attacking some enemy. I thought he was a candidate for a mental ward."

Back in his bedroom, Rock locked the door, but heard no more sounds. When he woke up at 10AM, Derek was frying bacon and eggs. "Hi ya, sleepyhead," he said. There was no mention of the previous night, and the slashed painting was gone. Derek's dark mood had passed.

Sober, Derek was "adorable once again," as Rock told Willson, "but I don't think I'll be shacking up with him again."

In 1948, Rock went to see Derek in *Knock on Any Door*, in which he was cast as Nick ("Pretty Boy") Romano, an unrepentant killer opposite Humphrey Bogart.

He'd later appear in some notable films such as *All the King's Men* (1949), but most of his career in the 1950s would be devoted to crime dramas, westerns, pirate adventures, or costume epics such as *The Adventures of Hajji Baba* (1954).

"I wasn't surprised to see him cast as the unhinged John Wilkes Booth in *Prince of Players* (1955)," Rock later said.

As his screen career faded, Derek become more famous for marrying glamourous young starlets who included Ursula Andress and Linda Evans. He'd become even better known as the Svengali to his last wife, Bo Derek. She appeared as Dudley Moore's sexual fantasy in the Blake Edwards movie, *10*, in 1979. She became a sex symbol, her cornrow hairstyle evolving into a national fad.

When Rock co-starred with Linda Evans in the 1984 TV series, *Dynasty*, only months before he died, his AIDS-ravaged appearance provoked a nationwide scandal, which will be explored later in this book.

***

For yet another 1950 release, Rock was given tenth billing in a "tits-and-sand" Arab adventure, *The Desert Hawk*, directed by Frederick de Cordova. It would mark the first of four movies in which he would appear with the Canadian actress, Yvonne De Carlo. A beautiful brunette with blue-gray eyes, she was "Queen of the Bs" at Universal. Originally, she'd been signed to a contract with Paramount as a possible replacement for Dorothy Lamour, who was getting tired of that sarong.

De Carlo's breakthrough role had come when she was cast in *Salome, Where She Danced* (1945). Producer Walter Wanger defined her as "the most beautiful girl in the world." She also became known as the "Queen of Technicolor," although flame-haired Rhonda Fleming also held that title.

Rock liked De Carlo, but not her view of women. She antagonized females in a 1976 interview when she said: "I'm all for men, and I think they ought to stay up there and be the bosses and have women wait on them hand and foot and put their slippers on and hand them the pipe and serve seven-course meals, as long as they open the door, support the woman, and do their duty in the bedroom."

In *The Desert Hawk* (1950), De Carlo was cast as Princess Scheherazade, who is forced to marry the cruel ruler, Prince Murad (George Macready). Through a mistaken identity, she is sold on the slave market to the handsome, dashing Desert Hawk himself (Richard Greene). Universal "hawked" the film by focusing publicity on De Carlo "as a slave in the palace of 1000 delights."

Given tenth billing as an Arab commander,

In *The Desert Hawk* (1950), in which Rock had only tenth billing, the dashingly handsome Richard Greene played the lover of Yvonne De Carlo.

But in De Carlo's next picture, *Scarlet Angel*, Rock would play leading man to the international beauty hailed as "The Queen of Technicolor."

Rock detested his role in *The Desert Hawk*, and urged all of his friends not to see it.

93

Captain Ras, Rock said, "I was supposed to protect the princess, but didn't do a good job of it."

"I can't bear to watch *The Desert Hawk*," Rock said, years later. "That goes for all those early movies of mine. Either as an Arab or an Indian, I looked like a tongue-tied galoot."

Although De Cordova liked Rock personally, he agreed with him. "I don't think you'll win an Oscar for *The Desert Hawk*, and I also won't as its director."

He later said, "Rock knew how bad he was. To his credit, he urged me to reshoot some scenes, but I told him I was working against the time clock on a low budget. The only way I was going to reshoot a scene with either Tony Curtis or Rock was if their dicks popped out of their pantaloons."

Rock attended the film's first screening with De Cordova. When it was over, Rock turned to him and said, "No critic will hail me as Valentino's replacement as the desert sheik."

***

The most elusive of the straight men Rock pursued in the early 1960s was fellow actor Jeffrey Hunter at the dawn of his acting career in Hollywood.

Born in New Orleans, he and Rock were about the same age. He didn't have a southern accent because he'd grown up in Milwaukee. During World War II, he'd joined the U.S. Navy. After his discharge, he'd studied theater at Northwestern University, later taking a graduate course at UCLA.

There, he was spotted by a talent scout, which led to a contract with 20th Century Fox that lasted throughout the 1950s. He became friends with another good-looking contract player, Robert Wagner. Each was evaluated as suitable for the same roles.

Hunter entered Rock's orbit when he began to hang out at Schwab's Drugstore with him, along with John Derek and Tony Curtis.

As Rock told Henry Willson, "It was Jeff's piercing eyes that first attracted me. He has that clean-cut, all-American look that's so wholesome you want to eat him alive."

He invited Rock for a screening of his first film, *Julius Caesar* (1950), in which he appeared with another newcomer, Charlton Heston. This film received very limited distribution and, of course, is not to be confused with the more celebrated 1953 version of *Julius Caesar* that had starred Marlon Brando.

After the screening, Rock invited Jeffrey for dinner at a little-known restaurant in West Hollywood, where, except for one woman, all the other patrons were male. "I was hoping that Jeff would take that as a clue, but he didn't seem to."

"I feel my film career has ended before it even began," Hunter said.

"You weren't all that bad," Rock assured him. "You should see me in one of my walk-ons."

Later, he told Willson, "We drank and then drank some more, and I made a pass at him, but he didn't receive. Could he be that naïve? I may have been misinformed, and I have not a shred of evidence, but I thought he was having an affair with Wagner. "

POOL PLAY: Robert Wagner with Jeffrey Hunter. When the gay gossip columnist, Mike Connolly, saw this photo, he told Henry Willson, "I think it depicts Wagner at the point of climax as he sodomizes Hunter."

"Later on," Rock said, "I learned that he was dating this cute little actress, Barbara Rush. They'd get married that year (1950). Barbara and I would make two movies together, beginning with *Magnificent Obsession.*"

Wagner and Hunter later became co-stars, appearing together in such films as *A Kiss Before Dying* (1956); *The True Story of Jesse James* (1957), and *In Love and War* (1958).

"Where Jeffrey was concerned, the race was on," Rock claimed. "I had not given up on him. My luck changed when I invited him for a tequila-soggy weekend in Tijuana."

On the way there, Rock boasted about the women he was seducing at the time. His claims, during this bisexual era of his life, were more or less true, but they were a decoy for the real reason he was luring Hunter to points South of the Border.

Later, Rock delivered a detailed account to Henry Willson of his weekend adventure in Mexico with Jeffrey Hunter. "We didn't go to the bullfights or do any of the tourist things," Rock admitted. "We headed out for a night on the prowl. I took him to some titty bars, where two good-looking gringos like us were surrounded by *putas*. Before midnight, I took him to one of the notorious sex shows. One featured this really hot guy who came out barechested, wearing only a matador's tight-fitting pants. He stripped them off and proceeded to screw this blonde, perhaps an American girl, who had porcelain-like skin. Jeff was getting hot…and hotter."

"At around 2AM, we headed back to our dump of a hotel. I was happy to see our cozy double bed. I stripped off everything. Perhaps not wanting to appear a sissy wimp, Jeff did the same. I liked what I saw, more than liked, actually."

"When he fell safely asleep in his drunken coma, I moved in on him. At first I met with minor protest, but he'd been horny all night, so he decided against his better judgment to give in to me. I got my man, but he didn't reciprocate—not even with a kiss goodnight."

According to Rock, "I wanted to continue our intimacy the next day, but he was having none of that."

"Let's forget that last night ever happened," he told Rock. "If you want to remain my friend, I trust it won't happen again."

"If that's your wish," Rock said. "But don't blame me. Blame yourself for being such a god damn good looker."

***

Set for a 1950 release, Rock's last film for that year was *Shakedown*, a crime *film noir* directed by Joseph Pevney and starring Howard Duff, Brian Donlevy, Lawrence Tierney, and Bruce Bennett. The leading ladies were named Peggie Castle and Peggy Dow.

Universal thought so little of the film that the studio did not renew its copyright, which is now in public domain.

Shakedown was one of the lesser efforts of producer Ted Richmond. During the course of his long life (he died in 2013 at the age of 103), he would produce far more prestigious films, the best-known of which was *Papillon* (1974) with Steve McQueen and Dustin Hoffman.

Pevney, the son of a Jewish watchmaker in New York, made his showbiz debut in vaudeville as a boy soprano in 1924. During his career, he'd direct everybody from Joan Crawford and James Cagney to Debbie Reynolds. He would helm Rock in future films.

The star of the picture, Howard Duff, had been cast as an unscrupulous

When not "boffing" Ava Gardner, Howard Duff took time out to hang with Rock.

96

newspaper photographer, Jack Early, a larcenous con artist and black-mailer. Brian Donlevy, as racketeer Nick Palmer, doesn't like to be photographed. He pays Early to take pictures that will frame his one of his henchman, Colton, as portrayed by Tierney.

Early (Duff) double-crosses Palmer (Donlevy) and informs Colton (Tierney) that his boss plans to frame him. Shortly afterward, Palmer is killed by a car bomb. Early becomes famous for taking a picture of the event. Eventually, Early himself is murdered by Colton, but just before he dies, he manages to snap a picture of his murderer in the act.

"I'd heard that Universal wanted to build up Rock for future leads, but I saw no evidence of that," Pevney said. "In *Shakedown*, he plays a nightclub doorman. All he had to do was open the door for Donlevy, and he couldn't even do that until after a dozen or so rehearsals. He had a southpaw but the door had to be opened on the right. I was sure that after *Shakedown*, he could get a job as a doorman." He was being sarcastic, of course.

According to Pevney, "Rock had only one line to deliver: 'Good evening, sir.' But he just couldn't get it right. Admittedly, it wouldn't require the acting skill of John Barrymore at his peak to pull off a line like that. When Rock finally got it right, the crew applauded. To make a bad situation worse, Rock showed up in a door-man's uniform that didn't fit. He stood 6'4" and his pants ended somewhere north of his ankles. Finally, wardrobe found a pair of pants that fitted. *FI-NALLY!*"

"After the film was wrapped, I was certain that I'd never use Rock in another picture," Pevney said. Then, with a sigh, he continued: "But then I got a memo ordering me to cast Rock in two more of my pictures, *Air Cadet* and *Iron Man*."

Under the name of Herman Brix, Bruce Bennett became a temporary screen Tarzan. He later co-starred with Joan Crawford as her husband in *Mildred Pierce* (1945)

In *Shakedown* (1950), he co-starred with Rock and they became close friends. In time, he would introduce Rock to Ronald Reagan, laying the groundwork for what eventually developed into an enduring friendship between Rock and the future U.S. President.

***

It has never been revealed how Rock became friends with Ronald and Nancy Reagan. After Rock's death in

1985, Reagan acknowledged their friendship by issued a widely distributed statement of mourning for their departed friend.

Their friendship began during the filming of *Shakedown*. Rock's colleague, Bruce Bennett, had introduced him to Reagan.

Rock had met Bennett during their filming of *Undertow*, yet came to know him better during the filming of *Shakedown*. At that point, Bennett's career was on a downward spiral, despite having successfully played Joan Crawford's husband in *Mildred Pierce* (1945). Rock had seen Bennett when he'd been billed as Herman Brix, the star of *The New Adventures of Tarzan* (1935).

One night over dinner, during the filming of *Shakedown*, Bennett told him that the author of the books on which the Tarzan franchise was based, Edgar Rice Burroughs, had selected him for the role of Tarzan way back in 1931. Shortly thereafter, Bennett sustained a serious back injury during his engagement as an uncredited football-playing extra during the filming of *Touchdown* (1931). As a result, the role of Tarzan in that early 1931 film had gone to Johnny Weissmuller.

Bennett would eventually be cast as Reagan's brother in *The Last Outpost* (1951), a Civil War yarn released by Paramount.

[At the time, Bennett was also having interchanges with Reagan, based on his status at the time as President of the Screen Actors' Guild. The organization was campaigning for the establishment of a strong pension plan for SAG members, as well as a health and welfare fund.

Bennett invited Rock to a speech Reagan was delivering to SAG members at an old movie house in Los Angeles. After the speech, Reagan joined the two actors for dinner.

Rock later told his friend, Tony Curtis, "I found Reagan very personable, very friendly, but reserved in a kind of way. It was like he was holding back, not wanting to get that intimate with anyone."

At that time, he was dating both Doris Day and starlet Nancy Davis.

"Ronnie seemed to like me, and it was the beginning of a decades-long friendship that was always enduring but never cracking the surface anywhere. Nancy took a real liking to me, however, and always

The former MGM starlet, Nancy Davis, poses with her husband, Ronald Reagan, who was struggling to find "a second act" (his words).

saw that I was invited to their parties when she married Reagan."

"I heard that Nancy, back in the late 1940s, was quite a girl about town,"
Rock said. "The men spread the word that she was a 'deep-throater.'"

"I think I turned her on a bit. She was always telling me how handsome I was.
At dinner parties, she always seated me next to her."

"After I made Pillow Talk *(1959) with Doris Day, I met Nancy two months*
later at the home of William Holden. She told me that she admired my work in that
romantic comedy. But then she paused before saying, 'I adored you, but I have
never seen the allure of Doris Day. She's got this awful singing voice. I prefer Jo
Stafford and Dinah Shore.'"

"I figured that Nancy was still jealous that Doris got to seduce Reagan before
she got him," Rock said. "But Nancy won out in the end by getting pregnant with
Patti. Ronnie, being the honorable guy he is, married her. The rest is one for the
history books."]

After Bruce Bennett finished his work on *The Last Outpost,* he met with
Rock to share some exciting news, relaying that his career was back on
track.

"I've just read this great script. The director, Fred Zinnemann, called
me. He's promised me what will be my greatest role yet in a western, the
male lead in *High Noon* (1952). I'll be appearing opposite Grace Kelly."

Of course, as the world knows, Gary Cooper got the part instead, winning a Best Actor Oscar for his performance.

***

Ever since Henry Willson had introduced Rock to his other favorite
client, Rory Calhoun, Rock had continued to see the ex-con turned movie
actor for an occasional one-night stand. The white heat of their intense
month-long affair had dimmed in its intensity.

As Calhoun told him, "It doesn't matter if it's a man or a woman. As
long as it's got a hole, I'll plug it."

One night, Rory phoned Rock with a surprise invitation. Errol Flynn
had seen one of bare-chested publicity photos that Universal had distributed of Rock and wanted both of them to come to his home on Mulholland
Drive for the weekend. The swashbuckling star had just returned from
India, where he'd filmed *Kim* (1951), based on the Rudyard Kipling novel.

Like Tyrone Power, Flynn had been one of Rock's all-time matinee
idols, ever since, as a kid in 1938, he'd been enthralled when he'd seen him
on the screen in *The Adventures of Robin Hood.* Rock accepted the invitation.

Before he met Rock, Flynn had racked up a huge list of sexual conquests, which he boasted ranged in number from 10,000 to 12,000. Many

of the names sexually associated with Flynn were from the A-list, and included three of the richest people in America: Aviator Howard Hughes; tobacco heiress Doris Duke; and Woolworth heiress Barbara Hutton. Other conquests derived from around the world: Laurence Oliver in London to Evita Perón in Buenos Aires. Along the way, Flynn managed to work in such stars as Lana Turner, Joan Bennett, Ann Sheridan, Hedy Lamarr, and Shelley Winters, to name only a few. Sometimes, during the filming of one of his pictures, he'd been known for sexual dalliances in his dressing room with as many as four different starlets at the same time.

When Rock arrived at his home, Flynn was most gracious, giving him a fast kiss on the mouth before embracing Calhoun. The established matinee idol was not a disappointment to Rock, although he found that up-close-and-personal, he wasn't quite as dashing as he'd been on the screen. His long years of dissipation were showing in his face, which makeup still concealed on camera. "It was his charm that won me over," Rock said. "He was oozing with it, a gracious, witty man and rather smart, too. He'd read a few books."

Before dinner, he offered both Rock and Calhoun an *apéritif*. Served in a crystal glass, the beverage had been a gift from the Maharajah of Brunei, and was viewed as the most powerful aphrodisiac in the world. According to legend, the recipe had come down through the centuries from Cleopatra, who had served it to Marc Antony, and it included crushed pearls and specks of gold.

Even though he'd served him the drink, Flynn was somewhat skeptical of its claim. "Frankly, I always find that a bit of cocaine rubbed on the tip of your prick before intercourse is more effective."

As the evening progressed, Flynn paid tribute to the fresh good looks of Calhoun and Rock. "It's not altogether comforting to know that a new

A high-testosterone threesome: Errol Flynn (left), Rock Hudson, and Rory Calhoun (right).

coven of handsome young men have descended on Hollywood to replace the likes of Ty Power and me. My face no longer is the one to launch a thousand ships like Helen of Troy. But it's still the face of an actor who can sell millions of tickets to those crappy flicks that that son of a bitch, Jack Warner, forces me to make."

After dinner, drinks were served on the patio by Flynn's houseboy, who seemed to look at his "master" with love in his eyes. It was obvious that the teenager adored his boss.

Flynn leaned back in his chair. "That drink from the Maharaja seems to be getting to me," he said. "How about you guys?"

"I'm game," Rock said.

"As you know from my track record, I'm always up for it," Calhoun boasted.

Once inside Flynn's bedroom, the star decided to try his hand at directing. As Rock described to his friend, Mark Miller, "Errol took charge and told us what he wanted us to do to him and what he wanted to do to us. It should have been on camera. I would have been a great blue movie."

"When we weren't making love, we drank and he told us amusing stories about his early days at Warner Brothers," Rock said.

Flynn related a hilarious story about what transpired during his filming of *The Adventures of Don Juan* (1949). For some reason, he called this film "a two-hour piss-take."

According to Flynn, "As rumor had it, and rather accurately, I fucked all the young men hired to perform as Don Juan's fencing students. After all, I was playing the great lover. What did those guys expect?"

He related that his art director, Edward Carrere, told him that "when I was photographed from the side, my 'protuberance,' as he called it, was too obvious. Then he suggested I get one of the homosexual costumers to 'tuck it away for me.' I didn't do that. Instead, I went to Perc Westmore, the best makeup man in Hollywood, and asked him to make this phallic thing for me that stretched sixteen inches."

"The next day, with the phallus tucked into my pants, when I faced

Rock Hudson spent an idyllic weekend in Palm Springs with a blonde-haired script girl, Betty Abbott, the very hip niece of the famous screen comedian, Bud Abbott.

Regardless of the event, Rock could always count on her to be his "arm candy."

Uncle Vince *[director Vincent Sherman]* he almost fainted. My co-star, Viveca Lindfors, screamed."

"However," he continued, "it had the opposite effect on my male co-star, Robert Douglas. He fell in love with me, and I've been banging him ever since."

Flynn said that when the picture was released, Hedda Hopper wrote in her column "that in some scenes, I looked intoxicated. She's my next-door neighbor. I stormed over to her front door and masturbated, slinging semen all over it as the bitch stood stunned at the window."

As their weekend of debauchery came to an end on Monday morning, Flynn kissed both Calhoun and Rock goodbye. "The kiss was at least as passionate as he'd delivered to Miriam Hopkins in *Virginia City* (1940) when she was cast as a dance hall girl," Rock said.

His parting words to Rock were, "You've got to become a regular at my parties, sport. When some of the guys get together in my jerk-off room, you're going to be the big boy on the totem pole."

***

In 1950 and 1951, in addition to his numerous male lovers, Rock also dated women, frequently receiving press coverage for his manliness as a result. It began when he was seen about town escorting an attractive, blonde-haired script girl named Betty Abbott, the niece of the comedian, Bud Abbott, one of the era's best screen comedians. *[As part of their widely billed act, Abbott & Costello, he usually played straight man to fidgety Lou Costello as they moved, comedically, from one explosive minefield to another.]*

When Betty introduced Rock to her famous relative, the comedian told him, "My job is to feed Lou, my sidekick, the set-up lines and let him take the pratfalls."

Columnists beefed up a romance between Betty and Rock, but it was greatly exaggerated. "We went out on a few harmless dates—and that's all, folks!" he told his friends.

In 1951, one woman entered his life and would remain there, on and off, until her death in 1972. She was the voluptuous Marilyn Maxwell, who got her start at the age of sixteen singing on the radio. Offered an MGM contract in 1942, she became one of the "Popcorn Blonde Bombshells" of the 1940s, competing with such stellar attractions as Betty Grable, Lana Turner, and Veronica Lake. Maxwell's hair was a platinum blonde like Jean Harlow's had been in the 1930s.

Four years older than Rock, she was tall, shapely, and, as the press dubbed her, "one of the best sweater-fillers in the country." He was drawn not only to her sex appeal, but to her quick intelligence and zany humor. "She was a funtime gal, and we hit it off from the beginning."

She'd begun a romance in 1943 with Frank Sinatra, which threatened his marriage to Nancy. At one point, the jealous wife confronted Maxwell at a party that Nancy had hosted at her home, kicking her out of the house but not before demanding the return of a diamond bracelet Sinatra had given her.

In one of her films, *Lost in a Harem* (1944), Maxwell performed a song entitled, "What Does It Take to Get You." One line in the lyrics stated, "I can even get as far as second base with Frank Sinatra."

Rock Hudson escorts Marilyn Maxwell for a night on the town. He later said, "She was the only woman I ever loved. I proposed marriage to her, but she turned me down."

Fans and entertainment-industry insiders knew what "second base" meant: Sinatra had met Maxwell in 1940 when she was an engaging and highly visible cheerleader—along with Lana Turner, Ava Gardner, and Virginia Mayo—for his softball team, The Swooners.

Maxwell's affair with Bob Hope became much more open than her trysts with Sinatra. In fact, some people referred to her as "Mrs. Bob Hope." Although married to singer Dolores Reade, Hope was often seen in public with Maxwell—that is, when he wasn't seducing Paulette Goddard, Betty Hutton, or his sarong girl, Dorothy Lamour.

As Hope's frequent partner in those "Road" pictures, Bing Crosby said, "He's a fast man with a squaw, but a slow man with a buck."

As Hope himself said, "I was lucky, you know. I always had a beautiful gal in my bed—and the money was good."

Maxwell had gone on those USO tours with Hope to entertain U.S. servicemen during both World War II and the Korean War.

Rock had been attracted to her after seeing her in only one role: In *Champion* (1949), she had co-starred with Kirk Douglas, playing his girlfriend opposite his character of an unscrupulous boxer who punches his way to the top.

Rock told friends, "On our first date, I discovered that Marilyn and I talked the same language. She understands my frustration of trying to climb every rung of the Hollywood ladder until I reach the top, but fearing—almost knowing—I'll never make it to the top."

She told him, "As kids, we think it's glamourous to be a movie star, but, as you already know, making a film is tedious, boring work. Some crews work together to make a great picture, but with every movie I've been in, it's every man for himself. From what I've seen, it's everybody working against everybody else."

As Rock freely admitted, their second date turned sexual. "What turned me on was that in the middle of the act, she seductively whispered in my ear that I was not only better than Frankie boy...but bigger! That brought out the latent heterosexual in me."

***

In his biography, *Tyrone Power, The Last Idol,* author Lawrence Guildes wrote: "Around 1952, Linda Christian and Tyrone Power were drawn into a morally liberated group of film people, who had swimming pool parties *cum* drinking parties, and the gatherings became very sexual by midnight. These groups exist in France, in Italy, and possibly in every country where there is a large film industry and a great many amoral people. Tyrone, who always kept his side affairs very much apart from his marriages, now crossed over the line, apparently quite willingly."

At the time, Power's marriage to starlet Linda Christian was coming unglued.

Edie Goetz, Louis B. Mayer's daughter, said that Power was often a guest at her parties. "He was a terrible flirt. He made light of it, but he flirted with anyone, even me, even though I was in love with my husband."

[Edie's husband, William Goetz, a film studio executive, was actually a close friend of Power. Without any evidence, rumors spread that Power was involved in a ménage à trois *with the Goetzes.]*

Rock always remembered the first party he attended at the home of Tyrone Power and Linda Christian. They had invited a medley of about three dozen other guests, both men and women.

Couples who swing: Tyrone Power and Linda Christian

Most of them were unknown to Rock, who kept looking for big names. Many of the guests were either Italian or Mexican, some working in the studios, but others expatriates or international visitors. Nearly all of them seemed to be friends or acquaintances of Christian, the starlet that Power had married in Rome in 1949, in the aftermath of the very emotional breakup of his affair with Lana Turner.

Power didn't seem much involved with, or concerned about, Christian's friends, and he and Rock sat in a remote corner of the party, near the pool house. Mostly, he was worried about the downward slide in his career as he entered the 1950s. "I'm afraid the scripts I'm being offered by Fox are routine or even bad. I need a big hit, and I don't know where it's coming from. If I get one, I'll try to see that you get cast opposite me. Perhaps we'll play rivals in love with the same girl. That's always a good story. Women especially go for pictures like that."

"I'd better mingle with Linda's guests—or else she'll give me hell later. Stick around. I'm inviting you for a sleepover. It'll be just the two of us."

"I'm looking forward to that," Rock answered.

For the next two hours, Rock wandered among the guests. He decided not to strip down and join the skinny dipping in the pool.

The only person Rock found to talk to was the singer, Mario Lanza, a newly minted friend of the Powers, who was being hailed as the American Caruso. In fact, he was set to star in the 1951 release of *The Great Caruso.*

Rock later said, "He was conceited beyond belief. His ego knew no bounds."

As Lanza stood surveying his prospects for the night, he confided to Rock that his life-long obsession with womanizing had begun during his stint in the U.S. Army. "It began in Texas where a guy could line up a dozen *putas* from across the border. Only three bucks per pussy. There are three things I'm addicted to—food, wine, and women."

He told Rock that during the war, his dream girl had been Betty Grable. "I used to masturbate to that famous pin-up picture of her. I never got to screw her, but her husband, Harry James, hired me to star in this CBS-TV special, *The Shower of Stars.* Betty

At a party at the home of Tyrone Power and Linda Christian, Rock had a long talk with singer Mario Lanza, who was making *The Great Caruso* (1951). He spent the evening talking about his great sexual prowess, claiming that on occasion, he could seduce a dozen women at one time.

came to my dressing room, and at least I got a blow-job out of it." [*That program included the television debut of Mario Lanza, who was rewarded for his appearance with $40,000 and two Chrysler automobiles.*]

It was getting around midnight when Power returned to Rock's side. Christian had already disappeared with "Mr. Apollo," an Italian muscleman the Powers had met in Rome. He had come to America as part of an attempt to get cast as the next Tarzan.

Rock really liked Power. As he admitted to George Nader, "It's not so much about sex, although it probably is for him, but I like being around him. Actually, I want one day to have his star power. When I was growing up, Tyrone Power was the kind of guy that could make audiences swoon—men envied him, women wanted him."

Power took his hand and led him away to his upstairs bedroom. By that time, all the guests had either gone home or else paired (or trio'd) off, some of them headed to the poolhouse for an orgy.

Rock never went into a lot of details about his love affair with Power. Unlike what he tended to do with his other conquests. He was uncharacteristically close-lipped about his idol.

Nader once asked him why, and was told, "Ty is a man who likes his privacy."

[*Power's hidden sex life has been speculated about in books. A clue was provided when Kenneth Anger, in the European edition of Hollywood Babylon, that exposé of Hollywood, suggested that Power liked to indulge in coprophagia (feces eating). His longtime trick, Scotty Hanson, denied that.*

However, two of Power's closest friends, actors Charles Laughton and Monty Woolley, were "outed" as devotees of that perversion. Power often spent time with them, in England, New York, and Hollywood, thereby throwing suspicion on himself.]

Later in his life, Rock did throw a flicker of light on his long and complicated relationship with Power when he told Tom Clark, "I went along with some excesses with Ty, which I would not do with anyone else. He was a great guy and a loving, generous man, and I did not want to judge him too harshly. We must never judge people for their needs, particularly when we don't understand them. Perhaps it has something to do with some traumatic experience in his childhood. How would I know? I'm not a fucking shrink. I will say this: He wanted to degrade himself for reasons that lurked deep within his soul."

"Seeing that beautiful man, that wonderful human being, degrade himself was painful to watch. I was always loyal to him, right up until the very end. Death came far too early."

***

Rock left the Power's home at around 3AM, driving back to his own house, where he slept until around noon.

Then, the phone on his nightstand woke him up with its persistent ringing. It was Power on the other end. Thanking him for the previous night.

"I'm the one who should thank you," Rock said.

"I fell asleep in your arms, but when I woke up, you were gone," Power said.

"Absence makes the heart grow fonder," Rock responded.

"Let's not get corny until later in the day," Power said. "Linda liked you a lot, at least what she saw of you. She really didn't get to talk to you very much. She wants you to come over this Friday night for dinner at around eight. It'll be just the three of us, not the usual crowd of Mexicans and Italians who hang out at our place. She's part Mexican, and she used to live in Rome—hence, her crowd."

"As you gathered, we don't adhere to our marriage vows any more. I was once going to leave her, but I found out she was pregnant. She gave birth to a girl."

"I'll be there," Rock promised.

"It's very casual," Power said. "Just wear jeans and a tight-fitting T-shirt. Don't bother with underwear—you won't need it."

As he put down the receiver, Rock interpreted that final remark as very suggestive. What did his friend have in store for him? He knew, of course."

He'd read a lot in the gossip columns about Christian. She'd had an extended affair with Errol Flynn, but then, who hadn't?

In Hector Arce's biography of Tyrone Power, he described Christian as "a Madame du Barry born two hundred years too late. All her life, she'd been trained in the art of pleasing a man. Bright and shrewd, fevered with the desire to be somebody, the chief blind spot in her makeup was her inability to distinguish fame from notoriety."

Press agents had labeled her as "The Anatomic Bomb," and a journalist had described her "catlike green eyes, her sensuous mouth, and her tall, voluptuous body."

On that Friday night, during his first private talk with Christian, Rock was invited to the edge of her pool for a drink. She had to explain that dinner would be an hour late because Power was on the phone upstairs, part of a long discussion with his boss, Darryl F. Zanuck.

"They take a steam bath every day at Fox after work," she said. "Zanuck told me that he was the straightest man in Hollywood, but that looking at Ty in the nude has almost stirred up long-suppressed homosexual desires."

"Ty can do that all right," Rock said.

She looked at him with a cynical gaze. "I'm sure you're already aware of that." Then she settled back, seemingly to appraise him. Perhaps his jeans were too tight, but he thought that's how Power had wanted him to dress.

"You may not know my husband very well," she said. "He has long periods in which he descends into dark moods. At those times, he wants to lock himself away. Sometimes, he can go for days, preferring to be alone, to avoid any human contact. Of course, I'm not sitting at home doing my knitting. We both have permission to 'roam the ranch,' and he calls it. So when he goes into one of those depressions, I hit the town for some fun."

"Sounds like a great marriage," Rock said. "In fact, you've just provided a blueprint for any marriage I might be forced to endure."

"I know," she said. "These unsophisticated Americans. Always believing that a person, most definitely a woman, should settle down, be a good wife, and mother to her husband's kids. These *gringos* know nothing of Roman society, where the morals aren't so damned strict."

"Ty doesn't like to be tied down," she continued. "I think he'd have run off months ago, but then I told him I was having a baby. She's in the far side of the house tonight, asleep with her nanny. We keep her locked away at night. She doesn't have to know what her parents are up to."

"That's the best way to raise her, I'm sure," Rock said. "What's out of sight need not bother her."

"It's not a perfect marriage, of course, because Ty has a lot of deep-rooted problems, He seeks relief in bizarre ways at times. Perhaps you're already aware of that."

There was an awkward silence before she said, "I was able to take him from the arms of Lana Turner, and she's a movie goddess. She's still lamenting him as the lost love of her life. I'm not shedding any tears for her. The bitch can have almost any man she wants…and she's had most of them. So losing Ty doesn't mean she'll be alone."

At no point did she ever ask Rock about his life before coming to Hollywood, or what had happened to his career since he'd arrived.

But she did speak of her own childhood, as if still troubled by it.

She was born in 1923 in Tampico, Mexico. Her maternal grandfather had owned a copper and silver mine; her maternal grandmother had been a beauty of Spanish and French descent. Her father was a Dutch-born engineer who worked for Shell Oil developing new oilfields. When she was a year old, his job sent him, with his family, to Venezuela.

She recalled going to school in Maracaibo, near the famous oil lake. "I know how to speak both Spanish and German. The town was a lovely place of flowers, endless sun—color everywhere."

She went on to say that her father was sent, again with his family, to supervise oil production in Iraq. They eventually settled in Haifa, at the time, part of Palestine under the British mandate. "I was sent to the German school there, which was filled with boys who were members of the *Hitler Jugend*. There was a big blown-up portrait of the *Führer* on the wall, and we had to sing Nazi songs."

"The day started with our teacher screeching *'Heil Hitler!'* The class raised outstretched arms in a Nazi salute."

"I was defiant. True to my Dutch heritage, I yelled *'Heil Wilhelmina!'*"

"The teacher punished me by striking my fingers, hard, with a ruler. I guess I was too defiant. One day, six members of the *Hitler Jugend* grabbed me after school and forced me off to this secluded area. I was repeatedly raped and left lying on the ground bleeding. Before they left, each of them stood over me and urinated on me."

"What a god damn awful story!" Rock said.

"After my 'deflowering,' you'd think I would have abandoned sex forever. But I didn't. In fact, I was driven to it. Perhaps in some mixed-up way, I see having sex with men as some sort of punishment. Sick, isn't it?"

"I don't judge, I don't condemn. Too many people do that already."

At that point, Power entered the patio. "What's the matter with you two?" he asked, jokingly. "I thought you'd be getting into it by now, and I could walk in and join the scene."

Rock stood up to embrace him.

"Let the fun begin!" Power said.

***

The next morning, Rock's home phone rang at 10AM, awakening him from a deep sleep. He'd gone to bed at 6AM. In the wake of his *ménage à trois* with Mr. and Mrs. Tyrone Power, he thought one of them might be phoning. "Hi, lover," he said in his sleepy voice. "What's up? After last night, I'm not!"

That, of course, was meant as a *double entendre*.

There was an awkward silence that lasted a moment before he heard the booming voice of the film director, George Sherman, who had been assigned to helm him in his next picture, action/western named *Tomahawk*

(1951).

"Do I play another Indian like I did in that James Stewart movie?" Rock asked.

"Hell, no! You're a soldier who falls in love with an Indian maiden."

"Why don't you call it *The Squaw Man?*"

"Don't be a smart ass. Cecil B. DeMille used that title back in 1931. I'm shipping your ass to the Black Hills of South Dakota. Van Heflin and Yvonne De Carlo are the stars. Lodgings will be tight. I've assigned you to bunk with our second male lead, Alec Nicol."

"Never heard of him," Rock said.

"You will. Before the end of the location shoot, I'm sure you two studs will be asshole buddies. It gets cold at night in those Black Hills!"

Chapter Five

ROCK AND GUY MADISON INTRODUCE BEEFCAKE TO TINSELTOWN

Campy and Queeny: "Odd Couple" Matings with Liberace & Tallulah Bankhead, *Dah-ling*

"I knocked them off, or is it knocked them up, one by one," Rock claimed. Top: Alex Nicol (left) and Guy Madison. Bottom: James Best (left) and Richard Long.

Before Rock flew out of Los Angeles, an agent

from Universal delivered a movie magazine to his mailbox. In it, he'd been configured as the focal point of an article that asked, "So, you'd like to be Mrs. Hudson? Here's how to handle Hollywood's Big Rock!" He read some woman reporter's fantasy of what it would be like to be Rock Hudson's wife. "Dream on, bitch!" he said, tossing the magazine.

Tomahawk (1951) would be Rock's first extensive location shoot. On the plane to South Dakota, the film's producer, Leonard Goldstein, gave him the script to read. As Rock later said, "I had a hard time finding my part. That's how small it was."

He'd been cast as a Yankee soldier who falls for an Indian maiden, Monahseetha (Susan Cabot) during the Civil War.

Goldstein had continued—despite the lackluster roles and performances—casting Rock in pictures he'd produced: *I Was a Shoplifter, One Way Street,* and *The Desert Hawk.* This would be the second movie he'd make with Yvonne De Carlo.

As Rock told his friends, "I don't know if Goldstein has the hots for me, or whether he's been ordered by Universal to keep me working, since I'm under contract."

As Rock stepped off the plane after it landed in Rapid City, there was a touch of autumn in the air. In the distance loomed the Black Hills. Crew members and second-tier members of the cast were transferred by bus to the town's most prominent hotel. The main stars had not yet arrived.

Rock was assigned a room with a double bed and was told that a fellow actor, Alex Nicol, would be checking in to share the quarters with him in two days. In a phone call to Mark Miller in L.A., Rock said, "I hope my roomie is not a pig but some hot stud, preferably blonde or blondish."

The publicist from Universal, Rick Warren, a short little guy with a bad skin condition, knocked on his door and entered. For a moment, Rock was horrified, thinking that he was his roommate.

A new theater was opening in Rapid City that night, and Warren had come up with the idea that the stars and second-tier actors in the picture should be introduced from the stage for publicity purposes.

He said that Van Heflin, De Carlo, Jack Oakie, and Preston Foster, along with the director, George Sherman, had already arrived on the day's last flight in from California, and that they'd agreed to appear. Rock was panic-stricken, as he'd never appeared on stage before a live audience. "You've got to do it," pimply skinned Warren ordered.

Backstage that night, Rock had a "kiss-kiss" reunion with De Carlo and was introduced to the three male stars. Each of them appeared before the packed house, where De Carlo received the loudest applause, including wolf whistles.

Rock appeared last, with Warren virtually having to push him onto the stage. "Ladies and gentlemen," Rock said in a cracked voice. When further words seemed to clog in his throat, Oakie ran out onto the stage to rescue him.

"Ladies and gentlemen," he said: "This is Rock Hudson. He plays a wooden Indian in our movie." The audience burst into laughter.

"I was a god damn zombie," Rock later recalled. "It was one of the most embarrassing moments of my life. The prospect that I would one day appear in plays before a live audience seemed as remote as Mars."

Back in his lonely hotel room, he studied a scenario of *Tomahawk* written by Daniel Jarrett. The actual screenplay for this Technicolor western was by Sylvia Richards, based on a threatened Indian uprising in Wyoming (not South Dakota) in 1866. With the discovery of gold in the Black Hills *[The Black Hills Gold Rush reached a peak between 1876 and 1877]*, soldiers moved in and built Fort Phil Kearny on the Bozeman Trail, on land that had been previously ceded to the Sioux by an earlier treaty.

Van Heflin played Jim Bridger, a frontier scout who tries to prevent an all-out war with forces assembled around the Sioux leader, "Red Cloud" (as portrayed by John War Eagle, veteran of dozens of TV and big-screen westerns) and his braves.

In an earlier conversation, De Carlo had told him that she was not pleased with her role of Julie Madden. "I could have called it

Susan Cabot...Rock's "squaw" in *Tomahawk* (1951)

in," she said.

She invited Rock to dine with her, along with Foster and Heflin. She told him that her affair with a stunt man, Jock Mahoney (aka Jacques and/or Jack Mahoney), was all but over. *[In 1962-63, Mahoney would go on to become one of the many actors playing Tarzan on the big screen.]*

Over dinner, it became obvious that she was going to warm her bed with Heflin during those cold autumnal nights. Rock was still waiting for his bedmate.

Heflin had never impressed Rock as a romantic leading man, even though he was a talented actor. He had been best showcased as the boozy, philosophical lawyer in *Johnny Eager* (1942), a role that had brought him a Best Supporting Actor Oscar. Rock had gone to see the picture only because it co-starred Lana Turner.

Obviously, De Carlo didn't agree with Rock's assessment of Heflin.

Unlike Rock, who had frozen on the stage, Foster had broken into show business on Broadway. Rock knew the actor, noted for his "mustachioed machismo," had appeared in movies, but he couldn't recall one. He was cast in the role of Colonel Carrington of the Union Army.

The next morning, Rock chatted with George Sherman, who was to direct him. He was known for churning out "B" westerns, including six pictures with the singing cowboy, Gene Autry. "You act just as good as Autry," he told Rock, although he didn't know if that were a compliment. Sherman would also have ten collaborations with John Wayne, Rock's future co-star. "You look more macho than Wayne," Sherman said. "Have you ever noticed that on screen he walks like a fairy, but gets away with it?"

That afternoon, Foster introduced him to Ann Doran as "my wife." *[She was his wife only in the movie.]* Doran told him she'd appeared in "hundreds" of silent films under an assumed name because her family thought all actresses were whores. This strong-willed woman from Amarillo, Texas, would in time appear in 500 films and 1,000 teleplays, but she would be remembered mainly for playing James Dean's domineering mother in *Rebel Without a Cause* (1955).

At long last, during a quiet moment when Rock was resting in his hotel room, a receptionist called to say that his roommate, Alex Nicol, was on his way upstairs.

Rock experienced a moment of dread until Nicol walked into the bedroom carrying his only suitcase with a duffel bag thrown across his shoulder. As Rock later told Miller, "That Alex is one hot guy—blondish, with blue eyes, very handsome, but not as a pretty boy. He fills out those blue jeans and is muscular but not in the weight-lifter category. I had to warn Jumbo to stay down."

Nicol was new to Hollywood. Sherman had discovered him in New York, which led to a contract with Universal.

Over beers—many beers—in the bar downstairs, Rock was captivated by his new friend, happy to be sharing a room with him. He learned that he'd gotten married two years before, to Jean Fleming, so he was assumed to be straight, unless all those beers elicited a gay streak in him.

Rock knew that Nicol had recently appeared as one of the Marines in *Mister Roberts* (1948) on Broadway. "I was also the understudy for Henry Fonda, but he never missed a performance, even on the night his wife died."

He wasn't too happy with his present role, that of a cavalry officer, Lt. Tob Dancy, who hated Indians. "I'm very tolerant of all people."

Nicol was eight years older than Rock, but he had lied to Universal and shaved four years off his actual age. "Actresses do that all the time. Why not me?"

He also said that his father had been an arms keeper at Sing Sing, and that he'd spent five years in the U.S. Army, serving with the 101st Cavalry.

The two men returned to their room at around 11PM. Since he'd been traveling all day, Nicol stripped off his clothes before heading for the shower. "At least he wasn't the modest type," Rock later told Miller. "He had all the equipment in all the right places. I was falling for him."

Rock was lying nude on their bed when Nicol came back into the bedroom, drying himself off. "I sleep bare-assed naked," he told Nicol.

"I'll do the same," he answered, crawling into bed beside him.

"Nothing ever happened!" Rock later confessed. "The stud went right to sleep. After all, it had been a long day. I got lucky the following night."

When Nicol and Rock met at 7PM the next evening in the hotel bar, the actor seemed more relaxed. Rock was aware that some guys on the set had spread word that he was homosexual. Nicol did not seem put off by that.

If anything, he made a confession to Rock: "Half the guys at the Actors Studio are homosexuals, guys like Marlon Brando and Monty Clift. Many of these guys are quite brilliant, and a struggling actor can learn a lot from them. If you want to go with the flow, you hang out with them. It's no reflection on a guy's manhood if he gets his cock sucked. If anything, it proves you're a real man, because homosexuals go only for the most masculine."

"You're my kind of man," Rock said.

In bed that night, Nicol said, "I've known right from the start you wanted me. I'm not naïve. Okay, it's yours."

"I don't need that in writing," Rock said, moving toward him. As he later told Miller, "Alex is 95% straight. I decided to go for the 5%. And I did, night after night."

Shortly thereafter, Rock learned that both he and Nicol had been cast in the same upcoming movie, *Air Cadet* (1951). "At least for the duration of that film, Alex's wife would have to share her man with me."

***

For its release in Great Britain, *Air Cadet* (1951) was given the much better title of *Jet Men of the Air*. This saga from Universal was the dramatic war tale of young men training to be jet fighters, with Rock cast as the unnamed "Upper Classman."

As he later admitted, "I bellowed to the young recruits on camera, telling them 'to drop everything when an upper classman comes around.' The harsh words I spewed out were only for the benefit of the camera. At night, I was a lot gentler, especially during sex with some of actors playing the cadets."

In this, his tenth movie, although his name appeared on a movie poster for the first time, it was positioned after the names of an array of other stars: Stephen McNally (as Major Jack Page); Gail Russell (as his wife); Janet Page; Alex Nicol (as Joe Czanoczek); Richard Long (as Russ Coutler); and Charles Drake (as Captain Sullivan).

As he would later confess to friends Mark Miller and George Nader, "Never before and never after the filming of *Air Cadet* would I experience such a feast of young, hot, gorgeous men. With one exception, all of them were ostensibly straight. But, as you know, that has never stopped me."

His series of affairs began when he decided to drive from California to the location shoot at the Randolph Air Base in San Antonio, Texas. He'd hooked up with a young actor, Robert Arthur, who had been assigned a small role. This son of Washington State had been working in films since 1945, playing teenagers or young adults.

Renting a car, with Arthur in the passenger seat, they headed out, driving east toward Texas, combining a sightseeing tour with the necessity of actually getting there.

Both actors discussed their past and future career moves. Arthur would soon appear in the Billy Wilder film, *Ace in the Hole* (1951), starring Kirk Douglas. He'd just made *Twelve O'Clock High* (1949), a taut World War II drama about American flyers stationed in England. "I fell in love with the star, Gregory Peck, one handsome guy. But what good did it do me? I could look but not touch."

Arthur had also appeared in an uncredited role in *Mildred Pierce* (1945), which had brought Joan Crawford her first and only Oscar. "Crawford and Ann Blyth, playing her daughter, might have fallen for Zachory Scott on screen, but it was Scott who visited my bed at night."

At a roadside motel, Arthur and Rock spent their first night together, and continued their affair until they reached the set of *Air Cadet*. After they got there, Rock became enveloped with affairs "with more studly men."

[In his later years, Arthur became a strong civil rights advocate for gay seniors, and a member of the Log Cabin Republicans.]

***

On his first day on the set, Rock had a reunion with Stephen McNally. In their previous film together, *Winchester '73*, McNally had had fourth billing, but in *Air Cadet*, he was the star, playing the leader of a Lockheed F-80 Shooting Star jet aerobatics team.

His onscreen rival was portrayed by Richard Long, who falls in love with McNally's onscreen wife, as portrayed by Gail Russell.

After the filming of *Air Cadet* was wrapped, McNally said, "I think I was the only male in the cast Hudson didn't seduce."

During filming, in a housing scheme that reflected the rooming shortage on the set of *Tomahawk*, Alex Nicol had been designated once again as Rock's roommate. Rock also had a reunion with James Best, whom he had most recently seduced on the set of *Winchester '73*.

For the third time, Rock appeared with Charles Drake. According to Rock, "He always gave me wide berth. I think he feared I was going to overpower him and rape him."

"Alex once again proved a reliable lover, and I really dug him," Rock confessed after returning to Hollywood. Nicol had just played a prisoner of war in *Target Unknown* (1951), in which he had appeared with Best. "James told me you came on to him when you guys made that western," Nicol said to Rock.

"I did more than just come on to him," Rock confessed. "Since that secret is out of the bag, let's

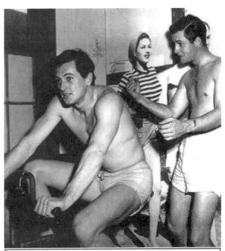

Why is Richard Long (right) sneaking up on Rock, and what does he have in mind?

117

lure him into our little den one night."

Three nights later, Best spent the night in bed with Nicol and Rock. "This time, he was an easy target, and put up no resistance. And he did more than lie back and enjoy it."

Soon, the director, Joseph Pevney, learned of what was going on. He told the producer, Aaron Rosenberg, "What in hell is Hudson auditioning for, a role as the Whore of Babylon? I'm really getting fed up with him. He was awful when I had to work with him on *Shakedown*. I doubt if he's improved any since then."

Pevney's patience with Rock ran out after only a few days of shooting. Perhaps in retaliation for his promiscuity, and chronically unhappy with his performance, he drastically cut his role so that he would disappear early in the picture. "It all became too much," Pevney told Rosenberg. "Seducing the leading male actors, except for McNally, was one thing, but taking the husband of Gail Russell and causing our leading lady to have a breakdown was more than I could take. Imagine what Gail must have felt!"

The director was referring to the recent arrival of Guy Madison on the set as part of a visit to his new wife (Russell). An explosion followed.

Before that, however, problems associated with another of Rock's entanglements (Richard Long) emerged, too.

***

On the set of *Air Cadet*, Rock also became embroiled with Richard Long, who had the fourth lead. Two years younger than Rock, the handsome, personable, and charming young man grew up in Rock's home state of Illinois, but moved to California in 1944.

The fifth of six children, Long was the son of a commercial artist, who struggled to feed and clothe his family. He had never planned to become an actor, even though most of his schoolmates at Hollywood High were dreaming of doing just that.

A talent agent from Universal had spotted and told him, "A male beauty like you should be in pictures."

Long had been propositioned by several young gay boys in his class, and he thought this was just another come-on. To judge by his opening statement to Long, the agent obviously was interested in more than just getting the student a film contract. But he came through with a contract, nonetheless. It is not known what Long, if anything, gave the agent in return. But he soon found himself playing the son of Orson Welles and Claudette Colbert in *Tomorrow Is Forever* (1945).

Long's real fame came when he was cast as the good-looking, well-educated son of *Ma and Pa Kettle* (Marjorie Main and Percy Kilbride) in that hit film series about these zany hillbillies. He later told Rock, "I feel trapped in this series, and I want out. Marjorie Main—an otherwise lovable old dyke—is the greatest scene stealer in the history of films."

Even though Rock was engaged in other affairs at the time, Long soon became the object of his affections. He was not only attracted to his looks, but to his sensitivity and magnetism. From all signs, he appeared to be straight, which Rock viewed as "merely a challenge." He wanted to see more of Long, and he invited him, and the young actor accepted, to be "my workout partner at the gym."

Soon the two young men were working out together. Rock liked what he saw and managed to lure Long into his bed. As they got to know each other, he found out that this was not Long's first homosexual experience. The gay British actor, Roddy McDowall, had been the first to seduce him after inviting him to one of his parties, where he'd met a young Elizabeth Taylor. McDowall also introduced Long to Merv Griffin, a young, reasonably handsome actor and singer. As he confessed to Rock, "Merv fell in love with me, and I didn't want that. I would never enter into a relationship with a man, and I plan to get married as soon as the right girl comes along."

"That's a line I use myself," Rock said.

Long talked with Rock about how important it was, for the sake of their careers, to be seen dating young wannabe female stars. He suggested that sexy Terry Moore might be available, if not otherwise engaged with Howard Hughes. "If not Terry, perhaps Debbie Reynolds or Mamie Van Doren."

***

There was yet another sad story that played out during the making of *Air Cadet*. This one swirled around Gail Russell, its alcoholic leading lady.

Director Joseph Pevney introduced Rock to her, but she had no interest in talking to him. During the filming, he noticed that John Wayne sometimes visited her on the set, disappearing into her

Gail Russell competing with Rock for the love of her husband, Guy Madison.

119

dressing room.

At this point in his life, Rock didn't formally meet "Duke." Years later, Rock joked, "When I met Gail, she had been Wayne's leading lady. But by the late '60s—irony of ironies—I would be The Duke's leading lady."

[Rock was referring to their co-starring film for 20th Century Fox, The Undefeated (1969), in which he would play the second lead opposite Wayne.]

Russell, a beautiful brunette, began appearing in movies during the final months of World War II. Paramount had signed her as a contract player while she was still in high school.

***

At one of Henry Willson's pool parties, Rock had met the dashingly handsome Guy Madison. Clad in skimpy swimwear during their first talk by the pool, both of them had checked each other out.

Madison confessed that he was under tremendous pressure to get married. In 1949, *Modern Screen* had run an article on him: "The handsome actor, Guy Madison, talks about a flagstone walk, a barn, and four kids, but he refuses to mention a little item called a wife! There ought to be a wife!"

Within weeks, Willson rushed Madison into a marriage with Gail Russell. The agent felt that as the wife of one of his bisexual screen studs, she'd be "safe," since she was also a known bisexual, having sustained affairs with such actresses as Dorothy Shay, a Florida-born popular recording artist known as the "Park Avenue Hillbilly."

Willson believed that Russell would be understanding about Madison's affairs with men, especially his months-long involvement with Rory Calhoun, another of Willson's prized stallions.

Less than a month after his marriage, Rock began his own affair with Madison, a former telephone lineman before he joined the U.S. Navy. On leave from a naval base in San Diego, and still dressed in his sailor whites, Madi-

"Henry Willson told me I was even more beautiful than Rock Hudson," Guy Madison claimed.

120

son had caught the eagle eye of Willson, always on the hunt for fresh male flesh. "He was dazzlingly beautiful," Willson said, "perhaps the most beautiful young man in Hollywood in the 1940s. He was also polite and charming. I couldn't wait to get him out of that sailor's uniform."

Madison (known at the time as Robert Moseley of Bakersfield, California) was "discovered" in a bar by Willson, the agent working as a talent scout for producer David O. Selznick.

"We've got to change your name for the marquee," Willson told him.

The newly renamed Guy Madison later told Rock, "At first, he named me "Rock Madison,' but decided to save the name 'Rock' for another actor who might come along. He took the name 'Madison' from the Dolley Madison Bakery across the street." [The former first lady spelled "Dolley" with an E.]

Willson arranged to have Madison appear in that 1944 tear-jerker, *Since You Went Away*, starring Claudette Colbert. Madison made a stunning appearance as a sailor in a scene with Jennifer Jones and Robert Walker. [*The Jones/Walker marriage had crumbled when she admitted to having an affair with Selznick, who later married her.*]

When *Since You Went Away* was released, one newspaper reported, "Teenage girls fell out of the balcony when Guy Madison came onto the screen." Willson had discovered a new star. At the premiere of the picture in New York, he was mobbed by screaming bobbysoxers, the kind Frank Sinatra was drawing at the time.

With his sun-bleached hair, Madison was definitely Rock's type. During an afternoon they spent together beside Henry Willson's pool led to an invitation from Rock to accompany him to one of the bedrooms upstairs.

"The kid generates sexual heat," Rock told George Nader. He's a hot little number, and I devoured him. It seems Guy surrenders his body to half our brothers in Hollywood. Of course, when Rory (Calhoun) isn't out fucking some dame, he calls Guy and he comes running."

Madison became the poster boy of World War II, the male equivalent of Betty Grable, whose famous pinup of her back side and "the world's most beautiful legs" decorated the insides of lockers from San Francisco to Bataan.

"He was drop-dead gorgeous," Willson said. "Rock and Guy helped introduced a new concept in male movie stars. It was called 'beefcake,' as opposed to 'cheesecake.' I practically invented it."

"Before actors like Rock or Guy came along, most male stars did not have great, prize-winning physiques, Lex Barker (Mr. Tarzan) excepted, of course. Just look at any old movie," Willson said.   "I   launched many a career by having one of my guys pose shirtless," Willson said.

"Take that so-called gentle giant, Cint Walker. He could have become Mr. Universe."

"My guys, at least most of them, took off their shirts for the movie mags, and when I got lucky with a chosen few, they dropped trou for me."

Nader later claimed, "Rock, Rory, and Guy often went on so-called hunting trips together. They enjoyed threeways. No animals were ever killed, and I don't think they carried rifles. Let's face it: Each guy was so sinfully good looking that they should be outlawed. All three were Hollywood boys, and the whole damn world knows about Hollywood boys. On hunting trips, the guys went off together to enjoy a meat dinner, definitely not rabbit or deer."

"I loved screwing Guy," Rock confessed. "He was a bit cocky when I met him. After all, he'd been the darling of the bobbysoxers, and it had gone to his head. However, I tamed the fucker… Taught him who's boss. I made him my bitch."

Months would go by before Rock saw Madison's wife on the set of *Air Cadet.* "Every now and then, when she thought I wasn't looking, I saw her staring at me. I think she'd heard stories that I was shacking up with her husband. But she never said anything to me. A lot of gossipy idiots accused me of driving her to drink. But I knew differently. She was hitting the bottle long before she met me, and was drinking during the making of *Air Cadet.* Amazingly, the camera didn't pick up on this."

"Guy told me he never loved her, and that the marriage was a sham. He said he married her because the fan magazines kept asking, 'When is Guy Madison going to get married?'"

"That is, when the same damn magazines weren't asking, "When is Rock Hudson going to get married?"

***

"Here I am, trying to build myself up as a romantic lead, and those fucks at Universal have cast me in a new movie, *The Fat Man,*" Rock complained to Henry Willson. "I'm lean and mean, hard as a rock, and appearing in a film with a name I hate. The only homosexuals who will go see it are those guys who get off on fatties."

He was relieved, however, when he read the script. He didn't have to gain a hundred pounds to appear in the fat role. He was cast as a (physically fit) ex-con instead.

Universal's movie poster proclaimed, "Now radio's great detective is the screen's super sleuth." Based on a radio series by Dashiell Hammett, Universal cast the portly J. Scott Smart, reprising his radio role as Brad

Runyan. A running joke in the film involves scenes where this overweight detective struggles to get in and out of his small MG.

A native of Pennsylvania, Smart had held down thirty jobs, from shoeshine boy to coal shoveler on a boat. Throughout much of the 1930s, '40s, and early '50s, he broadcast into America's homes, playing so many different characters over time that he became celebrated as "The Lon Chaney of Radio."

For his role in *The Fat Man*, Rock worked once again with di-

Rock kisses Julie London in *The Fat Man* (1951). Obviously, he was not cast as the obese detective.

rector William Castle, who had cast him in a bit part in his second movie, *Undertow*. After helming him in his first scene, Castle said, "You've picked up speed, kid."

The *film noir* was produced by Aubrey Schenck, who'd been a New York attorney until he submitted a script to 20th Century Fox. When it was accepted, he segued his career into that of a film director, turning out second-rate fare which was often entertaining, and included the ridiculous *Robinson Crusoe on Mars* (1964).

Rock found his movie wife, Julie London, charming and enchanting. She was a singer, known for her smoky, sensual voice and her languid demeanor, often the inspiration to many a female impersonator. She told Rock, "I sound so intimate in song because of my 'oversmoked' voice."

By 1955, she'd record her alltime hit, "Cry Me a River," which remains a classic even today.

Rock told her that while he was in the Navy, his bunkmate carried around a pin-up picture of her as the girl he wanted to come home to.

At the time, she was married to actor Jack Webb, who was playing William Holden's friend in the classic, *Sunset Blvd.* (1950).

Months after *The Fat Man* was released, a future co-star, Jeff Chandler, asked Rock what he thought of the movie. Rock delivered a terse review: "It came and it went."

***

Decades later, Rock did not want to talk about his early days in Hollywood, when he was labeled "a star fucker." And according to Tom Clark, his longtime companion, there was one affair that Rock, more than any other, never wanted mentioned. It began the night Rock wandered into Ciro's to hear the piano playing of the newly hailed entertainment sensation, Liberace.

The flamboyant Liberace startled the audiences of Las Vegas by appearing as a lavish replica of a pink flamingo, "I've had Elvis Presley. I've had Rock Hudson. After that, every other man is downhill for me."

On that night at Ciro's, Rock was accompanied by a tall, good-looking cowboy, who had dubbed himself "Hank Durango." No, he was not from Henry Willson's stable, although he had tried to be. He had nicknamed himself "The Durango Kid."

Apparently, shortly after they arrived, Durango headed for the men's room and "put on a show" at the urinal. Rock waited and waited, but he didn't return. One of the better-heeled homosexual guests had undoubtedly made off with this midnight cowboy.

Unfazed by his friend's disappearance, and alone at a table in the audience, Rock ordered another drink and sat back to watch Liberace, clad in a black tuxedo, play such favorites as "Boogie-Woogie."

After the show, Rock went backstage to congratulate Liberace for putting on such a good show and to tell him what a fan he was. Both performers were still on the verge of national fame or notoriety.

As was later revealed, the gay entertainer was enthralled by Rock's appearance. The wannabe star was at the peak of his youth, beauty, and masculinity. He was the physical ideal for a Hollywood heartthrob. Men in the early 1950s didn't refer to other men as beautiful, unless they aroused suspicions, but Liberace found Rock beautiful. "The thing about beautiful men is that they create a primal longing," Liberace told his new friend, Debbie Reynolds. One can't seem to tear one's eyes away from them."

Liberace invited Rock to his hotel suite for a 'nightcap." Even though still a bit naïve, Rock instinctively knew what "nightcap" meant.

At first, as Rock remembered it to Clark, Liberace talked about his own hopes and dreams. He believed that supper clubs like Ciro's or the Stork Club in New York were dying out. "Entertaining 600 people a night is one thing, but I crave bigger audiences," he was quoted as saying. "I want more money, more fans, and that elusive goddess, FAME."

Liberace went on to claim that the patrons at Ciro's didn't come to listen to an entertainer, "but to make out or to get drunk."

Finally, he seemed to take some interest in Rock and his career. He'd learned that Henry Willson was trying to launch him into movie stardom. "Surely, he gave you that name of Rock—sounds like something Willson would come up with. Unless, of course, he was referring to a certain appendage of yours."

"That, too," Rock said, not too modestly.

"I see," Liberace giggled. "Many have to change their name in show business. I've had a number of names. Would you believe 'Lee Chefroach' for a brief spell?"

Rock went on to compliment him for his piano playing, eventually admitting, "I play the piano a little bit—but nothing like you."

"Let's face it: Nobody plays the piano as good as I do."

After their second bottle of champagne, Liberace directed Rock into his bedroom, where he asked the young actor to perform a striptease.

Rock later claimed, "I knew what he wanted. The pudgy types always want one thing. He complained a lot about the pain of my entry. But he soon got used to it and couldn't get enough."

Liberace wanted Rock to spend the night and, during the next two weeks, invited him back, although Rock didn't visit every evening.

"The first time I ever had sex, it was with a football player for the Green Bay Packers," Liberace confessed. "Men are my kind of people. Some people say fucking saps your creative energy, but I don't believe that. I think it's a very healthy thing. A healthy sex life keeps you young and vital."

***

In later years, Liberace's companion and chauffeur, Scott Thorson, doubted the rumor of an affair between Rock and his lover.

"Rock wasn't Lee's type," he told a reporter. "They were too much alike. They both had giant egos. They were both stars. Men like that can't tolerate equals. Had Lee and Rock ever met, I think they would have disliked each other. They moved in completely different circles., socially and professionally."

Thorson was wrong on many counts. Rock was hardly a star when Liberace seduced him, only a bit player.

Daren Asbury Pyron, Liberace's biographer, wrote; "Thorson's incredulity notwithstanding, such an affair did occur, by Hudson's own admission. Hudson, along with author John Rechy (*City of Light*) and Thorson himself, was an exception to the general rule of kiss, don't tell."

In an interview with Boze Hadleigh, who later wrote a book, *Hollywood Gays*, Rock admitted his affair with Liberace, which only lasted a few weeks—"a fling, fun while it lasted."

As Pyron claimed, "Neither Liberace nor Rock Hudson stuck to types. A 'meeting of the minds' is not critical when two randy men turn each other on. Indeed, the absence of natural compatibility can even encourage and intensify a relationship, even as it dooms it, too."

"Liberace and I shared an interest in classical music," Rock said. "His piano playing knocked me out. But he was quite patronizing even then, and he treated everyone like his *protégé.*"

Pyron agreed that Liberace was not Hudson's type, but Rock didn't always date the "type" of partner he preferred. In fact, many people go through life without seducing their "types," especially if they are out of reach. Often, spouses marry against type, forming marital unions with the person they can get—not the one they dream about.

On subsequent visits to Liberace, Rock remembered bits and pieces of their talks.

The musician delivered a prediction of possible stardom for Rock, telling him, "You can become a matinee idol, a real screen god like Robert Taylor, Cary Grant, Tyrone Power, or Errol Flynn. Glamour, celebrity, stardom—that's what we both crave."

"When I went to the pictures as a boy, I saw people who had everything," Rock said. "It was a world of enchantment up there on the screen, and I wanted to be a part of it. I went to the movies to escape from the dreariness of life. Now I want to be in the movies, helping other people escape from fantasy."

"The world out here is the very symbol of artificiality—and that's why I want to be a part of it," Liberace said. "In spite of my flamboyant exterior, deep down, I'm still a simple boy from Milwaukee."

"Like hell you are," Rock answered. "I've explored you deep down. Let's face it: You're a bitch in heat when I get hold of you."

"True, true, but let's not get dirty."

Rock drifted out of Liberace's life as fast as he'd entered it. Too many other lovers, more to his type, were around the corner.

Months later, Liberace confessed to his friend, Merv Griffin, "I got Rock back when he was a struggling actor and playing an Indian in the movies." *[He was referring to the release of* Tomahawk *(1951).]* "In fact, that's quite a tomahawk that the big lug carried around with him."

"I know," Griffin said. "Been there, done that."

After director Joseph Pevney read the script for the Universal release, *Iron Man* (1951), he phoned the producer, Aaron Rosenberg. "I've heard that you've asked Rock Hudson to play a boxer, the second male lead?"

"I can and I will," Rosenberg answered. "One day, Rock Hudson is going to be the biggest star at Universal."

There's a problem...He's a southpaw," Pevney said.

"That's okay—he's in training now."

Both of the film executives were acutely aware of Rock: Pevney had previously directed him in *Shakedown,* and Rosenberg had produced *Air Cadet.*

During preparations for his role, Rock was not only taking boxing lessons with a semi-pro, but was enduring grueling workouts with a trainer, Frankie Van, who told him he needed to broaden his shoulders and make his forearms bigger. "Your ass is perfect. So are your legs."

After six weeks of intensive training, Rock went from 202 pounds to 195. At the end of six weeks, he stripped off his gym shorts and posed nude for Van, who endorsed his new look with: "You've done it! But I'll say this, kid. There's one part of you that doesn't need any more development."

"Thanks for the compliment," Rock said.

As a test to ensure that Rock could handle the part, Pevney hired a professional boxer to go two rounds with Rock. Van had told him to "look left, look right, look left-right, and then give the sucker a left hook."

On the second punch, Rock knocked out the other boxer, and then held up both his arms in a victory salute. The role was his.

Jeff Chandler and Evelyn Keyes, as Coke and Rose Mason, played a man and his wife. Stephen McNally, with whom Rock had recently worked, was cast as the gambler who lures him into the ring.

In *Iron Man* (1951), Rock Hudson (right) pounds Jeff Chandler onscreen. Offscreen, he continued that pounding.

The other co-stars included Joyce Holden, Jim Backus, and James Arness.

The stars were ordered to report to a special screening of the original, 1931 version of *Iron Man*, a film with the same title and plot. It had starred a young Lew Ayres along with Jean Harlow, who played his gold-digging wife.

In this latest reworking of the script, Chandler was cast as an ambitious, poor, well-intentioned, but emotionally immature Pennsylvania coal miner-turned-boxer consumed with inchoate rage who can't control his killer instincts when he steps into a ring with another boxer. According to the plot, crowds flocked to see him and to boo him, and sports reporters wrote of his "murderous rages in the ring."

Like Rock, Chandler trained hard for his role. "It's my chance to step up there in a class with Kirk Douglas and Robert Ryan. And that's pretty fast company."

He was referring to *Champion* (1949), which had starred Douglas as an unscrupulous boxer who punches his way to the top, and also *The Set Up* (also 1949), which had starred Ryan in an inside probe of the corrupt world of boxing.

Rock was cast as Tommy ("Speed") O'Keefe, who has to enter the ring with the murderous Coke.

Rock bonded with his co-star, Evelyn Keyes, who had played Scarlett O'Hara's younger sister in the iconic 1939 classic, *Gone With the Wind*. Throughout her life, she'd always been gay-friendly, and would later become a close pal of Tab Hunter, who described her as "full of piss and vinegar."

When Rock met her, she was divorcing director John Huston. "I didn't know why I married him in the first place. He was almost ugly: Deep pouches under his eyes made him look perpetually sad. Generous mouth, good teeth, weird posture which made his back curve forward, a bit hunched over. A real queer nose that was once flattened by a boxer. He had a way of talking, leaning in wrapping his melting caramel voice around you in an appealing Pied Piper tradition."

"God, you're articulate," Rock said. "I wish I was."

Born in Port Arthur, Texas, Keyes grew up in the port that was home to Lyndon B. Johnson's favorite bordello. She'd had an active love life, though she expressed a wonder: "What would have happened to me if I'd had a size 38 bra instead of a more modest 34?"

When Rock met Chandler, he was the biggest star at Universal, a position that Rock himself would seize in a few years. The attraction between the men was instant, Although Chandler was gray-haired, he was only seven years older than Rock. His hair had turned gray at an early age. Universal tried to get him to dye it, but he refused.

Rock, as he later told his friends, found him ruggedly masculine. As he later confided, "Jeff and I are great in bed together. We know how to reach each other's hot spots. There is only one difference between us. I have 2 ½ inches more, and foreskin. He was born to a Jewish family in Brooklyn. Incidentally, in high school in Brooklyn, he took the virginity of one Edythe Marrenner. We know her as Susan Hayward."

Chandler had just co-starred as the Indian chief, Cochise, in *Broken Arrow* (1950), for which he was Oscar nominated. The star of that picture was James Stewart, who was also the lead in two pictures he'd eventually make with Rock. Chandler became the first actor playing an American Indian to be nominated for an Academy Award.

A bisexual, Chandler had had a wartime romance with a soldier when he'd served mostly in the Aleutians. After his discharge, he'd married Marjorie Hoshelle, but continued to have affairs with both sexes.

Two days after they met, Rock and Chandler were engaged in "real man-on-man sex," as Rock called it. "Our affair became so hot, so intense, that it would soon burn out." He recalled that one scene called for them to bathe together in adjoining showers, Army barracks style.

The cameraman told them to strip, promising that he would film them only from the waist up. Eventually, the sequence was viewed as too homoerotic and cut from the final release. However, the photographer didn't keep his promise, and made a film clip of them frontally nude, washing their (respective) genitals. That clip was later configured into a "Hollywood Blue" movie.

During the film, Rock was brought into Chandler's very private world. After their first week, he confessed to Rock that he was a cross-dresser, and wanted him to take him, dressed as a woman, out as a date.

"Are you sure?" Rock asked. "You're a beautiful man, but might not look so good as a woman."

"I want to do it," Chandler said. "We'll go to remote places where no one will recognize us."

At one seedy bar out in San Fernando Valley, Chandler went to the women's toilet. During his absence, the barmaid said to Rock, "Honey, you can do better than that bull dyke. Like me, for instance,"

"She's got a lot of money, and pays well," he said.

"Oh, I see."

Iron Man drew mixed reviews, *The New York Times* defining it as "standard for the course of boxing movies. *Iron Man* is not in the blue-blooded company of Kirk Douglas' *Champion*. The bouts are exciting enough, but the punches, which are fairly hard and straight, are telegraphed."

In contrast, however, and for the first time, Rock's acting got some praise, albeit faint. ▪

***

Rock would make two movies, beginning with *Bright Victory* (1951), with his co-star, John Kennedy of Massachusetts. Originally, when that actor made his debut in show

In *Bright Victory* (1951), Julie Adams, one of Rock's alltime favorite leading ladies, has a moment of tender compassion for Arthur Kennedy, who is going blind.

business, he used that name (i.e., his birth name), but the increasing fame of another "John Kennedy from Massachusetts" forced him to switch to his middle name. Hence, forever after, he billed himself as "Arthur Kennedy."

Light-haired and of medium build, he was viewed in looks as "the Average Joe. In spite of his appearance, he brought a dynamic quality to almost any role he played on the stage or screen. *Bright Victory* would bring him his only Oscar nomination, but he was beat out by Humphrey Bogart for that actor's performance in *The African Queen*.

As a screen actor, Kennedy had first been discovered by James Cagney, who cast him as his younger brother in *City for Conquest* (1940).

Rock sensed that *Bright Victory* was going to be a critical success, and he was disappointed that he'd been assigned such a small role within it, that of Corporal John Flagg. "I was in only the first nine pages of the script," Rock said. "They got rid of me *pronto*."

All the actors assigned to the film knew from the beginning that *Bright Victory* would be Kennedy's picture.

The Canadian director, Mark Robson, was on a roll, having recently turned out three critically acclaimed movies, each released in 1949: *Champion* with Kirk Douglas; *My Foolish Heart* with Susan Hayward; and *Home of the Brave*, with James Edwards and Lloyd Bridges, one of the first dramas to deal with racism in the U.S. Armed Forces.

In *Bright Victory*, Robson assembled an extremely talented cast. He positioned Kennedy as Larry Nevins, an American sergeant blinded by a German sniper in North Africa during World War II. His part was that of a bigot, facing an uncertain future, who becomes strengthened by his ordeal. He is befriended by another blinded soldier, Joe Morgan (James Edwards). Not knowing that his new friend is black, Nevins later makes a racial slur which temporarily disrupts their friendship.

The female lead of the nurse, Judy Greene, was played by Peggy Dow, who would soon retire from films to marry a millionaire oilman from Tulsa. Rock had already made two films with her, *Undertow* and *Shakedown*, during which she dated his friend, Tony Curtis. In *Bright Victory,* she falls in love with Nevins.

The third lead was essayed by Julie (aka Julia) Adams, in the role of Chris Paterson. She would also be featured with both Kennedy and Rock in an upcoming James Stewart movie, and she and Rock would play the leads in an upcoming film as well, shortly after her marriage to the screenwriter, Leonard B. Stern.

She told Rock, "I was 'just a Little Girl from Little Rock,'" she said, ironically parodying the famous line from a future film with Marilyn Monroe and Jane Russell, *Gentlemen Prefer Blondes* (1953).   Adams   had been crowned *Miss Little Rock* in 1946.

Also in the film was a ruggedly handsome actor from San Francisco, Richard Egan. He would later star as Elvis Presley's older brother in *Love Me Tender* (1956), and he would also star opposite the by-then fading star Jane Russell in two of her last pictures—*Underwater!* (1955) and *The Revolt of Mamie Stover* (1956).

"I might have gone for Richard," Rock confessed to Henry Willson, "but it didn't happen. When I cozied up to him, he tried to convert me into becoming a Roman Catholic."

When Rock met Egan, he had just co-starred with Joan Crawford in *The Damned Don't Cry (1950).* Rock asked him, "With Miss Crawford, did you or did you not?"

"I did not!" Egan answered. "That honor went to Steve Cochran and David Brian."

***

Anthony Mann had directed Rock in his small role in *Winchester '73,* starring James Stewart, and he must have liked working with Rock, since he'd just cast him in the next Stewart film, *Bend of the River* (1952).

One of Mann's most recent pictures was *Devil's Doorway* (1950), starring Robert Taylor. Ironically, he was also directing Taylor's estranged wife, super-star Barbara Stanwyck, in *The Furies* (1951).

Taylor was heading to Rome to film the latest MGM spectacular, *Quo*

Vadis (1951), in which Elizabeth Taylor and Sophia Loren (as a joke) would appear as extras.

Mann decided to throw a farewell party for Taylor, and Rock counted himself lucky to receive an invitation to the going-away gala. He had not seen his former flight instructor in Illinois since the war.

When they'd parted, Taylor had promised that he'd keep in touch, but that didn't happen. When Rock got to Hollywood, the only point of contact Rock had for the star was the fan mail department at his studio, MGM.

He wrote three times, but got no personal answer. His letters were thrown into Taylor's bag of fan mail. However, some secretary sent him an 8" x 10" glossy with a machine-generated autograph as a response to every letter Rock wrote.

As he complained to Henry Willson, "I didn't want Bob's god damn autograph. I wanted to screw him."

At Mann's party, Rock noticed that Taylor and Stanwyck were working different sides of the room. At no point did he see them talking to each other.

He wanted to approach the star, his former lover, but found him always surrounded by people. After all, the party was in his honor.

A break finally came when Taylor headed for the bar and Rock decided that he, too, needed a drink.

Taylor stepped up the bar and ordered a scotch and soda. Coming up beside him, Rock did the same. After ordering, he turned to Taylor, who looked at him for the first time.

"Remember me, teacher?" Rock asked.

At first, Taylor looked puzzled. "I can't say I do. Have we met?"

"You were my flight instructor back in Illinois," Rock answered. "Perhaps the years have changed me a bit."

"Oh, brother! Those years have been kind. You look terrific! I remember now. Everything's coming back!"

Rock had changed his physical appearance. He was much bigger now, noticeably more confident, and his teeth had been fixed. He also speculated that Taylor had had so many lovers, he couldn't remember all of them. Of course, he certainly remembered the two goddesses with whom he'd recently had affairs, Ava Gardner in *The Bribe* (1949), and a very young Elizabeth Taylor, cast as his wife in *The Conspirator* (also 1949).

"Let's take our drinks out onto the terrace for some catch-up time... and some privacy," Taylor said, leading the way as Rock followed.

In the moonlight, out on the terrace with the palms swaying in the night breezes, Rock realized that the star was a bit drunk, especially when his hand reached out and fondled his crotch.

"Who can forget that?" Taylor asked.

"I'm more experienced now," Rock said. "Want some more?"

"Do I ever!"

As Rock would later confess to George Nader, "We expected to be interrupted at any minute by somebody coming out onto the terrace. So we got down right away to business."

Taylor invited him to drive with him to Palm Springs for the long weekend before he had to fly to Italy.

They exchanged phone numbers, and Taylor promised to pick him up the next morning at 6AM.

At this point, two other couples came out onto the terrace, and Taylor immediately switched the conversation to shop talk. "You won't believe this, but that son of a gun, Mann, forced me to play a Shoshone Indian in *Devil's Doorway* (1950), body paint and all. I hope I'm not laughed off the screen. John Wayne doesn't have to play an Indian."

"I'm sure that will happen to me sooner than later," Rock said.

[He was right: In 1954, he would star as Taza, *Son of Cochise.]*

After the party, when Rock returned home at 2AM, he phoned Nader and woke him up to tell him some of the details.

"You're moving up into the bigtime, kid," Nader said. "Keep me posted. Now get off the god damn phone so I can get my beauty sleep. Love ya, babe." Then he hung up.

Rock must have realized that he needed some beauty sleep too, since he had an early call with Taylor for the drive to Palm Springs.

***

That long weekend with the fading matinee idol of the 1930s was characterized by a lot of nudity, both in and out of the bedroom, and in and out of the pool. "The next time I meet Bob Taylor, he would not forget me again. I saw to that," Rock later told Nader.

When Taylor had made love to him years before in Illinois, since both of them were in the Navy at the time, he was very reserved. But as civilians, years later, and in the seclusion of a private villa, he opened up more to the younger star. He enthralled Rock with tales of pre-war Golden Age Hollywood, during which he'd co-starred with Joan Crawford, Garbo, Vivien Leigh, Katharine Hepburn, Irene Dunne, and even his own wife, Barbara Stanwyck.

He spoke of painful times, too, especially his most recent appearances in Washington before the House Un-American Activities Committee, in front of which he was interviewed as a friendly witness, outing (some said,

133

"betraying") communists in the film industry.

He also discussed his early days at MGM, when an acting coach suggested that he abandon the entertainment industry and return to his family's farm in Nebraska. He went on to complain about his contract. "I'm the biggest star in the world who works for the lowest paycheck."

Now, at the debut of the 1950s, Taylor was also concerned—along with Gary Cooper, Ronald Reagan, Tyrone Power, and Errol Flynn—by the hordes of potential new stars getting off buses at L.A.'s Union Station every day.

"I talked to Clark Gable only last week," Taylor said. "We both know that MGM is pink-slipping its old stars every day. Gable fears he'll be next. Let's face it! He's no longer the King of Hollywood."

"Mother Time is catching up with me," Taylor said. "No one's defined me as 'The Pretty Boy of Hollywood' in a long, long time. That label more appropriately belongs to you."

"I know time's a bitch, but I think you still look magnetic," Rock said.

"If that's what you really think, why not take my hand and lead me to bed where I expect you to perform unspeakable acts," Taylor said, with a smile.

"I'm game! C'mon along!"

On a lazy Sunday afternoon, Taylor gave the young actor a lot of career advice, and both of them spoke of changing times and the upcoming threat of television. "I hear MGM might show a lot of my old movies."

"Maybe you'll generate a new fan base," Rock said.

Early Monday morning, before they departed for Los Angeles, Taylor gave Rock some additional career advice and a warning: "It's imperative for both you and me to lead a private life that shields our desires. You've got to be careful. Beware of blackmailers. They come on so honest, trustworthy, and friendly, but the fucking bastards have one aim—and that's to either embarrass and expose you or else receive a big payoff. I've been threatened many times. Please be extra careful."

"It's shit to have to live in fear all the time for just leading the life you want," Rock said.

"But it's the price of fame," Taylor added. "Of course, everything in life has a price."

***

After Taylor returned from Rome, where he made *Quo Vadis* with his co-star, Deborah Kerr, he phoned and got together with Rock on several other occasions, always in Palm Springs, and always in secrecy. They were never seen out in public together.

Then one day, he read in the papers that Taylor had married a beautiful German-born actress, Ursula Thiess. Eventually, the couple would have a son and daughter together.

As Rock watched Taylor's career decline as he aged, he worked in mostly European pictures with very limited market share in the U.S. They included such pictures as *The Day the Hot Line Got Hot* (1968).

For his future career, Rock noted that as movie roles went dry, such stars as Ronald Reagan found new life on television. In Reagan's case, that included hosting *The General Electric Theater.* Taylor also moved into television, hosting *Death Valley Days* on TV from 1966 to '68 during the final months of his life.

Rock was sorry to read of the tragic ending of Robert Taylor from cancer. Eventually, he lost control of his body, and spent his final days in pain, anguish, agony, and regret, dying in a hospital bed on June 8, 1969.

A few million of his mature fans from the 1930s, many of whom had idolized him, had already been long departed.

***

Here Come the Nelsons (1952) doubled as both a general release movie and as a pilot for the upcoming *The Adventures of Ozzie and Harriet.* The hit TV sitcom would air from 1952 to 1966. The American public watched Ozzie and Harriet rear their boys on TV, steering them through key moments of their youth under the scrutiny of a television audience.

Before starring with Rock, the Nelsons had been hailed as "Radio's Favorite Family." The billing of the movie pilot starred Rock in fifth position after Ozzie, Harriet, David, and Ricky.

Others in the cast in-

Here Come The Nelsons (1952) depicted the fantasy version of one of America's most dysfunctional families. Harriet told Rock that her son Ricky (right) had a crush on him.

cluded starlet Barbara Lawrence, with talented supporting players: Sheldon Leonard, Jim Backus, Gale Gordon, and Ann Doran.

The director was Frederick de Cordova, with Aaron Rosenberg producing.

Rosenberg had already produced three films with Rock: *Air Cadet, Iron Man,* and *Winchester '73.* In reference to Rock, Rosenberg said, "I thought the big lug had potential, if only he could get over his fear of acting. He seemed terrified before stepping in front of a camera. He needed to relax more, and I knew that would come with more experience, which I was giving him in minor roles. In spite of his limited screen exposure, he was already a magnet for teenage girls and gay boys, who collected bare-chested publicity photos of him."

Rock was a familiar face to De Cordova, too. He had helmed him in the comedy *Peggy,* and in the "tits-and-sand" movie, *The Desert Hawk.* "Rock and his buddy, Tony Curtis, were trying desperately to become better actors, and to get more substantial roles," said De Cordova. "Until then, their parts were mostly shit. Rock always pleaded with me to reshoot his scenes, always claiming, 'I could do better.' I had to turn him down. I operated on a rapid time schedule with a starvation budget for production. I didn't have time to reshoot scenes with my major stars, much less with an actor in a minor part."

"Don't get me wrong: I appreciated his concern about wanting to improve his skills. He persisted and before too long after doing the dumb part with the Nelsons, stardom was his."

Rock was shocked to learn how far the Nelson family were from their idealized roles on radio and TV. Ozzie was an actor, bandleader, director, and producer. He presided with an iron fist over what was said to be the most dysfunctional family in Hollywood. As an authoritarian figure, he dictated every aspect of the lives of his growing boys.

As author David Halberstam wrote: "Ozzie was a workaholic who stole the childhood from his sons. He insisted they skip college to work in the TV series."

Unlike her husband, Harriet "won my heart," Rock said. "She was one of the most gay-friendly women in Hollywood."

She admitted to Rock that she'd begun smoking when she was thirteen and had once been married to an abusive comedian. As Harriet Hilliard, she was a singer who was performing in vaudeville until hired by Ozzie, a saxophone-playing bandleader.

"She was a lot of fun to hang out with," Rock said. "Unlike her proper radio and TV persona, she loved a dirty joke, and I knew plenty of them. Both of us enjoyed quite a few cocktails, and she could outdrink the best of men. Fortunately, Ozzie was always away on some business deal, allowing her to let loose."

She shocked him one night when she told him that her younger son, Ricky, had developed a powerful crush on him. "Let the kid down easy," she advised. He's only eleven, and these first loves can be so painful. He's got it bad for you, and I just know you'll be kind when you have to break the poor boy's heart."

***

The novelist and journalist, Denis Brian, described actress Tallulah Bankhead, a Southern belle from Alabama, as "a husky-voiced, strikingly lovely young starlet who shocked, attracted, repelled, and fascinated."

But by 1953, she hadn't aged well since her birth in 1903.

Brian also wrote: "She sniffed cocaine, kissed women, stole rivals' lovers, stripped in public—all the while gathering devoted, deliciously scandalized legions of fans on her skyrocket to fame."

What's wrong with the picture? She did more than kiss women. If they were still around, you could ask Greta Garbo, Marlene Dietrich, Katharine Cornell, Eva Le Gallienne, Hope Williams ("she had a boy's body"), Laurette Taylor, Billie Holiday, Mercedes de Acosta, Beatrice Lillie, Nazimova, and Hattie McDaniel (Scarlett O'Hara's "Mammy").

Writer Robert Gottlieb, in *The New Yorker* magazine, described Tallulah as "hectoring, demanding attention, catastrophically self-destructive, a personality more than a star, a celebrity before the phenomenon of celebrity had been identified."

It was the gay Welsh playwright and actor, Emlyn Williams, who said, "Tallulah's voice was seeped as deep in sex as the human voice can go without drowning."

Perhaps another gay playwright, Noël Coward, said it best: "Tallulah Bankhead was actually Humphrey Bogart in silk panties—that is, when she bothered to wear panties, which she rarely did, especially when turning cartwheels to amuse guests at any party, no matter how formal."

The indomitable Tallulah Bankhead always lavished praise on Rock Hudson. She told Mike Wallace, "Rock is a two-hander and a half, *dah-ling*."

It was 1953 at the Sands Hotel in Las Vegas when producer Jack Entratter came up with a new act. He wanted to book Tallulah for a live performance in a nightclub. Management agreed to a salary of $20,000 a week, the highest she'd ever been paid for a performance.

Rock had listened faithfully to her when she'd hosted *The Big Show* on radio, and he was anxious to see and hear her in the flesh. "She's my kind of woman," he told friends. "She's as outrageous as I secretly want to be."

On Broadway, there were predictions that Tallulah would fall flat on her face in Las Vegas. Tallulah herself was worried that she'd bomb. In fact, on her opening night at the Sands, she broke out in shingles. Her voice became so hoarse it sounded like she was croaking. Nevertheless, she pulled it off, and the audience loved her. She walked on and immediately delivered a galvanic, "OHHHHHHHHHH...MY GAAAAAAAAWD!"

For her opening remark, she said, "*Dah-lings*, I never thought I'd be the shill for a gambler's joint."

Onstage, she did her impersonations of famous stars, a particularly devastating one of Ethel Barrymore. She even danced the Black Bottom and sang her standard, "Bye, Bye Blackbird."

She read from Dorothy Parker's *The Waltz* to prove that she was still an actress. This was the same show that Rock would fly in to see three nights later. Although he missed opening night, Mae West showed up, as did Eddie Albert, Lucille Ball, Desi Arnaz, Monty Clift, and Marlene Dietrich.

Merv Griffin was the opening act for Tallulah, singing the hit songs of the day, many of which he'd sung before on radio. He secured Rock a front-row seat, and he laughed raucously throughout the show.

Tallulah had agreed to meet with him after the show, and a private table was reserved for them in the bar.

When Griffin brought Rock and Tallulah together, both of them seemed enchanted with each other. He would later refer to her as "The Queens' Queen." She would later tell Griffin, "He's drop-dead gorgeous, but thick as two bricks."

Despite the reservations each member of the famous pair might have had with each other, they formed an unlikely friendship and became known as "the odd couple."

Rock called on her every time he flew east to New York. He loved the way she talked, throwing convention to the wind. He was astonished to hear her say, "I don't know what I am, *dah-ling*. I've tried several varieties of sex, but the missionary position makes me claustrophobic, and all the other positions give me either a stiff neck or lockjaw."

"*Dah-ling*," she said at one point to him. "They say cocaine is habit-forming. I know that it is not. I've been snorting it for years."

Griffin left before midnight, and Tallulah invited Rock to her suite "for a nightcap."

At around ten the next morning, Griffin arrived to escort Tallulah to the office of their producer, Entratter, to discuss aspects of their act.

He arrived right on time and was greeted by actress Patsy Kelly, who had fallen on hard times and was now serving as Tallulah's "lady-in-waiting," as she called it. She directed him to the sofa in the living room of the suite. "Make yourself at home. Jerk off! Do whatever you want. Tallu will be out soon. I'm hitting the sack for a few more hours." She was obviously hung over.

In a few minutes, Griffin heard sounds emerging from the master bedroom. Its door opened and, to his astonishment, Rock emerged nude and at "half mast," as he phrased it.

"You and Tallulah?" Griffin asked. "I can't believe it. President Eisenhower in her bedroom, I could believe, even Queen Elizabeth and Tallulah in a lesbian tryst. But you two?"

"Stranger matings have occurred," Rock said. "Tallulah wouldn't be the first fag hag I've fucked. It was Joan Crawford. Besides, she's a lot of fun. The sex is just a mercy fuck on my part. I want to thank you for hooking me up with her."

After that weekend in Las Vegas, Rock became an on-again, off-again fixture in the final years of Tallulah's troubled life.

***

Bend of the River, a 1952 Western, would mark the second collaboration between James Stewart and director Anthony Mann, who had starred him most recently in *Winchester '73,* giving Rock a small part in that film as well. This time, Stewart would be cast as Glyn McLyntock in a far less heroic role—that of a cowboy with a shady past. He'd been a border raider during the Civil War, but now wanted to live down the regrets of his past.

Rock was cat as Trey Wilson, a quick-on-the-draw professional gambler who is traveling west to the newly opened Oregon Territory, hoping for a new start in life. He helps Stewart retrieve stolen supplies for the wagon train settlers.

He didn't have that much to do in the movie except "pose and pout," in the words of one biographer. His best scene comes near the end of the film, when he is wounded but bravely smiles through his pain. The leading lady, Julie (sometimes billed as Julia) Adams played Laura Baile, one of the pioneers on the wagon train. Despite her emotional commitments to the character played by Stewart, she offers Rock comfort. At the end of the film, Rock bonds with his own true love. Once again, Rock would be in a movie produced by Aaron Rosenberg, who had just cast him as the brassiere salesman in *Here Come the Nelsons*. Rock's star was rising, as shown by his status as the fourth lead after Stewart, Arthur Kennedy, and Adams. Both Kennedy and Adams had starred with him previously in *Bright Victory*.

Based on the 1950 novel, *Bend of the Snake*, by Bill Gulick, *Bend of the River* had Stewart playing a tough, cynical, and sometimes ruthless adventurer. He had once escaped a hangman's noose and wore a bandanna around his neck to disguise the scars left by the rope. In his new role, he was a scout for a wagon train filled with pioneers hoping for a new life in Oregon.

Rock on horseback posed for this publicity picture for *Bend of the River* (1952). It was hailed as the sexiest picture of a cowboy ever to appear in an American western.

As such, he is not the typical cowboy like Gary Cooper or John Wayne. He is living with dark shadows and looks grubby, not scrubbed clean like so many other cowboys in other Westerns. Mann advised Stewart not to take a bath until the film's end and to wear a dirty shirt and to "let the stubble grow."

Along the trail, as his "caravan" plods westward, Stewart rescues a notorious cowboy, Emerson Cole (Arthur Kennedy), who is about to be lynched by a mob. Ironically, since this is a movie, not real life, this is the same man who had previously rescued Stewart from a hangman's noose.

There is the predictable attack on the wagon trail, this time by five Shoshone Indians who wound Laura (Adams) with an arrow. Cole and McLyntock ride to her rescue.

Adams told Rock, "I'm mere window dressing. As you know, it's mandatory to put a pretty girl in a Western, so that she gets rescued by a cowboy."

***

James Stewart and his co-stars, including Rock, flew into Portland for the world premiere of their film. In the typical fashion of that era, the event began with a parade through town, with the stars riding in convertibles, with Stewart prominently positioned in the leading vehicle.

Rock waved to the crowds, later joking, "For the first time in my life, I knew what it feels like to be the Queen of England. I couldn't believe it, but along the route, a number of young girls kept screaming, 'We want Rock!' I didn't think I was hearing right."

The parade route ended in front of a movie house, where a badly constructed wooden platform had been accessorized with colored lights and a microphone. Stewart came out first and received respectful applause. In that voice familiar to movie audiences worldwide, he thanked the people of Oregon, but was almost drowned out by screams of "WE WANT ROCK!"

Universal had hired "shriekers," evocative of those bobbysoxers who had greeted Frank Sinatra. Henry Willson had also hired of number of his own. The crowd soon became a screaming, cacophonous armada of male and female fans.

The adoring crowd, paid or otherwise, practically stormed the hastily built wooden platform, and it started to collapse. A phalanx of cops moved in to rescue the stars, hustling them into the theater.

Back in Hollywood, Rock spoke candidly to Ronald Bohning, a reporter for *Variety*, about what had happened.

"This adulation went to my head. It was like I was floating on a cloud. Stewart was a movie idol, and I felt the crowds wanted me—and not him. It must have been really hard on him. Perhaps he realized that the baton had passed on to a new generation of young men. I'm sure if I lasted in the business, the same thing would happen to me one day.

"I couldn't sleep for most of the night. When dawn came, I got up, got dressed, and ordered breakfast at this workman's diner. No one recognized me. I walked down the street and found bare-chested publicity pictures of me in the window of every store. Morning workers passed me by. Not one god-damned person recognized me. Where were all those adoring fans?"

"I learned a sad lesson that day. Those mob scenes don't mean a damn thing.

141

If you try to grab onto fleeting flame, you'll soon learn she's a fickle goddess. You reach out to grab her, but you're reaching for nothing but air."

As if to compound the bitter lesson Rock had learned that day, he received more bad news a few hours later. Apparently, Stewart had learned that many of those screaming Rock fans had been pre-arranged and paid, either by Willson or by Universal.

He called Rock a "son of a bitch," informing Mann, "I'll never work with that double-crossing bastard again. I don't want that fucking asshole from Chicago within ten feet of me—ten miles would be even better."

***

For promotions of *Bend of the River,* Universal sent Rock, Lori Nelson, and Julie Adams on a grueling promotional junket through the Northwest, mainly in Washington and Oregon, the setting for the film. Gail Gifford, a publicist for Universal, was the tour's chaperone. Wanting to save money, Universal worked its contract players from dawn to midnight, having them appear in public and subjecting them to endless, usually superficial, interviews from the press.

For the first time in his career, Rock had to give many interviews, which he loathed, especially when a reporter inquired about his private life. He left the suggestion that he and Nelson "are an item."

In spite of all the pressure, he was a good sport throughout, and Nelson and Adams found him an ideal traveling companion, "always laughing, always full of fun," Adams said.

When *Bend of the River* was released, it received poor reviews and did not do well at the box office. Over the years, however, its fame and critical respect have grown. By 2008, the American Film Institute nominated it as one of the Top Ten Western films of all time.

When Rock flew back to Los Angeles from Portland—the final stop on the promotional tour and site of the film's premiere—he arrived home exhausted from the ordeal.

Good news was on the way: After all his struggles and disappointments, stardom had arrived at last.

Waiting for him at his house was news that he had been selected as the male lead opposite Yvonne De Carlo in her next picture. From that point on, he would have star billing in nearly all his future films, only occasionally being demoted to second billing.

There was more: One night at the home of friends, he met the man he wanted to move into his house, "So I can have him every night."

Chapter Six

THE BARON OF BEEFCAKE
(ROCK BECOMES A DASHING LEADING MAN, "RAW MEAT FOR SHE-WOLVES")

Rock Services the Studio Chief, His Director, And His Live-In Male Beauty at Night

Rock became the entertainment industry's go-to man for demonstrative love-making on screen. Above, Rock "gets down" with actress and sex kitten Yvonne De Carlo, playing a "scarlet saloon girl gone legit." in this steamy scene from *Scarlet Angel* (1952), a Civil War period piece.

It was a lazy Sunday afternoon on the beach at Venice, where Henry Willson often languished in his eternal search for his next stud. He could always change his name, put him through a rigorous workout in the gym, pose him for beefcake pictures, and then try to launch him into stardom, as he had for Guy Madison, Rory Calhoun, and Rock himself.

The partially clothed Willson was packing up his gear and was a little drunk from too much Budweiser in the sun when he looked at what was coming down the boardwalk.

"He was a dreamboat walking," as Willson later told Rock's friends, Mark Miller and George Nader.

In Willson's description, "The young man was well muscled, but not overly so. More of a swimmer's physique. He was more than six feet tall and was shirtless, wearing a pair of tight-fitting jeans that advertised his considerable assets. His blonde hair was streaked by the sun, and his face looked like it had been sculpted by that Italian fag who did the nude statue of David in Florence."

As he neared Willson, the agent stared into his striking blue eyes. "They were the bluest of the blue, the kind that handsome Nazi soldiers had,…you know, the ones that dropped the pellets into the gas chambers. But instead of a Nazi, this kid could have posed for a recruiting poster for the Army, an all-American, corn-fed boy from the fields of Iowa or one of those states you flew over *en route* to New York City."

The "walking streak of sex," was known as Jack Navaar. He had fought in the Korean War when he was drafted into the U.S. Army. After his tour of duty, he sailed with his Army buddies into San Francisco. He told his fellow soldiers, "I'm heading for Hollywood, where I'm going to make myself available for all offers."

"You mean *all* offers?" his friend asked.

"You've got that right," he answered. "It beats harvesting corn, plowing fields, and shoveling horseshit from the barn back home."

In Venice, Willson wasted no time in introducing himself to Navaar, and telling him he was a talent scout, always on the lookout for a star of tomorrow. "You've got the looks, and we can always teach you how to act."

It didn't take Willson long to lure Navaar into his automobile for the ride back to Hollywood.

After dinner and drinks, Willson invited him to sleep over for the weekend. "I hope you understand our deal. I always like to audition a young man before signing him to my stable. By the way, I hope you don't mind. I'll have to change your name to Rand Saxon. Now it's getting late. Time for your audition. You do get my point, don't you?"

"I got your point before you invited me into your car," Navaar said. Then he stood up from the sofa and began to unbuckle his jeans.

"Hold that for the bedroom," Willson said. "I want you completely bare-assed for this workout."

The curtain goes down on what happened next.

The next morning, in his kitchen, cooking breakfast for his new discovery, Willson phoned Nader. "Last night, I met God's gift to all cocksucking size queens. He's Rock's ideal type. You know, I've become Rock's pimp these days, trying to hold onto my best client by pimping for him on the side. I suggest you and Mark set up a dinner and invite my boy, Jack Navaar, over to meet 'The Rock.'"

Before Nader called Navaar to invite him for dinner, the young Army veteran had met a beautiful brunette and had made a date with her. He'd encountered her at Schwab's Drugstore at the magazine rack. This was the drugstore where Lana Turner was allegedly discovered but really wasn't.

Navaar had to cancel that date after Nader invited him over to the house he was sharing with Miller to present him to Rock Hudson. According to Navaar, "I couldn't wait to meet him. I'd seen his picture in the fan magazines, but had not actually seen one of his movies. But I read that he was cast in a new picture with that love goddess, Yvonne De Carlo, and I'd seen three of *her* movies."

On his way to the Miller-Nader home Navaar later admitted, "I was nervous as hell, meeting a movie star, a genuine movie star."

Nader and Miller agreed that Navaar lived up to Willson's billing. He was sitting with Rock's friends in their living room, having a beer, when the doorbell rang. Miller ushered Rock into his living room, where the new man was introduced.

Other than shaking his hand, Rock, during the early part of the evening, paid little attention to Navaar. He seemed full of fun and told riotously funny stories about his experiences working on *Bend of the River* with James Stewart. Navaar sat in the corner, feeling left out. He didn't have any Hollywood stories to tell, except the one about getting picked up on the beach by Willson.

When Miller rose to check the roast in the oven, Navaar trailed him into the kitchen. "I don't think Rock digs me at all. Maybe I should leave."

"No, stick around," Miller said. "Rock's been checking you out all evening. Quick, furtive glances. He's probably falling in love."

By the time dinner was served, Rock began to devote most of his attention to Naavar, asking him about serving in Korea, his previous life in the Midwest, even his dreams of becoming an actor.

That night, Miller and Nader kissed both Rock and Navaar goodbye, as the two men headed together out the door and into Rock's sunflower-yellow convertible for the ride back to his home at Avenida del Sol, where Preble had not yet moved out all his possessions.

"I've got this new hi-fi system, and we can test it out," Rock said. "A whole new batch of records have arrived."

After an hour of listening to music, Rock invited him out onto his terrace overlooking the Hollywood Hills and the lights of Los Angeles in the distance.

As Navaar would later tell Willson, "Suddenly, Rock just seemed to envelop me in his arms and started kissing and kissing, never stopping for the longest time. I enjoyed every minute of it, even though I'm basically straight."

By 2AM, Rock and Navaar were in bed, beginning his most enduring affair to date.

The next morning, Rock treated Navaar to his breakfast specialty, which he dubbed "Greyhound Bus Station Eggs."

Later that day, Rock asked Navaar to give up his small apartment and to come live with him, warning that they had to be secretive about it, except with their friends, since exposure of his homosexuality could ruin his burgeoning career.

"That's okay by me," Navaar said. "I wouldn't want word to get out about me being a fruitcake. That might keep me from even getting cast in a movie, too."

As the weeks passed, Rock and Navaar showed up for dinner with Nader and Miller two or three times a week. As Navaar confessed to Nader, "I came from a broken home that's breaking up once again, and Rock is, like his name, solid for me. He makes me feel loved and secure, and no one ever did that for me before."

One afternoon, Bob Preble showed up to retrieve the rest of his possessions, and it was only then that Navaar learned he'd been Rock's live-in lover. He was now dating a woman named Yvonne Rivero and planned to marry her.

Once Navaar learned that, he confronted Rock that night with his first demand—and it was a big one. He claimed he could no longer live in the house and make love in that double bed where Preble had once slept with Rock.

But instead of a big fight, Rock gave in to his demands. Within two weeks, he had rented a larger, two-story home on Grandview, and Navaar moved in with him there.

Willson never got "Rand Saxon" an acting job, but in the meantime, placed him in a blue-collar position working for Hughes Aircraft as a mechanic on the night shift.

That lasted only one week, before Rock demanded that he quit. I want you here when I come home at night. I want you available for weekend trips to Palm Springs or for jaunts to Laguna. I'll take care of all your expenses."

"I don't know," Navaar said with some hesitation. He knew that Hollywood was populated with "kept boys," and he didn't want to join their ranks. But he finally acquiesced and quit his job.

Soon, "Rock & Jack," as they came to be known, were driving up to Arcadia twice a month to call on Rock's mother, Kay, who was now into her third and final marriage, this time to a man named Joseph Olsen.

Many a stepfather or a loving mother might object to their son arriving with a male lover. But both Kay and Olsen were very supportive of the relationship, and often drove down from Arcadia to visit Rock and Navaar.

Kay liked Navaar so much, she nicknamed him "Cookie," and began to prepare his favorite dishes that his own mother used to cook for him.

"As long as it's fried chicken, corn on the cob, and mashed potatoes with lots of brown gravy, the boys didn't complain," she said.

She even called Cookie "My new son-in-law," telling him, "You make Rock happy. I'm so glad you've come into his life. Maybe he'll settle down and stop all this gadding about with God knows who."

Rock was making $200 a week from Universal, the most money he'd ever made, and he had plenty to spend on presents for Navaar for his 23rd birthday. He'd been saving up and purchasing clothing, including two cashmere sweaters and two dress suits, stashing them in his dressing room at Universal until the occasion came.

Navaar had never received such gifts before, and he became even more devoted to Rock after that birthday. When presenting the gifts to him, Rock had kissed him, telling him, "The best for the best."

Rock didn't know what his reception would be, and was a bit leery, when he and Navaar got into the yellow convertible to drive to Santa Monica to meet Navaar's mother. She welcomed Rock like he was her own son, and later told Navaar, "You've nailed a real catch. Some guys have all the luck. Not me. You did a hell of a lot better when it comes to snaring men than I do. My marriage is breaking up."

As the weeks went by, his mother became such friends with Rock that he even paid for her divorce. His generosity didn't end there. He often gave the mother money to help support herself and his lover's two younger sisters.

Not all was bliss in the Grandview home. Rock often had to go out on studio-arranged dates with starlets like Debbie Reynolds for publicity purposes, and Navaar was waiting alone for him at home.

He was still troubled by being a "kept boy," and sexually, he still had a strong desire to make love to a woman. But for Rock's sake, he tried to suppress such urges.

One night, Rock came in and demanded sex when Navaar was not in the mood. As he told Willson, "He didn't take 'no' for an answer. He practically raped me, but I felt I had to give in to him. After all, he was paying my bills. I was his sex slave, if you want to put it that way. Bought and paid for."

"Rand Saxon" still wanted to launch himself into the movies, so Rock offered to pay for his acting lessons. He had publicity shots made, none of which has surfaced to date. They are probably out there in some forgotten box, joining thousands upon thousands of other wannabes who never made it.

Navaar's days were lonely except when Miller would call. He didn't like it, but Miller referred to the two of them as "Hollywood wives." He did like going to have lunch with him at the Beverly Hills Hotel. They usually saw a movie star or two, and on one occasion, spotted Lana Turner dining with Howard Hughes.

The Nader/Miller and the Hudson/Navaar *ménages* often double dated, meeting in out-of-the-way places where they would not be photographed.

"In spite of his bisexual claims, I think Jack really came to love Rock," Miller said. "As for Rock, he was in his prime. Even with the handsome blonde stud in his bed at night, he still played the field. My God, that guy in the early 1950s could have sex four or five times a day. He was one damn sperm factory."

Navaar was friendly with Miller and Nader on the surface, but at home with Rock, he tried to undermine their friendship. Rock sensed that he was jealous of Nader. In spite of denials from both Nader and Rock, Navaar suspected they had once been lovers at the beginning of their friendship. Willson confirmed that.

Nader and Rock had gone boating, and they still spent a lot of time together. Once they sailed to Catalina Island when Miller was involved in business back in Los Angeles. Nader and Rock spent a long weekend in a modest motel with a double bed.

In Navaar's appraisal, both Rock and Nader were oversexed. They were extremely handsome, had great bodies and flaunted their endowments. In fact, when Nader had posed for publicity pictures in a tight-fitting bathing suit, his "mound" had to be air-brushed to make it a bit less prominent.

In spite of occasional squabbles, Rock liked his domestic relationship with Navaar. His close friendship with Miller and Nader continued, too. He said, "Over the years, various lovers of mine have tried to break up my relationship with George and Mark. But they never could. With those two guys, I was committed to hang in with them until death do us part. Lovers would come and go, but I expected that the only time we'd part would be when one of us was on our deathbed."

Without meaning to, Rock had predicted part of the scenario associated with his own demise.

***

Edward Muhl is a relatively mysterious figure in the saga of Rock Hudson, but in so many ways, he was the one production chief who really launched him into worldwide stardom. Henry Willson had only gotten him established with bit parts or minor supporting roles.

Born in 1907, Muhl was eighteen years older than Rock and director of production at Universal from 1953 until he retired in 1973.

Producer Carl Laemmle had hired him as his secretary at Universal back in 1927. Very ambitious, by 1937, Muhl had worked his way up from typing letters to producing films.

After the war, in 1947, Universal merged with International, run by William Goetz and Leo Spitz. In the newly reconfigured Universal International, Muhl was appointed as vice president and general manager.

In 1953, he was named general production executive under Goetz, but later that year, he was made head of production, replacing both Goetz and Spitz, who had jointly run Universal for seven years.

Muhl's ascension to power ushered in the heyday of Universal, based on successful films that starred, among others, Doris Day and Lana Turner. He pushed Universal into doing many pictures in Technicolor, a wise choice in the case of Rock because it showcased as never before what was referred to in the magazines as "his male beauty."

In his new post, Muhl had the power to dictate male leads and to decide which star to promote and which wannabe he didn't, letting many a contract expire in the TV-crazed 1950s, when movie audiences shrank.

Rock soon heard rumors that Muhl was calling many young male stars under contract to come to his office for private meetings, during which he told his secretary that he was not to be disturbed.

He was following the same routine that Darryl F. Zanuck did at 20th Century Fox and Harry Cohn did at Columbia, except whereas Zanuck and Cohn demanded that female hopefuls be delivered to them, Muhl preferred to seduce males.

Scott Brady had been one of Muhl's early favorites, as had Richard Long, Alex Nicol, and James Best. He reportedly found Jeffrey Hunter particularly delightful. Hugh O'Brian and Steve Cochran were among his alltime studs.

Privately, Tony Curtis admitted, "A lot of us in those days had to unzip our pants for Eddie Boy. He didn't require us to do anything but stand there while he serviced us on his knees. I can't count the number of young guys who paid visits to his office when he put up the DO NOT DISTURB sign. Some of us went on to become stars; others fell by the wayside."

"Rock and I were among the lucky few: The visits were most often in the afternoon, because Eddie Boy at night was at home with his loving wife and children, kissing them instead of his Beefcake Brigade. So, he was a married man. That doesn't mean a thing in Hollywood. Some of the best cocksuckers in Hollywood are closeted and married."

As he heard more and more about Muhl's seductions of young men, Rock wondered when his summons would come. It finally did when Muhl's secretary called with a request for Rock to meet him in his office that Friday afternoon at 4PM for a discussion about the direction of his career.

For the appointment, Rock donned a T-shirt and a pair of tight jeans with no underwear, encasing his feet in a pair of red leather boots.

Inside the studio chief's office, Rock realized immediately that Muhl wasn't his type, but what did that matter? Before he got to Rock's weapon, Muhl used his own most powerful weapon, which consisted of tantalizing Rock with news that he was going to make him a leading man, casting him opposite Yvonne De Carlo in her next picture, *Scarlet Angel* (1952).

He told him that the screenplay had already been written by Oscar Brodney, and then promised to give Rock a copy to take home to study over the weekend.

He explained that the latest version of *Scarlet Angel* was actually a reworking of the 1941 Universal picture, *The Flame of New Orleans* that had starred Marlene Dietrich opposite Bruce Cabot, Errol Flynn's former lover and roommate.

As Rock would later tell Willson in a detailed description, the seduction didn't occur right away. Muhl led him to the Universal screening room, where he ordered the projectionist to show *The Flame of New Orleans*.

"Imagine yourself in the Cabot role," he instructed Rock.

As anticipated, during the screening—in fact, about twenty min-

150

utes into the picture—Rock felt Muhl's hand come to rest on his crotch.

At the end of the picture, Muhl suggested that they retire to Rock's dressing room. "He followed me with his tongue hanging out," Rock graphically told Willson.

Rock thought he'd be ordered to undress, but he only had to remove his shirt, which was mostly unbuttoned anyway. Muhl reserved for himself the honor of unbuckling Rock's jeans, pulling them down to his knees.

"He gave me the world's best blow-job," Rock admitted. "After all, he'd had a lot of experience. He later told me I was the best he'd ever had, and that I had the biggest cock at Universal."

[For Rock, this was just the beginning. Once filming began, and for years to come, Muhl demanded many matinee performances from Rock, who participated willingly. "I delivered load after countless load, and he continued to want me after other male actors came and went. I was always his favorite, or so he said. For my contribution, I was made the leading man in film after film at Universal, until I became its biggest star. "It didn't have anything to do with a casting couch, because I was always standing. It was Muhl who was on his knees."

***

Rock was usually called to Muhl's office on a working day at the studio. But one Saturday, he was asked to come to the studio at 3PM for a meeting in his dressing room.

When he got there, Muhl was waiting for him, explaining that he wanted a studio photographer to take some beefcake pictures of him for his private collection.

Rock assumed that he was going to be asked to pose in the nude, and he was willing to do that. Anyone who had attended any of Willson's Sunday afternoon pool parties knew he was an exhibitionist.

When the photographer arrived, Rock realized that Muhl had another idea. The photographer brought five posing straps, the kind models used in all those physique muscle magazines of the 1950s. There was a choice of various colors, including shocking pink and chartreuse.

When Rock was asked to strip in front of the photographer, he assumed that he was or had been one of Muhl's conquests. He was good-looking enough, or, as Rock later said, "I realized that this was not the kid's first time at the rodeo."

When the yellow posing strap was on, Muhl knelt before him, removed his penis from the strap, and fellated him a bit before replacing it.

When Rock later saw the pictures, he said, "My God, I was busting out all over. That little strap could hardly contain me."

After the session with the photographer, Muhl remained behind in Rock's dressing room. As Rock recalled, "That was the first and only time I was fully un-dressed for one of my sessions with Muhl. On this particular afternoon, he sought out both my pouch AND my rosebud. He really dug me. I got a little nervous, though, when he told me he'd fallen in love with me."]

It was twilight time when Rock, with the script of *Scarlet Angel* in the front seat with him, pulled into his driveway.

Grabbing the script and rushing inside, he called out, "God damn it, Jack, where in the hell are you? I've now become a fully fledged movie star, the real thing. I'm going to become the biggest star in Tinseltown."

***

As dozens of photos from movie magazines from the early 1950s reveal, Rock was always willing to strip down for beefcake photos for his fans. Such was the case when *Photoplay* sent Douglas Greene, a photographer-journalist, to interview Rock and to get pictures of him to use for a layout.

Rock ordered Jack Navaar to go out grocery shopping, to pick up his clothes at the cleaners, to buy enough liquor to restock the bar, and not to return until after Greene had left. "I don't want the article to be about my homosexual love nest."

When Greene arrived on Rock's doorstep, he was stunned. Obviously, the editor at *Photoplay* knew what he was doing. Greene was his type, with broad shoulders, a tall, trim physique, blonde hair and blue eyes, not unlike Navaar himself. To Rock, he looked like the brother of Tab Hunter.

From their first flirtatious talk, Rock assumed that Greene was a homosexual who found him sexually appealing. "It was 'goo-goo eyes' time," Rock recalled.

Greene had heard that Rock was not shy about showing off his manly assets. A friend of his had attended one of Henry Willson's pool parties.

Rock was in jeans and a T-shirt when he'd answered his doorbell. After the interview, Greene asked Rock if he'd pose for some beefcake shots. Rock agreed and invited him into his bedroom, where he laid out three pairs of skimpy shorts. "You decide which ones you want me to wear," he suggested as he stripped completely nude.

The photographer noticed that Rock was rising to the occasion. Before the shorts were selected, Greene was down on his knees servicing Rock, which led to further intimacies in bed.

When it was over and a grateful Greene had departed, Rock knew that he'd be guaranteed an extensive layout in *Photoplay*.

When other reporters approached him for interviews, he grew tired of one oft-repeated question: "Do you sleep in the nude?"

Greene had not asked that, but most young stars at the time were getting used to it. Marilyn Monroe had a response: "I never sleep in the nude. I go to bed with a spray of Chanel No. 5."

When Charles Delson arrived from *Modern Screen* and asked that question, Rock responded sharply: "Hell, yes, I sleep in the nude!"

"Aren't you worried about a fire in the middle of the night, and you have to run out the door?"

"If that happens, I'd run out jaybird naked and the firemen would be presented with another hose."

"That's bragging," Delson answered. "You know I can't print that."

"It's for your ears only," Rock said. "Actually, I can't for the life of me understand why the reading public gives a damn about what a star wears to bed...or doesn't wear. To me, that would be of interest only to the person in bed with you."

"I think a more interesting question would be, 'Who are you sleeping with tonight?'"

"I didn't dare ask that," Delson said. "But just who are you sleeping with tonight?"

"I haven't made up my mind yet, but the invitations are from Marilyn Monroe, Yvonne De Carlo, and Ava Gardner."

"My God, Mr. Hudson, you know I can't print that either."

"Let's just keep it our little secret."

***

Sidney Salkow, a director from New York, accepted a daunting assignment to helm Rock Hudson in his first starring role. His co-star would be Yvonne De Carlo, with whom he'd already appeared in smaller parts in two of her pictures, *The Desert Hawk* (1950) and *Tomahawk* (1951).

Scarlet Angel, a 1952 Technicolor adventure film, was set in bawdy New Orleans in 1865, the final year of the Civil War.

For his appearance in *Scarlet Angel*, newcomer Rock was paid a fraction of what the movie's reigning diva, Yvonne De Carlo, received. Depicted above as a scheming, willfully scarlet saloon girl, she was years away from the role that made her famous with TV audiences, Lily Munster, matriarch of a clan of benign monsters in *The Munsters* (1964-66).

Fans thought *Scarlet Angel* was a reference to De Carlo, but it was the name of a disreputable tavern in the French Quarter of New Orleans. Sailors arriving in port were warned not to go there, "where the gambling is as crooked as the saloon gals."

Salkow cast Rock as Frank Truscott (nicknamed "Panama), the dashingly handsome sea captain of the *Atlantic Star*. On his first night at the Scarlet Angel, he spots a scheming, gold-digging saloon girl, Roxy McClanahan (De Carlo), as she steals a customer's wallet before training her greedy eyes on Rock.

Salkow had been told that Rock had no acting talent and to expect nothing but a wooden performance. But De Carlo cautioned that if a director showed patience, Rock would do whatever he wanted—or at least try hard.

A former dialogue coach, Salkow helped Rock more with his delivery than any other director. Following De Carlo's advice, he had patience with him and began to elicit the performance he wanted.

Salkow was rather daring in the layout of some of his scenes. As a Major in the U.S. Marines during World War II, he'd been wounded while filming a newsreel on the deck of an aircraft carrier during a blazing kamikaze attack from suicidal Japanese pilots.

"Sidney was no blowhard, like some directors—Otto Preminger comes to mind," Rock said. "He was more of a *'churn 'em out'* director—no masterpieces, but entertaining 'programmers,' fast-paced, cheaply produced, and made to fill the first half of a double bill. He was somewhat cynical about his career."

The plot of *Scarlet Angel* has De Carlo, born on the wrong side of the tracks, clawing her way to the top of the social ladder. Along the way, the cynical saloon girl falls for Rock's character, which the script had defined as "a diamond in the rough."

Their romance gets off to a rocky start. Panama (Rock) tells her, "There's a certain thing called class—and you just

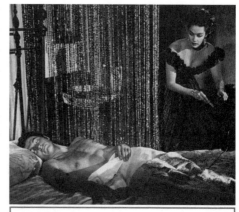

Omnisexual, ambisexual Rock was becoming all things to all moviegoers. In this publicity still from *Scarlet Angel* (1952), released during the most uptight years of the uptight 50s, the predatory and "out for the money scarlet woman" Yvonne De Carlo attempts to pilfer something as she surveys the partially dressed, hardbodied Rock of movie-goers' dreams.

haven't got it."

The biggest expense for the production was De Carlo's paycheck of $50,000 per picture. Rock, meanwhile, was still drawing his $200 a week, despite his status as a leading man.

"Rock was playing leads now," De Carlo said. "He'd come a long way since *Tomahawk*, and was no longer awkward before the camera. I was a bit late coming to the conclusion, but working with him on *Scarlet Angel*, I knew that bigtime stardom awaited him, if not for his talent, then for his looks. Too bad he batted for the other team, because I could have gone for him bigtime."

Scarlet Angel was the film that certified Rock as "The Baron of Beefcake." In London's *Daily Mirror*, journalist Donald Zee helped to promote that reputation:

> *"Today's Hollywood looks at the man first, the muscle next, the mind last. Beefcake has arrived. Cheesecake is no longer a monopoly. The bulging expanse above the masculine waist is being howled for by the she-wolves, so it's being rounded up all over the place! The bobbysoxers wolf-whistled at Tony Curtis, they were ecstatic over Burt Lancaster. But now there's a boy they've stripped to conquer all. The studio says Rock Hudson is going to make a fine actor, but at the moment, most of his talent is in his torso."*

***

Until 1951, Rock had never seen a movie starring the hot new acting sensation, Montgomery Clift, not even his stunning performances in *Red River* (1948) opposite John Wayne; or in *The Heiress* (1949) with Olivia de Havilland.

Yet even without seeing any of his movies, Rock was already jealous of him—and of that other sensation, Marlon Brando.

In fan magazine after fan magazine, he'd read of the sheer beauty of Clift's face—described as tortured, sensitive, and emotive. After *Red River*, according to a *Movieland* poll, Clift had been hailed as Hollywood's hottest new star. That magazine claimed that Clift had his choice of film roles, and that, "He has a face that brings fans to tears." *Photoplay* frequently touted his charms as well. In the aftermath of the first essay that that magazine had devoted to Clift, it was deluged with fan mail.

Film historian Anne Helen Petersen wrote: "Clift's sexuality, like those other fifties idols, Rock Hudson and Tab Hunter, was carefully concealed from the public. But that didn't mean that the gossip press didn't hint at something different, something *queer*, in the broadest sense of the word, about him."

Magazines ran articles about him under such provocative headlines as: *"IS IT TRUE WHAT THEY SAY ABOUT MONTY?"* and *"MONTY CLIFT: WOMAN HATER OR FREE SOUL?"*

"Whatever the relationships Clift may have had, he was circumspect. Petersen wrote: "Unlike Rock Hudson, whose affairs were very nearly exposed to the entire nation by *Confidential*, Clift never made the pages of the scandal rags. He was 'lonely,' yet with the help of his refusal to live in Los Angeles or participate in café society, he was able to keep his private life secret."

In 1942, when Tallulah Bankhead had starred in the Thornton Wilder comedy, *The Skin of Our Teeth*, in which Clift had appeared, she was asked if he were homosexual.

She answered, "I don't know, *dah-ling*. He never sucked MY cock."

One afternoon, Rock accepted an invitation to drive with George Nader and Mark Miller to Hollywood Boulevard to a movie house showing *A Place in the Sun* (1951), co-starring Clift with Elizabeth Taylor and Shelley Winters, whom he murders during the course of the film. Rock found the performances dazzling, especially the love scenes between Taylor and Clift. That movie launched her as a sex siren, and Clift as a superstar.

Nader later claimed that Rock was depressed as they ordered dinner at a drive-in. "How can I equal that?" he asked. "Me, the wooden lug in movie after movie."

His two friends tried to reassure him, but later admitted that Rock became even less sure of himself when all three of them went to see Marlon Brando perform on the screen as Stanley Kowalski in *A Streetcar Named Desire* by Tennessee Williams. Both Brando and Vivien Leigh, his co-star, would be nominated for Oscars that year. Although Vivien carried off her second Academy Award, Brando lost to Humphrey Bogart in *The African Queen*. Clift was also nominated for his performance as the tortured murderer in *A Place in the Sun*.

Montgomery Clift, an actor with a style that was different from that of Rock, who was subsequently offered a roster of roles that Rock might have envied.

According to Nader, after seeing Marlon Brando in *A Streetcar Named Desire*

(1951), Rock became even more emotionally upset. "The guy brings this raw sensuality to the movies, the likes of which I've never seen before," Rock said. "He's vulgar, like a fucking animal up there, but still as sexy, magnetic, a force to behold, and as good looking as Satan waiting for us at the Gates of Hell."

The press echoed Rock's sentiments, referring to Brando as "spectacularly, ruinously handsome, the kind of look that gives grown women the shivers." Hedda Hopper called him "Hollywood's New Sex Boat." Another female reporter wrote: "He's exciting! Marlon Brando! He's coarse, he's depraved! Marlon Brando! *He's male!*"

Rock lamented to his friends, "If that is how acting is going to be in the 1950s, I'm gonna become a god damn footnote. I can't perform like Clift and Brando. At best, I might develop into a sort of Clark Gable. But I doubt it."

Almost obsessed with Clift and Brando, Rock would go to see every film each of them made, especially their co-starring performances in *The Young Lions* (1958).

One afternoon, Rock received a surprise invitation from Merv Griffin for dinner and drinks with Clift. He was startled to learn that Clift was living in Griffin's home, a setup that Griffin's agent, "Bullets" Durgom, had arranged. "Monty moved in with me when he found the noise 'deafening' at the Château Marmont," Griffin said. "He's in Hollywood to star in Alfred Hitchcock's *I Confess* (1953), a film about a priest who hears a murder confession but is later accused of committing the crime himself."

As Griffin told Rock in reference to *I Confess*, "Clift promised me a role in it."

[Clift lived up to his promise, but Hitchcock ended up casting Griffin in only a voice-over.]

Rock just assumed that Clift and Griffin were lovers. After accepting the invitation, he called his casual friend, Roddy McDowall, who seemed to know everything going on in Hollywood's gay community.

"Merv told me he went to bed with Monty once," McDowall said. "He claimed that Monty is no Rock Hudson. He said he was confronted with a small piece of foreskin, and he couldn't do much with that. Since Monty is so inadequately

Merv Griffin, closeted homosexual and boy singer during the last-gasp days of the Big Bands.

157

endowed, he hates being called a sex symbol. That's a hard reputation for any guy to live up to. Women handle it better. Monty wants to be a serious actor, not a male sex symbol. You dear, Rock, will have to take up that banner."

Before arriving at Griffin's home, Rock had been warned that Clift was physically battered and bruised. A few days before, he'd driven to Hitchcock's home for a reunion with Olivia de Havilland, to help convince her to accept the female lead in *I Confess*.

Despite his blandishments, De Havilland ultimately turned down the role, the part going to Anne Baxter.

Returning home drunk, Clift had crashed into a tree and was terribly bruised, but with no broken bones. Not wanting Clift to be caught at the scene of the accident, Griffin, in a report he made to the police, claimed that Clift's car had been stolen "by young joy riders."

When Rock was introduced to Clift, he looked as if he'd barely survived a brutal fight in a boxing ring. But he had sobered up and was rather articulate.

"I might have been jealous of him," Rock said, "but he was generous as to my own career. I told him how intimidated I was by all the emerging new actors, especially those from the Method school, competing with me."

"Method actors will not dominate the movies of the 1950s," Clift predicted. "Only some of them. I think the day has come for the pretty boys, the so-called 'Beefcake Brigade' to come along and to appeal to younger audiences seeking date movies, those not especially tuned in to the 1940s John Garfield, Edward G. Robinson, Humphrey Bogart, or James Cagney, much less to Brando and me."

Clift also claimed that, "I think Henry Willson has got his finger on the pulse, the rise of the pretty boy, Tab Hunter and the like. I understand you're one of the stallions in Willson's stable."

Rock admitted that he was, but quickly added that he didn't plan to remain in the stable forever. "There's too much bullshit to put up with," he said. "I'd like to be given a chance to act instead of hearing, 'Take off your shirt, Rock,'"

***

Jack Navaar had gone to Santa Monica for the weekend to spend time with his troubled mother. Confronted with the option of accompanying him, Rock decided not to go and was home alone when his doorbell rang at 1AM. He'd just gone to sleep in the nude. Wrapping a towel around himself, he headed for the door, where, before opening it, he demanded to know who it was.

"It's Monty!" came the plaintive voice.

Rock let him in and discovered that he was very drunk but that he'd managed to arrive unharmed at the house on Grandview. Rock invited him in and even poured him a drink by request, although it was obvious that he'd had more than enough.

After an hour of listening to Monty's almost nonstop monologue, Rock suggested that both of them had better get some sleep.

As he told Nader, "Suddenly, he was on the carpet, on his knees, begging me to make love to him."

"I need someone to love me," Clift beseeched Rock. "I'm desperate to be loved."

Rock admitted that in bed, Clift was "incredibly passive and couldn't get an erection. There wasn't a lot there to erect. Finally, I just turned him over and fucked the hell out of him. He complained about the pain, but I think he loved it. The pain turned to pleasure. He woke up at noon."

Over coffee, no breakfast, Clift told Rock he was flying to Hawaii to make a movie, for release in 1953, in which he would play a soldier during the Japanese attack on Pearl Harbor.

"What's it called?" Rock asked.

"From Here to Eternity."

It would have been beyond Rock's wildest imagination to realize that in a few short years, he'd be one of the key players in the most traumatic event in Clift's life, one that would change him forever.

***

Ted Richmond, who had produced the movie *Shakedown*, in which Rock had had a minor part, phoned him at home with the news of his latest casting. *Has Anybody Seen My Gal?*, eventually released in 1952, was set in 1928, a romantic comedy in which Rock was to star with Piper Laurie.

"In this one, she gets star billing," Richmond said. "But you're the male lead."

Rock was disappointed to learn that, but didn't say anything. At least he was the main actor.

"You're moving up in the world, kid," Richmond assured him. "Look how fast you've risen to leading man status."

Actually, Laurie had been a friend of Rock's ever since the two of them had made a screen test for Universal, each of them hoping to be signed to a seven-year contract. They had been given scripts for the screenplay *Thunder on the Hill*. She was seventeen at the time, and feared that the part called for an older actress.

She admitted that she and Rock had a hard time keeping a straight face, since some of the lines seemed ridiculous. One, in particular, stood out. She had to say to Rock, "I love you like this, all stirred up with fire in your eyes."

After the test, she told him, "Just what a typical American teenage girl would say to her date."

Waiting to see if they'd get contracts, Rock became a frequent visitor at Laurie's apartment. She remembered him always showing up at dinner time. "He was always broke and always hungry, a hell of a big eater."

Rumors of a romance flared when they showed up together at a costume ball in 1952. He came dressed as a cannibal, with a fright wig, bronze-colored body makeup, and beads dangling prominently around his manly chest. They were photographed together countless times, once with Elizabeth Taylor petting the live baby piglet resting adorably, and as an "accessory," in her lap, always with her fervent hope that that that was all he was doing.

ROCK'S BIG BREAK! He's handsome, he's malleable, he's cooperative, he's photogenic, and he's wholesome-looking. Here he is, the perfect boyfriend, with Piper Laurie in postwar America's ode to happier days, *Has AnybodySeen My Gal?*

When news arrived that both of them had been signed by Universal, Laurie wrote: "We were joyous, moved to tears, and thrilled for our futures. To celebrate, I went out that night with three gorgeous guys, not only Rock, but my friend Bob Richards, and James Best, another contract player."

Unknown to Laurie, Rock and Best had been having an affair, although Best remained basically straight.

As stated in Laurie's memoirs, "Rock and I spent a lot of time hanging out together, and we always had a good time. I had no inkling of his sexual preference. I didn't think about it. There was no particular chemistry between us, and he never made a pass at me. I just figured I wasn't his type."

***

Over a lunch at the Universal commissary, Rock came face to face with the one director who would deliver him worldwide stardom, making him for a time Hollywood's biggest box office attraction. He was the Danish director, Douglas Sirk, who had earned a stellar position in Nazi cinema under the baton of Josef Goebbels, Hitler's Minister of Propaganda who had controlled UFA Studios.

Sirk had been born in 1897 in Hamburg to Danish parentage, his father a newspaper reporter. He'd had a distinguished career as an actor in Europe, often performing in plays by Shakespeare, including a memorable *Hamlet*. At Hamburg University, he'd attended a lecture by Albert Einstein. By the 1930s,

Showing skin at a costume ball: Piper Laurie as Circe (the Greek temptress) with her piglet. Rock (right) is almost unrecognizable as the Wild Man of Borneo.

he was one of the leading stage directors in Germany, enjoying great success with such plays as Brecht's *The Threepenny Opera*.

In 1937, he'd fled Germany because of his objections to Nazi control and because he had a Jewish wife, Hilde Jary, who might otherwise have been earmarked for the gas chambers.

By 1942, Sirk was in Hollywood, working for Columbia. One of his first pictures was the anti-Nazi movie, *Hitler's Madmen*.

As Rock remembered it, "Sirk's eyes seemed to light up when I came into the commissary. He'd only seen publicity pictures of me before. Other directors such as Joseph Pevney thought I was a crappy actor, but somehow, Sirk dug me, perhaps more than dug. He complimented me on my physique and good looks several times over hamburgers."

"We both knew that *Has Anybody Seen My Gal?* was a piece of nostalgic fluff, and that he deserved more serious material. But other screenplays were on the way. We had to get through this nonsense first."

During the first week of shooting, Rock had to wear a raccoon coat, typical of college boys in the 1920s. "It was god damn hot, not only the weather, but because of all those lights. After the scene, I went to my dressing room, stripped down, and jumped into the shower."

As Rock later relayed to Henry Willson, "Suddenly, the plastic shower curtain was pulled back and there stood Douglas looking at me, especially at one part of me."

"Go on, Rock," he said in a commanding voice like that of a director. "I've been dreaming of seeing you like this since we first met. You are truly descended from the Gods. I'm going to make you the biggest star in Hollywood. You certainly are equipped for it."

"Then he ordered me to soap up one part of me. I knew what that meant. By the time I'd stepped out of the shower, he was waiting with a big bath towel, and I rewarded him with my biggest erection. Showtime!"

The German director, Douglas Sirk, was one of the key players who helped turn Rock into a super star. Away from the camera, Sirk often came to Rock's dressing room to "worship" him.

As he'd later relate, "Doug explored every crevice. I'd just had a bath, but I got another one. He was hungry. He told me that other male stars at Universal didn't have what I had. It was all very flattering. A stream of endless praise when his mouth was not otherwise engaged."

Rock had more or less expected that the events of that afternoon would happen. Although Sirk was married, he was known around the lot as a closeted homosexual... perhaps not so closeted.

In David Bret's biography, *Rock Hudson*, he revealed that Sirk had been similarly involved with several of the young male stars at Universal. "He was regarded as a kindly, benevolent, Sugar Daddy."

Months before he'd seduced Rock, Sirk was known to have visited the dressing rooms of many of its male stars, notably Tony Curtis. He told friends, "The guy knows the penile measurements of most of us guys at Universal."

Sirk had seduced many actors, not just those at Universal. Others included Jeffrey Hunter, Scott Brady, Jeff Chandler, James Best, Alec Nicol, Richard Long, Robert Francis, Hugh O'Brian, Steve Cochran, and later, George Nader and Troy Donahue. He kept a diary of his conquests, which was later discovered—buried in a box of unused scripts—in his office when he departed Universal. Rock topped the list with the most favorable notations.

At one point, later in his life, a reporter asked Rock to explain his link to Sirk: "He was like a Dad to me," Rock answered, not adding that if the relationship were, indeed paternal, it was tinged with touches of incest.

"When you're scared and new and trying to figure out this thing, suddenly, this older man can reach out and say, 'There, there, it's okay.' Mr. Sirk is a great teacher. Working with him is like being enrolled in an acting class. You're urged to give everything you can as an actor. He was the first to make you realize that you don't rush. You don't hold back, but let it come out. Don't hammer. React instead of act. He was the first good director I worked with, an invaluable experience."

Raoul Walsh, who had frequently touted his early discovery of Rock, was furious when he read that statement. "I'll do one more picture with him just to bust his balls."

***

Has Anybody Seen My Gal?, scripted by Samuel Hoffman, was just one of six films in which Rock would appear for a 1952 release. The original story by Elanor H. Porter brought back the flapper era of the Roaring '20s when young people danced the Charleston and skirts were on the rise. The title was taken from that hit recording by the California Ramblers.

The veteran actor, Charles Coburn, interpreted the role of Samuel Fulton, a lonely and curmudgeonly millionaire, actually the richest man in the world. He decides to leave his vast fortune to the family of the late Millicent Blaisdell, the only woman he'd ever loved who dumped him. Her memory lived on until, late in his life, he decides to act.

He opts to travel to the small Vermont town where her family still lives, disguising himself as a poor old boarder seeking a room, and in need of a job. He ends up working as a soda jerk with Rock, who played the role of Dan Stebbins, an impoverished soda jerk. He's in love with the latest incarnation of "Millie" Blaisdell (Piper Laurie), the daughter of Lynn Bari and Larry Gates, who were cast as Harriet and Charles Blaisdell. In addition to Millie, they have a handsome son, Howard (William Reynolds playing a snotty teenager), and a very young daughter, Roberta (Gigi Perreau), the smartest of the lot.

The socially ambitious mother wants her daughter Millie to marry Carl Pennock (Skip Homeier), a creepy, skirt-chasing rich boy.

Actually, Rock's role is not very good. He appears angry in many scenes, as when Laurie temporarily throws him aside for the rich boy. He's handsome enough, but his role is not really sympathetic.

The usual complications follow, with the predictable results that get resolved in the end. Before it was changed, the film's original title had more appropriately been set as *Oh Money! Money!*

On the set, Rock rendezvoused once again with Laurie.

163

He joked with her. "I read in a gossip column yesterday that you bathe in milk and live on flower petals to maintain your luminous skin."

"Like hell I do," she answered.

In lieu of attracting strong, meaty roles, she had become a decorative leading lady for a salary of $100 a week. In time, she would star with Tony Curtis miscast in Arabian Nights Adventures or with Francis "The Talking Mule."

A reviewer would later point out that "Piper Laurie seemed to be glumly enduring her ordeal in *Has Anybody Seen My Gal?* But she's not all gloom and doom—in fact, she's the 'cat's pajamas' when she walks down a street of primary colors in her tight sweater and flapper skirt."

Another noted that "Universal seems intent on casting Piper Laurie in silly fluff and out-and-out garbage, either with Tony Curtis or Rock Hudson."

***

A relatively forgotten film today, *Has Anybody Seen My Gal?* deserves at least a footnote in Hollywood history because it was the movie that brought Rock Hudson and James Dean together as lovers.

As an extra, Dean walks into Rock's soda fountain where Coburn, in his role as an incognito but millionaire titan of industry, is working in disguise as the soda jerk. As noted earlier in the film, he is actually the richest man on earth.

In 1920s garb, Dean is attired in a red bow tie, a straw boater hat, a collegiate sweater, and white pants.

He rakishly places his order at the counter. "Hi Gramps! I'll have a choc malt, heavy on the choc, plenty of milk, four spoons of malt, two scoops of vanilla ice—one mixed with the rest and the other floating."

In response, Coburn quips, "Would you like to come in Wednesday for a fitting?"

The comedy was Dean's last movie in Hollywood before he relocated to New York to study at the Actors Studio and to star in a string of teleplays, including a

Before he was a *Rebel Without a Cause*, Hollywood bad boy James Dean made a brief, sassy appearance in this flapper fluff as the town's most irreverent teenager.

role with Ronald Reagan. When he eventually returned to Hollywood, he would do so as a star in *East of Eden* (1955).

Unlike Laurie, Dean already knew about Rock's sexual preference, having once attended one of Henry Willson's all-male Sunday afternoon pool parties.

Rock remem-

That newfangled thing, the Charleston—everybody's doing it, Piper Laurie (left); Rock Hudson; the richest man in the world (as portrayed by Charles Coburn, third from left); and Gigi Perreau, who vied with Natalie Wood for child roles.

bered the bit player and invited him to lunch, later claiming, "I found him kinda cute, a bit weird, but worth a fling at least if I couldn't get William Reynolds."

Over lunch, Dean shared his plans for New York and even asked Rock if he'd like to go with him.

"Hell no!" Rock answered. "I'll stick in Hollywood where I plan to become the biggest god damn movie star there is."

After lunch, Rock invited Dean to his dressing room because he had no more scenes that day. His invitation was a blunt as Dean himself: "I like to fuck and get fucked. How about it, kid?"

"You're on, Big Boy!"

"As a couple, we didn't exactly invent sex, but after our mating, sex would have to be spelled in the future as sexxx. That's a triple x." [*Rock confided this to Willson, who had failed to lure the young actor into his stable.*]

Rock delivered a "blow-by-blow" description of his fling with Dean to Roddy McDowall, who also knew him.

For the next ten days, Dean hung around the set, even though he was no longer needed.

In the 1960s, a reporter asked Rock what his memory was of working with Dean way back in 1952.

"Yeah, I ran into the kid, who had a very small role. He had slicked back, wavy hair, very neatly combed—that's all I remember."

Actor Nick Adams had a different memory. Adams arrived at Rock's house at 5PM one Saturday. He'd been hired to tend bar, agreeing to appear shirtless at an all-male party. He was also told to wear his hustler jeans with a bleached-out crotch to show off his endowment.

He headed for the living room to set up the bar. To his surprise, he discovered both Rock and his friend, James Dean, lying nude together on the sofa.

***

Walking down a corridor at Universal, Rock met George Sherman, who had directed him in *Tomahawk.* "You won't believe this," Sherman said. "But Errol Flynn is arriving at Universal today to make a film, *Against All Flags*" (1952).

"You mean, Jack Warner has released him?"

Sherman quickly filled him in on all the gossip: After putting up with the antics of his superstar for eighteen years, Warner appeared ready to break the relationship at the expiration of his contract with Flynn.

The studio had suffered lawsuits, rape charges, all sorts of erotic adventures, alcoholism, drug abuse, contractual disputes, bad behavior, and repeated "sabotage" that caused production costs to soar.

"There were even battles about how Flynn showed too much genitalia, thanks to those green tights he wore in Sherwood Forest," Sherman said.

Flynn was no longer the box office draw he was during the late 1930s and throughout the war years.

"If you make money at the box office, studios will even suppress a murder rap," Sherman said. "When Cary Grant was caught sucking off a studly stockroom boy in the men's room of a department store, it was hushed up."

"That's what I hear about Flynn," Rock said. "No lines at the box office, no new contract."

Flynn was not only declining physically, but he'd made a number of foolish decisions, both financial and in career moves. He'd foolishly turned down *King Solomon's Mines* (1950), the role going to Stewart Granger and the picture getting nominated for best of the year at the Academy Awards. In lieu of that, he chose to film *Kim* (also 1950) in India, a movie based on a weak interpretation of the epic Rudyard Kipling novel. Many critics found it "vapidly exotic...a dud."

Despite his highly publicized troubles, the name of Errol Flynn still spelled magic for Rock, as did the name of another fading matinee idol, Tyrone Power. Rock still remembered how, as a boy, he'd been powerfully attracted to Flynn on the screen as he dashed about in *Captain Blood* (1935), *The Charge of the Light Brigade* (1936), and *The Private Lives of Elizabeth and Essex* (1939), the latter with the intimidating Bette Davis, who loathed the actor.

166

Rock hadn't seen Flynn since he went to England to shoot *Kim*. He wrote a note and asked a messenger boy to deliver it to Flynn's dressing room.

At 3PM, Flynn got him on the phone, inviting him to his dressing room after work. Arriving at 6PM, Rock was greeted by Flynn in his underwear. "Come on in, sport," he said, flashing his famous smile. Once the door was closed, Flynn said, "Give me a kiss as only you know how. I haven't had a real man kiss me in months."

That kiss led to other maneuvers, and Rock and Flynn passed an hour on the sofa doing some heavy love-making.

In the afterglow, as a nude Flynn poured some liquor, he congratulated Rock on climbing up the rungs of the ladder to leading man status. "You finally broke through, as I knew you would."

That evening, Rock dropped into the home of his friends, George Nader and Mark Miller, to update them on "my latest adventures with Robin Hood."

Rock was to some degree shocked at how virulent Flynn had become in his attacks on Hollywood. "I've had it," he'd said. "The IRS is hounding me night and day. Teenage girls come out of nowhere claiming I raped them and even go so far as to find a crooked lawyer to file lawsuits against me. I'm fed up with all the *Confidential* exposés. The most recent one has me deserting my new wife, Patrice Wymore, and heading for a bordello."

"Ex-wives, ex-mistresses, ex-boyfriends who try to blackmail me—it's all been too much."

"I can see that," Rock said. "You've got what I'm still striving for—big-time stardom—but it doesn't sound all that thrilling once you get there."

"You've got that right, sport," Flynn said. "You're a sitting duck the more high-profile you become in this rotten town."

***

On the set of his latest picture, a 1952 Technicolor Western, *Horizons West,* Rock greeted Julie Adams. "People will talk," he said, "if we keep running into each other like this." He'd recently made *Bend of the River* with her and James Stewart.

Outwardly, although Rock was all smiles and good humor, he was inwardly seething with anger. Just as he thought he'd be given no more second male leads, the producer, Albert J. Cohen, had awarded the star role in that film to Robert Ryan, followed by Adams and Rock in second and third billing, respectively.

Rock had seen the movie poster, wherein his effigy had appeared in the lower right-hand corner of the ad, looking blandly innocuous and unsexy, wearing a Western shirt and a ten-gallon hat. In contrast, the illustration of Ryan had been configured with exaggerated muscles, posing shirtless and with a phallic-looking pistol as Adams clings to him seductively. "Here I am," said Rock, "the 'Baron of Beefcake,' and it's Ryan who gets to be the pinup boy."

At the time, Rock was unfamiliar with the film's director, Budd Boetticher, and was not looking forward to being helmed by him. *[If Boetticher had any reputation at all in the film colony, it was for directing low-budget Westerns. At the time he met Rock (1952), he'd already churned out* The Cimmaron Kid, Bronco Buster, *and* The Red Ball Express.*]*

Rock concealed his resentment and worked smoothly with Boetticher, especially when he learned that the director had cast him as his number one star in the upcoming film, *Seminole* (1953).

In a nutshell, *Horizons West* was the story of Dan Hammond (Ryan), who returns home to Texas after the Civil War, along with his brother Neil (Rock), who desperately wants to run his small ranch. But brother Dan has grandiose ambitions of founding a vast empire in Texas, the way the ruthless Cord Hardin (Raymond Burr) was doing.

Hardin's wife (Adams) begins to fall in love with Dan, as he becomes a power figure in the state, rustling horses and grabbing up ranchland.

Along the way, he makes many enemies, including his brother Neil, who by now has become the major lawman in Austin. The theme of sibling rivalry segues into a bitter and menacing showdown between the brothers.

"To say that my two male stars, Ryan and Hudson, didn't get along would be an understatement," Boetticher said. "It was like the meeting of two stud bulls with only one cow in the pasture, to put it in Western terms."

Like his director, Ryan, too, was a son of Chicago, who, onscreen, usually portrayed ruthless villains and hardened cops. The same height as Rock (6'4"), he had a muscular build.

The best assessment of Rock's costar was articulated by reporter Ty Burr. In reference to Ryan, he wrote:

168

"You notice the eyes first. Hard as marbles, dark as death. They can send a chill through the cheapest of 1950s 'B' movies. Beneath those eyes is a prow of a nose, then a mouth that can broaden in fraudulent welcome, or, more likely, twist into a metaphysical sneer. He has the looks of a screen idol, radiating Black Irish glamour. Women tend to

Courtly, patriarchal, macho, and dapper, Robert Ryan (left) interacts with Rock Hudson in this scene from one of the younger actor's breakthrough films, *Horizons West*.

act goofy when he is in the room. Not only that: He can act."

Horizons West marked Rock's 18th movie in four years. At the wrap, Boetticher told a reporter, "Rock Hudson is a big shitkicker type of guy, bashful in a cinch. He's got a winning smile. He suffers through the serious scenes with great pain, especially a role that calls for real acting. He blows most of his lines, and we have to reshoot. He's filled with apologies for slowing down production. Call me crazy, but I'm giving him the lead in my next picture. He's not an actor. He's a movie star in the making, and often that's a profession unique in itself, having nothing to do with a real actor."

***

One night over dinner with Jack Navaar and a coterie of male friends, Rock commented on a certain irony going on at his home studio. "Those matinee idols of yesterday, Errol Flynn and Tyrone Power, my friends, have both landed at Universal after their contracts expired at Warners and Fox."

Flynn was making *Against All Flags,* and Power was doing a costume drama, *Mississippi Gambler* (1953), a film produced by Ted Richmond, who had been one of Rock's producers. Not only that, but Power would be co-starring with two of Rock's former leading ladies, Piper Laurie and Julie Adams.

After Rock visited Power in his dressing room, he later recalled the experience to his friends: "I gathered Ty in my arms and gave him a great movie star kiss. He didn't faint. I stripped him, tossed him on the sofa, and fucked hell out of him."

Later, during the afterglow, they talked. Although Tyrone detested costume dramas, Universal had offered him $250,000, plus 50% of the profits.

He didn't like his role, that of a gambler "good at cards, ready with his fists, and handy with the ladies." Later, the critics blasted it, but the public flocked to see it.

He claimed that Zanuck, out of past loyalty, might have renewed his contract, but "It was time to go, I felt. I'm a free agent now."

Power also discussed his deteriorating marriage to Linda Christian. Rock had attended enough of their notorious parties, which turned into orgies around midnight, to know that they were sleeping around with other partners. He occasionally went to their Saturday night adventures, although usually finding them "too straight for my tastes." He preferred Henry Willson's all-male pool parties.

During the first week of Powers' shoot, when Rock wasn't needed one afternoon on his own film set, he phoned Power but didn't get him. He wandered over to his set. Richmond told him that Power had finished his scene and was in his dressing room. When he knocked on the door, he heard Power call out, "Who's there?" When he learned that it was Rock, he yelled, "I'm coming!"

That turned out to have a double meaning.

Power eventually opened the door with a towel wrapped around his waist. On the sofa lay a voluptuous woman covered with a sheet.

He introduced her as Anita Ekberg, a big-bosomed Swedish actress, who was an extra on *Mississippi Gambler*.

The trio chatted pleasantly for a few minutes before she dressed and exited. She didn't seem at all embarrassed at getting naked and having had sex with the star of the picture. Rock figured that since she was from Sweden, she was more sophisticated about sex than most American women at the time.

She kissed Rock goodbye on both cheeks, but gave Power a long, lingering kiss.

Little did Rock know that she'd soon be an extra on one of his own upcoming films, where he'd get to know her a lot better.

***

Raoul Walsh, the fabled director of *The Lawless Breed* (a film eventually released in 1952), greeted Rock with a firm handshake followed by a bear hug. "Welcome to the set, ya big lug!" he said. "I never thought you'd go anywhere in the movies, not really."

"You mean this time I don't have to paint your house, mow your lawn?"

"No more. You've come up in the world. If I had known, I'd never have sold your contract to Universal for peanuts."

Before shooting began, Rock spent three days with Walsh going over the script and rehearsing some of his lines, partly because he was known for flubbing scenes repeatedly.

On the third day, Walsh introduced Rock to the film's producer, William Alland, who had high hopes for *The Lawless Breed.*

The producer and director went over every one of Rock's scenes, with Walsh doing most of the talking. The Technicolor western was based on the life of the outlaw, John Wesley Hardin, a gunslinger and gambler, who was released from a Texas prison in 1896, after serving 16 years of a 25-year sentence.

In the film, his previous lawless background is explored in flashback. Cast in the role of Hardin, Rock is set to marry Jane Brown (Mary Castle), an orphan girl he was brought up with—that is, after he's made a fortune at the gambling tables.

She is killed, and he later marries and runs away with a saloon girl known as "Rosie" (Julie Adams).

When he finds a cardsharp cheating him, he kills him in self-defense when the man pulls a gun on him. Regrettably, the man he kills is a member of the Hadley family, led by Ike (Hugh O'Brian). They are set on revenge. During a cattle drive to Abilene, Hardin, in self-defense, kills another Hadley.

For six years, Hardin and Rose, pretending to be brother and sister, live in hiding under assumed names in Alabama. He's eventually caught and sent to prison.

For the scenes depicting Hardin's homecoming sixteen years later, Walsh had hired the best makeup man in Hollywood, Perc Westmore, to age him, adding wrinkles and a gray wig.

When Rock, as Hardin, returns home, he finds his son on the verge of following in his father's footsteps, but he steers him clear from a life of gun-slinging violence.

[*The Lawless Breed became one of the top box office hits of 1953.]*

In *The Lawless Breed* (1952), Rock, hiding from the law, pretends to be the brother of Julie Adams. But in the boudoir, the love he gives her is not brotherly.

***

Near the close of filming of *The Lawless Breed*, Rock received a call from the publicity department of Universal. "Time for a studio date, Rock Baby!" said Nelson Striker. "We've lined up for you to escort the poor man's Marilyn Monroe."

According to the blonde starlet, Mamie Van Doren, "The young guys and dolls who survived at Universal in those days were the ones who really worked hard to carve out a career."

Along with countless thousands, and rivaled by, among others, Jayne Mansfield, Van Doren was viewed as a Marilyn Monroe clone in the 1950s. "Perhaps Rock and I worked harder than most. That meant making ourselves available for 'studio dates.'" That was a way of getting publicity for both the man and woman, although secretly, they might despise each other. Or it could be a real friendly date. Take, for example, Tab Hunter, who was gay, dating Debbie Reynolds. At least they were friends, not lovers."

Being familiar with all that, Mamie wasn't surprised when she received a call from Al Horowitz, the chief of publicity at Universal. He wanted Rock to escort her to the annual *Photoplay* awards slated for a night in February 1953. She'd heard that the studio knew he was gay, so she didn't have to worry about his coming on to her.

In her 1987 memoirs, she devoted the entire Chapter One to the night Rock Hudson dated her. Before the date, Mamie lunched with an unidentified friend at the Universal commissary. Her friend warned her that she was being used to camouflage Rock's homosexuality.

"Of course, I know that," Mamie responded. "You think I don't know that it rains in Indiana in the summertime? It's publicity for Rock, but it's also publicity for me, and I need all I can get. So it's a fair trade-off."

"You'll be as safe with him as you'd be on a date with your mother," the friend predicted. As it turned out, she was no fortune teller.

On a studio date arranged by Universal, Mamie Van Doren, the studio's "Atomic Blonde," was escorted by the dashing new star, Rock Hudson. She was falsely told that he'd be "harmless."

172

At the time, Mamie was living with her parents. Rock arrived at her home, piloting his convertible to her remotely located residence in San Fernando Valley.

When Mamie appeared at her door to welcome Rock, he seemed stunned by her outfit, which had been borrowed from Universal's wardrobe department. As she recalled, "I felt a little silly in that garb. I looked like the queen of the prom." She'd been given a beaded dress with a strapless bodice and a flared skirt "with a football field of crinolines."

She later expressed surprise at how macho he was, a style which apparently wasn't part of her conception at the time of gay men. Of course, she lived in an era where it was commonly assumed that homosexual men were effeminate. In a more enlightened era, America now knows that gay men come in all stripes, even the most macho, well-muscled, and most heavily endowed on the planet—and that included Rock Hudson.

At the time he dated Mamie, Universal executives, especially Edward Muhl, was afraid that news of his lover's sexuality might be exposed in the notorious scandal rag of the day, *Confidential* magazine.

It was a chilly night, and Mamie was "goose-pimply" riding in that convertible to the Beverly Hills Hotel, site of the awards ceremony. Emerging from the convertible, Mamie and Rock headed for the entrance. Behind ropes, fans—mostly teenaged girls—were screaming, "ROCK! ROCK! ROCK!"

"I wasn't very well known at the time," she said. *[In years to come, film festivals would be held in her honor.]*

The waiter assigned to their shared table in the Crystal Room ushered Mamie and Rock to their seats. Much to their surprise, they'd been placed at the same table with Joan Crawford and her date.

Mamie did not identify the handsome young man, but others later reported that her date was Stephen Crane, the World War II husband of Lana Turner, and the father of her daughter, Cheryl Crane, who would later become involved in the fatal stabbing of Johnny Stompanato, Lana's gangster lover.

It was obvious that Crawford had been drinking heavily, though Crane was holding back, perhaps wanting to stay sober enough to drive her home and seduce her, something that Crawford demanded of all her young escorts at the time.

Unknown to Mamie at the time, Rock had already seduced Crawford. Although regarding Mamie with hostility, she was very flirtatious with Rock that night. That shocked the blonde starlet, since her mother, back in South Dakota, defined Crawford as her favorite movie star, and had even named her daughter after her. *[Mamie's birth name was Joan Olander.]*

At a nearby table sat Gary Cooper, who had met Rock when he was positioned as an escort for his wife, Rocky. Coop was enthralled with his date for the evening, Grace Kelly, with whom he'd co-starred in his most memorable western, *High Noon* (1952).

A drunken Crawford seemed threatened by all the new and successful faces at the tables that surrounded her. "Shit!" she said in a loud voice. "Shit to all of them." Then she turned to Rock. "Whole god damn room is filled with newcomers if you ask me. Right, Rocko?"

"You've got that right, Miss Crawford," he answered.

When she made her next pronouncement, she turned and aimed it directly at Mamie, no doubt threatened by the young blonde beauty. "Lots of pretty faces with nothing going on behind them." Then she signaled her waiter for another drink. "Few fucking real stars like me left in this whole god damn rotten town. Maybe John Wayne, but that's about it. Fucking new stars...that's what these newcomer hussies are like. That's why they got here tonight...*fucking!*"

Mamie controlled herself during Crawford's drunken rant, but she was horribly disappointed with the aging screen goddess who had started dancing the Charleston in silent films of the late 1920s.

One of the highlights of the evening was the appearance of the cowboy star, Tex Ritter, who sang the title song from *High Noon*. Later, John Wayne and Maureen O'Hara were awarded honors for their co-starring roles in *The Quiet Man* (1952), set in Ireland.

Crawford seemed all right with that. But when Marilyn Monroe was named "Newcomer of the Year," her fury burst out.

In a gold gown with deep *décolletage*, Marilyn, like Mamie, had borrowed a particularly daring dress from wardrobe, a garment obviously two sizes too small. As was later learned, she didn't wear panties. As columnist James Bacon described her wiggly walk up to the stage, "Her breasts undulated, and her *derrière* looked like two puppies fighting under a silk sheet."

She strutted onto the stage with her mincing walk to face Dean Martin at the podium. He broke into a hip-swinging dance, as his partner, Jerry Lewis, in the audience, leaped onto the top of his table and "hooted like a chimpanzee," in the words of one writer.

From her position at Rock's table, Crawford was enraged by Marilyn's entrance. Loud enough that the tables next to her could hear, she said, "I've got tits, too, but I don't have to juggle them all over the room." [*Miss Crawford forgot to mention that she'd made porn films during her early years in showbiz before getting a contract with MGM.*]

The next day, Crawford denounced Marilyn for "offending the nation" with her shocking appearance. She even criticized the sexy red dress she'd worn in *Niagara* (1953), her latest film.

The day after that, Marilyn shot back, "I was playing a slut in *Niagara*. Sluts often wear red dresses." Then, perhaps knowing what a notorious mother Crawford was, she said, "In spite of her criticism of me, I have always admired Miss Crawford as a loving mother."

To escape from Crawford's rants in the Crystal Room, Mamie excused herself to go to the ladies' room. There, although three women were filing out, she became aware of a woman who remained behind the closed door of the stall beside her, struggling with her floor length dress as she attempted to raise it up so she could urinate.

When each of them emerged from their respective stalls, Mamie was shocked to see Marilyn herself. They each knew each other slightly.

As they each made adjustments to their makeup, and as Mamie had lavishly complimented Marilyn on her award, the "newcomer" turned to her. "So Mamie, I hear you're screwing Jimmy McHugh."

"No, Norma Jeane," Mamie answered. "The old bastard is just my agent."

"You look smart enough to screw the right men in this business," Marilyn said. "That's how you get ahead—I should know. Good luck, girl!"

At the door, she paused. "In case you don't know, Norma Jeane doesn't live here anymore. One final word…" Then she held up her award. "After tonight, I've sucked my last cock unless I want to."

While Mamie was in the toilet, and just after Crane, too, headed for the men's room, Crawford slipped Rock a note. It said, 'Call me…I'm ready for a repeat performance."

At the end of the ceremony, in his convertible with Mamie, Rock headed back to the San Fernando Velley, passing the area where he lived. At her door, Mamie expected a kiss on the cheek, but he asked if he could come inside for a cup of coffee.

In the kitchen, as she was rustling up the ingredients for the caffeine he'd requested, she felt Rock's hands on her bare shoulders. As she recorded in her memoirs, "He turned toward me and kissed me. Not a smack on the cheek, but a passionate kiss with his body pressed against mine. I could feel him

Buxom Mamie Van Doren found that Rock was three times as big as Elvis Presley, but "too quick on the draw" for her.

175

hardening. Soon, we were breathing heavily and pawing each other."

"As we necked, we slowly sank to the kitchen floor. I was still in that beaded gown. The next morning, mother would find beads scattered all over. I was lying half on top of Rock helping him unzip his fly. Out popped a whopper That boulder that his agent named him for must have been a big one. He was very well endowed."

The next scene that took place was like an episode in a sex comedy that the Production Code wouldn't allow. Rock had a hard time finding the target, fighting his way through a sea of crinoline. On the waxed linoleum, she attempted to direct him, and finally managed, just in time. Breathing heavily, he announced, "I'm coming." He was right about that, splattering the crinolines.

After a cup of coffee to sober up for the drive home, he asked if he could have lunch with her in the commissary the next day.

She agreed, and showed up at 1PM when the dining area was crowded. Rock was sitting alone at a table waiting for her. A "cowboy," one of the handsome studly extras, was sitting with his back to Rock at a separate table.

Rock welcomed Mamie and gave her a light kiss.

During the course of the lunch, columnist James Bacon and a reporter, Harrison Carroll, of the Los Angeles *Herald-Express*, stopped by their table, and Rock introduced them to Van Doren, whom they had never met before.

After the reporters had gone, Rock invited the blonde cowboy at the table next to them to join Mamie and him. It became apparent to her that the two men were lovers. After a while, she felt left out of the conversation and wandered off after thanking him for lunch.

She had to return that beaded dress, minus a lot of its beads, to the wardrobe department. She hoped the mistress in there would not discover all that sticky, gooey stuff trapped between the folds of its crinoline.

***

Seminole, Rock's last film from the busy year of 1952 was a Technicolor adventure story set in 1835 in the wilds of Florida. Filming would take place in the untamed Everglades National Park, a locale fraught with dangers. Rock would jokingly refer to the film, eventually released in 1953, as "Semolina."

His contract at Universal was com-

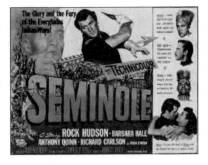

ing to an end, and he had not been notified whether Universal planned to renew it. One afternoon, he was summoned to the executive offices, where Edward Muhl awaited him. First things first: As was his custom, the studio chief got down on his knees, unzipped Rock's fly, removed his penis, and fellated him, as he had so many times in the past.

After Rock zipped up, Muhl told him the good news: His contract was going to be renewed. No longer working for starvation wages, he would be given $1,000 a week, with an escalation clause granting him $4,000 a week as the months progressed.

"Who loves you, baby?" Muhl asked.

In 1952, during the Eisenhower era, that was a vast sum of money, with enormous buying power.

After Rock made *Peggy* (1950) with Charles Coburn, the fan mail began pouring in. By the summer of 1952, he was receiving 1,800 fan mail letters a month, rising to 2,100 by September. At year's end, he was filling up mail-bags, with 4,000 fan letters a month when he was commissioned to play the lead in *Seminole*.

Once again, Budd Boetticher was the director, having recently helmed him in *Horizons West*. The leading lady in *Seminole* was Barbara Hale, with Anthony Quinn cast in the second male lead. Richard Carlson played the villain of the piece, with Rock's friend, Hugh O'Brian, cast as an Indian.

On the verge of major stardom, Lee Marvin was given a minor role, as was James Best, who had been Rock's on-again, off-again lover for some time, an affair that had heated up particularly during the making of *Air Cadet*.

The entire cast and crew were flown to Florida for location shooting. O'Brian and Rock spent two days in Miami before reporting for work. In the film, O'Brian had to play the role of a menacing Indian, Kajeck.

Rock told him, "Tonight at our hotel, I'll rehearse you for the role. Me, heap big Indian chief—you, squaw!"

"You've got the roles reversed," O'Brian said. "Me, heap big Indian chief, you, white woman captured on wagon train I turn into squaw."

Arriving in the Everglades, Rock told O'Brian, "I hope one of those big

Rock with Barbara Hale in *Seminole* (1952). The Indian chief played by Anthony Quinn is his major competition.

'gators isn't hungry."

The story of *Seminole* unfolds when Florida was just a frontier territory, its interior a wilderness. The U.S. cavalry was sent to protect the early settlers from attacks by Indians. As Lt. Lance Caldwell, a tall, handsome, and dashing cavalry officer, Rock is ordered to Fort King, a military outpost in north-central Florida, which has been under assault from a Seminole uprising. The movie opens at his court martial trial where he's been accused of murder. If found guilty, he will face a firing squad. He is allowed to tell his story, and the film moves into flashback:

Upon his arrival at the fort, Caldwell wanted to maintain peace with the Seminoles, but his commanding officer, Major Harlan Degan (Carlson), has other plans, as he seems hell bent on a massacre of the Indians.

Caldwell had a reunion with his childhood sweetheart, Revere Muldoon (Barbara Hale), who runs an outpost selling supplies to the settlers. He is still in love with her, but she's also involved with Osceola (Anthony Quinn) in an unlikely romance. In a plot that's a bit contrived, Caldwell had been friends with Osceola, back when he was known as "John," and the two men had served in the Army together. John quit the Army, returned to Florida, and became Osceola, the leader of his Seminole tribe.

O'Brian was cast as Kajeck, an Indian who wants to oust Osceola and become the tribal leader himself, waging war on the U.S. troops. He is barely recognizable, outfitted as he is in tribal costume, war paint, and wearing his hair in an outrageously spikey, sinister-looking Mohawk.

Over Caldwell's protest, Degan orders his troops to stage a raid on a Seminole camp deep in the Everglades, although his men are untrained. They walk into a trap, and most of the soldiers are killed.

In honor of his long-ago friendship, Osceola rescues the wounded Caldwell, and takes him back to the Indian encampment, with orders to nurse him back to health.

Muhl had demanded that Rock show his torso in every film, and he does so as a wounded soldier. Muhl instructed all directors, "Rock is known as the Baron of Beefcake, and I want him to keep that title."

Casting directors needed an actor who wasn't self-conscious about his body. Rock, shown here buff, trim, and muscled amid Native American artifacts on the set of *Seminole*, fit the bill.

Caldwell persuades Osceola, under a white flag of truce, to go with him to Fort King to negotiate peace terms. But Degan betrays him and tosses him into a bamboo-covered pit dug into the ground in the courtyard of the fort. In the dead of night, Kajeck slips into the camp, crawls down into the pit, struggles with Osceola, and murders him. Caldwell tried to rescue him, but Kajeck escapes. Caldwell is found with the dead chief and is accused of his murder.

After relaying his story at his court martial, Caldwell is framed and has to face a firing squad. But at the last minute, Kajeck arrives at the camp, demanding the body of Osceola for burial. He admits that he was the murderer, and Caldwell is set free. Subsequently, he picks up his romance with Revere for a happy ending.

Rock worked well with his fellow actors, including Barbara Hale, a native of Illinois, like himself. A former model,

Like Rock himself, his co-star in *Seminole*, Barbara Hale, depicted in this publicity photo from 1945, became more famous (and richer) from her work in television than for anything she ever did on the silver screen. In her case, widespread recognition derived from her performance as Della Street in the long-running TV series with Raymond Burr, *Perry Mason* (1957-66)

she'd been appearing in films since 1943 opposite such stars as Frank Sinatra, Robert Mitchum, James Stewart, and James Cagney. She'd played Al Jolson's wife in *Jolson Sings Again* (1949), starring Larry Parks.

Of Mexican and Irish descent, Quinn had been born in Mexico. He was not only an actor, but a painter, writer, and, in time, a director. Rock was surprised that he'd accepted such a small role in *Seminole*. Previously, he'd won Best Supporting Oscar for *Viva Zapata!* (1952) with Marlon Brando.

By 1947, he'd appeared in more than fifty movies, playing virtually any role—an Indian, a Filipino freedom fighter, a Chinese guerilla, an Arab chief, a Mafia don, and a Hawaiian tribal leader. Although married to Katherine DeMille, the daughter of Cecil B. DeMille, Quinn was a notorious womanizer. He told Rock, "My goal is to impregnate every woman on the planet."

[Quinn would father his last child in 1993 at the age of 78.]

Lee Marvin had been cast in *Seminole* as Sergeant Magruder. Rock could never have predicted how fast he'd zoom up the rungs of the Hollywood ladder into major stardom.

Rock would go on to appear with Marvin in his upcoming picture, *Gun Fury* (1953), released the same year as *Seminole*.

The movie poster for *Seminole* was Rock's favorite to date. The upper part depicted him battling an Indian, the lower part showed him in a love scene with Hale.

Seminole did much to enhance Rock's macho reputation, one critic hailing him as "Filmdom's next John Wayne."

In spite of *The New York Times* labeling *Seminole* "a swampy melodrama," it did reasonably well at the box office.

***

Rock hadn't seen James Best in several weeks, and he arranged for him to be his roommate on location during the filming of *Seminole* in the Everglades. Lodgings for cast and crew were in a dreary motel with a greasy spoon café on the edge of the national park.

In *Seminole*, Best had the small role of an enlisted man in the cavalry named Corporal Gerald. In one dramatic scene, Rock has to jump into quicksand to rescue him. In another, when Best is wounded by the Seminoles and carried on a stretcher, Rock tenderly looks after the wounded young man.

Theirs had been a different dynamic when the two had previously worked together on such pictures as *Air Cadet*. Best always maintained that he was straight, and Rock more or less had to force sex upon him. Now, he was the one who eagerly pursued Rock, who was using him as a convenient outlet for his sex drive during filming.

A photographer-reporter from *The Miami Herald*, Stephen Curry, journeyed to the location for a layout for its Sunday supplement, *Fun in Florida*. *[Rock, fully aware that he'd be the centerpiece of some bare-chested scenes as a wounded man in the picture, wanted to be properly tanned for the shoot. For the magazine layout, he and Best dressed up in skimpy swimwear and were photographed relaxing by the motel pool.]*

This was a rare departure for Rock,

'Jes two cowpokes whilin' away the hours together with a guitar...

Rock Hudson (left) with James Best on the set of *Seminole*.

as he usually went to great lengths not to be photographed with one of his male lovers, as opposed to his (widely photographed) dates with women.

To many readers of the photo layout, the pictures appeared innocent enough for that time. But when the photograph was seen in Hollywood, a hip town, it raised more than one eyebrow.

The caption was provocative: "In the Florida location for Rock Hudson's latest picture, 'The Baron of Beefcake' strips down for a sunbath. His loyal companion is James Best, *The Cimarron Kid,* one of his latest movies."

What made the photo so provocative was that Best was resting on his elbow gazing lovingly into Rock's handsome face.

When he returned to Hollywood, Rock told friends, "Sex with the long, lean, and lanky guy was just great, but I've got to end it. Back in Hollywood, I've got too many others to seduce."

In spite of repeated calls from Best, Rock did not return those calls. The two actors never appeared together in another movie.

***

One afternoon, Rock received an emergency call from George Sherman, who was directing Errol Flynn in *Against All Flags* (1952). Sherman had helmed Rock in *Tomahawk.*

Rock learned the bad news: His swashbuckling friend had slipped on the wet deck of a "pirate ship" and had broken his left ankle. The picture had five more days until it was wrapped, and Flynn would be in every scene. Sherman said he was shutting down production until Flynn recovered, his doctor estimating it would take five months before his plaster cast could be removed.

Rock had visited Flynn's set several times. In *Against All Flags,* Flynn had been cast as an 18th Century naval officer, Brian Hawke, who attacked the pirates of Madagascar. His injury had occurred on February 1, 1952, during a sword fight with stuntman Paul Stader.

It was four days before Rock could get in touch with Flynn to visit him. It was the stricken actor himself who phoned Rock one afternoon at Universal, inviting him to his home on Mulholland Drive.

He learned that Flynn was in residence there with his latest wife, the actress Patrice Wymore, and his eleven-year-old son, Sean. The boy's mother was the French actress Lili Damita, Flynn's first wife.

Rock accepted the invitation to visit his home, and he drove up the mountain to the swashbuckler's dream house, which he had designed himself. Rock was always surprised that Flynn's retreat from the world looked like the home of a conservative upper class family in the Connecticut countryside.

He continued to be honored that in the 1950s, Flynn had chosen him as one of his best pals. Their initial sexual intimacy had morphed into male bonding.

At the door, he rang the bell and was somewhat startled to see Sean Flynn opening it. Rock had been a very shy eleven-year-old. Not this boy. "Hot damn!" he said. "Rock Hudson in the flesh. I can't believe I'm meeting THE Rock Hudson." He held out his hand.

"Hi, kid," Rock said. "I'm here to see your dad."

Rock was mildly surprised that the boy was still holding his hand. "You're my idol. Don't tell dad, but you're my favorite movie star. I saw *Seminole* three times. I thought you were fantastic in *Scarlet Angel*. One day if you want to, I'll show you my bedroom. It's plastered with publicity pictures of you."

It didn't take Rock long to realize that this was the first case of idol worship he'd ever experienced. He was very flattered. Sean was going through a phase of adulation that Rock himself had experienced when watching the movies of Tyrone Power and Flynn himself in the late 1930s.

Rock Hudson Erotic Fire

182

Chapter Seven

ROCK AS BOX OFFICE DYNAMITE

Fans Morph Him Into "A Magnificent Obsession," Phallic Symbol, and Lust Object

By the time Rock was cast opposite Jane Wyman in *Magnificent Obsession* (1954), the Oscar-winner (*Johnny Belinda*) was already a screen legend. The ex-Mrs. Ronald Reagan had always been a very private person, Marlene Dietrich calling her "A mystery no one has ever bothered to solve."

As she worked with Rock, she gradually fell in love with him, later telling her best friend, Loretta Young, "Nobody told me he was attracted to men, especially my new husband, Fred Karger."

"**Get the hell in here, sport,** and pay homage to a fallen idol."

That was Errol Flynn's greeting to Rock, as he was ushered into the older star's bedroom by his son, Sean. He was lying in his underwear with his leg in a plaster cast, suffering from a broken ankle. Sean was ordered out of the room under protest. He wanted to stay with Rock, his idol.

As Rock chatted with Flynn, he took in the view of his body. In his early forties, he was in fairly good shape after a life of dissipation. He was still good-looking and still possessed a charisma that had enthralled millions around the world. But he had health issues, and not just a broken bone. That impediment, combined with a career in decline, resulted in his movies doing not very well at the box office.

Flynn poured out his concerns to Rock, often taking his hand for reassurance. "I'm making pictures I'm not proud of," he said. He cited *Rocky Mountain* (1950); *Kim* (1951); and *Adventures of Fabian* (also 1951), which he described as "the dullest picture extant."

"I knew when Jack Warner gave me *Mara Maru* (1952), that the bastard had little regard for my career at this point. On the set of *Against All Flags,* they're using footage from the original. Frankly, sport, I'm turning more and more to the bottle," Flynn said. "Gone are the days of my sexual adventures, like those I had with you. In the bottle, I somehow can maintain that delusion between my glory days in the late 1930s and the harsh reality of the 1950s setting in."

"I know I'm killing myself, fucking up my brain and liver, but I drink to escape the pain, the true mark of an alcoholic. Don't let it happen to you, sport."

"Before my time is up, I'm sure I'll have a few more sexual adventures—it's in my blood. But there's a slowing down by the time you reach the November of your years."

"Jack Warner assigned me to Universal, telling me, 'Flynn, you're more trouble than you're worth.' I've delayed production at Universal for five months."

Rock tried to reassure him that a big comeback picture awaited him. "You've got too much talent. You're still magic on the screen. You're due for a lucky break."

"If that were true, that would be such a delight, but, as you may have noted, that's not the usual way a movie star's life descends."

He told Rock that he planned to be out of the country for many months, taking advantage of the break that the Internal Revenue gave movie stars who

Errol Flynn, diehard swashbuckler, in *Against All Nations (1952)* shortly before the fall that put him out of commission.

Rock, on the verge of playing a swashbuckler in *Sea Devils*, found him instructional.

worked in pictures abroad for periods of more than eighteen months. "I'm not only escaping the IRS for back taxes, but I'm working hard to avoid ex-mistresses, ex-boyfriends, and ex-wives seeking back alimony, and frivolous lawsuits from teenaged girls for allegedly having raped them."

At the end of Rock's three-hour visit, Flynn was growing tired. "I'm about to doze off. Give me a good night kiss and drop over as many times as you can while I'm lying here unable to walk. You won't have Errol Flynn to hang out with for many more years. You'll have to carry on in my swashbuckling tradition and become the Errol Flynn of Universal."

"No one can ever fill those green tights like the master himself, Robin Hood—or should I say Captain Blood?"

"At this point in my life, the answer is neither. Those lusty days of mine are gone forever."

Weeks later, when Rock encountered Mickey Rooney and talked about Flynn, the pint-sized actor said, "Errol woke up one morning, looked in the mirror, and decided he was not Robin Hood any more. I think he's begun a long, slow death."

***

Director Raoul Walsh had been impressed with Rock in *The Lawless Breed*, and he decided to cast him another time, awarding him the male lead in *Sea Devils*. The picture would be released by RKO, which was owned at the time by Howard Hughes.

Yvonne De Carlo, Hughes' sometimes girlfriend, would get star billing over Rock, however. This was the fourth and final film he'd make with the beautiful brunette, aka "the Queen of Technicolor." Their previous films had included *The Desert Hawk, Tomahawk,* and *Scarlet Angel.*

Meeting with Walsh, Rock was given a copy of Victor Hugo's 1866 novel, *Toilers of the Sea (Les Travailleurs de la mer),* which was mostly set on the Channel Island of Guernsey where the Parisian novelist had spent fifteen years in exile. Rock struggled in his attempt to wade through the novel. The vastly altered screenplay by Borden Chase was easier to digest.

As Gilliatt, Rock would play a fisherman-turned-smuggler, a social outcast who falls in love with a beautiful woman, Drouchette. Exactly

who is this mysterious female? Is she a French spy, or perhaps a secret agent working for the British?

The action occurs in 1800 during the Napoleonic Wars. France and Britain had been at war since 1798, and *Sea Devils* takes place during what came to be known as the War of the Second Coalition.

Gilliatt agrees to transport Drouchette to the French coast in his ship, known as the *Sea Devil. En route,* he falls in love with her.

Complications ensue, including flamboyant barroom brawls, romance on the high seas, plenty of intrigue, and—most dramatic of all—a battle with a giant octopus, the action highlight of the film.

Cast and crew were flown to the Channel Islands, where shooting took place on both Guernsey and Jersey.

During filming, Rock got his chance to live up to his title of Baron of Beefcake, as he appears shirtless in some scenes, especially at one point when he is tied up. De Carlo competes with him in the flesh department, wearing a shoulderless gown with plunging *décollétage.* Walsh seemed to be defying the censors, hoping to let his actors appear as minimally dressed as the Production Code allowed.

De Carlo later, in her memoirs, commented on Walsh's vague directions. Just before filming one of the scenes, he told her, "Yvonne, don't forget. Rock is injured. Take out the cooking sherry and give him a good swig of it. If that doesn't work, get under the covers with him. That'll cure him. ACTION!"

Later, during her private discussion of those directions with her co-star, both she and Rock interpreted that as a homophobic slur. She later wrote that Walsh privately spoke of his anger at "all the birds flocking around Rock."

"Birds?" she asked.

"You know what I mean," he answered. "Birds of a feather flock together."

He was referring to the coterie of young gay men who had flown to the

We see that it's bondage, but could it be love? Two views of Rock inter-relating with Yvonne De Carlo in *Sea Devils* (1953).

Channel Islands from London to accompany Rock during the shoot. When the star had first arrived in London, in anticipation of the debut of filming in Jersey and Guernsey, he discovered that he'd developed thousands of gay male fans. He'd invited six of them, each a blonde and well-built, to go on location with him.

Cast and crew moved on to St. Malo on the northern coast of France for some final scenes. On one windy morning, Walsh was in a boat with his cameraman, shooting a scene with Rock and some men in an adjoining craft. A strong wind gust blew in, capsizing the director's boat. Although his cameraman swam to shore, Walsh was in trouble.

Rock jumped into the cold water and rescued him, hauling him to shore like a skilled lifeguard. After that, Rock redeemed himself, and Walsh even tolerated "the flock of birds" from London.

After his near-drowning, Walsh shut down production for a few days to recuperate. Rock and "The Birds" wandered off to a neighboring town for "fun and games." De Carlo was rescued by Prince Aly Khan, who showed up to take her on a tour along the coast of Normandy.

Walsh was disappointed with the final cut. "*Sea Devils* didn't live up to the Hugo novel because the bastards at RKO kept cutting down on my budget. That didn't allow me to film scenes I wanted. I had to take a lot of short cuts. But what the hell!"

***

Rock was away from home so much that Jack Navaar began to wonder if they were indeed lovers or just two men who occasionally got together. He complained, "You're rarely here. Maybe you could drop in at your own home for a visit some night."

On occasion, he could be seen driving around Hollywood alone in Rock's convertible. Navaar didn't feel comfortable having Rock support him financially, but he stuck it out. At night, he usually prepared a home-cooked dinner, but on many an occasion, Rock didn't show up to eat it. Often he returned home at around 10PM or much later, claiming he'd been held up at Universal.

Willson summoned Rock to his office for a private meeting, with the intention of warning him that with stardom approaching, he would have to make some big changes in his life. He even suggested the

Beefcake á la Roque. A publicity still from *Sea Devils* promotes Hudson as a rogue in the style of Errol Flynn.

unthinkable: Rock might have to get married. "You know, to the kind of gal who will let you slip around and get dick on the side, since that's something she can't supply. She'll be your arm candy at any premiere or big event where there are photographers."

"Of course," he continued, "you'll have to provide for her financially to keep her trap shut. Hell, I was about ready to marry Margaret Truman until her asshole of a father, that stubborn Missouri mule, butted in. He was on to me. Perhaps that nellie faggot, J. Edgar Hoover, gave the President the lowdown on me."

"You do aim high," Rock said. "The president's daughter, I mean…"

"I'll be on the lookout for a wife for you—perhaps a lesbian, if she doesn't look too butch."

***

Director Raoul Walsh met Rock over lunch at the Universal commissary. He seemed pleased with the results of their last picture, *The Lawless Breed*. "I watched it, kid, once again, the other night. I think you're beginning to learn how to act, something I never thought was possible."

"I like action movies, and I've come up with a dilly," Walsh said. "It's called *Gun Fury* (1953), a 3-D Western, since 3-D seems to be our best hope to lure people away from their TV sets and back into movie houses. The film is going to be shot in the desolate Red Rocks terrain of Sedona, Arizona."

Rock learned that he would star in it as Ben Warren in a screenplay by Irving Wallace. The producer, Lewis J. Rachmil, a New Yorker, had acquired the rights to the novel, *Ten Against Caesar,* by Kathleen B. George and Robert A. Granger, on which the screenplay had been based. The producer's name was unfamiliar to Rock, who learned that he had recently produced a string of William Boyd's Hopalong Cassidy B-westerns.

Gun Fury's screen writer, Wallace, was on the dawn of be-

Gun Fury (1953) was the last film Rock made with director Raoul Walsh, who had first put him under contract.

In this routine Western, Rock starred as a soldier-turned-pacifist who turns violent only when a tough gang of roughnecks kidnaps his *fiancée*, Donna Reed.

188

coming one of the bestselling novelists of the 20th Century. But when Rock was introduced to him, he was still struggling.

Rock began to read what Wallace had created for him.

Since Universal had had no immediate script for him, Rock was on a "loan-out" to Columbia for the production of *Gun Fury*. The story takes place right after the Civil War. As Ben Warren, Rock plays a former soldier who is now a pacifist and doesn't carry a gun. He takes a stagecoach ride with the girl he hopes to marry, Jennifer Ballard (Donna Reed).

The stagecoach, however, is held up by a gang of desperadoes led by Frank Slayton (Phil Carey). After the holdup, Rock is left for dead, and Slayton makes off with Jennifer to a desert hideout. Rock is not dead, but recovers, and he arms himself and sets out to rescue Jennifer and to take revenge on Slayton's cutthroats.

The two leading supporting actors were Lee Marvin, cast as Blinky; and Neville Brand as Brazos. Estella Morales is a "hot tamale" señorita, played by Roberta Haynes. She is dumped by her lover, Slayton, who prefers Rock's *gringa* fiancée (Reed) instead.

***

A phone call came in from San Francisco for Rock at his home. It was from Tyrone Power, who was on tour during the summer of 1953 with the Pulitzer Prize-winning play, *John Brown's Body,* based on an epic poem written by Stephen Vincent Benét in 1928. Charles Laughton was directing Power in the lead, backed up by Raymond Massey and Judith Anderson.

Power wanted Rock to fly to San Francisco to attend the Saturday night performance, and he eagerly accepted. "I'll be on the next plane."

"Don't worry about a hotel," Power told him. "There's plenty of room in my double bed."

Before leaving Los Angeles, Rock had a bitter argument with Jack Navaar, who wanted to go to San Francisco, too. At one point, the dispute became so heated that Navaar threatened that he would not be there when Rock returned. Storming out the door, Rock didn't believe him.

He arrived in San Francisco and reached the theater fifteen minutes before the curtain rose. He was ushered into the star's dressing room, where Power closed the door and bestowed on him a long, lingering kiss. When a knock on the door summoned him for the opening curtain, Power told Rock that he could see the play from backstage.

From a seat in the wings, Rock was surprised to discover that Laughton had cast this period piece with his actors clad in contemporary clothing. He thought Power was mesmerizing on stage, as was Anderson.

However, his illusion about her was marred when she gracefully exited in yellow chiffon only to run to a corner backstage where she hawked and spat.

At a cast party that evening, a reporter from a San Francisco newspaper asked Rock what he thought of the poetic play. "I have always been one of Tyrone Power's most ardent fans," he responded. "I thought he was brilliant in W. Somerset Maugham's *The Razor's Edge* (1946). He really shocked the world when he played that alcoholic carnival barker in *Nightmare Alley* (1947). He showed the critics he was not just a pretty face. His features seem chiseled by a sculptor, and he has his marvelous, seductive speaking voice."

Fearing that he'd sounded to gushy, Rock continued: "Power is America's answer to Sir Laurence Olivier."

Frankly, *John Brown's Body* had gone over Rock's head. After returning to his home in Los Angeles, he admitted to Navaar that he didn't understand most of it. Amazingly, in spite of that, Rock in 1976 would assume Power's role and tour twenty American cities performing in *John Brown's Body*.

***

In an Arabian Nights fantasy, *The Golden Blade* (1953), his fans would find Rock cast for the final time with his co-star, Piper Laurie. But a lot had changed in his career since he'd made *Has Anybody Seen My Gal?* with her. As proof of his rising star power, he now had star billing over her.

Nathan Juran was set to direct Universal's "Golden Couple" as enhanced with such supporting players as Gene Evans, George Macready, and Dennis Weaver, the latter as "Rabble Rouser." Rock had worked with Weaver before.

Rock had met Juran when he was an art director on *Winchester '73*, in which Rock had starred with James Stewart. After meeting with him, Rock told friends, "He was mostly concerned with my wardrobe as an Arab. As for Piper, he ordered her to take dance lessons for her one big number."

Rock's ego was diminished when he learned that he'd gotten the role only because Tony Curtis had rejected it.

Rock liked the movie poster which pictured him shirtless, both during fight scenes and during lovemaking in scenes with Laurie, whom one critic defined as "a fetching little redheaded minx."

In the role of the fearless Harun, a young and adventurous Basranian, Rock arrives in Baghdad during its golden heyday. He's here to avenge the death of his father, who, on his deathbed, gives him a medallion that belonged to his murderer.

Looking for bargains in a secondhand clothing shop in a souk, Harun comes across the magical Sword of Damascus. It can cut through iron, and Harun is impervious to injury whenever he wields it. In the shop, he meets Princess Kariruzan (Laurie), who is disguised as a boy. But whereas Katharine Hepburn might have pulled that ruse off in the Pre-Code 1930s, no one looking at Laurie in the more heavily censored 1950s could ever mistake her for a male. Based on the ridiculous assumption that she's believable as a boy, Harun (Rock) suggests that later, they might go "a-wenching."

After the gender confusion is resolved and she reveals herself as the princess, he learns that she's working to combat a band of evil schemers plotting to overthrow her father, the Caliph (Edgar Barrier).

Macready was cast as the sinister Vizier Jafar, a crooked aide to the Caliph. He wants his dim-witted son, Hasdi (Gene Evans), to marry the princess, even though, by now, her heart belongs to Harun.

"In several scenes, I used Errol Flynn as my role model, swinging from chandeliers, smashing in doors, stabbing guards," Rock said.

One reviewer interpreted him as the worst swashbuckler in movie history, asking, "Where is Errol Flynn now that we need him?"

He also utterly bombed in a dope-smoking dream sequence that left many viewers hysterical. John Rich, the movie's screenwriter, gave him such lines as (to Laurie): "When I was your age, I'd already tasted the nectar that lies in the kiss of a pretty damsel."

Rock performs in a series of action events drawn from the pages of *One Thousand and One Nights*, which was somehow combined with the myth of King Arthur and the Sword of Stone. Since it's a movie, expect our dashingly handsome adventurer to triumph against all odds and win the hand, and the kisses, of the beautiful princess.

Reviews were bad and often vicious, dismissing the picture as a campy romp. "If you're over ten years old, you'll laugh at most of it," one reporter claimed. Another critic dismissed it as "juvenile drivel, strictly Saturday afternoon fodder for the teenybopper. It's no match for other swashbucklers of the same period, and, again, no stretch for Rock Hudson."

***

Fresh from the bed of Tyrone Power, the buxom Swedish actress, Anita Ekberg, arrived on the set of *The Golden Blade* to interpret the role of one of the handmaidens in the palace of the Caliph. Another handmaiden role went to Kathleen Hughes.

Almost from the first day, she'd trained her eagle eye on seducing Rock, having heard that he was "the greatest swordsman" at Universal, both on and off the set. She met him when she, too, had to take lessons in elocution, dancing, and horseback riding, along with acting classes.

On her first available weekend, she invited him to go horseback riding with her in the Hollywood Hills. They returned early Monday morning after spending their nights in a remote motel.

Rock later said, "Other than Marilyn Monroe, Anita is the sexiest woman I've ever met." The comparison was apt. In just a few months, Ekberg would be billed as "Paramount's Answer to Marilyn Monroe."

Her breakthrough role would not come until 1961, when Fellini cast her in *La dolce vita* as the unattainable "dream woman" of the character played by Marcello Mastroianni. Her cavorting in Rome's Trevi Fountain became one of the most iconic scenes in the history of cinema. Lex Barker, the former screen Tarzan and the divorced husband of Lana Turner, played her boyfriend.

Years later, with her film career over, she was discovered running a used car lot in Rome. Reporters still sought her out, as she gave brutally frank interviews, "reviewing" both her former lovers and people she detested.

"If you want to know my biggest thrills, I'd name Errol Flynn, Frank Sinatra, Victor Mature, Sterling Hayden, and Lex Barker. A special Oscar goes to Rock Hudson. I don't know how young men accommodated him. A woman's plumbing seems more suited for his appendage than some boy."

The Swedish actress, Anita Ekburg, had only a small and somewhat silly role in *The Golden Blade*, but she later became famous for cavorting in the Trevi Fountain in Fellini's *La Dolce Vita* (1960).

***

For his final film at Universal in 1953, Rock was cast as the lead in *Back to God's Country,* set in the late 19th Century in the remote northwestern regions of North America. Based on a story by James Oliver Curwood, the movie had first been shot in harsh winter conditions in Alberta, Canada, in 1919, and was reworked for another and much better silent movie in 1927 right before the advent of the Talkies. Rock's version was the creation of screenwriter Tom Reed.

Before filming began, Rock tried to obtain copies of the two movies that had gone before, but was unsuccessful.

Once again, Joseph Pevney, who had never considered Rock a true actor, was assigned to direct him, having done so before in *Shakedown, Air Cadet,* and *Iron Man.*

He protested to producer Howard Christie, wanting to star Jeff Chandler instead. "Don't be a fool, Joe," Christie had responded. "My boss and your boss, Ed Muhl, is in love with Rock. He assigns his boy star parts."

"I didn't know that, I mean, the stuff about the casting couch."

"Well, you'd better believe it," Christie said. "Now let's get on with it. It's gonna be one hell of a hard shoot in the snowfields of the north."

Unlike Pevney, Christie had been more or less supportive of Rock ever since he'd produced *Seminole* in which he'd starred. Rock had recently seen Christie when he was producing *Against all Flags* with Errol Flynn, a movie he was to shut down after the star broke his ankle.

When Rock met with him again, the director feared that his own future looked bleak—and it was. Universal, in the months ahead, assigned him the direction of such "popcorn movies" as the Ma and Pa Kettle comedies, or else the farces with Abbott and Costello.

In the latest version of *Back to God's Country,* Rock was cast as the skipper of a schooner, *Flying Moon.* In his role of Peter Keith, he is a married man wed to Doris (Marcia Henderson). Together, they arrive by ship in a far northern seaport with a cargo of pelts.

Earlier in the film, viewers are introduced to the villains of the movie, Steve Cochran as Paul Blake, and Hugh O'Brian as Frank Hudson. They are seen viciously killing an Eskimo, beating his sled dog, and stealing his map, which they hope will lead to a gold mine.

The chained dog—a magnificent Great Dane—survives and is

whipped daily. One day, the dog will wreak revenge on Cochran.

Cochran and O'Brian conspire to keep Rock's schooner docked until the waters ice up, making departure impossible until spring. Cochran also has his eyes on Rock's wife. Simultaneously, it's revealed, the character played by Cochran is also deeply involved in some master/slave homoerotic relationship with O'Brian, who, like the dog, will wait his turn to strike back.

Cochran kills the cook aboard Rock's schooner and persuades its crew to abandon ship. Rock hunts his drunken crew members down and brings them back. While he's away,

Marcia Henderson with her movie husband, hunter, trapper, animal lover, and able-bodied seaman, as portrayed by Rock.

Cochran attempts to rape Rock's wife, but she fights him off.

Meanwhile, O'Brian secretly forges a will that will result, he hopes, in inheriting all of his partner's money, but Cochran discovers a copy. For this betrayal, Cochran kills O'Brian, the ultimate triumph of a "master" over his "slave."

Rock returns from his search for his crew and fights Cochran in a brutal scene that was dangerous to shoot. His character is seriously injured and his leg is (agonizingly) broken. As the plot thickens, it emerges that he and his wife, along with the loyal Great Dane and an Eskimo guide (who, it turns out, betrays them), have to travel to a fort hundreds of miles away to get medical attention.

The party sets off through the snowfields, mushing their huskies toward the remote fort and (presumably) a doctor. Across a savage wintry landscape of snowfields, Rock, in agony and with his leg broken, is strapped to a dogsled.

As the sled ride across the Far North unfolds, the most dramatic scenes are revealed. Rock and his party are attacked by wolves, but escape to survive both an avalanche and betrayal by their Eskimo guide, always with Cochran, intent on killing them, in hot pursuit. Their loyal Great Dane, however, remembering how Cochran had killed his Eskimo master and kept him chained and whipped, daily, in captivity, ultimately attacks him, sinking his fangs into his throat and ripping out his jugular.

As his female co-star, Rock had wanted a big-name star, but got a minor actress, Marcia Henderson, instead. Her reputation was small, although she'd played Wendy in *Peter Pan* on Broadway. Universal was hoping that co-starring her with Rock might shoot her into stardom. It didn't.

When Rock met her, she was in the throes of divorce and was conducting affairs with both Frank Sinatra and Bing Crosby. When Pevney told Rock that, he said, "Maybe she's a music lover."

The villains, Cochran and O'Brian, were well known to Rock. He'd been friends with O'Brian since high school, and worked with him in both *The Lawless Breed* and *Seminole.*

Although Rock didn't personally know Cochran, he had been mesmerized by his screen presence, telling his friends that "Cochran is the sexiest man in the movies."

During shooting in the remote wilds of the north, Rock had wondered what he'd do for sex. Then an idea occurred to him. He'd request Steve Cochran as his cabin roommate and see what developed during those long, cold, wintry nights.

***

Steve Cochran was a former cow-puncher, railroad worker, department store detective, and carpenter. He'd been born in Eureka, California, eight years before Rock entered the world.

He was rejected for military service during World War II, but performed in plays at a variety of Army camps across the country. This led to Hollywood,

In *Back to God's Country,* Steve Cochran represented brooding sexuality and unbridled evil as the "Villain of the Far North."

Above, he attempts to rape Marcia Henderson, cast as Rock's wife. Below, in a separate scene, he shoots Hugh O'Brian, his homoerotic partner.

195

where Samuel Goldwyn realized his potential as a "walking streak of sex." His swarthy good looks and tough-guy demeanor led to a series of films in which he was cast as cutthroats, gangsters, and menacing lovers.

Although he was often referred to as a Hollywood pretty boy, the phrase "ruggedly handsome" would have been more appropriate.

In 1946, he starred in one of the biggest box office attractions of the era, *The Best Years of Our Lives,* in which he was cast as the sleazy boyfriend of Virginia Mayo. At her home in Thousand Oaks, California, shortly before her death, Ms. Mayo confessed to Darwin Porter that their love-making had continued off the screen as well.

The actor/comedian, Danny Kaye, "developed the hots for me" (Cochran's words) and cast him in three of his movies: *The Wonder Man* (1945); *The Kid from Brooklyn* (1946); and *A Song is Born* (1948).

Mae West selected Cochran over Kirk Douglas as her leading man in the stage production of *Diamond Lil* (1948). He also became her off-screen lover. As he once remarked, "I've been known to throw a mercy fuck to an aging diva from time to time or to plug a gay boy for an occasional variation."

Rock had most recently seen Cochran in *Storm Warning* (1950), co-starring Ginger Rogers and Ronald Reagan. In it, Cochran was cast as the abusive husband of Doris Day in this tale of the KKK in a small Southern town.

When Rock met him, he had made *The Damned Don't Cry* (1950). As he told Rock, "Joan Crawford couldn't get enough of what I've got swinging."

In Hollywood, Cochran could often be seen riding around on his motorcycle. He kept an odd assortment of pets, including a goat, a monkey, and his large German Shepherd who was said to play the piano.

His sexual prowess soon became a Hollywood legend: James Ellroy, the Los Angeles crime writer, made references to him in two novels, *American Tabloid* and *L.A. Confidential.* The actor was alleged to have one of the largest penises in Hollywood, and was nicknamed "Mr. King Size" when not being referred to as "The *Shvantz.*"

The first night Rock bunked with Cochran, the older actor seemed to realize his intentions. Their cabin had a wood-burning fireplace, and Rock made sure it was toasty warm. Cochran showered and came out of the bathroom with a towel wrapped around his waist.

As he sat on the sofa, he was on ample display. The slippage of his towel was deliberate, not accidental. After a few beers, he dropped the towel altogether, inviting Rock to join him in a double bed. After the lights were extinguished, as Rock later told his friends, "Cochran invited me to go on and enjoy myself."

As the days passed, Rock noted that his new bunkmate starting drinking in the afternoon. "Steve seemed haunted by demons. He didn't share his fears with me, but often spoke of other things. One night, he told me his dream life would be as a sultan in a harem composed of girls ages thirteen to fourteen, nothing older."

As Rock later relayed to George Nader and Mark Miller, "It was dirty, rotten, filthy sex, as vile as it gets—and what fun it was."

Cochran had an ulterior motive in warming Rock's bed at night. Over dinner on their third evening together, he told him that he planned to form his own film production company. It became obvious that he wanted to use Rock's emerging star power to help him get launched, and he talked about it incessantly, except for taking time out for love-making.

Rock had no intention of telling him that he would not participate, but he waited until both of them returned to Los Angeles. Cochran phoned him several times, wanting to meet with him and talk over his plans to establish and promote Robert Alexander Productions. After several failed attempts to reach him, Cochran no longer called.

From a distance, Rock watched as Cochran's career and his production company headed south. He starred in a string of low-budget movies through the 1950s, including *The Beat Generation* in 1959.

In June of 1965, Rock was shocked to read of Cochran's horrible death at the age of 48. He'd gone sailing off the coast of Mexico with three females, ages 14, 19, and 25. Each had been promised a role in his upcoming movie.

He died while his 40-foot schooner, *The Rogue,* was sailing off the coast of Guatemala. The girls didn't know how to pilot the craft, and for ten days, they remained adrift at sea with his rotting corpse aboard. Finally, the schooner drifted into the port of Champerico, Guatemala, where they were rescued.

It was believed that the actor had died of a lung infection, although rumors surfaced for years that he had been murdered, perhaps by poisoning, but no evidence ever emerged that was convincing.

***

Rock didn't want the lead in *Taza, Son of Cochise,* a film whose plot unfolded three years after the end of the bloody Apache Wars (1849-1886). After reading the story line by Gerald Drayson Adams, Rock said, "I've got to look into the eyes of Oona, my future squaw, and say *'unga, bunga, wunga.'*"

He had dinner one night with Marilyn Maxwell, who was his sometimes lover when she wasn't involved with Frank Sinatra. He poured out his distress at having to play another Indian role, as he considered it roughly equivalent to his performance as Young Bull in *Winchester '73*, in which he'd worn pigtails, war paint, and a *faux* nose.

"Until you reach super stardom, you've got to take whatever shit they throw at you, or else you'll go on suspension," she said. "That's the way it works for contract players, as you know. One night at a party, when Spencer Tracy chatted with us, I remember he said, 'Learn your lines the night before, show up on time, and don't bump into the furniture or trip over a rug."

Even in France, movie viewers said "Ooooh-la-la!"

"Besides," she said. "You'll be half naked throughout most of the film, and that will guarantee box office. Those gay makeup boys over at Universal will love putting makeup on that award-winning torso of yours."

The next day at wardrobe, after he was made up and dressed as Taza, he observed his image in a full-length mirror. "I look like Joe College with a long wig and sepia makeup. It's a joke! I fear this will be the silliest film ever made."

A viewing in 2017 by latter-day fans prompted one of Rock's fans, Sarah Davenport, to exclaim, "Rock was not all that bad. He has some good moments on the screen, and at no point does he appear ridiculous as Taza...or laughable. In a nutshell, I found him convincing as an Indian brave."

The film was shot on location in Moab, Utah. At times, the scenic backdrop of the Arches National Monument Park was more fascinating than the action going on in front of it. Released at the time of the 3-D craze sweeping across America, Taza was Rock's second and last movie shot in that medium. It also marked his second and last role as an Indian brave.

When writer George Zuckerman took over the script, he made the movie a bit more realistic. In a cameo at the beginning of the movie, Jeff Chandler, Rock's former cross-dressing lover, was cast as the dying Cochise, a role he'd played on the screen before. He wants to leave a legacy of peace to his son, Taza.

Taza's brother, Naiche (Bart Roberts), is more warlike and yearns to take on the U.S. cavalry in combat.

Taza's love interest is Oona, the role going to Barbara Rush, with whom Rock would work again. The two stars became friends, perhaps because she was not aware that he had made love to her handsome husband, actor Jeffrey Hunter.

Although the script is not historically accurate, Taza, born in 1843, was a real person, the leader of the Chiricahua tribe. In September of 1876, he visited Washington with a delegation of Apaches, fell ill there, and died of pneumonia.

Taza (Rock) with his beloved (Oona), as played by Barbara Rush.

The film marked a turning point in Rock's career. Douglas Sirk had previously helmed him in "that flapper movie," *Has Anybody Seen My Gal?*, but this was the first time he'd teamed up with producer Ross Hunter. That director/producer team would push Rock into superstardom in the immediate future with such box office triumphs as *Magnificent Obsession* (1954) and *Pillow Talk* (1959). A closeted homosexual, Sirk was already having infrequent sex with Rock when he cast him as Taza.

Meeting him for the first time, Ross Hunter said to Jeff Chandler, "I fell in love with Rock the first time he walked into my office."

Born to a German-Austrian family with Jewish roots, Hunter had gotten his start acting in "B" musicals in the

Rock Hudson, a noble savage

1940s. Bored with that, he eventually worked his way into film production. By 1951, Universal hired him to helm Chandler and Maureen O'Hara in *Flame of Araby*. From there, Hunter would go on to turn out light-hearted comedies, musicals, and melodramatic tearjerkers like *Imitation of Life* (1959) starring Lana Turner.

Many critics dismissed him, but not movie audiences. He claimed, "I gave the public what they wanted—a chance to dream, to live vicariously, to see beautiful women, jewels, gorgeous clothes, melodrama, perhaps a bit of soap opera at times."

Hunter invited Rock to dinner at Chasen's, later asking him to visit his home for a nightcap. Rock accepted, telling George Nader and Mark Miller, "I knew what was coming, and I had to go along with it. This guy could really make me a star, especially teamed with Sirk. I knew that on location I would have to prostitute myself before him, but what the hell."

Hunter's first night with Rock evolved into a life-long passion. He would go on to sustain a long-term love affair with Jaques Mapes, a set designer, but Hunter always maintained, "Rock was my single greatest thrill."

Before Rock set off to Utah with Sirk and Hunter, he had to drop by the office of studio chief, Ed Muhl. "He wanted to get down on his knees and worship me as a farewell."

On the set, Rock worked smoothly with Rush, who had won a 1954 Golden Globe Award as the most promising newcomer of the year, based on her performance in *It Came From Outer Space*.

Near the end of the filming of *Taza, Son of Cochise*, Rock learned that Sirk and Hunter planned to cast him in the movie that would make him a superstar.

***

Barbara Rush may never have known that Rock had made love to her handsome hunk of a husband, Jeffrey Hunter.

In the dialogue of *Taza, Son of Cochise*, they'd gone "*unga, bunga, wunga.*"

Jeffrey Hunter with his wife, Barbara Rush.

Jack Navaar and Rock had one of their biggest fights when Rock refused to allow him to accompany him to Utah. There was a reason. At Universal, Rock had been introduced to Lance Fuller, whom he described as "a handsome hunk from Kentucky." He was a contract player at Universal, but was mostly appearing in uncredited roles as was the case with his role in *Singin' in the Rain* (1952). The year Rock met him, he would also have a small part in *Cattle Queen of Montana* (1954), co-starring Barbara Stanwyck and Ronald Reagan.

Three years younger than Rock, he was married to actress Joi Lansing, but that union seemed on the rocks. Actually, Fuller liked man-on-man sex.

During the location filming of *Taza*, Rock arranged for Fuller to bunk with him in a log cabin Universal had rented for him. Rock, the star, and Fuller, the bit player, practically fell in love during the making of the movie. As Rock later told Miller and Nader, "If I didn't still have Jack in the house, I would have moved in Lance. He's very smart, vulnerable, with hard thighs that lead to glory."

Fuller had broken into movies in 1943 at the age of fourteen. He was cast in *Frankenstein Meets the Wolf Man*.

On long, windy nights, Fuller shared his hopes and dreams of stardom, which had eluded him up to now. At one point, Fuller and Rock discussed living together—that is, if he could ease Navaar out the door.

But there were signs of trouble. At time, he drank too much, which brought out an aggression in him totally different from what he exhibited when sober. Once, when he went with Rock to a roughneck bar, he almost attacked a cowboy who might have seriously injured him. Rock restrained him and got him out of the tavern.

After their return to Hollywood, Rock continued to see Fuller, but very infrequently. As the '50s moved on, his hoped-for film career stalled, and he began to appear on television in such series as *The Rifleman* and *77 Sunset Strip*.

In 1968, Rock heard that he had attacked a police officer in Los Angeles, who then shot him in the chest. The actor was in critical condition at a local hospital. Rock visited him three times until he pulled through. After his release, Rock never saw him again. Although he would become involved in more violent incidents in the future, he would live out the century, dying at the age of 73 in Los Angeles after a long illness.

Lance Fuller...wannabe movie star, Rock's future lover, and a neurotic with a violent temper.

***

Douglas Sirk wanted to be known as the hottest director at Universal, and Ross Hunter preferred to be its biggest money-making producer. It seemed natural that the two men would team up once again after their success with having starred Rock in *Taza, Son of Cochise.*

It was Hunter who first emerged with a project, after watching Loretta Young and Jeff Chandler emote in *Because of You* (1952), helmed by Rock's former director, Joseph Pevney.

This trite, forgettable film did good box office. Hunter conceived of the idea of re-teaming Young and Chandler again in a remake of the 1935 film, *Magnificent Obsession* that had starred Irene Dunne and Robert Taylor. Based on the 1929 novel by Lloyd C. Douglas, the movie made a matinee idol of Taylor.

But when he was presented with the story line, Chandler didn't want to reappear in a woman's picture with Young, evaluating the plot as "too soppy." Young also rejected it, claiming, "Irene Dunne is my best friend, and I want the picture to remain as one of her biggest triumphs, without my going and spoiling her cinematic glory."

Despite those setbacks, Hunter presented Sirk with Douglas' novel, but the director returned it. "I couldn't get halfway through it, finding it muddled and confused. I don't see a picture in this." He then referred to the plot—as depicted in the novel—as "a stewpot of trashy soap opera kitsch, and a crazy storyline where the main character, Bob Merrick, almost overnight goes from sinner and a selfish rogue to a male saint."

Still committed to the project, Hunter waited until Robert Blees completed the screenplay and then handed it to Sirk. The 1935 version was also screened for him. Responding, Sirk finally understood: "Now I get it," he said. "I'll do it. I think this awful story might translate into box office if we get the right leading woman and man."

After a session of considering various middle-aged actresses, the two men decided on Jane Wyman, whose career had begun to decline even though she'd received critical praise for her 1961 role in *The Blue Veil.*

At the time, both Wyman and her ex-husband, Ronald Reagan, were having careers

Producer Ross Hunter was one of the most influential men in Hollywood in making Rock a super star.

"Along the way, Ross developed the hots for me" (Rock's words).

202

heading south. At the time, Reagan had only $9,000 in the bank and was the MC of a burlesque show in Las Vegas.

Sirk and Hunter pitched the story to Wyman, who had seen the original, and she responded that she'd love to interpret the role of Helen Phillips, its leading lady. She had only one requirement, demanding veto power over her co-star.

Sirk and Hunter saw an immediate problem. Their boss, Ed Muhl, was continuing to "service" Rock, who had gotten angry at the studio chief when he forced him into playing *Taza, Son of Cochise*. Muhl tried to make up for it by granting him the next major heartthrob role the studio had.

Rock had never heard of *Magnificent Obsession,* but after the story line was explained to him, he wanted to do it.

Wyman had never seen one of Rock's movies, so Hunter screened *The Lawless Breed* for her. She approved, telling him, "My God, that's one handsome man. I find him magnetic on the screen. Give him the role."

Hunter didn't tell her just how "magnetic" he found Rock to be as well.

Rock had to go through a series of screen tests, and photographed extremely well in close-ups with his "sincere, loving brown eyes."

Adjustments had to be made from the original script, wherein Dunne, born in 1898, had been obviously older than Taylor (born in 1911). She had a daughter, but in the new script—in which Wyman would be married to an older man—the circumstances were altered, and the daughter was reconfigured into a step-daughter from an earlier mar-

Douglas Sirk and Ross Hunter informed Rock he'd have to perform love scenes with Jane Wyman on camera in *Magnificent Obsession*.

"What they didn't tell me was that I'd have to make love to her off-camera as well," Rock said.

riage.

Wyman was about ten years older than Rock, but didn't look it. The pair, when photographed together, made more convincing lovers, in Sirk's view, than Dunne and Taylor.

The plot was far-fetched. Rock would play Bob Merrick, a reckless millionaire playboy, who had dropped out of medical school after inheriting his father's fortune. One day, in spite of warnings about choppy waves, he took his speedboat out for a spin around a lake, but crashed, injuring himself. Rushing to the scene, the police commandeered the town's only resuscitator from the home of Dr. Wayne Phillips, a beloved surgeon at the local hospital. During the interim, the doctor had a heart attack, but the resuscitator was not nearby, and he dies.

After his release from the hospital, Merrick alienates the doctor's widow by falling in love with her. This causes another tragedy when Merrick makes advances toward her, and she jumps out of the car only to be hit by an oncoming vehicle, which blinds her.

Later, Merrick leaves a party drunk and crashes his car at the home of Edward Randolph, an eccentric painter and the best friend of Dr. Phillips. This artist had previously been rescued and greatly aided by the late doctor, whose philosophy is explained to Merrick. It alters his self-centered ways forever.

Randolph claims that if one adopts a policy of helping and healing others in distress, and not expecting any reward, it can become an obsession: "A Magnificent Obsession."

The good doctor has given away most of his money, leaving his widow financially insecure.

Merrick abandons his wicked ways, undergoes a radical change to both his personality and his values, and tries to help others, secretly funding Helen's recovery and paying for her trip to consult a doctor in Switzerland.

Before she goes, however, he encounters her on the beach, where he identifies himself as a medical student named Robby. Gradually (and still blind), she falls in love with him.

In Switzerland, despite their role as specialists, her doctors fail to restore her sight. and Merrick flies there, revealing himself as the man who had been involved in the accident which had originally caused her to lose her sight. She accepts his marriage proposal, but later, dazed and confused, she flees to Mexico with her nurse and companion, Nancy Ashford (Agnes Moorehead).

In the meantime, Merrick become a neurosurgeon. He eventually learns that Helen is dangerously ill, suffering from a brain tumor. He flies to her side and performs a delicate surgery that not only removes the tumor, but restores her sight. They can now live together happily ever after. The ending, in its era, left many members of the audience sobbing.

Wyman had famously played a deaf mute in *Johnny Belinda* (1948). Now, as an actress fiercely devoted to her craft, she needed to know how a blind woman maneuvers. To do so, she met with blind people, noting how they walked and moved without knocking things over or groping wildly in the air.

The veteran actress and formidable personality, Agnes Moorehead would co-star in both films that Rock made with Jane Wyman.

Otto Kruger was Randolph, the eccentric, philanthropic artist, and Barbara Rush was cast as Joyce Phillips, Helen's stepdaughter.

The weekend before shooting began, Rock and Jack Navaar, along with Mark Miller and George Nader, drove down to Laguna Beach for some surfing on big waves.

The two couples arrived at the beach with inflated rubber "inner tubes" from the wheels of cars—devices used by many surfers at the time instead of the more traditional surfboards seen in the beach movies of the 1950s.

After Rock had been in the ocean for about twenty minutes, a giant wave suddenly rose up out of the seabed and hurled Rock ashore, where he crashed against his namesake, a big Rock. He screamed in pain as his collarbone shattered.

The police and an ambulance were summoned, a medic shooting Rock with novocaine to ease his pain before he was rushed to a hospital, with sirens blasting and red dome lights flashing.

For about a week, he was forced to lie on his back. He told Navaar, "I'm going crazy. I can't turn over." Finally, after a week, he summoned his doctor. "I can't stand this cast anymore." He ordered him to remove it, broken collarbone or not, claiming, "I have a big picture to shoot, the breakthrough of a lifetime."

Doctors wound an Ace bandage around his arm and chest in an attempt to hold his shoulder in place. He was warned, however, that this was likely to create a calcium deposit—"a big lump"—and that perhaps it would cause him pain on and off for years to come.

Although other executives were urging Muhl to replace Rock, he stubbornly refused. "*Magnificent Obsession* belongs to Rock even if we have to shut down production for three months until he recovers."

In an interview with *Photoplay*, Rock admitted, "This is the toughest and most complex character I've ever played on the screen." He added as an afterthought, which was not printed, "I hope I don't fuck it up."

To his friends, he expressed a fear that appearing with such formidable talents as Wyman and Moorehead "would leave me hanging out to dry."

Muhl had issued long-standing orders that all of Rock's films should in-

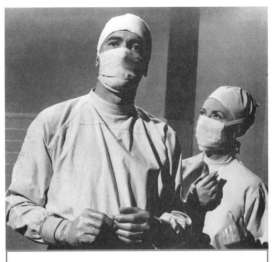

Even a movie star can become a surgeon, especially if he's handsome wearing surgical scrubs and a mask.

Photo above shows Rock, about to perform brain surgery on Jane Wyman.

clude at least one scene depicting him shirtless, as a means of maintaining his reputation as "Baron of Beefcake."

After some thought, Sirk figured out how to work that into *Magnificent Obsession*. He accomplished that based on the understanding that surgeons frequently strip off their shirts before donning their surgical smocks, and such was the context in which Rock got to appear "topless" in one of the film's scenes. Actually, the inclusion of this scene evoked hisses from the film's preview audience, who thereby implied that Rock was "showing off" before performing some life-threatening surgery.

***

In *Magnificent Obsession*, Rock played alongside Barbara Rush. He knew her well, having already performed with her in *Taza, Son of Cochise*. In that film her character, that of an Indian squaw, had fallen in love with him.

In this latest film, however, her character would express everything except love. Rush played Wyman's stepdaughter, who blames Rock's character for the death of her father.

Discounting their animosity in *Magnificent Obsession*, Rush was optimistic during a press interview in which she emphasized, "Rock and I would be romantic again," she said, "when we make *Captain Lightfoot*

(1955) in Ireland.

Character actor Charles Bickford had originally been cast as Randolph, the artist. But the delay in production caused by Rock's surfing accident force him to drop out to co-star with Judy Garland in *A Star is Born* (1954). Consequently, Otto Kruger took over the role. He often played villains, such as in Alfred Hitchcock's *Saboteur* (1942). The white-haired, long-faced actor had begun working in silent films way back in 1915.

Moorehead was delighted to be working with Wyman again, having recently co-starred with her in *The Blue Veil*. She was one of the finest actresses in Hollywood, having launched her screen career in *Citizen Kane* (1941). She could play virtually any role, including, in the words of one critic, "biddies, crones, *grandes dames,* intimidating moms, and spinster aunts."

When Moorehead and Rock came together, rumors circulated that she was a lesbian and that Rock was gay. The only time she might have "outed" herself with Rock was when she told him, "You take care of the boys; and I'll handle the girls."

Ironically, her greatest fame came when she played the role of a matriarchal witch, Endora, on the hit TV series, *Bewitched* (1964-72). Her sometimes co-star, Paul Lynde, was quoted as saying, "The whole world knows that Agnes is a lesbian—I mean classy as hell, but one of the alltime Hollywood dykes."

On the first day of filming, Hunter had told both Rock and Wyman, "I want this to be a three-hanky movie. I'm the world's champion crier myself. That's why I'm so good at producing junk like our movie. Call me the 'Sultan of Soap Operas.'"

***

On the West Coast, the sneak preview of *Magnificent Obsession* was screened at the Four State Theater in Encino. Navaar and Rock decided to go, slipping in as the titles were shown and sitting in the back row. Rock didn't want to be recognized.

Throughout the film, Rock nervously shifted his body and seemed in agony. At the end, before the house lights were switched back on, he rushed out of the theater. Caught up in the crowd, Navaar got detained, reaching their car about ten minutes after Rock. There, he found Rock in the front seat, weeping. "You didn't like it?" Navaar asked.

Rock looked at him, still sobbing. "That's not it! After tonight, I know I'm going to be a star, a really big star. That scares me to death."

The film's official West Coast premiere was staged on May 11, 1954, a red carpet event at the Westwood Theater. Universal offered to supply Rock and even Navaar with studio dates, but Rock rejected the offer, preferring to show up with his longtime companion, script girl Betty Abbott. Along with her, he invited his mother, Kay, and his stepfather, Joe Olsen, who showed up in a rented tux. Navaar was assigned a starlet, Claudia Boyer, as his date.

Heading down the red carpet, Rock spotted Navaar's mother and two daughters standing behind the ropes. He rushed over and kissed both of them before rejoining Abbott as her escort. As he did, some heckler yelled out, "FAGGOT!" The creep was drowned out by teenage girls screaming "ROCK! ROCK! ROCK!"

Wyman showed up with her dashingly handsome husband, bandleader Fred Karger, whom Rock had first gotten to know during a location shooting on Lake Arrowhead. It would be weeks after the release of the movie that Rock's role in the lives of Karger and Wyman became known—and mostly just whispered about—not appearing in any publication.

At the premiere, the gossip columnist Louella Parsons asked Rock if he were going to marry Betty Abbott, his date for the evening. "We're not engaged," he answered. "But we're very good friends."

Wyman faced the press: "After working with Rock Hudson, I predict he's going to be the biggest thing to hit the movies in the 1950s and maybe far beyond. He can't help but be big at the box office, considering his looks and charisma on the screen. The camera just adores him."

She left out the fact that in some scenes, he'd flubbed his lines, calling for anywhere from thirty to forty retakes. In all cases, she was endlessly patient with him.

As she recalled years later, "If I could sit patiently for hours listening to Ronald Reagan rant about politics, I think I could endure anything with the patience of Job."

Rock also talked to the press, praising his co-star. "A lot of my critics thought I'd go on playing a doorman, an Apache, a soda jerk, or a cavalry officer for the rest of my life. Things can change overnight in Hollywood. Jane was a wonderful girl to work with, a real pro, and she helped me a lot. You know she calls me 'The Great White Hope?' I just love her."

Navaar had been promised that he and his date would sit up front with Rock, but Universal's publicists had other plans. He and Boyer were hustled off to the rear, where they joined Ann Sheridan and the set designer, Jaques Mapes, who was Ross Hunter's lover.

This seating arrangement infuriated Navaar, and in many ways marked the beginning of the end of his love affair with Rock. At the party that followed the screening, at La Rue's, Navaar refused to even speak to

Rock, who was being repeatedly congratulated by the Hollywood elite.

The explosion between Navaar and Rock reached a flash point when they got home. Navaar seemed anxious for a confrontation. "So you're a bigtime movie star. A big fucking movie star. What am I? The jerk sent to the back of the bus? Go fuck yourself tonight. I'm not doing it, bigtime movie star."

***

The initial gross for *Magnificent Obsession* brought $5.2 million into Universal's coffers, and may ultimately have made $10 million when foreign grosses were tallied. Fan mail for Rock arrived in bags, as he zoomed up as America's newest heartthrob and the third biggest box office star in the country.

For her efforts, Wyman received another Oscar nomination, although she lost to Grace Kelly for her performance in *The Country Girl*.

Bosley Crowther, of *The New York Times*, had never found any merit in Rock as an actor, but even this acid-tongued critic wrote, "The manly, strapping Rock Hudson gives a fine, direct account of himself, and is the film's only surprise."

Not all critics were as kind. Doug McClelland wrote: "Rock Hudson is comic strip handsome, thrashing about with no special distinction, his scenes lined up with all the depth and subtlety of great colored blocks."

For the most part, Wyman got praise from the critics, one of them claiming that her performance "was in appealing contrast to Miss Dunne's pristine languor."

In 1954, *Modern Screen* named Rock, "The Most Popular Actor of the Year," and *Look* magazine cited him as "Hollywood's Top Male Star, liquid gold at the box office."

With all that acclaim, he was bitterly disappointed to learn that his next picture was a "B" movie adventure story. But Muhl insisted that the deal had been cemented before the success of *Magnificent Obsession*.

***

During its filming, Jane Wyman had bonded with Rock and, in the words of director Douglas Sirk, "took him under her protective wing."

She was a genuine, deeply committed pro, having worked in films since 1932, when she'd been a Goldwyn Girl in *The Kid from Spain*. Hers had been a long, hard-fought road from that uncredited introduction in films to super stardom, but she'd traveled it.

Her husband, the bandleader, Fred Karger, was away on tour when she began working with Rock. She started inviting Rock to her home at night, not only to prepare dinner for him, but to go over his scenes.

Gradually, she began to make romantic overtures to him. As he would admit later, "Jane was not a big sexual turn-on for me. Neither were Joan Crawford or Tallulah Bankhead. But I did my duty. At least Jane was more alluring than those grand ladies."

One night, dinner led to her bedroom, where she found him a skilled lover. She wanted that bout repeated during the days and evenings ahead. She later told her friend, Joan Blondell, "Rock is a much more accomplished lover than I'm used to."

She had already gone on record, giving her evaluation of the sexual prowess of her former husband, Ronald Reagan. "He's as good in bed as he was in his movies," she proclaimed.

One night, Rock arrived unannounced and drunk at the home of Henry Willson, his agent. He looked distraught and complained of his aching, still-mending collarbone. His eyes were bloodshot, and he had an early call that upcoming Monday.

Willson was already aware that his relationship with Jack Navaar was on life support. He was also aware of his evening intimacies with Wyman.

"She's making sounds like she's falling in love with me," he told Willson. "I'm not ready for that. But I don't know how to ease out of the relationship. Maybe when Karger returns to Hollywood, I'll escape."

"Go gently with her," Willson advised. "She's a big star, and there is talk of re-teaming the two of you in other pictures. Now is not the time to piss her off. I'd advise you to continue with stud duties at least for a while. So far, you've been doing great with career advancement, shacking up with your boss, Ed Muhl; your director, Douglas Sirk; and your producer, Ross Hunter. Why not add your leading lady to the list?"

The following week, Roddy McDowall, Rock's friend and confidant, learned more about Rock's affairs than Willson. Rock knew that his agent— based on his dislike of possibly infuriating Wyman— would be furious if he learned the full story.

"At first, I think I brought out the mother instinct in Jane," Rock said. "She's married to Fred Karger, as you know. He's a very good-looking guy, and I know why Marilyn Monroe fought to keep him as her lover, but lost out to Jane."

"But things got a little sticky with Fred," Rock admitted to McDowall, "when he joined us for location shooting at Lake Arrowhead. When Jane was otherwise occupied, Fred and I began to hang out together. You may know this already, since you seem to know every time a cockroach walks across Hollywood Boulevard. Fred is bisexual."

As filming beside the lake progressed, the sexual dramas and innuendoes became more intense. Although whispered about on the set of *Magnificent Obsession,* news of Rock's affair with Wyman were not revealed in the press. Through an informant, Hedda Hopper, however, heard that something was going wrong, and in her column, she reported that Wyman's marriage to Karger was on the rocks. In a few weeks, she would be reporting that the musician had moved back into the home of his mother, where mother and son had once housed a struggling Marilyn Monroe, giving her spending money.

When she learns that her husband (in this case, Fred Karger, left) is sleeping with her leading man (Rock Hudson) what's a screen diva (Jane Wyman) supposed to do?

Neither Hopper nor her rival in gossip, Louella Parsons, learned what role Rock played in Wyman and Karger's ultimate divorce.

Temporarily, they reconciled in an uneasy truce, and Karger moved back in with her. Shortly thereafter, both performers, along with Rock, flew to New York for the premiere of *Magnificent Obsession.* The Kargers were given a suite at the Waldorf Astoria, with Rock in his own suite a few doors down.

According to Rock, as relayed to McDowall, "It happened for the first time when Fred and I went boating together and found a secluded spot along a riverbank. Fortunately, we brought a blanket. At least I know why both Marilyn and Jane have the hots for him. I also learned that he's still seeing Marilyn on and off when Joe DiMaggio is not around."

"Your having a broken collarbone doesn't seem to have diminished your sex life," McDowall said.

"Sex helps me forget my pain," Rock said. "Sometimes, sex is for my pleasure. At other times, I'm nothing but a male prostitute. As far as that goes, hundreds of fan letters are pouring in from people who write about how much they want to make love to me. I feel I've become a phallic symbol to the world."

"You can't use that line," McDowall cautioned. "It belongs to Errol Flynn."

Until Rock met Karger, Rock had never heard of him, but he quickly learned that he was well known in Hollywood circles. He'd had numerous affairs with other stars, including Judy Garland. He was rumored to have had sexual trysts with "boys in the band" (his band), with a fondness for saxophone players.

In years to come, Monroe insisted that her own fondness for saxophone players be mentioned as a line within her 1959 movie, *Some Like It Hot*.

Karger was the son of Maxwell Karger, a producer and director from the early days of MGM. Born to Hollywood royalty, he had led the life of a privileged child, meeting some of the greats of the silent screen when he was a boy.

He was fond of telling stories of how, as a boy, Rudolph Valentino had given him a lusty kiss on the lips, and that all he got from Charlie Chaplin was a lollipop. Mary Pickford had promised to make him a child star, but didn't, and the silent screen comedian Buster Keaton had given him a baby rattlesnake which bit him.

One night at a party, during the filming of *Magnificent Obsession*, Rock had gone to a gathering, where he chatted with Shelley Winters, whom he'd met on the set of *Winchester '73*. She had been Monroe's roommate in the late 1940s. The gossipy dame from Brooklyn told Rock, "I see Marilyn from time to time. She tells me that even though Joe DiMaggio is in her life, Karger is the only man she's ever really loved."

One night, Rock had asked Karger why he'd married Wyman and not Monroe. He answered, "I didn't think Marilyn would be the proper mother for my daughter."

"That's reason enough, I guess," Rock said.

***

Rock, Wyman, and Karger flew to Manhattan for the East Coast premiere of their film, and registered into their respective suites at the Waldorf. The trio attracted much attention when they entered "21," which, of course, was familiar to celebrities from Hollywood. The evening had gone pleasantly enough, although Rock could not help but notice the tension between the married couple.

The following day, it was decided that Karger and Rock would work out together at an exclusive health club on Manhattan's Upper East Side while Wyman would visit one of New York's best hairdressers, preparing for their widely publicized premiere that night.

All of them agreed to be back in their suites before 6PM to get ready for the gala event, which was expected to attract an elite crowd of other celebrities.

Intent on keeping her appointment at the hairdresser, she left the suite she shared with Karger first, as he remained behind, packing a small bag for the gym. Rock had already arrived in their suite with his own gym bag.

Out on the street, twenty minutes after leaving the Waldorf, Wyman realized she'd left a diamond bracelet—one of her most expensive pieces of jewelry, the most valuable Reagan had ever given her—on the top of a vanity back at the hotel. She hurried back to her suite, fearing that one of the maids might steal it.

She hurriedly entered the suite, believing that it was empty. Suddenly, she heard noises coming from the bedroom. When she opened its door, she saw Karger and Rock, each completely nude, making love. Karger was on his back, and he was the first to see her as Rock mounted him.

"Oh, my God!" Karger shouted. It was a case of *coitus interruptus.*

Grabbing a sheet, Rock quickly exited into the bathroom, slamming the door behind him.

Glaring at her husband, Wyman grabbed her bracelet and hurried out the door, leaving the men alone. She didn't know what happened to them after that, or what they said to each other.

When she returned from the hairdresser, she found Karger getting dressed in his formal wear. Rock was gone. She wouldn't see him until the premiere.

At first she said nothing. Karger later confided to Rock what her reaction was.

"You've got to understand, honey. Both Douglas Sirk and Ross Hunter have told me that Rock is going to be the biggest star in Hollywood in just a year or so. I had to give in to him. He came on strong. With him headed for super stardom, he could get me assigned as musical director on one of his hit films. I was doing it for career advancement...*for us,* darling.:"

Presumably, she assumed her most convincing mask of sophistication and tolerance. "It's okay. Rock is very seductive. I, of all people, know that!"

"You mean...?" He looked flabbergasted.

"I mean just that, my husband," she answered. "I had him before you. We'll have to ask him which of us he prefers."

"I can't believe this is happening," he said.

"I'm flying back to the Coast alone," she said. "I hope you'll understand. Now get out and let me get dressed so we can put on our smiles as Mr. and Mrs. Jane Wyman on the red carpet."

After Wyman returned to Los Angeles, Karger remained behind at the Waldorf for four days. Since she had abandoned their suite, he moved in Rock. There was another shocker yet to come. After his final day in New York, he returned to the hotel at 7PM from publicity duties. He had spent much of the day signing autographs.

Back in their suite, he found Karger on the sofa wearing only his jockey shorts. After some intense kissing, they chatted.

Sudden, a woman appeared at the door to the bedroom. For two brief seconds, Rock feared that it might be Wyman. But it wasn't.

Entering the suite was Marilyn Monroe, attired only in panties and a brassiere, concealing her nudity with a coat.

"Marilyn!" Rock said. "I didn't know you were in New York. Come in. I'll order champagne."

She rushed to his side, giving him a wet, lingering kiss, then doing the same for Karger. "Long time no see."

"Let's all get dressed and go out on the town," Rock awkwardly suggested.

"You'll obviously have to change for the evening, so come on into the bedroom," Marilyn giggled. You, too, Freddie. It's still early and life is short. There's nothing wrong with three young people having some fun."

Loosening his tie, Rock headed for the bedroom as Karger followed. "So which of us is gonna be Lucky Pierre tonight?"

Back in Hollywood, Rock couldn't resist telling George Nader and Mark Miller some superficial details about the three-way with Monroe and Karger. But he never revealed the most intimate details of what actually happened, despite the urging from his friends.

"I'll let you draw your own conclusions," he told them.

[After their interactions in New York, Wyman never resumed her affair with Rock, even though she would co-star with him in one more picture and—on camera, at least—make love to him more than once. She proved the degree to which she was a professional by remaining on friendly terms.

Her divorce from Karger was granted in 1955. Ironically, she remarried him in 1961, divorcing him again in 1965.

After they parted, the ill-matched couple never saw each other again. Both Wyman and Karger also faded from Rock's life after she co-starred with him in All That Heaven Allows, *released only one year after* Magnificent Obsession.]

Chapter Eight

Rock Enjoys the Trappings and Dangers of Movie Stardom

Orgies with Tyrone Power, A Love Affair with "My Italian Stallion," & A Sexual Tryst with Lana Turner

To Conceal His Scandal-Soaked Private Life, Rock Courts Henry Willson's Bisexual Secretary, Phyllis Gates

In *All That Heaven Allows,* Universal was hoping to repeat the box office success of *Magnificent Obsession* by the reteaming of Rock Hudson and Jane Wyman as lovers, in spite of the obvious difference in their ages.

A true professional, Wyman could play love scenes with Rock, even though she'd walked in on him in a New York hotel suite, making love to her young husband, Fred Karger. She, too, had had a fling with Rock, but now that was but a memory.

According to his closest friends, George Nader and

Mark Miller, with the sudden arrival of stardom, Rock Hudson seemed to undergo a personality change.

"The shy young man we'd first met was now filled with self-confidence in the way he greeted people on the phone, ordered a drink at a bar, or even how he entered a room," Nader claimed. "All eyes would be trained on him now, whereas in the past, he might have been ignored as a nobody, or some out-of-work actor looking for a job. Now, he had star presence, something his early directors might have thought was not possible."

Invitations began to arrive for him from the elite of Hollywood, summoning him to A-list parties. Even Marion Davies, the longtime mistress of press baron William Randolph Hearst, invited him to her swanky parties, as did Dolores Del Rio of the porcelain skin.

He became a faithful guest at the home of Ronald Reagan and his second wife, starlet Nancy Davis, whose film career was near its end. Jack Warner welcomed him to the parties he hosted for the Hollywood *über-élite*. Joan Crawford still requested him as an escort, and even Gregory Peck invited him over for dinner. Louella Parsons wanted to know more about his private life, plus answer the eternal question: *"When Is Hollywood's Most Eligible Bachelor Going to Find a Wife?"*

His list of escorts expanded to include not just Marilyn Maxwell or script girl Betty Abbott, but bigger names like Crawford and Judy Garland.

There was much speculation in fan magazines about how Rock still maintained his bachelor status. The October 3, 1955 issue of the widely read *Life* magazine ran Rock, wearing western garb, on its cover. The caption read "ROCK HUDSON, HOLLYWOOD'S MOST HANDSOME BACHELOR."

During the Eisenhower era, a man nearing the age of thirty—and still not married—was inevitably a source of homosexual rumors.

Fan letters continued to pour in from teenagers across America. But a new type of mail began to come in. Word always travels fast along America's homosexual underground, and even the most isolated gay man knew by the mid-1950s that Rock was a member of their tribe.

Suddenly, pictures and love letters began to arrive from young men posed in skimpy bathing trunks or even nude, with erections, soliciting Rock for a date. He rushed home in the late afternoon to sort through those letters, often ignoring the others within the deluge.

Henry Willson, Rock's agent, grew increasingly worried that Rock's launch into super stardom would place him in a dangerous position of either being blackmailed by one of his tricks, or else exposed in one of the scandal magazines, especially the biggest of the lot, *Confidential*, with its four million avid readers. As Humphrey Bogart said, "We always read it, but claimed that the cook brought it into the house."

At Universal, Rock's salary was increased. He was presented with a new wardrobe by studio chief Ed Muhl, and he even got a monogrammed dressing room. Universal's Publicity Department churned out fanciful stories about their new macho man, a coveted date among Hollywood's rising starlets.

Time defined *Confidential* as a "cheesecake of innuendo, detraction, and plain smut." First published in 1952 under the editorial direction of Robert Harrison, it created panic in Hollywood. Who would be exposed next?

Rock was an avid reader, discovering headlines that read—ERROL FLYNN & HIS TWO-WAY MIRROR; ROBERT WAGNER IS A FLAT TIRE IN THE BOUDOIR; ARE THE DUKE AND DUCHESS OF WINDSOR REALLY MARRIED?; WHAT LEX BARKER NEVER TOLD LANA TURNER; DOES DESI ARNAZ REALLY LOVE LUCY?; and LANA TURNER AND AVA GARDNER SHARED A LOVER.

Readers also learned that June Allyson, America's Sweetheart of the 1940s, was a nympho; Rita Hayworth a neglectful mother; Liberace was gay; Bing Crosby a wife beater; Ava Gardner had an affair with Sammy Davis, Jr.; and Lizabeth Scott's name had been listed in a call girl's address book.

"Rock and I lived in constant fear that our gay private life would be exposed in one of those rags," George Nader said. "Every time *Confidential* came out, we rushed to the newsstand with our stomachs churning. Which star or stars would be exposed next? It's amazing that Rock, who fucked around a lot, was never outed, only whispered about. He must have had a guardian angel riding saddleback. Or else he'd made a pact with the Devil."

In Samuel Bernstein's book, *Mr. Confidential,* devoted to publisher Robert Harrison, he wrote: "Rumors swirled around the press offices of Universal that a monumentally damaging story was going to break. It was about Rock Hudson, the he-man of the studio, star of their smash hit, *Magnificent Obsession* and their Great White Hope. According to gossip, he was to be revealed as a Swish. The breathless sighs of women (and men) in the dark all over the country whenever he stripped off his shirt pointed to the fact that Hudson would be a major star."

"By any measure, it was astonishing that Rock was never exposed in *Confidential*," Bernstein claimed. "By the standards of the day, his sexuality was openly known around town, and he was a guy who really liked to sleep around. He was a hunk, in his 20s, and horny as hell, so why not? It isn't a value judgment. Documentation would have been ridiculously easy. All it would have taken was sending Fred Otash (the master Hollywood detective) to follow Rock around for a few nights at best."

Learning of this upcoming *exposé*—somebody, somewhere, would surely talk for that kind of money—Willson went into overdrive. He firmly believed that Rock was set to become the most popular movie star in the world. An *exposé* by *Confidential* could derail his chance.

Willson decided to make a deal with Harrison. He would throw his second most valuable client, Rory Calhoun, under the bus. He turned over evidence to them that, as a teenager, Calhoun had been arrested, convicted, and jailed for armed robbery and car-jacking. He even offered access to his police mug shot, taken by Salt Lake City (Utah) law enforcement at the time of his arrest.

BEFORE AND AFTER: The dashingly handsome movie star, Rory Calhoun, spent part of his young life in a prison cell.

In a spectacular betrayal of his client, Henry Willson agreed to expose Calhoun to keep *Confidential* from outing Rock (a more profitable client) as a homosexual.

At the time, Calhoun was appearing in two pictures with Marilyn Monroe, including *How to Marry a Millionaire* (1953), although in that movie, he went for Betty Grable and not Monroe. He was reported to be having an affair with Monroe on the set of her latest picture, *River of No Return* (1954).

Confidential hit the stands with a picture of Calhoun on its cover. Amazingly, the exposure of his previous indiscretions did not derail his career. If anything, it made him a hero in Hollywood. Parties were given in his honor, and television producers vied for his services. He also got more movie offers than he could handle.

He freely admitted, if asked, "Yes, I was a car-stealing juvenile delinquent."

Ultimately, it would be Tab Hunter whom *Confidential* would Out as a homosexual.

Some sources falsely reported

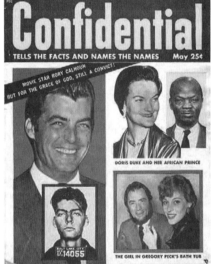

When the *Confidential* exposé of Rory Calhoun hit the newsstands, sales figures soared by an extra million copies.

that it was Nader who was eventually exposed as a homosexual, but that was not true. Nader retired in 1972 without ever having to endure such exposure. He became known as a homosexual only after he and his lover, Mark Miller, inherited Rock's estate in 1985.

***

Rock had little regard for his next movie, *Bengal Brigade,* eventually released in 1954. Configured as a Universal Technicolor adventure story, it was set in British-occupied India in 1857 at the outbreak of the Indian mutiny. His female stars included the Titian-haired Arlene Dahl and a stunning beauty, Ursula Thiess, who had survived her war-ravaged native Germany, where she had managed to rescue her one-day-old baby from a blazing, fire-bombed hospital.

Its director was Laslo Benedek, a name unfamiliar to Rock. Its producer was Ted Richmond, who had also husbanded two other films with Rock—*Shakedown* and *Has Anybody Seen My Gal?*. Its screenplay was by Seton I. Miller, who had both written and directed *Fighter Squadron,* Rock's first Hollywood film in which he'd had a bit part.

Miller didn't seem to remember that Rock had made a brief appearance in his first film. He also wasn't that impressed with *Bengal Brigade's* director, Benedek, who told Rock, "In my day, I worked with such strongmen as Howard Hawks and Michael Curtiz."

Rock was cast in the unlikely role of Captain Jeffrey Claybourne, a British officer with the Bengal troops. He does not attempt a British accent.

At the opening of the movie, he was Court Martialled from his regiment based on a charge of disobeying wrong-minded orders. To his dismay, he soon realizes that his duty to his men isn't over. He is lured into wild adventures, including a fling with a flame-haired beauty and an Indian girl who falls in love with him. There is an uprising, plus betrayals, palace intrigue, exotic dances, all this high drama leaving Rock at the end of the film facing a firing squad. However, since it's a movie, the audience knows that in the final thirty seconds, our hero will be ripped directly from the jaws of death.

Cast and crew did not go on location to mysterious exotic India, and it shows. *Bengal Brigade* has a "back lot" look, having been churned out on Hollywood sound stages.

The 1950s movie star, Arlene Dahl, was hailed as one of the great beauties of Hollywood. Born in Minnesota to Norwegian parents, she'd begun to prepare for an acting career as a child by taking elocution and dancing lessons

219

and appearing in amateur theatrical productions before becoming a model.

Rock envied her, and not only for her beauty. She had married two of the hottest matinee idols in Hollywood, beginning with the former screen Tarzan, Lex Barker, in 1951, divorcing him in 1952. He'd gone on to marry Lana Turner. The year Rock met Dahl, she'd marry Fernando Lamas, fresh from the bed of Lana herself. He was the Argentine heartthrob known for wearing tight pants to show off his endowment. Later, he would marry "The Mermaid," MGM swimming star Esther Williams.

The second female lead of *Bengal Brigade*, German-born Ursula Thiess, cast as the Indian girl, Latah, was getting ready to marry Robert Taylor. Rock was certain that she didn't know that the matinee idol had made love to him on several occasions, beginning when he'd been his flight instructor back in Illinois in 1944.

Thiess had recently been dubbed "the most beautiful woman in the world."

Rock's co-star in *Bengal Brigade* was one of the most beautiful film goddesses of the 1950s, Arlene Dahl.

He was rumored to have asked her, "When your husband, Lex Barker, reached a climax, is it true he let out the Tarzan yell?"

Although born a German, Ursula Thiess was made up to look like an Indian maiden in *Bengal Brigade*. Unknown to her, she and Rock had something in common: *Matinée* idol Robert Taylor.

When Rock heard that, he told her, "Bob has been called the world's most beautiful man. I think it's right that you two beauties mate."

"When Bob and I started dating, the press reported that at least he'd met someone prettier than himself," Thiess said.

Thiess found Rock "a sensitive, cooperative young actor, always ready to give a helping hand. He showed, like Bob, great admiration for character actors, possibly feeling trapped in his own good looks, as he knew Bob did. I appreciated his ever-present gallantry to me."

Unlike *Magnificent Obsession*, Rock did not get good reviews, one critic claiming he was "badly miscast as the British Army officer working to thwart a Sepoy rebellion in India." Or, as another critic put it, "Rock Hudson valiantly tries to impersonate an English officer."

Tyrone Power had enjoyed one of the most diversified arrays of A-list lovers in Hollywood. But his most enduring relationship was with Smitty Hanson, a tall, extraordinarily handsome, blonde-haired young man well known for his impressive endowment. Power's relationship with him stretched over a period of twenty-one years, ever since he'd met him at 20th Century Fox one afternoon. He took him home with him that same night, and he became Power's most favored "trick."

Like Rock's lover, Jack Navaar, Hanson was bisexual. There is evidence that during Power's marriage to Linda Christian, Hanson urged a three-way. The first time he put forth that suggestion (i.e., Tyrone Power in a sexual interlude with Linda Christian and Smitty Hanson) Power exploded in anger.

In contrast, when Hanson suggested a three-way with himself, Power, and Rock Hudson, Power readily agreed. "Now we're talking, boy!"

Hanson always maintained, especially after Power's early death, that, "Ty was basically gay but had affairs with girls from time to time, with an occasional marriage."

Hanson was not dependent on Power for money, and therefore managed to avoid accusations of being a kept boy. He had two other jobs, the more profitable of which involved pimping for closeted gay male movie stars. He had also emerged as a reliable custodian of movie star mansions, looking after them while their occupants and/or owners were abroad, perhaps making a movie. In some cases, stars were gone for up to eighteen months at a time as a means of avoiding income tax.

To be discreet, Power and Hanson often used one of these mansions for sexual trysts away from the prying eyes of gossipy Hollywood. They also staged all-male orgies at various homes.

When Power arranged an evening that included both Rock and Hanson, Rock drove to the home of Gregory Peck, who was in Europe making a movie at the time. As always, he shared details of that night with George Nader and Mark Miller.

"Smitty had some of the best weed smuggled in from Mexico, and all three of us got high and stripped buck-assed naked," Rock said. "Smitty and I had a lot more swinging than Ty, anatomically speaking. Ty and I made love like regular people, if you could call gay sex regular. But Smitty knew techniques he claimed had been handed down over the ages from Kama. He told me that that was the Hindu god of Love. My god, what he could do with a feather. He drove me crazy. He'd perfected this anal suction technique. He held me in his grip until he got a second offering from me—it was incredible! In other words, Ty was great for kissing, Smitty for fucking."

After that *ménage à trois*, Rock was invited to at least two of their orgies staged at other vacated star mansions. When gay male stars like Peter Lawford and Alan Ladd were invited to these orgies, Hanson always arranged for an array of handsome young men to be on hand to mate with them in the bedrooms upstairs. Most of these young men had come to Hollywood to be movie stars themselves, but had ended up hustling instead.

Although Rock never saw one of them at a Hanson orgy, he told him that Cary Grant and Victor Mature were two of his best customers. Hanson's links to these superstars were first revealed in Hector Arce's best-seller, *The Secret Life of Tyrone Power*. He didn't name Grant or Mature, but described one of the participants as "a leading action hero," and the other, "one of the immortals of the screen."

Through indiscreet gossip, word of these orgies reached the ears of both Louella Parsons and Hedda Hopper, but, of course, they never wrote about them.

Rock remembered attending an orgy in one of the canyons of Beverly Hills. He was never told who currently owned the house, but it was believed to have been built by one of the great vamps of the silent screen, perhaps Gloria Swanson or Pola Negri.

Hanson was indiscreet about providing Rock with additional private details about Power's indiscretions than Rock wanted to know.

"Ty has me set him up with young men, but on occasion, he'll order me to bring in a young starlet. He'll have me seduce the girl, but in the middle of the act, he'll yank me off her and fellate me to climax. That seems to turn him on more than anything else. He claims he gets off on the smell of a young man in heat."

Hanson also privately expressed a belief that Power's long hours of partying and heavy drinking were taking a toll on both his looks and his body.

***

As Rock approached his 30th birthday, the fan magazines began turning up the heat. Both Rock and Willson had despaired at reading the inevitable headlines: WHY HASN'T ROCK HUDSON MARRIED?

The agent faced two big goals and set out to attain them, knowing it would take some scheming. He had to get Rock married off, preferably to a "lipstick" lesbian. He also had to break up his relationship with Jack

Navaar and get him moved out of Grandview.

In the meantime, tension at the Hudson/Navaar household grew worse day by day. There wasn't a night that passed without an argument. "I admit I was jealous," Navaar later recalled. "After all, I had had a dream of being a big star, but my career never got off the ground. People were clamoring for Rock, both men and women, and I knew he was cheating on me. He kept coming home later and later, always drunk. He seemed to have the same lame excuse that he had to escort Joan Crawford to some event, which I knew was not true. He wasn't dressed to take out an immaculately groomed creature like Crawford."

Rumors were persistent that he was involved with another pretty boy, Farley Granger, whom producer Samuel Goldwyn had discovered and put under contract.

Both Rock and Navaar had gone to see Alfred Hitchcock's *Strangers on a Train* (1951), in which Granger had been cast as a tennis star who gets involved in a double murder conspiracy, colluding with a psycho played by Robert Walker.

After exiting from the movie theater, Rock and Navaar had gone to a diner to eat. Navaar later claimed that Rock had spent most of the meal raving about how gorgeous Granger looked in those tennis shorts. Both men knew that he was rumored to be gay. Within weeks, Navaar heard another rumor that Rock was slipping around for secret trysts with Granger. That was confirmed late one Saturday afternoon when Navaar eavesdropped, hearing Rock setting up a rendezvous with him for later that evening.

The evening before Rock was scheduled to fly to Ireland to begin work on his latest film, *Captain Lightfoot,* Navaar spent a good part of the day preparing a special dinner for him. At 8PM, Rock phoned and said that he'd been held up at Universal in talks about the upcoming movie.

Navaar didn't believe him. He knew that his lover's most prized possession was his record collection, a cluster of LPs devoted to the work of his favorite singers: Dinah Shore, Doris Day, Ella Fitzgerald, Peggy Lee, Jo Stafford, and Nat King Cole. Over the phone, Navaar delivered an ominous threat: "I'm going to take your record collection and, one by one,

Samuel Goldwyn's "golden boy," Farley Granger, brought sexual thrills to every star from Shelley Winters to Rock Hudson.

toss them down the hillside in our backyard. I'm going to continue to do that, two or three of them every ten minutes until you get your overworked ass back here."

Driving as fast as he could, Rock sped back to Grandview to rescue what remained of his records.

Navaar never revealed exactly what happened next, after Rock stormed back into his house, and then raced into the backyard, where Navaar was tossing his records. All he would say was, "What happened between Rock and me that night should have landed both of us in the hospital. I just hope his pretty face recovers before the beginning of shooting."

At 5AM, with his luggage already packed, Rock headed out the door while Navaar was still asleep. He did not leave a note. Leaving his yellow convertible in the driveway, he took a taxi to the airport.

Perhaps he did not know it at the time, but he would never see Navaar again.

***

A petite, pretty secretary, Phyllis Gates, hailing from Minnesota, was set to enter the life of Rock and Navaar. "She would drive the final nail into Navaar's coffin," Willson said, never afraid to use a *cliché*. "As for Rock, it would considerably alter the course of his life...for the worse, I might add."

But just who was she? When she burst onto the Hollywood scene, generating masses of publicity, no one knew much about her. Most of her "pre-Rock" life was shrouded in mystery, and her "post-Rock" years were filtered as a cover-up, especially her so-called autobiography, *My Husband, Rock Hudson,* published in 1987. Its subtitle was *The Real Story of Rock Hudson's Marriage to Phyllis Gates.*

It wasn't the real story, but a version that Gates wanted the public to believe. Instead of shedding light on her real story, she distorted it and hid the facts.

In the same year Rock was born, Gates had grown up on a farm 130 miles southwest of Minneapolis, her parents of German and Norwegian origin. The first language she learned around the house was Norwegian

Henry Willson's secretary, Phyllis Gates, was the "lipstick" lesbian he'd been searching for to marry Rock Hudson to conceal his homosexuality from his adoring fans.

with a scattering of German.

In high school, she learned typing and shorthand, based on the hopes of a career as a secretary. After graduation, she found a job working for six engineers in Minneapolis. After a few months, she grew bored and began working as an airline stewardess, as they were called in those days.

On her first visit to New York, she splurged and stayed at the Windsor Hotel at 58th Street and Sixth Avenue. The next morning at breakfast, she sat at a table next to two young men, the bigger and handsomer staring at her from time to time.

Finally, he got up and asked if he and his friend could join her, introducing himself only as "Marlon," his friend as "Wally."

She enjoyed bantering with them and became so friendly that she accepted their invitation to show her New York. It was her first trip here. At this point in her autobiography, she began to fudge the details. After an exhausting sightseeing tour and lunch at the Russian Tea Room, Marlon invited her to his apartment, just around the corner. Wally bowed out.

Marlon took her back to his unkempt quarters, where he introduced her to Russell, his pet raccoon.

In her autobiography, Gates drew a curtain around what followed, leaving out the detail that he seduced her.

He did tell her that he was an actor. But it was only the next morning when Wally and Marlon breakfasted once again with her, and after they left, that she learned who they were. Her girlfriend, who was sharing her room, saw them together.

"My God, I didn't know you knew Marlon Brando."

As amazing as it sounds, Phyllis had never heard of him, despite his great success with Tennessee Williams' *A Streetcar Named Desire,* both on stage and on the screen in 1951 with Vivien Leigh in an Oscar-winning role. "That was his friend, the comedian Wally Cox," her girlfriend said.

[The first time Rock (the actor) met Brando (the superstar) at a party in Beverly Hills, introductions were not needed, as both of them knew who the other was. Brando's opening greeting to Rock was, "I fucked Phyllis before you did, and probably did a better job of it."

Rock would not forget that jab, and he got "my sweet revenge" (his words) later, when he appeared in a movie with Brando's second wife, Anna Kashfi, in a secondary role.]

Gates liked New York so much, she moved there, getting a job as a secretary to Maynard Morris, a "fussy, high-strung man," who was a show business entrepreneur. She detested working there, admitting she knew nothing about show business. "When Darryl F. Zanuck called Morris, I didn't know if I should put through the call or not. He might not be important."

Ironically, on February 13, 1953, her life was about to change. Stepping off the curb of a sidewalk in Manhattan, she was hit by an oncoming car. She woke up in the emergency room of a hospital with a leg broken in four places and two breaks in her pelvis. Her injuries included a concussion and internal bleeding. Some of the skin on her left cheek had been scraped away when she was thrown onto the pavement.

Emergency surgery was needed. After months of recuperation, she received a $10,000 settlement back in an era when that was considered a large payment.

With that new-found money, she decided to move to Hollywood to try her luck there. On the afternoon of the day that she moved into the chic Beverly Hills Hotel, she purchased a red Ford convertible. But those thousands of dollars from her settlement soon ran out, and she applied for a job as a secretary. Her new boss turned out to be none other than Henry Willson, Rock Hudson's agent.

As she remembered, Willson was always rushing in and out. Whenever he had any free time in the office, he performed a dance for her, complete with bumps and grinds like a parody of a burlesque dancer. She began to meet his clients, most of them young men wanting to become the next Tab Hunter or Rock Hudson. Her job was to weed out the "losers," selecting only "the hot ones" to send into Willson's office. She was surprised to learn that he also handled younger clients like Natalie Wood or older ones like Ann Sothern and Jeanette MacDonald.

One memorable day, Rudy Vallee, the crooner with the quavery voice, a singing sensation of yesteryear, arrived during a meeting that Willson was conducting with the gay singer, Johnnie Ray, who had recently released a hit record, "Cry." Willson was discussing Ray's upcoming appearance in *There's No Business Like Show Business* (1954), co-starring Marilyn Monroe and Ethel Merman.

"Willson could be bitchy about people he didn't like, often referring to the men as 'that queer,' or to the women as 'that bitch,'" Gates said.

As the days went by, Willson's gaydar picked up vibes that Gates was a lesbian. That was confirmed when she was seen Saturday night in a lesbian bar in West Hollywood. His mind began to work, as he came to think she might make the perfect wife for a "lavender marriage" with Rock. His mind was also churning with other schemes, one of which involved Jack Navaar.

***

226

After Gates had worked for Henry Willson for eight months, she asked if she could take a two-week vacation, ostensibly to visit her family in Minnesota. He reluctantly agreed, claiming that in most cases, a vacation wasn't granted until an employee had been on the payroll for a year.

The next day, he came up with an idea, informing her that a friend of his was also heading for the same region of the Midwest, and, as a means of saving the cost of air fare, he could drive her to Minnesota and back.

At first, she was reluctant to drive across the country with a strange man, but Willson assured her that Jack Navaar was a perfect gentleman, omitting any mention of the fact that he was Rock's live-in lover. At this time, Rock was away on a tour of Europe, with the understanding that he'd be flying to Dublin soon to begin shooting *Captain Lightfoot* (1955).

A luncheon was arranged between Navaar and Gates, and the two of them got along smoothly, laughing and joking by the end of the meal.

Navaar invited her to go with him to the beach at Santa Monica, and that was followed by dinner at a drive-in. She was very impressed with his car, which was the latest luxury model Lincoln, property of the Ford Motor Company. Actually, the car didn't belong to Navaar. It had been lent to Rock, with the understanding that the star would drive it around as part of a publicity campaign.

That upcoming weekend, another beach holiday—this time to Laguna—was arranged for Navaar and Phyllis, during which they were joined by Mark Miller. Like Rock, George Nader, Miller's lover, was also away on location.

Miller and Navaar speculated, after the time they spent with her, that Gates was a lesbian, perhaps bisexual. Their suspicion was confirmed that night, when she invited them to take her to Camille's, a tavern that catered to a mixture of gay men and lesbians. On that night, most of the patrons were women, kissing and dancing together. Deserting her male companions, Gates was seen talking to an attractive redhead who looked no more than nineteen. Without saying good night, she disappeared with the young women for the remainder of the weekend, showing up for work on Monday with no explanation.

Navaar admitted that he developed a powerful crush on Gates because of her "marvelous laugh and incredible personality." He, too, was claiming bisexuality, in spite of his long-standing relationship with Rock.

One Friday afternoon, Navaar and Gates set out together for Minnesota, having agreed to share motel rooms as a means of cutting down on expenses. It was only months later that Navaar realized that Willson had engineered the trip to "alienate me from Rock."

On their first night on the road, they had more than a few drinks in a local tavern before adjourning to their shared bedroom in a nearby motel. As Navaar later remembered, "I was on top of her within an hour. After we'd made love, I was convinced that she was bi-."

In her autobiography, Gates identified Navaar as "Bill McGiver," describing him as "good looking, blonde, of medium height, and with a pleasant personality." She denied that she'd had an affair with him.

Merrily they rolled along, singing songs, listening to the radio, and telling jokes—"the dirtier the better." Before arriving at the home of Gates' family in Minnesota, he had identified himself as "Rock Hudson's roommate." She was flabbergasted. Even though he was Willson's most valuable client, she had never met him.

Her family was most impressed, and all of them came out of the house to greet Rock's roommate and to lavish praise on the emerald-green Lincoln.

Then Navaar was off on a 150-mile trip to his own hometown for a reunion with his family. After a week, he returned to pick up Gates. They headed together to Kansas City, where she used to be based as an airline stewardess (aka "flight attendant"). She knew the town well.

On their first night there, she took him to a lesbian bar named Jilly's, where she picked up a very beautiful young girl who seemed no more than twenty. By 11PM, Gates whispered to Navaar that the girl, whose name was "Arlene," had agreed to spend the night with them in their double bed.

After that, the fun-loving couple headed west, picking up a handsome young hitchhiker outside of town. He, too, was heading for California. He introduced himself as Bud Henderson, a 25-year-old ex-U.S. soldier who wanted to go to Hollywood to break into the movies. For the rest of the trip, he, too, shared their motel bedrooms, and they also fed him, as he had only fifty dollars in his pocket.

She gave him Willson's business card, suggesting that he drop in Wednesday afternoon for an interview with her boss, a real star-maker, who had already created such movie idols as Tab Hunter and Rock Hudson.

"He really goes for guys built like you are. He'll get you auditions and will probably change your name. Of course, you'll have to sing for your supper."

"That I can do," he said, "like a canary. I'll do anything to break into the movies."

At the end of the trip, Gates never saw Navaar again. Once, when she mentioned him to Willson, he snapped at her. "He's no longer one of our clients. Case closed."

***

Before he had to report to work in Ireland, Rock had time to visit cities on the Continent, traveling to France and Italy before stopping over in London.

For his companion, he opted to travel with the script girl, Betty Abbott, who had been widely photographed with him when he'd escorted her to the glittering premiere of *Magnificent Obsession* in Hollywood. The couple had long been rumored to have been lovers, and many speculated that they were on the verge of marriage, viewing their shared Continental jaunt as a "pre-honeymoon." They would never marry, but in the 1950s, she became known as "The Second Mrs. Rock Hudson."

Rock flew to Paris with Abbott, but once there, he began a series of one-night stands with handsome young Frenchmen, in reference to whom he later jokingly said, "I learned the finer points of French kissing, which extends beyond the mouth."

He became a patron of the gay bars on the city's Left Bank. When Parisian newspapers announced his arrival, he was also invited to exclusive parties, attending only a few of them.

At one, he was introduced to the famous gay author, Jean Cocteau, who invited him to his home outside Paris. Rock pleaded off. But Cocteau did introduce him to the most celebrated French singer of her era, Edith Piaf.

Back in America, he told friends, "She propositioned me, but I turned her down gracefully, claiming she was too short and I was too tall. Our bodies would not be compatible for lovemaking."

In Paris, Rock and Abbott rented a car for the drive to Cannes, where he created a sensation on the beach in a skimpy male bikini, attracting a flock of admirers, including some young men he took back to his suite at the Carlton.

After Cannes, they headed east toward the Italian frontier with visits to Florence and Venice, before the final leg of their trip, the Eternal City of Rome.

On his second night there, Rock dined with Tennessee Williams and Anna Magnani. The playwright told him he would have been ideal in his film, *The Rose Tattoo* (1955), but it had already been cast with Burt Lancaster playing opposite Magnani.

"Both of them kept sending hungry signals that they wanted to devour me, but I cleverly pretended not to notice," Rock said. "After dinner, Magnani went from table to table, gathering up leftovers to feed to the hungry,

229

homeless cats of Rome. In a taxi, I escorted them to the Colosseum to let them off, before I fled into the night to a hot pickup bar deep in the heart of Trastevere."

The bar was crowded with young Roman males and a lot of visiting American men eager to meet them. Italy was still recovering from the lingering horror of World War II, and many expatriate homosexuals from America rented apartments in Rome. Their numbers included such authors as Tennessee Williams and Gore Vidal. "The supply of young men was endless, as a quick stroll along the Via Veneto would reveal," Vidal said. "You had your pick of the beauties."

Although the Trastevere bar, the Tivoli Gardens, had a bevy of men who intrigued Rock, one stood out from all the rest. As Rock moved outside to enjoy a glass of wine in the garden of the bar, his eyes locked onto those of one young man who smiled at him.

Rock smiled back. That was all the invitation the Adonis needed to approach Rock and extend his hand, holding onto Rock's for a long moment.

His name was Massimo (no last name given), and he had been born in Rome, reportedly from parents who came from the port city of Bari, the capital of the Apulia (aka Puglia) region of southeastern Italy. He was deeply tanned, with black curly hair which he'd bleached blonde. His English was limited, and he chatted with Rock for about thirty minutes before Rock hailed a taxi to haul his conquest back to his suite at the Excelsior Hotel, opening onto the Via Veneto.

Massimo remained in that suite until Rock had to fly off to London. They depended on room service for food and drink. As Rock would later relay to George Nader and Mark Miller, "Massimo was the single greatest sexual thrill of my life. He didn't just make love, he made love like he meant it, leaving no surface of the body unmolested."

He was not always the most articulate of actors unless he was particularly inspired, as he was during the delivery of his description of Massimo: "Behind all that muscle and hardness was a sweet, sensitive guy who knew both how to give pleasure and how to receive it. As lovers, we were equally balanced. He has velvety skin, a bull's neck, a square jaw, a perfect face, and buttocks sculpted by Michelangelo. Balls like eggs and genitalia that matched those centurions depicted in the erotic frescoes I saw in the ruins of Pompeii. What a guy! He couldn't get enough of me, and I certainly couldn't get enough of him. Massimo belongs in the Pantheon of Roman Gods."

It was all Rock could do to tell Massimo goodbye, and the young man made it more difficult for him by pleading to Rock to take him to London and then on to Ireland.

Rock warned him that he couldn't, because he feared exposure of their relationship in the press. "I have to be careful," he told Massimo. "A lot of reporters are trying to expose me. That could ruin my career."

Before parting, Rock gave him a thousand dollars and promised he'd send more money from time to time. Massimo wanted to be an actor in Italian films, but roles were few and far between. When a job offer came in, it was for a low-paying extra.

"Until we meet again," Rock promised with a farewell kiss in the privacy of his suite. "Massimo was crying as I left, and en route to the airport, I already had begun to miss my Italian Stallion."

Little did Rock know at the time, but he was embarking on his longest and most enduring love affair, a relationship that would survive horrific downs but also glorious highs as the years drifted by.

It was only after Rock died that Massimo spoke of him, and then only rarely. "If Rock ever screwed around with a woman—and that is one damn big 'if'—I'm sure it was a quickie, and not extended lovemaking. I'm sure that after a brief encounter, he would be off to resume the chase for the next blonde-haired young man. As for sexual endurance, he was the Ben-Hur of the chariot race."

Massimo's final comment about their relationship, to a reporter in Rome, was blunt: "Rock Hudson could be unspeakably vulgar. He cheated on me all the time and sometimes treated me like shit. Would I go through all that again? You bet!"

***

Rock arrived in Ireland, his first visit to that country, to film a period adventure piece, *Captain Lightfoot,* a CinemaScope production in Technicolor. The screenplay was by the American novelist, William Riley Burnett, who had also written the novel. He was better known for his classic crime novel, *Little Caesar,* which had been adapted for a movie in 1930 starring Edward G. Robinson.

Set in the early days of the 19th Century, the picaresque drama revolves around Michael Martin (aka Captain Lightfoot), who robs the wealthy in the foothills around Dublin. He is a sort of Robin Hood of the Emerald Isle. In this "galloping romance," as it came to be known, Rock had never been photographed more dashingly, especially when he's attired in what he defined as "my foppish drag." Never again would he appear in such lavish costumes.

He was reunited with Barbara Rush, his leading lady cast as Aga Doherty, and looking ravishly beautiful despite her recent divorce from Jeffrey

Hunter. *[Hunter had been a lover of Rock's.]* Rush had been cast as Rock's squaw in *Taza, Son of Cochise*, and also played Jane Wyman's stepdaughter in *Magnificent Obsession*.

The movie was shot at the Powerscourt Estate in Enniskerry, County Wicklow, and around Clogherhead in County Louth. Rock and Rush were backed up by some talented actors, notably "the grand old man of Britain," Finlay Curry, cast as Callahan. Born in Edinburgh in 1878, he was no stranger to epic adventures, having made two such movies with Robert Taylor, including *Quo Vadis* in 1951, and *Ivanhoe* in 1952, the latter with Elizabeth Taylor and Joan Fontaine.

As Captain Thunderbolt, Jeff Morrow was a name already familiar to Rock. He'd heard him on radio in the title role of Dick Tracy, and he'd recently completed *The Robe* (1953) with Richard Burton. Morrow was often parodied as "The Cro-Magnon Man" because of his prominent brow.

"In *Captain Lightfoot*, I could 'swashbuckle' with the best of them," Rock said. "Lucky for me I saw all those Errol Flynn movies when I was a boy. My buddy, Errol, taught me how to play it."

The second female lead, that of Lady Anne More, was played by Kathleen Ryan. She was hailed as one of Ireland's greatest beauties, the subject of Louise la Brocquy's most striking portrait, *Girl in White*.

Both the film's director, Douglas Sirk, and its producer, Ross Hunter, were at the Dublin airport to welcome Rock when his plane landed. They took him for a celebratory dinner at the city's finest restaurant, still basking in the glow of their recent success with *Magnificent Obsession*.

As Rock later told friends, "I had to do Douglas that night and Ross the next morning. It was a good thing I didn't bring Massimo. When those guys finished with me, I had to have enough energy left to perform all those action shots."

Shooting lasted for around three months, and Rock began to long for one of his favorite foods, pizza. His dialogue coach, Charles FitzSimons, told him, "There is no pizza in Ireland," which was not true.

Rock revealed how resourceful he was. The news vendor who brought the daily papers had married a Neapolitan woman, and Naples was the home of pizza. It was arranged for Rock to visit his home one night, with the understanding that his wife had baked three savory pizzas for the two hungry men. Later, he discovered an Italian restaurant in Dublin.

One night, after Rock had performed "stud duty" (his words) for Hunter, the producer told him that he would produce Rock's next two films. They included a film adaptation of the novel, *Tacey Cromwell*, for which he was negotiating with Lana Turner to co-star opposite him. *[After many permutations, it would eventually be released with Rock but without Lana in 1955 as* One Desire. *The other would reteam him with Jane Wyman in a melodramatic love story,* All That Heaven Allows *(also 1955).]*

In *Captain Lightfoot*, Rock is seen making love to his leading lady, Barbara Rush. Rumors swirled that the two planned to be married.

"At the beginning of the shoot, it was not Barbara getting screwed by me, but my director and producer," Rock told friends.

The tour of Europe that Rock had recently completed with Betty Abbott did not go unnoticed by gossip columnists. Privately, many Hollywood insiders claimed that Abbott was just for show to deflect from Rock's obsessive cruising in Paris, Cannes, Florence, Venice, and, ultimately, Rome.

One columnist wrote, "Rock Hudson believes in fun babes, not those Method actresses who want to make films with messages. He believes in a good night kiss on the first date, virtually demanding it, and he's leery of two careers in one marriage, which would rule out all those actresses chasing after him like Marilyn Maxwell. However, he feels the future Mrs. Rock Hudson has to be hip to the perils of show business. Many observers feel that Betty Abbott, a script girl, and a relative of comedian Bud Abbott, would be the ideal choice for the matinee idol when he gets ready to settle down."

There was even speculation that he might run off and marry Barbara Rush when her divorce from Jeffrey Hunter came through.

***

During the making of *Captain Lightfoot*, Rock became involved in one of his most torrid affairs, but it wasn't with Betty Abbott or Barbara Rush. It was with the studly Tommy Yeardye, who in time would become famous as the co-founder of the Vidal Sassoon empire.

Five years younger than Rock, Yeardye had grown up in poverty in Ireland, but all that Irish stew and potatoes had turned him into a hulking muscleman who stood as tall as Rock and was nicknamed "Mr. Muscles."

In time, he would become the lover of both Rock Hudson and Dinah Dors, who was hailed as Britain's answer to Marilyn Monroe. A blonde bombshell, she was a favorite pinup of G.I.'s during World War II, the British equivalent of Betty Grable in America. Dors once described Yeardye as "Fists like bricks, eyes like green emeralds, and the cock of a horse."

As a teenager, he had worked his way to London, where he began to earn money as a gigolo for rich English women and as a hustler "for size queens," as he so graphically stated it. He eventually became an actor (more like an extra), and a stuntman.

In Ireland, Douglas Sirk and Ross Hunter began searching for a stunt double for Rock, and after reading one of their advertisements, this hulking, 200-pounder showed up at their studio. Both Hunter and Sirk "auditioned" and then hired him before Rock got a look at him.

Rock would always remember the late morning when Hunter introduced him to Yeardye. "Hi, I'm Tommy Yeardye, your new double."

"His handshake was like getting your hand trapped in an iron vise," Rock said. "He was one powerhouse of a man."

"He not only gave me a bearish grin, but a bearish hug," Rock said. "We got acquainted real fast...and how!"

"Over dinner that night, Yeardye informed Rock that Sirk had told him that he matched Rock in every department."

"You mean, in *every* department?" Rock asked flirtatiously.

"If you don't believe me, try me out tonight. I've been auditioned by both Sirk and Hunter. Why not by the star of the picture, too?"

"Why not?" Rock said. "You're on, buster. It's Showtime!"

Their night together in bed was followed by repeat performances that

The sex goddess of Britain, Dinah Dors, was photographed after a night of "pounding" by her lover, Tommy Yeardye, a bull of a man, a Rock was soon to discover.

234

continued frequently throughout the remainder of the shoot. "The guy matched me in every way—same height, size, and weight. In one department, we were almost identical. That almost never happens to me." This confession was later made to George Nader and Mark Miller. "Sirk and Hunter broke Tommy in for me."

"He whispers sweet nothings in your ear, which helps you tolerate the initial pain that soon turns into the most exquisite pleasure. At the finale, there's an eruption of Mount Vesuvius."

"We had to part after filming ended in Dublin, but I told him, 'We'll meet again.'"

"That we will do," Yeardye responded, "even if I'm shacked up with some blonde bimbo."

***

During Rock's sojourn in Ireland, life at Grandview, back in Los Angeles, had heated up. Navaar had been entrusted with the protection of Rock's home and property, but despite his obligations, he had driven Rock's Lincoln to Mexico with some male friends. During his absence, Grandview had been broken into and looted.

Perhaps it really had. Or perhaps Henry Willson had staged the robbery as a vehicle to foment discord between Rock and Navaar.

It was late at night when a call came into Rock's lodgings in Dublin from California. Rock answered the phone sleepily. Willson had nothing but trouble to report. In addition to the robbery, he revealed that Navaar had staged orgies at Grandview, in the process attracting "the trash of the town."

There was another detail to add, and Willson did just that, knowing how much it would infuriate his client. He claimed that Navaar had taken the Lincoln and driven "some woman, I don't know who," on a cross-country trip to the Middle West, shacking up with her in various roadside motels.

Willson had already instructed Phyllis Gates that she should never mention the name of Navaar to Rock, with the understanding that inevitably, she was bound to meet him, since she was his secretary. "For God's sake, don't let him know that you guys drove together to Minnesota in his Lincoln." Gates had promised to keep quiet.

On hearing the news about Navaar, the robbery of his house, and the trashing of his possessions, Rock exploded in fury. His agent had never heard him so angry.

"Kick the fucker out of my house...and I mean tonight, right now, in fact," Rock shouted into his end of the phone. "I trusted him. Look where that got me. Stop his weekly check. Make sure you get the keys, both to my cars—and that includes the convertible as well as the Lincoln. Station a security guard at my house when he moves out so I won't lose any more of my possessions."

Navaar recalled that when he drove back from Tijuana, Willson was already at Grandview, putting the house in order again with the assistance of a maid and another worker.

Willson immediately ordered Navaar to pack up and leave. Navaar later recalled, "I knew then that I was dead meat. I didn't know what lies he'd told Rock about me. I felt the cards stacked against me. Rock was probably alienated from me for all time. I knew I wouldn't be able to repair the relationship, and a part of me didn't want to. I just wanted to disappear from all of their lives, and I packed up and headed out the door, but not before throwing the keys in Willson's god damn face."

"I had less than fifty bucks in my pocket and nowhere to live. Thanks a lot, guys! I never saw Rock again. The time had come to stop living in someone else's shadow and become my own man. I eventually became a building contractor in San Diego, married a beautiful woman, and we had three kids. Goodbye Rock. Goodbye forever."

When Rock returned to Grandview, everything was in order, and there was no trace of Navaar. He decided then and there that it was too dangerous for him to live with a male again, risking an *exposé* in *Confidential*.

As the years went by, Rock sustained numerous affairs, even a marriage, but for a long time, no other male would reside in his home on a permanent basis. In time, as his box office pre-eminence collapsed and his best movies were behind him, he decided that "the heat is off" and he became more relaxed.

***

Two evenings after his return to California from Ireland, he sat alone on his terrace. Home alone, he was glad that Navaar was no longer in his life. During the past few months, Navaar had become as demanding as a nagging wife. Relieved to be free again, he celebrated the many options available for him in both his personal and professional life.

Under a moonless night sky, he nursed a drink, smoked some cigarettes, and pondered his future. The silence was interrupted by a phone call. The evening was about to become one of the most memorable of his life.

He picked up the receiver, thinking it might be Mark Miller, phoning him with an invitation to dinner at the home he shared with George Nader. He was shocked to hear Lana Turner on the other end of the line. As they talked, he realized that she did not remember having met him many months before at a Hollywood party, where she had been drunk and angry, loudly denouncing her third husband, the tin plate heir, Bob Topping.

Unlike what she'd sounded like at the time of their first meeting, the voice coming over the receiver was smooth, seductive, sensuous, and velvety. She told him how excited she was to be co-starring with him in their upcoming film, *Tacey Cromwell*. "Ross Hunter hand delivered the script to me, and I'm excited by it. I accepted the role. In some way, it brings back memories of my co-starring with Clark Gable in *Honky Tonk* (1941). How ironic that I'll be working with an actor acclaimed as 'The New Gable.'"

"You're not as excited as I am to be Lana Turner's co-star," he told her.

"When *Honky Tonk* was released," Turner told him, "the papers claimed that when Gable kissed me, it made screen history. Let's make screen history again."

"I'm your man," he answered.

She told him how much she'd enjoyed his stunning performance in *Magnificent Obsession*. "How I envied that bitch, Jane Wyman, in her role. I could have done a much better job. Jane Wyman is not the kind of woman Bob Merrick would have fallen in love with. I'm his kind of woman, as you'll soon see."

Then she invited him to her home, and he eagerly accepted. "I'm here all alone—no husband, no daughter, no mother hanging around to judge me."

He showered and dressed, gargling several times and trying on three separate outfits before deciding what appearance he wanted to make. Ultimately, he decided to go casual. Concluding that she wasn't much of a home-maker, he stopped along the way and picked up some take-out food from a Chinese restaurant.

At her home in Brentwood, clad in white shorts, a white blouse, and white high heels, she answered the door herself. "She was a vision of the murderous Coral in *The Postman Always Rings Twice* (1946), looking as gloriously enticing as she did back then."

The following day, he would describe in detail his evening with THE Lana Turner.

She was luscious, seductive, and charming. It

When Rock went to see Lana Turner in *The Postman Always RingsTwice* (1946), he fell in love with her image on the screen.

In Hollywood, he got the real thing.

237

had been many years since she'd competed with Betty Grable as the pre-eminent pinup girl for G.I.s during World War II. But she had held up very well and looked far younger than her years.

Ever since he'd seen *They Won't Forget* way back in 1937, and even though he'd been just a boy at the time, he had been enthralled by her undulating walk down the street in that movie. She'd worn a clinging sweater in which the shape and size of her bouncing breasts were clearly revealed. Overnight, she had become America's "Sweater Girl."

She had emerged as SEX personified, as she bounced along the sidewalk during the opening moments of that film, her character *en route*, early in the film, to being brutally raped and murdered.

As Rock later reported to Miller, "If I were really straight, I mean full-time straight, I would want Lana Turner for my wife. Imagine waking up with Lana Turner in your arms!"

"If I didn't already have George," Miller responded, "I'd rather wake up with that new kid on the block, Robert Wagner, in my arms."

There was little talk of *Tacey Cromwell,* but a lot of chatting about their personal lives. Of course, he shared only a "limited hangout" with her. She seemed in need of reinventing herself. "I don't want to go down in Hollywood history as just some distant memory of the love goddess of the 1940s. I want to continue to make the type of picture that will lure the couch potatoes away from their TV sets and into movie palaces."

Turner was also interested in co-starring with some of the leading men who were fast rising in the new decade. "Let's face it: Robert Taylor, Gable, and Errol Flynn are getting a bit long in the tooth for matinee idols. Soon, they'll be playing grandfathers. I, however, am not ready for mother roles yet, and certainly not ready for character parts."

"You look as good as you did when I first saw you opposite Gable in *Somewhere I'll Find You* (1942)," he told her. "That's when I fell in love with you."

"I shudder to think about the making of that movie," she answered. "Gable's wife, Carole Lombard, died in a plane crash during a war bond tour. He was a total wreck, so much so that everyone doubted he'd ever finish the movie."

After dinner and a few drinks, she suggested that since it was getting late, he should sleep over, and leave after breakfast the next morning.

"I think that would be a swell idea," he said. She led him into her boudoir and handed him a red silk robe. "Why don't you pull off your clothes and get comfortable while I get ready for bed, too."

She disappeared for a long time into her bathroom/dressing room. She finally emerged in a black *négligée*. He had already stripped and put on the robe, but left it open. "As he would later recall, "Everything I had was on parade."

Her eyes quickly took in the vision. "Seeing is believing," she said. "If I hadn't known Lex Barker and Fernando Lamas, I wouldn't believe that men come in that size."

"Let's have some fun," he said, dropping his robe and moving toward her.

With his friends, he didn't go into clinical detail about what happened next. He did admit, however, "I was insatiable, and so was she. So many stars in private don't live up to their screen image. Lana, however, in person is just what you get on the screen. She made me feel great, like a real man. She demanded fulfillment—and that's what she got."

The next morning, after he'd showered and had breakfast, she walked him to the door. "We'll have wonderful, glorious times making this movie together, except for a fear I have."

"What's that?" he asked.

"I fear that during the making of our movie, I'll fall hopelessly in love with you—and my life is far too complicated now."

***

Rock was stunned when director Jerry Hopper greeted him on the morning of his first day of rehearsals for his newest movie. First, he was told that Universal considered the title *Tacey Cromwell* "not commercial enough." Conceived as a western epic produced by Ross Hunter and formatted in Technicolor, it had been retitled *One Desire*, and scheduled for release in 1955. This would have been Hunter's first teaming with Lana Turner. *[He would later cast her in her "comeback" picture,* Imitation of Life *(1959).]*

Then Rock was informed by Hunter that Lana had had "artistic difficulties" with the film's director (Hopper), and that she had been replaced at the last minute by Anne Baxter. Although at first, Rock was disappointed, he was also glad to be working with Baxter, whom he considered "a real pro," later claiming "she taught me a lot."

He had first seen Baxter in the role of Sophie opposite Tyrone Power in *The Razor's Edge* (1946). Her performance had won her an Oscar as Best Supporting Actress.

She had also starred as the scheming Eve Harrington in one of Rock's all-time favorite films, *All About Eve* (1950). Its other star, Bette Davis playing Margo Channing, and Baxter, too, were each nominated as Best Actress that year, thereby splitting the Academy's vote and effectively canceling each other's chances of winning. In the end, Judy Holliday won the Best Actress award that year for her performance in *Born Yesterday.*

When Baxter was introduced to Rock, she looked him up and down. "I don't usually like to work in movies with actors better looking than I am. First, Tyrone Power. Now Rock Hudson.:" She'd been fitted with an elaborate, scarlet-colored, saloon-girl gown.

"You look glamorous in that Mae West drag," he told her.

Baxter had recently divorced actor John Hodiak. As Rock told George Nader, "At this premiere, I once stood next to Hodiak at a urinal. Now I know why he's called 'Mr. Beer Can.' I know why Anne went for him, but so did Lucille Ball, Judy Garland, and Hedy Lamarr. I was told that his former co-stars, Robert Taylor and Van Johnson, also lusted for him, and I heard that he was most cooperative in servicing people regardless of their gender."

Rock had never worked with Hopper before, although he would soon be helming him in an upcoming film, *Never Say Goodbye* (1956). When Rock shook his hand, he said, with a smile, "I thought you only directed Charlton Heston movies. He's the bastard who stole all the good parts from me back in our school plays."

He was referring to Hopper having directed Heston in *Pony Express* (1953), *Secret of the Incas* (1954), and *The Private War of Major Benson* (1955).

The character in the novel on which the film had been based was named "Gaye," but Universal ordered an immediate change. "We can't have our biggest box office attraction being referred to as 'Gaye' in a movie," Ed Muhl ordered from his executive office. He was still insisting that Rock pay him frequent visits for a "zipper unfastening."

During his most recent visit, he had told Rock, "The film's name states my passion exactly—*One Desire*, and that's for you, ya big lug."

It was only at rehearsals that Rock learned what the movie was about. He

Anne Baxter and Rock pose as screen lovers in *One Desire*, but it was just make-believe. "Anne was a great pal," he said, "and she got to Tyrone Power years before I did."

had never bothered to read Conrad Richter's best-selling novel, *Tacey Cromwell.*

As the movie opens, Rock, cast as Clint Saunders, is a card dealer in a notorious gambling house, which is run by Tacey Cromwell (Baxter) and McBain (William Hopper), who is in love with her. There's a complication: She's in love with Rock. Although he is not ready to settle down, she begs him to take her as he heads west to seek fame and fortune in a copper-mining town. There is some baggage to take along—Rock's little brother, Nugget.

Out West, in a frontier town, she wants to forget her shady past and gain respectability. The *One Desire* of the title refers to her attempts to escape the circa-1900 stigmas associated with her scarlet past. The film is most effective in depicting the intolerance of an early American frontier town. Tacey and Nugget live in a small house, and Rock, staying in the town's one hotel, comes over every evening until they are married.

During the course of a day, Rock meets the leading society lady of the town, Judith Watrous (Julie Adams), who sets out to take him away from Baxter. She'll do whatever it takes, as her father, Senator Watrous (Carl Benton Reid), soon realizes.

She hires a detective to investigate Baxter's past as a gambling hall hostess-cum-prostitute. In the meantime, Baxter has taken into her home not only Nugget but an orphan girl named Seely (Natalie Wood).

But based on the detective's report she's declared an unfit mother and forced to give up her children. Without letting Rock know, she heads back East to hook up with McBain (William Hopper) again at the gambling house.

In the meantime, Rock enters into a loveless marriage with Adams and becomes the president of the local bank, living in a grand house.

But true love will win out in the end. There is no need for a divorce. In a fit of anger, Adams throws a gas lamp at Rock, who flees from the house. While he's gone, the gas ignites the curtains, and his scheming wife is burned alive.

Baxter, by the way, happens to have returned to town, and in the wake of Adams' death, reclaims not only Rock but the children, too. After all the drama, heartbreak, flames, and betrayal, the film's ending is, in-

ONE DESIRE: Rock as a croupier in a gambling house: Movie goers interpreted his stance in this photo as sexually provocative, holding out promises of fast money and fast times.

deed, happy.

Adams told Rock that she was delighted to be playing a bad girl on the screen. By now, she'd co-starred with him in three other movies, including *Bend of the River*, *Horizons West*, and *The Lawless Breed*.

Rock and Natalie had something in common: Both were clients of Henry Willson's. Not only that, but he was also the agent for Robert Wagner, the man she would, years later (in 1957) marry. Somewhat provocatively, Rock asked Wood, "Do you think Robert has to lie on Henry's casting couch like I did?"

Respectable as a president of the local bank, Rock, onscreen, has entered a loveless marriage with Julie Adams, perhaps mirroring the one he'd soon enter with Phyllis Gates.

"I don't know, and I don't want to know," she answered. "It conjures up a most unattractive picture. Let's face it: Henry's a beast!"

During the early scenes of the movie, Natalie needs to play a young tomboy, a girl who's about seven years old. She was sixteen at the time, and Jerry Hopper didn't think she'd be convincing in a part that young. For her auditions, she showed up in pigtails and without makeup, and she got the role.

For her, the fun part was when she got to play an older version of Seely: "I've been the Pigtail Kid in Hollywood for so many years. I want to grow up."

She remembered that her favorite moment on the set was when she appeared, late in the film, as a nineteen-year-old, with her hair upswept, glamorously made up, and dressed in a wasp-waisted hoopskirt.

"Rock let out a wolf-whistle loud enough to be heard in Honolulu," she said. It was the beginning of a life-long friendship between the two. They became confidants, never lovers.

In time, he heard all about her marriage to Wagner, her divorce from him, and her remarriage to him in 1972, after her divorce from him in 1962, and Wagner's "interim marriage" to another woman in between.

She also filled him in as her lovers came and went: Warren Beatty, Elvis Presley ("he's lousy in bed"), James Dean, David Niven, Frank Sinatra, Nicky Hilton, Dennis Hopper, Audie Murphy, Steve McQueen, and "my biggest thrill," John Ireland.

At the time she co-starred in *One Desire*, she was still a virgin, or so she claimed to Rock. "She was very flirtatious with me, wanting me 'to make her a woman.' I could have taken advantage, but I didn't. Weeks later, I learned that her mother was urging her to lose her virginity. Her own mother! Could you imagine that?" Natalie later confessed to him that her mother had selected the young actor Nick Adams to "deflower" her daughter.

Often, during the shooting of *One Desire*, Ross Hunter, took an hour or so off in the afternoon to visit Rock in his dressing room. Hunter's passion for his star continued unabated.

Rock would have preferred William Hopper, the closeted gay son of homo-hating Hedda Hopper. Instead of sex, the two men—each sharing secrets associated with living in the Hollywood closet—bonded.

A coy ingenue, Natalie Wood, in *One Desire*.

She was attracted to Rock, but told him, "If you want to take my virginity, you're too late. Mother has already gotten Nick Adams to do that."

One night over dinner, Hopper confessed that as a contract player during the late 1930s at Warner Brothers, he had fallen in love with another handsome young contract player, Ronald Reagan. "It was unrequited love. We made several films together, and sometimes on location, we bunked together. When Ronnie stripped down, he told me I could look but not touch."

The future U.S. President told director Nick Grinde, "It's a burden being the dreamboat of Hopper's sexual fantasies. I feel more comfortable when I share the bed of Lana Turner or Susan Hayward, with Jane Wyman lurking around the corner."

Hopper and Wood were slated to co-star in their next picture, in which he would play her father in *Rebel Without a Cause* (1955) starring James Dean.

In spite of its mixed reviews, *One Desire* did reasonably well at the box office. Several critics cited its fine acting, the costumes, and especially the dramatic climax when Adams in burned to death, and Baxter's gambling hall palace also goes up in flames.

The New York Times was less enthusiastic, referring to the movie as "nothing more than a plodding, old-fashioned soap opera triangle that spectators may find themselves simply tuning in, eyes closed, to the familiar trail of events, dialogue, and musical effects."

***

During the filming of *One Desire*, speculation continued as to why Rock, nearing the age of thirty, had not settled down and gotten married.

The unwanted publicity reached a crescendo when Louella Parsons in her widely circulated column, published a provocative article in the summer of 1954. It was headlined ROCK HUDSON: WILL HE PUT HIS CAREER AHEAD OF MATRIMONY?

The column was loaded with innuendo, and only a sexual dimwit couldn't surmise that its intention was to make clear that Rock was a closeted homosexual.

The onslaught of speculation associated with his lack of a wife continued, as fan magazine after fan magazine raised the same question over and over again. In an article in *Movie-TV Secrets,* a reporter wrote, "Rock Hudson is handsome, personable, intelligent, and a top-salaried actor. So what's wrong with him where the fair sex is concerned, we ask?"

Almost daily, Henry Willson badgered Rock with demands that he get a wife—"The sooner the better"—before he was exposed in print.

"If you can't find a wife of your own, preferably a beautiful lez, I'll dig one up for you."

Rock had remained Willson's most important client, but his pert, pretty new secretary, Phyllis Gates, had not met him, although she'd made love to his lover, Jack Navaar, without him ever finding out. When she had come to work for Willson, Rock was away in Ireland filming *Captain Lightfoot.*

Then, one breezy morning in October of 1954, Rock strolled into Willson's office. She was at her desk, typing a letter to Jack Warner.

She looked up at this tall, handsome stranger as he approached her. "Hi, I'm Rock Hudson."

Her life was about to change for all time.

As she recalled that fateful day, "Rock had the longest legs I'd seen on any man. They stretched from Hollywood to Denver. He sure wasn't dressed like a movie star, showing up in blue denim slacks, a plaid cotton shirt, and a pair of Indian moccasins with no socks."

Following the instructions she'd been given, she told him to go right into Willson's office. She was rewarded with Rock's by now famous smile.

After he signed some papers for Willson, he came back into the outer office, passing Gates and smiling again on his way out, but without saying anything.

When Willson buzzed her, she entered to take dictation. First he asked, "So what do you think of the one, the only, the daunting Rock Hudson?"

"Fantastic!" she answered. "A dreamboat, every woman's heartthrob."

A few nights later, Willson invited Gates for drinks at a popular watering hole of the stars, the Cock 'n Bull. He'd never done that before. About fifteen minutes later, Rock entered the bar, heading toward them but stumbling over a chair and nearly falling down.

"He's a fucking movie star, but still as awkward as hell," Willson whispered to her.

After some aimless chit-chat, mostly Hollywood gossip, Willson invited both of them to dinner at Frascati's. When he excused himself to make one of his endless phone calls, she found small talk with Rock difficult.

At the end of dinner, she perceived that so-called "meeting" with Rock had been a disaster, and she expected never to hear from him again. "We simply had nothing in common, nothing to talk about."

It came as a total surprise the following day when he phoned and invited her for dinner that Friday night, adding, "Without Henry."

She turned to her best friend, Pat Devlin, her office assistant, "Imagine me going out on a real date with THE Rock Hudson, called by some the most desirable man on the planet. Me, a barefoot little farm girl from the cornfields of Minnesota."

Despite her lean budget, she went out and bought a simple but chic black dress, obviously a rip-off of *couture* by Chanel. But two hours before Rock was due at her door, he phoned and canceled, asserting that Willson had ordered him to grant an interview with *Photoplay*. She was miffed, but recognized that business (and publicity) came first.

He called two days later, again with apologies, and asked for another chance. Once again, he broke that date at the last minute, too.

With some reluctance, she agreed to yet a third date with him, and once again, he canceled on her at the last minute, claiming "something has come up."

The next morning, she confronted Willson. "I'm through with Rock Hudson, your 'Mr. Big Movie Star.' How inconsiderate! Tell the damn hot shot not to call me again."

This occurred during the Christmas season. Quite by chance, she ran into Rock a few days later on the sidewalk as both of them were shopping. He was with a companion, whom he introduced as "Craig," with no last name.

She would later describe him as having blonde hair, a suntan, and being "incredibly handsome with eyes the color of the Pacific." What she did not know at the time was that this young man was Rock's idealized type. He wished her a Merry Christmas and promised to call her.

There has been confusion as to the identity of this blonde Adonis. One biographer suggested that "Rock was with a lover who might have been William Reynolds," who was set to appear once again with Rock in his upcoming movie, *All That Heaven Allows*.

It was not Reynolds. There is no proof that Reynolds and Rock were ever lovers, although he frequently commented on what a handsome young man Reynolds was. He'd married actress Molly Sinclair in 1950 and remained with her until her death in 1992.

The mystery man was actually Craig Hill, a Los Angeles-born actor, who was the live-in lover of Rock's friend and fellow actor, John Carlyle. Details of Carlyle's life and loves were published in his autobiography *Under the Rainbow, An Intimate Memoir of Judy Garland, Rock Hudson, and My Life in Old Hollywood*, first published in 2007.

Initially, Rock had had a brief affair with Carlyle. Later, Rock had moved in on Hill, whom he later described as a "fatally good-looking mother fucker."

Carlyle, Hill, and Rock were each represented by Henry Willson.

Hill had first appeared on the screen in the memorable *All About Eve* (1950), co-starring Oscar nominees Bette Davis and Anne Baxter. He played Baxter's leading man in the play-within-the-movie *Footsteps on the Ceiling*.

Rock's former co-star in *One Desire*, Baxter, said, "I would have gone for Craig myself, but when I heard he was making the Sunset Strip rounds with Willson, I decided he played for the other team."

After that, Hill had appeared in *Cheaper by the Dozen* (1950), starring the prissy Clifton Webb. Hill later admitted to Rock, "I allowed Webb to have his way with me, although I detested him."

Rock admitted, "That's how I got my start, kid. It's what a guy has to do in Hollywood."

Hill had followed that appearance with a role in Sam Fuller's war drama, *Fixed Bayonets* (1951), co-starring Richard Basehart. He'd also played one of James Cagney's lieutenants in the 1952 remake of *What Price Glory*.

When 20th Century Fox dropped him, he was put under contract at Rock's home studio (Universal) and signed for *The Black Shield of Falworth* (1954), where Rock first met him and had a fling with him, before Hill moved in with Carlyle.

As amazing as it sounds, before Carlyle, Hill had had a fling in Las Vegas with none other than Marlene Dietrich, who was also appearing in the gambling mecca. As Carlyle wrote in his memoir, "Dietrich nursed him through a bout of the flu and cooked good German food for him when she was staying at Billy Wilder's guest house. Then she dumped Craig in favor of an older, more cosmopolitan actor, Michael Wilding, who, of course, went on to marry Elizabeth Taylor."

There is no evidence that Carlyle ever found out that Rock and Hill were carrying on an affair behind his back. Willson even claimed that Rock and Hill had fallen in love, and at one point, Rock wanted Hill to come and live with him. But that didn't work out. However, the two young actors staged sexual trysts until Hill, with his screen career faltering in America, went to live in Barcelona and made some Spanish language films.

***

After encountering Gates on the street shopping, Rock did phone the next day and invited her to dinner at the Villa Nova. "I hope you won't cancel at the last minute," she said.

"I'll guarantee with my blood that I'll show up. Forgive me for having to bow out previously at the last minute. Blame it on Willson and those damn interviews."

From her closet, she removed the black Chanel rip-off and readied herself for a glamourous evening, her first real date alone with him. But it didn't work out as she expected. Apparently, Willson heard about it and showed up to join them at table.

"Those two guys had one gay old time, laughing, talking, joking, spreading gossip, mostly from Willson who seemed to know who was doing whom all over town. I felt left out."

Rock seemed to be aware of how disappointed she was after Willson "invaded" their space. He called the next day, inviting her for a night of dinner and dancing at L'Escoffier, a chic restaurant within the Beverly Hilton. She'd long heard of the club, as it was frequented by Elizabeth Taylor, Joan Crawford, Ava Gardner, Frank Sinatra, and Lana Turner, many of them showing up with rotating partners in their romantic or sexual sagas.

Right on time, Rock arrived on Gates' doorstep. This time, he was dressed like a movie star, in an expensive, well-tailored suit he'd purchased at Savile Row in London. It was accessorized with gold cufflinks, a tasteful necktie, and alligator shoes, this time with socks. After a dinner of prime rib, they were drawn to the dance floor and the music of Joe Mashay and his talented band. As she'd later proclaim, "He was the best dancer I'd ever known, enveloping me gently in his arms." What she didn't mention in her memoirs was that most of her former dance partners had been women.

The perfect gentleman, Rock delivered her safely to her doorstep and didn't insist on coming in for a nightcap, the usual line of a Hollywood wolf.

He gave her a warm kiss on the lips and quietly departed into the night. Unknown to her, he had set up a midnight date with one of Willson's latest discoveries. A good-looking, well-built former truck driver, like Rock himself, the newly christened "Rick Cummings" would, in time, go back to his home state of Ohio having decided that he didn't like casting couches.

Rock later told Willson, "Cummings is a great name for this kid. Hell, where did you find him?"

"He was working as a masseur at a bathhouse in Venice," Willson confessed, "giving massages to guys who insisted that he remove the towel from around his waist."

The next afternoon, Gates answered her doorbell to find Rock standing there with a fragrant, freshly cut Christmas tree. He brought it inside and returned to his Buick convertible to fetch the decorations he'd purchased earlier in the afternoon. They spent the rest of the day decorating the tree and enjoying her home-cooked food, which he pronounced as "better than Kay's, but for god's sake don't tell Mother I said that."

It was December 23, 1954, a date she described in her memoirs as the first time Rock slept over and seduced her. She resorted to purple prose in describing the event. "The first kiss lasted a long time, and I didn't want it to end. His big hands were amazingly gentle as he began to explore, and I fell completely under his spell."

"He had a magnificent body," she wrote. "The love act itself was sublimely passionate, although it ended sooner than I would have liked. I figured that Rock had been very excited."

[Many women, not just Mamie Van Doren, reported that Rock was "quick on the draw" (Marilyn Maxwell's appraisal). Rock would penetrate a woman and reach a quick climax, leaving her feeling unfulfilled. In marked contrast, many young men claimed that he liked to spend hours in bed with them.]

After that night of passion, or at least what passed for passion, he phoned the next day and asked if he could spend Christmas Eve with her. "I'm all alone and have no place to go," he lamented. "Craig Hill and John Carlyle had family plans, and Mark Miller and George Nader were out of town. The prospect of spending Christmas Eve with Henry Willson was not his idea of how to do it."

For Christmas Eve, he invited her to this cozy little candlelit *trattoria* off Sunset Boulevard, a spot deemed appropriate by movie stars who were dating "off the record."

On this particular night, whereas the patrons of the other tables were in a festive mood, he seemed rather moody. She had never seen his sullen side before. But by the time the check arrived, his spirits had perked up. This renewed sense of energy led to another sleepover and another bout of love-making, which once again ended far too quickly for her taste.

As Christmas dawned, and after the opening of the presents each of them had purchased for the other, he invited her to drive with him to

Pasadena for Christmas dinner with his mother and stepfather, Kay and Joe Olsen.

The Olsens were gracious, although Kay seemed reserved around her, devoting all of her attention to Rock. Gates had mistakenly assumed that Kay would be delighted that Rock showed up with a woman, although on three separate occasions, she mentioned how much she missed the visits of Jack Navaar. What Gates didn't tell the congregants at the table was that she, too, missed Navaar, finding him a more enduring and satisfying lover than Rock himself, a secret she revealed to her best friend, Pat Devlin.

Kay doted on her son, anticipating his needs before he requested something. She carved a turkey leg for him, telling Gates "It was always my baby's favorite."

During the course of the dinner, she learned that he had never officially changed his name to Rock Hudson, and that he was still legally known as Roy Fitzgerald.

Driving back to Gates' home, Rock confided in her: "I wish Kay would treat me more like a mother than a fan."

***

One day, right before the noon lunch hour, Rock's Buick convertible pulled up in front of Henry Willson's office building. Rock jumped out of the car and raced inside, finding Gates typing a letter. "He came in, all beams and smiles, like he'd just discovered gold in Alaska. I'd never seen him so excited. Even though I was at work, and Willson was out of the office, he demanded that I close down the office and come with him to see his new discovery."

"I found the house of my dreams," he told her, "after looking at almost thirty other homes. Something was wrong with all of them, but this place I found is just perfect. The moment I spotted it, I knew it was where I wanted to spend the rest of my life. When I walked through the door, my mind was immediately made up."

En route to the property, he confided, "Ever since I was a little boy, I never liked any of the places I've lived, especially in Illinois with my first stepfather."

She later recalled, "His enthusiasm continued. It was as if he'd won his first Best Actor Oscar."

On the way there, they had to pass along all the "bird streets"—Robin, Mockingbird, Flicker, and Oriole before he turned onto Warbler Place and drove up a steep driveway.

Surrounded by towering pines, the house looked like a hunting lodge in the Tyrolean Alps. Its special feature was a steel gate that opened or shut with the press of a remote control.

"This will keep out my fans. At Grandview, they were coming onto the property and even trying to look through my windows. Here, I can find the privacy I need."

Under a shingled roof, the house was painted barn red. Inside, the aura was very masculine, with a few wood furnishings and burnished floors of grooved oak that formed geometric patterns. In one corner was a bar, and a special feature was a brick-built, floor-to-ceiling barbecue big enough to roast an ox. Upstairs were two rather small bedrooms with one bathroom. The backyard opened onto an ivy-draped hillside that rose 300 feet. Into it, a network of footpaths—each of them accented with steps crafted from cross-cut slabs of tree trunks—had been carved into the slope. She remembered the site as "scenic as a postcard."

"The owner wants $32,000, and Henry has arranged for Universal to advance me $38,000, the extra money to be used for furnishings."

Inside the house, he asked her, "What do you think of it?"

"I love it, so unusual and so unlike the homes everybody else lives in."

She was stunned by what he said next: "Come live with me here. Quit your job with Henry. I'll take care of you."

[She later said that she was thrilled with the offer, but didn't want to quit her job, which she liked. She was not certain that he was asking her to live with him because Willson had ordered him to do so as a means of avoiding charges of homosexuality. Then there was the question of love. He'd never told her he loved her, and she was unsure of her own mixed feelings.

There was another problem, too: During the Eisenhower era, no movie star lived with a woman without marriage; otherwise, there would be a scandal.

Years later, Phyllis said, "I considered calling my memoirs What's Love Got to Do With It?"]

She avoided giving him a direct answer. She knew that she and Rock might fool the public, but in Hollywood a marital union with Rock would be interpreted as a lavender marriage—i.e., a union framed and conceived as a means of camouflaging homosexuality. The marital union of actors Alexis Smith and Craig Stevens was a good example of this type of arrangement.

"You're sweet, Rock," she told him. "but living together is another matter. Let's hold off a bit and think about it some more before jumping into something we might regret."

"Perhaps you're right," he answered, "but the invitation remains open."

That night, he didn't ask to come into her apartment for a sleepover, but told her he had another appointment. "I'll call you tomorrow." Then he departed without a customary kiss.

The next day at Willson's office, she confided to Pat Devlin what Rock had proposed, asking her advice. "You know you're just being used. But since you like girls, and he likes boys, it might be the perfect arrangement. Call it an 'accommodation.' He might marry you, a lavender marriage. They're commonplace in this town."

"Frankly, I think this was Willson's idea right from the beginning," Devlin told her. "Why don't you live together and see if you guys are compatible. If he marries you, think about it. You'd be Mrs. Rock Hudson, married to one of the biggest box office names in Hollywood. There would be a heap of advantages. Besides, if it doesn't work out, think of the alimony. You could sue the hell out of him and live comfortably in the arms of some beautiful woman for the rest of your life—all on Rock's money."

***

It was only later that day, based on one of Willson's casual remarks, that she learned where Rock had gone after leaving her at the door to her apartment. He had driven to Willson's for an all-male party.

John Carlyle was there with his lover, Craig Hill (Rock's secret lover), along with an array of handsome young men, each desiring to become a movie star. After exchanging hugs and (chaste) kisses with Carlyle and Hill, Rock "went on the hunt for big game," according to Carlyle. "And no one was better than Rock at bagging his man."

"Our boy had this uncanny knack for making a conquest. He preferred straight men. Actually, most of the men at Willson's parties were straight, but in their early days they made themselves available on the casting couch. The straighter they were, the more Rock wanted to seduce them."

"That guy could charm the most heterosexual into bed," Carlyle said. "It was amazing. He would turn on the seductive charm. Of course, all of the guys were wannabes, looking for a break wherever it might come. The big movie star knew how to make these guys feel important. He flattered them, he made them think their every utterance should be written down for posterity. He held out hope that there might be a role for them in his next picture."

"One thing I could say about Willson: He knew how to assemble the best array of male pulchritude in Hollywood. On any given night, you could encounter a smattering of Rory Calhouns, Robert Wagners, and a few Guy Madisons and Tab Hunters. At least two John Saxons, a Mike Connors type, a few dressed like cowboys in Robert Fuller drag, even a challenger for Clint Walker's title of 'Gentle Giant.' In other words, the greatest assemblage of gorgeous men on Planet Earth. Don't tell me Rock would rather be in the arms of Phyllis Gates. Get real, girl!"

"After Rock seduced one of these studs, they would return to the beds of their girlfriends or young wives. Perhaps some of them would never have sex with another man. Read the Kinsey Report. While making *Captain Lightfoot* in Ireland, Rock confessed to me that he'd seduced about a dozen 'Irish blokes' among the camera crew and a pair of twins he met in a gay pub in Dublin. He didn't care if they were young husbands or else engaged to marry some Irish lassie—in fact, if they were, that was a turn-on for him."

Two days after Christmas, an item appeared in Mike Connolly's column in *The Hollywood Reporter*. He was Willson's close friend and a major source of inside news. Author Gore Vidal once described him like this: "He was your average drunk Irish Catholic queen, who was pretty venomous when in his cups and good company outside them."

Connolly revealed for the first time that "Rock Hudson is having hideaway dinners with Phyllis Gates, the pretty little secretary of talent agent Henry Willson, who has a knack for discovering hot new talent. He made a star out of Rock Hudson, who was a truck driver."

Gates knew, of course, that Willson had planted the item, and that she was being used to promote Rock's heterosexuality. So what? Such an item was also concealing her own notorious past, details of which Rock would soon discover.

***

After the big box office success of *Magnificent Obsession* (1954), it seemed inevitable that Universal would reteam Jane Wyman with Rock in an upcoming picture. To fulfill this goal, Ross Hunter, as producer, and Douglas Sirk, as director, also teamed up again to produce *All That Heaven Allows* (1955), the story of a May-September romance between a wealthy widow, Cary Scott (Wyman), and her tall, handsome, virile young gardener, Ron Kilby (Rock). At the time, Wyman was forty-one and Rock had recently turned twenty-nine.

When she had first starred with Rock, she was unaware of his sexual preference, and had fallen for him, even though she'd been married at the time to musician Fred Karger, Marilyn Monroe's former lover.

Since their joint appearance in their first film together, even though Rock's star had, by now, risen over Hollywood bigger and brighter than her own, Hunter and Sirk decided to let her retain her star billing. Their decision was in part influenced by the Best Actress Oscar she had won for playing the deaf mute who is raped in *Johnny Belinda* (1948).

Since their first movie together, Rock had become the most written-about male movie star in Hollywood, topped only by Marilyn Monroe among the women. Rock Hudson fan clubs had sprouted up everywhere. He was known internationally, especially in Western Europe.

As filming began, Rock looked much younger than his years, and at her age, Wyman was very well-preserved. Most of her contemporary female stars seemed to have an expiration date stamped on their foreheads, and most of them were sitting at home waiting for the phone to ring.

Not Wyman. Not only was she continuing to make movies, but she had ventured into television, hosting 49 episodes of *Jane Wyman Presents the Fireside Theater* (1955-58). *[More or less simultaneously, as a means of salvaging his faltering acting career, her former husband, Ronald Reagan, was hosting* General Electric Theatre *(1954-62).]*

Before filming began, Wyman met with Sirk, having heard rumors that he was sustaining an ongoing affair with Rock. Because of that, she felt she could confide something personal to him, thinking he might understand. She revealed that in New York, she had walked into her suite at the Waldorf Astoria, to discover Rock making love to her husband, Fred Karger.

"That is a problem," Sirk answered. "You and Rock will have to appear in love scenes together. That might prove difficult. Thanks for the heads-up."

"Don't worry," she said. "I can put aside personal feelings, regardless of Hudson's betrayal. I won't be the first actress in Hollywood who has to pull off that stunt. At this point in my movie career, I need another hit—and I aim to have one. Hell, I would even play a love scene with Nancy's Ronald Reagan if the script called for it."

The first day Rock appeared on the set, he approached Wyman, giving her a kiss on the cheek. "Great to be working with you again. We really created a sensation in our last picture."

"Let's do it again, and get down to business without getting into personal stuff," she answered. "I know what you're feeling right now. I had to make a lot of silly, stupid pictures before I broke out."

"People treat me different now," he said. "Sometimes they just look at me in awe. Hell, I believe that if I let out a fart, I'd be told how sweet it is. It seems that everybody I meet these days thinks I can walk on water."

"I don't," she answered sharply.

"I didn't think you would, after what happened in New York. But Jane, let's forget about Freddie boy. He's just trying to find himself. Lots of fucked-up feelings going on inside him. You must understand that in Hollywood, these things happen more often than you know."

"Don't kid yourself, buster," she said. "You forget, I hit Hollywood in 1932 in an uncredited role in *The Kid from Spain* when I played a Goldwyn Girl. I've seen plenty. I've even had a husband or two that I concealed in my bio. And I've lived to see my former husband marry the starlet once hailed as 'The Fellatio Queen of Hollywood.'"

***

All That Heaven Allows, inspired by an original story by Edna and Harry Lee, was based on a screenplay by Peg Fenwick. In it, Wyman was cast as Cary Scott, a wealthy widow living in an affluent section of a New England town, its social life centering around a snobbish country club.

Her two college-age children, Ned (William Reynolds) and Kay (Gloria Talbott), are home from school. They want their mother to marry Harvey (Conrad Nagel), as does her best friend, red-haired Sara Warren (Agnes Moorehead). She is not in love with him. He's not in love with her, either, but he could offer companionship. Their respective "fires of autumn" burn on low flames.

Cary upsets not only her children, but her curtain-twitching neighbors when she falls in love with her studly young gardener. Right from the beginning, she finds him intelligent, sensitive, down-to-earth, idealistic, leading a Thoreau-inspired *Walden Pond* lifestyle on the distant fringe of their gossipy, narrow-minded, and mean-spirited New England town.

During their first luncheon together, he presents her with the sprig of a golden raintree, telling her that the tree can only thrive near a house of love.

Wyman accepts the gardener's invitation to visit him at his home. They drive together through autumnal countrysides of reds, golds, and yellows, brilliantly filmed in Technicolor by Russell Metty. Rock is converting an old mill into a home. At one point, she is frightened by a bird and falls into his arms as they share a romantic gaze. Before long, she's in an intimate embrace, receiving her first kiss from him. She becomes flustered and confused, but is starting to fall in love with this wonderful man, who seems almost too good, loving, kind, considerate, and romantic to be real.

At one point in the unfolding drama, Ron invites Cary to meet his friends. They are warm, down-to-earth people, radically unlike her judgmental friends from the country club.

Charles Drake and Virginia Grey were cast as Mick and Alida Anderson. The husband used to be an advertising executive, but when he met Ron, he abandoned that lifestyle for a more pastoral venue. In a subsequent dialogue, Alida makes it clear how happy they are living together, having been directly inspired in their lifestyle choice by Ron (aka Rock).

When they learn about their mother's growing passion for this "lower class gardener," both of Cary's children are horrified, especially her son, Ned, who is home during a break from his studies at Princeton. He fears his mother's romance will besmirch the dignified memory of his late father.

Contemptuously, Ned dismisses her romance with Rock, suggesting that she's just falling for a good-looking set of muscles. Although she is clearly bored with the claustrophobic confines of this provincial town, Ned promises to buy her a television set to keep her company.

Vapidly, daughter Kay espouses her Freudian theories of attraction, then expresses her preference for Harvey as a suitable match for her widowed mother. She talks about how wives in ancient Egypt were walled up with the bodies of their dead husbands, presumably to service the departed in their after-lives.

Cary faces a dilemma: Should she follow the dictates of her heart and take Ron as her lover? Or should she surrender to convention and abandon him, acquiescing to the wishes of her children and her community? At least for a while, she breaks off her relationship with the gardener, sacrificing her own happiness in favor of their prejudicial dictates and mores.

The moody, melancholic passion of this soap opera story

Bored older woman, hot younger man...In *All That Heaven Allows* (1955) Jane Wyman and Rock repeat the theme they successfully developed in *Magnificent Obsession,* this time with a counter-culture, Bohemian twist.

is enhanced by Frank Skinner's haunting, Chopin-esque musical score. It was made during the dying days of Golden Age Hollywood, when so-called women's pictures were on life support.

Originally, Sirk wanted to film an ending that left Ron's future in doubt. When he falls down the side of cliff, does he survive and later recover? Hunter demanded a happy ending, and, as producer, he got it.

In the final version that was released, Cary decides to return to Ron and visits his home, but he's not there. As she drives away, he spots her faraway car from a snow-covered hillside, where he has gone hunting. Seeing her, he races toward her, but plummets down the slippery slope and is seriously injured.

Later, she learns of the accident, his doctor telling her that Ron has suffered a dangerous concussion and cannot be moved. She rushes to his side and whispers to him that she's come back. The final shot is of a little deer wandering away, heading back to its forest home. FADE OUT.

***

When reporters came onto the set, Wyman put up a brave front. "After working with Rock this second time around, I'd say he's going to be the biggest thing the industry has seen in the 1950s."

When Sirk read that remark, he kidded her. "Rock's got the biggest thing all right."

"Oh, you damn size queens," she responded, walking away in a huff.

As Wyman was leaving Universal one afternoon, she ran into her estranged husband, Fred Karger, who was just arriving. At first, she felt he might be coming to see her, perhaps begging for a reconciliation, but that was not why he was here. Their divorce decree would not come through until December of 1955.

She asked him why he was here, and he used the excuse that Rock was hiring him and his band to play at this big Hollywood party he was tossing. "A lot of stars will be there, and he wants the music to be great."

Wyman had not been invited.

"Put on a great show," she said before walking off.

After learning that Karger was still romancing Rock, Wyman told Sirk, "During the making of *Magnificent Obsession*, I got actually screwed by Rock before he discovered my husband. Now, on our latest movie, I'm getting screwed by him in a different way."

She never saw Karger on the lot ever again, but was told that he sometimes parked across from the gate at Universal, sitting in his car waiting for Rock to get off from work. She was painfully aware that they were still having an affair, even though both men denied it.

"Don't worry," Sirk assured her. "Their romance will die soon enough. Rock is very promiscuous. He'll be moving on to his next conquest."

"I don't know why I'm even concerned with him," she said. "After all, I'm about to divorce him. He's free to do what he wants."

"I think you still have some love for him," Sirk said. "Here's my advice. When his flirtation with Rock blows over, why don't you remarry him? You're both older and wiser the second time around. That often happens between a man and a woman."

"That is about the dumbest idea I've ever heard, and I've heard some doozies. I'll never remarry that jerk."

"Jane, my darling girl, you're protesting too much."

[Jane Wyman remarried Fred Karger in 1961, divorcing him in 1965 for the final time.]

***

Upon the release of *All That Heaven Allows*, it did respectable box office, but without the soaring success of *Magnificent Obsession*. Most critics, however, dismissed it as "another soaper" from the Hunter / Sirk team.

Ed Muhl, Rock's sometimes lover at Universal, debated that he might get more life out of Rock and Wyman by reteaming them in a series of comedies. And although Muhl's core idea eventually became a reality, the final products ultimately featured Doris Day as Rock's leading lady instead of Wyman.

In reference to *All That Heaven Allows*, Bosley Crowther, in *The New York Times*, wrote, "The script was obviously written to bring Jane Wyman and Rock Hudson together again, since they made a popular twosome in *Magnificent Obsession*. Solid and sensible drama plainly had to give way to outright emotional bulldozing and a paving of easy clichés."

The Pink Triangle, an underground gay newspaper that flourished briefly for one summer, heaped praise on *All That Heaven Allows*. "What more can you want? Brilliant color of an autumnal landscape, thundering music, biting social commentary, and Rock Hudson, the most gorgeous man in the world and the sexiest actor ever to appear in Hollywood history."

"As for the matinee idols Rock replaced: Flynn looks like shit these days, with puffy eyes, and Ty Power is also developing lines under his eyes. Gable should be playing grandfather parts. Robert Taylor is looking more and more like our fathers."

The film had to wait several decades before it faced a reappraisal by critics. Today, it is viewed as a critique of the social conformity of the Eisenhower Era (i.e., 1953-1961). Filmmakers Rainer Werner Fassbinder and Quentin Tarantino praised it—in fact, it was the inspiration for Fassbinder's brilliant and critically acclaimed "experimental" film, *Ali: A Fear Eats the Soul (Angst essen Seele auf;* 1974). The plot of that German-language film explored the toxic fear and loathing that arose after an elderly German woman develops a love affair with a Moroccan migrant worker in postwar Germany.

All That Heaven Allows remained influential even as a satire: It was spoofed by the *avant-garde* director John Waters in *Polyester* (1981), in which Tab Hunter had to make love to the comically flamboyant drag queen Divine.

In 1995, *All That Heaven Allows* was selected by the Library of Congress for preservation by the United States National Film Registry as "culturally, historically, or aesthetically significant."

"Rock Hudson is in my movies because he is a handsome cipher," said Sirk. "If an actor has too much personality, he projects what he wants to project. With too much uniqueness, he is always himself, never Everyman. With Rock, female audiences can project their feelings and desires onto him, and men can assign to him their own hopes and fears—that is, those men who aren't in love with his screen image. Most Hollywood stars are symbols, not individuals. This keeps actors from getting in the way of the story, for movies are just illustrated, breathing stories."

Years later, Rock made a final comment about Wyman. "She's had the same girlish hairdo for decades, the one with the bangs. Or, as they call her in England, 'the girl with the fringe.' But she's not a girl anymore, and it's beginning to look a little grisly."

Chapter Nine

Now That He's a Bigtime Movie Star, Celebrities Flock to Rock

Chiefly Elizabeth Taylor, Monty Clift, and Fleetingly, Garbo, Sinatra, and Truman Capote

Michael Wilding "Worships" Rock, Who Takes Up with Norman Bates (Tony Perkins)

Call it an interlude in Rock's life. Opposites are said to attract. Such was the case when Rock picked up a young hitchhiker named Tony Perkins, who was in Hollywood making a movie with Gary Cooper. "My fling with Tony was brief before I delivered him back to Tab Hunter."

After arriving at Idlewild Airport for a short vacation in New York, Rock took a taxi to the Waldorf Astoria. Ed Muhl, in charge of production at Universal, had arranged for the studio to pay Rock's tab, writing it off as a publicity junket. Rock wasn't enthusiastic about the press and public relations associated with his trip: He wanted all his clandestine activities in New York to go unpublicized.

Before he departed from Los Angeles, he visited Muhl at his office for another "locked door" conference. He always felt embarrassed passing through the pool of secretaries *en route* to Muhl's office, as he suspected that they were fully aware of what was going on behind their boss's closed and locked door.

After zipping up, and as he was heading out the door, Muhl called him back and handed him the first draft, written by Charles Hoffman, of his next picture.

It was "another sudsy melodrama" entitled *Never Say Goodbye* and eventually released in 1956. Muhl told him that Universal was hoping to attract the same audience, lots of women, who had flocked to showings of *All That Heaven Allows.*

As the studio chief revealed, Rock would be the star of the picture. There would be no A-list leading lady, as had been the case with Jane Wyman. "All the other players will depend on your star power."

"Just who will be my leading lady?" Rock asked.

"Cornell Borchers?"

"That's not exactly a household name," Rock said, sarcastically.

"She's good, a German actress touted as the new Ingrid Bergman. You surely saw her in *The Big Lift* (1950) with your buddy, Monty Clift."

"That's the one Monty picture I missed," Rock said.

At the Waldorf in Manhattan, Rock enjoyed a luxurious bath in a tub once used by the Duke of Windsor.

After drying off and putting on a robe, he phoned Montgomery Clift, who had asked him to look him up when he arrived in town. The actor seemed delighted to hear from him and invited him to a pre-dinner cocktail party at his home. He was asked to arrive at four o'clock so they could have a private talk.

En route to Clift's apartment, Rock hoped it was not for a seduction, as he remembered sex with the actor as a most unsatisfying experience.

Looking disheveled and unshaven, Clift answered the door in his underwear. As Rock remembered it, "Monty's face looked as it did in *A Place in the Sun* (1951) with Elizabeth Taylor. It was so earnest, those big eyes pleading for understanding. He was nervous, actually shaking. He'd obviously been drinking."

As the two very different actors talked, Clift poured out his disillusionment with Hollywood. "Those bastards out there on the Coast are offering me every script going into production. I've turned

Montgomery Clift and Elizabeth Taylor graced the screen as the doomed lovers in *A Place in the Sun* (1951). She told Rock, "I've never loved a man as much as Monty. As strange as it might seem, it has absolutely nothing to do with sex."

all of them down. One is called *East of Eden,* a John Steinbeck thing. I turned down *The Country Girl* with Grace Kelly, the role going to William Holden. Not for me. I wanted to return to Broadway. I've left tickets for you for *The Sea Gull,* you and your date, whoever he is."

Clift told him that he liked living in New York City. "I'm a very private person, and I don't want to end up in the scandal rags. There are too many prying eyes in Hollywood, notably those despicable old hags, Parsons and Hopper. Here I keep looking for love and never finding it.

After about an hour, Clift excused himself, heading for the shower and to get dressed for his party, to which he'd invited some of the city's theatrical elite.

As the guests began to arrive, Rock was amazed at those invited, some of whom he had previously encountered "when I was a nobody."

Times had changed. Now, each of the A-list guests treated him differently, each showing respect for his new status in Hollywood.

"What a difference a day makes," he later said. "Days, hell! It took me years of playing all those dumb parts like *Taza, Son of Cochise* to get where I am."

Through the door walked a radiant Elizabeth Taylor, whom he'd met before. Her husband, Michael Wilding, according to Dorothy Kilgallen's column, had been left behind in Hollywood. Her escort was Roddy McDowall, whom Rock knew casually. The British actor and former child star had always come on to him, but Rock had never been interested, considering him too effeminate.

Although Rock had been introduced to Elizabeth before, she did not remember him. She now paid him the attention and respect that a fellow movie star deserved. He remembered her as "warm and gracious." He stared into her violet eyes, finding her most appealing.

She suggested that when he returned to Hollywood that he hook up with Clift and come over to join Wilding and her for dinner at her hilltop home. He gladly accepted the invitation.

"You know what? We might go beyond a dinner," she said. "Maybe co-star in a picture together. If we did, and if some critic claims you photograph more beautifully than me, I'll cut off his balls."

"I'm sure that will never happen," he said, "but I can dream."

Since nearly every guest had another engagement beginning around eight o'clock, either for dinner or the theater, introductions and chats were brief. In walked Frank Sinatra, whom he'd never met. Sinatra and Clift, as two lost souls, had formed an unusual friendship during the filming of *From Here to Eternity* (1953) in Hawaii.

"Hey, kid, glad to meet you," Sinatra said to Rock. He did not bother to introduce the blonde starlet who accompanied him. Obviously, Ava Gardner was not in town. "I've been hearing great things about you. You're going places."

"I don't care how far I might climb, I'll never reach your heights," Rock said.

"That may be true," Sinatra said. "But once you climb to the top, and are adored by millions, Hollywood likes to knock you down from the ladder."

Late arrivals at Clift's party included Greta Garbo in sunglasses. She was accompanied by a mannish-looking woman dressed in men's clothing.

At first, Garbo was surrounded by admirers, but when she went to sit down, alone, in a corner, Rock approached and greeted her, recalling the time, so long ago, when he'd chatted with her at the Château Marmont. To his surprise, she remembered him. "I've seen your picture with Wyman," she said. "You performed very well."

"It was a bit daunting performing in *Magnificent Obsession*," he said, "following in the footsteps of Robert Taylor. I saw *Camille* (1936) with you and Bob two times."

"I remember it well," Garbo answered. "Back when Bob was so beautiful but also so dumb."

Suddenly, he turned around to confront the author Truman Capote. On his arm was a blonde, whom he introduced as Christine Jorgensen.

Rock knew immediately who she was. Half the world knew that this former G.I. named George had become a woman, thanks to surgical procedures starting in 1951 in Copenhagen. The boy, who grew up in the Bronx where he was repeatedly raped by street gangs, was the first American transgendered woman to gain international renown. She had become an instant, albeit notorious, celebrity.

Both Capote and Jorgensen gushed over Rock's recent movies. Each of them flirted with him, telling him how "big and gorgeous" he looked both on and off the screen.

***

With "Tales of Manhattan" to relate to his friends, Rock flew back to Los Angeles, but it was several days before he phoned Phyllis Gates.

He'd read Charles Hoffman's script of *Never Say Goodbye*, which was to be shot at

Greta Garbo...only chance encounters.

262

his home studio (Universal), and which would eventually be released in 1956. He viewed it as a Technicolor "turgid tear-jerker," but was delighted to see it become one of the year's big box office hits, according to *Variety*.

On the first day back at the studio, he was greeted by its director, Douglas Sirk. "I've missed you," he whispered into Rock's ear.

"We'll get together later this afternoon," Rock promised. "I've been saving it for you."

"Yeah, I bet," Sirk said.

At that point, its producer, Albert J. Cohen, approached, and Sirk introduced him to the film's leading man. Cohen told Rock something he didn't know: Their movie was based on an Italian play, *Come Prima, Meglio di Prima*, by Luigi Pirandello, a playwright unfamiliar to Rock.

Christine Jorgensen, the world's most famous transsexual, wanted Rock to co-star as her leading man in a movie.

He learned something else that surprised him. *Never Say Goodbye* had already been filmed back in 1945, when Merle Oberon and Charles Korvin played the lovers. Rock asked Sirk to arrange a showing of that film for him, and he did, Rock finding it a "sudsy soaper" like *All That Heaven Allows,* and directly evocative of *Magnificent Obsession*. It was the story of a man and his wife who are separated for twelve years, but then unite in the end.

In *Magnificent Obsession,* Jane Wyman, while fleeing from Rock, had been hit by a car, blinding her. Later, after his character "reinvents" himself as a doctor, he restores her sight.

Author Truman Capote said he was thinking about writing a script to co-star Rock with Marilyn Monroe, predicting the duo would be the hottest screen team in history.

In *Never Say Goodbye,* the leading lady is also hit by a car. Cast once again as a doctor, Rock performs the successful surgery on her.

Sirk invited Rock to lunch in the commissary to meet his leading lady, Cornell Borchers. "I brought her over from Germany." Over lunch, he learned that she was actually from Lithuania. "I thought Cornell here would be ideal cast in all those parts that used to go to a young Ingrid

Bergman."

Rock found her polite, but cold and distant. After she'd departed, he told Sirk, "It's going to be difficult for me to melt Miss Iceberg in our love scenes."

George Sanders, who had famously married and divorced the blonde Hungarian bombshell, Zsa Zsa Gabor, played the second male lead. The reputation of this Russian-born bisexual actor had preceded him.

Sanders invited Rock to lunch, and he reluctantly accepted, hoping that Sanders wouldn't make a pass at him. As it turned out, he was a fascinating wit. "I don't like nightclubs, and I don't like women. They're boring. Hollywood girls are too beautiful—so beautiful you can't actually believe they are real. And who in hell wants to fall

In another sudsy soaper, *Never Say Goodbye*, Rock was cast opposite Cornell Borchers, who was touted in Hollywood as "The New Ingrid Bergman." That she was not, as it turned out to be.

in love with a woman who is unbelievable? Frankly, I find the greatest aphrodisiac is money."

"I find it pleasant to be unpleasant—but never to you, dear boy."

Sanders evaluated his own assets when he claimed, "I have the most perfect legs in Hollywood, and I work hours trying to keep them in shape. Had I not had fantastic talent as an actor, which I demonstrated so well in *All About Eve* (1950), I think my legs alone would have made me a movie star."

When he suggested that Rock join him for a weekend in Laguna, he politely declined. He certainly knew that Sanders wasn't completely homosexual, as he was known for hetero affairs which had ranged from tobacco heiress Doris Duke to Marilyn Monroe, from Hedy Lamarr to Lucille Ball.

A few days later, Sirk announced to Rock and the rest of the cast that he had to leave the production because Universal had problems with other films that needed "immediate surgery." However, he promised Rock that he'd be on the lookout for another screenplay that would duplicate the success of *Magnificent Obsession*.

Sirk was called back for a final "doctoring" of *Never Say Goodbye* after Rock's work on the film was completed. Sanders and Sirk were the best of friends, and Sanders successfully pleaded with him to reshoot three of his pivotal scenes.

During Sirk's absence, the new (interim) director assigned to *Never Say Goodbye* was Jerry Hopper, who had recently directed Rock in *One Desire* opposite Anne Baxter. Rock worked smoothly with him, but later said, "He was not memorable in any way."

In the recycled, time-worn plot, Rock was cast as an army doctor, Michael Parker, in postwar Vienna. There, he meets and falls in love with an entertainer, Lisa Gosting (Borchers), whose on-stage partner is Victor (Sanders). Parker falls in love and marries her, and the couple have a daughter. However, based on some mysterious miscommunications amid the vagaries of the Cold War, he begins to suspect that she is still carrying on an affair with Victor.

One day, she travels into the Soviet zone of Vienna to see her father. But when she tries to cross the border back into the U.S.-occupied zone, she is detained by Soviet authorities and subsequently "disappears."

The years go by—twelve, in fact—and Rock is now living in America with his daughter Suzy (Shelley Fabares). She has been told that her mother died in Austria years ago.

Quite by coincidence, so common in the movies, Parker encounters Lisa in a nightclub, where she is still performing with Victor.

Fleeing from Parker, Borchers has a car accident, but as a surgeon, Rock performs an operation on her and helps her recover. Although she's reluctant to return to his home with him, she desperately wants to meet her daughter.

At home, Suzy resents her, thinking that she is her father's new wife. But in time, Lisa wins her over, and husband, wife, and daughter settle into a house of love after all those years have passed when they were apart.

Phyllis Gates went to see *Never Say Goodbye* and dismissed it as "another Universal potboiler aimed at capitalizing on the studio's most valuable star."

Rock said, "It's a good thing Phyllis is not a movie critic." Earlier, on February 7, 1955, he had invited her to a preview of *Captain Lightfoot*. According to Phyllis, as published in her memoirs, "He looked heavenly in his military uniform, but the movie was nothing to shout about."

Rock Hudson and Elizabeth Taylor "circled" each other for months in Hollywood before becoming lifelong friends.

After Rock flew back to Los Angeles from New York, Montgomery Clift arrived a few days later and phoned him, telling him that she had invited both of them to dinner at the home she shared with Michael Wilding. "She remembers you from my party in Manhattan and wants to get to know you better," Clift said.

"I'm very flattered," he said. "I'll pick you up and drive you to her place."

By the summer of 1954, Elizabeth and her British actor husband had moved into a high-tech house, built of steel and adobe, at 1375 Beverly Estate Drive, high above Benedict Canyon Drive in Beverly Hills.

As Rock would learn later that evening, the house was also shared by four dogs, two of which were "spoiled poodles" (Rock's words), along with five cats and two ducks. He was surprised that Elizabeth allowed this menagerie to roam freely throughout the house. "None of the animals was housebroken, so guests had to watch where they stepped. Gee Gee, one of her dogs, was allowed to lick her baby son. She told Rock, "A dog's saliva is the purest thing in the world, a true disinfectant."

This was the first party he'd attended with Elizabeth where she spent most of the evening talking to him. Once again, she suggested that they might one day star in a picture together, even though he was under contract to Universal, and she was "serving out a slave contract at MGM" (her words).

"Monty told me he's madly in love with you," she said. "You are the true passion of his life."

"He must have been drunk when he told you that." Rock said. "He's not in love with me. Nor me with him. That was just something to say at the moment."

"Actually, I'm madly in love with Monty myself," she said. "I have been ever since we made *A Place in the Sun* (1951) for George Stevens."

British actor Michael Wilding, husband of Elizabeth Taylor, invited Rock to go for a moonlit walk in their garden. He wanted to do to Rock what he did to Stewart Granger during the war.

"That's one of my favorite pictures," he said. "That closing scene where you must tell him goodbye forever in his jail cell broke my heart," he said. "You two were dynamite together."

"But our love affair was doomed from the beginning. Monty prefers your plumbing to mine."

She also told him that Clift visited their home almost every night. "Michael tolerates him, and Monty dotes on our baby son. He named him 'Britches.' By the way, I'm pregnant again. Louella Parsons is suggesting that it really is Monty's child since it's hardly a secret that Michael and I are estranged. We no longer sleep in the same bed."

"Too bad," he said. "I've heard rumors."

"Tell me about them," she said.

"It's going around that you, Michael, and Monty are engaged in a *ménage à trois*," he said. "I didn't know such a fancy word until I got to Hollywood. Back in Illinois, we called it a three-way."

"Nothing could be further from the truth," she said. "Gossip is the price of stardom. As your star rises higher, you'll find that to be true."

"Actually, my marriage to Michael has devolved into a brother-sister relationship," she confessed. "A scarlet woman like me should never have married an older man. Actually, I'm not scarlet. Color me purple!"

"That's the color to describe me, too. I don't want to settle down. I want to play the field. It's more fun."

"I think this is going to be the beginning of a beautiful friendship, as Claude Rains and Humphrey Bogart vowed in the closing reel of *Casablanca* (1943)."

And so it was.

***

Whether he was in love with him or not, Clift still demanded sex from Rock, who obliged but confessed to his friends, "My heart isn't in it. But we do go to some hot parties. I mean, he knows everybody."

One such party they attended was at the home of Stewart Granger and his wife, Jean Simmons, both Britishers. Clift told Rock that for a while, the Grangers and the Wilding had lived under the same roof. According to Clift, "Stewart (Granger) and Michael (Wilding) are each bi-, and they've continued the affair they'd inaugurated way back during World War II in London."

"Does Elizabeth know this?"

"Of course she does. So does Jean. You'll find Londoners are very sophisticated about such arrangements. They're not as provincial as we

Americans from the Midwest."

Arriving at the party, Rock found its hosts, Granger and Simmons, most gracious. Both Elizabeth and her husband, Michael, kissed him on the lips, which came as a bit of a surprise to him. Rock was introduced to Elizabeth's gay secretary, Dick Hanley, who flirted with him.

It was Hanley who would later describe some of the guests at this intimate Hollywood party: "Rock and Jean would meet for the first time. Stewart and Michael have been lovers since dinosaurs wandered through London. I felt at some point that both Elizabeth and Michael, on different occasions, would seduce Rock, because it was obvious that each of them was attracted to him. Who wouldn't be? So was I. And I'd heard that Rock occasionally got off on a woman."

"Victor Mature showed up solo," Hanley continued. "He and Elizabeth had been lovers. Mature is bi-, you know. From the way he related to Rock, I knew he was going to go after him at some future date. Richard Burton, Elizabeth's future love, showed up with Lana Turner, who had once had an affair with Mature, too. Burton and Lana had signed to make *The Rains of Ranchipur* (1955) together, on the location for which they would have an affair. That was a remake of *The Rains Came* (1939) with Tyrone Power, whom Lana was still claiming as the love of her life."

Also according to Hanley, "I was shocked when Lana came up to Rock and gave him a long, lingering kiss. Obviously, those two had made it together. Maybe Rock is bi-, not gay. I hope you can follow all this. In a nutshell, everybody had fucked everybody else, or was about to. Ah, Hollywood. Only I got left out in the cold."

***

The following week, Elizabeth once again invited Clift and Rock to dinner at her hilltop home. But two hours before Rock was scheduled to pick up Clift and drive him there, Clift phoned him with regrets: "I've got the runs. Something I ate. I phoned Bessie. She wants you to come on alone, since she always wants somebody over for dinner so she won't have to be alone in the house with Michael."

Driving up the steep hillside road leading to her house, Rock arrived right on time and was greeted by Wilding. The only other person present was the nanny, who was in another wing of the house looking after their young son.

That night, Rock realized just how capricious Elizabeth was. Just after his arrival at her house, she had phoned her husband, claiming she was busy at the studio and that she couldn't make it for dinner. Consequently, and despite the invitation she had previously extended, Rock would have to dine alone with Wilding, whom he didn't really know.

As the evening unfolded, Rock found him witty, charming, and a most gracious host. "He was very honest and forthright, speaking of how successful his film career had been in England and how it had stalled after his move to Los Angeles."

Wilding maintained a dim view of Hollywood. "My first and most lasting impression of this Tinseltown is that of living in a cell and working in a factory."

He spoke with bitterness about his recent role in *Torch Song* (1953), wherein he played a blind pianist accompanying singer Joan Crawford in her comeback picture at her former studio, MGM.

"The director told me that my job, as the character I played, was to soften the abusive, bitchy nature of this formidable *grande dame*," Wilding said. "An impossible task. I'm probably her only leading man she didn't fuck."

He even spoke honestly about his deteriorating marriage to Elizabeth. "I feel I'm just a boring old appendage who can't even pull his weight as a breadwinner."

Knowing that Rock was gay, he talked about Hedda Hopper, claiming that she had warned Elizabeth not to marry him. "The bitch said I was gay and cited my affair with Stewart Granger. I should sue the cow. Stewart jokes about it. He told me, 'We've got to stop holding hands in public.'"

Rock had already read about Wilding's many affairs with women, who, it was alleged, had included Ingrid Bergman, Paulette Goddard, Rita Hayworth, the Woolworth heiress, Barbara Hutton, and Marlene Dietrich.

In London, Dietrich told a reporter, "Wilding claims he cannot live without me and then he goes and fucks *[her exact word]* Elizabeth Taylor. It must be her huge breasts. He likes them to dangle in his face."

After drinks on the outdoor patio around the pool, Wilding suggested that since it was a hot night, Rock might want to cool off by going for a swim. "You don't need to worry about a bathing suit. We're here alone—and we're both men."

By now hip to Hollywood husbands, Rock slowly stripped before him, as Wilding sat sipping his drink and admiring the unveiling.

As Rock would later confess, "It was a bit of a turn-on for me to know that the man married to the most beautiful woman in the world really wanted ME."

After letting Wilding absorb the visual impact of his body, Rock jumped into the pool and swam three laps.

When he emerged, Wilding was waiting with a large pink bath towel.

As Rock later relayed to Henry Willson, "He dried off every inch of my body, paying particularly loving attention to one part of my anatomy. Naturally, I rose to the occasion."

After he'd finished fellating Rock, Wilding rose to his feet. "Don't tell anyone, but Hedda Hopper was right!"

***

Later, when Elizabeth and Rock became confidants, she told him the real truth about where she'd been on the night when she didn't show up to the dinner she'd invited him to. "I've met the love of my life," she confessed. "He's dashing, he's handsome, a great lover, and his name is Kevin McClory."

Later, Rock had lunch with McClory, whom he found attractive and charming and obviously in love with Elizabeth. He said that director John Huston had hired him to work on *The African Queen* (1951), alongside Humphrey Bogart and Katharine Hepburn. He also discussed a close friend of his, author Ian Fleming.

"He has created this wonderful character of a sexy spy, James Bond. The character has unlimited cinematic possibilities. Physically, you would be fantastic as James Bond—if only you could imitate a British accent."

***

Phyllis Gates became angry at Rock when he waited for several days before phoning her. His excuse was, "I've been too busy." When they did get together for a dinner, she found him "a total mess."

"When he wasn't working, he was impossibly bored," she claimed. "He had no hobbies and hated golf. He said he felt like a lumbering jackass on a tennis court. He did like to go to the beach with this wild set of guys. He never introduced me to any of them. Talk about skimpy bathing suits. Those jerks he hung out with might as well have been nude."

"Rock came over about two nights a week, and I cooked dinner for him. He was a meat-and-potatoes kind of guy. On some nights, he called out for pizza. One night, he spent about ten to fifteen minutes talking in the yard to this well-built pizza delivery man. I don't know what was going on."

"Rock had a dual personality—at one point laughing and joking, and then he would descend into a dark mood where nobody could reach him. I think at those times, he was overcome with a self-loathing."

"On rare occasions, he'd invite me for dinner with Mark (Miller) and George (Nader). Those guys liked to play charades, a game I hated. Rock and Nader were actors, and Mark had had experience in the theater, so I couldn't compete against them. It didn't seem fair."

Rock gave up his Shoreham apartment and moved into his new home on at 9151 Warbler Place, off Sunset Boulevard. From his previous digs, he hauled in two mandatory furnishings, his king-size bed, suitable for up to four friendly bedmates, and his hi-fi set. He played records endlessly. "Sometimes he drove me crazy when he would play one recording over and over again," Gates said.

"I don't know where he went on other nights of the week," she said. "He never said anything, but claimed he was conducting business. He did give a lot of interviews to magazines, since he was the hottest property in Hollywood. But he got tired of being asked when he was going to get married."

"One magazine writer after another wanted to know when he was going to settle down with a woman and produce some Rock Juniors running around his new home," Gates said.

She would later claim that she was "terribly lonely" whenever Rock went on location. Henry Willson doubted that. "She spends at least two or three nights a week in the lesbian bars," he claimed. "Rock liked blonde boys, and Phyllis preferred cute little redheads. Piper Laurie would have been her fantasy girl, but Piper walked the straight-and-narrow path."

When Rock came back into town, Willson kept him abreast of Gates' nocturnal adventures.

"I'm glad to hear that," Rock said. "It sounds like we can work out an accommodation in a living arrangement. She can follow her desires, and I can go after what I want. Occasionally, I can throw her a mercy fuck. I don't want to get married to anyone. I'm having too much fun as a single man."

"You've got to stay out of trouble, kid," Willson warned him. "The scandal mongers are after you. You're getting bigger every day. I see an Oscar in your future. But the vultures are circling, wanting a piece of your flesh."

***

Call it an interlude in the life of Rock Hudson. The reason he wasn't spending much time with Phyllis Gates, his excuse for which was that he was usually busy most evenings "with business," was because a new young man had entered his life. He would not remain there for long, but while he did, Rock sustained a passionate involvement with Anthony

Perkins.

He was the son of a famed character actor, Osgood Perkins, who had died when his son was five. Representative of an adolescent archetype typical of movie characters of that era, the handsome young man was seven years younger than Rock.

It all began after Rock had spent a night at the Château Marmont, a popular and relatively elegant choice for off-the-record sexual trysts, a temporary abode for everyone from Greta Garbo to Grace Kelly.

Rock had spent the night with a muscular, exceedingly handsome blonde-haired young man, known only as "Danny." Although he had arrived in Hollywood with the intention of breaking into the movies, the only job he could find was as a gas jockey at a filling station in Santa Monica. Rock had flirted with him while he was pumping gas into his convertible. An arrangement was sealed when Danny said, "I get off from work at ten if you want to drive by. But it's not for free."

"I didn't think it was," Rock said.

"By the way, did anybody ever tell you that you look like Rock Hudson?" Danny asked.

"I get that all the time. I guess so, although I've never seen any of his movies. I'm an architect from Orange County."

At the agreed-upon time, he picked Danny up and drove him to the Château Marmont for the night. Rock later told his friends, "He charged more than the going rate and wanted fifty dollars. He was certainly worth it."

Danny left early the next morning. Rock went down to the hotel's garage to drive away. Across the street from the Château, he spotted a tall, skinny young man who had a certain appeal for him, even though he wasn't Rock's usual type. Rock later said, "I wish all my friends would get it out of their heads that I go only for blonde-haired, well-built studs."

The young man had his thumb out, trying to hitch a ride. Rock stopped his car and asked him where he was going. When he gave the address of Allied Artists Picture Corporation, Rock told him to get in.

"Hi, I'm Tony Perkins."

Rock looked at him carefully. "I've seen you. You played the gawky boyfriend of Jean Simmons in *The Actress* (1953), that George Cukor film. I know Jean."

"One and the same," Perkins said. "I've come to Hollywood to make *Friendly Persuasion* (1956), a Civil War drama, with Gary Cooper. I'll play a gentle farm lad, a pacifist distressed to learn he's forced to enlist in the Army where he might have to kill other men in battle."

"I'm Rock Hudson," he said.

"The whole world knows who you are," Perkins answered. "I've seen six of your movies. You're very good, a real different type from me. I don't think any director will offer me one of your macho roles."

"Do you believe that opposites attract?" Rock asked flirtatiously.

"I don't know, but I sure would like to find out," Perkins said.

"Why don't we meet tonight at around seven at the bar of the Marmont? I could meet you there."

"That would be fine with me, but I've got to tell you," Perkins said. "I'm not a guest there. I can't afford it. Until I get some more money, I'm staying in this janitor's room across the street and sleeping on a cot. Cukor asked me to stay with him, but that's not my scene."

That evening, both men were on time for their rendezvous at the bar of the Marmont. As a means to that end, Rock had to cancel a previous dinner date he'd arranged with Gates. For that promised event, she had already planned a menu and shopped for ingredients.

As Rock later told Henry Willson, "This Perkins kid has a lot of boyish charm. From the moment he hopped into my car, he sent out the right signals, even though he's terribly shy. But once you get him into bed, he's not that shy. In other words, I didn't have to break him in."

"How was the sex?" Willson always wanted to know that.

"Tony has this specialty. He fills his mouth with the hottest water he can stand. He then goes down on you. He calls it a 'hot flash.'"

"He's a beanpole, a bit awkward," Rock said. "Wears a buttoned-down Brooks Brothers shirt and aviator glasses. In some ways, he looks like a New England prep school student. He also reminds me of that little doggie in the window, pleading with a prospective owner, 'Buy me. Buy me.'"

Perkins told Rock, "I'm having a hard time in Hollywood. I find it a giant swampland filled with alligators."

In time, Rock would learn that Perkins was the lover of Tab Hunter, who said, "Tony had a boyish quality. There was a lot of tension lurking in him. He slouched around with his hands shoved deep in his pockets, and he jiggles his foot unconsciously—a nervous twitch."

Rock and Perkins went out on a few dates, but to obscure places, sometimes darkened jazz clubs. "At times, I think we inhabit different planets," Rock said. "He talks a lot about the theater in New York, and the serious roles he wants to play in films. Much of what he talks about bores me."

Mark Miller agreed that Rock's affair with Perkins seemed doomed from the beginning. "He was too New York-oriented for Rock, too East Coast. It was his attitude. Frankly, as Rock told me, he became annoyed at how intelligent he was, his god damn sensitivity you could scoop up with a shovel."

After their sixth night together in two weeks, Perkins warned Rock, "You must not fall in love with me. If you do, I won't always be there for you. You see, I'm not sure I want to live my life as a homosexual. I'm still trying to figure out just who I am, and I'm not there yet."

"Okay, kid," Rock said, not disguising the slight sarcasm in his voice. "I'll restrain myself."

"I quit seeing Tony when I left to shoot *Giant*," Rock claimed. "Over the years, we sometimes ran into each other. No mention was ever made of our time at the Château Marmont. By the time I got to Texas, I found my date book overloaded. Tony later spread the word that I was a male whore. Well, if you have the name, why not play the game?"

Friendly Persuasion opened across the country, mostly to critical acclaim. Perkins received an Oscar nomination for Best Supporting Actor and was hailed as "the new James Dean."

Rock admitted, "I'm jealous and why not? The kid's just starting out, and already he's getting raves."

As time went by, Rock heard more and more disturbing reports about Perkins. One night, a hustler Rock had "rented" told him he'd once tricked with Perkins. "He got into the bathtub and had me piss on him. Easiest twenty dollars I ever made."

The pop artist, Andy Warhol, claimed, "Perkins likes to pay hustlers to climb in through his bedroom window, tie him up, and then rape him."

Author Truman Capote said, "Tony is a sadist. At some point when he has sex with a guy, he wants to see blood. He *IS* Norman Bates."

The gossipy author was referring to Perkins' landmark role in Alfred Hitchcock's classic, *Psycho* (1960). He would be forever identified with that role, much to the detriment of his career.

According to Capote, "For about two years after seeing that horror film, I was afraid to step into the shower without locking my bathroom door and window. I will always remember Tony for his cobra-like smile."

[Anthony Perkins died of AIDS on September 12, 1992.]

Tony Perkins in the final scene of Alfred Hitchcock's *Psycho* (1960)

Chapter Ten

GIANT

A Lesbian Author, A Gay Leading Man, A Sultry Bed-Hopping Violet-Eyed Beauty, & A Bisexual Rebel Bring a Sprawling Saga of Texas and Its Oilmen to the Screen

How Hollywood's Fading Matinee Idols Schemed
for the Role of Texas Rancher Bick Benedict,
& How It Was Eventually Awarded to

ROCK HUDSON

A trio of conflicting alliances, Elizabeth Taylor, Rock Hudson, and cigarette-smoking James Dean.

Hollywood was abuzz with the news that director George Stevens was going to make an all-star spectacular film of the year, the screen adaptation of Edna Ferber's best-selling novel, *Giant*, peopled with an amazing cast of characters living, thriving, feuding, and fighting for love and glory in the Lone Star State.

Now at the peak of his acclaim, California-born Stevens was a deeply respected kind of Renaissance figure with a career that had included stints as a director, producer, screenwriter, and cinematographer. As the head of the U.S. Army Signal Corps during World War II, he'd made newsreels of the Allied landings on the bloody beaches of Normandy. Later, he'd filmed the liberation by U.S. troops of the notorious concentration camp at Dachau.

He'd already won the Best Director Oscar for his 1951 *A Place in the Sun*, starring Elizabeth Taylor and Montgomery Clift, and he'd been Oscar-nominated for his direction of the 1953 Western, *Shane*, starring Alan Ladd and Jean Arthur.

The male lead in *Giant* was the character of Bick Benedict, patriarch of a Texas dynasty, married to a liberated woman, Leslie Benedict. The second male lead was that of Jett Rink, an upstart ranch hand-turned-wildcatter. *Giant* also featured many lesser roles for which established stars would compete.

Bick is a strapping, tall, and handsome Texan, the owner of the sprawling Reata Ranch that's almost the size of New Hampshire. The cattle baron is proud and a bit of a chauvinist in that he treats women like second-class citizens, perhaps granting Mexicans third-class status.

The casting of *Giant* proved a superhuman effort for Stevens. It seemed that every actor and actress in Hollywood wanted one of the three leads. Adding to the frenzy, many minor stars competed for roles in the supporting cast.

The director believed that many actors could effectively be cast as Bick Benedict. More difficult would be finding an actor who could portray the brassy young wildcatter, Jett Rink. Stevens thought that role, with the right actor, might become the highlight of the film.

Ferber described Rink as "a character threatening sexual danger. He was a brute, savage, dirty, belligerent, irresponsible, sadistic, a sullen, loutish kind of boy who bore a grudge

against the world."

"He was all right when he behaves himself," she wrote. "But when he drinks, he goes kind of crazy. He's a kind of genius, Jett is. He'll probably end up a billionaire—or in the electric chair. Put him in a car and he goes crazy."

It was almost as if she were describing James Dean, whom she'd never heard of at the time.

The character of Rink was based on the life of a Texas oilman, Glenn McCarthy (1908-1988), hailed both as "The King of the Wildcatters" and "Diamond Glenn." At the age of eight, he'd been a waterboy for oil drillers, earning fifty cents a day. But he grew up fast, and between 1931 and 1942, he struck oil in Texas nearly forty times. His was a rags-to-riches story, a virtual cliché of a Texas oil millionaire. He became a symbol of Texas opulence itself when he opened the landmark Shamrock Hotel in Houston on St. Patrick's Day in 1949.

Years later, the tyrant, J.R. Ewing, in the hit TV series *Dallas,* was said to have been based on McCarthy.

The most flamboyant oil wildcatter in the flamboyant history of Texas: Glenn McCarthy

Many actors came to mind for the role of Rink, beginning with Charlton Heston and going on to Cornel Wilde, Anthony Quinn, and Jack Palance. Stevens, at least for a day, considered the singer/actor Gordon McCrae, who was known for his musicals such as the lead he played in the Broadway hit, *Oklahoma!*.

To avoid stereotypes, Stevens decided he didn't want to cast actors who had appeared in Westerns before. One night, he came up with the idea of offering the role to Richard Burton. "I thought his voice had the music of his native Wales in it. He would be no Western cliché like John Wayne or Gary Cooper."

As it turned out, Burton was not available. "It would have been a challenge to me

Edna Ferber: She didn't like Texans, and Texans didn't like her.

277

as an actor," he said. "Having a Welshman speak with a Texas drawl."

[Later, after Burton learned that Elizabeth Taylor had been cast as Leslie, he ran into Stevens one night at Chasen's in Los Angeles. In the men's room, he whispered to him, "I'm sorry I wasn't free to play Jett Rink. It would have given me a chance to introduce Elizabeth Taylor to my Welsh dick."]

Unable to get Burton, Stevens reversed his decision and turned to an actor who already knew how to handle a Western. He offered the role to Alan Ladd. Unknown to the director, Ladd at the time was despondent to the point of suicide. He was drinking heavily and living through a personal hell that was exacerbated by fear of a blackmail attempt from a hustler who was threatening to tell all to *Confidential* unless he came up with $10,000 in cash.

Stevens had interacted smoothly with Ladd during the filming of their blockbuster, *Shane.* With that in mind, he sent him the first draft of the script for *Giant.*

Ladd read the script that night and eagerly telephoned Stevens the next morning. "I'm your Bick Benedict!"

Stevens was aghast. He hadn't told Ladd that he wanted him for the lesser role of Rink.

"There's no way in hell I could make a midget like Ladd play a tall, strapping Texan," Stevens told his aides. "Stand him on crates to make him taller?"

Stevens got back to Ladd with, "No, no, Alan, I want you to play Jett Rink!"

"I'm not going to play that shit," Ladd said. "A flamboyantly corrupt Texas oil millionaire who begins life as a dirty little punk? Not for me, buddy."

He hung up on Stevens, but two years later, he told a reporter, "Turning down the role that went to James Dean was one of the biggest mistakes of my career."

What Ladd had rejected, James Stewart went for in a very big way, even though Jett Rink would be a radical departure from the good guys he usually played on screen. Perhaps that change of pace was the reason he wanted to star as *Giant's* corrupt ranch hand.

Nothing illustrated "New Hollywood" vs. "Old Hollywood" better than the rivalry for roles between James Dean and James Stewart. Stevens called it "The Battle of the Two Jimmy's."

Stewart was pushing fifty (actually, he was forty-seven at the time) when he campaigned for the role of Rink. From the beginning, Stevens didn't want him. "If he were twenty years younger, he could have handled it with that drawl of his, his beanpole physique, and his shy, gulping manner," Stevens said. "Being in a Western was no problem. He'd come to personify the American West as much as John Wayne. I could make a younger actor old with makeup, but there was no way I could make Stewart a young man—even with all the makeup in the world."

"It was one of my greatest embarrassments to have to call Stewart and turn him down for the role," Stevens said. "After all, he was one of the greatest of all screen actors. I didn't feel so bad for him, however. After all, he'd just had a hit opposite Grace Kelly in Alfred Hitchcock's *Rear Window* (1954)."

Hollywood reporters went to work trying to cast the movie for Stevens. More and more columnists claimed that the role of Jett Rink should go to Montgomery Clift. Even the director thought the casting would be perfect, except for Clift's personal demons. He was known to be drunk for days at a time, and there were rumors of a heavy dependence on drugs.

When Stevens discussed Clift with Jack Warner, the studio chief said, "There's not only a lethal combination of drugs and liquor, but he's also living the tormented life of a faggot."

Actually, the final decision was made by the studio's insurance underwriters. Warner was told, "Clift is too god damn risky. We won't insure him."

When Dean heard through his lover, Arthur Loew, Jr., that the role of Jett Rink "might suit you as tight as a rubber on your dick," he rushed out and bought the paperback edition of *Giant*, which he read cover to cover in three days. He later told Loew, "That's me, boy. I'm Jett Rink. If I grab that role, I can escape being typecast as a sinister adolescent."

Loew promised to approach Stevens and to pitch him for the role of Jett. To Dean's dismay, he learned that the director had already sent the script to Marlon Brando. Once again, these two Method actors would each be in consideration for the same role. Eventually, however, Brando sent the script back, rejecting the part as "too small."

"I finally decided the role should go to Dean," Stevens said. "The guy had been hounding me for days to get that juicy part. I called him to tell him to transform himself into a Texas ranger. 'The role is yours,' I promised him."

Stevens believed that he would be ideal in the opening scenes, when Jett Rink was a young rancher. But since, during the course of the movie, he has to age into a drunken, battered 45-year-old for the film's final scenes, the director worried that he might not pull them off, even with heavy makeup and graying hair.

Actually, he'd been aware of Dean's acting ever since he'd watched his teleplay, *A Long Time Till Dawn*. He told a reporter, "It was the first time

OF COURSE WE KNOW THAT ROCK HUDSON WAS ULTIMATELY REWARDED WITH THE ROLE, BUT WHO ELSE WAS CONSIDERED TO PLAY BICK BENEDICT IN *GIANT*?

Gary Cooper, Clark Gable, and Sterling Hayden

John Wayne, William Holden, and Alan Ladd

Robert Mitchum, Gregory Peck, and Forrest Tucker

that I ever watched anxiously during the credits so I could find out who this brilliant, sensitive actor was."

After Stevens had *East of Eden* screened for him, he congratulated Elia Kazan. "I found the kid's performance mesmerizing," Stevens said. "I was sorry I lost your boy, Brando. I'd wanted him to play Jett Rink. But getting Dean might be even better."

What appears in the background was just a facade. Built in Burbank and reassembled on the arid flatlands of West Texas, it seems like a mirage in this iconic photo of the impudent millionaire-to-be, as played by James Dean.

"Working with Jimmy will be an experience you'll carry with you to your grave," Kazan said. "I'll say no more."

Stevens, even at this early stage in the compilation of *Giant,* was already hearing rumbling suspicions that Dean might carry some baggage with him. As expressed so colorfully by biographer David Bret: "Jimmy was already being hailed as a lost cause, a cock-hungry schizophrenic, a pre-'Brat Pack' *prima donna*, whose only truly happy, but not entirely sane moments occurred when he was creating merry hell."

***

During his selection of candidates for Bick Benedict, the male lead of *Giant*, Stevens was bombarded with phone calls from William Holden, Gary Cooper, and Clark Gable. At least a dozen other Hollywood males also made their voices heard.

Lying on different massage boards at their gym, John Wayne told Forrest Tucker, "I'm gonna play Bick Benedict."

"Like hell you are!" Tucker shot back, as he lay nude on a board waiting to get a massage. "That role calls for a Texan with a big dick." He then ripped off Wayne's towel. "As you can plainly see, my Moby Dick is six times the size of yours. The role is mine."

Hailed as "The Blonde Viking God," Sterling Hayden said, "Tucker is usually too drunk to play the part. I'm the right size for Bick Benedict...in every department."

Robert Mitchum was also lobbying for the role. After meeting with Stevens, he told his friends, "I've practically got it wrapped up. I can just see the billboards now—ROBERT MITCHUM AND GRACE KELLY STARRING IN *GIANT.*

He was therefore shocked when he learned that Stevens was considering him for the role of Rink instead of Bick Benedict.

Late one afternoon, a call came in for Stevens from Ross Hunter, the producer of *Magnificent Obsession* (1954), the tear-jerker that had starred Rock Hudson with Jane Wyman. "I want you to consider Rock for this part. He's going to become the biggest macho male star since Gable."

Although his decision was not final, Stevens at the time was more or less leaning toward casting William Holden in the lead. He was a big, good-looking guy

George Stevens said, "Rock Hudson was a great guy to work with, but that Dean boy was a real shit."

who'd won the Best Actor Oscar for *Stalag 17* (1953), the same year Audrey Hepburn had won as Best Actress for *Roman Holiday* with Gregory Peck.

Stevens considered uniting Audrey Hepburn with Holden once again in *Giant.* He'd heard that they had been offscreen lovers as well.

If not Hepburn, then Grace Kelly. Holden and Kelly had had great chemistry in *The Country Girl* (1954), which had brought her a Best Actress Oscar. Stevens knew that Holden and Kelly had also been involved in a torrid love affair during the making of the movie, and he felt that together in *Giant,* they'd light up the screen.

Then there was Ross Hunter's suggestion of offering the role of Bick Benedict to Rock Hudson...

***

Brimming over with excitement, Henry Willson phoned Rock with the good news: "George Stevens is considering you as the lead in *Giant.*"

"What's that?" he asked. "Some sci-fi horror shit? What do I play? A fifty-foot monster? No thanks."

"For crissake, dumb ass," the agent responded. "The role is of a big Texan rancher based on the Edna Ferber novel about the Texas oil boom. It's a great part, a real saga. Practically every actor in Hollywood wants the part. Only last week, Stevens interviewed Gregory Peck."

"I've never heard of *Giant,*" Rock said. "I guess I don't read *Variety* enough."

"Our biggest problem is to get your cocksucker friend, Ed Muhl, to allow Universal to release you to Warners. I heard that Jack Warner is willing to pay Universal a million dollars to get you for six months."

"I think I can persuade Ed," Rock said. "I won't tell you how."

"As if I don't already know," Willson said. "This role could bring you an Oscar!"

An appointment was arranged for 2PM the following afternoon in Stevens' office. Rock knew very little about the director, other than he'd helmed two of his favorite movies, *A Place in the Sun* and *Shane*. Willson also told him that he'd directed such big name stars as Katharine Hepburn, Spencer Tracy, and Cary Grant.

Unknown to Rock, Stevens had previously ordered a screening of *Magnificent Obsession*. He'd also ordered *The Lawless Breed* screened for him. In that one, Rock had to age decades during the course of the film. He'd be required to go through an equivalent aging process in *Giant* if he got the role.

Rock arrived right on time for his appointment, and was politely ushered into Stevens' office. He'd dressed up in Western gear that included a pair of red leather boots, blue jeans, a flannel shirt, and a ten-gallon hat.

"You sure look like you could impersonate Bick Benedict," Stevens told him, evaluating him with his eagle eye.

The director and the actor talked for about two hours. Stevens later said, "I was surprised that Rock had not read the novel and knew absolutely nothing about the role. With him, I'd be starting from scratch. I was still leaning toward Bill Holden, but Rock might bring a freshness to it that Bill couldn't."

Before leaving, Stevens told Rock, "If I give you're the role, and I'm not sure that I will, it'll mean you beat out Gary Cooper and Clark Gable. Not bad for a newcomer, wouldn't you say?"

"Indeed I would," He gave Stevens a firm handshake and acted super macho. Stevens promised, "you'll have my decision in two weeks. But I've got to get Universal to release you."

"I'll start to work on Ed Muhl right now," Rock promised.

He phoned Muhl that very afternoon. Instead of his usual visit to his office for a sexual tryst, he invited him to accompany him to Palm Springs for the weekend. Muhl eagerly accepted, making up some excuse to his family.

When Rock returned to Hollywood the following Monday, he phoned Willson. "Ed has agreed to lend me out if Stevens will give me the role. Boy, did I give him a workout. Usually, Ed settles for a blow-job in his office. But I gave him the full treatment in Palm Springs. He claims he's fallen madly in love with me."

As the days went by, Rock was a nervous wreck, waiting to hear from

Stevens. He was disappointed when he read in Louella Parson that Stevens had agreed to cast Holden in the role. He'd read that item at 10AM over his morning coffee, which tasted as bitter as he felt.

But by 2PM, a call came in from Stevens. "You're my Bick Benedict. I just had a quick lunch with Bill Holden. I hated to have to turn him down, but somehow, I think you'd be better. And I just got off the phone with Ed Muhl. He's convinced that after you've made *Giant,* you'll return to Universal a bigger star than ever."

Rock later recalled that on the afternoon his casting was announced in the press, he'd been a nervous wreck and wanted to sweat it out in the steam room at the studio. He stripped down and entered the sauna nude, only to discover an equally nude William Holden lying on a towel covering a slab of marble.

Rock would later describe the encounter to Elizabeth Taylor: "Here I was, the new star of Hollywood, confronting an aging star with my better body, bigger dick, and a more awesome presence. I felt embarrassed for him."

Holden quickly threw a towel around himself and exited from the sauna. On the way out, he said, "I wish you all the luck in the world, kid. Go for it!"

"I didn't gloat," Rock later said. "By then, I was wise to the ways of Hollywood. I knew that when I became fifty, I'd enter some sauna and confront a young, buffed body belonging to some new hotshot being billed as "the next Rock Hudson."

***

After Rock had been cast as Bick Benedict and James Dean as Jett Rink, Stevens set about deciding which of the many actresses in Hollywood should be cast as Leslie Lynnton Benedict.

Many actresses wanted the coveted part. Stevens' co-producer, Henry Ginsberg, "came up with the dumbest casting idea of all," (Stevens' words). "He wanted Marlene Dietrich."

"Are you out of your mind?" Stevens asked Ginsberg. "She could play the Benedict grandmother if such a role existed. The Kraut is as old as Gable, Spencer Tracy, and Gary Cooper. For all I know, she was born at the close of the 19th Century. Besides, she's a Kraut. We want an American girl who grew up on a horse ranch in Maryland."

Producer David O. Selznick phoned Stevens with another idea. He wanted him to cast his wife, Jennifer Jones, predicting, "She'll win another Oscar." She had won in 1943 for her performance in *The Song of Bernadette.*

"I don't have to tell you that Jennifer is the finest motion picture actress in Hollywood."

Yeah, but I'm the god damn director of the picture," Stevens said. "If I cast Jennifer, you'll try to direct my picture. NO WAY. Besides, your wife is too syrupy for the role."

[Ironically, Rock and Jennifer Jones would co-star together in Ernest Hemingway's A Farewell to Arms *in 1957.]*

With Rock, over lunch one day, Stevens discussed his possible roster of leading ladies.

He admitted that he'd already offered the film's female lead to Eva Marie Saint, but she had to turn it down because she was pregnant. "Therefore, my choice was narrowed down to either Grace Kelly or Audrey Hepburn."

"Either of them would be swell," Rock said.

"Swell? Are you kidding? Either of them would be terrific. I tell you what: I'll fly you to New York and arrange for you to meet both of them. Perhaps then you can help me make a final decision, depending on your chemistry with either of them..or both."

***

Rock was leary and more than a bit nervous when he flew to New York to meet with both Grace Kelly and Audrey Hepburn, two of the most talked about actresses on the planet, each at the pinnacle of her film success. Stevens had arranged for him to meet Kelly first.

Ever since the 1952 release of *High Noon* with Gary Cooper, she had been a spectacular draw at the box office. She'd gone to Africa with Ava Gardner and Clark Gable for the filming of *Mogambo* (1953). In 1954, she'd had a banner year, celebrating the release of four major-league films. They included her appearance with Ray Milland in *Dial M for Murder;* with James Stewart in *Rear Window;* with William Holden and Bing Crosby in *The Country Girl;* and the more disappointing *Green Fire* with Stewart Granger.

She'd had affairs with her leading men, and almost broke up Milland's marriage. Author Gore Vidal, who knew her, said, "Grace always lays her leading men. She even managed to get a rise out of "oh, so gay' Cary Grant when they made *To Catch a Thief* (1955).

Grace Kelly...tiring of making love to grandfathers.

285

Age didn't seem to matter to her. Let's face it: Gable and Coop were both born in 1901. They were practically babies from the 19ᵗʰ Century. Several critics have attacked the casting of Grace with all of yesterday's matinee idols."

When she'd read Edna Ferber's *Giant*, she immediately wanted to play the female lead if she could get Dore Schary to release her from MGM, a studio to which she was under contract. *[He had replaced Louis B. Mayer as the studio chief.]* "Schary doesn't like me at all," Kelly had protested.

In New York, during a phone call with Rock, she invited him to her apartment on Fifth Avenue, across from the Metropolitan Museum, at 2PM.

She answered the door herself, and he found her looking lovely, even radiant, dressed simply in a blouse and slacks, with no makeup.

She showed him around her new apartment, which, as she explained, was being decorated by George Stacey, with plenty of input from her. "I'm buying antiques on Third Avenue, a task that's helping me to dispel my demons."

"You have those, too?" he asked.

"For the first time in my life, I'm putting down roots somewhere other than Philadelphia," she said. "In Hollywood, I have acquaintances, but in New York, I have friends."

"I hope you'll come to consider me in that category one day."

"We'll see," she said.

She spoke to him of how important it was to her to play Leslie Benedict. "She's a liberated woman, battling the prejudices of super macho Texans. I want to be more than scenery in a movie. That's what I felt I was in *Mogambo*. In *Green Fire*, MGM is promoting me in ads as a bosomy, green-draped lady. There's no green dress in the movie. Again, I might just as well have been part of the scenery."

He told her how much he admired her work, and that he longed to star in *Giant* with her.

"I recently saw you with Jane Wyman in *Magnificent Obsession*," she said. "You were marvelous and so handsome on the screen. And in person, too. We'd be the perfect combination. You're only four years older than me. I checked your birth date. At least I wouldn't be ridiculed by critics who mocked me for making love on screen to grandfathers."

"I don't know if Schary will release me," she said. "He wants me to co-star in this western, *Jeremy Rodock*, with Spencer Tracy. Back to grandfathers again. Hell, he's even older than Coop and Gable."

She also revealed that she was under consideration for an MGM movie, *Something of Value*, about the Mau Mau uprising in Kenya. "There's a strong role for the leading man and a black actor. The female role? Weak."

[There was a certain irony in the possible casting of Kelly. Had she accepted that role, she would have faced Rock, along with Sidney Poitier, as her co-stars.]

As Rock admitted when he returned to the West Coast, Kelly did not invite him to spend the night. "She ushered me out by seven o'clock. She had to change and make up her face. But at the door, she gave me a long, lingering, and passionate kiss, holding out a promise for our future together."

As he was leaving her apartment building, he ran into David Niven arriving. He nodded and shook hands with Rock. "Discretion is always advised," he said, before stepping into the elevator.

Somehow, gossipy Walter Winchell heard of Rock's visit to Kelly's apartment. In his column, he wrote that "Grace Kelly is getting serious about Rock Hudson"

Before Rock left New York, he phoned Stevens, claiming, "Grace and I would have great chemistry on the screen."

"Too bad," Stevens said. "I just talked to Schary. He's not going to release her. Better hustle your ass over to see Audrey. I've already set it up."

Even though he never got to work with Kelly, she and Rock became friends, and he visited her on occasion after she married Prince Rainier and ruled over the Principality of Monaco.

***

Audrey Hepburn was appearing on Broadway in the Jean Giraudoux play, *Ondine,* based on a 19th Century fable about a supremely sensitive water nymph who comes to earth and falls for a knight, as played by Mel Ferrer, her husband in real life.

Sitting by himself, Rock had sneaked into the theater and had taken a backrow seat after the lights went dark.

To him, the highlight of the play, which he didn't really understand or appreciate, was when Hepburn, in the third act, appeared in a fishnet body stocking, with strategically positioned *faux* seaweed covering her vital zones. A murmur arose from the audience, who seemed to think she was nude.

As pre-arranged by George Stevens, Rock went backstage at the 46th Street Theater and was ushered into Hepburn's dressing room.

After taking her bows, Hepburn came in to greet Rock, extending a delicate hand and beaming at his praise, which was not sincere, for her performance.

He would forever remember his first impression of her. "She was rapturously beautiful with a quick wit and a bubbling personality. She was an exquisite creature, but had absolutely no sex appeal, with a pencil-thin body."

She looked up at him with doe eyes and moved with splendid grace as she went behind a screen to change out of her costume into street clothes. She was like some American princess, and it was obvious why she'd been cast as a princess in *Roman Holiday* (1953).

Audrey Hepburn..."too much of a stretch for me to be riding the range in the Lone Star State."

At one point during their conversation, Ferrer came into the room. He'd recently married her and seemed very possessive, even resentful of Rock's presence. "I have reservations about Audrey going to Texas and playing the wife of a rancher. Texas…I hear that's where they eat rattlesnakes for breakfast. *Giant* doesn't sound like the proper vehicle for Audrey."

"It's a great role for a woman," Rock said, not having read what the part entailed. Ferrer was very dismissive and told Hepburn he'd meet her later. He left without saying goodbye to Rock, and he hadn't even shaken his hand when introduced.

Rock continued discussing the role with her after complimenting her on her serene beauty. "Please," she said. "Ava Gardner and Elizabeth Taylor are glamourous, and I don't fit into their category at all. In fact, I think the character of Leslie Benedict would not look like she's just emerged from a beauty parlor. I would play her as a natural woman, trying to blend into a desert wasteland."

"Perhaps," he said. The more she talked about it, telling him how she'd play it, the more he felt she might conflict with Stevens, who had strong ideas of his own.

He'd read so much about her that he almost couldn't believe he was talking about co-starring with her in a movie. As critic Walter Kerr had said of her stage appearance, "Audrey Hepburn is every man's dream of a nymph." Orson Welles had claimed that she was the "patron saint to anorexics." Director Billy Wilder proclaimed that "she will single-handedly make bazooms a thing of the past. Titism will die."

"Having previously agreed that he would accompany her from the theater back to her hotel, he walked across town and rode the elevator with her to her suite. When they got there, she immediately entered the bedroom and then re-emerged into the living room, where she announced "I'm so sorry, but Mel is exhausted and had to retire."

He was surprised to see the suite filled with what were obviously her personal possessions. "I always travel with twenty large trunks," she said, "containing some of my art and a lot of my personal possessions. I like to make any place I stay, even a hotel suite, a slice of my home. When I'm ready to go, I pack everything back into my trunks and ship them to my next destination."

"How very clever of you," he said. "A real homebody who re-creates her home wherever it might be, even if she goes to Texas."

"Physically, you and I would not be evenly matched on the screen," she said: "I would look like a flat-chested midget standing next to you. I can't imagine how our bodies would fit together during love scenes. You might end up looking like a child molester."

"Perhaps we should rehearse right now and see if it would work," he said.

She smiled indulgently. "I like a man who talks dirty. I'm not as prim and proper as I look. I am always portrayed as a saint. I'm not. By all counts, I should never have made it as a movie star. Perhaps a ballet dancer, not a film star. At each stage of my career, I lacked the experience. The role of a Texas cowgirl would certainly be a bit of a stretch for me."

She offered him a drink, but chose not to have one herself. "I must be frank with you," she said. "What I'm about to say in no way demeans you as an actor. But when I expressed an interest in playing Leslie Benedict, I had the impression that William Holden was going to play my husband. As you know, we've already demonstrated chemistry on the screen. Perhaps you saw us together in *Sabrina* (1954).

"I did indeed," he answered. "The two of you were dynamite. As for you and me, we are both actors, and I assume we could simulate passion not personally felt."

"Well said. Actually, I think you have the most obvious sex appeal of any actor in movies today. Bill's sex appeal is more subtle. If anything, my fear of starring with you is that some nasty critic will say, 'Why would Rock Hudson fall for a *gamin* who looks almost like a boy?'"

He observed her closely, fearing something was wrong. In spite of a hacking cough, she continued to smoke one cigarette after another, as if she were under some kind of intense pressure. He feared her new husband was dominating her unfairly. But she was not one to share the details of her intimate life with a stranger.

As she stood at the door of her hotel suite, wishing him a good night, she promised to phone Stevens and discuss the role with him. "You'll know soon enough if we're going to be a team."

He took her hand. "Until we meet again."

On July 9, *Ondine* closed on Broadway. She'd had a series of two-hour telephone discussions with Stevens, and received a letter from him.

My dear Audrey,

Our talks have been filled with a certain tension, even though I find you en-chantment itself. But I fear it is the kind of enchantment that would be wasted in the wilds of Texas. I respect your views about how you'd play Leslie. How-ever, your point of view is not shared with me. It gives me great pain, but I must withdraw my offer.

***

When Rock heard that it was all but final that James Dean would be cast as the flamboyant wildcatter, Jett Rink, in *Giant*, "he went into panic," according to Phyllis Gates. "He feared that Dean would steal the picture right out from under him."

Rock might be a box office star, but Dean seemed to be getting all the praise after the release of *East of Eden* (1955) based on the John Steinbeck novel. Even before its release, there was a buzz of excitement about the performance that Dean was delivering in *Rebel Without a Cause* (also 1955).

During several tense days, Elizabeth Taylor told Rock she knew that the role she coveted, that of Leslie in *Giant*, was almost beyond her reach. George Stevens, who had directed her so brilliantly in *A Place in the Sun*, "seemed to want every other actress in Hollywood, but considered me chopped liver, I guess. But I want that part, and I'm going for it. Imagine a script that calls for me to transform myself from a beautiful young bride to a grandmother. Oscar, you've got Elizabeth Taylor's name written on your ass!"

When it became clear that Grace Kelly would not be available, Eliza-beth jumped with joy and headed for Benny Thau's office to beg him to have MGM lend her services to Warner Brothers.

There was still one problem: MGM didn't want to lend her. "I had to go on a sitdown strike...well, almost," she said to a reporter. "Dare I say blackmail in certain quarters? No, don't print that...it wasn't exactly black-mail."

Then, she engaged in a big brawl with Thau. "I think he wanted me to play Lassie's mother—or some such shit—in a sequel."

She finally won out, "but my bruises were black. I got no extra money. MGM took it all for the loan-out."

When at last they became convinced that Elizabeth was the right ac-tress for the part, the executives at Warner Brothers offered $250,000 for her services, even though her contract called for her to make only $100,000 a year from MGM at the time. MGM pocketed the difference.

The filming of *Giant* had to be delayed because of Elizabeth's pregnancy, which gave Dean the chance to finish shooting *Rebel Without a Cause* and Rock the chance to complete his work at Universal, where he was called back to reshoot some scenes on *All That Heaven Allows.*

Giant was budgeted at $2 million, a huge sum back then, but it would end up costing more than $5 million.

For Elizabeth, the challenging role of Leslie Benedict would be a landmark in her career, having made "all those rubbish movies" for MGM. Other than being saddled with a new baby, and a husband she wanted to dump (Michael Wilding), she had to also face the newest problem in her life: She'd fallen in love with Kevin McClory.

***

In pre-production since 1953, *Giant* went into full gear in May of 1955. By that time, George Stevens had cast the other (secondary) roles. Once he had signed Elizabeth Taylor, James Dean, and Rock, he went about casting the supporting players. Many actors and actresses wanted to play the character parts, everyone from Ramon Novarro, the star of the silent screen, to Angela Lansbury.

Stevens selected one of the most talented casts ever assembled.

Carroll Baker and Dennis Hopper were cast as the children of Bick and Leslie Benedict. Baker played Luz Benedict II, and Hopper was Jordan ("Jordy") Benedict III.

Baker was both a pinup girl and a dramatic actress, going from playing naïve *ingénues* to brash and flamboyant women. She would be forever identified with Tennessee Williams' thumb-sucking *Baby Doll* (1956), for which she would be nominated for a Best Actress Oscar.

At the time Rock met her, she had married Jack Garfein, a Holocaust survivor whom she'd met at the Actors Studio. To marry him, she converted to Judaism.

Another graduate of the Actors Studio, Hopper, born in Dodge City, Kansas, had just appeared with Dean in *Rebel Without a Cause.* When Rock met him, he concluded, "Hopper is even crazier than Dean. Everybody is raving what a brilliant actor he's going to become. I'm yet to be convinced."

Carroll Baker...shifting alliances

Hopper's fame lay in his future when he made his directorial film debut in *Easy Rider* (1969) with co-star Peter Fonda. He appeared on screen wearing then-radical long hair and a mustache.

With a skeptical eye, Rock later read various appraisals of that film. A reporter, Ann Hornaday, claimed, "With his portrait of counter-culture heroes raising their middle finger to the uptight middle-class hypocrites, *Easy Rider* became the cinematic symbol of the 1960s, a celluloid anthem to freedom, macho behavior, and anti-establishment rebellion."

Dennis Hopper..."Both Jimmy and Rock came on to me."

Cast as Bick's macho sister, Mercedes McCambridge "was one tough dyke," according to Rock. In the movie, she wore a cowboy hat given to her by Gary Cooper.

Mercedes McCambridge with James Dean. "Jimmy and I were best buddies."

She resents Leslie, but dotes on Jett Rink. She had won a Best Supporting Actress Oscar for her role in *All the King's Men* (1949), in which Broderick Crawford had played a notorious Louisiana politician based on Huey Long. She would also be nominated for another Supporting Actress Oscar for her role in *Giant*.

McCambridge had just finished playing opposite Joan Crawford in the campy *Johnny Guitar* (1954). She worked again with Elizabeth as a tarantula mother in *Suddenly, Last Summer* (1959).

A former child actress, Jane Withers played Vashti Hake Snythe, a neighbor of the Benedicts. Her husband in *Giant* was Mort ("Pinky") Snythe, played by Robert Nichols. He was also a singer and dancer, facing a career that would span seven decades. In 1949, he had appeared with Cary Grant in *I Was a Male War Bride*.

As Bick's Uncle Bawley, character actor Chill Wills was a Texan born and bred. He'd become known for supplying the distinctive voice of Francis, the talking mule, in a series of movies. He had a deep Texas twang. "I taught Rock how to speak like a Texan," he bragged.

Rock soon learned that Wills loathed Jews, homosexuals, Mexicans, African Americans, and New Yorkers.

Earl Holliman, a former "Louisiana boy, poorer than a jackrabbit," played Bob Dace, the husband of Judy Benedict (Fran Bennett), the other daughter of Bick and Leslie.

Other roles were filled by the doomed Sal Mineo, cast as the Mexican-American, Angel Obregón II, who goes off to war and comes back in a coffin.

The Australian actor, Rod Taylor, was cast as Sir David Karfrey, the British diplomat, who ends his budding romance with Leslie when Bick arrives on the scene.

After he'd rounded up his "Texas posse," as Stevens called them, he summoned the press to a conference at Warners to present the cast. Both Rock and Elizabeth were chatting pleasantly, as their friendship was blossoming. But soon they realized that Dean was going to upstage the stars. He arrived late.

Rock looked on with disdain as he appeared in a threadbare red flannel shirt, tattered cowboy boots, dirty blue jeans, a Stetson, and a cowhide belt with a large silver buckle that he claimed had once belonged to Roy Rogers.

A cigarette dangled from the corner of his mouth, and he wore very dark sunglasses, which he refused to remove. He told reporters, "I had a hell of a fucking night, and I've got bags under my eyes."

Rock and Dean had a reunion. He hadn't seen him since they'd had a brief fling when he had a very small one-line role in *Has Anybody Seen My Gal?*

He introduced Dean to Elizabeth, and was shocked at how rude he was to her. He'd heard that she had lobbied for Montgomery Clift to be cast into his role.

After the press conference, Elizabeth invited the cast to a party at her home before shooting began.

Sal Mineo...Rock's bedmate.

***

George Stevens rented a bus to take the cast of *Giant* to the hilltop house of Michael Wilding and Elizabeth. She'd also invited Gore Vidal, whom she'd met at

Rock Hudson, Carroll Baker, and Chill Wills. "Each of us liked to lasso different coyotes," Wills said.

293

MGM. He would later become the screenwriter for her movie, *Suddenly, Last Summer* (1959), based on the play by Tennessee Williams.

Vidal had long been intrigued by Rock's screen image and by rumors that he was gay. Although having nothing to do with *Giant*, he solicited an invitation to party within the Wilding home just as an excuse to meet Rock.

From across a crowded room, he was intrigued by Rock in the flesh, and he wanted to get to know this tall, handsome, muscular actor known for his easy-going nature and his sexual magnetism.

Later, Vidal would work on the screenplay for a remake of *Ben-Hur* (eventually released in 1959) in which he'd urge MGM to cast Rock in the lead. The original version of the film had been one of the biggest and most profitable hits of the silent screen in 1925, when the gay actor, Ramon Novarro, played the male lead.

Vidal had heard rumors that Rock had seduced Jane Wyman during the filming of *Magnificent Obsession.*

When he got to talk to Rock later that evening, he found the actor, without pretensions, speaking with candor about his life in Hollywood. Until then, Rock had never heard of Vidal, but Elizabeth told him he was an up-and-coming screenwriter and a novelist who had once written a controversial homosexual novel, *The City and the Pillar.*

At some point, Rock invited Vidal to a midnight pool party at the home of his agent, Henry Willson. Vidal eagerly accepted the invitation.

Once there, the author found at least three dozen young men in various states of dress or undress, including some wearing those flimsy *caches-sexes* ("sex hiders"), popularized on the French Riviera. Others were parading around completely nude.

Rock emerged from one of the dressing rooms wearing conventional bathing trunks and introduced Vidal to Willson. The politically inclined Vidal talked about Margaret Truman with Willson, knowing that he had dated her.

He later wrote, "Henry Willson had a hawkish nose evoking a bird of prey sniffing out his next meal, plus a protruding lower lip that implied a deep capacity for petulance. He's also, like Dorothy Kilgallen, a chinless wonder."

At 2AM, Rock invited Vidal into one of Willson's second-floor bedrooms. Vidal later told his best friend, the set designer and TV producer, Stanley Mills Haggart, "We had to go the oral route. There was no way I was going to let him put that club in me."

Vidal later said, "My relationship with Rock could be broken down into two epochs—the pre-*Giant* period and the post-*Giant* period. We made it together at least three times before he left for Texas. I more or less convinced him that Tennessee Williams and I were going to perhaps urge that he be cast in one of those southern dramas."

After he got back from Texas, I phoned him several times, but he didn't return my calls. However, when he heard I was working on a screen play for *Ben-Hur*, he became friendly once again—how like an actor!"

But that's a story for another day.

Gore Vidal...wanted Rock for *Ben-Hur*.

***

Rock had never heard of Edna Ferber until he was cast as the lead in *Giant*. He later learned that Doubleday had published her epic about Texas in 1952, and it had sold 25 million copies.

The novel had enthralled thousands of Americans, but not many Texans. As John Barkham in *The New York Times* wrote: "Miss Ferber makes it very clear that she doesn't like the Texas she writes about, and it's a cinch that when Texans read about what she has written about them, they won't like Miss Ferber either."

In reference to a saga that sprawled across three generations of sweeping historical changes, critic Robert Tanitch wrote: "The Lone Star State was turned into a symbol, a giant symbol, for all that was the least estimable in America: Its money-grabbing materialism, its thick-skinned self-interest, its profligacy and vulgarity, its low-browism, its snobbery and racism, its narrow-mindedness, its self-satisfied isolationism, and its spiritual impoverishment."

Marghanita Laski in the *Spectator* claimed that "Edna Ferber can always be relied upon for a good story interwoven with fascinating information and sound moral judgments on the shortcomings as well as the virtues of her country and its history."

Born in 1885 in Kalamazoo, Michigan, Ferber was a lesbian who never married. She was the daughter of a Hungarian-born Jewish storekeeper. Throughout her life, she was never linked with another person sexually, although many of the characters she created had passionate involvements. She once told a reporter, "Being an old maid is a great deal like death by drowning—a really delightful sensation when you ceased struggling."

Many of her novels had been adapted to the screen, including *So Big* (1924), for which she won the Pulitzer Prize. Barbara Stanwyck, with Bette Davis in a minor role, had brought it to the screen in 1932, and Jane Wyman had starred in the remake in 1953. Ferber's novel, *Show Boat* (1929), was adapted into a celebrated musical, a tale of life and love along the Mississippi. It was remade twice—first with Irene Dunne in 1936 and again in 1951 with Kathryn Grayson and Ava Gardner.

Cimarron (1929), another of Ferber's novels, had also been a big hit in the movies, starring Richard Dix and Irene Dunne in a chronicle of frontier life in Oklahoma. It was remade in 1960, and starred Glenn Ford.

Even after he was awarded the male lead in *Giant*, Rock still resisted reading the novel, but he paid special attention to the screenplay by Ivan Moffat and Fred Guiol. The two writers had faced the daunting task of reducing the 447-page novel into a 178-page script, which they completed in April of 1955. Shot in Technicolor and released by Warner's in 1956, *Giant* had a running time of 198 minutes.

Moffat was a British screenwriter and the grandson of the famous Edwardian actor and theatrical producer, Sir Herbert Beerbohm Tree (1852-1917). *[A brilliant actor long associated with London's Haymarket Theatre, and an influential visionary in the entertainment industry of his day, he arranged some of the first filmed versions of segments of Shakespearean plays.]*

As such, Moffat was an odd choice as author of a screenplay about Texas. He'd met George Stevens in World War II during his filming of the activities of the U.S. Army in Europe. After the war, Moffat followed Stevens to Hollywood, assisting him at Paramount.

There, he became known for his high-profile affairs, notably with Elizabeth Taylor and later with Lady Caroline Blackwood. His gay friend, author Christopher Isherwood, said, "He's so pretty and bright-eyed, it's no wonder he's in bed with some woman every night."

Another odd choice to adapt Ferber to the screen was Fred Guiol, who had worked at the Hal Roach Studios for several years and was known for directing many of the Laurel and Hardy movies. Although a sort of "odd couple" writing team, Moffat and Guiol would be nominated for an Academy Award for Best Adapted Screenplay of 1955.

In the saga, Bick Benedict was a tall, handsome, Texas rancher who travels to Maryland (actually, Virginia was used in the film) to purchase a prize black stallion. Here, he meets the beautiful daughter, Leslie Lynnton, of the Maryland horse breeder.

At dinner, she (coyly) asks him, "Why aren't you married, Bick?" Fan magazines on both coasts had been asking Rock that very question.

After a whirlwind romance, Bick marries Leslie and takes her back to his sprawling Texas ranch, Reata, which covers nearly 600,000 acres.

Stuck in the middle of nowhere, Leslie immediately runs into conflict with Bick's older sister, Luz (as played by Mercedes McCambridge), who rules Reata like an empire. Luz becomes instantly jealous of her brother's wife, all the while maintaining a special affection for Jett Rink, the hired hand, as a kind of surrogate mother to him.

After settling in, Leslie is appalled at some of the living conditions and lack of medical facilities for the Mexicans who live in the neighborhood. She intervenes, much to the annoyance of Bick. Unlike the women of Texas Bick has known, Leslie is intelligent, high-spirited, and relatively liberated.

Luz dies early in the film after falling from "War Winds," her horse. When she digs her spurs into his flanks, he bucks her off, killing her. In her will, she leaves a small piece of the Benedict Ranch, that portion that belonged to her, to Rink. Bick is unable to persuade Rink to sell the land back to him.

In time, Rink discovered oil on the land he has inherited, and becomes a millionaire. In the meantime, he has fallen in love with Leslie. Bick, too, strikes oil on his land and becomes rich like Rink. Both men revel in their newfound roles as oil barons.

Much to his horror, it's revealed that Luz II, the daughter (as played by Carroll Baker) of Bick and Leslie, is sustaining an affair with the much older Rink. Not only that, but his son, Jordy, marries a Mexican girl, and dreams of becoming a doctor instead of a rancher.

The most dramatic scene in the film occurs near its end, when the *nouveau-riches* of Texas turn out to honor native son Jett Rink. For Dean, playing the character who had reached middle age was his most challenging episode. Stevens was obviously worried on the day the sequence was shot. He feared Dean might not have the skill to pull off this scene even with fake graying hair and makeup that aged him.

It is revealed that for his home state, Rink had constructed an airport and a glamourous hotel (a clear reference for those in the know to Houston's Shamrock Hotel), where the reception honoring him is to be held.

Rink arrives late…arrogant, isolated, and drunk, evoking memories of Howard Hughes. In a belligerent mood, he tangles with Benedict's family, which leads to an altercation.

Bick (Rock) lures him into the vast wine cellars of the hotel, but as he faces Rink, planning to fight with him, he sees he's in no shape to duke it out. Instead, Bick knocks over a rack of wine which, in a domino effect, topples row after row of expensive vintages. "You're all through," he shouts at Rink before storming out.

When Rink finally reaches the podium, where he has been asked to make a speech to the distinguished guests, he'd too drunk. He can only slump over and pass out as the horrified audience heads for the exit doors. Rink now faces the lonely stateroom where only he remains. He slurs through an emotive little speech, but no one is there to listen.

George Stevens selected Marfa, Texas, for location scenes for *Giant*. Positioned within a three-hour drive southeast from El Paso and about sixty miles north of the Mexican border, it was a drought-stricken little town where daytime temperatures sometimes rose to 120° F.

The cast and crew of *Giant* swelled the population of Marfa to 3,000. Many locals rented their homes to them and camped out in tents during the filming.

On Main Street stood one hotel, El Paisano, and two movie houses, each showing Mexican films. Technicians had erected the grandiose façade of a three-story Victorian mansion, the abode of the Benedicts, for $200,000. Built in Burbank, it was shipped east to Texas and re-assembled. Since Marfa lies in a part of West Texas without oil wells, Warners had to erect derricks that gushed ersatz crude.

Stevens set about creating harmony in the town by employing some 200 locals, thereby easing tensions between the town and its invaders. The local newspaper, *The Big Sentinel*, had denounced Ferber's novel, defining it as "superficial and derogatory to Texans."

For the big barbecue scene, Stevens invited a lot of Texas millionaires to participate, winning their support, since they wanted to see themselves in the film, not realizing that it was mocking and satirizing them.

One of the cast members, crusty Chill Wills, knew Marfa well, having made a film there in 1950 called *High Lonesome*, in which he co-starred with John Drew Barrymore.

The saga of *Giant* moves through the rise and failing fortunes of Texans, with side detours into moral dissipation, racism, miscegenation, the oppression of women, oil well conflicts, and the changing social scenario of Texas itself. The movie's subplot involves the war between the longtime Texas aristocracy and the *nouveau riche* wildcatters whose oil wells have "come in big."

Even before shooting began, Stevens assigned Pat Hinkle to help Rock and Dean master the Texas drawl and the "lock-hipped swagger of a wrangler." Nicknamed "Texas Bob," he bonded more with Dean than with Rock. On weekends, he invited Dean to travel with him into the enveloping desert to shoot rabbits and coyotes. Hinkle tried to teach both Dean and Rock rope tricks, which Dean eventually mastered, and which Rock did not.

Rock picked up much legend and lore about Old Texas from this cowboy, who had been born in Brownsville, at the state's southernmost tip.

"We were so poor, we could afford only a tumbleweed for a pet," he told Rock.

Because of the severe housing shortage in Marfa, only a few members of the cast were granted the privilege of living alone, privately and without roommates, in a house of their own. The best of the rented homes went to Elizabeth Taylor. Her husband, Michael Wilding, remained, for the most part, in California with their children.

Rock was assigned lodgings in a rented house that he shared with Dean and Chill Wills. Wills had his own bedroom, and Rock and Dean would sleep in a small room with twin beds. The building's only bathroom was shared by all three of them.

When Rock arrived there, he introduced himself to Wills, who invited him for a beer in the kitchen. The folksy, shaggy-haired actor had gotten his start singing in medicine and minstrel shows before abandoning them and heading to Hollywood.

Soon, he was appearing as a sidekick cowboy in Westerns or else as a backwoods rustic equivalent to the role he'd been assigned in *The Yearling* (1946) with Gregory Peck and Jane Wyman. That same year, he appeared as a roughshod but good-natured "diamond in the rough" with Judy Garland in *The Harvey Girls*.

In his raspy, homespun voice, Wills enthralled Rock and Dean with tales of growing up in Texas, the effect of which deepened his understanding of the character he was playing.

As they talked, Rock felt he was getting close to understanding the mentality of a dyed-in-the-wool Texan. Wills had been born in Seagoville (now a suburb of Dallas) in the hot summer of 1903.

Wills would later describe to Forrest Tucker and John Wayne, among others, what it was like living in small quarters with Dean and Rock. "The walls were paper thin. For the first week or so, those two pretty boys were as happy as a pig in shit. Those creaky bedsprings got a lot of workout."

[In 1987, Elizabeth Taylor told *Star* magazine that, "In the beginning, I thought Rock and Jimmy were two lovebirds. When I was with the both of them, I felt like an uncomfortable third party. But that was to change very soon.]

"Jimmy and Rock were two such very different kind of men and polar opposites as actors," Elizabeth said." It seemed inevitable that their fucking would soon turn to feuding. It was a short honeymoon before war was declared."

At one point, after watching Rock emote in a scene, Dean gave him some acting advice: "The trick is, you've got to put some teeth in your ass."

"Thanks for the tip," Rock said sarcastically. "I'll treasure it always."

While still living with Rock, Dean made calls to one of his best friends, Eartha Kitt, the African American singer. He was always very candid with the woman he called his soulmate.

"During the first week or so, Hudson couldn't get enough of my ass. But he has turned on me. There's nothing real about him. He and Marilyn Monroe are nothing but Hollywood products. If Tinseltown wasn't on the map, Hudson would still be a truck driver, getting blow-jobs at seedy truck stops. I'm moving out!"

On the day he left, he told Wills, "Hudson is trying to queer me and make me his bitch. My ass is sore. He's too big."

Dean resented the enormous buildup that Warners was giving Rock. One press release trumpeted, "The prize acting plum of the year, one which has often been reported in the grasp of a number of Hollywood's top male stars, goes to a dark horse, Rock Hudson, who has never once been mentioned in the spirited competition. Hudson will be co-starring with the beautiful Elizabeth Taylor, with newcomer James Dean in a small supporting role."

During their filming of *Giant*, Rock appeared on the cover of *Life* magazine, headlined as "Hollywood's Most Handsome Bachelor." *Life* speculated about why the twenty-nine-year-old had never gotten married, telling its readers that it was about time he explained to his fans why.

Rock and Dean had completely different approaches to acting. Dean was from the Marlon Brando/ Monty Clift/ Rod Steiger/ Eli Wallach school of (Method) acting, and Rock was from the "erotic hunk of beefcake academy" whose members also included Tab Hunter, John Derek, and Guy Madison.

When Dean was forced to act out a scene with Rock, he referred to his colleague as "a lump of dead wood." In retaliation, Rock called Dean "that little scruff."

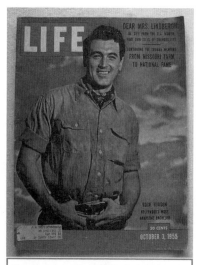

When Rock got to know Elizabeth more intimately, he confessed to her, "I want sex, real man-on-man sex, but I don't go in for this kinky stuff. Dean wants to get into that claw-footed, old timey bathtub we have, and then he

On October 3, 1955, a handsome, dashing Rock Hudson appeared on the cover of *Life* magazine, where he was heralded as the most handsome bachelor in Hollywood, an apt title.

But the question kept nagging him: "Why hasn't he gotten married?"

begs me to piss on him. He also likes me to burn his ass with my cigarette butt—shit like that. I'm not into all this sicko crap."

Rock also told Elizabeth, "Dean is the kind of guy who could make mad, passionate love with you one minute. Then, after he shoots off, he starts complaining about your acting. It's amazing."

After moving out, Dean's behavior around Rock remained erratic. Dennis Hopper was already familiar with his antics, having worked with him on *Rebel Without a Cause*. One day, as the two actors were passing by Rock's trailer, the tall actor came out the door.

"Suddenly, Jimmy ran toward him and leaped into his arms and began French kissing him," Hopper said. "This went on for about a minute or so before Rock pushed him away. Rock retreated back into his trailer. I asked Jimmy why in hell he'd done that."

"Because he's a fairy," Dean answered.

Stevens was well acquainted with Elizabeth, having directed her in *A Place in the Sun*, but he'd never helmed Rock or Dean. He found Rock relatively compliant, "always on the mark, always knowing his dialogue, and carrying out my instructions perfectly."

In contrast, he found his working relationship with Dean much more difficult, defining it as a "rapport of challenge."

Stevens was a perfectionist, demanding that a small scene be reshot sometimes as many as fifty times. Several times, Dean shouted back at him, "I got the god damn thing right on the first take."

Weeks later, when Stevens was editing the final version, he realized that he'd shot 25,000 feet of film, and used only 7,500 feet of it.

In a memo to Jack Warner, Stevens complained about Dean, citing his "tardiness, his unmanageableness, his soaring resistance to reasonable demands, differing from what I have in mind, and his depleting the morale of the entire company. My impression is that *Giant* is a George Stevens Production, not a James Dean Production."

In protest, Dean said, "I can't get my ideas of Jett Rink over to Stevens. I know Jett better than Stevens does. He just won't listen to me. He's trying to keep me from making a truly great picture instead of a mediocre Western."

"The cocky little bastard accuses me of interfering with his work," Stevens claimed. "I accuse him of jeopardizing my movie. I'm the son of a bitch running this show, not some snot-nosed cocksucker from Indiana who takes it up the ass."

During another call, Dean complained to Eartha Kitt about Rock. "How can I create a character working with someone so plastic? I feel nothing from him. I also have no support from Elizabeth in her later incarnation as she's maturing. They are not maturing with me. They are the same from beginning to end; only their hair has been grayed. You can't be an old person by aging your face with makeup and by putting some gray stripes in your hair. You have to imagine old. You have to become old."

"George Stevens wanted everything to be as big as the state of Texas itself," Rock said. "That went from Dimitri Tiomkin's musical score to William C. Mellor's panoramic cinematography."

"George puts me at ease," Rock said. "His effect on me is almost hypnotic. He puts the whammy on you, and after that, you feel you've got to do what he tells you to do. His instincts are always right on target. He never goes around claiming he discovered a star like some directors do. When you're as big as George, you don't need to wear braces on your ego."

Rock told Professor Ronald Davis, "I've fallen in love with George Stevens, and, of course, I don't mean that in a sexual way. He gave me such power as an actor. I've never felt like that before. Through him, I've come to trust my own talent as an actor. He's given me confidence I never had before."

Stevens heaped praise on Rock. "He's going to be big. In *Giant*, he's better than Gable in *Gone With the Wind*. He's every bit as good as Humphrey Bogart and Gregory Peck. Of course, he's not quite Fredric March yet, but then who in hell is?"

Carroll Baker said, "From the start, Jimmy wasn't happy playing a role with third billing after Rock and Elizabeth. He wanted to take some of the wind out of Rock's sails, and that wasn't hard for a trickster like Jimmy to pull off. Rock would rehearse a scene and have it down pat. Then Dean would improvise, come up with something not in the script. Rock hated that. Jimmy was using scene-stealing tips he'd learned at the Actors Studio.

Both Elizabeth and Rock were trained in the old Hollywood tradition. It was a combination of Texas oil mixed with Hollywood champagne, a mixture that didn't blend. Jimmy had a relatively small part, and he was determined to make the most of it."

Rock complained to Stevens: "Dean sucks all the air out of the room. He leaves you with nothing, the selfish bastard."

As filming progressed, Rock noted that Dean was growing more eccentric and irresponsible. He took de-

Elizabeth Taylor, called a "penitent Madonna worshipping at a crucifixion before who else but James Dean, Jesus Christ reincarnate."

light in horrifying Stevens, Rock, Elizabeth, and the rest of the cast by roaring around on his motorcycle, performing stunts on the seat and handlebars.

Once, he lured Elizabeth onto his cycle and went careening at breakneck speeds off along mountain trails across the river from the sets. Rock was talking to Stevens when Dean returned with his passenger. "Elizabeth looked terrified," Rock said.

Stevens confronted Dean. "You keep pulling shit like that, and I'll see that you never work another day in Hollywood."

"Hell with you!" Dean said. "You order me on the set at six in the morning, and then you make me rot in the sun all day and you don't even use me. You can't ruin me. I'm gonna be bigger than you, you motherfucker!" Then he stormed off.

After the first two weeks of filming, Stevens said, "Dean never understands that Jett Rink is only part of the film, not the central figure. In his first two movies, he was the primary focus. But I have two other stars: Rock Hudson and Elizabeth Taylor."

When Stevens attacked Dean's performance in front of Rock, the actor became very sullen, addressing the director as "Fatso." He also began to show up late, once going an entire day without making an appearance and holding up production which, of course, ran up costs for Warners.

Reflecting later on the turmoil he suffered from Dean, Stevens said to Rock, "All in all, it was a headache to work with him. He was always pulling and hauling, and he had developed this cultivated, designed irresponsibility. It's tough on you, he seemed to imply, but I've got to do it my way. From the director's point of view, this is not the most delightful sort of fellow to work with. Anyway, he delivered his performance, and he cracked himself up."

By the end of the shoot, Rock would have completed the third most heralded role of his career, the other two being *Magnificent Obsession,* where he starred as Bob Merrick, and the upcoming comedy, *Pillow Talk,* when he played the sex-obsessed Brad Allen.

***

Within the modest house that had been assigned to her, Elizabeth lived across the street from the lodgings of Rock, Dean, and Chill Wills. After Dean moved out, Rock began to spend his nights with Elizabeth.

He told a reporter from Dallas, "I'm crazy about her. She's the only woman I know who makes me dizzy. She's so much fun, and oh so beautiful. I think she gets tired of people always talking about her beauty and her violet eyes. One night when I was raving about how gorgeous she was, she went to her bedroom and emerged as Minnie Mouse. What a dame!"

Elizabeth recalled, "In Texas, Rock and I hit it off right away. The heat, humidity, and dust in Marfa were so thoroughly oppressive we had to bolster our spirits any way we could. So we stayed up drinking all night and luckily were young enough and resilient enough to go straight to the set in the morning with fresh complexions and with no bags under our eyes. During our toots, we concocted the best drink I've ever tasted—a chocolate martini made with vodka, Hershey's syrup, and Kahlua. How we survived, I'll never know. Between takes the next day, we often had to flee to the honey wagon to throw up."

"Rock and Elizabeth were like kids again," claimed Stevens. "They indulged in a kind of baby talk, and they liked to play pranks on each other, tossing water at each other from our rapidly dwindling supply."

Rock and Elizabeth became so affectionate they started calling each other by nicknames, "Bessie" and "Rockabye."

She told her assistant, Dick Hanley, "Rock has become my second best friend—no one will replace Monty as Number One."

In Texas, Hudson and Elizabeth discovered nachos, devouring them along with a massive consumption of alcohol. "Then they staged belch-and-fart contests," Dennis Hooper said.

On the set of *Giant*, Elizabeth had to battle her weight problem. All those nachos and chocolate martinis she consumed with Rock were obviously fattening. But Stevens complained that she compounded the problem with her midnight snacks, which consisted of homemade vanilla ice cream drenched in fudge and peanut butter, preceded by a series of mayonnaise sandwiches, "which I just adore."

For about ten nights, Rock seduced Elizabeth. Actually, she was the aggressor. She'd later tell Roddy McDowall something he already knew: "Rock is really endowed, and I mean really. As a lover, he's very efficient and eager to get on with it. For me, it's over before it begins. We've decided to be great friends, not lovers. No woman will ever succeed in igniting his enthusiasm in bed, and of that, I'm certain."

***

At first, Jimmy and Carroll Baker sat together whispering conspiratorially. "Our main diversion was making fun of Rock and Elizabeth," Baker later said. "We were cruel and cutting."

During their first two weeks in Marfa, whereas Elizabeth and Rock spent nearly every evening together, Jimmy was frequently seen bonding with Baker, whom he'd known from the Actors Studio in New York.

Rock constantly complained to Elizabeth about Stevens. "He gives Dean all the close-ups, and I'm left out in the cold."

Elizabeth and Rock feared that Jimmy was stealing the picture. Both actors set out to woo Baker into their cabal. In that, they succeeded, and subsequently, Jimmy stopped speaking to her, feeling betrayed.

"Dean got the ultimate revenge," Baker said. "He succeeded in stealing Elizabeth from Rock and me. The dirty rat wanted Elizabeth for himself, and I went into a state of mourning. Elizabeth went off every evening with Jimmy, ignoring Rock and me. The tables had turned."

During the final three weeks of the shoot, Elizabeth temporarily deserted both Rock and Baker. [*Her friendship with Rock would be recharged after Jimmy's untimely death.*]

The film's cast and crew were shown the daily rushes in a battered old movie theater that had closed down with the coming of television. Most of the participants preferred to sit on the theater's ground floor, but Elizabeth and Jimmy usually retreated upstairs, to the balcony, where they were alone. She brought popcorn from her house to share with him.

"They were like two lovebirds," Chill Wills said. "I never could figure out these switch-hitters. One night, Jimmy is taking it up the ass, and on another night, he's pounding pussy. You figure."

Throughout the filming of *Giant*, Elizabeth was plagued with various illnesses, some of which required hospitalization. The first of her health emergencies began in July of 1955, when she developed a severe sore throat and could not deliver her lines. That was almost immediately followed by a bladder infection and thrombophlebitis, a blood clot in a vein of her left leg. She blamed its flare-up on Stevens for "making me wear those tight breeches."

Dr. John Davis examined her and asserted that she suffered from "a congenital anomaly of the spine." To alleviate the pain in her lower back caused by a dysfunctional sciatic nerve, she took heavy doses of Novocaine.

One scene in *Giant* called for Elizabeth "to do a lot of jumping and twisting on a bed." Her always-sensitive back exploded in pain again, as she suffered a ruptured intervertebral disc. She was shot with Novocaine and Hydrocortisone and also given Demerol and Meticorten. "I was a god damn walking pharmacy," she claimed.

Unlike Rock, Stevens didn't believe in any of her illnesses, calling them "psychosomatic." On August 12, she returned to the set on crutches.

Rock was always at her side, and at one point, he was seen carrying her in his arms to her dressing trailer.

Dean had campaigned for Stevens to cast his sometimes lover, Sal Mineo, in the small role of Angel Obregón II, the son of poor Mexican immigrants. Jimmy said, "Sal has the look of the angels." The director agreed and cast Mineo. *[Mineo had no scenes with Dean onscreen.]* They'd been lovers on the set of *Rebel Without a Cause*, and the Italian-American actor retained powerful emotions. He had bought a rebuilt Mercury like the car his idol had driven in *Rebel*. He had also taken to wearing a red jacket similar to the one Dean had famously worn in that film.

"My father made coffins for the Bronx Casket Company, where he was a hand-finisher and later, a foreman," Mineo said years later, in Manhattan, to Darwin Porter. "Near the end of *Giant*, I join the Army and leave Texas, only to be sent back in a coffin. Since my dad made coffins, I tried to get Stevens to use one of his since it was my coffin in the film, but he turned down my offer."

"I did not have to go to Texas because my scenes were shot at Warners in Burbank. But I went there anyway, to see what was happening and with the intention of shacking up with either Jimmy or Rock—or maybe both, if I got lucky."

"When I got there, I found out that Jimmy had moved out of the house with Rock, and that big, muscular son of a bitch was looking for another boy ass. I volunteered and he got mine."

"I didn't think I had a chance, because the rumor was that he preferred tall, blonde-haired and muscular guys who looked like Steve Reeves. Here I was, a 5'8", raven-haired 120-pound, olive-skinned WOP from the Bronx."

"But he really came on to me and invited me to spend the night with him in a bed recently vacated by Jimmy. What a pounding I got that night! He nearly split me open, and I loved it. I got to spend two of the most glorious weeks of my life in bed with Rock until he discovered this cowboy in Marfa. Into that little bedroom went the cowboy. Out went Sal Mineo."

"Jimmy broke off his friendship with me when he heard I'd slept with Rock. We later made up. I'd planned to get involved with him again, since we'd been cast together in the boxing movie, *Somebody Up There Likes Me*. Of course, that was not to happen. Into my life walked Paul Newman instead."

"The last time I saw Jimmy, I almost didn't recognize him," Mineo said. "It was on the Warners lot. I was coming out of the commissary as he was going in. This old man with gray hair, a mustache, and hunched shoulders passed me by. Well, almost passed me by. He stopped and groped my salami. I was about to punch him out when I saw through the makeup. It was Jimmy. He grabbed me and embraced me. He promised to call me real soon."

"It was a day in late September. That phone call never came in. The next thing I heard, he was dead."

***

Stevens called Dean's first shot with Elizabeth on June 3, 1955, "a day that will live in infamy in the annals of cinema history." It was filmed on an open set at the Worth Evans Ranch, which Stevens had temporarily rented. It was the site of the famous scene where Dean was depicted with a rifle hoisted over his shoulders—he called it "my crucifixion pose."

Time and time again, he flubbed his lines. Watching the proceedings, Dennis Hopper said, "That was one nervous queen. He was fucking up big time with another queen (i.e., Elizabeth) of Hollywood."

In front of at least 250 onlookers, Dean ruined take after take by freezing up. A total of sixteen shots failed. Suddenly, he broke from the set and walked over to a wire fence in front of the assembled population of Marfa, some of whom had skipped school to attend this first ceremonial film shoot. As everyone looked on, including Rock, Dean unzipped his jeans and hauled out his penis. Shock waves were heard from the 250-plus crowd as Dean took what he called "a horse piss."

He later told Hopper, "I knew if I could piss in front of some two thousand (sic) people, I could do anything. I'm a Method actor." He returned to the set and did the scene perfectly in one take. Leaving the set, he turned to Elizabeth, "I'm cool, man. It's cool."

Elizabeth later told Dick Hanley, "Jimmy and I in Texas were at first very suspicious of each other. We circled each other like two animals of prey. To him, I was just another Hollywood star, all bosom and no brains. To me, he was a would-be intellectual New York Method actor. We were not prepared to dig each other at all."

"But after a while, we found we were just two human beings, and we became intimate friends that involved tender, loving sex in the beginning, none of that kinky shit that Rock talked about. But, as in the case with Rock, we decided that we could hold each other, protect each other from the cold winds, but as friends, not as lovers."

Evoking Rock's relationship with Elizabeth, Dean engaged in playful games with her. "Two kids on the playground," Stevens called their intimacy.

307

However, during moments of manic giddiness, Dean had a tendency to go too far. One day, he grabbed Elizabeth, picked her up off her feet, and turned her upside down so that her skirt fell over her head, exposing her "unmentionable" regions to photographers.

Rock watched the scene in horror, later telling Stevens, "I wanted to go over and slug him for treating Elizabeth like that."

As she later told Stevens, "Fortunately, unlike Marilyn Monroe on most occasions, I wore my panties that day, or else my twat would be hanging on every bathroom wall in every man's toilet in America."

To Elizabeth, Dean always remained a mystery, but she came to love him. "Sometimes, Jimmy and I would sit up until three in the morning, talking, and he would tell me about his past life, his conflicts, and some of his loves and tragedies. And the next day it was almost as if he didn't want to recognize me, or to remember that he had revealed so much of himself the night before. And so he would pass me and ignore me, or just give me a cursory nod of the head. And then it took him a day or two to become my friend again."

He told Elizabeth, "I would have been shot down by some yellow boy in Korea, but I escaped the draft—blame my flat feet, bad eyesight, and butt-fucking."

Years after her love scenes on and off the screen with Rock in *Giant* were completed, Elizabeth Taylor talked to Peter Lawford about the making of the movie while both were vacationing in the Swiss resort of Gstaad.

"Maybe I should have divorced Michael Wilding and married Rock. We could have made it work, perhaps by inviting a young man on occasion to share our bed."

***

On the set of *Giant* in Texas, a studio underling rushed Elizabeth the latest edition of *Confidential* magazine, which ran the headline: WHEN LIZ TAYLOR'S AWAY, MIKE WILL PLAY. It detailed the night Wilding picked up two female strippers at a club in Hollywood and brought them back to the home he shared with Elizabeth in Beverly Hills. In the scandal's aftermath, Elizabeth told Rock, "Whether it's true or not, a woman can't let an indiscretion break up a marriage."

Of course, considering the dramas of her own affairs, she was in no position to chastise Wilding.

Flying to Texas with their two sons to check up on Elizabeth, Wilding was greeted with a blaring headline—MICHAEL WORRIED ABOUT LIZ AND ROCK.

When Wilding arrived in Marfa, he went to find Elizabeth, perhaps to remind her she was a wife and mother. Not finding her, he was told that she was last seen driving off with Rock.

"Where in hell do you drive to in this one-horse town?" he asked.

Instead of Elizabeth and Rock, Wilding encountered Dean. "I have to be very frank with you," Dean told Wilding. "I've fallen in love with your wife. She's going to divorce you—and marry me. But, remember, you had your chance. Now it's my turn."

On his first night in Marfa, Wilding stayed at Elizabeth's rented home, but she didn't return that night.

He claimed that he was still in love with Elizabeth, "but I found the daily tremors of living with such a volcanic creature more and more difficult. After my failure to make it as a star in Hollywood, I felt like James Mason in that role of a has-been in *A Star Is Born*."

Elizabeth and Wilding quarreled throughout his stay in Marfa, and he soon flew from El Paso back to Los Angeles, taking their two sons with him.

"By then, I knew the marriage was all but over," he said. "All that remained was bringing down the final curtain."

Rock talked briefly with Wilding right before he left Marfa. He denied that he was the man who had driven off with Elizabeth on the night of Wilding's arrival. "Perhaps it was Dean."

Wilding confided, "My marriage is all but over. It was a hell of a ride."

***

For the filming of the opening scenes in *Giant*, which both Ferber's novel and the screenplay had identified as a horse farm in Maryland, Rock had flown to Virginia, settling into Charlottesville.

He left Phyllis Gates behind, asking her to oversee the decoration of his newly purchased home. While in Virginia, he called her only once before he headed to Marfa, Texas, for more location shooting.

He was rarely in touch with her during his time in Texas, and she heard rumors that he was having affairs with both Dean and Elizabeth. In a phone call, he admitted his distaste for Dean, but did confess to spending every evening with Elizabeth. "Don't get the wrong idea. We're just drinking buddies. She can hold her liquor better than me."

During the last week of the shoot, he had Henry Willson arrange Gates' transportation to Marfa. She recalled setting out "to that god-forsaken hole…the heat, the dust, the rotten food…and James Dean, a *poseur* and malingerer." (Yes, those are the words she used.)

In the dry, stifling heat, it was Dennis Hopper who came to meet her at the train station. He said that Rock would hook up with her that evening because he was filming two scenes that day.

As she later said, "Dennis hailed this 'Dust Bowl' taxi, and we headed for El Paisano Hotel, where a room had been reserved for me. I was not to stay at Rock's rented house—that was made clear."

"Dennis dropped me off and made a quick exit," Gates said. "He was a good-looking kid, and I suspect that since Dean had moved out of Rock's house, he'd taken up with Dennis, who was more Rock's type than Sal Mineo."

Before he left her, Hopper confessed, "I want to be an actor, and Rock is encouraging me. He told me I might become 'the next James Dean.'"

Rock arrived at his future wife's hotel at around 6PM, welcoming her to Texas and calling her by his nickname for her, "Bunting."

In her memoirs, she claimed that he immediately hauled her into bed and made love to her. "He was overwhelming, as passionate as he'd ever been."

That was what she wrote. What she told Willson back in Hollywood differed.: "He was in and out so fast I didn't know what was happening. Rock still doesn't believe women are capable of having an orgasm."

Afterward, he took her to this seedy old movie house to sit through the dailies. One scene had been shot forty-eight times, and Gates did not notice much difference. Rock explained to her that Stevens wasted "miles and miles" of film trying to get a scene just right.

After the screening, she was introduced to Elizabeth, whom Gates described as "a flawless beauty."

Elizabeth smiled weakly but politely and then introduced Gates to Dean, who gave her a weak handshake and quickly departed.

Rock walked Gates back to her hotel, but did not come upstairs again because he had an early morning call.

The next morning, as she was leaving the hotel, she encountered Dean spinning a lariat in front of El Paisano. "He invited me for a bowl of hot chili for breakfast."

He seemed angry with both Rock and Stevens, but had nothing but praise for Elizabeth. "Rock is very jealous of me because she likes me more than she likes him. She is torn between the two of us, having to divide her time."

During breakfast, Gates overheard Jane Withers breakfasting at the next table. She told Chill Wills and Mercedes McCambridge, "I don't know why Rock shipped *her* to Texas."

After five days, during which Rock visited her room only one more time, she returned to Los Angeles with him by train.

Upon their arrival at the train depot, a writer for the *Hollywood Reporter* confronted him.

Gates was shocked at how candid he was in discussing Dean. "I didn't like Dean particularly," he confessed. "Chill Wills and I stayed in a rented house with him for a while. He was hard to be around. He hated George Stevens, didn't think he was a good director, and he was always angry and full of contempt for everything. He never smiled. He was sulky, had no manners. It was rough doing a scene with him. Actors should give and take with each other. With Dean, it's all take, no give."

***

Back in Hollywood, Elizabeth continued her friendship with Dean, and also "recharged the batteries in my love for Rock, who was going through a troubling time and needed me."

As influenced by his agent, Henry Willson, Rock was pondering marriage to Phyllis Gates, his lesbian secretary. Rock continued to live with the fear of exposure of his homosexuality.

"Michael and I visited Jimmy at least three times at his little house in San Fernando Valley, and he came to see us," Elizabeth said. "He seemed engulfed in loneliness. The first time he invited us for dinner, he heated up two cans of beans—and that was that. We sat and talked and listened to his music."

On another night, he invited Elizabeth for a ride in the pride of his life, a new Porsche Spyder nicknamed "Little Bastard."

He took her for a spin through Beverly Hills and rode up and down Sunset Boulevard. He turned left onto Hollywood Boulevard, passing Grauman's Chinese Theater. When they passed the theater with its cement castings of the hands and feet of various stars, he told her he was considering having a cast of his erect cock impressed into the cement instead.

The next day, he dropped in at her home to tell her goodbye, claiming that he was driving his Porsche, accompanied by a friend, to the road race at Salinas. The date was September 30, 1955. He would die later that day.

"Whatever you do, Jimmy, be safe—just be safe," she cautioned him.

***

At Warner Brothers in Burbank, Stevens invited some of his stars, including Rock, Elizabeth, and Carroll Baker, to watch the rushes for *Giant*. At one point, there was an urgent ringing of the telephone. Stevens got up to answer it. Then the cast heard him say, "No, my god. When? Are you sure?"

As Baker remembered it, "The picture froze. The lights shot up. We turned and looked at George. The phone dangled in his hand. He was white and motionless. Death was present in that room. 'There's been a car crash,' he said. 'Jimmy Dean has been killed.'"

An hour later, Rock and Elizabeth learned the painful details.

At 5:45pm, Dean and his passenger, Rulf Wütherich, a German immigrant who knew members of the Porsche family, were speeding Dean's Porsche Spyder during their approach to an intersection of Highways 41 and 466, one mile east of Cholame in San Luis Obispo County.

Some reports claimed that Dean was going 120 miles an hour when he saw a black-and-white Ford sedan making a leisurely left turn onto the highway. It was too late for him to stop to avoid a collision with Donald Turnupseed, a student at California Polytechnic.

The student escaped with a broken nose. Dean's passenger, Wütherich, was thrown clean out of the car. He suffered a broken jaw and other injuries, but, unlike Dean, he survived.

In contrast, Dean's head was almost severed from his body. He was DOA at Paso Robles War Memorial Hospital. The doctor who signed his death certificate had called Warner Brothers in Burbank.

As Gates remembered it, Rock spent most of that evening sobbing over Dean's death. "I hated his guts, and I wanted him dead. Now that it has actually happened, I'm filled with remorse. It's like I actually willed him to die."

He confessed to her, "I was jealous of him because I was afraid he was stealing the picture from me. I've been wishing him dead ever since we left Texas. And now he's gone!"

"It was days before Rock overcame his black depression," she claimed.

"I tried everything I could to break through to him. I reasoned with him, I argued that there was nothing to blame himself for. It had been an accident, that's all, a brutal accident. He couldn't be reached. He was overcome by guilt and shame, almost as though he himself had killed Dean. I felt lonely, shut out from his innermost feelings. Frightened, too, because his mood was so unrelenting. What kind of love did we have, anyway, if I was unable to comfort him?"

In the aftermath of Dean's death, Rock rarely spoke of Dean again, claiming, "I don't like to talk about the dead."

In 1983, he gave an interview to Professor Ronald Davis:

"Jimmy was certainly an effective actor. I never worked with an actor who had so much concentration. He had a lot of faults. I didn't particularly like him, but that didn't matter. He was very effective in the role of Jett Rink, especially when he played a younger man."

"I keep thinking of Monty Clift. If he had done the part, he would have acted the bejesus out of the role. Especially as an older man near the close of Giant. *Dean didn't pull it off as an older man. He was, after all, still a kid. I kept thinking if Monty had played Jett Rink, as Elizabeth originally wanted, there would have been nobody else in the movie. He was that brilliant!"*

***

In the aftermath of Dean's death, Wilding sat up until dawn with Elizabeth, "who sobbed the night away." Not respecting her grief, Stevens demanded that she show up for work the next day to shoot a final scene.

"That sod!" she shouted at Wilding. "The heartless sod!"

Although she could barely manage it, Elizabeth arrived on time on the set. She was still given to crying fits, but she stumbled through the scene as best she could, with a lot of help from her makeup artist. At the end of the day, she turned to Stevens. "This is the last time I'll ever work for a god damn ghoul like you!"

The next day she collapsed, complaining of abdominal pains. An ambulance was rushed to the set and, with dome lights flashing, took her to the hospital. She stubbornly remained there for two weeks, delaying some retakes and holding up production, which faced mounting costs because of her absence.

Before his death, during the filming of Dean's final scenes, he had mumbled and in some cases had been virtually incoherent. Stevens called back Nick Adams, Dean's former lover, who could do a perfect imitation of his voice, for dubbing the sound track, where appropriate, of Dean's words.

In Los Angeles, Elizabeth, along with Rock, pressed their hands and footprints into the freshly poured cement in the forecourt of Grauman's Chinese Theater.

In October of 1956, the cast was flown to New York for its world premiere at the Roxy Theater at Times Square.

Elizabeth attended with Mike Todd. She was divorcing Michael Wilding and had fallen for this dynamic producer. Rock came with Phyllis.

By this time, a weird cult had formed around the image of the late James Dean. Thousands of his fanatical fans believed that he had not died, but that he was going to make an appearance at the New York premiere of a movie that had helped to make him famous.

Shortly before the screening, Stevens hosted a reception for the film's cast. The director warned everyone that there might be a problem associated with security at the premiere. The New York Police Department had assigned extra men to the premises, and wooden barriers had been erected to restrain the throngs. Fears involved the possibility of a riot because of the hysteria engulfing the fans, mostly those who had come to worship the deceased actor.

In advance of the premiere at New York City's Roxy Theater, Todd had presented Elizabeth with a pair of ten-thousand-dollar diamond earrings. The crowd outside the theater grew and grew until it stretched for several blocks. As Elizabeth and Todd emerged from their long black limousine, a roar went up as fans pushed against the police barricades.

Carroll Baker and her husband, director Jack Garfein, walked directly behind Elizabeth and Todd. As Baker remembered it, "The fanatic Dean cult were nearest the red-carpet aisle leading into the entrance. Those closest to us were thrashing against the barriers, letting out menacing, eerie cries; they had red, distorted, lunatic-like faces. The sight of them filled me with revulsion a moment before the premonition of danger gripped me."

In front of them, Todd, too, was aware of the danger, and he was shoving photographers and reporters aside to make a pathway to safety for Elizabeth. It was as if he was trying to create a tunnel for her to escape.

Baker then described the pandemonium that followed. "There was an explosion of human bodies across the barricades and a stampede of howling maniacs trampling each other and rushing the actors."

Photographers were knocked down along with their cameras. Some of the fans even knocked over police officers, whose caps often went flying through the air. Jane Withers was nearly trampled to death.

The fans tore at Elizabeth, grabbing her hair and trying to rip off pieces of her gown. Todd yelled at them, "Stand back."

A screech went up. "My earring!" shouted Elizabeth. "I've lost one of my earrings!"

"Forget the god damn earring." Todd shouted at her. "I'll buy you another pair."

The manager of the Roxy appeared, and ushered Elizabeth and Todd into his office, where he offered them a brandy to steady their nerves. Rock joined Elizabeth. His shirt was in shreds, and his jacket had disappeared, along with his wallet.

Rock was horrified at the audience in Manhattan. "For most of the film, there was this loud booing of me on the screen. I was, after all, playing a bigot. I wanted to flee from the theater. But when I took on a worse bigot in a restaurant when he refused to service Mexicans, the audience burst into wild applause for me. Only then did I realize they weren't booing me, but the bigot I had played."

A week later, Todd escorted Elizabeth to the Los Angeles premiere at Grauman's Chinese Theater. Rock arrived with Phyllis on his arm. As promised, Clark Gable showed up with Joan Crawford, and Tab Hunter came with Natalie Wood.

Mike Connolly, the Hollywood columnist, noted the "saddest sight of the evening. A much- humiliated Gable, once the King of Hollywood, showed up. He had lobbied for the role of Bick Benedict, but George Stevens rejected him."

Many guests sympathized with Rock over the loss of Dean. He thanked him.

The last comment Dean had made about him before his fatal car crash was when he told Hedda Hopper, "I'll never make another movie with Rack (sic)."

At the party, Barbara Stanwyck approached Rock. It is not known if she knew that her former husband, Robert Taylor, had made love to him. She said, "Of all the actors, and that includes Elizabeth Taylor, you were the only one who aged gracefully and believably."

Giant became the highest-grossing film in the history of Warner Brothers until the release of *My Fair Lady* in 1964.

***

Most of the reviews generated after the premieres were raves. Posthumously, Dean was singled out for special praise. And, as with all movies, there were occasional attacks.

Isabel Quigly in the *Spectator* claimed, "James Dean more than fulfills his early promise. Small and cocky, writhing, with self-consciousness, with guile, with the pangs of poverty, ignorance, social ineptitude, the quintessence of everything youthful, impossible, impressionable, frustrated, and gauche—and yet a 'personality,' someone that matters beyond his pathetic presence—his performance in the first half (later, he is asked to grow old, and cannot manage it), would make *Giant* worth seeing, even if it were five hours long."

Lindsay Anderson in *New Statesman* and *Nation* delivered this: "The acting is moderately adequate by Rock Hudson, good by Elizabeth Taylor, and virtuoso by James Dean, whose Jett Rink is a willful and brilliant variation on the character he made his own, and died for—the baffled, violent adolescent, rejected by the world he rejects. The middle-aged Jett Rink he could not manage: a matured, hopelessly corrupt character was beyond him."

Time magazine stated: "He created the finest piece of atmospheric acting seen on the screen since Marlon Brando and Rod Steiger did their 'brother' scene in *On the Waterfront.*"

At the time of the Academy Awards in the spring of 1956, *Giant* was a strong contender for an impressive string of other awards as well. It was nominated for Best Picture; Stevens for Best Director; both Dean and Rock for Best Actor; and Mercedes McCambridge for Best Supporting Actress. Only the director, George Stevens, won.

"George deserved his Oscar," Rock claimed. "He is one of the all-time greats, and he had me do things I never thought I could do. He got me to do scenes his way, and made me think it was my idea. If nothing else, he could trick a performance out of me."

Ironically, the award for Best Picture that year went to Michael Todd for *Around the World in 80 Days*. He would become Elizabeth's third husband.

Many critics claimed that Dean would have won if he'd been nominated as Best Supporting Actor, which he really was. He and Rock split each other's votes.

As it turned out, Anthony Quinn won that year as Best Supporting Actor for his performance in *Lust for Life*, and the Best Actor Oscar went to Yul Brynner for *The King and I.* Also nominated for Best Actor, along with Dean and Rock, were Kirk Douglas for *Lust for Life* and Sir Laurence Olivier for *Richard III.*

After the release of *Giant,* Rock was shocked, even humiliated, when a *Photoplay* poll had Dean topping the list as America's number one star, even though dead. Dean was still receiving 8,000 fan letters a week at Warners. "Not bad for a dead man," Rock told Henry Willson.

In 2005, *Giant* was selected for preservation in the U.S. National Film Registry by the Library of Congress. It was viewed as "culturally, historically, or aesthetically significant."

***

There was a footnote to Rock's involvement with members of the cast of *Giant* that did not appear on the radar screen.

Rod Taylor, the Australian actor, was five years younger than Rock and was super macho and devastatingly handsome in a rugged sort of way. When Rock met him, he had divorced his first wife, model Peggy Williams, a union that had lasted for only three years. It would be nearly a decade before he would marry again.

Stevens had cast Rod in the role of a British baron, Sir David Karfrey. From the moment Rock was introduced to him, the two men formed a bond that would last for years.

Rod had been born in a suburb of Sydney, the son of a steel contractor and a commercial artist. His great-great grand uncle, Captain Charles Sturt (1795-1869), survives in the annals of Australian history as a rugged British explorer of Australia's vast interior in the 1820s.

Before coming to Hollywood, Rod had worked in radio and on the stage in his native Australia. He had been the voice of Tarzan on radio, and was frequently seen on the stage at Sydney's Mercury Theatre.

His dream was to go to Hollywood and become a movie star. When Rock met him, he'd already appeared in seven movies, including an uncredited role in *The Virgin Queen* (1955), with Bette Davis, and more prominently as the boyfriend of Debbie Reynolds in *The Catered Affair* (also 1955), once again starring Davis.

Another Taylor, Elizabeth, was the first to learn about Rock's affair with Rod, and soon, he was joining Rock and herself for chocolate martinis. Even when Rod was not needed in Marfa, Rock asked him to come and live with him in the small room vacated by Dean. Elizabeth collectively referred to the two actors as "Rod & Rock."

Both Rock and Elizabeth would help Rod in his future film career. He would be cast in her 1957 *Raintree County*, and Rock would do him one even better, lobbying to have him as his co-star in the 1963 *A Gathering of Eagles*.

Rick chided his agent, Henry Willson, for not signing a contract to represent this Aussie. "With his name of Rod, people in Hollywood will think you named him. Incidentally, Rod is a very apt name for him. He likes it doggie style."

317

After Rock had married and divorced Phyllis Gates, he moved to Malibu, where he lived with Rod along the Pacific Coast Highway. These two "handsome hunks" (as Willson defined them) went for swims in the Pacific whenever they could, which was most of the time.

"In many ways, Rod and I were the perfect match—too bad he liked beautiful models, female, that is," Rock said. "I even advised Elizabeth to give Rod a whirl."

Whether she did or not is not known, but she did get him a key role in her movie, *The V.I.P.s* (1963), in which she co-starred with Richard Burton and Louis Jourdan.

Rod's Malibu "romps" with Rock were not revealed in print until Tia Scalia, as co-authored with Sterling Saint James, released a biography of her well-known sister, Gia, entitled: *Gia Scalia—the First Gia.* But except for his romantic involvement with Rock, Rod, as far as it is known, pursued the life of a rampant heterosexual.

Biographer John Parker noted: "As Rock's close friends knew, he was especially adept at getting a man into bed, regardless of his heterosexual or homosexual qualifications. Cameramen, tough and manly, had been charmed into his rooms and surprised even themselves by having sex with him. When Hudson was on the warpath, using his well-known catchphrase, 'Wanna have some fun?', he was skillful and practiced at luring his quarry."

***

Back in Hollywood after filming *Giant,* Rock cursed the endless questions from reporters about his marital status. He gave his stock replay: "I'm too busy to get married and settle down. Besides, the right girl hasn't come along yet."

An article in *Life* magazine was headlined THE SIMPLE LIFE OF A BUSY BACHELOR—ROCK HUDSON GETS RICH ALONE.

Almost daily, Willson urged him to marry Phyllis.

"I don't love her, and I never will," Rock said.

"Hell with that!" Willson ordered. "Marry her anyway! In Hollywood, they're called lavender marriages!"

Chapter Eleven

ROCK LAUNCHES HIS SEVEN-YEAR REIGN AS KING OF HOLLYWOOD

He's Hailed as the World's Most Desirable Male

PHYLLISGATE!
His Embarrassing Lavender Marriage to his Gay Agent's
Lesbian Secretary

In an ill-fated marriage to mask his homosexuality, Rock Hudson married Phyllis Gates, a well known patron of Hollywood's lesbian bars. Here, they are seen on their wedding day (left) and at home acting like "a pair of lovebirds" a week later.

With the release of *Giant*, Rock became the uncrowned "King of Hollywood," a reign that would last for seven years. He became the number one box office attraction in the world. Almost daily, he received offers to star in major film projects.

A reporter noted: "No man is considered more desirable than Rock

Hudson. His male beauty is without a serious challenger. Robert Wagner is handsome (not a great body); Tony Curtis is sorta cute; and Tab Hunter is a pretty blonde. But Hudson oozes masculinity, a sex symbol of the ages, with a body far superior to the matinee idols of yesterday: Clark Gable, Tyrone Power, Errol Flynn, and Robert Taylor."

Back in Hollywood, Rock asked Phyllis Gates to give up her job as secretary to Henry Willson, but she was enjoying it too much, despite complaints about her meager paycheck.

Rock mocked and trivialized her duties at Willson's office, referring to her as "the pimp's assistant."

He was referring to the young men that Willson supplied on demand to directors or producers. At least that's how it started. He soon learned that not all the powerbrokers wanted a man (or boy) for the night. Many of them preferred desirable female starlets anxious to break into the movies. For a time, Willson had pimped for Howard Hughes, who liked "a boy one night, a girl the next" (Willson's words). Hughes broke off from Willson when, one night, the date Willson had arranged for him arrived with her stern, unfunny mother.

On some occasions, Willson used his young studs, many of them bisexual, to service the wives of producers and directors. Their husbands seemed to approve, as it gave them the chance to run off for the night for nocturnal adventures of their own.

"What Henry was doing was a form of blackmail as well," Phyllis later wrote. What she left out of her memoir was that the duties associated with her job involved rounding up young (female) starlets, some of whom she "auditioned." It was only later, in the final stages of the disintegration of their marriage, that Rock learned that.

Phyllis didn't want to abandon her post in Willson's office because of the intriguing sexual opportunities it afforded her.

When Rock did call Phyllis, it was to invite her to the home of an estranged couple, Elizabeth Taylor and Michael Wilding. "She and Mike are still together, perhaps for the sake of their sons, but they sleep in different rooms," Rock said.

She didn't know how to dress, but he told her it would be informal. She showed up in low heels, slacks, and a blouse. When Elizabeth emerged from the house to greet them, she dazzled her guests in a "lavender gown that matched the color of her eyes and with tons of diamonds" (Phyllis' words). She proceeded to ignore her British husband throughout the course of the dinner that followed.

The following week, Rock extended an invitation to Elizabeth and Wilding to dine at his newly decorated home. It included a home-cooked dinner by Phyllis.

Elizabeth had a hearty appetite, Wilding less so, and Phyllis received many compliments on her cuisine. Elizabeth asked her if she might teach her how to cook. "First, I need to know how to boil water."

Rock insisted on Phyllis preparing her chocolate *soufflé* for dessert, and Elizabeth went into the kitchen with her to see how it was done.

Ed Muhl, now that Rock was back in town, continued to extend favors, sending over an entire case of French vintage wine, compliments of Universal.

While the women were otherwise occupied in the kitchen, Wilding invited Rock to walk out to the pool area with him. At first, he spoke of how his film career had stalled since he'd arrived in America. "My role in that unintentionally funny soaper, *The Egyptian* (1954) was painful for me to watch. No wonder Brando turned it down. My only comfort is that finally, some of my early British films are being shown on American TV. It gives me some dignity to know that many Americans are watching them and will not think I'm a complete ass."

Rock knew what he wanted, and Wilding steered him over to the poolhouse. Rock reached to unzip his pants, but Wilding blocked his hand. "I like to do that myself. It's more thrilling when I reach in and remove the prize."

***

Although Phyllis had moved into Rock's new house, she still maintained her apartment on Fairfax Avenue for her own private affairs. Rock was rarely at home, always claiming, "I have business to attend to tonight."

One afternoon, he drove over to Willson's office, where he found Phyllis typing behind her desk. He presented her with a small box, which she opened to find a white diamond ring with a white-gold band. He insisted she wear it.

Later, she said that at the time it seemed "like a proposal of marriage, but that never came. I was less than thrilled. Was it an engagement ring— or not?"

He began to include her on weekends with two different gay couples— either George Nader and Mark Miller or with John Carlyle and Craig Hill. Both Carlyle and Hill were still under contract to Willson. Hill told Rock that, "Henry has threatened to drop us if we continue to live together, but despite his threats, John and I are going to remain a couple anyway."

Rock was always sending Carlyle and Phyllis out on errands. Hill and Rock would remain by the pool. Rock was continuing his affair with the handsome young actor, but doing so ever so discreetly.

Many of Rock's attempts to merge Phyllis into the gay context of his private life were unsuccessful. According to Phyllis, "In Palm Springs, we couldn't sleep in the same bed, because Rock was a bed hog, crowding me out. I ended up on the living room sofa, listening to Craig and John make love in their bedroom. All I got from Rock was a 'good night.'"

In Hollywood, Rock used Phyllis as "arm candy" (his words) when he had to show up with a female as his date for certain parties. She remembered two occasions where they jointly attended parties at the home of Ronald and Nancy Reagan. "When I came in with Rock, Nancy just doted on him. It was obvious she was mad about the boy. She virtually ignored me."

Even though Phyllis was living with Rock, he remained a mystery to her. She recalled that one morning at 2AM, there was a loud pounding on the door. He got up to answer it, telling her not to get involved. "I'll handle this."

Then she heard angry voices—Rock's and some unknown man's—coming from the living room. Eventually, the front door slammed, and Rock drove off, presumably with the stranger. When he returned about an hour later, he confronted her angry demand, "Who in hell was that?"

"That was some creep who used to be my roommate," he told her. "He's demanding money from me. To get rid of him, I gave him what cash I had in the house and drove him back to Sunset to dump the fucker."

In Mike Connolly's column two days later, she read: "A big, big male star is in the hands of blackmailers, mainly because of one silly escapade."

She knew who that "big, big star" was.

For the next few days, she heard Rock talking privately in his little study at the far side of the living room. He seemed worried, very depressed, and she kept wondering who this blackmailer was and what incriminating evidence he had on Rock. She asked for more details, but he told her he didn't want to talk about it.

Sometimes, there were strange phone calls long after midnight, and on three different occasions, Rock drove off in the early morning hours, obviously to meet someone.

Could it be another threatened exposure in *Confidential*?

The pressure seemed to be building until one night, he took her to dinner at Frascati's. "Let's get married," he urged. "I want to get married right away. Willson has agreed to arrange everything."

She didn't like to be rushed, and wanted to postpone a marriage for a month or so, but he insisted that it was vital for him to be married as soon as possible.

Rushing to make last-minute arrangements, she asked her close friend and *confidante*, Pat Devlin, to be her maid of honor.

For Rock's best man, he phoned his schoolboy friend in Illinois, Jim Matteoni. He had never spoken of him to her before. He was now married to Gloria, and was the father of two children.

"To Jim, I'm Roy Fitzgerald." Actually, that was still his name. As he explained to her, "Rock Hudson is just my stage name. You'll become Mrs. Roy Fitzgerald."

She wanted to invite her parents, but there was no time. She was surprised that he didn't invite his own mother, Kay Olsen. Phyllis later learned that her husband, Joe, was recovering from surgery and would not have been able to come to the wedding even if invited.

She never understood why Rock did not invite George Nader and Mark Miller to the wedding. "He was with them all the time, but for some reason, he didn't want them to see him marry me. When I asked him about it, he said, 'They can read about it in the papers.'"

The date was November 9, 1955, at Santa Barbara. Universal sent a cameraman to record the event for publicity pictures to be released around the world. The ceremony took place at the Trinity Lutheran Church, with the Rev. Nordahl B. Thorpe officiating. Both Phyllis and Rock asked that the word "obey" be removed from their vows.

Willson had selected gardenias as the focal point of the floral arrangements. Phyllis didn't like gardenias, nor did she like the brown dress purchased by Rock for her to wear.

She later wrote, "Henry delighted in pouring rice down my bosom, and Rock was convulsed."

Immediately after the ceremony, Willson placed calls to Hedda Hopper and Louella Parsons. Before that, he coached the newlyweds in what to say to the two leading gossip columnists of Hollywood. The agent also called Jack Diamond, head of publicity at Universal, to release news about the nuptials to the wire services.

As Phyllis later wrote, "Rock was charming, always acting. He did more acting with me than he did at Universal. He never loved me. I know that now."

In her confession, she omitted something crucial: She was not in love with him, either.

Willson had arranged a honeymoon cottage at the Biltmore Hotel in Santa Barbara, overlooking the ocean. She noticed that it had twin beds, the usual double bed having been removed earlier in the day. After dining and a lot of drinking, they retired to the cottage shortly before midnight.

He emerged from the bathroom in his pajamas, told her he was exhausted, and went immediately to sleep.

The next morning, when the papers arrived, virtually everybody in the film industry, many of whom knew Rock, had commented on their union, sometimes anonymously.

Debbie Reynolds, who had "studio-dated" Rock, said, "When he got married, the whole industry laughed itself silly." Rock's former lover, Tony Curtis, referred to the Hudsons as "the odd couple—Rock is gay, Phyllis is a dyke. People will go far to have a movie career in Hollywood." Rock's former leading lady, Arlene Dahl, said, "It was not a marriage. It was an arrangement." Mamie Van Doren claimed, "Rock did what Universal demanded he do."

Before the end of the month, Rock would be making a movie with Robert Stack, his friend and former co-star. Privately, Stack told friends, "If the public knew of all the arranged marriages in Hollywood, they would shit their pants. I mean some really big macho stars have lavender marriages. But I can't name them. I would be sued if I did."

Sheila Britton, a hairdresser and one of Phyllis' former girlfriends, said, "Phyllis told reporters she was madly in love with Hudson. She didn't tell me that. I would have laughed in her face."

Jim Matteoni drove them to the airport that morning. Rock and Phyllis sat together in the back seat. She felt he was putting on a show for his schoolboy friend from Illinois.

Rock kept staring at her wedding band and telling Matteoni how happy he was—"how madly in love." But once Matteoni drove off, Rock became moody and had almost nothing to say on the flight to Miami, where they would spend the night before heading for their honeymoon in Jamaica.

***

Henry Willson's carefully laid plans for Rock's honeymoon ran afoul in Miami Beach when the newlyweds found that no reservation had been made for them at the Saxony Hotel. An insurance convention had booked most of the good rooms, and the desk clerk assigned them to a closet-sized, rawboned bedroom on the eighth floor opening onto garbage cans in the rear. Rock didn't want to call attention to himself, but Phyllis intervened with the desk and got them a larger, oceanfront bedroom.

It was very late at night when they retired, and they didn't go down to breakfast in the café until 4PM the next day. In a rented baby blue Cadillac convertible, they rode up and down the beachfronting highway, taking in the sights.

Over a crabmeat dinner at The Lighthouse, Rock warned her, "When we get back to Hollywood, you'll hear a lot of silly rumors about me, none of them true. I'm a big star now, and as any major film actor can tell you, once stardom comes, so do all sorts of monstrous rumors."

In a memoir far into her future, she wrote that she and Rock spent the night in bed making passionate love. "It was the best ever, not brief and hurried, as it had been. I drifted into a deep sleep, knowing in my heart I had never been so happy in my life."

That's not how Rock remembered the night when he returned to the West Coast. He told Willson, "I felt trapped in this marriage, like a caged animal. I deliberately provoked an argument with her, so I could make up an excuse to be by myself for a walk on the moonlit beach. I didn't return for three hours."

"I went to the gay cruising grounds I'd heard about. Within half an hour, I met a good-looking blonde kid visiting the beach with his parents from New Jersey. He and I got along great, and soon we were heading for a secluded spot on the sands, where we made wild, passionate love. That was the highlight of my honeymoon so far until I reached Jamaica."

The next morning, the ill-suited honeymooners flew to Montego Bay on the northwestern coast of Jamaica. This time, their reservations were in order. Willson had booked a bungalow for them at the Half Moon Club, a luxurious hideaway which lay 6½ miles from the international airport. A hotel limousine was waiting to transfer them to the resort. There was no press to greet them, and their privacy seemed relatively assured. Actually, Rock was not that well known in Jamaica at the time.

After a rest, the honeymooners wandered across some of the nearly 400 acres of grounds before changing into their bathing suits for a swim in the waters off the white sandy beach. It was beginning to resemble a typical honeymoon of any couple from the U.S. mainland.

On their first night at dinner, they headed for the resort's more formal restaurant, where they danced to the music of a Jamaican band. Rock struck up a conversation with a friendly couple at the next table. The playwright, George Axelrod, along with his wife Joan, had read about Rock's recent marriage, and recognized him at once.

He had never heard of Axelrod until he identified himself, claiming, "I have a hit on Broadway. *Will Success Spoil Rock Hunter?*, starring Jayne Mansfield."

"My God!" Rock said. "You wrote that? I'm planning to stop in Manhattan on the way back to Los Angeles just to see it. I have only one complaint: Why didn't you name it Rock Hudson? It would have been my only chance to see my name in lights on Broadway."

"My original title was, indeed, *Will Success Spoil Rock Hudson?* But your damn agent, Henry Willson, threatened to sue me. So I used Tab Hunter's last name instead."

During their time together in Jamaica, Rock and Axelrod became friendly, and he learned more about the playwright. He was becoming known for the crafting of sexually frank farces that included *The Seven Year Itch* (1952), which later became a movie starring Marilyn Monroe.

Axelrod would go on to adapt the William Inge play, *Bus Stop,* into a film, released in 1956, that once again starred Monroe. In it, Rock wanted to play the role of the lovesick cowboy, but was not available at the time of its filming, the part going to Don Murray.

Axelrod would also write the screenplay for *Breakfast at Tiffany's* (1961), based on the novella by Truman Capote. Originally Capote, or so he claimed, had written the story with Rock and Marilyn in mind, but that casting didn't work out, the star parts going to Audrey Hepburn and George Peppard.

There was one final role that Rock lobbied for and didn't get. Axelrod wrote the screenplay for *The Manchurian Candidate,* a thriller, released in 1962, about an assassination and Cold War paranoia. That choice role went to Frank Sinatra.

Over lunch one afternoon, Axelrod said that during the dates Rock planned to be in Manhattan, Moss Hart was throwing a big bash for Broadway actors and for visiting stars from Hollywood. "I'll get you an invitation from Moss, and I'll also get you the best seats in the house to see *Rock Hunter.*"

On their third day in Jamaica, Rock hired a guide recommended by the hotel. Phyllis never knew what his real name was, as Rock nicknamed him "Mandingo." He was as tall as Rock but his physique was much bigger. He could have passed for white, "with eyes as green as emeralds" (Rock's words). He'd been born to an Irish mother in Jamaica and her mulatto boyfriend who had deserted her before childbirth.

On the first day, he took them shopping at the local Crafts Market near Harbour Street in Montego Bay. There, they bought Panama style *jipijapas* straw hats for protection from the fierce sun.

During his honeymoon in Jamaica, Rock chose not to warm the bed of his new bride, but made off with their handsome, well-muscled tour guide, whom he nicknamed "Mandingo."

326

The next day, Phyllis was surprised when Rock suggested that the activities planned for that day would be too rugged for her, telling her to stay at the hotel. He then left with Mandingo in his Jeep.

Together, they explored Doctor's Cave Beach, opening onto the waters where schools of tropical fish weaved in and out. The next day, again without Phyllis, they went rafting on the Great River, followed by another day without Phyllis of horseback riding in the mountains.

She was, however, invited the following day when they returned to the heart of Mo Bay for lunch at the Pork Pit, where they were served the native specialty, jerk pork and jerk chicken. Rock and Mandingo devoured the meal, ordering steamed, freshly caught fish as well. That night, however, Phyllis came down with a case of "*turista*" and remained sick for the next two days.

Commissioning the hotel's staff to look after and care for his new wife, Rock and Mandingo sailed that morning in a rented boat to an almost deserted island just east of the town of Falmouth. There, they found a little beach bar built of driftwood, plus a small native hut rented out for off-the-record sexual trysts. The owner of the bar made daiquiris from the local fruit and cooked jerk lobster for them. Rock and Mandingo didn't return to Half Moon until around midnight. He found his wife in a sour mood and understandably so.

On the last day of their honeymoon, Phyllis woke up feeling better. She heard Rock taking a shower, and, clad only in a black *négligée,* entered the bathroom. Through the translucent shower partition, she saw him lathering every part of his body. Impulsively, she dropped her *négligée* onto the tile floor and opened the sliding partition, stepping inside with him. He was holding up his face to the spray.

When he became aware of her presence, he jumped out of the shower. "It's all yours!" he shouted. "I'm through!"

She later claimed that she felt "lost and abandoned. I was also horrified. It was the last days of our honeymoon, and I wanted to spend it with him. But he and that guide had planned a Jeep ride into the mountains. He'd already had dinner somewhere when he returned to the hotel that night and collapsed into bed since we had an early morning flight to Idlewild in New York."

He had not been completely truthful with Axelrod. Until that invitation came through from Axelrod, he had not planned a stopover in Manhattan.

In Manhattan, since their suitcases contained clothing suitable only for the tropics, Rock took her to Saks on Fifth Avenue to buy clothes suitable for late autumn/early winter in New York, and formal wear for Moss Hart's chic upcoming party.

George Axelrod had alerted the press about the arrival of Rock at the Belasco Theatre to see *Will Success Spoil Rock Hunter?*, whose title had been inspired by his name. He and Phyllis were ushered to the best seats in the house to watch an outrageous Jayne Mansfield, backed up by two talented actors, Walter Matthau and Orson Bean.

In what was defined as a Faustian comedy, the play was about a magazine writer who sells his soul to the devil (incarnated as a larcenous literary agent) with the goal of becoming a successful screenwriter.

Mansfield, as a vapid blonde sex symbol, was obviously impersonating an exaggerated lampoon version of Marilyn Monroe. Her character of Rita Marlowe had "oh-so-kissable lips" and a mammary display of an overly endowed woman who obviously believed in showing more than less.

After the play, Axelrod escorted both Rock and Phyllis backstage to meet the star. She remembered the occasion: "Mansfield virtually tossed those knockers at Rock. Perhaps she'd heard that he'd once fucked her rival, Mamie Van Doren, and she wanted a chance at my husband. When I was introduced to this caricature, she didn't even look at me."

Mansfield wasn't modest during a self-assessment she delivered to Rock: "I'm the toast of Broadway," she claimed. "I hope I said that right. But I have no desire to be a Broadway star. I want to be a movie star, worshipped by millions. You'll lobby your director to cast me as your next leading lady."

"Don't you think the Production Code would censor us?" he asked.

"We certainly would burn up the screen—that's for sure. Just imagine it! Me, as my voluptuous self and you as the male version of me. Of course, we'd need to wear as few clothes as possible. You'd need to do more than take off your shirt. I'd love to see you on camera in a snug pair of jockey shorts—not those stupid boxers most actors wear in movies."

Then she asked Rock if he'd es-

A mammary Jayne Mansfield in *Will Success Spoil Rock Hunter?*

She wanted Rock as her leading man in a series of romantic sex comedies.

cort her to supper at Sardi's after she changed into her street clothes. "You can bring this girl if you must," she said, indicating Phyllis.

In half an hour, she appeared again in a pair of tight-fitting scarlet toreador pants and a very low-cut leopard-skin blouse that revealed all of her breasts down to the nipples. Staggering out the door in a pair of red, backless Springolator heels, she took Rock's arm, bypassing fans *en route* to a taxi. "These fans demand that I dye my naturally brown hair a silvery moonglow, and we have to give them what they want."

Phyllis was a mere tagalong as Mansfield and Rock entered Sardi's. Diners stood up to applaud them. "Tonight, dear, you and I are the most beautiful, most stunning, and sexiest couple in all of Manhattan."

As drink orders were taken, a fan presented Mansfield with the February 1955 issue of Hugh Hefner's *Playboy* (it contained her nude centerfold) for an autograph. "Are you and Rock dating?" the fan asked, ignoring Phyllis.

Mansfield giggled. "I'm a big girl and I have to have a big guy." Then she snuggled up against Rock.

Throughout the supper, it was hard to talk or eat because of the constant interruptions of people approaching their table. Most of them wanted Mansfield's autograph, although a few also requested Rock's signature, too. "There's a problem in playing comedy," she told him. "I've been advised that if I'm too funny, I will no longer be sexy."

"I can't imagine you not being sexy," he said.

"Everyone is always comparing me to Marilyn," she said. "Would you believe that bitch wanted to come to opening night in an attempt to steal my thunder?"

"When it comes to competing blonde stars, I can believe anything," he answered.

"Originally, I tried to find a job as a model in ads," she said. "I was hired by General Electric to pose with a dozen other girls around a swimming pool. But I was fired because I looked too sexy."

At long last, the evening ended, as she made her way out of the restaurant on Rock's arm, with Phyllis trailing behind. Axelrod had arranged for a limousine to take them back to their respective hotels.

Before exiting from the vehicle, Mansfield reached over and gave Rock a long, lingering kiss. "Let's get together in Hollywood. We could become a hot new screen team. The world's sexiest woman starring with the world's sexiest man. Good night, big guy." Then she got out of the car. Never once had she addressed Phyllis.

As the limousine pulled away, she erupted into sarcasm: "What a fun evening *that* was."

The following night, Rock escorted Phyllis to Moss Hart's glittering *soirée*, a social event that had attracted the theatrical and literary elite of Manhattan. Truman Capote was one of the first of the guests to greet Rock and embrace him. Rock seemed distinctly uncomfortable in his presence. As was usual for that time of the evening, Capote was drunk: "So this is the little wren you married?"

Capote then introduced Rock to Bennett Cerf, publisher of Random House. "In about twenty-five years," Cerf said to Rock, "I'd love to publish your memoirs."

Tennessee Williams approached with a long cigarette holder between his teeth. He graciously invited Rock and Phyllis to visit him in Key West.

Rock chatted briefly with Claudette Colbert, who introduced him to Kirk Douglas, who in the future would be his co-star in a movie. Anne Baxter came up to Rock and gave him a passionate kiss. She hadn't seen him since they'd co-starred together in *One Desire* (1955).

A bit tipsy, the English actress/*comedienne*, Bea Lillie, came over to Rock and congratulated him on his recent successes. "If I liked men, I could go for you."

Celebrities paraded in front of him, Oscar Hammerstein telling him, "If you could sing, I'd cast you in a Broadway musical."

Henry Fonda shook his hand. Rock congratulated him on his performance in the film version of *Mister Roberts* (1955). He found this distinguished actor rather quiet, unmannered, and straightforward, just as he was on the screen. Yul Brynner approached and suggested they should co-star in a film together.

From across the crowded room, Marlon Brando came over, at first paying attention only to Phyllis. She later wrote, "What a momentary thrill." She wondered if he'd remember their sexual encounter. He did, indeed, kissing her lips. Then he retreated into a corner of the room, spending the rest of the evening in an animated chat with Rock. After leaving the party, Phyllis asked Rock what they were talking about.

"He discussed his bisexuality with me. Right now, he said he's having this fling with James Baldwin."

"And who in hell is that?" she asked.

"He's this black writer...or something," Rock answered.

***

After he returned to Hollywood, Rock thought that by marrying Phyllis, the attention of the magazines focusing on his private life would let up. It did not. Almost daily, he was called upon by Henry Willson to bring her out to pose for domestic pictures beside the fireplace, at the dinner table, in a cozy living room scene talking as their dog looked on, having a cup of coffee with her arm interlocked with his, even giving her a piggyback ride.

After coping with an almost daily barrage of this, he snapped at one reporter who had asked what he and Phyllis did at night.

In disgust, he said, "I have her strip nude and dance for me on top of our coffee table."

There is strong evidence that marriage changed her, as it did Rock. But he also faced another major change in his life—and that was bigtime stardom.

In *The Life of Rock Hudson*, an American Legends edition by the "Charles River Editors," several people on the staff claimed, "All this renewed attention went to Rock's head. Phyllis quickly learned that she didn't recognize the man she'd married. He insisted on having his way on everything, about where he ate with his friends or who came to visit and at what time. He also started ignoring and even avoiding the press, becoming increasingly secretive about his private life. The only person Hudson didn't try to control was Phyllis; he simply ignored her, often not knowing or caring where she was."

Two months after their marriage, Rock admitted to George Nader and to Mark Miller, "Phyllis was a lot of fun before we got married. From the day of our wedding, that was all over. A white piece of paper changed everything. She became the wife of a movie star. She had to have a new dress for every occasion, and she had to wear mink, not fox. It's not going to work out—I just knew it."

The question remained: What did this married couple do for sex during the short time they were married?

Scotty Bowers, who used to supply studs or beautiful girls to the rich and famous, revealed what was going on in his 2012 memoir, *Full Service*.

He claimed that Rock had been one of his customers since he hit town in the late 1940s. He also wrote, "Phyllis was a very nice person and one hundred percent lesbian. I knew her well. Over the years, I arranged many tricks for her. She liked her female partners slim, dark-haired, and young."

Bowers referred to their marriage as a publicity stunt and defined all those portraits of a loving couple as shams. "They slept in separate rooms and never had anything remotely close to a physical relationship."

He also noted that as time went by, "Rock cruised the streets nightly, picking up strangers for sex and bringing them home."

***

After his honeymoon, back in Hollywood, Rock learned that Douglas Sirk, his director and sometimes lover, had cast him in his next film, *Written on the Wind* (eventually released in 1956), with Lauren Bacall as his leading lady.

The very next day, he received a phone call from Bacall. She congratulated him on his marriage and invited him to dinner. "When I give my next party, I'll invite your wife—forgive me, I forgot her name—but this time, I want to talk business. If you don't mind, please come alone. Bogie, of course, will come down to meet us."

He accepted and left his house the following evening without telling Phyllis that she'd been excluded from the Bogart home.

When he rang the Bogart family's doorbell, he was surprised to see Humphrey Bogart himself—wearing pajamas and a silk bathrobe—opening the door.

Although Rock masked it, he was shocked at the condition of Bogart's health. There had been rumors that he was seriously ill, and he looked like he was deteriorating rapidly. Perhaps it was cancer. He had just completed his last motion picture, *The Harder They Fall* (1956), in which he'd been cast as a washed-up sportswriter horrified by the corruption in the fight game.

Come on in, kid," Bogie said. "Have a drink. All liquor is half price until nine o'clock." He extended a withered hand to Rock, who had just gotten a taste of his host's dry wit. "Betty will be down in a minute."

"Forgive me, who is Betty?" Rock asked.

"Betty Bacall, damn it. That's her real name. Everybody in Hollywood calls her Betty. And don't, for God's sake, call me Bogie—I hate that name. Call me Mr. Bogart or bastard, I answer to both."

Bogie, who had been born in 1899, sat on the sofa drinking and talking to Rock during the waning months of his life. "I'm sorry I can talk only about women," he said. "Not men. I don't go that route, never did, although I had many offers in my early days. The idea of putting a cock in my mouth or taking it up my ass is beyond my wildest fantasy."

"That's good to hear," Rock said, not knowing how to react to such a remark. Was he being insulted by a homophobe?

"Someone told me you once fucked Marilyn Monroe?" Bogie asked.

"You know it's not right for a gentleman to kiss and tell."

"I checked out Monroe's bosom at this event when I sat at the same table with her," Bogie said. "Frankly, I'm not a great bosom man myself. What about you?"

"I admired Audrey Hepburn in *Roman Holiday*," Rock answered.

"I've had enough women in my day," Bogie said. "Bushels of them, even three wives before I hooked Betty. Now I've settled down. Wife number four."

"Number one for me," Rock said.

"Women are funny creatures," Bogie said. "Just because they have that little triangle between their legs, they think they can get away with anything. What do you think?"

"Just because a man has a big cock, some guys think the world is theirs," Rock said.

"You're talking Sinatra, of course," Bogie said.

"Sinatra, among others."

"If you're one of those 'others,' and I suspect you are," Bogie said, "I must warn you. Starring in that picture with Betty, you must keep it zipped up. I feel there has to be a bond between a man and his wife. Even if your partner doesn't know about it, the relationship will be less open if you cheat. Something real between a man and a woman will be broken."

"I'll take that under consideration in my own marriage," Rock falsely promised.

At that moment, Bacall came down the stairs. Rock had never been particularly attracted to her on the screen, but she looked immaculately and enticingly groomed. She greeted him with a charming smile, extending her hand. "Welcome. What have you gents been talking about while I was getting ready?"

"Cocks and pussies," Bogie bluntly said.

"Which category won

Robert Stack (left), Rock, and Dorothy Malone emote in *Written on the Wind.*

Since his first movie role in *Fighter Squadron* in 1948, Rock and Stack had been bosom buddies and rumored lovers. Rock admitted to Stack, "Instead of the clean-living hero in *Written on the Wind*, I'd rather have been cast in your role as the rich drunk and latent homosexual."

out?" she asked, eyeing both men. "I suspect that each of you came up with a different answer."

"Now, Betty, let's not start the evening off being provocative," Bogie cautioned.

Rock learned quickly that Bacall was not one to waste time on idle chit-chat. She quickly got to the point about why she'd invited him here.

"About this *Written on the Wind* thing they want us for," she said. "I've read the script three times. I'm married to Robert Stack, but he has a weak sperm count. You're secretly in love with me. But Stack's sister, Dorothy Malone, has the hots for you. I get pregnant. Stack thinks you're the father. He beats me up, gets a revolver and plans to kill you. Malone struggles with him, the gun goes off. He's dead. You and I flee from Texas."

"You've nailed it," he said.

"Frankly," she said, "Stack and Malone get the scene-stealing roles. I think our characters are rather dull."

Over dinner, Rock had a hard time adjusting to the dialogue in the Bogart household. He didn't know when Bogie was serious or joking.

Rock managed to get through the dinner with a minimum of embarrassment, although Bogie seemed to be trying to make him uncomfortable.

Over a nightcap before departing, Rock once again sat on the sofa in the Bogarts' living room. "I've warned this stud here to keep it zipped up when he makes that silly little melodrama with you," Bogie said to Bacall. "I'm reading between the lines, but I think that the Stack character is really in love with *your* character, Rock. Perhaps if you could throw him a fuck, it might cure his impotency."

"I'll pass that suggestion on to Douglas Sirk," Rock said.

"Bogie stood up, announcing it was time for him to retire. Rock thought the evening was at an end when it wasn't. Bogie asked Rock if he'd escort his wife to the Cocoanut Grove, where she wanted to hear Frank Sinatra sing.

"I'd be honored," Rock said.

"Frankie is a member of my Rat Pack," Bogie said. "Fellow members include Dean Martin, Sammy Davis, Joey Bishop, and Peter Lawford."

"I'm the den mother," Bacall said. "Shirley MacLaine is an honorary member."

During the making of *Written on the Wind*, Rock in private acted as a "beard," concealing Lauren Bacall's adulterous affair with Frank Sinatra.

Rock shook Bogie's hand. "Good luck, kid," he said. "Times are changing here in Hollywood. A whole new group of babies are taking over from us old farts. Some of them are even being billed as the New Bogie. If you run into one of those bastards trying to steal my thunder, tell the shit that the old Bogie isn't dead yet."

"I'll do that," Rock promised.

Rock and Bacall shared a ringside seat sitting through a performance of Sinatra in concert. He joined them at the end of the show, and was exceedingly friendly to Rock, having recalled meeting him back in New York. "Thanks, pal, for bringing Betty tonight. I may need you to do me that same favor on other nights, too."

"Glad to," Rock said.

Rock gave Bacall a kiss on the cheek before exiting, promising to see her on the set of *Written on the Wind* Monday morning.

On the way out of the club, he realized he'd just confirmed a rumor buzzing around Hollywood. Lauren Bacall was having an affair with Frank Sinatra behind Bogie's back. As Rock later told friends, "She has to get it somewhere, I guess."

***

Rock's next film, *Written on the Wind*, became one of his memorable. Filmed in Technicolor at Universal for a 1956 release, it was produced by Albert Zugsmith and directed by Douglas Sirk, starring Rock in the lead, supported by Lauren Bacall, Robert Stack, Dorothy Malone, and character actor Robert Keith.

Robert Wilder, the American novelist, playwright, and screenwriter, had penned the novel back in 1946. Before that, in 1942, he had also written the novel, *Flamingo Road*, which had been made into a film in 1949 starring Joan Crawford.

There had been an initial interest in filming *Written on the Wind*, but it had lingered on the shelf for a decade since the family of tobacco heir, Zachary Smith Reynolds, had threatened a lawsuit. The novel was obviously based on the mysterious death of the young North Carolina man who had married the celebrated and older torch singer, Libby Holman, whose best friend was Montgomery Clift.

[The youngest son of tobacco magnate, R.J. Reynolds, Smith was a 20-year-old playboy, rumored to be a closeted homosexual, who had nonetheless fallen in love with Holman, then a Broadway musical comedy star, and married her in 1931. At an alcohol-fueled July holiday party in 1932, at the family's estate in North Carolina, Holman had announced that she was pregnant. That led to an argument

and accusations. Rumors circulated that Reynolds was impotent.

No one is certain what happened next. A shot was heard, and the staff discovered Reynolds bleeding and unconscious, with a gunshot wound to his head. Authorities initially ruled the shooting a suicide, but the coroner's office later defined it as a homicide. That led to an indictment of Holman and Albert Bailey, a friend of Reynolds and the supposed lover of Holman.

However, the Reynolds family, fearing a scandal and the airing of their dirty laundry, intervened and had the charges dropped.

Holman gave birth to her only child, Christopher Smith Reynolds, nicknamed "Topper," on January 10, 1933. Topper died on August 7, 1950 after falling while mountain climbing on California's highest peak, Mount Whitney.

The tragedy was first brought to the screen in the 1935 movie, Reckless, starring Jean Harlow, William Powell, and Franchot Tone, the husband of Joan Crawford.]

Ignoring threats of a lawsuit, with the justification that a lot of time had passed since the death of the Reynolds heir, Zugsmith, a film producer, director, and screenwriter, decided to defy the Reynolds estate and bring the scandal to the screen once again. The year before, he had produced *Female on the Beach* (1955), starring Crawford and Jeff Chandler. Each of those stars had been lovers of Rock. During the production of Rock's latest film, *Written on the Wind*, Zugsmith was also acquiring the rights to *The Tarnished Angels*, in which he would re-cast Rock, Stack, and Malone.

Based on Robert Wilder's novel, the screenplay for *Written on the Wind* was by George Zuckerman, who had also written the screenplay for *Taza, Son of Cochise* (1954), in which Rock had starred. [*Rock forever after had referred to it as "that god damn movie where I had to play an Indian.]*

From the first rehearsal, it was obvious to Bacall and Rock that their two supporting players, Stack and Malone, had the flashy roles and that they—the stars—had been saddled with parts that were relatively demure, within a drama whose setting had been moved from North Carolina to Texas.

Rock was cast as Mitch Wayne, a geologist who worked for the oil company owned by Kyle Hadley (as portrayed by Stack). They had been best friends since childhood. Whereas the novel had depicted them as homosexual lovers, the Production Code of the 1950s insisted on the obliteration of any depiction of homosexuality on the screen.

In every scene he's in, Mitch (i.e.,

Libby Holman, the most scandal-soaked heiress of the Flapper Age, depicted here "between murders."

336

Rock) is the strong, steady influence, in vivid contrast to Kyle, (Stack) who's the insecure, alcoholic offspring of a Texas oil baron, Jasper Hadley, as played by Robert Keith. He could play any role from a psychopathic killer to a no-nonsense cop.

Spoiled by inherited wealth and crippled by personal demons, Kyle has been told he has a low sperm count and might not be able to father a child. His sister Marylee (Malone) is a self-destructive, alcoholic nymphomaniac who is desperately in love with Mitch, who does not return her love.

The plot heats up when Kyle impulsively marries Lucy Moore (Bacall), a New York executive secretary, and brings her to live at the family estate in Texas. Soon, Mitch (Rock) begins to fall in love with his best friend's wife, Lucy (Bacall). When she announces her pregnancy, Kyle wrongly assumes that Mitch is the father.

Seeking revenge, Kyle takes his pistol and aims it at Mitch. Marylee struggles with her brother over the weapon, which accidentally goes off, killing him.

From the beginning, Rock had been sexually attracted to Stack, who assured him he was straight. He maintained to Rock that a straight man and a gay one could be the best of friends without ever having sex. They often slept in the same bed together and even swam nude together, but Rock had never made any sexual overtures to Stack.

However, that would change during the filming of *Written on the Wind*. Stack invited Rock to drive with him to Palm Springs for the weekend. During a drunken evening there, Stack confessed that he had not been truthful with him, and outed himself as a bisexual, telling Rock, "I want you."

That night, Rock's long-standing sexual interest in Stack was explored, as the two men become lovers, not only throughout the remainder of the filming, but for years to come. The fact that Stack eventually married didn't interfere with their secret trysts. *[In 1956, Stack wed Rosemarie Bowe and would still be married to her at the time of his death in May of 2003.]*

During the shoot, Stack was excited by his role, telling Rock, "I see an Oscar in my future. I've never had such a strong part. If *The Lost Weekend* (1945) brought Ray Milland an Oscar for playing a drunk, my role of Kyle is a sure winner for me."

"Sirk told me yesterday that he suspects my best scenes are played off-screen," Rock said. "I think he's jealous."

Rock had long admired Malone—"She has the most soulful eyes of any actress in the business"—ever since he'd seen her in the classic *film noir*, *The Big Sleep* (1946), starring Humphrey Bogart, in which she'd played a bespectacled bookstore clerk. According to Malone, "I'm loving playing a juicy, drunken soap opera vixen, an oilfield heiress pursuing Texan studs."

Malone had just completed *Sincerely Yours* (1955), in which she laughably played the love interest of Liberace. Around the same time, she was sustaining a torrid affair with the bisexual actor, Scott Brady. Ironically, Rock had seduced both men, two very different types.

Bacall attended a screening of *Written on the Wind's* final cut with Rock, but dismissed the movie, referring to it as "a soap opera beyond soap operas, a masterpiece of suds." Rock, in contrast, liked it.

As one reviewer noted, "Hudson is charming and manly, but he plays a relatively pallid and tame second fiddle to the emotional pyrotechnics and confrontational *tours-de-force* that Stack and Malone pull off."

A usual critic of Rock's films, Bosley Crowther of *The New York Times* wrote, "The trouble with this romantic picture is that nothing really happens, the complications within the characters are never clear, and the sloppy, self-pitying fellow at the center of the whole thing is a bore." (He was referring to Stack, not Rock.)

TV Guide later defined the film as "the ultimate in lushy melodrama, Douglas Sirk's finest directorial effort, and one of the most notable critiques of the American family ever made."

For their efforts, Malone won the Best Supporting Actress Oscar, and Stack was nominated for Best Supporting Actor. To his forever chagrin, he lost to Anthony Quinn for his brief appearance as Gauguin in *Lust for Life* starring Kirk Douglas as Van Gogh.

In 1998, Roger Ebert of the *Chicago Sun-Times* wrote: "*Written on the Wind* is a perverse and wickedly funny melodrama in which you can find the seeds of *Dallas, Dynasty,* and all the other prime-time TV soaps. Sirk is the one who established their tone, in which shocking behavior is treated with passionate solemnity, whole parody burbles beneath."

Written on the Wind was named as the BBC's *Top 100 Films of All Time* and praised as "the quintessential film of the 1950s."

***

As was revealed in several sources, the great French singer, Edith Piaf, had a reunion with Rock when he was filming *Written on the Wind.* He'd met her before in Paris and found her very flirtatious. Originally, he'd gone to see her in Hollywood at the exclusive Mocambo Night club on Sunset Boulevard, a Brazilian-themed venue. The crowd had been sparse the night Rock had attended. Meeting him for a drink after the show, Piaf complained, "The Americans don't understand me and my music. They like

Judy Garland instead. They don't seem to know what to make of a personality like me."

Piaf was in Hollywood during the filming of *Written on the Wind,* and she asked Rock if she could visit the set to watch an American movie being made.

During her stay in Hollywood, Piaf made three visits to the set, as both the cast and crew crowded around her. Lauren Bacall told her, "You are enchanting," and Robert Stack said, "No one sings quite like you. That haunting big voice of yours comes from a remarkably little body."

"Big things come in small packages," she replied, kissing him on the lips. "French men are wonderful lovers, but you and Rock seemed to represent a woman's fantasy of tall American men. They may not be the most skilled of lovers, but they are so beautiful, one hardly complains."

Rock invited her to dinner, which later led to an invitation to visit her for the night in her suite at the Château Marmont.

He was eager to report the events of the night not only to his agent, Henry Willson, but to a few of his best friends, including Mark Miller and George Nader. He was gone all night and didn't return until the next afternoon.

Phyllis had prepared dinner for him the night of the Piaf seduction. He didn't show up and didn't phone, so the next evening, she went out on her own to her favorite lesbian bar and left no note.

In her suite, Piaf spoke in the same raspy, tobacco-hardened voice she used in her memorable songs. He had long collected her records, including his favorites, *La vie en rose,* and *Hymne à l'amour.* She told him, "I am a woman who cannot live without love."

"Edith and I made a Mutt and Jeff combination," Rock said, jokingly. "At 6'4" inches, I towered over her 4'8" frame." He went on to affectionately refer to her as "My Little Sparrow."

He knew that seduction was in the offing with her from the beginning of that evening, and that he would be following a long list of lovers ranging from Marlene Dietrich to John Garfield, whom she'd fallen in love with when she saw him on the screen in *The Postman Always Rings Twice* (1946) with luscious Lana Turner.

She revealed that during World War II, she'd set up residence in a Parisian whorehouse, since it was heated. *[Whereas the occupying Nazis didn't allow Parisians to have heat, they did heat the rooms where the German soldiers seduced the prostitutes of Paris.]*

She told him that she'd been virtually raised by

The Immortal Piaf, symbol and archetype of Paris itself.

whores, since her mother had died and her father left her in her grand-mother's whorehouse when he went off to enlist in the French Army during World War I. "Growing up with whores—who were wonderful to me—I came to realize that when a boy called for a girl, she came to him without complaint. It was expected of her."

Eddie Constantine, an American actor who worked in French films and became one of her many lovers, said, "Men have done her so much harm when she was young, I think she was taking her revenge by seducing all possible men, including me."

She could also be self-deprecating, complaining that the American ideal seems to be Marilyn Monroe. "I'm hardly a sex symbol in this country with my sagging breasts and droopy buttocks."

In response, Rock picked her up off the sofa and held her in his strong arms. "I think you're adorable, and I'm going to make love to you"

And so he did.

***

After a night with Edith Piaf, Rock reported that he would always re-member her tiny, babylike ears—"very kissable." He also said her skin was smooth and almost translucent. "Those hands traveling over my body were so small, so loving. At one point, she kissed the inside of my palms, little birdlike kisses. If I had any complaint, it was a lingering smell of some hor-rible, crude soap she'd used. Apparently, she'd developed a fondness for this particular brand of soap during the Nazi occupation of Paris."

The next morning, over a continental breakfast with French croissants, she said, "I wish I had been a virgin when you took me to bed last night. You are the man I would like to have surrendered my virginity to."

During her whirlwind concert tour of Los Angeles, simultaneous with her involvement with Rock, Piaf also turned to Scotty Bowers, who, when not providing "play for pay" to men and women throughout the entertain-ment industry, also supplied sexual partners of any gender to the Holly-wood elite.

For a period of about a month, Bowers, too, conducted an affair with Piaf, reporting its details within his 2012 memoir, *Full Service*. Rock agreed with Bowers' appraisal of the French singer: "During sex, she would say sing-songy things in French, purring in a low, sugary kind of way."

According to Bowers, "I thought she was sexy as hell. She wasn't ex-actly pretty, but had an interesting face. She was a sad person, who seemed to be on the verge of tears all the time."

Elizabeth Taylor and Montgomery Clift were co-starring together in *Raintree County* (1957), which was MGM's attempt to come up with a hit equivalent to *Gone With the Wind* (1939). In it, Clift played a small-town Hoosier who makes the mistake of marrying a Southern belle right before the outbreak of the Civil War.

In Los Angeles, the afternoon of May 12, 1956, had been hot and sweaty. At the Hudson home, Phyllis was filled with complaints: "You never empty the ashtray, and you drop your clothes all over the house, and I have to pick up after you. You don't shower enough. Your armpits smell. Also, you don't brush your teeth. You want them to look yellow in Technicolor?"

That final remark inspired him to rise from the sofa and brush his teeth.

The most frequent of her constant complaints focused on her claim that he gave her only a hundred dollars a week, with the understanding that he expected it to pay not only for their food, but all her personal needs, too, including dry cleaning and hairdressing.

Rock was clearly bored, but he perked up when a call came in from Elizabeth. Spontaneously, with very little advance notice, she had decided to host a dinner party whose menu would consist exclusively of take-out food. "Michael (Wilding) has been lying on the sofa all afternoon complaining of pains in his lower back. I told him I'm the only one entitled to back pains. Actually, he gives me a pain in the ass."

"I think Monty and his lover, Kevin McCarthy, are coming, and I've invited Edward Dmytryk, our director on *Raintree.* J. Edgar Hoover will probably have us investigated as commies for hanging out with him. Of course, your wife is invited, too," she said. "What's the name again of that dear little thing?"

She lowered her voice. "I have a secret to share. I'm also inviting this handsome gay priest, Father George Long. He told me he'd more or less fallen in love with Monty watching him play a priest in *I Confess* (1953). He's a hunk. His favorite word is 'fuck.' If you play it right, I think you would go for him more than Monty."

She had phoned Clift three times that day, begging him to come to her party, even though he didn't want to. He complained that the road to her home was too dangerous to navigate at night.

At MGM, Dore Schary, the studio's chief, informed his assistant, Benny Thau, "I don't want Monty to become another roadkill casualty like James Dean. While he's making *Raintree County,* hire a chauffeur for him, a full-time driver for our druggie star."

But on the night of Elizabeth's house party, Clift had dismissed his driver because he did not plan on going out that evening.

As regards the dangerous access to her house, Elizabeth agreed with Clift, admitting "I live in a crow's nest with a murderous drive up to it, a real cork-twister."

McCarthy was in Hollywood filming what later became a cult sci-fi classic, *Invasion of the Body Snatchers* (1956).

All of them gathered at Elizabeth's party, where Clift and Rock agreed she was serving "piss-warm, pussy pink rosé," between recordings by Frank Sinatra and Nat King Cole.

The gay priest didn't show up that night. Elizabeth told her guests, "Monty and I look just gorgeous in *Raintree County*,"

Later, on the terrace with Rock, she gossiped about Robert Stack, with whom he had starred in *Written on the Wind*. "I had him, darling, before you got him," she confessed. When Clift and Rock talked privately in the kitchen, Clift told him, "I didn't want to come here tonight. I'm tired, I'm depressed, and I take medication to make me sleep. I haven't slept much in the last four nights. I can't hear any more about the troubles those two are having in their marriages. Bessie Mae pours out all these complaints against Michael, and then I get an earful from him about what a bad wife and mother she is."

Phyllis later claimed, "The party was not a success. Elizabeth and Rock ignored me, having their private jokes. Monty appeared drugged and out of it. Wilding never got up off the sofa, because of his bad back. McCarthy told me he was a serious actor but needed the money so he made this 'silly little science fiction thriller.'"

According to Phyllis, "At one point, Clift got into an argument with Dmytryk, claiming he had cut three brilliant scenes which he'd improvised and which were not part of the script. I felt like I'd stumbled into the wrong gathering. I was just extra baggage Rock hauled in."

Clift was the first to announce that he was "dead tired" and was leaving. McCarthy also claimed he had an early plane to catch and needed to depart. All the guests thanked Elizabeth, and Rock followed the two actors out the door, planning, at Elizabeth's urging, to return for a nightcap.

Outside in the driveway, Rock urged

Kevin McCarthy with Dana Wynter as they try to escape having their bodies kidnapped in *Invasion of the Body Snatchers* (1956).

Clift to get into his back seat and let him drive him off the mountain back to his home on Dawn Ridge Road. But Clift refused, saying, "I am perfectly able driving myself."

"I was tempted to slug him and throw him into the back seat and drive him home anyway," Rock said. "I spent years regretting my decision not to do that."

Clift appealed to McCarthy to guide the way for him. "Otherwise, I'll be driving in circles all night." His friend agreed, but loudly warned Clift not to drive "too closely on my tail."

McCarthy later recalled what happened on that fateful night: "I looked into my rearview mirror, and I saw Monty approaching too close to my vehicle. I thought he was playing chicken with me. I put my foot on the gas and went faster when his own car seemed almost on top of me. We both made the first turn, but the next one was treacherous. We were careening, swerving, and screeching. There were no streetlights. I saw his car weave from one side of the road to the other. Then I heard this terrible crash. A cloud of dust appeared in my rearview mirror."

Braking and then parking off to the side, McCarthy got out of his car and rushed to the scene of the accident, where he discovered his friend had crashed into a telephone pole. His Chevrolet, as he described it, was "an accordion-pleated mess."

He peered into the dark interior, noting that the motor was still running. Reaching through the front driver's-side window, he managed to turn off the ignition. He smelled leaking gasoline, and feared that the car would burst into flames.

In the dark, he could not see Clift's body. Unknown to him at the time, Clift had fallen (or been hammered) into a fetus-like position under the steering wheel.

Incorrectly, McCarthy surmised that Clift had been thrown out of the car, but he couldn't find any trace of it. Meanwhile, the car hung precariously above the ravine.

He desperately needed to get to a phone, but he had noticed that all the houses nearby were under construction and unoccupied. The Wilding home seemed the only one finished. He raced up the hill, panting for breath. Passing through the Wilding family's garden gate, he pounded on the door and repeatedly rang the doorbell.

It was Wilding who answered the door. "Monty's dead!" McCarthy shouted. "An accident!"

"Go home, Kevin," Wilding said. "The party's over." He seemed to think his guest was playing some kind of sick joke on him.

From inside the house emerged a scream. It was Elizabeth. She believed McCarthy. First her friend, James Dean….now, Clift.

***

Elizabeth immediately phoned for an ambulance and placed a frantic call to Dr. Rex Kennamer, a Los Angeles physician known as "the doctor to the stars." Outside, near the base of her house, Rock urged her to stay back, but she refused. "No, god damn it! Monty needs me!"

At the wreckage, Rock tried to pull open the driver's side front door, but it was too smashed in. In the meantime, Elizabeth was able to open a rear door wide enough to slip in and climb over the seat to the front. She became a kind of Mother Courage, cuddling Clift into her arms as Rock looked in with a flashlight.

Clift's head looked like it had smashed into the steering wheel. The windshield was shattered. He was bleeding profusely—so much so that it looked like his face had been halved.

"Rock was the strongest man in our party, and he eventually got that smashed door open, and came in to help me," Elizabeth said.

She had on a pink scarf, and her white dress was blood-soaked. "I remember ripping off this scarf and using it to help stop the flow of blood. All my previous revulsion about blood left me. I held his head, and he sort of came to. He became almost lucid for a moment. Of course, he was still in shock. A tooth was hanging on his lip by a few shreds of flesh, and he asked me to pull it off because it was cutting his tongue."

Later, according to Elizabeth, "Suddenly, he was gasping for breath. He motioned that one—maybe more—of his teeth had broken away and had lodged in his throat. I reached with two fingers and removed the teeth from his windpipe so he could breathe. I was living through the most ghastly night of my life—yes, the most ghastly."

"The damn ambulance must have gone via Idaho, since the driver had gotten lost," she said. "Dr. Kennamer drove up before the emergency crew. He guided Rock in gently removing the body from the car."

By this time, photographers and reporters had been alerted by calls to the police. They rushed to the scene, wanting to sell photographs of Clift with his face a bloody pulp.

Elizabeth yelled to Rock to prevent them from taking pictures and, along with McCarthy and Wilding, he formed a wall to shield the victim from their sight and from their cameras.

As Rock remembered it, "I heard Elizabeth deliver the foulest language I'd ever heard, and I'd been in the Navy during the war."

She screamed, "You sons of bitches. I'll kick all of you in the nuts, you shithead bastards."

One of the photographers had heard that Clift had been decapitated. "I want to get a picture of his head detached from the body." Rock punched him in the nose, bloodying it.

After being guided on a stretcher into the back of the ambulance, Clift passed out. Elizabeth sat by his side, holding his hand and telling him how much she loved him. "By that point, his face had

Wreckage from the car accident that disfigured (and almost killed) Montgomery Clift.

swollen until it was almost to the sides of his shoulders. He looked like a giant red soccer ball."

Phyllis had joined Elizabeth in the ambulance in case she could be of help, whereas Rock, with Wilding and McCarthy as his passengers, followed the ambulance down the winding hillside road.

Edward Dmytryk remained within Elizabeth's home, finally getting Dore Schary on the phone, telling him that production on *Raintree County* would have to be shut down. "At this point, I'm not sure Monty is going to live. If he does, his face will be pulp, and he may never face a movie camera again."

Ever alert to production and costs, the studio chief and the director began discussing a replacement. "You say Hudson was on the scene? He'd look great in a costume picture with Elizabeth. They were fabulous together in *Giant.*"

"Aren't we being a bit ghoulish?" Dmytryk asked.

"I'm running a god damn studio, not a hospital ward for actors who smash up their cars. I knew this could happen. That's why I hired a chauffeur for the damn faggot."

At the hospital, blood-soaked Elizabeth held herself together only until Clift entered the operating room, and then she became hysterical. For comfort, she ignored Wilding and allowed Rock to put his strong arms around her during the horrible ordeal that followed.

"By dawn, all of us left the hospital when we learned that Monty was out of danger," Rock said. "We were told we could visit him the next day, and that his jaws would be wired."

Dr. Kennamer had told them what had happened, claiming "he came close to dying."

As was revealed, Clift suffered acute facial lacerations, a perforated eardrum, four fractured ribs, a split lip, a broken nose, broken teeth, a crushed jaw and sinus cavity, and a severely dangerous concussion.

Elizabeth preferred that Rock drive her home, with Wilding and McCarthy relegated to the back seat.

In the front seat with Rock and Phyllis, Elizabeth turned to Rock. "I want to hide. Monty almost died. I feel so guilty. If I hadn't insisted he come to my house, he'd be asleep in his bed. I know this night will haunt me for the rest of my life."

***

In the immediate aftermath of Clift's accident, Rock had a bitter dispute with Phyllis when he learned she'd talked to the press. Somehow, as it turned out, she'd spoken to a reporter. Perhaps without meaning to, she'd confided that Clift had not wanted to drive up that tortuous road to Elizabeth's house on the night of the accident. Phyllis was not trained to deal with cagey reporters.

During the next few days, Elizabeth was bludgeoned by the press. One reporter wrote, "*The Girl Who Had Everything [a reference to her 1953 movie with co-star Fernando Lamas]* wants her own way—or the highway."

Rock tossed the newspaper at Phyllis. "Now you see what you've done. I forbid you to talk to the press again."

Both Elizabeth and Rock were the first visitors allowed to see Clift in his room at the Cedars of Lebanon. Despite their horror, they put up brave fronts.

During her exit from the hospital, Elizabeth told Rock, "It was all I could do not to let out a scream. My God, his head is as big as a pumpkin at Halloween—and far more grotesque. His jaws are wired. He'll have to have a series of operations to reconstruct that once-beautiful face and his teeth. He has to lie in traction suffering from whiplash."

On his second visit, Rock confronted the formidable Libby Holman, who immediately launched an attack on him. She hardly could blame him for Clift's accident, holding Elizabeth responsible for that, but she had gone to a screening of *Written on the Wind*.

Rock was not very familiar with her previous scandals, although he'd been told that his movie was based on the mysterious death of her young husband, the tobacco heir, Zachary Smith Reynolds, in 1932.

The scandal had not only ruined Holman's singing career, but had made her a social pariah for the remainder of the 1930s.

"You bastards, for some stupid movie, have brought back all that pain and suffering to me," she angrily charged. "What are you trying to do? Just as I had almost recovered, you dredged up all that horror from yesterday and exposed it to millions of people."

"I'm sorry, Miss Holman. I had no idea," Rock said.

Elizabeth later learned that Holman was smuggling martinis to Clift within his hospital room, and he was drinking them through a straw. She complained to Rock. "His doctors warned him against alcohol, fearing it will sabotage plans for the reconstruction of his face."

Aware of Holman's streak of lesbianism, she referred to her as "that dyke murderess."

In turn, Holman denounced Elizabeth, calling her "that god damn heifer in heat."

Elizabeth and Rock learned to bring mushy food to Clift, who detested the hospital's offerings. At the Farmers Market, Rock shopped for favorite treats—guacamole and overripe bananas. Clift was having a hard time swallowing.

She told Rock that she nearly cried seeing how hard it was just to get some baby food in him.

One afternoon, Clift confided to Rock, "I've got to recover my face to report back to work on *Raintree County*. I owe it to Bessie Mae."

She was holding out, threatening to not finish the picture without him.

Rock desperately wanted to keep a secret from Clift: Dore Schary had asked him to stand by to reshoot Clift's scenes and to re-craft the picture with Elizabeth.

Once, during a hospital visit, Rock encountered the second most-formidable woman in Clift's arsenal, Mira Rostova, his longtime acting coach. Born in St. Petersburg in Russia, she went over every scene, line by line, before he even faced a director.

Rostova knew better than to blame Rock for the accident, but she attacked Elizabeth in front of Clift, calling her "that beautiful witch" and claiming that "Monty gave in to her demands, risking his life just so he could attend one of her silly little parties. She's a selfish bitch."

Clift did not reply.

As the days and weeks passed, Clift's recovery and reconstruction work progressed at a rate that was faster and more successful than anyone had expected. Even his doctors were amazed.

On Clift's second day back at his dreary little rented house on Dawn Ridge Road, Rock dropped in for a private visit, bringing with him some very ripe papayas. In the kitchen, he made a papaya milk shake for his recovering friend.

Rock agreed with Elizabeth's assessment: She had told him, "Monty's once lustrous eyes are as dead as those fish on ice sold at the Farmers Market."

Clift had a swimming pool, which he could not use. When Rock asked Clift if there was anything he wanted or needed, he said, "I do have one request: It would mean a lot to me. Would you strip down so I can take in your nudity, then go for a swim, emerging like Neptune in his glory?"

Rock did what Monty had requested, Clift telling him, "I can at least take delight in your male beauty."

At times, Clift appeared half dead, as he was taking a large number of morphine-based painkillers. One afternoon, Rock found Clift in a sad condition, horribly depressed. "I know my beauty will never be restored," he lamented. "What's left for me? To star in horror movies?"

Clift took his fingers and ran them over Rock's handsome face: "Once, I was called the most beautiful male movie star in Hollywood. Now you will have to carry that banner."

Rock was out of the country when news reached him that Clift had returned to work, starring opposite Elizabeth in *Raintree County*. Although in pain, he finished the film "for Bessie Mae."

Eventually, Rock got to see it, and was shocked to see how Clift looked in the second half of the movie. It had been touted as "the second *Gone With the Wind*," but it hardly lived up to that promotion.

Author Ellis Amburn accurately summed up Clift's new look on the screen: "When Monty Clift recovered, he was scarcely recognizable, appearing pinched and withered. The famous gullwing eyebrows were now shaggy thickets, the left side of his face was almost paralyzed, the once heroic jawline was soft and mushy. His eyes looked dead, no doubt due to pain, bewilderment, and massive doses of barbiturates."

Rock himself privately gave his own view of the new Monty Clift: "One half of what was once the screen's most expressive face is now dead and gone, a distant memory."

***

On November 9, 1956, Henry Willson decided to celebrate Rock's rise to stardom and his marriage to Phyllis Gates. *[It had survived a year.]* For weeks in advance, he had planned a lavish party at his home on Stone Canyon Drive, sending out invitations to the elite of Hollywood.

For this spectacular *fête*, he ordered that his swimming pool be covered and converted into a dance floor. Carefully, he arranged for an elaborate buffet catered by Chasen's, and he hired the Bernie Richard orchestra, a popular group at the time, to provide the dance music.

Wardrobe mattered, so, for Phyllis, Willson purchased a stunning red gown from Dior at a chic shop in Beverly Hills, and commissioned a tailor to make a new tuxedo for Rock, using his star's money, of course.

On the night of the party, he stationed a beaming Rock with Phyllis at his front door to welcome the A-list guests. She compared the event to a wedding reception.

Unlike most of Willson's parties, this one was only for male/female couples. Among the first to arrive were Rock's friends, Ronald and Nancy Reagan. Jane Wyman, Rock's co-star in two box office hits, was not invited because Nancy was jealous of her husband's former wife.

Tap-dancing Ann Miller arrived on the arm of hotelier Conrad Hilton, followed by director Mervyn LeRoy as the escort of Lana Turner, whom he'd cast in her first movie, *They Won't Forget* (1937). Katharine Hepburn and Spencer Tracy were honored guests, but Sinatra, at the last minute, cabled his regrets.

The co-stars of *It Should Happen to You* (1953), Judy Holliday and Peter Lawford, made a cuddly twosome, and they were trailed by Clifton Webb and his mother, Maybelle.

In the most spectacular *haute couture* of the evening, Anita Louise arrived with her husband, Buddy Adler, the 20th Century Fox executive. Rock congratulated him on the success of *From Here to Eternity* (1954). Adler flattered him, telling Rock he had wanted him to play the male lead—the lovesick cowboy—in *Bus Stop* (1956) opposite Marilyn Monroe.

A former head of production at Rock's studio, Universal, William Goetz, showed up with his wife, Edith Mayer, the daughter of Louis B. Mayer, the ousted former head of MGM. "Call me tomorrow," Goetz told Rock. "I have this great script I want you to read. It's called *Sayonara*. The lead would be ideal for you."

Mayer's replacement, Dore Schary, entered the foyer with his wife, Miriam Svet, a noted pianist and a painter of renown. As a gift, she had brought one of her small paintings, which she presented to Phyllis and to Rock, who were most grateful.

Mike Connolly, the columnist and magazine reporter, was the next guest to arrive. Appearing in the hall with his "date," Jayne Mansfield, in plunging décolletage. Later, she would have a "wardrobe malfunction" beside the covered-over pool. Rock always

Right after his wedding to Phyllis Gates, Rock urged her to get on the phone: "Tell it to Louella. Tell it to Hedda. I want the whole god damn world to know that Rock Hudson is no longer a bachelor."

avoided trying to be alone with Connolly. "When he got drunk, he was always trying to feel me up."

Connolly was privy to most of Hollywood's darkest secrets, which he could not write about. *Newsweek* once described him "as probably the most influential columnist inside the movie colony."

William T. Orr and his wife, Joy Page, the stepdaughter of Jack L. Warner, greeted Phyllis and Rock. They each congratulated Rock on the box office success of Warner's *Giant*. That studio's chief executive had launched Warners into television production and would turn out such hit series as *Maverick* and *77 Sunset Strip*.

Later, during a talk with Orr, Rock told him that while he was in the Navy, he and his fellow sailors had seen one of Orr's training films, *Three Cadets*. "It warned us of the dangers of untreated venereal disease."

"For those movies, I had my pick of stars: Alan Ladd, William Holden, and Ronnie Reagan over there at the far side of the pool. In a whisper to Rock, he said, "Ronnie should have seen the film. While he was in the Army, he got gonorrhea."

The last guests to arrive were from England: Diana Dors, the British blonde bombshell, and her escort. Standing about twenty feet away, Jayne Mansfield gave her an icy stare. On Dors' arm was super macho Tommy Yeardye, Rock's former lover in Ireland during his filming of *Captain Lightfoot* (1955).

Phyllis was surprised at how warmly the two men greeted each other, since Rock had never mentioned him to her before. Dors flashed her an artificial smile, later referring to her as "Rock's little mouse."

Before the party ended, Rock managed to dance with nearly every woman at the party, paying particular attention to the older ladies, all of whom seemed enchanted with him. He was aware of the power most of them had over their well-connected husbands in the film industry.

The gala broke up at 2AM, and Rock and Phyllis profusely thanked Willson for the event, which everyone agreed had been a great success.

Without Phyllis, and without telling her where he was going, Rock returned the following night to Willson's home for another party. This one was limited only to male guests.

Showing up this time, Rock had a man on his arm, Yeardye. He had not gone to Las Vegas with Dors, who had flown there to meet with casino owners about future gigs at one of their clubs.

A close friend of Willson's, Mike Connolly, was there, assuring Rock, "I gave your party a great writeup, but this other little party of Henry's will just be our secret." Appraising Yeardye from head to toe and back again, he asked, "And who is this divine gift to all cocksuckers?"

When introduced, he said, "Oh, yes, Diana Dors' boy. I adore you—not her. She stood by that commie, Charlie Chaplin."

About thirty-five young men showed up to feast on Chasen's leftovers from the night before.

For Connolly's "Party Favor," Willson had invited a good-looking, very masculine Italian. Before Willson introduced him to Rock, he whispered, "He and the Oscar statuette have something in common, and I'm speaking measurements. If you'd like, I can fix you guys up at some future date. For references, ask Ava Gardner, Janet Leigh, or Zsa Zsa Gabor."

"What, no men?" Rock asked.

"Try Clifton Webb or Cary Grant," Willson answered.

"What's his name?"

"Johnny Stompanato."

***

By the time Rock made a cameo appearance in Universal's *Four Girls in Town* (1956), he was firmly established as the top box office champion of the world. He had beat out John Wayne, who came in second, followed by Pat Boone, Elvis Presley, Frank Sinatra, Gary Cooper, William Holden, James Stewart, Jerry Lewis, and Yul Brynner. Not one actress was among the top ten, although Marilyn Monroe and Kim Novak had each been on an equivalent list the year before.

Also cast in *Four Girls in Town*, John Gavin was being groomed as "the next Rock Hudson." Both actors were represented by Henry Willson.

Born John Golenor of Mexican and Irish descent, Gavin was the scion of an influential family of landowners. During the Korean War, he'd served in the U.S. Navy. Returning to America, he never planned to be an actor until a friend, Bryan Foy, a "B" film producer, lured him into the studio to take a screen test. Universal determined that Gavin had somewhat the same looks of its major star. He was as tall as Rock and conformed to the *cliché* of tall, dark, and handsome.

Willson told friends, "John is just as virile, just as strapping, and just as good-looking as Rock, and both of them would be ideal in the same role. Of course, I never got to find out if Gavin possessed the same endowment as 'The Rock.' I forgot to ask his wife."

As the agent for both Gavin and Rock, Willson no longer operated independently. He had accepted an executive position at Famous Artists Agency, controlled by Charles Feldman. Willson said, "Perhaps they wanted me, but mainly they wanted 'a piece of The Rock.'"

Apparently, Rock did not feel threatened by this competition and, even though Gavin was being dubbed "Rock Hudson Jr." Rock agreed to pose for publicity pictures with him aboard Rock's sailing boat, *Khairuman,* named for the character Piper Laurie had played in *The Golden Blade* back in 1953.

[Rock eventually got rid of his boat because vandals kept consistently painting such slurs as FAGGOT or QUEER on the sides of the vessel.]

Gavin told Rock, "I never wanted to be an actor. I was lured into it. When I had to face the camera, I was really afraid and I was just plain awful."

"You're taking a page from my own life," Rock said.

He had first seen Gavin on the screen in *A Time to Love and a Time to Die* (1958), based on the novel by Erich Maria Remarque. It was an intensely dramatic story of a German soldier set against the backdrop of World War II. Gavin drew comparisons to Lew Ayres' breakthrough role in *All Quiet on the Western Front* (1931), also based on a novel by Remarque.

Universal dubbed Gavin "our New White Hope," and columnist Hedda Hopper predicted "John Gavin will take the public by storm in this new picture." None of that happened, and the drama didn't fare well at the box office.

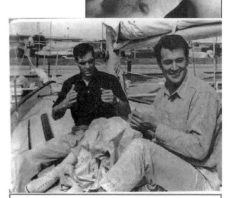

Gavin's debut was directed by none other than Douglas Sirk. "I found John as mesmerizing on the screen as Rock. So did Ross Hunter. That's why both of us cast him in *Imitation of Life* (1959) opposite Lana Turner. Those two became the most gorgeous pair on the screen. Hunter reportedly was "besotten" with Gavin, but never made any attempt to seduce him.

Gavin's career, despite the favorable predictions, never took off like Rock's. He did make a number of prominent appearances, including starring as Julius Caesar in Stanley Kubrick's epic *Spartacus* (1960) and in the Alfred Hitchcock thriller *Psycho* the same year. Other films had him co-starring with Doris Day in the 1960 thriller *Midnight Lace,* and with Susan Hayward in a remake of *Back Street*

Like Rock, the strikingly handsome actor, John Gavin, could pose for beefcake, too. He was billed as "The next Rock Hudson." But Rock didn't seem threatened by this competition, and even invited him to go boating with him to Catalina.

352

(1961), the Fannie Hurst soaper. "My God," Hayward said. "John looked more glamorous than I did."

In time, Gavin became president (from 1971 to 1973) of the Screen Actors Guild, a post once held by Ronald Reagan. Reagan in 1981 appointed him U.S. Ambassador to Mexico, a post he kept until 1986.

***

Rock's close friend, George Nader, was the star of *Four Girls in Town*, which both men knew was "a silly little piece of fluff," produced mainly to show off the beauty of some international starlets. It was the story of four star-struck girls who arrive, camera-ready, it seemed, at Universal Studios.

The package was pulled together by Aaron Rosenberg, who had last featured Rock in the James Stewart picture, *Bend of the River* (1952).

On set, Rock had a reunion with Julie Adams, with whom he had last worked on the set for *One Desire.* As one of the other four girls referenced in the title, Marianne Koch (sometimes billed as Marianne Cook), was a German actress from Munich.

Before meeting Rock, Koch had starred in the haunting thriller, *Night People* with Gregory Peck. In time, as roles became harder to find, she appeared in a number of "spaghetti westerns."

Also beautifying the scenery was Elsa Martinelli, an Italian actress and former model. Her first big break in films came in *The Indian Fighter* (1955), with Kirk Douglas. In it, he leads a wagon train through warring Indian country. Douglas had spotted her face on the cover of a magazine, finding it "compelling."

Gia Scala, the fourth girl in the Nader film, would become embroiled in Rock's life by the end of the 1950s.

***

George Nader and Julie Adams as they appeared in his latest film, *Four Girls in Town* (1957).

Usually, Adams was a leading lady for Rock. Nader urged director Jack Sher to let him appear in a bathing suit scene. "Like my friend Rock, I've also got a body to exhibit."

One of Henry Willson's clients, Grant Williams, a New Yorker, had been cast in a minor role in *Written on the Wind,* on the set of which he'd first met Rock. He told Willson, "I find the kid really hot, very masculine, exceedingly attractive—just like I like 'em."

Williams was six years younger than Rock, and Willson had signed him after auditioning him on the casting couch. "He's mouth-watering… you won't be disappointed," Willson claimed.

It wasn't until Williams was cast in *Four Girls in Town* in the role of Spencer Farrington, Jr., that Rock turned on his charm and made overtures to seduce him. He found him such an easy conquest, he invited him to spend most of a week at a rented cottage in Laguna Beach, a rental for which producer Ross Hunter held the lease.

Rock lied to Phyllis, telling her he was involved in an extended location shooting for *Four Girls in Town,* even though Rock's appearance in the film lasted only five minutes, during which he played himself. He could always tell his wife, "They cut several of my scenes," in case she ever saw the picture.

At the beachfront cottage, after a lobster dinner and a walk on the beach, Williams and Rock became lovers, beginning a relationship that would extend for many years. Rock set out to learn what he could about his new sidekick, as he liked talking to him.

Born to a Scottish father and an Irish mother, Williams, like Mark Miller, had wanted to be an operatic tenor more than he did an actor. In time, he would perform five seasons at the New York Opera.

During the course of their first sexual marathon in Laguna, Williams gave Rock an autographed photo of himself from when he served in the U.S. Air Forces during the Korean War.

After his discharge, he'd enrolled in the Actors Studio in New York, which led to small roles on Broadway and on television. A talent scout for Universal spotted him on the *Kraft Televison Theater* in 1954 and signed him to a two-year contract.

When Rock returned home Sunday night from Laguna, he confronted an angry Phyllis, who made all sorts of charges against him, accusing him of being a liar and a cheat. He retaliated: "And what did you do, hang out in all the lesbian bars?"

Relenting somewhat, Rock promised to return home faithfully to dinner every night of the following week, but did not keep that vow. That very Monday night, when Williams in-

The picture was entitled *Four Girls in Town*, but after meeting the handsome actor, Grant Williams, who was also in the film, Rock suggested that it be retitled *Four Girls (and a Boy) in Town*.

vited him to his apartment, he accepted, staggering back to his house at midnight.

Rock was still seeing Williams for sex when he filmed his breakthrough role in the science fiction film, *The Incredible Shrinking Man* (1957). Later, Rock jokingly told Willson, "I knew Grant before he shrank."

The movie was a success, getting good reviews, but, as Rock sadly noted, it didn't launch Williams into stardom.

After two years, Universal dropped him, but Warners signed him in 1960. Many of his future roles were on television, though occasionally, he appeared on the big screen. In 1961, Rock was seen escorting both Troy Donahue and Williams to a screening of *Susan Slade*, in which Donahue had been awarded the lead, with Williams in a small role,

At the time, there were rumors that Rock was increasingly developing a fondness for three-ways. Another client of Willson with the same last name as Grant, Van Williams later confirmed that Rock preferred three-ways and tried to lure him into several.

Rock was still involved in a relationship of sorts with Grant Williams in 1963, when he went with him to see *PT 109*, a World War II action yarn based on Lt. John F. Kennedy's experiences in the Pacific as the captain of a PT boat sunk by the Japanese. The picture was released in June of that year, and the President was assassinated that November.

Williams told Rock that "Jackie Kennedy has always had this crush on Warren Beatty, and she wanted him for the lead, but the fucker turned down the role. Then Paul Newman wanted to play it, but JFK thought he was 'too Jewish.'"

[Grant Williams died relatively young, at the age of 54, having succumbed to peritonitis. Ironically, that was also the year of Rock's death. Grant never married.]

***

After the release of *Giant*, Rock's marriage to Phyllis began to fall apart. "He wasn't interested in marriage," she claimed. "All he ever thought about was his career or going out on his nightly adventures, never explaining where he'd gone or what he'd done. He would come in at two or three o'clock in the morning, having to get up before the crack of dawn with almost no sleep to report to the studio."

During the first months of their marriage, it had been different. "He seemed to want to show me off to all of Hollywood. It was like saying, 'Hey, guys, I'm married. All those rumors about me aren't true. Look, I've got a real live girl on my arm. She's pert and pretty."

For a while, their marriage had included a series of glittering events where photographers were on hand to record their entrances. They usually included the opening night of major performances by stars appearing at his favorite night club, the Cocoanut Grove. He attended performances by Harry Belafonte or Lena Horne, and Phyllis and Rock had danced to the romantic music of Freddie Martin and his band.

Phyllis later recalled their first Christmas together: They'd been invited to the home of Humphrey Bogart and Lauren Bacall during the period when Bacall was co-starring with him in *Written on the Wind*. Rat Packers dropped in: Sammy Davis, Jr., Frank Sinatra, and Peter Lawford. Judy Garland showed up and sang for them. "She kissed Rock like she'd known him for quite a while, I suspect intimately from the way she acted. I cried when she sang *Over the Rainbow*."

"Judy was followed by Noël Coward on a visit from London, singing 'Mad Dogs and Englishmen,' and June Allyson performing some number—I forget," Phyllis said. "She's not a great singer. The bitch flirted with Rock. I heard she was a nympho."

"I was a country girl among the sophisticates," Phyllis said. "For three minutes, I got to chat with Katharine Hepburn and Spencer Tracy. If they'd ever had something around 1940, it was over now. Scotty Bowers, who supplied tricks for the stars, told me he provided girls—'no blemishes, please'—for Hepburn and young studs for Tracy."

"Bogie seemed to adore me," Phyllis said. "He told Rock I was too good for him."

Within a year, she said, "Rock and I visited Bogie once again. He had to be lowered down on this dumbwaiter and wheeled into the living room. He could still banter with guests, still giving out the insults, but he was frail, weak, and dying from cancer."

She recalled, "I was surprised at how many of the stars made a pass at me. The first time it happened, a slightly drunk Sinatra approached me. 'How about getting together for a little fun?' he asked. 'I'm sure you're not getting that much from Rock.'"

Robert Stack and his wife, Rosemary, invited Rock and Phyllis to their vacation home in Palm Springs, an Andalusian-style house built around a large, plant-filled patio. "Bob practically grew up among Hollywood royalty and he and Rock had great fun together," Phyllis said. "While there, I heard rumors that Rock and Bob might have more going on than a friendship, but I didn't want to believe that."

Back in Hollywood, the Stacks invited the Hudsons to their elegantly furnished home on St. Pierre Road in Bel Air. There, she was introduced to John Wayne, with whom Rock would one day co-star in a picture.

"Wayne was very nice to me, congratulating me on snaring Rock. He was so much shorter than I thought. He looked so imposing on the screen. Joan Crawford was at the party with some handsome young man who looked a hundred years younger than she was. I was surprised that she and Wayne didn't speak. When I was a girl in 1942, I saw them together in *Reunion in France.* They stayed on opposite sides of the room, didn't cross over."

That night, when Rock took his wife home, he told her why. Crawford had been quoted as saying, "Get John Wayne out of the saddle—and you've got nothing."

Now that he was a big star, Rock got invited to all the A-list parties. "We were entertained by Jack and Mary Benny, Claudette Colbert and Joel Pressman, Irene Dunne and Francis Griffin, the Cary Grants, the Gregory Pecks, even Clifton Webb. "Webb didn't have a wife, of course, so his domineering mother, Maybelle, filled in for him," Phyllis said. "Jack Warner invited us over to his lavish home. Ed Muhl, who ran Universal, entertained us at his family home. Unlike most of our hosts, he seemed to resent me and monopolized Rock for most of the evening. Later, I heard rumors about Rock and him."

Muhl might not have paid Phyllis much attention, but other hosts or guests continued to make passes at her, all the while pretending to be Rock's friends. "One night, we were invited to this beautiful party at the home of George Burns and Gracie Allen," Phyllis said. "George, of all people, made a pass at me, and believe me, he was serious. My God, I read he was born in 1896."

But then one day, all A-list parties disappeared from their communal calendar, and Rock no longer took her out. When she asked why, he said, "By now the whole damn town has seen I've got a wife. Isn't that enough?"

She claimed he was always in a bad mood when he come home, and at one time, he accused her of rendering him a prisoner, defining his marriage as a kind of "house arrest."

"He almost deliberately provoked a fight," she said, "and then he'd storm out the door and be gone all night. Sometimes, he stayed gone a day or two and never called, not a word. Then he began to freeze people out. Loretta Young phoned, but he rejected her invitation. He also turned down Barbara Hutton, the Woolworth heiress."

"He was always going over to see George Nader and Mark Miller. At first, he invited me, but after a while, he started going over there by himself."

"I was seeing a psychiatrist, a woman, and she urged me to get Rock to come in for testing. I finally talked him into it, and he went through some personality profile tests. She later told me, 'Your husband has the emotional development of an eight-year-old.'"

***

In 1956, Colonel Dean Hess, a minister from Ohio, published his war-themed autobiography, *Battle Hymn*, based on his experience as a fighter pilot in the U.S. Air Force during World War II. Both Ross Hunter and Douglas Sirk read it, deciding it would make a marvelous film in color and CinemaScope.

During the course of the war, Hess had accidentally dropped a bomb on an orphanage in Nazi Germany, killing 37 orphans. Ignoring their own murderous exploits, the Nazis denounced Hess in every media outlet they could find, asserting "the pilot's hands will be stained forever with the blood of those harmless innocents who did not get to live out their lives."

Hunter purchased the film rights for Universal, but did not immediately see it as a vehicle for Rock, envisioning it instead as an ideal property for Robert Mitchum. Hess, however, was horrified at the casting, objecting to Mitchum on moral grounds because of his arrest and short jail term after having been caught in a marijuana bust in the late 1940s.

Then, whereas Sirk thought the heroic role would be ideal for Robert Stack, Hunter demanded that Rock be cast, and, as producer, he overrode his director.

Taking great liberties, screenwriters Vincent B. Edwards and Charles Grayson used the autobiography only as inspiration, eliminating many of the events associated with World War II and focusing instead on Col. Hess, as portrayed by Rock, re-enlisting in the Air Force during the Korean War. In that later conflict, as depicted within the autobiography, Hess had trained pilots in South Korea to fight the communist menace.

In *Battle Hymn's* final cut, during his tour of duty, Hess, as portrayed by Rock, is made aware of orphaned war refugees coming onto the military base to raid the garbage cans for some morsels of food. After a lot of plot complications, he rescues the orphans, directing an effort to evacuate the homeless waifs to safety. At the end of the war, Hess (i.e., Rock)

In this idyllic movie poster advertising *Battle Hymn*, a war movie set in Korea, Rock Hudson and Martha Hyer look like a fantasy version of a soldier and his loving wife on the homefront.

Hyer remained Rock's least favorite leading lady...that is, until he met Julie Andrews.

358

returns to his ministry in Ohio and the arms of his loving wife, Mary (played by Martha Hyer).

The cast included some veteran character actors, with Dan Duryea in the third lead. He had known Rock since he'd worked on pictures with him that included *One Way Street* and *Winchester '73*. In Rock's view, "Dan Duryea was the best actor to play a villain in all of Hollywood."

Or, as one critic expressed it, "A sly man, he creeps up on malice as if it were to catch a cat, and he is unable to prevent a giggle cracking his high-pitched voice: a door-to-door salesman just waiting for bored housewives."

Dan DeFore was cast as Captain Dan Skidmore, one of Hess's Air Force comrades. DeFore was a corn-fed boy from a large family of seven children from Cedar Rapids, Iowa. He'd been working in movies since 1936, and Rock had seen him in *She's Working Her Way Through College* (1952), starring Ronald Reagan and Virginia Mayo.

When Rock told Phyllis of his latest role in *Battle Hymn*, he shocked her by proclaiming, "I love war. It's so exciting."

When she reminded him of its horrors, he dismissed her protest: "I don't think about that. I had great fun serving in the Navy—the male bonding, the camaraderie."

Of all his leading ladies, Martha Hyer, whom Rock dubbed "The Ice Queen," was his least favorite. Born into wealth in Fort Worth, Texas, she in time would convert to Judaism in 1966 when she married producer Hal. B. Wallis. Today, she is mostly remembered for her role as Gwen French in *Some Came Running* (1958) co-starring with Frank Sinatra, Shirley MacLaine, and Dean Martin. Hyer was nominated for a Best Supporting Actress Oscar, but lost to Wendy Hiller for *Separate Tables* (1958).

Hyer later told the press, "I didn't enjoy working with Rock Hudson. He was a shallow little boy, who may have grown tall but never grew up. Self-centered and spoiled, he could never communicate on any level that did not relate to himself."

Because of the *Battle Hymn's* low budget, location shooting would not take place in Korea, but in Nogales, Arizona, which had a similar landscape. Phyllis and Rock got into yet another argument when he refused to take her with him to the Southwest. As he told Nader, "For sex, I will rely on cowboys. Arizona is full of them. I should do very well. After all, I'm Rock Hudson!"

After the release of *Battle Hymn*, Bosley Crowther of *The New York Times* was rather dismissive. "Perhaps the most candid comment to be made about Universal's *Battle Hymn* is also the most propitious, so far as its box-office chances are concerned. That is to say, it is conventional. It follows religiously the line of mingled piety and pugnacity laid down for standard idealistic service films. What's more, it has Rock Hudson playing the big hero role. And it is in CinemaScope and Technicolor. Wrap them up and what have you got? The popular thing."

In *Battle Hymn,* the caramel-colored Anna Kashfi, born in Darjeeling, in the Himalayan foothills, then part of British India, had the second female lead.

Cast in the film as a Korean woman, En Soon Yang, she runs a shelter for Korean orphans uprooted by the ravages of war in 1950. Colonel Hess (Rock) aids her in providing for and ultimately evacuating the homeless waifs. She falls in love with him, not knowing that he is a morally upright minister and already married.

Kashfi's origins remain mysterious, as she gave conflicting accounts over the years. Her real name was Joan O'Callaghan, and she may have been of Irish descent. Or was she of Indian descent? Perhaps she was "half Indian."

During the shoot, Rock showed little interest in her. She found him "courteous but reserved. When I heard of his confused personal problems, (a reference to his homosexuality), I felt a sense of pathos, as if he were burdened with that cross unwillingly." She wrote that assessment in a memoir.

But when he learned that Kashfi was dating Marlon Brando, and was about to marry him, Rock began to devote a lot of attention to her. As he admitted to friends, he'd been obsessively interested in Brando, and felt threatened by his superior acting.

The interior scenes for *Battle Hymn* were shot in Hollywood, after cast and crew returned from Arizona. Brando visited the set several times, ostensibly to spend time with Kashfi, but, as she noted, he spent far more time talking to Rock than to his bride-to-be.

"The two men huddled in a corner somewhere," Kashfi claimed. "From a distance, their conversation appeared quite animated. Personally, I think Marlon wanted to keep his own talent, but preferred it to be showcased in a body like Rock possessed. He always wanted to be tall. Once, when I was near them, I

The battling Brandos: Marlon with Anna Kashfi.

After seducing Rock, Brando said, "I wish I had your body, especially what's hanging."

Rock shot back, "I wish I had your talent."

heard them sharing their very different experiences with James Dean."

One day, when Kashfi didn't need to report to work, Louella Parsons dropped by the set, looking for an item for her column. She had learned that Brando was dating Kashfi. The columnist shared her opinion of Brando with Rock. "As far as I'm concerned, Mr. Mumbles can drop dead. He has the manners of a chimpanzee, the gall of a Kinsey researcher, and the swelled head of a Navy blimp."

One day, Phyllis came onto the set, and Rock introduced her to Kashfi. The two women bonded and soon became friends. As stated in Kashfi's memoirs, "I learned that Phyllis was in the throes of a personal crisis, and she confided in me that her marriage to Rock was coming apart. She claimed that her husband was having a number of affairs with men, and he was almost never at home."

"He just trots me out when he needs a trophy wife to show off to the press," Phyllis claimed.

At the time, Rock still lived deep in the closet, but Brando had been more open about his bisexuality. "I have seduced men, and I am not ashamed," he once said. His lovers had ranged from Tennessee Williams and Wally Cox to Marilyn Monroe and tobacco heiress Doris Duke.

He'd told Rock, "Should sex and desire die in me, it would be the end. It doesn't matter if I have almost never been happy with a woman."

Kashfi confided to Phyllis, "Marlon is not well appointed. He screens that deficiency by undue devotion to his sex organ."

Brando had once famously said, "I've never been circumsized, and my noble tool has performed its duties through thick and thin without fail."

One Saturday afternoon, Kashfi and Phyllis agreed to go on a shopping trip together. Kashfi kissed Brando goodbye and headed out the door for her rendezvous.

Right after a late lunch, Phyllis complained of a splitting headache and decided to go home. Having lost her shopping companion, Kashfi drove back to the house she shared with Brando and came into the living room. As she later told Phyllis, "I looked out at the patio, and I saw both Rock and Marlon sunning themselves by the pool. They were talking and holding hands. I decided not to intrude. Of course, I had never seen Rock in the nude before. But seeing him side by side with Marlon, I realized that God did not create all men equally. I got short-changed. I skipped out of the house and didn't return until 7PM. Rock was gone. Marlon made no mention that he had entertained your husband."

***

361

Phyllis was unaware that Rock even knew Grace Kelly when he invited her to go with him to attend a banquet honoring the future Princess of Monaco. A magazine was presenting her with an award for being one of the world's most popular stars.

After the ceremony, Grace approached Rock, who introduced her to Phyllis. "You live on one of those 'bird streets,' don't you?" Grace asked.

Phyllis confirmed that they did, and Grace said that she was renting Gaylord Hauser's home in the same neighborhood. "Why don't the two of you drop in for a nightcap?"

Rock claimed that he knew the home, and they agreed to meet there within an hour.

Later, over drinks, Phyllis remembered Grace spending a lot of time talking about astrology. She seemed as interested in it as Nancy Reagan.

The press had been filled with rumors of her romance with Cary Grant during the time the pair had filmed *To Catch a Thief* (1955). "Cary and I have astrological signs that are most compatible," she said.

The surprise of the evening came when she announced that she was going to marry Prince Rainier of Monaco, giving up her film career. She had already told Rock that she would not be able to co-star with him in his next picture, *Something of Value,* to be shot in Africa.

Rock's schedule did not permit him to attend what was hailed as "The Wedding of the Century" on April 19, 1956, in Monaco.

***

One night, Rock and Phyllis were awakened by a loud pounding on their front door and the persistent ringing of their doorbell.

He rose from bed, found his silk robe and rushed to the door, but didn't open it. "Who is it?" he shouted, fearing some unwanted invasion.

"It's Elizabeth fucking Taylor!" she shouted. "Let me in!"

He opened the door to find a disheveled Elizabeth standing there in the dim light of the porch. She barged inside. "I've left Michael *[Wilding]*. I'm moving in to avoid the press. My luggage is in the car."

Chapter Twelve

WHEN ROCK'S MARRIAGE CRASHES, HE FLIES TO ITALY TO STAR AS A HEMINGWAY HERO

Love Scenes with Jennifer Jones, Onscreen, by Day, & with a "Roman Romeo," Offscreen, at Night

Fighting the Mau Mau for Something of Value in Kenya

Rock Faces Blackmail and Extortion from the Mob in L.A.

Producer David O. Selznick overhyped the novel, *A Farewell to Arms*, a love story between a soldier and an army nurse set against the backdrop of World War I in Italy. He told Rock it would be bigger than his *Gone With the Wind* and would no doubt win him a Best Actor Oscar.

Selznick made Rock nervous during love scenes with Jennifer Jones (Selznick's wife). "He hawkeyed our every move," Rock claimed.

Elizabeth Taylor hid out at Rock's house for five days and night. She'd moved out of her home with Michael Wilding, but called him every day to make sure their nanny was taking care of her sons.

She was avoiding the press, who never found out where she was. Producer Mike Todd, her new boyfriend, visited her every day, bringing special foods and, on two occasions, a diamond bracelet. One night Rock noted she seemed more delighted with the chili from Chasen's than she was with the bracelet.

When Todd wasn't there, Rock found his former co-star from *Giant* in a very confessional mood. They relived many of their heavy drinking sessions in Marfa, Texas, during their filming of *Giant*. Phyllis felt left out of their bonding and often retreated to bed early.

No one was more interested than George Nader and Mark Miller in learning the most minute details of Elizabeth's mysterious sojourn in Rock's house. The press was reporting that she had entered a sanitorium after a suicide attempt.

One night, she spoke candidly about her brief fling with the doomed James Dean: "We had a little twinkle in bed with each other on occasion."

He asked her, "You mean, water sports?"

"As I said, a little twinkle for each other."

She made another very personal confession, which didn't surprise him because it had already been rumored. She claimed that during her affair with Frank Sinatra, he impregnated her. "Frank's manager picked me up in a limousine and drove me into Mexico to this dirty little crap-hole where I had an abortion."

At times, in speaking of her failed marriage to Wilding (1952-1957), she broke down and cried. "He's lazy, not ambitious at all, and I was the breadwinner of the family. I began to think he was just using me. We quarreled all the time, until I finally gave up hope for him. I think he's a loser, and I like winners like Mike Todd."

"That story broke while we were in Marfa, the one about how Michael entertained two strippers at our home. Of course, I couldn't hold that against him, as I was fucking around a lot in Texas, as you of all people know so well. My biggest criticism of him is that he was such an Englishman. In spite of my birth, I'm the most American woman in Hollywood. No Deborah Kerr, this gal!"

She claimed she'd made a big mistake when she had invited Wilding to a screening of Judy Garland's *A Star is Born* (1954). "It was like we were watching a story torn from the pages of our own lives. I was the rising young star, and he was the doomed Norman Maine, an alcoholic whose star had already set in the West. After the screening, he told me, 'All I have left is to walk into the Pacific and drown like Norman Maine. Food for sharks. I feel like a displaced person, not wanted on the voyage with the paying passengers, but assigned to some little closet off the furnace room.'"

She also confirmed that whenever her divorce from Wilding became official, she planned to marry Todd. "He's the most take-charge man I've ever known. After the alcoholic violence of Nicky Hilton, and that boring couch potato I'm married to now, I'm going to run off with a man who wants to 'take a big bite out of life,' whatever in the fuck that means."

"He's outrageous to me, calling me Lizzie Schwartzkopf and often slapping my ass, telling me to take off a few pounds."

"One of my favorite movies was *A Free Soul* with Norma Shearer," she said. "It came out in 1931, a year before I was born. When I did the remake, *The Girl Who Had Everything* (1953), I ordered that the original be screened for me at MGM. One line that Shearer uttered appealed to me. She saw her future 'with a new kind of man and a new kind of world.' That's what I want for myself."

On the third night of her stay, she revealed that she'd been offered the female lead in Rock's next picture, *Something of Value (1957)*, to be shot in Africa. Grace Kelly had turned it down.

After reading the script, Elizabeth told Rock, "I want to escape the press, and Africa would be a good place to hide out. But you and Sidney Poitier have all the best scenes. I'm more of an African wallflower, waiting for the Mau Mau to come and rape me. But I've talked it over with Mike—Todd, that is, not the other Mike—and he refuses to let me go. Even though we're not married, he's already running my life."

At the end of her stay in their house, Elizabeth thanked the Hudsons for their hospitality, giving Phyllis a piece of jewelry, which she later sold. Rock loaded Elizabeth's luggage into the trunk of Todd's car, as he sat impatiently behind the wheel.

Rock was out of touch with Elizabeth when her divorce in Acapulco came through in January of 1957. She immediately rushed into a marriage to Todd.

As she later told Rock, "Debbie Reynolds was my matron of honor, and Eddie Fisher was his best man. It was a super production, complete with African drums pounding out jungle rhythms, and strolling violinists dressed like gauchos. A groaning buffet table: guacamole, tortillas, hot tamales, burritos, three huge suckling pigs. I ate so much I farted all night. Thank God Mike didn't want rear door sex on our wedding night."

"Before he collapsed into bed that night, Mike told me he saw the world 'as a place to plunder, with me emerging as his most prized loot.'"

***

As Rock's marriage to Phyllis continued to deteriorate, she complained constantly of his premature ejaculation. That is, when he had sex with her at all, which he rarely did during the final months of their ill-fated marriage.

She even complained of her lack of a satisfactory sex life to George Nader. "He reaches a climax right away without giving me a chance at orgasm. At first, I tried to be sympathetic about his condition, but I'm left completely frustrated."

"On some occasions, I ask him to try again, but he laughs off the suggestion. He asked me, 'Who wants to eat *hors d'oeuvres* after a big dinner?'"

She also confessed to Nader that he had once complained, "All women are dirty, reminding me of a cow."

"After that, at even the suggestion of having sex with him, I scrubbed and scrubbed, terrified that he might detect a vaginal odor," she said.

Nader's advice to Phyllis was "Hit the lesbian bars. You'll find satisfaction there. You're a good-looking woman and should have no problem picking up some hot chick."

"You're right. I never had any trouble doing that."

After he left her, Phyllis often mocked Rock to her friends, who spread her complaints and her gossip. "This guy would strip nude, hide his genitals between his legs, and leap around the living room pretending to be a ballet dancer. I could do nothing but laugh at him. Imagine one of those dancing hippos in *Fantasia*."

***

Universal's CEO, Ed Muhl, Rock's lover, made a deal with MGM, who wanted to lease him for a starring role in *Something of Value* (1957) a story of the Mau Mau uprising in British colonial Kenya. Before flying to Nairobi, Rock was offered an all-expense paid vacation in Italy and France for two weeks, and he took Phyllis with him.

Before the first leg of the trip—a stopover in New York—Phyllis pleaded with him to stop off in Minnesota to visit her parents, Mr. and Mrs. Leo Gates, and to meet her friends and family. She traveled ahead of him to the agrarian hamlet of Montevideo, Minnesota, 130 miles west of Minneapolis, and three days later, Rock flew to Minneapolis, where he rented a car and drove to their family home.

There, he was received "with open arms" (Phyllis' words) by her parents. When news of his arrival spread, dozens of young people gathered in their front yard, demanding that he come out and sign autographs.

He didn't want to go outside with them, as he hated signing autographs, but she appealed to him, "You're the biggest thing to hit this town since sliced bread." Despite being forced into it, he was most gracious to his fans.

Mrs. Gates told the local newspaper, "I'm so happy for my daughter. My son-in-law is so friendly and loving, especially to children. He's also so tall, so handsome, and such a big movie star. Phyllis is the luckiest girl in the world!"

After Minnesota, the Hudsons flew away to New York City, where, on their first night, he took her to a performance by Rex Harrison and Julie Andrews of *My Fair Lady*. Onstage, they played their Broadway roles of Henry Higgins and Eliza Doolittle.

Backstage, Andrews was most gracious to Rock, although years later, they would feud with each other during their filming of *Darling Lili* (1970).

On Rock and Phyllis's second night in Manhattan, Edna Ferber invited them to dine with her at The Colony. She told Rock, "When I saw you in *Giant*, I told everyone that you are my Bick Benedict come to life from the pages of my novel."

At Idlewild, they boarded an Air France plane to Paris, her first trip abroad. Muhl's staff had booked a suite for them at the deluxe Plaza Athénée, which had housed everyone from Rudolph Valentino to Charlie Chaplin and Gloria Swanson.

As Phyllis entered the lobby of that very chic hotel, she was amazed to discover the most expensive prostitutes in Europe waiting to be picked up by millionaires. "Rock pointed them out to me. I wouldn't have known. Most of them were dressed in *haute couture* and were beautifully coiffed and groomed. They crowded around Rock, trying to set up a date."

He dined with her on their first night in Paris and even went the next day in a limousine that Universal had arranged for her sightseeing tour of Paris. But that night, he left her to dine in the hotel restaurant alone, as he disappeared onto the Left Bank. He explained that he had business meetings, but he didn't return to their suite until after 2AM.

As he later told Henry Willson, "I hit the gay bars across the Seine. Those pretty French boys went crazy when Rock Hudson, the movie star, walked through the door."

On their final night in Paris, Claude Terrail personally supervised their meal at the spectacularly famous Tour d'Argent, their table overlooking the floodlit flying buttresses of the Cathedral of Notre-Dame.

"I don't think Rock and I were ever more in love than that wonderful, romantic night," she later claimed.

Actually, after dinner, he sent her back to their hotel alone in that stretch limousine, as he headed for his favorite bar on the Left Bank, which also rented upstairs rooms for assignations. He was later seen disappearing upstairs with three handsome young Frenchmen.

***

After Paris, it was off aboard a flight to Rome, a city already familiar to Rock. Universal had a limousine waiting at the airport to haul them to the Grand Hotel where, within an hour, "the loving couple" had been scheduled as the main event at a press conference.

The moment they checked in, Rock received two urgent messages, one from the American author Gore Vidal and the other from "my Roman Adonis," Massimo.

Rock telephoned the handsome young actor first and headed out for Massimo's apartment, telling Phyllis he was visiting Gore Vidal. "He's working on the script for a remake of *Ben-Hur*." *[That film was eventually released, but without Rock, in 1959.]*

On her second evening in Rome, Phyllis returned at around 6PM from shopping along the Via Condotti. In their suite, she found a note from her husband, informing her that he had left for a conference that focused on *Ben-Hur.*

That night, he actually did visit Vidal's apartment, a notorious address where the author often staged all-male orgies. For their reunion, Rock brought Massimo with him, since he also wanted to get cast in *Ben-Hur.*

During their conversation, over drinks, Vidal admitted to Rock that, "I'm trying to queer up the script a little bit."

Vidal revealed that MGM producer Sam Zimbalist had originally supported Paul Newman as the male lead in *Ben-Hur.* "But Paul turned it down. He said his legs were too skinny for the costumes he'd have to wear. Brando was offered the role, too, but he said that after his 1953 appearance in *Julius Caesar* that he would never again appear in a swords-and-sandals epic. Burt Lancaster had other commitments. Finally, MGM came to you, Rock, the most ideal choice. You've got the best body of all of them."

A scriptwriter for *Ben-Hur*, Gore Vidal wanted Rock cast as the hero, with a heavy emphasis on homoerotic scenes, but the deal fell through.

Charlton Heston, Rock's long-ago friend from school, took the role instead.

The second male lead, the character of Messala, had already been assigned to Stephen Boyd, the ruggedly handsome Northern Irish actor, who was gay.

Vidal ran into a challenge during his

crafting of a script: Judah Ben-Hur and Messala had been intimate child-hood friends. Years later, they meet as strong-willed, testosterone-perme-ated adults, whose personalities and political allegiances have by now been clearly defined: Ben-Hur (a character eventually portrayed by Charlton Heston) is a land-owning, fervently patriotic Zionist Jew; Messala a haughty, aristocratic, and unscrupulous Roman officer.

At their reunion, after years of separation, the men soon quarrel bit-terly over the politics of their era, and the seeds are sown for a mutual loathing. Before the end of the film, their rivalry leads to Messala's grisly death in that famous chariot race.

"To explain all this hostility, I want to suggest that they were boyhood lovers. When they meet again, Messala wants to resume the love affair, but Ben-Hur turns him down, Messala boils with rage. Hell hath no fury like a horny Roman officer rejected in love, from a Jew, no less."

As outlined by Vidal that night, "A very reluctant William Wyler has agreed to go along with this homosexually derived plot device, providing that it is so understated and subtle that naïve audiences won't get it. Of course, all gay men will."

Rock thought the plot motivation, as defined by Vidal, was a splendid idea, and he assured everyone that as soon as an offer was made to Uni-versal, he was willing to star as Judah Ben-Hur.

Rock began some intense phone dialogues with Muhl at Universal. "I thought it was a done deal," he later recalled. "MGM offered Universal a million dollars for my services. I didn't know any actor in history who'd ever been offered that much money. When Elizabeth Taylor finally got a million for *Cleopatra* (1963), it made headlines."

Yet five days later, Muhl phoned with the bad news: "The money peo-ple at Universal aren't going to let you go," he said. "They want you to make a series of pictures for us which, as they are convinced, will make millions for Universal, far more than they could make off a loanout to MGM."

Rock was very disappointed, and he felt compelled to blame someone, his anger eventually focusing on Henry Willson. "He's behind this, I just know it," he told Phyllis, "Willson could have used his clout to get me *Ben-Hur*. Instead, he's spending too much time fucking the latest cute boys get-ting off the train at Union Station. Not today, but sooner than later, I'm going to fire the son of a bitch."

***

The *Ben-Hur* drama played out during what had been envisioned as

Rock's vacation in Rome. Their next stop was a limousine tour, first to Florence and then on to Venice, before a return to Rome.

Discreetly and on his own, Rock booked rooms for Massimo in both Florence and Venice, telling him, "I've got to do something for sex while I'm there. You've got to help me out."

Massimo was only too willing to go along, promising he'd be very discreet.

In Florence, it was the usual round of sightseeing and shopping. After the first day, Rock deserted Phyllis, who, in the limousine and with a guide, visited many of the city's churches and museums. After her limousine tour of the city, they had dinner together in the cellar restaurant, Buca Lapi, which had opened in 1880 in the lower levels of the Palazzo Antinori.

Their luxurious accommodations in Florence were at the Savoy Hotel, a lavishly (some said campily) neo-Baroque confection dating from 1896 and famously occupied by, among others, Vincent Price. On the side, Rock had booked Massimo into a much less opulent hotel near the railway station.

After dinner, Rock told Phyllis that he needed to walk and clear his head and that he wanted to be alone on his strolls. He returned to their suite, with no further explanation, at 3AM.

The next day, he left her to go alone in the limousine for a tour of more churches and statue-filled squares. Later, he admitted to Nader, "Massimo and I spent a lot of time making love and making up for all those weeks we'd been apart."

After Florence, the studio-financed limousine drove Rock and Phyllis east to Venice for more sightseeing and some gondola rides. They were booked into a suite at the very luxurious Gritti Palace, where Ernest Hemingway had once stayed.

Rock had been so pleased with Massimo's presence and performance in Florence that he booked him, not in a third-class hotel near the train station, but in a suite at the Danieli, a very grand and plush historic monument beside the Grand Canal. Built in the 14th Century by Doge Dandolo, it had been reconfigured as a "Hotel for Kings" in 1822.

Rock admitted that Phyllis had begun to get on his nerves, complaining constantly about his mysterious business meetings, and about how he frequently left her alone to explore the city. "You're not alone, god damn it! You've got a fucking guide! If you want to fuck someone, fuck HIM!" That was the afternoon that a gondola ride had been booked for them.

A photographer from a local newspaper snapped a photo of Rock with Phyllis in the gondola, "with Rock looking grumpy" (Phyllis' words).

After their stopover in Venice, they returned to Rome for the final days of their short vacation in Italy. Once again, Universal had a limousine waiting to take them to their shared suite at the Grand Hotel, although most movie stars stayed nearby at the Excelsior on the Via Veneto. "I guess they're afraid we'd run into Elizabeth Taylor or Frank Sinatra," Rock said.

On the first night of their return to Rome, they dined at the landmark Osteria dell'Orso, the most celebrated restaurant in Rome, dating from the 14th Century. Over the ages, it had fed everyone from Dante Alighieri to Mary Pickford and Douglas Fairbanks, Sr.

For their nightcap, they headed for a café on the fashionable Via Veneto, a venue that attracted a chic late-night crowd. Rock was surprised that no autograph seekers recognized him and sought him out. Phyllis cautioned, "I hear they're accustomed to American movie stars on this avenue."

As they were sipping their drinks, she was startled when a handsome and bleached-blonde young man—it was actually Massimo on a ruse—approached their café table and greeted Rock like a dear friend. She recalled that he wore an emerald green silk Italian suit with a red silk scarf around his neck.

Rock introduced him as a member of the Italian movie colony, explaining that he'd just made a movie with Anna Magnani, *Suor Letizia* (1957).

"She's heard that you're in town," Massimo said. "I'm having lunch with her tomorrow, and I just know she'd love to see you again."

"That sounds delightful," Rock answered.

"And, of course, I know she'd be delighted to meet your wife. What was your name again?"

Massimo knew perfectly well who Phyllis Gates was, as he'd had many arguments with Rock about her.

"I'll call in the morning after I've made the arrangements," Massimo said.

She noticed that he didn't ask the name of the hotel where Rock was staying. She controlled her fury until she was walking with Rock down the corridor of the Grand toward their suite. Then she exploded: "Who in hell was that silly little bleached-blonde fruitcake?"

At that remark, Rock impulsively smashed her face with his powerful open hand, bloodying her nose. She screamed and kept on screaming, loudly and hysterically. The blow had somehow broken the cord holding together her necklace, pearls from which went rolling across the floor. Bellboys rushed to her aid, two of them restraining Rock. He broke free and headed down the corridor, out of the hotel, and onto the street, eventually spending the night in Massimo's apartment.

She later admitted, "I cried myself to sleep that night. I couldn't believe he'd stuck me so hard. He'd never done that before. Obviously, I'd hit a real sensitive nerve with him about that Italian hustler."

There were other factors causing Rock's anxieties to bubble over: He'd spoken to Henry Willson that day, only to learn that Robert Harrison of *Confidential* was getting ready for another *exposé*, this one entitled ROCK HUDSON AND HIS ROMAN ROMEO.

This time, Willson managed to persuade *Confidential* to substitute publication of the Rock *exposé* for one that outed the homosexual relationship of Elvis Presley with Nick Adams. Their affair had allegedly transpired in both Memphis and in Hollywood.

As Willson relayed to Rock, "Once again, you've missed the bullet. You've got to drop this Massimo creep. Why him? You can have all the guys you want."

The next morning, Phyllis phoned the airline, booking an immediate flight back to Los Angeles. Rock's call came in for her at 8AM: "Forgive me, Bunting. I don't know what came over me. You know I have a violent temper, but I try to control it."

Nevertheless, she told him she was leaving. Within a half hour, he was in her suite. "He was actually crying, a big grown thing like him crying like a baby. He promised me it would never happen again."

He finally convinced her to stay and fly on to Kenya with him, as planned. She later told friends, "I know now that he was much more concerned with his career and a possible scandal. I'm sure all of the staff had heard of our bloody encounter. I was certain that at least one of them was trying to sell the story to the scandal sheets. He didn't want to face the headlines—ROCK HUDSON BEATS WIFE IN ROMAN HOTEL."

During their flight from Rome to Nairobi, they sat in adjoining seats, but had little to say to each other. She reflected on the status of their marriage: "The boyish man I married died back there in Rome. I was sitting beside a grown man, more demanding than ever, wanting to lead life on his own terms and not dictated by a wife. I think what he most desired was to be back in Rome with Massimo. It was a new and different Rock Hudson sitting next to me, one I did not like or respect. How long could we go on?"

***

Before reaching Kenya, Rock thumbed through Robert C. Ruark's big, brawny, and brutal novel, *Something of Value*, originally published in 1955. He read only the parts that pertained to his character. *Kirkus Review* claimed that Ruark's style was obviously influenced by the "rugged masculinity of Ernest Hemingway, but without any of his discipline."

Universal had paid Ruark $400,000 for the screen rights. Richard Brooks, the respected director, had adapted Ruark's material into a screenplay for a black-and-white film, the concept of which disappointed Rock, who had wanted the vibrant African setting to be presented in Technicolor.

The drama focused on the notorious Mau Mau uprising in British-controlled Kenya that raged between 1952 and 1960. It was a grisly conflict between blacks and colonial whites, widely publicized in Europe and the U.S. for its murderous attacks on settlers and their farmsteads. British troops, in collaboration with the Kenya Regiment (which included anti-Mau Mau black Africans who endorsed British rule) engaged in the bloody conflict. Its loyalties and boundaries shifted during the course of the hostilities, embarrassing publicity for the British, and the deaths of hundreds. Independence for Kenya was finally achieved in 1960, three years after the release of the film.

In the script, Rock was cast as Peter McKenzie, son of Walter McKenzie (as portrayed by Walter Fitzgerald), who had farmed his land since the early 1940s. As a boy, Peter grew up with Kimani Wa Karanja (as portrayed by Sidney Poitier), a native. The two boys were like brothers.

Peter's brother-in-law, Jeff Newton (Robert Beatty), frowned on such familiarities: "Blacks are blacks—not playmates," he proclaimed. His wife, Elizabeth (Peter's sister, as portrayed by Wendy Hiller), is later made to suffer horribly at the hands of the Mau Mau.

At one point, Kimani can no longer tolerate Newton's bullying. After a vicious slap, he runs away and joins the Mau Mau, enduring a horrendous blood-drinking ritual from his witchcraft-practicing father.

Peter (Rock) is set to marry his betrothed, Holly (Dana Wynter). They are away on safari when the Mau Mau attack the McKenzie estate, killing Newton and his two children and badly injuring Newton's pregnant wife, Elizabeth.

To retaliate against the raid, British forces bomb a Mau Mau encampment, imprisoning the tribesmen and torturing them.

By this time, Holly and Elizabeth have moved from the hinterlands to Nairobi, hoping to find a safe haven there.

Wanting to bring an end to the butchery, Peter (Rock) searches for Kimani, who by now, has taken a wife and fathered a child. Anti-Mau Mau vigilantes learn of their secret meeting and attack, killing villagers and Kumani's wife, although his child is saved.

Kumani believes that Peter has betrayed him and sets out for revenge, but dies unexpectedly after falling into a pit. Engineered for capturing a lion, its depths had been studded with upward-pointing bamboo spikes.

Near the end of the film, Peter rescues Kimani's infant and takes him off to rear him with his sister's son, hoping for a peaceful future.

The filmmaking "package" was put together by producer Pandro S. Berman, who'd made a name for himself during RKO's heyday in the 1930s, an era that witnessed the rise of Katharine Hepburn and the popularity of all those Fred Astaire/Ginger Rogers movies.

Although Berman had rejected the novel, *Gone With the Wind,* as the subject of a film adaptation, he functioned as the organizing force behind two other hit movies released the same year, 1939: *The Hunchback of Notre Dame* and *Gunga Din.* The gruff and darkly handsome Berman had met with Rock before his transit, with Phyllis, to Africa. During their meeting, Berman expressed disappointment that he couldn't get Grace Kelly or Elizabeth Taylor "to dress up" their movie.

Director Richard Brooks had arrived in Kenya weeks before Rock to scout for locations and to make final adjustments to his screenplay. Born to Russian Jewish immigrants, Brooks was both a director and a screen writer, having just helmed *Blackboard Jungle* (1955) with Glenn Ford. He'd also written the screenplay for *Key Largo* (1948) for John Huston, starring Humphrey Bogart and his wife, Lauren Bacall. In his immediate future, he would direct Elizabeth Taylor in *Cat on a Hot Tin Roof* (1958) and Burt Lancaster in *Elmer Gantry* (1960).

In the third lead, Sidney Poitier, a Bahamian born in Miami, would in time become one of the great male stars of classic cinema and the first African American to win a Best Actor Academy Award (for *Lilies of the Field;* 1963). Poitier's greatest success would come in 1967 with a trio of movies involving race and race relations: *To Sir, with Love; In the Heat of the Night;* and *Guess Who's Coming to Dinner?,* the latter with Katharine Hepburn and Spencer Tracy in his last film role.

The very talented director, Richard Brooks, helmed Rock in *Something of Value,* shot in dangerous Kenyan territory where foreigners were often abducted.

Instead of a beheading, they sometimes suffered a total castration.

Primarily a stage actress, English-born Wendy Hiller occasionally accepted movie roles. In 1959, she'd win the Best Supporting

Actress Oscar for *Separate Tables,* cast as the lonely hotel manager and mistress of the character played by Burt Lancaster.

Instead of Kelly or Taylor, Rock got Dana Wynter as his leading lady. She was a German-born English actress, whose best-known film became *Invasion of the Body Snatchers* (1956). When Rock met her, she'd just made *D-Day, the Sixth of June* (1956), with Robert Taylor, Rock's former lover.

Wynter had married the Hollywood divorce attorney, Greg Bautzer, the town's most eligible and desirable bachelor, having had a series of love affairs with Tinseltown's most glamourous stars, ranging from Joan Crawford to Lana Turner.

Rock interpreted Wynter as a strong anti-apartheid advocate.

***

Brooks was at the airport to greet Rock and Phyllis upon their arrival in Nairobi. "Welcome to Kenya. There's not a god damn thing here that won't kill you. The Mau Mau are still on a fucking rampage, even cutting off the dicks of some British soldiers they captured."

That was Phyllis' introduction to Brooks. That night she and Rock dined with him. Later, she told her husband, "Never again. He has the most vulgar mouth I've ever heard. No respect for a lady."

After dinner, Rock and Phyllis retired to their suite at the New Stanley Hotel, finding each of their twin beds covered with mosquito netting. "Malaria, you know," the bellboy said.

The next morning, Rock, with Phyllis, visited a local tailor, run by an *emigré* from Calcutta, with the intention of getting them suited with some safari outfits. "Me, heap big game hunter like Hemingway," Rock said.

The following day, he went off on location with Brooks, while Phyllis wandered alone around Nairobi. She inspected the local shops, most of them run by Indian merchants, selling everything from warthog tusks to zebra-skin rugs.

When she returned to the hotel, she met two wives of English soldiers, who warned her that she should never go out alone: "White women are often abducted and gang raped before they're mur-

In spite of their onscreen friendship ending in violence, Rock and Sidney Poitier befriended each other during the shoot in Kenya. The hotel manager didn't want to house the African American actor until Rock told him he was making $30,000 for three months of work.

"If he's making that much money, he can't be black," the manager said. "Poitier can have a room on your floor."

dered," one of the wives warned her.

After four days, Rock and Phyllis went by Jeep to the slopes of towering Mount Kenya for location shooting.

Jack Block, manager of the Mawingo Hotel, welcomed them and escorted them to their honeymoon suite, the most luxurious accommodation in all of Kenya. It was filled with Oriental rugs, a gigantic four-poster bed, and a terrace opening onto a panoramic view of Mount Kenya.

[In 1960, William Holden would purchase the hotel and reconfigure it as the Mount Kenya Safari Club. At presstime for this book, the place operates as the Fairmont Mount Kenya Safari Club Nanyuki.]

Early the next morning, Rock left for the shooting of an opening scene. He returned to the hotel that evening, terrified and sweat-drenched. "I was nearly killed when I stumbled across a black mamba. The bite of this snake is said to kill you instantly."

Rock with Dana Wynter, searching for *Something of Value.*

Rock later told Richard Brooks, "I'm sorry you couldn't get Grace Kelly or Elizabeth Taylor—better box office."

That weekend, Phyllis watched in dismay as Rock and Brooks went off on a full-day excursion into Mau Mau country, heading off into the mountains. When he returned that night, Rock confessed to her that they had gone to a Mau Mau encampment where tribal leaders were plotting their next raid.

"You could have been killed!" she protested.

"No, they actually were quite nice," he answered.

"Nice? You call rapists and murderers nice? Perhaps they are when they're not chopping off heads."

She knew that Brooks held her in contempt, having derisively relayed to one of the cameramen, "I'm told that Rock had to marry her to conceal his homo leanings. Surely he could have found something better than this little prune who runs in fright if a man utters the word 'fuck.'"

She detested Kenya and eventually managed a return to Los Angeles ahead of schedule, with the understanding that Rock would remain on site to finish his filming. On the day of her (early) departure, he drove her to the airport, where she boarded a plane to Stockholm. From there, she'd begin a flight over the North Pole to Los Angeles.

After bidding her goodbye, he waited in the airport's lounge bar for an hour for the arrival of an Alitalia flight from Rome. Disembarking from that flight was a blonde-haired Adonis, Massimo. Rock rushed to greet him. "The harridan is gone. I'm starved for love. Welcome to Africa, my man."

***

Something of Value opened to a disappointing box office. Bosley Crowther of *The New York Times* attacked the casting of Rock as a white African. "He runs through a range of stalwart poses that might be more viable on the Western Plains. Dana Wynter is slightly limp as his *fiancée*, and Wendy Hiller, Walter Fitzgerald, and Robert Beatty make a curious assortment of Kenya farm settlers. Sidney Poitier gives a stirring, strong performance as the emotion-torn black friend."

***

Back in Los Angeles with Phyllis, Rock resumed the closing chapter of what he privately assessed to his friends as, "my non-marriage to the dyke."

The fan magazines, however, continued to play up what they configured, in print, at least, as a happy and conventional marriage. In one article, Rock was quoted as saying, "Phyllis and I plan to have lots of babies. I was an only child, and I know how lonely that can be. I want my sons and daughters to have playmates growing up together."

He also claimed, "When day is done, I head for home, knowing Phyllis is there waiting for me with a home-cooked meal."

That was spectacularly inaccurate. He was rarely at home. Sometimes he called, claiming he'd be very late, citing a fan magazine interview or a business huddle with Henry Willson. On many a night, he didn't come home at all, asserting that he was too tired to drive and would sleep over in his dressing room at the studio.

In yet another magazine article, Rock proclaimed, "My Phyllis is even more vibrant and vivacious than the day I married her—what a gal!"

After his return from Africa, she found his dark moods descending more and more frequently. At times, he complained of feeling trapped within the walls of his home.

He often told her he needed to go for a long drive in the Hollywood Hills to clear his head. Then another development transpired within their marriage. While shooting interiors for *Something of Value,* their lovemaking ceased forever.

There was also a notable change in his wardrobe. One day, he brought home six pairs of blue jeans. Prior to this, he had never liked blue jeans on a man, unless he was in a Western. "You're a movie star with a wardrobe filled with beautiful clothes, often from Ed Muhl at Universal," Phyllis said. "Why do you want to dress like a bum?"

Rock ignored her. He soaked the half-dozen pairs of tight-fitting jeans in the bathtub, donned each of them, wet, and then went into his backyard. There, he lay down in the sun, drying the jeans to the contours of his body. He also poured bleach onto the crotch of each of the six pairs of jeans.

When she saw him heading out one night wearing a pair of the "doctored" jeans, her eyes focused on his crotch. "Why not go nude?" she asked, mockingly. "My God, those damn jeans completely outline your penis. Isn't that making things a bit too obvious?"

"If you've got it, flaunt it!" he told her before heading out the door.

She was furious, and after about two weeks, plotted her revenge. While he was at MGM completing his final scenes, she rounded up every pair of those jeans, hauled them into the backyard, and set them on fire in the incinerator.

When he returned home that night with plans to go out, he searched for his jeans before learning that she'd burned them. He was furious, denouncing her for nearly an hour. Then he stormed out of the house, and didn't see her for the next few days.

Perhaps each was aware that the end was near. "I really believed that he couldn't stand the sight of me," she said.

***

On many nights when she was home alone, calls came in from men, identifying themselves only by their first names—Jim, Ralph, Dave, Clint, or whomever. When she confronted Rock about the identity of all these men, he claimed, "Fans must have gotten my private number."

One caller was more persistent than the others, and he identified himself by his full name of John Steele. At least that's who he claimed to be.

As it turned out, that wasn't his name at all. He was the notorious Johnny Stompanato, the gangster henchman of hoodlum Mickey Cohen.

Rock was home one night when he called, and, while Phyllis was in the kitchen cooking dinner, he talked at length with Johnny, whom he'd met at a party hosted by Henry Willson. A rendezvous was planned for later that night in Johnny's apartment. Rock left right after dinner, telling

Phyllis that he had a business appointment, which she did not believe.

Unknown to Rock, Johnny was Hollywood's leading stud-for-hire with a roster of previous seductions that included both men and women. His first movie star seduction, back in the 1940s, had been Ava Gardner and later, Janet Leigh. From there, he went on to seduce Zsa Zsa Gabor, Errol Flynn, Clifton Webb, Spencer Tracy, Marilyn Monroe, Cole Porter, and even the sometimes girlfriend of both Rock and Frank Sinatra, Marilyn Maxwell.

During the early 1950s, police records in Los Angeles revealed that he'd been arrested eight times, based on charges ranging from suspicion of robbery to vagrancy. Mob Boss Mickey Cohen mocked the vagrancy charge. "When the cops took him in, Johnny had $5,000 in his wallet, all in one-hundred-dollar bills."

As a front, he ran the Myrtlewood Gift Shop in Westwood, a place known for selling contemporary wood carvings and crude pottery as fine art.

In time, Johnny didn't need to pursue petty crime, as he and Cohen stumbled upon a big money-making scheme. They began to blackmail Hollywood stars, male and female, by secretly photographing them in compromising situations having sex with him, a stud widely noted for his exceptionally large penis. He was nicknamed by his conquests as "Superman of the Boudoir."

Zsa Zsa told friends, *"Dah-ling,* it stretches all the way to Alaska."

Unknown to Rock at the time, Johnny had first been exposed in *U.S. Confidential,* a book written by Lee Mortimer who called him "a general stooge for Mickey Cohen, whose job it is to round up beautiful women to service visiting mobsters from Chicago or New York."

After her mother, Lana Turner, began an affair with Johnny Stompanato, her daughter, Cheryl Crane, described his appearance in a memoir: "B-picture looks, thick set. Powerfully built and soft-spoken. He talked in short sentences to cover a poor grasp of grammar and had a deep baritone voice. With friends, he seldom smiled or laughed out loud, and always seemed coiled, holding himself in."

She also described his wardrobe: "Roomy, draped slacks, a silver-buckled leather belt, and lizard shoes."

Before he flew to Italy to make *A Farewell to Arms,* Rock had three sessions with Johnny.

Extortionist, hustler, and play-for-pay con artist, Johnny Stompanato

He later told friends George Nader and Mark Miller, "It is the best sex I've ever had. This guy is not only good, he's super great! He should teach classes in love-making. He's a fuck machine and can go all night!"

In the months ahead, Rock would painfully learn that his second session of love-making with Johnny had been secretly filmed in clips that clearly identified the players. Their third encounter was also filmed, but with a difference. After Johnny had sex with Rock, he offered him a nightcap.

All that Rock remembered was falling into a deep sleep, waking up in a motel room at 10AM the next morning. He told his friends, "I was more exhausted than I thought I was. I slept like a log." What he didn't know was that he'd been extensively photographed in his drugged coma by Johnny.

When Rock revived, Johnny was gone, but he'd left him a note: "You'll be hearing from me. Johnny."

***

After lending Rock out to MGM for *Something of Value,* and before he leased him to 20th Century Fox, Ed Muhl wanted his major star to film a movie for his home studio, Universal.

He had acquired the rights to the 1935 William Faulkner novel, *Pylon.* Because of certain daring plot twists, the movie rights had not been purchased because the Production Code had gone into effect, and studios feared that the project was too controversial.

But Universal decided that for a 1957 release, the world had become more enlightened, and *Pylon,* its title changed to *The Tarnished Angels,* could at last go before the cameras.

Upon the release of the film, it was billed as THE BOOK THEY SAID COULD NEVER BE FILMED!

Once again, Douglas Sirk was called in as director, marking the last time he'd helm Rock. Sirk and producer Albert Zugsmith, who had turned out the highly successful *Written on the Wind,* decided to rehire the same stars; not only Rock, but Dorothy Malone and his longtime friend and occasional lover, Robert Stack. Character actor Jack Carson was given the fourth lead, the role of a mechanic, "Jiggs."

George Zuckerman adapted the screenplay from the Faulkner novel. He'd had great success with his *Written on the Wind.*

Set in the depths of the Depression, *The Tarnished Angels* featured Stack as Roger Shumann, a disillusioned and impoverished, once-celebrated World War I flying ace. He had evolved into a barn-storming stunt pilot at rural airshows with his parachutist wife, LaVerne (Malone) and worshipful son Jack (Christopher Olden).

Rock, in the role of Burke Devlin, plays an alcoholic, down-on-his-luck reporter dependent on loans from his editor. He's intrigued by the gypsy-like lifestyle of the former war hero, but is dismayed by how he treats his wife, LaVerne. Devlin is soon attracted to her himself.

In this convoluted plot, Stack (as Shumann) trades the sexual services of his wife to an over-the-hill business magnate Matt Ord (Robert Middleton) in exchange for one of his battered old planes.

Stack later admitted to pangs of remorse when the character he was playing onscreen "sold" the sexual services of his onscreen wife to a "dirty old man." He was thinking at the time about his real wife, Rosemarie, who was scheduled, any day now, to deliver their baby.

As Stack, years later, explained in his memoirs about a real-life event that transpired on the outdoor location of this film, "Suddenly, out of nowhere, an old plane was diving straight for the cameras," he wrote. "Behind it trailed a tatty old banner proclaiming, in letters four feet tall: IT'S A GIRL!"

"Rock had arranged with the hospital to send word immediately when my baby was born. He had then hired a stunt pilot and gave him instructions to tow the appropriate message behind the plane. It's a moment I've never forgotten. Anybody who tells you that Rock Hudson isn't a first-class gent had better put up his dukes."

Jiggs, the mechanic in the film, makes a decision that will lead to tragedy. He manages to repair the damaged plane to get it airborne, but it has reached its "expiration date." Once airborne, Shumann begins to experience difficulties with the motor, which gives out as he plunges to the earth, killing him in a fiery crash.

But LaVerne (Malone) and Devlin (Rock) don't end up as a loving couple at the film's end. He tells her goodbye as she heads to Iowa, without him, to rear her son, Jack.

Rock liked veteran actor Carson, a Canadian, who had appeared in some of his favorite movies, notably in such classics as *Mildred Pierce (1945)*, a film that brought Joan Crawford her one and only Best Actress Oscar.

Carson, on film, was

known for his wisecracking, smug cockiness. At the time he met Rock, he'd appeared in Judy Garland's *A Star Is Born* (1954), and had been designated to play Paul Newman's older brother, Gooper, father of all those no-neck monsters in the film adaptation Tennessee Williams' *Cat on a Hot Tin Roof* (1958).

***

The one cast member in *The Tarnished Angels* who most intrigued Rock was Troy Donahue, one of Henry Willson's latest discoveries fresh from his casting couch. He had nabbed a minor role in the film, playing Frank Burnham, an unscrupulous daredevil aviator.

Willson was billing him as "The Next James Dean," and, without embarrassment, Troy was seen about town in the same red jacket Dean had worn in his iconic film, *Rebel Without a Cause* (1955).

John Gilmore, one of Dean's best friends, met the young, blonde-haired, blue-eyed actor, saying, "Troy was a bright new face, or should I say, 'ass,' on Willson's meat rack. Everyone was aware of that. As Rock's agent, but also as his pimp, Willson worked behind the scenes to get Troy a role in Rock's latest film."

"Rock had reached such heights as a star that he could demand that one of the young actors in one of his films should also be able to get fucked, even if they were straight," Gilmore claimed. "As he went around Hollywood, he was often mistaken for Tab Hunter. Troy would say, 'No, I'm Troy Donahue, the straight one.' He was about as straight as a crooked road."

Born Merle Johnson, Jr., in New York, Troy was eleven years younger than Rock. Willson immediately changed his name, going first for "Paris Donahue," the mythical lover of Helen of Troy, but dropping the Paris and eventually settling on Troy instead.

After meeting Rock, Donahue said, "Acting is all I ever wanted to do. Ever since I was a kid, I read plays. My parents didn't want me to become an actor. They preferred something more stable—doctor, lawyer, Indian chief, anything but actor."

When Willson "sold" the idea of Troy to Rock, he said, "During the shoot, you can use him for sexual relief, so you won't be cruising everything in sight and running the chance of getting exposed in *Confidential.*"

Indeed, Rock was initially attracted to Troy, and even told Willson, "Great cocksucker, but he's another Princess Tiny Meat like Monty Clift."

"At least you can get off on him," Willson said. "After all those demonstrations of his oral talents, you can always turn him over and fuck hell out of him. Great ass!"

On the set of *The Tarnished Angels*, Rock began an affair with the good-looking blonde that lasted for several months.

Troy told Rock that it wasn't Willson who discovered him. "Initially, producer William Asher and director James Sheldon spotted me in a diner in Malibu. They got me a screen test at Columbia Pictures, but Harry Cohn hated it, saying I come off like a faggot. To make matters worse, I was so despondent I almost died. I lost control of my car and plunged forty feet down a canyon. Obviously, I survived. But it was a close call."

Troy admitted that he felt Willson was wrong in promoting him as the new James Dean even to the point of "wearing that damn red jacket. You know yourself, I'm nothing like Dean. After all, you made a picture with the fucker. I'll let you in on a secret: Instead of Dean, my goal is to become 'The Next Tab Hunter.'"

"In that, I think you'll succeed," Rock predicted.

And he was right.

For years, Troy tried to mask his bisexuality. When pressed, he admitted, "Rock saw me as his next trick, but I was one of the few straight men who resisted his unwelcome advances. I'm a sort of ladies' man."

Robert Stack, who knew Rock intimately, said, "Donahue's a liar. Everybody in the cast, including Dorothy (Malone) and Jack Carson, even Sirk, knew that Donahue was getting plugged two or three times a day. Rock was always oversexed."

***

Sirk had opted to shoot *The Tarnished Angels* in black and white to recapture the despondent mood of the Depression era. William Faulkner, a former screenwriter himself, visited the set several times, and had high praise for Rock's portrayal of his main character, the reporter. He later told the press, "*The Tarnished Angels* is the best screen adaptation of one of my novels ever made."

In general, however, reviews were poor, *Variety* calling it "a stumbling entry. Characters are mostly colorless, given static reading in drawn-out situations, with a story line lacking in punch."

That forever critic of Rock's movies, Bosley Crowther of *The New York Times*, claimed that *The Tarnished Angels* was "badly, cheaply written and abominably played by a hand-picked cast. The sentiments are inflated—blown out of proportions to the values involved. And the acting, under Douglas Sirk's direction, is elaborate and absurd."

But the years have gone by, and movie aficionados have come to appreciate the film more. That same *New York Times* featured an entirely different evaluation when critic David Kehr looked at it a decade later, defining it as "among Sirk's most self-conscious and artistically ambitious creations. This is bravura filmmaking in the service of a haunting vision. Yet there are moments of almost microscopic subtlety: The camera movements that express the moral reversal of the Hudson and Stack characters, one growing larger than the other; the infinite tenderness with which Hudson strokes Ms. Malone's hair, helplessly trying to comfort her after a shock."

Rating it four stars, *TV Guide* called it "the best-ever adaptation of a Faulkner novel, "echoing the same sentiments of the novelist himself. *The Tarnished Angels* was directed with passion and perception by Sirk. The acting is first-rate here, and the script is outstanding, full of wit, black humor, and occasional fine poetic monologues."

***

Instead of *Ben-Hur*, Rock was lured into accepting David Selznick's offer of a remake, scheduled for release in 1957, of *A Farewell to Arms,* based on Ernest Hemingway's semi-autobiographical novel of the same name.

Its first film version had been released in 1932 and had starred Gary Cooper as a soldier and Helen Hayes as a nurse in love with him.

Selznick had unrealistic hopes for this latest version. "It'll be bigger than my *Gone With the Wind.* I'm casting my wife, Jennifer Jones, as your leading lady. If we can pull this one off according to my vision, the Academy will be awarding Oscars to both of you."

Before he flew to Italy to begin filming, Rock encountered another Oscar, Oscar Levant, at a party. "Starring in a major motion picture can be as much fun as walking through a field of cow dung with glue on your shoes."

"Thanks for the tip," Rock said. "I've been warned."

The morning Rock was scheduled to fly out of Los Angeles for the debut of location shooting, a call came in from Montgomery Clift. "It may be too late to bow out now, but watch your step. Working with both Selznick and Jennifer Jones is a recipe for disaster. I'm still recovering not only from the wounds of my accident, where you helped rescue me, but from the bruises inflicted when I made *Indiscretions of an American Wife* (1953) with the two of them in Rome. Those two, especially Selznick, can drive you nuts."

Clift confessed that during the shoot, Jones had developed a crush on hm. "When she found out I went for guys, she became hysterical. She went into her portable dressing room and tried to stuff a mink stole down her portable toilet."

Rock had not read the Hemingway novel, nor did he plan to. However, Clift told him that whereas Jones was 38, the character of the nurse, Catherine Barkley, had been conceived by the author as a 24-year-old.

In Rome, Selznick arranged for Rock to meet with Jones to discuss their roles. She told him that she had long wanted to portray a Hemingway heroine. "I really lobbied to be cast as Lady Brett in *The Sun Also Rises* (1957) with that divine Tyrone Power. But, as you know, Ava Gardner made off with that role."

She also lamented that she had not gotten the female lead in *Giant* opposite him. "Elizabeth Taylor tried to pull it off—I'll give her that. But you were perfect."

She told him, "David thinks that the two of us will be dynamite on screen. After we finish this one, there may be offers for us to co-star in a series of romantic dramas."

The next day, Rock was given an updated screenplay by Ben Hecht, who was considered one of the best script writers in Hollywood. He'd even applied the finishing touches to *Gone With the Wind* while working, around the same time, on other scripts such as *Gunga Din* starring Cary Grant and *Wuthering Heights* with Laurence Olivier. "The year 1939 was one busy mother-fucker with all that."

He found Hecht a colorful character with a confessional kind of private talk. "The best thing for a future writer was to run away from home at the age of 16. I spent my teen years in whorehouses, police stations, courtrooms telling it to the judge, theater stages, jails, saloons, slums, madhouses, and at fires, murders, and riots. While running from the police, I'd duck into bookstores and read for hours."

Rock was both delighted and intimidated to have John Huston as his director. Over the course of nearly half a century, he would receive fifteen Academy Award nominations, winning two of them. As "The Ernest Hemingway of Cinema," he was Humphrey Bogart's favorite director, having helmed him in *The Maltese Falcon* (1941), *The Treasure of Sierra Madre* (1948), and *The African Queen* (1951), which brought Bogie an Oscar.

But when shooting began in Italy, Huston was no longer around. The director and the producer had not agreed on anything. Huston wanted "more Hemingway" in the script, whereas Selznick was ordering Hecht to reshape it into more of a love story between Rock and Jones.

He even objected to Rock's haircut, Huston preferring the shorter style of a soldier during the Italian campaign, whereas Selznick demanded longer hair, claiming it was needed to maintain Rock's sex appeal to teenage girls.

"They even fought over my Adam's apple, Selznick thinking it was too prominent and that it should be concealed by makeup," Rock said.

"God damn it," Huston said. "He's a man, isn't he? Men have Adam's apples."

Selznick told the press, "In Mr. Huston, I asked for a First Violinist and I got a soloist."

"When Huston and Selznick came together, it was a case of an immovable object meeting an irresistible force," Rock said.

Jennifer Jones' biographer, Edward Z. Epstein, wrote: "Huston was hardly a minnow in a shark tank, and not a man to cringe before the onslaught of a crunching producer. He'd crunched quite a few of his own!"

Huston complained, "Selznick wants to direct everything. What does that make me? His hired prostitute?"

Privately, Selznick confided to Jones and Rock, "I fired George Cukor on *Gone With the Wind* after two weeks, and I'm going to do the same with Huston."

He didn't have to, as the director resigned before he got the boot.

Selznick then hired director Charles Vidor (no relation to King Vidor). About the only thing Huston had in common with Vidor was that both of them had married Evelyn Keyes, "Scarlett O'Hara's Younger Sister" in *Gone With the Wind*.

When Rock met Vidor, the director asked him, "Are all those rumors about you true?"

"Hell, no!" Rock snapped. "All of them damn lies!"

Vidor had recently directed *Love Me or Leave Me* (1954) with James Cagney and Doris Day cast as the singer, Ruth Etting. "I think you and Doris would make the perfect couple in a romantic comedy," Vidor told him.

In Hecht's script, Rock played Frederick Henry, an American officer serving in an ambulance unit for the Italian Army during World War I, a role originated by Gary Cooper. After he's wounded, he's sent to a British hospital in Northern Italy, where a nurse, Catherine Barkley (Jennifer Jones) gives him tender, loving care. She's not only his nurse, but becomes his lover.

A friend, Dr. Emerich (Oskar Homolka), convinces the army that the patient's knee is more severely wounded than it is, so the newly self-defined lovers can continue their affair.

Eventually, Catherine discovers that she's pregnant, and their affair continues until the stern head nurse, Miss Van Campben (Mercedes McCambridge), discovers their secret and separates them. She evaluates the patient as fully recovered and declares that he can and should resume his duties on the front as an ambulance driver. In the interim, Catherine fears that her lover has abandoned her.

The third lead, Major Alessandro Rinaldi, was played by Vittorio De Sico, the noted Italian director. He had been acclaimed, among other achievements, for his 1947 film, *The Bicycle Thief*, an icon of neorealism on the screen.

[Although the 1957 remake of A Farewell to Arms would ultimately flop at the box office, De Sica's performance was praised. For it, he would be nominated for a Best Supporting Actor Oscar.]

In battle once again, Frederick is wounded and taken to the American hospital in Milan. There, he meets a sympathetic nurse (Elaine Stritch), who becomes aware that Frederick and Catherine are deeply in love with each other. She arranges for Catherine to be transferred to the hospital in Milan for a reunion with her lover.

The McCambridge character appears on the scene, discharging Frederick from the ward. Back in the field, once again as an ambulance driver, his commanding officers send him directly into the fury of battle to face the rampaging Germans.

Vidor re-created many savage scenes of war, not for the faint of heart. Among the grisly scenes were views of mothers weeping as they cuddled their dying babies in their arms.

After the notorious Battle of Carporeto, where the Italians and the German invaders waged war, Frederick and Major Rinaldi (De Sica) aid the local refugees fleeing the "Huns" from the north. After delivering assistance to the refugees, when Rinaldi and Frederick report to the nearest Army base, the Commandant there defines each of them as deserters from the Front, and his judgment is harsh: Each of them is sentenced to be executed by a firing squad. Rinaldi is fatally shot, but Frederick escapes by jumping into the river.

Fleeing from his pursuers, Frederick reunites with Catherine and they flee from Milan, escaping in a rowboat across the lake to the Swiss border. Inside neutral Switzerland, they self-identify as tourists.

Catherine's pregnancy weighs heavily on her, and she is forced to enter a hospital where their child is stillborn. She dies shortly thereafter.

At movie's end, Frederick wanders down a deserted street, a lost, lonely soldier, filled with despair and facing an uncertain future.

During the shoot, Rock and McCambridge had little to say to each other. During the filming of *Giant*, when she played his sister, "She wasn't very sisterly," he told Jones. "She and James Dean were always off somewhere conspiring against me."

He learned that McCambridge and Stritch were having a lesbian affair. When she was not otherwise engaged, Rock hung out with Stritch, finding her a lot of fun. He'd first seen her in the road show of *Call Me Madam*, which had brought Broadway success to Ethel Merman.

Rock recalled, "Elaine was hip, very flippant, a tough old broad who could tell a dirty joke better than any man I knew."

As the doctor in the movie, Homolka was a Viennese actor with a lot of success on the stage. He'd actually been a soldier in the Austro-Hungarian army during World War I. Usually, he was cast as villains, communist spies, or Soviet Bloc military officers. Occasionally, he broke free from typecasting and appeared in a comedy, including one, *The Seven Year Itch* (1955) with Marilyn Monroe.

***

Upon the release of *A Farewell to Arms*, reviews were universally bad. It marked Selznick's last sad swan song to Hollywood, over which he'd once reigned.

Variety wrote: "Miss Jones imbues the nurse with a sense of neurosis and foreboding, but she only sporadically rises to the full challenge of this super-difficult role. She frequently lacks warmth."

The New York Herald-Tribune claimed, "If there were a supreme Bad Taste Award for movies, *A Farewell to Arms* would win hands down. This smutty version of Ernest Hemingway's novel will set thousands of stomachs turning."

Nearly all critics cited Rock's performance as the soldier as being "wooden." Some movie goers laughed when Rock delivered his most embarrassing line after he learns that Catherine is dying: "Maybe this is the price for sleeping together."

Bosley Crowther in *The New York Times* wrote: "Selznick's picture lacks the all-important awareness of the inescapable presence and pressure of war. The key support to the structure of the theme has been largely removed by Ben Hecht's script and by a clear elimination of subtle thematic overtones. It is a tedious account of a love affair between two persons who are strangely insistent upon keeping it informal. As a pure romance, it has its shortcoming."

"The essential excitement of a violent love is strangely missing in the studied performances that Rock Hudson and Jennifer Jones give in the leading roles," Crowther asserted. "Hudson is most noticeably unbending, as if he were cautious and shy, but Jones plays the famous Catherine Barkley with bewildering nervous moves and grimaces. The show of devotion between two people is intensely acted, not realized. It is questionable, indeed, whether Hudson and Jones have the right personalities for these roles."

TV Guide called it "an overblown Hollywood extravaganza that hasn't improved with age. The chief virtue of this hollow epic is the stupendous color photography of the Italian Alps. Also enjoyable is De Sica's inspired performance, but it's not enough to offset the flagrant overacting by Jones and the wooden acting of Hudson."

Time Out New York described the film as "an inflated remake with surplus production values and spectacle. A padded Ben Hecht script and Selznick's invariable tendency to overkill are equally to blame."

Slant magazine awarded *A Farewell to Arms* two stars—out of a possible five. "To those willing to endure *A Farewell to Arms:* Don't be a hero! We have Selznick to blame for this bloated two-hour plus Technicolor remake, announcing from the larger-than-life opening credits set against epic shots of sunsets, mountains, and valleys that he's aiming for another *Gone With the Wind,* without compelling lovers at the heart of his grand-scale love story. It's all just a meaningless protracted spectacle."

After sitting through the movie in Key West, Hemingway said, "Rock Hudson is no Gary Cooper. You write a novel that you've viewed over the years as true and real. Then you see what Hollywood does to it. It's like pissing in your father's beer."

William Faulkner had praised Rock's performance as the reporter in *The Tarnished Angels.* But Hemingway, an even more famous novelist, interpreted Rock, as the American soldier, "soft and sappy."

***

Professionally shooting *A Farewell to Arms* in Italy was a horrendous ordeal for Rock. In spite of his scandalous previous sojourn (with Phyllis) at the Grand Hotel, he had selected it once again as his home in the Italian capital, this time bringing Massimo with him. They celebrated their long-delayed reunion, staying locked inside and ordering from room service for two uninterrupted days and nights. "We made up for lost time," Rock said in a phone call to Henry Willson, who began to plot ways to break up this romance, which was becoming fodder for gossip.

Some employee at the Grand tipped off the scandal sheets in Rome. One item reported that Rock was "auditioning" a Roman gladiator type for a bit part in *A Farewell to Arms,* even though the picture was already filled with extras cast as World War I soldiers. Massimo was identified in a tabloid as an actor friend of Anna Magnani and referred to as Rock's "Roman Romeo" and even "The Apollo of the Eternal City."

There was also bad news on the homefront: Phyllis had wanted to go with him to Rome, as she had once before *en route* to Kenya. But two days before departure, she became sick, complaining of food poisoning, perhaps from a platter of oysters she'd eaten in Malibu at a beachfront restaurant.

Rock really didn't want her to go, based on his preference for the company of Massimo, and the embarrassments of his earlier "Roman Holiday" with her. But he promised to send for her after she recovered.

On her third night alone, she phoned her doctor, who then came to her house, finding her bed stricken. He delivered her to St. John's Hospital, where she underwent a series of tests. When the results came in, it was discovered that she had a severe case of hepatitis, almost severe enough to threaten her life. She would have to be hospitalized, she was told, for at least three months.

Rock heard this news from Willson, who phoned him in Rome from Hollywood. "Thank God I stopped having sex with her," Rock said. "She might have infected me."

When cast and crew members asked if he were flying back to her side, he told them, "Phyllis does this on occasion. She puts on an act. Actually, she's as healthy as a cow." He later realized that using that bovine metaphor was indiscreet.

News of Phyllis's condition reached the press, and many reporters, especially Louella Parsons, were critical of Rock for not flying back to be at her bedside. Defiantly, he announced that he could not leave the production, because he was scheduled "in almost every scene."

***

In Hollywood, in a hospital, Phyllis was placed in an isolation ward because she was highly infectious. At first, doctors ordered intravenous feedings because she could not retain food in her stomach. In time, however, she began to digest light meals. When visitors were finally allowed to see her, they wore masks and hospital gowns.

Anna Kashfi, the disillusioned current wife of Marlon Brando, showed up, and, with Phyllis, they each gossiped about the failures and shortcomings of their respective husbands.

It seemed that Phyllis was not the only Hollywood wife having roman-tic troubles. Hjordis Niven, wife of the British actor, David Niven, was hav-ing minor surgery at the hospital, and when she was able, she, too, visited Phyllis' room.

She later reported that Hjordis had recently learned that her husband had had an affair with Errol Flynn in the early 1940s. "I guess it's what Hollywood husbands do," she said.

Ironically, Dolly Isley, the mother of Jennifer Jones, had suffered a heart attack and was in a hospital room two doors away from Phyllis. Selznick booked a ticket to fly his wife from Rome back to see her mother, and it was assumed that Rock would return from Rome, too, to visit his wife. But he did not. Nor did he call. Willson handled Rock's non-involvement, send-ing Phyllis flowers every three days with a forged note, supposedly from Rock.

After Jones visited her stricken mother at the hospital, she called on Phyllis, finding her desperately ill. She presented her with a tray of Eliza-beth Arden cosmetics. Phyllis pleaded with her husband's co-star, begging her, "Please, please, get Rock to fly home. I really need him here."

"I'll do whatever I can," Jones responded. "It all depends on this heavy shooting schedule we have. David can't afford to shut down production, even for a few days. I wasn't in every scene, but Rock was. That's why I'm here now, but I'm returning to Rome in the morning. I know Rock worries about you all the time."

Around this time, Willson himself was due for meetings in Rome, too. Before his departure, he persuaded Universal to release a statement to the press: It claimed that Rock was horrified to learn of the serious illness of his "beloved Bunting. As soon as Rock can break free of film production, he plans to fly to her side to see her through this ordeal. In the meantime, he is seeing that Mrs. Hudson gets the best medical care available in Cali-fornia."

At the time, Willson was more concerned with mitigating a potential scandal in Rome based on Rock's love life than he was with Phyllis' med-ical condition.

He came up with a scheme. To activate it, he called Troy Donahue, an actor he was aggressively promoting at the time, to fly to Rome with him. His aim involved using Donahue to break up Rock's romance with Mas-simo, which was becoming too well known and too public.

Donahue was eager for another reunion with Rock. Rock had already reported favorably on the blonde-haired young actor's oral abilities and, as an afterthought, added, "He's also a great fuck…Takes it like a man."

Willson and Donahue eventually arrived together in Rome, the agent booking a suite for himself at the Excelsior. Rock had already booked the suite adjoining his own, with full knowledge that an interconnecting door could be opened between them. It was in that adjoining suite where Donahue was installed.

Willson's plan to use Donahue as bait to get rid of Massimo didn't work out that way. On their first night, Rock opened the interconnecting door to Donahue's suite and invited him to join Massimo and himself. Their two-way became a three-way.

Not only that, but word leaked to the gossip columnists that Rock was staging Roman orgies in his suite, inviting the best-looking hustlers—many of them wearing colorful silk shirts unbuttoned to

Two actors from the stables of Henry Willson, each with improbable names (Troy and Rock), meeting as movie stars and international heartthrobs on the set of *The Tarnished Angels*

show off their David-esque physiques—prowling the Via Veneto at night. Their numbers were sometimes supplemented by Gore Vidal, who "shipped over" an assortment of his own favorite hustlers to join them.

Rock, already "accessorized" with two wannabe actors (Donahue and Massimo), was about to add to their trio. Arriving in Rome was the British bombshell, Dinah Dors. She was accompanied by her lover, Tommy Yeardye. To be discreet, she checked into the Excelsior alone, and proceeded without an escort to her suite, as she knew that the press would be following her.

Rock, meanwhile, made arrangements for Yeardye to occupy the adjoining suite, with Donahue, at the Grand Hotel. On his first night there, the three-way in these interconnected rooms evolved into a four-way. Rock would later report to Willson, "It was one of the most glorious nights of my wicked life. I was the Queen Bee."

The usually hip Dors seemed unaware that her boyfriend was having an affair with Rock. She remained friendly to him, even visiting him on the set of *A Farewell to Arms*. She flirted with Rock, and he assumed she wanted to have an affair with him, too, but he politely resisted her.

She told Yeardye, who later reported to Rock, "I heard he had sex with Marilyn Monroe. Why not me? I'm sexier, blonder, and far more beautiful than any old Marilyn Monroe."

***

In a weakened condition, Phyllis moved back into their house on Warbler Place, where she hired a full-time nurse. She was "tired all the time," she complained. Next door, a house was under construction, and she claimed that the constant hammering "is driving me crazy."

She phoned a real estate agent who arranged for the rental of a small beach house in Malibu. She

Dinah Dors visited Rock in Rome on the set of *A Farewell to Arms*. He turned down her sexual solicitation but not the come-on of her studly boyfriend, Tommy Yeardye.

moved in there with her nurse and Demi, her beloved poodle. She was also having sessions three times a week with a female psychiatrist, Dr. Dubois.

She ordered Willson to inform Rock that she'd temporarily changed her address. If he wanted to see her when he came back after nearly six months in Italy, he'd find her in Malibu.

When Rock returned to his home turf, Universal alerted him that he was receiving more than 10,000 fan letters a month, and that secretaries were answering his mail. A newsletter for his devoted fans, the *Hudson Herald*, was launched so that the public could keep abreast of his career moves. His female worshippers were cautioned, however, not to inquire about his private life, since he preferred "to keep private things private."

There were glowing reports about how much he'd missed his wife, who was ill, during his time in Italy. After seeing all the reports wherein many groups interpreted him as "the World's Most Desirable Male," he spoke candidly to a reporter, "I'm not perfect. I chew my nails. My eyes are a bit dull, a shoe shine brown, I eat all the wrong foods and worry constantly about putting on a pound or two."

He arrived back in Hollywood at a time when many stars had decided to take on *Confidential* and bankrupt its publisher, Robert Harrison, bringing an end to his scandal magazine. Harrison faced an ongoing series of libel suits originating from, among others, Maureen O'Hara and Dorothy Dandridge. The biggest was filed by Liberace, who was accused of "being mad about the boy," alleging that he had supposedly molested a hapless press agent. *[Eventually, Liberace settled that suit for $40,000 but later brought another lawsuit—this one for $25 million—against London's* Daily Mirror.*]*

In the United States, both Willson and Rock feared that Harrison's files on the stars would be subpoenaed and entered into court records.

Before Rock arrived back in California, Phyllis had taken a bold move without consulting her husband: She met with lawyers from a law firm named Morgan Maree, which represented such actors as Humphrey Bogart and David Niven. For months, she had suspected that Willson was stealing from Rock, even billing him for private expenses associated with his own lavish lifestyle.

In her memoirs, she revealed that Willson found out what she was doing, claiming that his "Machiavellian mind" had gone to work to destroy her and to spread gossip about her. "He knew I was behind the switch to the Maree firm taking over Rock's business affairs, though he was still retained as his agent for a few more months."

"He viewed me as a dangerous monster that he, like a well-meaning Dr. Frankenstein, had created." she wrote. "After that, he treated me almost as if I didn't exist."

Rock's homecoming was widely reported in the press, and he temporarily moved into Phyllis's cottage in Malibu. She wrote that he rushed to take her in his arms, claiming, "I missed you so much, Bunting. It was awful being stuck over in Italy without you."

"He took me into the bedroom," she claimed, "and we made love."

To Mark Miller and George Nader, Rock presented his own version of the reunion. "I was actually afraid to get near her, thinking she might be infectious, regardless of what her doctors said. Lovemaking was out of the question. Thinking of her as a walking germ carrier that might destroy my own liver was one big god damn turnoff."

"The moment I arrived in Malibu, the bitch began to nag the hell out of me. She made all sorts of accusations, even confronting me with Troy Donahue. She also asked if I had taken up with my 'Roman fruitcake,' a reference to Massimo."

The morning after their reunion, she told him that she'd met with officers of the Maree firm, who had told her that they wanted to take over the management of his business affairs. At first, she thought he'd attack her for doing all this without his knowledge, yet she found him very receptive. He told her, "I've known for years that Henry has been stealing from me. About time to put an end to it."

Both of them went to the Maree office, where Rock met with officers, who convinced him, "You're being robbed weekly." He signed the necessary documents to turn over management of his money and assets to Maree.

Back in Malibu, Rock was gone most nights, claiming that he was negotiating for another picture or giving fan magazine interviews.

One night, he invited Phyllis to dinner at a restaurant in Malibu. At that point, they occupied separate bedrooms. She didn't get to talk much to him that evening, as they were interrupted by his fans. When she did, she pleaded with him to start seeing her psychiatrist, hoping to save their marriage. He absolutely refused, claiming, "All I need right now is some god damn headshrinker."

Back home, their marriage almost ended that night. Rock had left the gate unlatched and her poodle, Demi, ran out onto the Pacific Coast Highway, where it was struck and killed by a truck. She discovered her pet as road kill.

After that, she claimed she could no longer live in Malibu, where Demi had been killed. Both of them returned to Warbler Place. She later reported that he was gone every night. "When he was home, he was moody and grumpy, and he seems to find fault with everything I do," she told George Nader, who still befriended her. "For months, he raved about my cooking. But now, he won't eat it. He accused me of fattening him up so other lovers won't be attracted to him."

"I don't know where he eats now, but he's losing weight and getting in shape for his next picture, to be shot in Hawaii. Perhaps it'll require beach scenes—I don't know…"

***

In the weeks after his dismissal as Rock's business manager, Henry Willson was still fuming over his major star's betrayal. He continued to blame it on "his dyke wife."

One evening, shortly before midnight, Willson placed a call to Rock's home. He was sleeping in the guest bedroom. He had just come in after "scoring a hit" on the beach in Santa Monica.

"I don't know how those fuckers at the Maree firm are taking care of business, but I don't think those jerks can handle the latest jam you're in," Willson said.

"What in hell are you talking about?" Rock asked.

"It's your buddy, Johnny Stompanato," Willson answered.

"Yes, I know, he's Mickey Cohen's henchman, but that doesn't affect me."

"Yes it does. I know you met Johnny at one of my parties. I should have warned you how dangerous he is."

"I didn't find him all that dangerous," Rock said. "We had some fun and games for three nights—and that was that."

"Not quite," Willson said. "Two hours ago, I was hand-delivered a package from one of Cohen's boys. It was filled with pictures secretly snapped of you, including several showing you having sex with Johnny boy. In some, you're positioned in all sorts of ways, naked and drugged. Johnny is demanding $25,000 for the negatives."

"What the hell! I had no idea. What happens now? Do I have to cough up that much money?"

"I heard the Maree boys have you on a tight budget," Willson said. "You don't have that much in your account, unless Ed Muhl wants to advance it to you against your salary."

"I don't know," Rock said. "I feel trapped. If those pictures get out, my career is ruined."

"Unlike the Maree jerks, I can get you out of this mess. We can hire the best private detective in Hollywood. Fred Otash. He told me that Johnny and Cohen make lots of money from blackmailing stars. Both men and women. Johnny blackmails without gender preferences. For $5,000, Otash can break into Johnny's apartment, where he's probably stashed the pictures."

"Then go for it," Rock said. "Sooner than later, god damn it."

"Who loves ya, baby?" Willson said before putting down the phone.

***

Fred Otash was one of Hollywood's most notorious detectives, usually on the wrong side of the law. He spent a lot of time arranging illegal abortions for the mistresses of movie stars, and he had been the chief investigator for *Confidential* magazine.

The "gumshoe" intimately knew the seedy side of Hollywood, which he'd first learned when he was a tough cop for the Los Angeles Police Department.

Stompanato, working with Cohen, was well known as a blackmailer of movie stars he'd seduced and secretly photographed. Otash told Willson that the minor stars paid him $10,000 for the negatives, whereas bigger stars, such as Cary Grant, "had to cough up $25,000."

While still a police officer, Otash knew Stompanato only casually. In his 1976 memoir, *Investigation Hollywood*, he wrote of how he and his partner, "Pinky" Meadue, had terrorized Stompanato one night.

The two cops were cruising Sunset Strip when they spotted the gangster's Cadillac ahead of them. "Let's have some fun with him," Otash told his partner, ordering him to drive directly alongside Stompanato's vehicle.

As he did, Otash stuck the barrel of a police shotgun out the window of his car and shouted, "Now you've had it, you motherfucker!"

Spotting the weapon, Stompanato ducked down but, as he did, he lost control of his vehicle. "It went over the curb and down over the hill off Sunset," Otash wrote in his memoir. "He could have been killed."

As they drove off, Otash and Meadue were laughing raucously, having interpreted the incident as "hysterical."

Otash told Willson he'd be delighted "to save Hudson's ass." He cited services he'd previously rendered to Bette Davis, Errol Flynn, Judy Garland, Frank Sinatra, and others, including Hollywood's most famous attorney, Jerry Geisler.

Henry Willson hired master detective Fred Otash, depicted above, to prevent Johnny Stompanato from blackmailing Rock Hudson with incriminating photographs.

Within three nights, Otash, along with an accomplice, broke into Stompanato's apartment and stole the negatives and photographs of Rock, along with some other incriminating candid shots of other movie stars. His pictures were handed over to Rock by Willson, who kept the other shots "for my own amusement."

Greatly relieved, Rock thanked Willson profusely for "saving my career."

Otash had not disappeared from Rock's life, however. Within a few months, he'd be hired by Phyllis to record her secret talks with Rock, a prelude to their divorce. During their candid talks, Rock had no clue she was having his voice—and hers, too—recorded.

***

Day after day, Phyllis kept voicing her complaints about Rock and he was also expressing his displeasure at everything, especially the small house in which they lived. "I feel in a cage with you," he charged. He began searching for a much larger house and found a Tudor-styled one set on two acres, but at $130,000, the property seemed more than he could afford at the time.

To cheer him up, she suggested he drive with her, along with her two friends, Pat Devlin and Steve Evans, to an arts festival and picnic in Laguna. During the outing, Rock was mostly sullen, but she chatted amicably with her companions.

The trouble began *en route* north with Rock at the wheel. He was going about eighty miles an hour and at one point, ninety.

She urged him to slow down. "Are you trying to kill yourself like James Dean?"

At that remark, he backhanded her, so hard her lip bled. As she had done at the Grand Hotel in Rome, she began to scream, shouting, "You bastard! How dare you!"

He struck her again across the mouth. Hysterical, she crawled from the front seat and lodged between Devlin and Evans, who comforted her. Finally, she stopped screeching.

The rest of the ride was in silence. Back at Rock's house, Devlin escorted her up to the bedroom to try to comfort her. Alone in the room with her, she urged Phyllis to file for a divorce as soon as possible.

The next morning, before Rock reported to Fox to loop some dialogue, she confronted him. "Just what kind of man are you? I'll tell you: You're not a man at all. As for your friends, all of them are silly and shallow."

Amazingly, after he'd completed his obligations to Fox, he invited her to fly with him to Hawaii where shooting was to begin on his latest picture, this one entitled *Twilight for the Gods,* slated for a release in Technicolor from Universal in 1958.

She agreed to go, even though he hadn't even spoken to her during the previous four days. She wondered if the invitation was part of a plot, hatched with Willson. Were the scandal sheets after him again, making it necessary for him to be seen with a wife?

***

It was in late September of 1957 that their plane landed in Honolulu, where the weather was beautiful. A limousine waited to take them to their honeymoon suite at the Royal Hawaiian.

Within an hour, film director Joseph Pevney arrived to have a drink and to invite them to dinner. Rock turned down the dinner invitation, but sat on their terrace, talking over the script.

Pevney had first helmed Rock in a bit part in *Shakedown* with Howard Duff, followed by *Air Cadet* and *Iron Man,* that latter with Jeff Chandler. By the time he directed Rock in *Back to God's Country,* Rock was a star and had the lead.

"I was so wrong about you," Pevney confessed. "You've become a star in spite of my prediction. An Oscar nominee, no less."

In *Twilight for the Gods,* Rock had been cast as the shabby-looking Captain Bell, a hard-drinking skipper who had been court-martialed and discharged from the Navy. Actually, the role called for a disheveled Humphrey Bogart the way he looked in *The African Queen* (1951). When Universal saw the first rushes, Ed Muhl phoned Pevney and threatened to fire him if he didn't have Rock "cleaned up and looking handsome as always."

Pevney ordered wardrobe and makeup to redo Rock's look, and—as captain of the broken-down *Cannibal,* which was barely seaworthy—he appeared quite glamorous.

After Honolulu, Rock, with Phyllis, the cast, and the crew, were flown to the island of Maui for the actual shoot. Here, Rock met his producers, Gordon Kay, who was known mainly for turning out "B" westerns for Republic and some two dozen Allan ("Rocky") Lane "oaters," as they were called, including *Carson City Raiders* (1948).

On Maui, Rock also met or else had a reunion of the motley crew of passengers, who were to be depicted aboard his brigantine. His beautiful leading lady, dancer Cyd Charisse, was cast as Charlotte King, fleeing a murder charge. First Mate Ramsay (Arthur Kennedy) openly defies his captain. Rock had worked on *Bright Victory* (1951) which had starred Kennedy, but times had changed: Rock was now the leading man.

Other passengers included a jovial island derelict, a show-biz entrepreneur, a prostitute, a washed-up opera singer, and a couple of refugees riding the stormy seas. As the ship sails along, the true character of each of these passengers is revealed.

Phyllis was still recovering from her long illness and felt weak, complaining of headaches. Rock, at night, cruised the beaches. He later told George Nader, "Outside of California, Hawaii has the best-looking men in the world, most often attached to the U.S. Navy. I met several of them, especially a guy from Louisiana, although Colorado and Kansas weren't bad, either."

He had long admired Cyd Charisse, the wife of singer Tony Martin. She'd married him in 1948 and remained with him until her death. Rock learned that even though she'd had polio as a girl in Amarillo, Texas, she in time recovered to become one of the best dancers in the history of the movies, especially when partnered with either Fred Astaire or Gene Kelly. She'd recently filmed *Brigadoon* (1954) with

Kelly and Van Johnson.

Rock was somewhat surprised when Charisse became friends with Phyllis—that is, on the days when his wife was feeling well enough to get out of bed.

Charisse later wrote in a memoir that Rock was "one of the nicest and handsomest men in Hollywood. However, our movie was the absolute worst of any film in which I appeared. Pevney took a good book—a bestseller—and did not know what to do with it."

During their conversations, Phyllis confided to Charisse: "I think there is no hope for my marriage. How I envy Tony and you, a loving couple. I'm going to leave Hawaii in a day or so. The only thing that remains in my marriage is the divorce and a financial settlement."

For the most part, reviews for *Twilight for the Gods* were poor, as was the box office.

Howard Thompson, in *The New York Times*, wrote: This unsurprising tale moves slowly, seems about a third too long, and generates little dramatic heat *en route.* For a tension-laced plot that should have whipped up some murderous desperation, the stormy waters included, tapers off to a pallidly optimistic conclusion. Miss Charisse is bland and beautiful, and Mr. Hudson simply looks discouraged, and well he should, for what kind of veteran sailor would airily float his charges out to sea in a death trap?"

Cyd Charisse and Rock make love on camera in *Twilight for the Gods.*

Offscreen, she warned him, "My heart belongs only to Tony Martin."

***

Flying back from Honolulu, Rock found that Phyllis was out shopping when he arrived back at their home. He immediately packed his luggage and moved out. He left a note: "I'm going to the Beverly Hills Hotel. Let's keep it quiet."

When she got home and read the note, her reaction was: "He wants to keep our separation secret, and he checks into the Beverly Hills Hotel?"

PILLOW TALK

WITH AMERICA'S BUBBLY
HAPPY-GO-LUCKY, LA-DI-DA
VIRGIN WHO REALLY WASN'T

Rock's Secret Life Is Threatened
As His Lesbian Wife Heads for the Divorce Courts

Before movies became more sexually explicit, this "footsie scene" between Doris Day and Rock Hudson in their romantic comedy hit, *Pillow Talk*, was viewed as risqué. Although in separate bathrooms, only a vertical line separated the nude hunk from the bubbly champagne blonde.

A tall man was seen pulling his car into the driveway on Round Valley Drive in Sherman Oaks and walking up to the door where he rang the bell. It was Rock Hudson, calling, unannounced, on Mark Miller and George Nader. Up to now, he'd always phoned in advance.

Their Dublin-born, red-haired housekeeper, who was a fan of Rock's, opened the door and welcomed him. "Mr. Miller's not at home," she said. "But Mr. Nader is reading a script out on his terrace."

Rock kissed her on the cheek and walked out there, taking Nader by surprise. He jumped up and embraced Rock, and within minutes the maid returned with late morning coffee.

After drinking a cup, Rock said, "I want to go to 'the Platform,' where I can talk freely."

That was Nader's name for a small outdoor deck built on a belvedere overlooking the valley below. He and Rock walked up stone steps to reach it. For the first few minutes, both of the men just took in the panoramic view. Rock didn't say anything, as if building up to something he wanted to confess.

Nader relayed to Miller when he came home that night, "Maybe it was my vanity, but at first, I thought Rock was going to tell me he'd fallen in love with me and wanted me to leave you and run off with him."

"You are vain," Miller cautioned. "That will never happen."

Finally, Rock began to open up and talk. "I tried everything to make it work," he said. "I thought of sharp razor blades cutting into my balls, of black widow spiders, of being handcuffed and dropped into a pit of vipers. Nothing worked. I'm telling you what I refused to tell my shrink."

Nader was confused, wondering exactly what his friend was confessing. Phyllis had complained of Rock's premature ejaculations, which Nader had never understood. He was fully aware of the rave reviews that Rock's female conquests had given him, including Joan Crawford, with whom both of them had already been intimate.

Nader had once told Miller, "If Rock could please a devouring Venus's-flytrap like Crawford, he could satisfy any woman."

Rock then delivered what Nader later called a bombshell: "I've left Phyllis for good. I've checked into a bungalow on the grounds of the Beverly Hills Hotel. Howard Hughes is in the bungalow next door. If you have to reach me, I've registered under the name of Mark George, obviously using the first names of you two guys."

"That's when our argument began," Nader said, weeks later. "I made the mistake of defending Phyllis."

He urged Rock to stay with her, if, for nothing else, the sake of keeping up appearances. "This is a bad time to leave, with all these *Confidential* libel trials going on, and tons of Hollywood scandals being aired. You could come in for a hit. She's given you a lot of publicity…I mean good heterosexual publicity, about what a great husband you are."

"I tried to make the marriage work," he said. "I offered to keep our marriage going, even by inviting a young man into our bed every night. She turned me down."

"You should have invited a young woman instead," Nader advised.

"Yeah, right! What a big turn-on that would have been for me. You two don't get it, do you?"

"I get it, all right," Nader said. "But I'm thinking of your career. Do you know what might be aired in a divorce court, especially if she gets a good lawyer? You might end up like Robert Taylor, paying Barbara Stanwyck alimony for the rest of his life."

"Not only that, but charges she might air in court could destroy your career, just as it's reaching its peak," Nader said.

It isn't known what happened next, but apparently Rock and Nader got into their biggest argument ever. He rejected all of Nader's advice, although he had come to visit him just to hear it. But Nader obviously wasn't telling him what he wanted to hear.

Rock turned to him. "Fuck you!" he shouted. Within minutes, there was the sound of the screech of tires as Rock, from behind the wheel of his car, roared away from the Nader/Miller home.

Over the next week, during his residency at the hotel, Rock refused to accept Nader's phone calls. Miller intervened, but Rock wouldn't speak to him, either. Eventually, he sent them a note: "Don't call me…ever! It's over! Stay away!"

Throughout the course of the next year, he never saw them.

Rock had wanted his break from Phyllis kept a secret, but the very next day, Louella Parsons, learning about it from some source, devoted a column to it. "The Hudson marriage has reached a snag, and he is living at the Beverly Hills Hotel under an assumed name. Their breakup might be one of those things that happen in the best of families—an argument and then the kiss-and-makeup reconciliation."

As occurred so often in her columns, the gossip maven got it wrong.

***

Eager to return to work, Rock was rushed into his next film for Universal, *This Earth Is Mine*, which was scheduled for a 1959 release. It was based on *The Cup and the Sword*, a novel by Alice Tisdale Hobart about a California wine dynasty who struggles to survive after Prohibition became the law of the land between two world wars. Hobart had also written a best-seller, *Oil for the Lamps of China*.

That film's executive producer was none other than Universal's chief of production, Ed Muhl, who, over the years, had continued to pay "oral tribute" to Rock, his major star, during sexual trysts with "my pet" (his nickname for Rock).

Muhl selected the noted director, Henry King, to helm the picture, and lined up a distinguished cast of co-stars. They included Jean Simmons, Claude

Rains, and Dorothy McGuire.

Rock was eager to work with King, who had previously directed such stars as Gregory Peck, Tyrone Power, Gary Cooper, Susan Hayward, Jennifer Jones, and Spencer Tracy. A son of Virginia born in 1886, King had begun appearing in Silents back in 1913. Three years later, he was a director. In time, he'd be twice nominated for a Best Director Oscar.

Although Muhl had already given Rock a copy of the novel to read as background for his performance, he opted to ignore it in favor of the film script by Casey Robinson. Robinson, known for turning out scripts for some of Bette Davis' most memorable movies—including *Dark Victory* (1939), *The Old Maid* (also 1939), and *Now, Voyager* (1942)—had been the pre-eminent screen writer at Warners. He had also written the scripts for *Captain Blood* (1935) for Errol Flynn, and *Kings Row* (1942), Ronald Reagan's best picture.

This Earth is Mine depicts the lives, loves, and vendettas of a California wine-making dynasty, the Rambeau family, and their struggle to survive when the bottling and sale of wine was outlawed. In many ways, Rock's film was a precursor of the hit TV series, *Falcon Crest* (1981-90), that co-starred Rock's former leading lady, Jane Wyman.

In the film, Elizabeth Rambeau (Jean Simmons), an English cousin, arrives in California in 1931 for a family reunion. She is viewed as "damaged goods" because of a torrid and widely gossiped-about affair she'd had in England.

In California, she learns that her aunt and uncle are setting her up for a prearranged marriage to Andrew Swann (Francis Bathencourt), a young man from another branch of the family.

Yet another cousin, John Rambeau (Rock), soon lets Elizabeth know that the proposed marriage is an attempt to consolidate the vineyards of the two branches of the family. Slowly, he begins to fall in love with Elizabeth himself.

Ruling over the dynasty is the aging Philippe Rambeau (Claude Rains), the family's patriarch, who stubbornly refuses to deal with bootleggers who are, during Prohibition, buying up all the grapes they can find.

Joining in the conspiracy to marry off Elizabeth is Martha (Dorothy McGuire), the daughter of Philippe,

Jean Simmons was Rock's leading lady in *This Earth Is Mine*. She was going through a personal crisis. Howard Hughes was pursuing her, and her husband, Stewart Granger, was threatening to murder the producer/aviator.

John's uncle.

The convoluted plot deals with lies, betrayals, blackmail, paternity disputes, gunplay (Rock is wounded), and a rampant wildfire.

It segués into a Hollywood ending after Rock drops a lit cigarette and ignites a wildfire that rages across the parched fields, destroying the Rambeau vineyards. At the end of Prohibition, with the understanding that the family can once again manufacture and sell its wine, John has to start all over again. Elizabeth appears with a cutting from a grapevine from her valley vineyard with the intention of planting it in his mountain vineyard. There is talk of melding the valley's softness with the mountain's strength to make a "good family." Then they fall into each other's arms, proclaiming undying love to each other.

Napa Valley was the setting for *This Earth Is Mine,* and many of its residents were hired as extras. But when the movie was released, audiences at the time seemed little interested in the epic of a wine-growing dynasty.

Variety claimed that the movie "completely lacked a dramatic cohesion. It is verbose and contradictory, and its complex plot begins with confusion and ends in tedium."

The critic for *The New York Times* also did not like the trials and tribulations of this clan of California vineyard owners. "Universal has come up with an ambitious family saga as handsome as it is hollow. It opened yesterday (June 27, 1959) at the Roxy, where the grapes stole the show."

Rock feared for his career. To remain at the top of the box office, he had to star in a triumph.

***

Back in Los Angeles, Rock had moved out of his bungalow at the Beverly Hills Hotel and had rented a furnished apartment in Crescent Heights.

Without alerting him that he was flying in from Rome, Massimo was the first person who knocked on his door. He'd bribed a desk clerk at the hotel, where Rock had left his new address with the understanding that his mail would be forwarded.

In a connection arranged through his friend, Anna Magnani, Massimo had obtained a work permit, hoping to find employment in Hollywood as an actor, even though his English was far from proficient. He didn't expect any help from Henry Willson, who had tried to break up his romance with Rock back in Rome. New in town, and confused by the shifting hierarchies of Hollywood, he clung to the hope that Rock, based on his star power, might get him cast in bit parts at Universal.

Rock was expecting a delivery that morning and was shocked when he opened the door to confront Massimo. Thus, in lieu of receiving his "Roman Romeo" into his open arms, he reluctantly allowed him to enter his apartment and stood near the door with him, not even inviting him to sit down.

That was far from what Massimo had expected. He had hoped that he would be sleeping in Rock's bed that night.

The Italian had arrived at the wrong time in Hollywood. Rock was lying low, hoping to avoid any association with the trial in Los Angeles of Robert Harrison, publisher of *Confidential* magazine. Harrison had been charged with a conspiracy to commit criminal libel and of printing lewd material. To his horror, Tab Hunter was drawn into the trial, and other stars, among them Maureen O'Hara, were suing for damages, as was Liberace, who had been exposed as being "mad about the boy," a reference to the press agent he'd tried to seduce. Rock feared that the magazine's file on him would be subpoenaed by the court.

In Rome, there had already been published rumors about Rock and Massimo, and he didn't want the same thing to happen to him in Hollywood, especially not at a time like this, when he felt especially vulnerable.

"You told me in Rome you loved me," Massimo protested, as Rock reopened the door, inviting him to leave.

"That was then and this is now. Go back to Rome. I can't help you here."

"But you made me feel I was special," Massimo continued to protest.

"Forget it! You were just one of the many guys I've screwed. It meant nothing to me."

In despair, during the weeks that followed, Massimo made the rounds of studios, leaving his address, which was a cheap motel in West Hollywood.

Willson learned of his arrival in California, and he feared that Massimo would sell an *exposé* of his affair with Rock to the scandal magazines and immediately contacted him with a warning to get out of town. "The heat's on," Willson said.

When Massimo refused to leave, Willson called master detective Fred Otash, who employed some ex-Marines, a sort of goon squad, to deal with potential blackmailers. Late one night, when Massimo was maneuvering his rented car into the parking lot of his hotel, three men set upon him, beating him severely and warning him that worse things were yet to come if he didn't leave California at once.

The next day, his hopes dashed, Massimo flew back to the relative safety of Rome.

***

Having not heard from Rock in weeks, Phyllis Gates, living alone at Warbler Place, decided it was time to seek a divorce lawyer. She called Jerry Giesler, the most famous divorce lawyer in California. When an appointment was arranged, she was surprised to find that his office was actually within his lavish home in Beverly Hills.

She would later claim he treated her like her favorite uncle as she poured out a litany of grievances about what an inadequate husband Rock was, including how he'd struck her and bloodied her nose on two different occasions.

After listening patiently to her complaints, Giesler's first question was, "How much money is Hudson worth?"

She claimed she didn't really know, since Willson had been managing his affairs, which had now been turned over to a law firm.

Giesler told her that he'd met both Rock and Willson before, explaining that the star and his agent had come to him in the aftermath of a threatened *exposé* in *Confidential.*

"Rock had attended a gang bang at Willson's home, and one of the guys there got it on with Rock and had gone to *Confidential* and tried to sell what he knew. I told those guys I couldn't do anything until they actually published something, and then I could file a possible libel suit, which might do no more than make unwanted (additional) headlines."

Phyllis, in her 1987 memoir, *Rock Hudson, My Husband,* revealed her state of mind around the time Giesler represented her. She wrote: "Was Rock a homosexual? I couldn't believe it. He had always been the manliest of men."

Of course, that was a complete lie. As Willson's secretary, she knew from the beginning that Rock was gay, and the only reason he was marrying her was to conceal that fact.

Debbie Reynolds, a friend of Rock's, read Phyllis' memoirs and said, "All of us who knew Rock and Phyllis laughed our way through her book. We knew of her lesbian affairs. Not since Joan Crawford and Marlene Dietrich published their so-called autobiographies has there ever been such a dishonest memoir. Phyllis should have entitled it *Lies & More Lies."*

Chapter 22 of her memoir was called "The Italian Affair." Although she doesn't name him, the handsome young Italian she refers to was Massimo. She claimed that when Rock returned home from Italy after filming *A Farewell to Arms,* she'd heard rumors that he'd had an affair while abroad. She quoted an unnamed friend who informed her of this.

"Who was she?" Phyllis had allegedly asked.

"It wasn't a she," the friend replied. "It was a he."

Phyllis reported in her memoir, and also bruited widely around Hollywood, that she was shocked at the news. Her public account of her "shock" was absurd, as she and Rock had had that violent confrontation at the Grand Hotel in Rome over Massimo, whom she'd met on the Via Veneto. In fact, she knew enough about Massimo that she urged Giesler to name him as the correspondent in her divorce. The attorney cautioned her, "You know that that would ruin your husband's career."

"That's the point," she answered. "Instead of facing two men in court, I'd end up with a bigger settlement, negotiated privately."

When Rock heard about her consultations with Giesler and her thirst for vengeance, he cut off all her charge accounts, which enraged her. Then she was notified that thereafter, she would receive only $1,000 a month as an allowance.

Word of this was leaked to the press. The next day, there was a knock on her door. She opened it to encounter Marlon Brando, who had once made love to her in New York. He claimed he couldn't stay, but handed her a check for $1,000 to help meet her expenses.

Around this time, she claimed that anonymous death threats were being phoned in to her, and she suspected that Willson was behind them.

Then, one morning as she was reading the paper, a headline struck her: JERRY GIESLER SUFFERS HEART ATTACK. The announcement made her realize that since Giesler had been incapacitated, she'd probably have to start all over again with a new divorce lawyer.

Within a few days, she was surprised to receive a phone call from Rock. He wanted to drop by his own house to pick up the rest of his personal belongings. He went on to tell her he'd rented a beach house in Malibu.

She was hardly the naïve woman she'd depicted in her fake memoir. She immediately phoned Fred Otash, whose skills she'd come to appreciate during her employment as Willson's secretary.

Ironically, Otash had been hired by Rock when Johnny Stompananto was trying to blackmail him. Now, she wanted Otash to secretly record her meeting with Rock, which she might use against him in a divorce case, or else as a bargaining tool in the negotiation of her financial settlement.

Otash sent William V. Lowe to the house on Warbler Place to install a listening device in Rock's house, with the understanding that he'd be secluded inside, behind a locked door, during Rock's visit, which occurred at 6:30PM on January 21, 1958.

Otash and Lowe already had lots of experience entrapping stars with secret recording devices. The crime novelist, James Ellroy, author of *L.A. Confidential,* once said "Freddie (Otash) was the kind of guy you went to if you wanted a picture of Rock Hudson with a dick in his mouth."

In Otash's own memoir, *Investigation Hollywood,* the detective devoted several pages to the actual transcript of Rock's dialogue with his wife. He did not name them, but referred to them as "STAR" and "WIFE." The chapter was entitled HOMOSEXUALS ARE ALSO MOVIE STARS.

[In the recording, Rock can be heard admitting that he'd had an affair with Willson when he was trying to break into the movies.]

At one point, Phyllis tells him, "Everyone knows you were picking up boys off the street shortly before we were married, and have continued to do so." That remark shot down the feigned innocence of her memoir.

Rock openly admitted that he'd picked up a young man for sex the day after he'd married her.

[Again, she contradicted her memoir by telling him that she knew everything that was going on in Italy, a reference to Massimo.]

"Can you deny that your pattern is that of a homosexual?" she asked.

"No, I can't deny it," he is heard saying.

"And that is why you never touched me?" she asked him.

[That remark lends credence to those who claimed that during their marriage, Rock never had sex with her, and that theirs had been a celibate lavender marriage from its inception. Perhaps she should have re-read Otash's Investigation, Hollywood *before dictating her own memoir to veteran Hollywood writer, Bob Thomas.]*

Reflecting on the secret recording, Otash later said, "I've always enjoyed this star on the screen, and his private life is none of my business—someone hires me to delve into it. That's a different situation. That's work. It's nothing personal."

***

For his appearance at the Academy Awards presentation on March 26, 1958, Rock was asked to sing a duet, "Baby, It's Cold Outside" with any woman star in Hollywood he preferred. Academy executives thought he'd select his former co-star, Jane Wyman, who was also a singer, having previously recorded with Bing Crosby.

It came as something of a shock when he suggested Mae West. He had fallen in love with her screen image in the 1930s when he was just a boy. As one Academy member said, "Rock brought the old gal out of mothballs, although she was still insisting that she looked like a gal of 28."

In possession of her private number, Rock made a call to West at her Ravenswood apartment, and from her he received the familiar invitation, "Come up and see me sometime."

As he recalled, "She was just plain and simply a sweet old lady who told me marvelous stories about her life."

No one in cinema history had ever described the indomitable Mae West in such terms. Actually, she didn't look simple at all, emerging in a champagne-colored *négligée* with a twenty-foot train. Wearing an elaborate blonde wig, and overly made up, she greeted him by looking him up and down, appraising him like a male sex slave on an auction block. "You must have eaten your Wheaties," she said. "They sure grow 'em big in Chicago. I, of all people, know how true that is."

She spoke of her early days in the 1930s when she'd arrived in Hollywood after a notorious but successful stage career on Broadway. "When I got here, I put the tinsel in Tinseltown. I was not a little girl from a little town makin' good in a big town. I was a big girl from a big town makin' good in a little town."

Rock Hudson and the indomitable Mae West appeared at the 1958 Oscar ceremony singing "Baby, It's Cold Outside."

It might have been cold outside, but "Rock & Mae gave the audience sexual fever," in the words of Hedda Hopper.

"Back then, unlike the gals in pictures today, I didn't have to take off my clothes. Men imagined what was underneath."

"I'm not shedding any tears over news that *Confidential* may be shut down," she said. "Those bastards even exposed my good friend, Liberace, as being gay. We both know that Lee doesn't have a gay bone in his body."

"I can't vouch for that," Rock answered.

"She gave him a knowing smile. "I know, dearie, Lee told me all about it. *Confidential* went after me, running an *exposé* about how I prefer…how shall I put this delicately?..'tan' boxers?"

"I suppose a Mandingo every now and then might cross our paths," he said.

She chuckled again. "The difference between a white man and a black man is that the black man does not leave a woman's bed until he has satisfied her."

"I'll have to take your word for that," he answered.

She excused herself for about twenty minutes, inviting him, during her absence, to admire the nude statue of herself prominently displayed in her apartment.

When she returned, she revealed that she might be considering a presidential bid in 1960, running against Richard Nixon and 'that old horndog,

Joseph Kennedy's son. My platform will be 'A Chick In Every Pot and a Man in Every Bed.'"

"A reporter phoned me yesterday and asked if I had any advice for teenage girls of today. I did: 'Grow up!'"

Rock adored West, although he was realistic enough to know that she had evolved into some campy, way over-the-top version of what she had been. Like a comedic version of Norma Desmond from *Sunset Blvd.*, she was loudly obsessed with memories of her long-ago glory days. She'd become a grotesque caricature of herself, an icon that female impersonators were fond of trying to capture onstage.

In reference to their upcoming duet at the Academy Awards, Rock recalled, "The minute we started rehearsing, I would break into giggles. We had a hard time getting through the complete song. When not making me laugh, she would take time out to share certain opinions. She thought all the sex queens in movie history from Theda Bara to Marilyn Monroe were pure bullshit. She said that if a gal didn't have a sense of humor to go with it, it wasn't worthwhile."

Mae West and Rock singing "Baby, It's Cold Outside," received the wildest ovation of the evening and delighted millions of television viewers. Backstage at the finale, West even suggested that the two of them should make a movie together.

***

In the weeks leading up to Phyllis Gates' filing for divorce, she claimed she was receiving many threats coming in over the phone, and that she actually feared for her life. She told friends, "Henry Willson will stop at nothing to protect his bread winner, Rock."

She became so afraid that she often slept over at a friend's house, fearing someone would break in on her at Warbler Place

Willson was worried that she would threaten him in a court hearing. As his former secretary, she'd learned that he'd slept with most of his male clients, whether they were gay or straight, including Rock in the early years.

Rock hired Greg Bautzer to represent his interests, as he was the best in the business, when not romancing glamour queens such as Lana Turner. Bautzer immediately hired a detective to gather incriminating evidence on Phyllis herself.

If she continued through with her threat to expose Rock in court, it was Bautzer's aim to expose her as a promiscuous lesbian who made pickups in lesbian bars in Santa Monica. Bautzer wanted to build up a case that she was a wife in name only to Rock, and that she'd only married him because she was a gold-digger, with the hope and intention of blackmailing him one day.

There was always the possibility that she might summon Massimo and name him as correspondent in her divorce trial. Not only that, but she rounded up eyewitnesses such as Pat Devlin who would testify that she witnessed Rock strike her as he was driving them back from Laguna.

Before his heart attack, Jerry Giesler had warned her that if she destroyed Rock's career, it might adversely affect his ability to pay alimony. "You'll be the one who ends up suffering, not have enough money to live on."

Before Rock moved into his furnished apartment in Crescent Heights, Bautzer had two men check the place from top to bottom to ascertain if it were bugged. Indeed, one of the men discovered that it had only recently been bugged, probably by master detective Fred Otash, who had been hired by Phyllis in anticipation of her upcoming divorce hearing.

On April 22, 1958, she filed her divorce petition, citing mental cruelty, giving specific examples of her husband's "brutal treatment of her that on occasion had resulted in physical violence."

It was revealed at the time of the divorce hearing that Rock was making $3,500 a week from Universal. The judge wanted to know his salary so that adequate alimony could be assessed.

The final hearing was slated during the hot summer of 1958. On August 13, both Rock, with "his high-priced lawyers" (her words), showed up at Superior court in Santa Monica. Both parties gave each other wide berth, and at no point did either of them make eye contact.

After reviewing the charges, Phyllis was represented by attorney James Smith, who argued her case in front of Judge Edward Brand. After hearing the charges, Brand granted her divorce on grounds of mental cruelty. He ordered Rock to pay her $250 a week for the next ten years. Not only that, but she got his home at Warbler Place, which was valued at $35,000. She also was allowed to keep all of the wedding presents they'd received, plus the Ford Thunderbird he'd given her, and seven percent of a film company he'd formed with Willson called Seven Pictures Corporation. She later said, "The income I accepted seemed paltry concerning Rock's earning power." The moment judgment was rendered, Rock was seen leaving the court with Willson at his side. That would be the second to last time she ever saw him.

She later claimed, "Rock sat petrified during the court hearing, knowing that at any minute I had the power to destroy his career. I chose not to. Both bastards, Willson and Rock, missed the bullet."

After the hearing, she complained of "post-divorce blues." No longer the wife of a movie star, there were no more glittering parties or premieres to attend, no more limos, no more getting the best table in any restaurant, no more charge accounts. "The party was over," she wrote.

Weeks after her divorce, she became sick and had to endure gall bladder surgery. She had not yet paid all her legal bills and now she faced horrendous medical expenses. When she recovered and returned home, she found the bills mounting. She called Rock's accountants to pay her medical bills, only to discover that Rock had canceled her health insurance.

There was more trouble ahead when she checked on whatever revenue Seven Pictures might have generated. She painfully learned that her share was nil, since whatever assets the corporation might have had had been transferred to Rock's new company, Gibraltar, of which she had no part.

In 1961, she sued Rock for having transferred her share, and he was forced to show up in court. It would be the last time she'd ever see him. At the trial, he was forced to pay her $135,000 in a cash settlement, plus $30,000 in legal fees.

One reporter showed up to ask him how he felt months after his divorce. "For me, Phyllis Gates does not exist."

He told friends, "Did I love her? You've got to be kidding. I loved her about as much as I find Marjorie Main sexy—and she's a dyke."

Throughout the rest of her life, Phyllis presented a dismal view of Rock to the world—that is, when she spoke about him at all: "To me, Rock seemed like that Laurence Harvey character in *Room at the Top* (1959), using people as stepping stones until he himself was totally corrupted, an empty human incapable of feelings."

Although they never saw each other again, Phyllis would reappear once again to threaten Rock. The money she'd been awarded ran out, and now she was threatening to ruin his career by writing a tell-about book, exposing his homosexual affairs.

***

After *This Earth Is Mine,* Rock waited impatiently for his next role. He wanted to take his mind off the wife he'd dumped. The call finally came in from Henry Willson. "Ross Hunter wants to cast you in a romantic comedy with Doris Day called *Any Way the Wind Blows.*"

"No way, José!" Rock said. "I don't do that Cary Grant *schtick*. And why Doris Day? You've got to be kidding!"

"For a while, they considered Debbie Reynolds," Willson said.

"Debbie's my friend, but she's a midget," Rock protested. "We'd be laughed off the screen."

In the next few weeks, although Rock had become convinced that he could convincingly play such a role, he worried that he and Doris would have no chemistry together on screen. "I bet she's as warm as a December night on an Arctic ice floe."

The project's title was changed to *Pillow Talk* and the Hudson/Day comedy became the biggest comedy of 1959. It also rejuvenated the career of Doris, and launched the coupling of Rock with Doris as one of the most memorable in Hollywood, ranking alongside that of Spencer Tracy with Katharine Hepburn, or William Powell with Myrna Loy.

On screen, Doris became a bouncy, fresh-faced blonde with a champagne-bubble glamour, clad in a chic wardrobe of two dozen costumes each designed by Jean-Louis.

Its director, Michael Gordon, was born to a middle-class family in Baltimore, and was making a comeback of sorts. He'd directed José Ferrer in his 1950 Oscar-winning interpretation of the title role in *Cyrano de Bergerac*. But after that, he'd been blacklisted during the communist witch hunt of the early 1950s.

After languishing without work and blacklisted for most of the 1950s, Hunter called Gordon back from oblivion to relaunch himself with *Pillow Talk*. After three long meetings with Rock, Gordon convinced him that he'd be sensational playing comedy, even though he'd never attempted it before.

Almost from the first day he met Doris, Rock bonded with her. Within a few days, she nicknamed him "Ernie," and he called her "Eunice." They formed a friendship that lasted until his death. By 1960 at the Golden Globe Awards, they were named the world's favorite actor and actress.

With Hunter, Marty Melcher, Doris' husband, was the film's co-producer. To get acquainted, he invited Rock to join Doris and himself for a weekend at their beach house.

"Marty spent most of the weekend telling me how wealthy he'd made Doris, with his oil wells and bond deals. He said he'd like to do the same for me, if I'd turn over my capital to him. I had heard, though, that he was a crook, so I begged off."

Thus Rock learned years before Doris that she'd married a swindler. Upon Melcher's death in 1968, he'd lost all the millions she had earned as a major-league entertainer over the years, and she was in debt.

Pillow Talk had a long gestation period. Writers Russell Rouse and Clarence Green had sold it to RKO in 1942, but it lay around for

414

three years until the writers bought it back, reselling it in 1947 as a play. In 1958, Melcher acquired the rights for Arwin Productions, and Universal agreed to distribute it.

Shot in Eastmancolor and CinemaScope, *Pillow Talk* features a supporting cast that included Tony Randall, Thelma Ritter, and Nick Adams.

Rock was cast as Brad Allen, a womanizing bachelor who, between seductions, composes music. Temporarily, he is forced to share a party line with Jan Morrow (Doris), an interior decorator. Every time she picks up the phone to make a business call, he's on the line wooing another conquest.

The battle of the sexes is on. When Brad actually sees Jan, after feuding with her telephonically, he's attracted to her and sets out to make a conquest of her. In her case, it'll be a challenge. She absolutely detests Brad Allen, so he pretends to be a naïve Texas rancher, a bit shy around women.

As Brad, he comes up with a scheme, suggesting to her that Rex, her new beau, might be a homosexual, although that particular word was forbidden on the screen. Instead, he says, "There are some men who are very devoted to their mothers. You know, the type that likes to collect cooking recipes and exchange bits of gossip."

Ironically, as a gay male in private life, Rock found himself impersonating a horny straight man on screen impersonating a gay male, the type who raises his pinky when having a drink.

The film's most provocative scene, and the one which got the most attention, was the bathtub scene. It's a double shot of each of them in their respective bathrooms in their separate apartments. Only a vertical line separates their supposed private moments within their (respective) intimate private spaces. In one scene, the camera angles and clip juxtapositions make it appear that they're playing footsies with each other in a kind of titillating foreplay.

Rock was most effective in his comic scenes with Tony Randall, who'd been cast as Jonathan Forbes, a millionaire who is also in love with Jan. Jonathan is Brad's old college buddy and currently an investor in Broadway plays (i.e., a theatrical sugar daddy). When Jonathan learns of Brad's

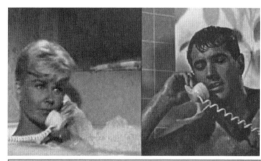

In their respective baths, Doris developed a monopoly on playing the standoffish, perennial virgin, but womanizing Rock, as Brad Allen, was determined to subdue her with his manly charms.

415

masquerade, he demands that he leave Manhattan and exile himself within his private cabin in the remote wilds of Connecticut to complete the music for a new Broadway show.

Unknown to Jonathan, "Rex" invites Jan to join him and she accepts. In fact, she seems coyly willing to surrender her virginity. But while she's isolated in the cabin with him, spotting some sheet music, she plunks the melody of a song on the piano in the living room and immediately recognizes it as a composition from Brad. He's not Rex after all.

After discovering Brad's true identity, she is enraged but also humiliated, because she was falling in love with him. Fleeing back to Manhattan, she is upset to learn that her company has been hired to redecorate his bachelor quarters. His instruction is to make the new interior an environment in which she herself would feel at home and comfortable.

She pulls a trick on him as an act of revenge. After the apartment has been redecorated, she invites him in to see it. She's turned the setting into a bawdy whorehouse with beaded curtains. Horrified at what she has done, he storms across the street to her own apartment building, barges in, and scoops her up in his arms.

In her pajamas, she is carried across the street to his apartment. He flings her onto his bed and announces his plan to marry her.

Of course, as in all romantic comedies, love prevails in the finale. In the last scene, four pillows appear on screen—pink, blue, pink, and blue—suggesting the baby boomers the two lovers will spawn.

After the first week of shooting, Doris confessed to Rock that she feared the way she was photographed, worrying that "I'll come off looking like Marjorie Main."

He assured her of her beauty, and told her how excited he was to be her leading man. As such, he'd join an array of actors including Clark Gable, Cary Grant, Ronald Reagan (she had an affair with him), Louis Jourdan, Jack Lemmon, David Niven, and James Garner, who had told her, "I'd rather co-star with you than with Elizabeth Taylor."

From left to right, the stars of *Pillow Talk* were Rock Hudson, Doris Day, and Tony Randall.

On screen, Randall is said to be pursuing Doris, but offscreen, the closeted homosexual was after "The Big Man" himself.

Ross Hunter later admitted, "I worshipped Rock. The whole world did. He knew what a sexy dude he was. But Doris doubted her sex appeal. I told her underneath all those dirndls lurked one of the wildest asses in Hollywood. When I told

416

her that, she said, 'I'm just an old-fashioned, peanut butter girl next door.'"

Randall, born to a Jewish family in Tulsa, Oklahoma, was five years older than Rock. He would achieve his greatest success on TV as part of *The Odd Couple*, the prissy Felix Unger, a character created by playwright Neil Simon. After *Pillow Talk*, he would star in the next two romantic comedies Rock and Doris made.

As a closeted homosexual who had married twice, Randall was very secretive about his private life. "Everybody knew Rock was gay, but only a secret few knew about Tony's secret desires," Hunter claimed.

In his tell-nothing memoir, *Which Reminds Me*, Randall wrote: "Any publicity an actor generates should be about his work, not himself. The public knows only one thing about me: I don't smoke."

Brooklyn-born Thelma Ritter never lost her Brooklyn accent, and was celebrated for her comedic roles, none better than when she was cast as "Birdie" in *All About Eve* (1950), earning a Best Supporting Actress nomination for herself. Before meeting Rock, she'd starred as James Stewart's nurse in Alfred Hitchcock's *Rear Window* (1954).

In *Pillow Talk*, she was hilarious as Doris' drunken housekeeper, who arrives for work every morning with an ice pack under her hat. For her performance, she received an Oscar nod as Best Supporting Actress, losing to Shelley Winters for her *The Diary of Anne Frank*.

The Academy overlooked Rock that year. Charlton Heston won for *Ben-Hur*, a role that had once been offered to Rock.

Cast in the minor role of Mrs. Walters, Lee Patrick, a long-established film star, had been in some of Rock's favorite movies, including *The Maltese Falcon* (1949), going on to appear in *Mildred Pierce* (1945) with Joan Crawford and in *Auntie Mame* (1958) with Rosalind Russell.

To his shock, Hunter had a hard time convincing theater owners that *Pillow Talk* might be a big hit. Time and time again, he met with resistance and was often told that "sophisticated comedies are out." Some theater managers even suggested that both Rock and Doris "were a thing of the past, overtaken by newer stars."

To compensate, he launched press tours with the cast, espe-

At the New York premiere of *Pillow Talk*, Rock entertained and charmed the two "tarantula divas," Gloria Swanson (center) and the formidable Tallulah Bankhead, who had already seduced him.

417

cially Doris and Rock, throughout the late summer and early fall of 1959. Recordings from both Rock and Doris were sent to radio stations.

Finally, Sol Schwartz, owner of the Palace Theatre on Broadway, opened *Pillow Talk* with a two-week run beginning on October 7. The Hollywood premiere was at the Egyptian Theater. From the East Coast to the West, it was a smash hit. Movie houses across America booked it, and it became the highest-grossing film of 1959.

At the world premiere in New York, Rock was seen escorting two grand actresses, Gloria Swanson and Tallulah Bankhead.

The next morning, he dreaded reading Bosley Crowther's review in *The New York Times*, expecting another attack from him. However, he defined it as "one of the most lively and up-to-date comedy romances of the year."

The *New York Herald Tribune* said, "*Pillow Talk* is a mélange of legs, pillows, slips, gowns, and a décor about as light as it could get without floating away."

Time magazine claimed, "When these magnificent objects go into a clinch—aglow from the sun lamp, agleam with hair lacquer—they look like creatures of the flesh more than a couple of Cadillacs parked in a suggestive position."

Box Office magazine, a publication which had had little, if any, kind words for his performances before that, wrote, "Hudson is as suave, self-possessed, and convincing as though he has been delineating lighter roles all through his distinguished career."

Redbook compared *Pillow Talk* to the 1934 *It Happened One Night*, which had brought Oscars to its co-stars, Clark Gable and Claudette Colbert.

Doris' role in *Pillow Talk* earned her her only Oscar nomination as Best Actress. The competition was stiff, including not only Audrey Hepburn in *The Nun's Story*, but Katharine Hepburn and Elizabeth Taylor, each for their respective performances in *Suddenly, Last Summer*. All of them lost to Simone Signoret for *A Room at the Top*.

Today, *Pillow Talk*, in the National Film Registry of the Library of Congress, is designated as "culturally, historically, or artistically important."

Pillow Talk represented a milestone in Rock's personal life. In October of

Onscreen, Rock and Doris played their love scenes with passion.

Offscreen, their mating in *Pillow Talk* became the seed of an enduring lifelong friendship.

1959, he ended his feud with George Nader and Mark Miller. All three of them attended a showing of *Pillow Talk* in Burbank. "Mark and I laughed all the way through it," Nader said. "We told Rock it was his best picture to date. Move over, Cary Grant. He was fifty-five. Time to start playing fathers."

***

"Tony Randall," according to producer Ross Hunter, "was one of the saddest creatures in private life, a homo-hating gay man like J. Edgar Hoover of the F.B.I."

The actor's great screen success had come in *Pillow Talk*, in which he played Doris Day's suitor. As seen today by more sophisticated audiences, Randall appears to be more interested in Rock Hudson than in the bouncy, chirpy, strong-willed blonde portrayed by Doris.

Indeed he was. Rock told his friends, George Nader and Mark Miller, that, "Tony came on to me real strong. I think he fell in love with me, at least a little bit."

One TV critic asserted that Randall always played it gay in *The Odd Couple*. "If Felix Unger isn't gay, I don't know who is. Those prissy characters he played were a 1950s and 1960s version of Edward Everett Horton, Franklin Panghorn, and Clifton Webb."

As a means of concealing his own homosexuality, Randall gave a number of interviews on the subject of homosexuality, all of them off-key and decidedly homophobic. One such interview, bizarrely entitled "Evening Out the Odd Couple," was printed in the September 17, 1972 issue of *After Dark*.

In the article, Randall described the time he escorted a group of friends to what he described as "an all-male house in Los Angeles."

"Oh, that was really bad, really bad. Just terrible Just disgusting! But also not good. Oh, guys sucking each other's cocks. There's nothing to watch in that. It confirms something I've always suspected about homosexuality—they don't like it. Those guys never got aroused. Whereas in today's modern straight porn, the kids really go at it. Yeah. Oh, it's awful to see great big guys...definitely not my bag. There's no such thing as homosexuality—it's just something invented by a bunch of fags."

In that same article, Randall went on to assert that he'd been bitterly attacked for an interview he gave in *Opera News*. In that piece, he complained about the "hordes" of homosexuals who went to the opera "to scream and squeal and support broken down sopranos. They're a self-appointed claque. This is absolutely true. Some guys that follow Bette Davis movies—and all that."

When Rock was shown a copy of this rambling and disjointed interview, he remarked, "Tony is a very funny man. But this is about the most ridiculous piece of shit I've ever read. Homosexuals don't like getting it on? Tell that to millions of gay men around the world. I no longer think Tony is smart. From that throat does not emerge the wisdom of the ages. But he certainly opened up that throat to me. I'd rank him as one of the best cocksuckers of all time, even better than Liberace—and that's a high compliment indeed."

In another notorious interview, Randall said, "Jack Parr was right. On nationwide TV he said, 'What's ruining television are those big productions—the fairies who come in and sing with the big balloons. It's the fairies who are going to ruin television. I myself always felt there are too many pansies on TV. Let's face it. The gay boys—I call them camera-swishes—are dictating what you see on TV. It's appalling. TV is going to pervert America's teenager boys to their perverse world. It's odd when you turn on the TV and don't see a limp wrist."

Rock also responded to that interview. "The limpest wrist on television belongs to Tony himself. If they were the same size, he and J. Edgar Hoover could exchange gowns."

Rock went on to say, "Tony once told me that he was caught sucking off a teenage boy in a New York T-room—that's a toilet—but the cop let him off because Tony was a riot in *Pillow Talk.*"

***

Rock had met the notorious Nick Adams on the set of *Giant* when he'd come to visit his friend and former roommate, James Dean. In fact, Nick had dubbed Dean's voice in a few scenes after he died in a car crash in 1955.

Up to now, Rock had avoided an involvement with Nick, who was known as a trouble maker and a "star fucker." His closest friends said he'd go to bed with any star—male or female—who might advance his career. It didn't matter to Nick as long as the fuckee was a star or possibly a director. He'd not only taken Natalie Wood's virginity, but had been sexually intimate with both James Dean and Elvis Presley.

Nick had interpreted the small role of "Chick" in *Rebel Without a Cause* (1955), and the handsome, blonde-haired actor would become the fourth member of the doomed young cast of that picture who would die young. That quartet included not only Dean, but Natalie Wood and Sal Mineo, too.

The biographer, Albert Goldman, wrote: "Nick Adams was forever selling himself: a property which, to hear him tell it, was nothing less than sensational, the greatest actor to hit this town in years. In fact, he had very little going for him in terms of looks or talent or professional experience. He was just another poor kid from the sticks who had grown up dreaming of the silver screen."

Born in the gritty, coal-mining town of Nanticoke, Pennsylvania, Nick was the son of Ukrainian immigrants. Eventually, after some bit acting parts, he enlisted in the U.S. Coast Guard and spent time in California during periods when his ship was stationed in San Diego. Occasionally, he auditioned for bit roles while dressed in his seaman's uniform.

On a 48-hour leave, he met Henry Willson in a gay bar. Rock's agent was impressed with his sun-bleached hair and by the way he filled out his Navy whites. He approached him. "I'm a talent scout for David O. Selznick. Do you want to be in movies?"

The answer was a resounding yes. "Movies were my life," he said. "You had to have an escape when you were living in a basement with a family who got by on thirty dollars a month. I saw all the Cagney, Bogart, and John Garfield pictures, the ones where a guy finally got a break. Odds against the world—that was my meat."

As Willson found out later that night, "Nick had another kind of meat—in fact, meat enough for the poor when he stripped off his Navy uniform. If he didn't make it as an actor, he could always hustle."

Nicholas Ray cast and then directed Nick in *Rebel Without a Cause* (1955) after putting him on his casting couch, a site recently vacated by Sal Mineo and James Dean. "Nick was as squirrelly as a leprechaun."

After leaving Phyllis Gates, Rock moved into a beach house built on stilts in Malibu, overlooking the gay beach. Rock casually ran into Nick one Saturday afternoon when he was cruising guys on the beach. "Nick wore a white bikini that made things rather obvious," Rock later told Willson. "I invited him home, and by Sunday night, he'd moved into my new place."

"Get rid of him!" Willson warned. "Col. Tom Parker had to pay *Confidential* a lot of money to suppress an *exposé* about Nick and Elvis. Elvis even moved Nick into Graceland. Elvis worshipped James Dean and took up with Nick when he came to Hollywood, since he was said to have been Dean's best friend."

Rock secured for Nick Adams a small role in *Pillow Talk*, where he pursues Doris Day, who views him as a jerk.

"Right from the beginning, Nick offered his services to Elvis," Willson said. "A guide to Inside Hollywood, a bosom companion, a homosexual lover. In case you didn't already know, Elvis is a bisexual. Nick told Elvis, 'If you want to meet movie stars, I know them. Want to fuck Natalie Wood? I can set it up.'"

And so he did.

Ross Hunter, based on Rock's urging and on Nick's sexual collaboration and cooperation, eventually cast the young Ukrainian in *Pillow Talk* too.

In the movie, Rock rescues Doris Day from the unwanted advances of Tony Walters, cast as the son of one of her clients. In a reprimand to the intoxicated young man, Rock, pretending to be a rancher from Texas, tells him, "In Texas, we say never drink anything stronger than you are—or older."

When Nick's career suddenly took off in television, he moved out of Rock's house in Malibu, but the two men stayed in touch and saw each other on occasion.

Nick had a few highs before his career went south. In 1959, he starred in the hit ABC TV series, *The Rebel,* cast as an ex-Confederate soldier with a sawed-off shotgun, nicknamed "trouble-shooter," toting it through various adventures in the old American West.

In 1963, he'd be nominated for a Best Supporting Actor Oscar for *Twilight of Honor.* He lost to veteran actor Melvyn Douglas for his performance in *Hud,* in which he had co-starred with Paul Newman.

In the 1960s, Nick's career declined as he appeared infrequently in TV episodes and low-budget films.

After leaving Rock, Nick continued to chase stars, hooking up with John Wayne after his friend, Forrest Tucker, introduced them. For some reason, Wayne bonded with the brash young man and was seen coming and going from Nick's house on 2126 El Roble Drive in Beverly Hills. According to Nick, "Everything I learned about how to play a Western character, I learned from John."

Nick found peace at last on February 6, 1968, after his lifeless body was discovered by his lawyer, Ervin Roeder, at his house. His corpse

A bare-chested Nick Adams is seen as the ex-Confederate soldier in the hit TV series, *The Rebel.*

As the columnist, Mike Connolly, said, "Nick shacked up with the A-list: James Dean, Elvis Presley, Rock Hudson, and John Wayne."

was propped up against the wall of his bedroom. An autopsy revealed that he had overdosed on a cocktail of the anti-anxiety medications Paraldehyde and Promazine. A coroner's report determined that the death was "accidental, suicidal, or undetermined." But reports of foul play continue to this day. No drugs or needles were found in his room. There was no suicide note.

Tucker claimed, "All of Hollywood knows Nick Adams was knocked off. It's hushed up—one of those things you dare not talk about because Hollywood likes to keep as many scandals from the public as possible. It's bad for business."

It was later speculated that Nick was killed by a goon employed by Col. Tom Parker. Nick had bragged that he was writing an *exposé* of his relationship with Elvis. He was halfway through the book at the time of his death, but a police search of his home found no manuscript.

Tucker, always outspoken and candid, also commented on Nick's relationship with John Wayne: "I know the Duke. He's a friend of mine ever since he got me cast in *Sands of Iwo Jima* (1949). Nick told me the whole story, and I'll go to my grave not telling it. What the fuck. No one would believe it. Not about Duke Wayne."

***

After Nick Adams, Rock's next big seduction came through an introduction by Elizabeth Taylor herself. Rock jokingly referred to her as "My Pimp." Mike Todd, who had become her third husband, discovered Van Williams, a handsome diving instructor, in 1956 in Hawaii. Because of his striking good looks, Todd urged him to come to Hollywood to try to break into the movies.

Williams arrived in Hollywood in 1958, but by that time, Todd had already died in a plane crash aboard the *Lucky Liz* over New Mexico.

Elizabeth wanted Williams to meet Rock, who could hook him up with Henry Willson, who was still his agent. Soon, Williams became one of "Henry's boys," after enduring an audition on his casting couch. He was straight and would eventually marry Vicki Flaxman in 1959, a union lasting until his death in 2016.

Elizabeth Taylor "pimped" the handsome, studly actor, Van Williams, to her dear friend, Rock.

After their introduction through Elizabeth, Williams and Rock went on a hunting trip together over the course of a long weekend, occupying a remote cabin. The invitation was extended after Rock learned that Williams' favorite pastime involved hunting and shooting geese, duck, and other animals. As Rock told Elizabeth after their return to Los Angeles, "Van learned at our remote little cabin what *my* favorite pastime was. I'll owe you one for the hookup."

Willson managed to get Williams a contract at Warners, after which he was cast in *Tall Story* (1960), in which he played a smug jock stepping stark naked out of the men's locker room shower, giving a young Jane Fonda an eyeful of him. Fonda was cast as a man-hungry coed, but it was her man-hungry co-star, Anthony Perkins, who seduced Williams in his dressing room, not Fonda.

Willson found it easier to get television roles for Williams than work in films, and the actor landed his first big break starring in the ABC TV series, *Bourbon Street Beat* (1959-60), set in New Orleans. An even bigger break came when ABC cast him as *The Green Hornet*, a TV series for the 1966-67 season.

After he abandoned acting, Williams became a successful businessman, with homes in Hawaii, Sun Valley, and Fort Worth.

Years later, he recalled his involvement with both Willson and Rock: "I called Henry 'the Fixer.' He arranged liaisons of guys with guys, women with women, and women with guys. He tried to fix me up with Terry Moore, but I didn't go for her."

He never admitted to an affair with Rock, but said, "He had an enormous sex drive. Henry had his standards, but Rock would sleep with anyone…well, almost, if the guy was young, gorgeous, well built, and preferably blonde. I fitted that bill."

"Rock demanded sex from any young actor Henry got cast in one of his movies," Williams claimed. "He didn't have time to cruise when making a film, and he wanted a guy on hand he could seduce in his dressing room."

***

Rock's penchant for pursuing straight men led to the inevitable conflict with the man's wife or girlfriend.

Gia Scala had appeared in small roles with Rock in *Four Girls in Town*, *Never Say Goodbye*, and *All This and Heaven Too*. In 1959, she'd married the aspiring American actor Don Burnett, who was tall and handsome and was labeled "a Rock Hudson lookalike." He stood six feet three, just one inch shorter than Rock himself.

She introduced Rock to her young husband, and they became friends, often going sailing together. In December of 2014, Tina Scala, Gia's sister, published a memoir entitled, *Gia Scala: The First Gia.* The publicity associated with it read: "With her beauty & movie star fame, handsome and famous men courted her, but the man she loved left her for another man."

Guess who that man was?

Five years younger than Rock, Burnett was a son of Los Angeles. Rock liked him at once. "Every actor I meet was born somewhere else, but you're a native," he told him.

Actress Gia Scala fell in love with a fellow actor, Don Burnett, and married him. But in time, the handsome hunk, hailed as a Rock Hudson lookalike, ditched Scala and went to live with Rock himself.

Burnett, Rock, and Gia Scala often went boating together. There is a picture of Rock and Burnett sleeping peacefully while Gia navigates the boat.

Burnett later described Rock as "very macho and physical—lots of swimming, running into the Hollywood Hills, plenty of sailing to Catalina Island. We even went scuba diving. Nights were filled with heavy drinking."

Burnett became the love of Gia Scala's life. She described him as "exciting and eligible husband material. It was Kismet."

[The marriage of Gia Scala to Burnett came crashing down in March of 1969, and her husband went to live with Rock. She heard rumors of their being together, and one night, enraged, she drove over to find her husband's 1957 Cadillac Coupe DeVille convertible in Rock's driveway.

Filled with fury, she stepped on her accelerator and plowed her car into the rear end of his vehicle. She did that three times in rapid succession before speeding off, and before the police arrived. Hearing the sound of the crash, Burnett screamed down at her from an upstairs window of Rock's house. He later swore out a restraining order against her. Rock did not welcome the publicity.

In time, Gia began to drink heavily, and her almost constant depression, combined with her alcoholism, led to the deterioration of her film career. At one time, she had appeared with Gregory Peck in The Guns of Navarone *(1961). Years later, meeting him at a party, she claimed, "Rock Hudson destroyed my happiness."*

On April 30, 1972, her nude corpse was found inside her home in the Hollywood Hills. At the age of 38, she had apparently died of barbiturate intoxication.]

***

Rock later joked to George Nader that he was going to write a tell-all autobiography when he had no more career to lose. "I'll have a title for each chapter. When I left Gates, and lived on the beach, I'll call that chapter 'Fucking My Way Through Malibu.' I haven't titled my chapter about my days living in Newport Beach."

He claimed that on a lucky day, he could pick up at least two or three men on the beach and invite them back to his Malibu house on stilts. "It seems that all of them wanted to go to bed with Rock Hudson."

But he explained it wasn't the dream factory he thought it would be, as most of them were "duds" when it came to all-out sex.

"Once they found themselves in bed with THE Rock Hudson, they were so intimidated they couldn't get a hard-on. All I could do was turn them over for a bang, but I wanted more."

At Newport Beach, he'd gone sailing every weekend to Catalina on a boat he'd purchased from his friend, actress Claire Trevor. "Often, I'd go sailing in the wind with my beach boy *du jour*, with more flesh waiting on the beaches of Catalina. What a life!"

Ed Muhl, after he retired from Universal, said, "Rock was right up there with Marilyn Monroe. Both stars used sex to broker business deals, and saw sexual intercourse as little more than a handshake."

Although *Confidential* was no longer around to send fear through him, Willson still warned Rock that he was being far too indiscreet, urging him to move away from the beach and find a more substantial residence.

When actor Sam Jaffe left for Europe for an extended stay, Rock drove to 9402 Beverly Crest Drive. There, he found the house of his dreams, which he would not only rent from Jaffe, but later purchase. Not knowing it at the time, of course, this was the home in which he'd die.

In the meantime, the 1960s were roaring noisily in on him. With them came social upheavals and political unrest, assassinations of key political figures, the Vietnam War, and the arrival on the scene of a sexual revolution with unrestricted sex on a mass level, often without gender preference.

Rock's career, at least for a while, was peaking, and the world seemed to be his until one day he woke up and it wasn't.

Chapter Fourteen

Rock Fires Henry Willson and Proposes Marriage to Marilyn Maxwell

More Doris Day! *Lover Come Back!*

Rock Plays Prince Charming to Grace Kelly in Monaco, in Her Royal Chambers

In *Lover Come Back*, Rock deceives Doris Day as he did in *Pillow Talk*. Deliberately wearing "the worst suit I'd ever worn on the screen," he impersonates an eccentric chemist who is afraid of women and may, in fact, be a male virgin. His aim, of course, is to get Doris, as his chief rival in the advertising world, to seduce him.

Rock's next film assignment was *The Last Sunset*, a western set for a 1961 release by Universal. It would co-star Rock alongside Kirk Douglas, Dorothy Malone, Carol Lynley, and veteran actor Joseph Cotten, as directed by Robert Aldrich.

Its screenplay by Dalton Trumbo had been adapted from Howard Rigsby's novel *Sundown at Crazy Horse*.

The novelist on whose work the screenplay was based protested that his original title was more provocative and a better choice than what was eventually used. *[Actually,* The Last Sunset *was certainly better than other titles suggested (and rejected) by Universal:* All Girls Wear Yellow Dresses, Trigger Talk, Shoe the Wild Sea-Mare, *and* Two to Make Hate. *"Have you ever heard more atrocious titles?" its co-star, Kirk Douglas asked.]*

Aldrich was a strong director, and whereas Rock rarely conflicted with him, agreeing with what was demanded of him, Douglas challenged him during the filming of almost every scene. After this project with Rock, Aldrich would go on to direct films that evolved into major-league hits, including *What Ever Happened to Baby Jane?* (1962) and *The Dirty Dozen* (1967).

Critic John Patterson summed up Aldrich's directorial priorities: "He's paunchy, caustic, macho, and pessimistic, depicting evil and corruption unflinchingly, and pushing violence. His aggressive and pugnacious filmmaking style, often crass and crude, but never less than utterly vital and alive, warrants—indeed will richly reward—your immediate attention."

The Last Sunset was the final movie Rock owed Universal under his old contract. During the shoot, he signed a new contract calling for two Universal pictures a year for $100,000 per picture. If he had time left, he could work for other studios.

The script by Trumbo was not one of his greater successes. Douglas had recently commissioned him to write the script for *Spartacus* (1960), thereby ending the writer's status as an unemployable outcast based on his alleged and widely publicized communist allegiances. Even during the depths of his disgrace, under a pseudonym, Dalton had written other successful filmscripts, notably *Roman Holiday* (1953), co-starring Gregory Peck and Audrey Hepburn.

With two superstars in the same movie, there arose the thorny issue of billing. Although Douglas' film production company was making the movie and theoretically, at least, in charge of the creative content, Universal was financing and distributing it. Consequently, Ed Muhl demanded that Rock get first billing, and Douglas acquiesced.

He later asserted, "I had a problem working with Rock. He avoided any kind of direct contact with me. I was aware of how difficult it must have been for him—his co-star was also his boss. I tried everything I could to make him comfortable. But he always had a strange attitude to me, never dealing with me directly. He would make demands to Universal, and some executive would then come to me and say, 'You have to do this and this. Rock demands it.'"

"It never occurred to me that he was a homosexual," Douglas said. "I don't draw a line between masculine and feminine. We all have both sides. And we need them, especially artists."

In his capacity as the film's producer, during his pursuit of a suitable female lead, Douglas sent the script to Lauren Bacall, with whom he had co-starred in *Young Man With a Horn* (1950).

[What was not generally known is that Douglas had taken her virginity in her pre-Bogart days during her stint as a model in New York City, when she was identified as Betty Bacall.]

Bacall brusquely rejected the script for *The Last Sunset*, expressing indignation that Douglas even offered it to her, although he could never figure out why. "She berated me for sending her the script. I said, 'Betty, it's the leading female role. You have Rock Hudson in love with you. He was in love with you in *Written on the Wind*. You have Kirk Douglas in love with you. That's nothing new for you. I think it's a good part.' Bacall rejected the role anyway."

After that rebuff, Douglas sent the script to Dorothy Malone, whose character had been in love with Rock in *Written on the Wind*. Malone immediately and enthusiastically agreed to star in it.

A supporting role went to Joseph Cotten, who had entered cinematic history through his association with Orson Welles' *Citizen Kane* (1941).

Another role went to Carol Lynley, a former child model in New York. She had graced the cover of *Life* magazine in April of 1957 at the age of 15. She'd appeared on Broadway and in the movie *Blue Denim,* a controversial stage play that had dealt with an unwanted pregnancy and subsequent abortion.

Character actors Jack Elam and Neville Brand were cast as villains who want to sell Lynley and Malone into white slavery.

Douglas was cast as the neurotic gunman, Brendan O'Malley, a lonesome, tormented cowboy who dresses entirely in black and makes blarney-like observations about life. Perhaps for the first time in a Hollywood Western, the plot involves the potential for incest, a conundrum that seems to encourage his character's eventual suicide. O'Malley faces a shootout with Dana Stribling (as interpreted by Rock), who has pursued him across the border and into Mexico for killing his brother-in-law, even though he has no jurisdiction to apprehend him South of the Border.

O'Malley (Douglas) has opted to visit his former sweetheart, Belle Breckenridge (Malone), with whom he'd had an affair sixteen years ago. He meets her daughter, Missy (Lynley), who, coincidentally, was born sixteen years ago. Belle is now married to an old drunk, John (Joseph Cotten), a garrulous and ineffectual gentleman rancher trapped in his nostalgia for Civil War glories past.

Herders and cowpokes are desperately needed to drive hundreds of cattle north into Texas. For his involvement in the migration, O'Malley demands a fifth of the herd. When Stribling (Rock) arrives on the scene, he agrees to join the ranchers, but only if he's designated as their trail boss. O'Malley, it appears, will travel northward with the herd, but only to Mexico's border with Texas, as he'll be arrested the minute he sets foot in U.S. territory.

Here, Trumbo turns up the heat: John (Cotten) is killed in a barroom brawl; Stribling falls in love with Belle, O'Malley develops the hots for Belle's teenaged daughter, Missy, and the group is attacked by Indians.

More trouble is on the way when a trio of nefarious bushwhackers join the group, supposedly as trail drivers. Their evil intentions are eventually thwarted.

Finally, with their cattle, the migrants reach the U.S. border, and O'Malley—against his better judgment—crosses into Texas. Although he plans to escape with Missy after getting paid, Belle reveals that Missy is O'Malley's daughter from their love affair sixteen years before—a thorny problem, indeed, soaked with the potentiality for father/daughter incest. Resolution to the dilemma comes in the aftermath of an armed confrontation between the "cowboy in black" (Douglas) and the vigilante sheriff (Rock), who guns him down (perhaps with Douglas's collusion as part of a suicide pact, the script is unclear) as the sun sets in the West.

The movie was filmed entirely in Mexico.

The critic for the *Hollywood Reporter* wrote: "*The Last Sunset* is a big, big Western. But like the men it cele-

Facing *The Last Sunset*, (left to right), Kirk Douglas, Carol Lynley, Dorothy Malone, and Rock Hudson.

Unknowingly, Douglas falls in love with his own daughter.

brates, it gives indications of being a dying breed. It is not an exciting picture, and is particularly disappointing considering the caliber of talent that went into its acting, writing, and directing."

***

Fearing that Rock might be "slipping away" as his most profitable client, Henry Willson wanted to break through with a spectacular deal that would keep Rock bound to his agency. Buoyed by the success of *Pillow Talk*, he devised a concept for a sexy, romantic comedy set in Italy. For years, Rock and Marilyn Monroe had each expressed a desire to make a movie together. Now, behind the scenes, Willson maneuvered her representative to get her signed as Rock's co-star.

Come September, eventually released in 1961, was a change of pace for director Robert Mulligan, better known for his humanistic dramas. Even as he was tangling with the problems associated with this new comedy featuring Rock, he was to some degree preoccupied with his next film, *To Kill a Mockingbird* (1962), which would become a legendary movie classic starring Gregory Peck as Harper Lee's Atticus Finch.

Mulligan and Rock blended together smoothly. His first direction to Rock involved telling him, "My technique is to rest the camera on your face quietly, unobtrusively, and let something happen. Then it's up to you."

When director John Huston heard that Mulligan wanted to cast Monroe as Rock's co-star, he phoned Mulligan for a candid, director-to-director talk. Around this time, Huston was on location helming Monroe in *The Misfits* (1961), having co-starred her with Clark Gable (in his last motion picture before his death) and Montgomery Clift (Rock's former lover; in fact, both "Monty and Marilyn" had been former lovers of Rock.)

In his dialogue with Mulligan, Huston complained about the potential chaos associated with both stars: "Monty is in even worse shape than Marilyn, I never know when they're going to show up, but I can bet either of them will be drugged."

Huston also claimed that Arthur Miller, Marilyn's then-husband and the author of *The Misfits'* screenplay, was tangling daily with his wife as their marriage crumbled. Like Gable, this would be the last movie she ever completed.

As a final warning, Huston revealed, "My two druggies are driving Gable into an early grave."

Robert Arthur, *Come September's* producer, would also produce Rock's next film, *Lover Come Back*.

When Rock set off for Italy to make *Come September,* he was thirty-five years old and had been acting in movies for more than a decade. To his closest friends, he expressed a desire to break out, perhaps make a film in France with sex kitten Brigitte Bardot. He knew in time his temples would turn gray, so he was even considering becoming a director as head of his own production company.

The dream of casting the temperamental Monroe faded quickly, much to Rock's disappointment. Mulligan, as director, cast Gina Lollobrigida as Rock's mistress, with a supporting cast that included Bobby Darin, Sandra Dee, and Walter Slezak.

Two years younger than Rock, Lollobrigida, the Italian bombshell, after placing third in the 1947 Miss Italy contest, had evolved into an international sex symbol, the rival of the more widely acclaimed Sophia Loren. Ms. Loren once, with touches of bitchery and venom, had told the press, "Lollobrigida's personality is limited, and she's good at playing a peasant, but incapable of playing a lady on the screen"

During the course of her career, Lollobrigida would emote onscreen with leading men who, in addition to Rock, included Burt Lancaster, Tony Curtis, Errol Flynn, Frank Sinatra, Anthony Quinn, Yul Brynner, and Sean Connery. Likewise, her loves would range from a rumored affair with Cuban dictator Fidel Castro to Dr. Christiaan Barnard, the South African surgeon who pioneered the first procedures for heart transplants.

During one of her meetings with Rock, she complained, "I get annoyed when people think I must be the same woman I portray on the screen."

Rock had seen only one film with his sexy leading lady, *Beat the Devil* (1953), in which Lollobrigida had co-starred with Humphrey Bogart and Jennifer Jones, Rock's former leading lady in *A Farewell to Arms.*

Huston, who directed the picture and shot it along Italy's Amalfi Coast, said, "Gina is like a modern apartment building with outside balconies."

Bobby Darin and Sandra Dee, who had not met each other before filming began, were cast as the young lovers. A son of New York's East Harlem, singer Darin was at home performing country, folk, swing, jazz, pop, and rock 'n roll, but was less successful imitating Elvis Presley.

432

He started out as a songwriter for Connie Francis, fell in love with her and proposed. She turned him down, later claiming, "It was the biggest mistake of my life."

In 1958, Darin had released his million-dollar *Billboard* topper, "Splish Splash," which was heard on radio stations across the land. That was followed by such megahits as "Mack the Knife" from *The Threepenny Opera,* as well as "Dream Lover" and "Beyond the Sea." For his role in *Come September,* he would win a Golden Globe award.

A seemingly innocent, virginal archetype (some say "caricature") of the 1950s, cute, perky Sandra Dee, of New Jersey has become a symbol of a bygone era of wholesome teen romances. Rock's frequent producer, Ross Hunter, had discovered her when she was only twelve. He cast her in *Imitation of Life* (1959) as Lana Turner's daughter. The box office grosser revived Turner's sagging career and made Dee a star. That was followed by *Gidget* (also 1959) which elevated Dee into a household name.

At the start of Dee's film career, Louella Parsons, in a statement that horrified her, compared her to Shirley Temple.

When Rock met her on the set in Italy, she was struggling with *anorexia nervosa.* She was loudly critical of her screen image as a teenage virgin. She immediately requested one of his cigarettes. "I smoke," she said, lighting up as part of her best Bette Davis impersonation. "I also drink. And, get this. I fuck!"

Puffing some more, she asked him, "Do you want to know who took my virginity?"

"I can't guess. It's really none of my business."

"My stepfather, Eugene Douvan," she claimed. "He was always mounting me. I'd call it rape."

By this stage of her career, Dee had already made a big film, *A Summer Place* (1959) for Warners, opposite Troy Donahue, Rock's former lover. Donahue and Dee were each receiving some 5,000 to 7,500 fan letters a week.

Donahue was considered briefly for the Darin role, but was rejected. During his most recent call to Rock, he had expressed another bitter disappointment: Elia Kazan had considered casting him as the lead in *Splendor in the Grass*

Young lovers Sandra Dee and Bobby Darin met for the first time on the set of Rock's latest film, *Come September.*

The first time he spotted her, before he had even spoken to her, he decided she was going to become his bride.

(1961), based on a play by William Inge. Shortly thereafter, Inge developed an overpowering crush on Warren Beatty, and persuaded Kazan to cast "the object of his affection" (Beatty) instead.

In preparation for her performance in *Come September*, before her arrival in Italy, Dee had given an interview to *Parade* magazine (June 1960) in which she proclaimed, "The last man I'm going to marry is a man in show business. They're selfish, unreliable, and make lousy husbands. The Hollywood type of marriage is not for me. I want all my children to have the same father."

Appearing as Rock's co-star in *Come September*, Gina Lollobrigida told him, "My whole life is one big, long battle to tell men I don't wish to take off my clothes. I cannot help the sexy way I look and that it drives men wild. Sex appeal I do not do on purpose. I do it sincerely. I am always dressed in my pictures."

In tribute to her assets, the French coined the term *lollobrigidienne*, meaning "curvaceous."

Darin was more enthusiastic about the concept of marriage. The first time he spotted Dee from a distance, he asked her makeup man, Jack Freeman, "What's that dame like?"

Freeman assured Darin that Dee was wonderful. "Why do you ask?"

"I think I might marry her." Darin replied.

The first time he met her, she was arriving on a boat, and he was standing on the pier wearing a sunflower yellow suit. As she approached, visible across the water, he called out to her, "Will you marry me?"

She shot back, "Not today!"

During the casting for *Come September*, the most visible role for a character actor went to a Viennese, Walter Slezak, who had starred in German-language films before migrating to the United States in 1930. He was often cast as a villain or a thug, most notably when Alfred Hitchcock hired him to play a Nazi U-boat captain in *Lifeboat* (1944) opposite Tallulah Bankhead. When Ronald Reagan became U.S. President, Slezak became quite famous because of the frequent screening of Reagan's most embarrassing cinematic mishap, *Bedtime for Bonzo* (1951), in which Slezak had co-starred.

Come September was shot on location in Rome and in the little resort town of Portofino, site of a villa owned by Rex Harrison, in the northeast of Italy, near Genoa. The cast and crew were lodged at the local *grande dame*, the Excelsior Hotel, in the larger neighboring town of Santa Margherita Ligure.

In the film, Rock was cast as Robert Talbot, a rich American businessman who owns a villa on the Ligurian coast. He has a Roman mistress, Lisa

Fellini (Lollobrigida), and he spends September (theoretically when the coast is at its most beautiful) with her every year.

She has, however, grown tired of being his one-month-a-year girlfriend and decides to marry a (rather dull and very staid) Englishman named Spencer (Ronald Howard).

Impulsively, this year Robert (Rock) has opted to vacation at his villa in July, not September. There, he discovers not only that his sometimes mistress is getting married, but that his *majordomo* and housekeeper, Maurice Clavell (Slezak) has transformed his villa into a summer hotel. It's presently housing a bevy of teenaged American girls, spearheaded by Sandy (Sandra Dee).

En route to his villa, Rock, driving in his expensive car, is taunted by four horny (American) teenaged boys. The hecklers include Tony (Darin), who soon trains his eye on Sandy. The young men camp outside Rock's villa and begin courting the girls staying at "the hotel."

Of course, after one farcical sequence after another, it all works out in the end, as we know it will. Robert marries his stylish and beautiful Italian mistress, and Tony gets Sandy, as indeed Darin did in real life, marrying Dee on December 1, 1960 before the release of the picture. Their troubled marriage would last until March of 1967.

As a child, Darin had suffered from recurring bouts of rheumatic fever, which left him in poor health for the remainder of his life. He died in December of 1973 at the age of 37.

During filming, Rock came to resent the press attention focusing on his co-stars. The Italian paparazzi pursued "La Lolla" as Gina was called. When news of the Darin/Dee romance broke, reporters swarmed onto the set to interview them. Rock was virtually ignored. Indeed, he had his own romance going on, but it was a dark secret as he spent his nights in the arms of his Roman Romeo, Massimo.

Released in CinemaScope in 1961, *Come September* did reasonably well at the box office, but nothing to equal *Pillow Talk*. Universal was demanding another repeat romantic comedy with Doris Day. He and Lollobrigida did not have any

On screen in *Come September*, Rock and Gina Lollobrigida, dubbed "La Lollo," played his mistress.

They are seen here on a motor scooter touring the scenic Italian coast. One Roman newspaper reported that during the making of the film, the two sexy stars had an affair. But another paper quoted her as saying, "Rock never made a pass at me."

435

particular chemistry on the screen, but the duo would be cast in one more comedy, three years hence.

Most critics dismissed *Come September* as a frothy comedy about the younger generation (Dee and Darin) vs. the older generation (Rock and Lollobrigida).

***

Flying into Rome, Rock hailed a taxi, which took him and all his luggage to the Grand Hotel near the city's railway station. By now, the staff there was familiar with his antics, having either seen or heard about his violent confrontation in an upstairs hallway with Phyllis Gates. Massimo, too, was also familiar with the hotel, having passed some nights there with Rock.

Rock's first call was to Massimo at his apartment. At first, his former lover was furious at him for rejecting him during his previous visit to Los Angeles, where he'd hoped to find work as an actor.

Rock pleaded his case, claiming that the heat had been on at the time because of the *Confidential* trial. He also claimed that at the time, Phyllis had hired a master detective to gather evidence of his homosexual involvements.

He finally convinced Massimo to stay with him during the shooting of *Come September*. Over breakfast the next morning, Massimo pleaded with Rock to get him a small role in his film. Rock claimed that the director, Robert Mulligan, had already cast all the parts. "There's always next time," Rock promised.

Rock wanted to keep a low profile during this visit to Rome, and Massimo knew all the hidden spots where they could go. They avoided the Via Veneto, preferring instead the tucked-away *trattorie* and clubs of Trastevere, where Rock had first met and picked up Massimo for a night of casual sex. One little restaurant with a courtyard was discovered along the Appian Way.

In spite of an affair that stretched over a period of twenty years, there is no known picture of Rock with Massimo, his "Roman Romeo."

One underground newspaper ran this photograph, with the top part of his head cut off, claiming it was Massimo, but there is no proof that it actually was. However, if it weren't Massimo, at least the body matched that of Rock's longtime lover.

To help Massimo recover from his disappointment for not appearing in Rock's movie, he gave him a thousand dollars in countersigned travelers' checks, promising that more money would be forthcoming.

When filming was transferred from Rome to Portofino, Rock invited his lover to drive there with him. When they got there, he stashed him in a *pensione* right in the center, while he stayed in a suite at the Excelsior in neighboring Santa Margherita Ligure.

During the location shooting, Rock was seen coming and going from Massimo's *pensione*, informing Mulligan that he'd rented a room there for use as his dressing room. The director didn't seem to care what he used it for.

Once source claimed that Rock had brief flings with four of the young men cast in minor roles, but this could not be confirmed. However, it appeared unlikely, since he was in bed with Massimo every night, allowing almost no time for a sexual rampage.

When *Come September* was wrapped, Rock had ten days before he had to fly back to Los Angeles. He invited Massimo to fly with him to Nice, where they rented a car and drove west to Cannes. There, he had booked a suite at the Carlton.

On their second day at the chic resort, Rock suggested they keep the suite, but pack some clothing in case Grace Kelly invited them to stay over in the principality over which she now presided as Princess of Monaco.

Previously, back in 1957, Rock had taken Massimo to Monaco, where he had been introduced to Kelly. A photographer there had snapped their photo, but editors cut Massimo out of the frame, showing an altered version with only Rock and Grace.

This time, the Princess invited Rock and Massimo to join her at the royal palace for lunch, claiming that her husband, Prince Rainier, was away in Paris. He was rumored to have a mistress there.

Over lunch, Kelly spoke candidly about her life. She told Rock she continued to regret she had not gotten to play the role of Leslie in *Giant,* the juicy part going to Elizabeth Taylor. "Actually, I flirted with the idea of playing the hooker in Elizabeth's film, *BUtterfield 8.* That

Rock and Grace Kelly, the Princess of Monaco, had an ongoing affair that lasted for many years.

She told her friend, Ava Gardner, "Rock truly lives up to his reputation as the world's most desirable male. When so many screen legends take off their trousers, they are so disappointing. Since you've sampled many of them, I don't have to name them for you."

would certainly have destroyed my squeaky clean image."

Rock's prediction that he'd be offered an extended invitation to overnight at the palace in Monaco was correct: The Princess invited them for a three-night stopover before Rainier returned.

"She flirted outrageously with him," Massimo said, "and spoke several times about his masculine charms. One day, when he left the table, she told me that she never believed all those rumors about his gay life. How she could she have said that in front of me, of all people!"

"She was always so feminine around Rock," Massimo claimed. "It was like she wanted to be coddled. She was so helpless. But it was just an act. She was a strong, independent, woman who knew exactly what she wanted, and set out to get it. She was definitely not 'Baby Grace,' some clinging, dependent female."

The highlight of their visit came for both men the next day, when in a Rolls Royce, they were driven to the French villages of Èze and La Turbie. "I noted that the villagers recognized her, but did not dare approach her," Massimo said. "They kept a respectful distance, but stared at us a lot."

Over a gourmet lunch at a table with a panoramic view of the coast, the Princess revealed that Rainier and Aristotle Onassis had first plotted that he should marry Marilyn Monroe as a means of increasing tourism to Monaco. "I was second choice," she admitted, whether it was true or not.

Confidentially, she spoke about how hard it had been for her to adjust to life in Monaco, and what a quarrelsome clan the House of Grimaldi was. She referred to her husband as "Rainier. His parents were separated at the time of his birth, and his mother ran off with an Italian doctor in the 1920s. His mother often complained about Rainier's father, saying that before he made love, he put on his crown."

She revealed that the Grimaldis had feuded with nearly every royal household in Europe. "That's why so few of them turned up at my wedding. The obese Aga Khan showed up laden with jewelry. He was in a wheelchair. Another obsese monarch, the deposed king of Egypt, Farouk, also attended, telling me that every morning he woke up, he feared that an assassin would kill him."

For three nights, Rock and Massimo were guests of the Princess at her palace. "She told us that for appearance's sake, we should occupy separate suites. And whereas I was confined to Siberia in a far wing of the palace, Rock occupied a suite near to hers. I can't prove it, but I believe that Rock slipped into her suite and made love to her for three nights in a row."

After Monaco, Rock drove Massimo west to Cannes. *En route*, Massimo accused him of "screwing Grace."

Rock adamantly denied it.

"Once we returned to our suite at the Carlton in Cannes, Rock's passion for me resumed...and how! He promised to be faithful to me in the future. Of course, that promise had the lifespan of a plucked wildflower."

***

"Marilyn Maxwell was a helluva broad," or so said Frank Sinatra, who "heavy dated" her during the 1940s, much to the annoyance of his faithful first wife, Nancy. "She's a great gal," said Rock Hudson, who resumed dating her when he returned to Los Angeles, after bidding Massimo goodbye in Rome.

One reporter claimed that Maxwell, an ex-band singer, was "every man's fantasy of what a movie star looked like, evoking Lana Turner." Tall and voluptuous, she was graced with white porcelain skin and platinum hair, with a smile "so inviting that only monks could resist her," in the words of Bob Hope, her longtime lover.

Rock had had an affair with her in the 1950s, which he resumed in the wake of his divorce from Phyllis Gates. Maxwell is often cited as proof of Rock's bisexuality, at least during his early days in Hollywood. The press labeled her "one of the best sweater-fillers in town."

For a while, Maxwell deluded herself, thinking Rock's fascination with gay sex was "a passing fad," but it wasn't. She considered Rock a "real heman," telling her friends that many of the most masculine Hollywood stars, including Clark Gable and Gary Cooper, had had sex with men in the 1920s. She even pointed out that John Wayne had, too, although his involvements may have been for career advancement. She once said, "Many of Henry Willson's pretty boys later got married, had children, and abandoned their gay pasts."

There was something infectious about Marilyn," Rock said. "Perhaps it was her zany humor. Sometimes, we'd roll around the living room floor, giggling and tickling each other. She could make me laugh even on the gloomiest of days. She could not only act, which she took se-

Of all the women who passed through Rock's love life—and there were far more than the public knew—only the blonde goddess, Marilyn Maxwell, "moved into a chamber of my heart" (Rock's words).

"For me, Lana Turner and Marilyn Monroe were passing fads. The other Marilyn (Maxwell) was the real thing."

riously, but was a good singer and dancer, too."

Although her affair with Rock stayed under the radar screen for the most part, she virtually broadcast her affair with Sinatra in the 1944 movie, *Lost in a Harem.* She performed a song entitled "What Does It Take to Get You?" which contained a line "I can even get to second base with Frank Sinatra." Movie audiences even back then knew what second base meant, and most of them had read in the columns about her link to Sinatra.

"Marilyn and I were crazy about each other," Rock confessed. "I even proposed marriage to her, but she turned me down."

What Rock didn't reveal was the reason for her rejection. According to the terms he demanded in their marriage, he wanted her to allow him to have affairs with men on the side. She claimed that she suspected she'd be too jealous to allow that.

Even though she rejected his proposal, one night after he'd seduced her, she startled him by saying, "Even though I won't marry you, I want to be the mother of your child. With a mama as gorgeous as me, and a papa as dazzlingly handsome as you, we'll have the most beautiful kid at Hollywood High."

He often spent lavishly on her, giving her a mink coat for Christmas, later finding out that Bob Hope had given her a roughly equivalent mink.

From 1954 to 1960, she'd been married to writer/producer Jerry Davis, with whom she produced her only child, Matthew. Rock became like a second father to him, affectionately calling him "Matt."

For Matt's sixth birthday, Rock tossed a party for him and his friends from school. He rented a merry-go-round for the event and hired clowns from Ringling Brothers to perform.

Davis often complained to his then-wife that she and Rock were spending too much time together. "I'd come home from work, and there would be six-foot, four inches of macho stud hanging out with my wife. God knows how many more inches of the guy were hidden. My friends laughed at me for viewing Rock as a potential threat, insisting that he was exclusively gay."

Maxwell called Rock "Big Sam," and he lovingly nicknamed her "Max."

"We could spend hours listening to records. She preferred the songs of the Big Band era, especially Sinatra, but also Doris Day."

She told her close friend, Jean Greenberg, "I was deeply in love with Rock. He always told me that he loved me dearly, but wasn't in love with me. What a difference!"

Throughout the 1960s, when Maxwell's career declined greatly, Rock often came to her aid financially. In 1963, he paid all her medical bills after she almost died from an ovarian cyst.

She picked up whatever acting jobs she could find, signing with ABC to appear in 26 episodes of a series, *Bus Stop* (1961-62) a drama about travelers passing through the fictional town of Sunrise, Colorado. After thirteen episodes, she bowed out of the series, telling Rock, "There wasn't much for me to do, except serve a second cup of coffee to a cowpoke and direct him to the head for a horse piss."

At the end of her career, she got roles in an occasional feature film, but they were third rate, including a tired Western, *Arizona Bushwackers* in 1968.

Near the end of her life, Rock told George Nader, "Marilyn and I have become soulmates, not lovers anymore."

When he was fifteen years old, Matthew came home from school and found his mother dead on the floor of their living room, having died two or three hours earlier of a heart attack. She was close to being fifty years old.

Rock was heartbroken. He rescued Matthew and took him to live with him at his new home, The Castle, until her estate could be settled.

Rock was among the pallbearers at her funeral, along with Frank Sinatra, Jack Benny, Bob Hope, and Bing Crosby. Rock paid all her funeral expenses.

His personal friend and agent, publicist David Olson, said, "For days, he was despondent and wouldn't even pick up the phone. He was drinking heavily. When he finally did come to the phone, he told me, "That's it for me. I'll never love another woman as long as I live."

That was one vow he kept.

***

Robert Arthur, who had produced *Come September,* put together another package (*Lover Come Back,* released in 1961) for presentation to Martin Melcher, the husband of Doris Day, to reteam the trio—Rock, Doris, and Tony Randall—from *Pillow Talk.*

A supporting cast would feature Edie Adams, Jack Oakie, and Ann B. Davis. Delbert Mann was tapped as the director, with a screenplay written in part with Stanley Shapiro, who had penned *Come September.*

Universal billed *Lover Come Back* as a "champagne chaser" to *Pillow Talk.* Rock's friendship with Day continued, but he didn't get along with Melcher. Neither did Henry Willson, who called him "Farty Belcher."

Willson thought he had solidified his role in Rock's life by getting him a million-dollar share of the profits. This increase in his compensation put Rock up there with the earning power of Cary Grant, Marlon Brando, and

Spencer Tracy.

Meeting with Day, Rock resumed his humorous, fun-loving times with her, except they came up with two new nicknames for each other—Zelda for her and Murgatroy for him.

Kansas-born Delbert Mann had never helmed Rock before, but he'd won a Best Director Oscar for *Marty* (1955), starring Ernest Borgnine. He earned his reputation directing some 100 live TV dramas, beginning in the early days of the little black box. In fact, he was credited with helping to bring TV techniques to the world of film in Hollywood.

He and Rock worked smoothly as a team, and he'd helm him again in *A Gathering of Eagles* (1963). He would also direct Day again in 1962 in *That Touch of Mink.*

Doris Day and Rock had to shoot three beach scenes in *Lover Come Back*. The scene above had to be reshot when one of Rock's big balls actually popped out from the confines of his bathing suit. The director ordered a more sanitized version.

In another segment, when she finds out who he really is, she suggests that they go skinny dipping after dark. When he does, she drives off with his clothes, leaving him stranded on the beach, nude.

Melcher made a rash decision not to recast Rock with Day in *That Touch of Mink.* He told executives, "Rock got too much credit for *Pillow Talk* and *Lover Come Back*. It was Doris, not Hudson, who made those two movies box office triumphs. Reviewer after reviewer cited him playing a Cary Grant role. For Doris' next picture, I decided to cast the real Cary Grant."

As it turned out, whereas Rock would have settled for a million dollars, Grant ended up costing the studio four million.

When Rock met Mann, he congratulated him on having directed one of his favorite films, *Separate Tables* (1958), which had been nominated for a Best Picture Oscar, starring Rita Hayworth, Burt Lancaster, and Deborah Kerr.

Lover Come Back would be the last film of Jack Oakie, who was cast as J. Paxton Miller, a randy business executive. Rock had previously appeared with Oakie in *Tomahawk.*

Rock found Edie Adams, cast as an ambitious show-girl named Rebel

Davis, highly entertaining, especially when she delivered her devastating impersonations of Marilyn Monroe. She had become famous on TV, thanks to her *schticks* with comedian Ernie Kovacs, whom she'd married, and with talk show host pioneer Jack Paar. Her cigarette commercials had made her one of the top three most recognizable TV celebrities. *The New York Times* summed up her body of work: "It both embodied and winked at the stereotypes of fetching chanteuse and sexpot blonde."

Horror of horrors. Imagine the humiliation of Carol Templeton when, after a drunken night, she wakes up in bed with her worst enemy and chief rival in the advertising world, Jerry Webster. She's wearing his pajama tops, and he's attired only in the bottoms.

The plot for *Lover Come Back* focuses on two rivals-cum-lovers, Day (as Carol Templeton) and Rock (as Jerry Webster). They work for competing advertising agencies, but their methods of winning clients are vastly different.

Day is efficient and hardworking, preparing charts and sample ads for her prospective clients, devising legitimate ways to sell their products. In contrast, in this spoof of Madison Avenue, Jerry is devious. His philosophy of advertising is, "Give me a well-stacked dame in a bathing suit, and I'll sell after-shave to the Beatniks!"

The character of Jerry (Rock) is defined and established from the very beginning, when he's delivered directly to his office by one of his busty *belles du jour* after an obvious night of sex and partying.

Rock and Doris, competitive rivals who know each other only by reputation, set out to woo a wealthy client, J. Paxton Miller (Oakie), a proud Southerner, the type who salutes the Confederate flag. In something approaching a parody of Madison Avenue's advertising world, Rock solicits his ac-

Fabulous, funny, glamorous, and brilliant at playing a dumb broad: Edie Adams

count with flattery, booze, and broads, and by letting the good times roll.

Once again, Randall plays Jerry's (i.e., Rock's) neurotic, wimpy employer who seems to spend all of his free time on his psychiatrist's couch. For him, the highlight of the movie occurred when Rock and Doris, as Jerry and Carol, are on the beach, filming a scene in their bathing attire. According to Randall, "There was one take where Rock leaned over and one ball come out of his trunks, and then back in again. We said,

All smiles in front of the camera, Doris Day and Marty Melcher had a disastrous marriage made in hell.

After his death, she learned painfully that he'd squandered all the millions she'd made during one of Hollywood's most successful careers, both in films and as a recording artist.

'Hey, play that again! We were just shrieking and screaming.' It nearly got in the picture."

When Rock heard Randall's crack, he told the director, "If there's one thing that Randall adores about me, it's my big balls."

Jerry has a good-time girlfriend, showgirl "Rebel" Davis, whom he has been manipulating with the prospect that one day, he'll make her the star of a TV commercial. He has pacified her long enough, and now, she wants to hold him to his promise…or else. He makes her "the VIP Girl" promoting a product that does not exist. After filming, he orders the cameraman to stash the footage far away out of sight.

But Ramsey (Randall), taking charge of an account for the first time in his life, releases it nationwide on TV screens, Demands for the product pour in from everywhere.

In desperation, Jerry turns to Dr. Linus Tylor (Jack Kruschen), paying him to create a product, any product, to meet the demand. In her attempt to grab the account, Carol goes to his laboratory, where she encounters Jerry (Rock). Mistakenly, she assumes that he is the eccentric scientist who invented the product that the ad world is suddenly frantic about.

As he did in *Pillow Talk*, Rock suddenly pretends to be somebody else. This time his impersonates the scientist who, according to false reports, invented the VIP sensation. Rock portrays him as shy, uncertain, and a bit afraid of women. It's all part of Jerry's plot to get her to play the aggressor in the seduction which the audience by now interprets as virtually inevitable.

He almost succeeds. Carol, in love and ready to rumble, is about to seduce him in her apartment with the intention of "making a man out of him." She's already taught him how to kiss. But a few moments before her carefully orchestrated deflowering, she receives a call from Ramsey, who tells her that her shy suitor is actually her dreaded nemesis, Jerry Webster.

Not revealing what she knows, she invites him for a midnight swim at an isolated beach 30 miles away. When he tells her he has no trunks, she assures him "you won't need them." After he strips down, she drives off with his clothes, leaving him naked on the beach. By morning, a van hauling furs pulls up at his hotel, and he gets out, rushing into the building clad only in a mink coat.

Carol goes before the Advertising Council to expose Jerry for promoting a product that does not exist. But he enters the scene triumphantly with VIP, sensational mint-like candies created moments before by Dr. Tyler, and invites one and all to sample them. One of the wafers, moviegoers learn, has the intoxicating power of a triple martini. Everyone, including Carol, gets drunk.

When she unexpectedly wakes up in bed with Rock in a motel room, she screams, in response to which Rock shows their marriage certificate. They had had sex the night before. She flees, demanding an annulment.

They are separated for nine months until he learns she is pregnant. He rushes to the hospital and, in the last minute of the film, he remarries her just as she is being wheeled into the delivery room.

Rock later referred to *Lover Come Back* as "one of my alltime favorite comedies."

Lover Come Back opened in February of 1962, grossing $440,000 in a single week, a big figure back then. Bosley Crowther, writing in *The New York Times,* had attacked Rock's movies for years. He wrote, "Mr. Hudson and Miss Day are delicious, he in his big sprawling way, and she in her wide-eyed, pert, pugnacious, and eventually melting vein. *Pillow Talk* was but a warm-up for this springy and spirited surprise, which is one of the brightest, most delightful satiric comedies since *It Happened One Night.*"

It matched *Pillow Talk* in box office appeal and did even better, grossing $8.5 million in the U.S. and Canada alone.

At Oscar time, *Lover Come Back* was nominated for Best Screenplay, an award which its screenwriters, Stanley Shapiro and Paul Henning, shared.

***

With an income beefed up by *Come September* and *Lover Come Back,* Rock decided he wanted to purchase the home he'd been renting from Sam

445

Jaffe.

He'd fallen in love with the spacious, U-shaped mansion with its red-tile roof at 9402 Beverly Crescent Drive, high up in Beverly Hills. He gave his small home in Newport Beach to his mother, Kay, and his stepfather, Joe Olsen.

The mansion cost $200,000, and he'd have to shell out another half-million dollars for the improvements and additions he wanted. At the time of his death, it was appraised at $3.5 million.

With balconies opening onto panoramic views, the 3½-acre property fronted three cliffsides. He moved in permanently with seven dogs, referring to them as "my mutts" and identifying the canines with such monikers as Jack and Jill, or, in the case of one German shepherd, "Pisser."

Inside, he decorated it in a super macho style that would have pleased Ernest Hemingway. Décor included African artifacts and zebra rugs he'd brought back from Kenya after filming *Something of Value*. Some of the ceilings were supported by rustic trusses crafted from artfully configured tree limbs. Marble fireplaces adorned the public rooms, and wrought-iron candelabra were positioned throughout.

Heavy wooden furniture, mostly mahogany, dominated the decors, with swords and tapestries adding to the massive, macho feel of the place. Elizabeth Taylor was one of the first visitors, calling it "Don Quixote decorating." The larger living room contained a huge black piano, where stars, often drunk, agreed to sing at some of his parties, none better than Judy Garland.

The house opened onto a large courtyard paved in red tiles fronting a 40-foot swimming pool, the setting of many all-male parties—clothing optional. At one end was a *pissoir* for those who didn't want to trek inside. At another end was a 20-foot barbecue where Rock sometimes cooked steaks, invariably so well done they were almost burnt.

Scattered about the courtyard were nude statues of young men from the Mexican artist, Victor Salmones. Beyond the pool was a greenhouse filled with orchids.

From the pool, a walkway, known as "Assignation Lane," zigzagged down one of the cliffs in a setting of flowers and trees. For those who wanted to get more serious than kissing, there were three well-equipped tents for love-making.

White stucco walls surrounded and enclosed the property, and it was entered through a massive wrought-iron gate that was electronically operated, by remote control, from the foyer. It was rarely locked, and Elizabeth asked why. Rock told her that if a handsome young man wanted to get in to see him, he didn't want him to wear himself out climbing over the walls.

Rock's favorite color was red, which he used lavishly, insisting that all his rugs be in that color. The exception was the kitchen, which he once painted lilac. That was in homage of a scene in one of his favorite movies, *Pillow Talk*. Doris Day, as an interior decorator, looks over some designs submitted by her (gay) male assistant. "Leonard," she says. "No one paints their kitchen lilac."

"I do!" he protests.

For the major guest room, which Rock called "the Tijuana Room," Marilyn Maxwell and he decorated it like a Mexican whorehouse, painting everything red. "It's only for serious fucking," he claimed.

The master bedroom, where he slept, was painted blue, his second-favorite color. The focal point of this 60' by 70' room was a massive four-poster, with a nude youth carved into its mahogany headboard. "My bed can sleep five comfortably, which it has done on many an occasion. After all, everybody wants to go to bed with Rock Hudson."

He also had a very large bathroom and huge shower, again suitable for five. The shower had a picture window opening onto a view, although he maintained the "real view" was what was only visible inside the shower. Towels hung from mounted elephant heads.

His favorite retreat was "The Playroom," where he stored his vast record collection, which took up one entire wall. He also installed both a jukebox and a movie screen, where he frequently screened *Giant* along with *Taza, Son of Cochise.* "It was a godawful picture, but many of my guests raved about my performance as Taza, not knowing that I was showing the film as a joke."

At one end of The Playroom, he had built a wooden stage with footlights, and it was here that his friends on holidays, especially around Christmastime, presented shows. On his first Christmas in The Castle, Mark Miller, appearing in drag as "Sylvia Casablancas," sang operas. At the end of his performance, he took a needle and pricked the big balloons that he'd used as breasts.

Rock borrowed costumes from the wardrobe department at Universal, so that he, George Nader, and two other men could appear as painted hookers from *Sweet Charity*. They delivered a hilarious rendition of "Hey, Big Spender." Rock wore a large blonde wig with cascades of curls, a low-cut beaded satin dress, his legs enclosed in fishnet hose, his feet in red "Joan Crawford fuck-me" high heels. He was the hit of the show, especially when he followed it with a striptease.

Despite repeated requests from Henry Willson to allow photographers from fan magazines to shoot the interior, Rock adamantly refused. "My home is off limits," he said.

He had to fly to Surinam to film his next picture, *The Spiral Road* (1962), and he needed to find a house sitter while he was abroad. Marion Wagner, the former wife of Robert Wagner between his two marriages to Natalie Wood, needed a place to stay temporarily.

She moved in, but after a week, she fired the housekeeper. She engaged a new one, Leatrice Lowe, nicknamed "Joy."

Approaching forty, she was an attractive African American woman who had, when she was 21, held the title of "Miss Cleveland." She moved into the large servants' quarters, which had two bedrooms.

When Rock met her, she offered to resign, but he immediately bonded with her, attracted to her quick wit. He was also drawn to her cooking, especially since she prepared his favorite dish, Southern fried chicken with gravy and mashed potatoes. His second favorite dish was deep-fried chicken with gizzards, which he called "gizzles." He was also enthralled by her deviled eggs and her chili pie, which he claimed, "gives me the best farts."

Before he threw his next all-male pool party, he asked her if she were offended by the sight of nude males.

"They're my favorite thing, *chile*," she shot back.

He agreed to pay her sixty dollars a week, an arrangement which remained in effect over the course of the next fourteen years.

"You never knew who was coming to dinner," she said. "One night, he told me to cook something real special, using only the finest linen and silver. I went all out."

It was good that she did. When she peeped into the hall, she spotted Rock greeting Grace Kelly and Prince Rainier.

***

Rock didn't want to get trapped in romantic comedies and was eager to star in *The Spiral Road*. Eventually released in 1962, it was a Universal film in Eastmancolor filmed on location in Surinam, a former Dutch colony on the northeastern Atlantic coast of South America. On location, Rock was reunited with Robert Arthur, the producer who had successfully nurtured the mega-hit *Lover*

Come Back; and Robert Mulligan, the director who had guided him through *Come September.*

John Lee Mahin and Neil Patterson adapted the script from the novel, *The Spiral Road,* by the respected Dutch author Jan de Hartog.

Mulligan had rounded up a supporting cast that included Burl Ives, Gena Rowlands, and Geoffrey Keen.

In a nutshell, *The Spiral Road* is about an atheist scientist's conversion to God after enduring horrendous experiences in the jungle. Even though the film was shot in the rain forests of Surinam, the action is supposed to take place in Java, also a former colony administered by the Netherlands.

Cast as Dr. Anton Drager, Rock travels to the impassable jungles of Java to study the effects of leprosy under Dr. Brits Jansen (Ives), who plays his role thunderously. Whereas the older man is a seasoned jungle physician, Drager is an opportunistic freshman medic, hoping to make a name for himself by capitalizing off Jansen's breakthrough research.

Philosophically, the two doctors are a mismatch, a sort of Odd Couple practicing medicine, a man of science vs. a man of God. In the film, Rock marries his long-suffering sweetheart, "Els" (Rowlands), stashes her in a good home in Batavia, and then heads off into the wild.

Jansen's best friend is William Wattereus (Keen), a Salvation Army captain who runs a jungle sanctuary for leprosy patients. His wife suffers from the disease.

When Jansen becomes suspicious of Drager's motives and discovers that he is secretly recording, with the intent to steal, the good doctor's experiments, he refuses to work with him any longer.

Drager drifts into an emotional decline, drinking heavily. Even though he's married, he takes up with a native girl.

When it appears that both his professional and private lives are in jeopardy, he goes up river to find a fellow doctor (Philip Abbott), who has been the victim of witchcraft, practiced by Burubi (Reggie Nader), a "shaman" who wants all the colonial doctors to leave his country. Drager becomes a victim of Burubi and is driven half insane. Eventually, he is forced to kill Burubi in self-defense.

When a search party dis-

Gena Rowlands and Rock, as they appeared in *The Spiral Road.* The two stars were completely unconvincing as a married couple.

covers Drager, he's lapsed into a coma. The whole ordeal has forced him to turn to God and abandon his arrogance and his previous self-definition as an atheist.

Hudson allowed himself to be photographed most unattractively during many sequences of this film. Rock Hudson fans point out the full growth of beard he sported at the end of the film. One reviewer claimed, "He looked like a caveman Alley Oop."

Bathtime for Burl Ives in *The Spiral Road*. For this scene, the veteran actor and singer stripped completely naked. "The sight of Ives nude was enough to turn me off men for life," Rock said.

Ives was the most colorful actor with whom Rock would ever work. He had previously played one of his favorite characters, Big Daddy, in Tennessee Williams' *Cat on a Hot Tin Roof* (1959). A former itinerant singer and banjo player, Ives and Rock came from the same state of Illinois. He shared many of his adventures on the road with Rock, including when he was arrested for performing the bawdy English folk song, "Foggy Dew." One of his most famous, and less controversial, minstrel songs was "Jimmy Crack Corn."

He'd hit a rough spot in his career in 1950 when he was blacklisted and placed on the Red Channels List. But in 1952, he cooperated with the House Un-American Activities Committee and was allowed to resume acting. His collaboration led to denunciations from some of his previous friends and cohorts: He was labeled a turncoat by many of his fellow folk singers, including Pete Seeger, who accused him of betrayal.

Ives and Rock also shared memories of working with the late James Dean. Ives had played the sheriff of Salinas in *East of Eden* (1955).

Gena Rowlands, whose career would span six decades, was famously married to John Cassavetes, and the acting duo would make ten films together, their union lasting until his death in 1989. She was twice nominated for a Best Actress Oscar, both for *A Woman Under the Influence* (1974) and *Gloria* (1980).

Critics came down hard on *The Spiral Road*. One writer called it "a story about love, leprosy, and lunacy in Java, making for an interminable movie-going experience, with Hudson at his most wooden."

Variety wrote, "Being uninspired, *The Spiral Road* is an uninspiring tale. Before Rock Hudson discovers God, the picture takes the devil's own time getting down to cases and its resolution. Hudson's arrogance and cynicism are played against a lot of bleeding hearts."

Over the years, however, *The Spiral Road* has picked up fans. Author Alvarez Albert called it, "A chilling overview of Western colonial arrogance, a compelling and often beautiful film adaptation of De Hartog's masterpiece. The superb cast easily sustains the epic scope and grandeur of the film, while the intelligent and artful script relates a story that is at once compelling and horrifying."

***

It wouldn't last for long, but in 1963, Rock's fan mail reached a volume of nearly 30,000 letters a week, with a large percentage originating with gay men, worldwide.

To take advantage of his continuing popularity, Universal was eager to rush him into another film. This time, they opted for a military theme, *A Gathering of Eagles* for a 1963 release.

Its Ukraine-born producer, Sy Bartlett, had also written the original story. With the help of director Delbert Mann, he rounded up a supporting cast that featured Rod Taylor as the second lead. Other cast members included Mary Peach, who played Rock's wife, plus Barry Sullivan, Kevin McCarthy, Leif Erickson, Robert Lansing, and Richard Anderson.

As a screenwriter, Bartlett had received his first credit at RKO back in 1933. By 1956, he had founded Melville Productions with Gregory Peck, who had starred in his script for *12 O'Clock High* (1949). *A Gathering of Eagles* evoked some episodes from the Peck movie. Because of his own military background, Bartlett was eager to launch the movie with Rock.

Mann had helmed Rock in *Lover Come Back,* and he wanted to show Hollywood that "I can do more than romantic froth with Doris Day and Rock Hudson."

Set in the deepest chill of the Cold War, the dramas swirling through the plot of *A Gathering of Eagles* technically, at least, took place during peacetime. Having survived his miscasting in *The Spiral Road*, Rock delivered one of his strongest performances.

Its setting focused on the Strategic Air Command (SAC), in which Rock played a U.S. Air Force officer, Col. Jim Caldwell.

As a SAC B-52 wing commander, he must shape up his unit in time to pass a grueling operational readiness inspection. The previous commander had failed to do that, and had lost his command. Caldwell is determined that the same fate would not await him.

He had recently married an Englishwoman, Victoria (Mary Peach), who is not happy as the wife of a military man. Caldwell became so tough in shaping his men, and bringing that toughness home at night, that her character feels confused and fearful as he exhibits a side of himself she'd never seen before.

Originally, Julie Andrews was slated to interpret the role, but Mann claimed, "She can sing, but she can't act." He'd rejected her, favoring this less experienced actress who had been born in South Africa.

After seeing the first rushes, the screenwriter, Robert Pirosh, came to Bartlett. (It was Pirosh

In *A Gathering of Eagles*, Rod Taylor (left) and Rock resumed their affair, launched when they'd lived together in a beach house in Malibu.

From the front, it's obvious that they were two of the handsomest men on the screen at the time. When the director, Delbert Mann, saw the publicity still of their rears, he said, "It's obvious to me why Rod and Rock are attracted to each other."

who had adapted Bartlett's original story into a screenplay. "Miss Peach and Rock just have no chemistry together," he complained.

In any summary of Rock's career, Mary Peach emerges as one of his least dynamic leading ladies, no competition for Elizabeth Taylor or Doris Day.

With the intention of adding authenticity, both Bartlett and Mann prevailed upon General Curtis LeMay, former head of SAC and Chief of Staff for the U.S. Air Force, to give unprecedented access to both the cast and crew to various SAC facilities that would otherwise have been off-limits. According to LeMay, "I wanted a film that would remind Americans that we did have weapons of mass destruction under tight control."

In the second lead, Rod Taylor was cast as Caldwell's former buddy from the Korean War, who is now a vice wing commander. Rock had met

Taylor when they had worked together on *Giant*. Later, they had become lovers. Taylor, for a period of his life, had lived with Rock in his beachhouse in Malibu for a few months.

During filming of *A Gathering of Eagles*, Rock invited Taylor to share his dressing room. "The whole cast and crew knew what was going on," Mann said. "Who could blame them? Both of them were handsome studs having a little fun."

Barry Sullivan played the base commander, Col. Bill Fowler, and Kevin McCarthy was cast as the fierce Major General ("Happy Jack") Kirby, the inspector general for SAC. Ironically, Sullivan had previously starred in a 1958 film called *Strategic Air Command*, so he was on familiar turf.

With McCarthy, Rock shared memories of their mutual friend, Montgomery Clift, and the horrible night he drove off that cliff below Elizabeth Taylor's house after all of them had convened for dinner.

Rock jokingly said, "We had enough actors playing military men that we could have invaded Mexico…at least."

In many ways, *A Gathering of Eagles* marked the beginning of the long road of Rock's decline as a top box office attraction. Reviews were unfavorable, as was attendance, the movie playing to many empty seats.

Unfortunately for its box-office receipts, whereas *A Gathering of Eagles* was sympathetic to the U.S. military, it was released in 1963 near the beginning of a decade noted for its anti-military protests. In vivid contrast, two movies shown the following year (*Fail-Safe* and *Dr. Strangelove*) each took a negative view of the military and a nihilistic view of American imperialism in general. Each of those "counterculture" films received rave notices and long lines at the box office.

***

The turbulent 1960s had arrived, and Hollywood was rapidly changing. Rock made one of the biggest decisions of his life, one that he had long postponed. He decided to fire his longtime agent, Henry Willson.

The 1950s, a decade heavily influenced by the presuppositions and aesthetics of Willson's pretty boys, including Tab Hunter and Troy Donahue, was nearing its end. In its place, the turbulent unrest of the 60s ushered in a new type of leading men, for the most part "anti-heroes" whom Rock referred to as "The Uglies." Into that category, he lumped Dustin Hoffman, Al Pacino, Robert De Niro, and Richard Dreyfuss.

"I feel like a dying breed," Rock told his new agent, John Foreman of C.M.A.

"Willson was a louse," Rock said. "I saw him get good parts for other actors, while I was given second-rate scripts. I told him to 'get out and beat the bushes for me.' He replied, 'He who beats the bushes gets bit by a snake.'"

When asked why he'd fired Willson, Rock said, "Big ego. He felt he knew everyone and everything. He did some good things for me at the beginning, but he got lazy. He never planned ahead. He sat back in his office and waited for the phone to ring with the offer of a picture for me. I'm tired of all the rotten scripts I'm getting. I need a picture with a big-name leading lady."

Sara Davidson, Rock's biographer, wrote: "Henry Willson was a master of illusion, devious and secretive, capable of being extremely kind and utterly heartless. Like the Trickster, he appeared to different people in different ways."

Tom Clark, Rock's companion throughout most of the 1970s, detested Willson, and the feeling was mutual. "Willson was a man with a vast, cruel ego," Clark charged. "He enjoyed the creation of a product more than the marketing of it. His genius was turning raw material into a marketable entity. He turned the rough, raw, unprocessed Roy Fitzgerald into the polished, urbane, handsome Rock Hudson. And then he practically ignored him."

An editor at *Photoplay* claimed, "Willson was devastated when Rock walked out on him. Rock had been his meal ticket for years. He not only rejected him as his agent, but as his friend."

He admitted to George Nader, "You of all people knew how I kept Willson on for so long. I was afraid he'd go to the tabloids and expose me as gay. Of course, it means we'll have to give up our mutually shared fuck pad."

He was referring to an apartment the two men rented at 2026 Cahuenga Boulevard, where they "auditioned" a string of young wannabe actors, far from prying eyes.

To his associates, Willson had for years maintained that "Rock will never leave me. After all, I made him a star. The stud will be forever in the debt of his daddy. Were it not for me, he would have been exposed by *Confidential* and his career would have ended before it got launched into the bigtime."

When news reached Willson that Rock had fired him, his secretary, Betty Butler, claimed that her boss flew into a violent rage. "At one point, he threatened to throw acid into Rock's face. He claimed that the star had become one only because of his pretty face." He told her, "I want to destroy the thing that made him a star."

His second threat involved calling tabloid writers: "I'll expose the son of a bitch as a fag."

Willson never carried through with these threats, but they were reported to Rock. "So that's what he's going to do. I've got to shake him and his reputation. Every time he sucks a cock, I get blamed."

James Bacon, the Hollywood reporter for the Associated Press, wrote: "When a big star like Rock Hudson leaves his agent, it can mean the death of his agency. Henry will never get another big star after Rock Hudson fired him."

The reporter was right. As time went by, Willson became an alcoholic, a pathetic figure around Hollywood. He descended into financial ruin. His days as a starmaker and his marketing of Troy, Rock, and Tab faded into movie history, a dying era, *Gone With the Wind*.

Rock saw Willson one final time when an aging, flabby, defeated man showed up at The Castle. He was broke and desperate, begging Rock to go to the bank with him and sign documents, using Rock's good credit to get him a second mortgage. If Willson didn't pay, Rock, as the co-signer, would have had to cough up the money.

Rock adamantly refused to do that, rightly figuring it was some sort of financial trick. To get rid of him, Rock wrote out a check for a thousand dollars and gave it to his former agent, who had more or less embezzled many thousands of dollars from his paycheck at Universal.

Later, Rock told Miller, "I've paid my dues to Willson, time and time again when he had control of my money, using it to finance his own lavish lifestyle back then."

Months later, Rock found out there had already been a second mortgage on Willson's home. Not only that, but a third mortgage, too.

In 1974, Willson, in failing health, moved into the Motion Picture Country Home, A retirement facility in Woodland Hills, California.

Before moving into the retirement home, Willson had to sell all his possessions, even his black Cadillac. By then, the banks had repossessed his home, site of many a lavish party in the 1950s.

In his new, much-reduced circumstances, Willson was given an allowance of one dollar a day. He converted it into dimes to use for phone calls.

One night, Robert Wagner, a former client of Willsons, arrived at his retirement home to participate in a charity event. He later described Willson to friends, calling him, "a bloated wreck who couldn't breathe, but wheezed. He looked very unkempt, and his heavy drinking had given him this huge, distended stomach."

Word reached Troy Donahue that his former agent, Henry Willson, who had made him a star, was dying from cirrhosis of the liver. On November 2, 1978, Donahue went to the retirement home to visit him. Willson had lapsed into a coma. "All I could do was sit by his bed for about ten minutes, holding his hand."

Death came later that night. He was 67 years old, but looked to be in his 80s.

Rory Calhoun, one of Willson's long-ago lovers, was one of the pall-bearers at his funeral. Rock did not show up, nor did he send flowers.

Willson was buried in an unmarked grave at the Valhalla Memorial Park in North Hollywood. No one purchased a headstone for him, although he'd always wanted one with the word STARMAKER chiseled in stone.

Rock Hudson would live for another seven years before facing his own horrible death.

***

The great director/producer, Howard Hawks, personally phoned Rock to ask if he'd star in his next film, *Man's Favorite Sport*, scheduled for release by Universal in 1964.

When Rock heard the title, he jokingly asked, "Will it get by the censors?"

"It's not that kind of sport, kid," Hawks told him. Then he candidly admitted that he'd already submitted the script to Katharine Hepburn and Cary Grant since it was an homage to, and had been inspired by, their screwball comedy classic, *Bringing Up Baby* (1938).

"Both of them turned me down," Hawks confessed. "After their rejection, I had the script reshaped as a possible vehicle for you and Paula Prentiss."

"Since you'll be directing it, I'll accept without even reading the script," Rock responded to Hawks. "That's the kind of faith I have in you."

Rock had long admired this son of Indiana, born in 1896, a man who'd begun his career in silent movies. Hawks had helmed many of Rock's favorite films, including *To Have and Have Not* (1944), and *Red River* (1948). Critic Leonard Maltin defined him as "the greatest American director who is not a household name."

The day after their phone conversation, the script, written by three different men, arrived on Rock's doorstep. He avidly read it, finding it filled with slapstick and sexual innuendo. Cast as Roger Willoughby, a well-known expert on fishing, Rock plays a salesman for Abercrombie & Fitch, spewing out advice for fishermen, both printed and oral.

But he has a secret: He has never been fishing. Not only that, he can't stand the smell of fish, and he can't bear the idea of eating one. Nonetheless, he is forced to enter a major-league fishing tournament through the machinations of Abigail Page (Paula Prentiss), a brash and obtrusive press and P.R. agent. She soon discovers his secret, and reacts with a condemnation of him as a "great big phony."

As in screwball comedy, the dialogue is fast, the humor broad. Deception abounds, and romance weighs heady in the air. Madcap diversions from the plot include Prentiss impersonating Cleopatra and a bicycle-riding bear.

A daughter of San Antonio, Prentiss was perhaps the tallest leading lady (5' 10") ever associated with Rock. She was married at the time to actor/director Richard Benjamin.

In private, Hawks had the final cut screened for him. Then he admitted to his associates, "as a screen team, Rock and Paula just don't click. Sometimes, a couple like Hepburn and Grant will come together and create magic on the screen. Not Paula with Rock. This will be their last picture together, and of that, I'm certain."

Rock, too, was disappointed with the final cut, expressing his own opinion about why it didn't work. "For me, in a comedy, the records tell us that I have to be the devil or the agitator, the one who plays the gag on someone else. I'm too big—apparently—to have the gag played on me, because the audience won't believe it. I played the buffoon in *Man's Favorite Sport*. The joke was too strong, the revenge too strong. I felt uncomfortable in the role."

He'd begun the movie with the greatest respect for Hawks. However, after working with him, he said, "He'd made brilliant films. But it was like he'd given up. And therefore, it was quite disillusioning working with him. All the jokes and comedic sequences in our films were repeats of episodes he'd done in other movies."

When Rock saw this publicity still from *Man's Favorite Sport*, he said, "Paula Prentiss fucked me over in that movie. My reaction to working with her is clearly reflected on my face."

Man's Favorite Sport performed reasonably well at the box office, grossing more than $6 million. Reviews for Rock were generally good, albeit tepid. One critic observed, "Rock was placed in the difficult position of having to impersonate Cary Grant. He had to repeat the nightclub scene from *Bringing Up Baby,* which Grant had brought off with such panache."

In his review, Robin Wood wrote: "Prentiss slips agreeably into Katharine Hepburn's shoes. Her bass voice is comically imposing. She's more consciously malevolent and charming than Hepburn in *Baby.* She is very good, but at times, one has the feeling that Hawks is importing a characterization on her instead of working with her."

***

During the filming of *Man's Favorite Sport,* Rock had a chance encounter with a handsome young man, Lee Garlington. He'd come to Hollywood hoping that his good looks would parley him into movie stardom. He'd ended up working as an extra on the Universal lot.

He'd heard extensive rumors that Rock was gay and was anxious to meet him. "He was the biggest movie star in the world, so I thought, 'Let me get an eye on him.' I stood outside his dressing room cottage at Universal, pretending to be reading a copy of *Variety.* It was probably upside down when he strolled by."

After making a good, hard appraisal, Rock continued his walk, but before turning the corner, he stared back rather intensely. That was it, the total extent of any interest he might have expressed at the time.

"Perhaps it was that long, lingering look he gave me," Garlington said. "It held out a promise for the future."

Almost a year would go by before he received an unexpected call from Mark Miller. Rock had obviously remembered the view of Garlington pretending to read *Variety,* and he had charged Miller with the task of procuring his contact information and paving the way for a date.

According to Garlington, "Hearing Miller on the phone convinced me that Rock had not forgotten."

"Would you like to meet Rock Hudson?" Miller had asked.

"I'd love it," Garlington had responded. "He's my favorite movie star."

An appointment was set up for the following evening at The Castle.

"I was terrified of actually meeting him," Garlington said, "but eager to. I arrived right at seven at his mansion, and I was shaking nervously. I'd never met such a big star before. Something deep inside me told me that my life was about to change."

Chapter Fifteen

ROCK BIDS *ADIEU* TO UNIVERSAL

Rock Meets a Handsome Stockbroker Who Becomes "The Love of My Life"

Making Screen Love to Doris Day, Gina Lollobrigida, & Leslie Caron

Rock was rarely snapped with one of his boyfriends, so this is a rare occurrence when he was caught on a night out with the handsome, well-bred Lee Garlington, who became a stockbroker "after I recovered from the bite of the acting bug."

Rock later told Mark Miller, "Lee was my ideal, the man who got away, the one man I truly loved above all others."

Intelligent, handsome, & well-bred, Lee Garlington joined hundreds of young men arriving in Hollywood with dreams of movie stardom. Those same dreams had filled Rock Hudson's head in the late 1940s. Except for a precious few, most of these young men would drift later into other jobs, some remaining in California, but many returning to their homes in Indiana or wherever.

Garlington was a lot smarter than many of the other dreamers, so he had prepared a "back-up plan" by becoming certified as an investment counselor and stockbroker.

When he met Rock, he was close to celebrating his 25th birthday, having arrived in California from his native city of Atlanta. He had completed his military service and was hoping to break into pictures. He did get an uncredited role as an extra in *The Virginian* (1962), a hit TV Western series, but other parts were hard to come by.

Rock had been very intrigued when he'd first spotted Garlington hanging out around his dressing room, but he had him checked out before making any overture to him. A detective learned that the young man was gay and that he had a male lover living with him in an apartment in Hollywood. But after a few months, their affair ended, and Garlington was free. Rock moved in on him, using Mark Miller to arrange a meeting at The Castle one evening.

"Now that I know he's not a spy for some scandal rag, I want him," Rock told Miller, his trusted confidant.

Garlington was anything but a hustler, and he insisted on paying his own way. Having abandoned his dream of movie stardom, he'd taken a job at a brokerage firm in Beverly Hills.

The young man later recalled his first night with Rock at The Castle. "I was frightened at being in the presence of the world's biggest movie star. He mixed us a tropical drink he'd learned how to make shooting a picture in Hawaii. It tasted good, and I got a little high, but not high enough to stop shaking."

"When he put the inevitable moves on me, I was too nervous to make anything happen. Apparently, this was a regular occurrence whenever Rock picked up guys. They were too awed by his fame to perform. To put it another way, I didn't rise to the occasion. I thought I'd blown my chance, since I was such a dud. I just knew there would be no second date. Rock had drawn a blank with me."

Photographed at The Castle, Lee Garlington was slow to begin an affair with Rock. But when it heated up, it became one of the most enduring in Rock's turbulent life.

To the stockbroker's surprise, Rock phoned the next day and set up another date. He pursued Garlington like a football captain in the 1950s going after a virginal Sandra Dee type, slowly

Unlike his other lovers, Garlington was independent and insisted on paying his own way, even if it meant Rock had to fly in tourist class.

gaining her confidence and putting her at ease before getting what he wanted.

"We listened to records—he had a great collection—and dined in obscure restaurants. We shared our dreams and talked about what we wanted out of life. I found him a kind, sensitive man. I was no longer nervous. Seductions followed, and it would go on and off for years to come."

Even though their relationship deepened, Rock refused to move him into The Castle. "He was always afraid of being outed," Garlington said. "It would have been career suicide back then, or even today. To Rock, his career was first and foremost. One night at a premiere, he introduced me to Paul Newman and his wife, Joanne Woodward. Newman gave me a knowing smile. He knew Rock's secret, and he sensed I was his lover. Rock never demanded I keep our love affair a secret. He just assumed I would be discreet."

At the premieres they attended, Rock and Garlington always had "arm candy" to escort, usually starlets hoping to get their pictures taken.

In the beginning, Garlington's 1963 Chevy Nova late at night would get parked behind Rock's Cadillac in the driveway of The Castle. "I was sleeping over and having sex with him, but we didn't want people to know, even his household. I would get up at six o'clock in the morning and let my car roll down the hill before turning on the motor, since I didn't want to make any noise. Later, I learned that Joy, his housekeeper, knew what was going on all along. She was very hip."

Not since his live-in lover, Jack Navaar, had Rock become so obsessed with a young man. Around The Castle, Rock was very casual, often going shirtless, wearing moccasins and a pair of chinos.

"We watched old movies in his den and listened to records. He had a collection of most of his movies. I watched him kissing his leading ladies on the screen, including Gina Lollobrigida. I would say to myself, 'Gee whiz, he kisses me in the same way.' That always brought a giggle to me."

Around Garlington, Rock was always in a good mood and full of humor. Garlington had heard of his dark, depressive moods, but he never was a witness to any of them.

Although their relationship in varying degrees would last on and off for years, Rock was not Garlington's ideal sexual partner. "Because of Rock's massive size, I felt he would be a very strong male figure in my life, one to dominate me. But he was a gentle lover. He smoked too much, drank too much, and allowed other people to boss him around. He had a lot of hangers-on he should have booted from The Castle."

Even though they were lovers, the two men were not faithful to each other. "I knew Rock was having affairs on the side, but so was I. Yet when he found out I'd had this guy staying in my apartment, he appeared devastated. He got drunk that night and actually shed tears. I hadn't meant to hurt him."

Six months into the relationship, Rock presented Garlington with a gold keyring, containing the key to the front door of The Castle so that he could come and go. It was inscribed: "At the end of the first quarter the home team was ahead, and at the end of the half the visitor is ahead. Damn it! R.H."

Between pictures, Rock liked to travel and invited Garlington to go with him. His young lover demanded that he pay his own way, which meant that the two of them had to fly in tourist class, not first class. Such was the case when they flew to Puerto Vallarta for a vacation. This was the town that Elizabeth Taylor and Richard Burton put on the map. In 1963, Burton filmed Tennessee Williams' *The Night of the Iguana,* starring Ava Gardner, there. Elizabeth liked Puerto Vallarta so much she purchased a villa in its historic core.

When Rock returned to The Castle, he learned that some female fan had broken in and spent a night in his bedroom. She opened his closets and perhaps searched through his drawers, but there was no sign that she'd discovered revealing pictures he'd taken of Garlington. "He was very shook up," Garlington said, "and felt very vulnerable."

When Rock had two free weeks, he invited Garlington to fly with him to New Orleans. Tanked up on martinis, he told Garlington one night, "I'm going to the studio and confess that I'm gay. I'm gonna say I have a lover, and if they don't like it, they can shove it up their asses."

Garlington said, "You're not going to do anything like that, and you know you're not. You'll sober up in the morning, and reason will return."

In tourist class, the two lovers flew to New Orleans together. Garlington's Southern family was well off, and his father, also in town at the time, had ordered a Lincoln Continental convertible to meet them at the airport.

They spent three nights together in New Orleans, enjoying the Cajun cuisine and the late night bars along Bourbon Street. They patronized Pat O'Brien's Tavern, downing Hurricanes, the specialty drink of the house. On the first night, a fan approached Rock, asking for his autograph. Then he turned to Garlington. "Are you somebody, too?"

"No, I'm a nobody who went nowhere," Garlington snapped.

After New Orleans, they headed out for a motor trip through Louisiana's plantation country, visiting antebellum mansions that had not yet *Gone With the Wind.* Stopovers for the night were at roadside motels. Garlington registered for both of them, while Rock sat in the car, not wanting to be recognized.

In time, the intensity of their affair drifted and lessened, and it was Garlington who went to The Castle to end it. "I decided it was time for both of us to move on. He got drunk that night, and I seemed to have really hurt him. He was such a sweetheart, and I still adored him. Why did I let him go? It was a mistake. I know that now. But I was young and immature, not really knowing what I wanted."

Their friendship lasted for another decade, and on occasion, they still made love to each other. In 1971, the two of them were spotted on Lake Louise in Canada, where they had rented a log cabin.

Garlington never saw Rock after 1972. By then, Tom Clark had taken over much of Rock's life. "I was frozen out," Garlington said. "Clark told me I had hurt Rock so much, I was not entitled to his friendship. If I had realized in 1965 what a wonderful man Rock really was, I would have hung in there. If that had happened, we might still be living together, and he would not have died like he did."

Garlington had an acute business sense, and he went on to a successful life and career. Tired of his role as a stockbroker, he launched a profitable medical electronics company, later selling it and investing his profits in real estate. Eventually, he returned to academia, where he earned a doctorate in psychology, working as a counseling coordinator at a community clinic.

Shortly before Rock died of AIDS in 1985, Garlington tried to contact Rock at The Castle.

Mark Miller came to the phone, explaining that "Rock was too far gone and would not be able to recognize me. It's best for you to remember the gentle giant the way he was."

**

Once again, and for the third and final time, Rock and Doris Day were reteamed in a new romantic comedy, *Send Me No Flowers* (1964) for Universal, still his home studio. Marty Melcher, Day's husband, insisted on being named as its executive producer, for which he was paid $50,000 for doing nothing.

Melcher didn't like Rock and objected to his being cast, preferring James Garner instead. But the bosses at Universal wanted Rock, hoping once again to score big box office as they had with *Pillow Talk* and *Lover Come Back*.

"Melcher was nothing but a conniving, thieving little shit," Rock claimed.

Norman Jewison, the director, had a very low opinion of Melcher, too. "He was a hustler, a shallow, insecure hustler. Without Doris, he would be driving a truck for the Teamsters. I never knew anyone who liked him. Perhaps even Doris didn't like him after a few months, but the brave soul hung in there until the bitter end."

Rock and Jewison were not alone in detesting Melcher. While he was making *Young at Heart* (1954), Frank Sinatra had banned him from the set.

The actual producer of *Send Me No Flowers* was not Melcher, but Harry Keller, who either directed or produced a number of B-Westerns, among other films, for Universal. When Rock met him, he'd just produced *Tammy and the Doctor* (1953). More than a decade later, he'd be associated with the more provocative *Kitten With a Whip* (1964), which lured masochists and sadists into movie houses.

A Canadian film director and producer, Jewison would eventually be nominated for a Best Director Oscar. One of the finest directors with whom Rock ever worked, he told him he wanted to escape frothy comedies and do more serious pictures.

After Rock's film with Day, Jewison helmed Steve McQueen in *The Cincinnati Kid* (1965). Three years later, he'd also direct him in *The Thomas Crown Affair* (1968). Rock complained, "Norman did more for Steve than he did for me."

He told Jewison, "I hate the script for *Send Me No Flowers*."

After the Day/Hudson comedy, some of Jewison's greatest hits lay in his future, including *In the Heat of the Night* (1971).

Send Me No Flowers had been based on a failed Broadway play of the same name by Norman Barasch and Carroll Moore. The filmscript was written by Julius Epstein. Along with his twin brother, Philip, and Howard E. Koch, Epstein had famously scripted the 1942 film, *Casablanca,* starring Humphrey Bogart and Ingrid Bergman.

Rock was cast as George Kimball, a hypochondriac living with his wife Judy (Day) in the suburbs. He's a pill popper, taking his temperature in the shower and imagining all sorts of illnesses.

Complaining of chest pains, he goes to see Dr. Ralph Morrissey (Edward Andrews). After examining him, the doctor pronounces him in the finest of health. However, in the next room he overhears the doctor talking, saying, "He has just a few weeks to live." Although the doctor is discussing another patient, George assumes that he's talking about him.

On his way home, George meets his best

friend, Arnold Nash (Tony Randall, in his third film with Rock and Day). He confides to him the "news" about his imminent death, and Arnold assures him that he will deliver a flattering eulogy at his funeral.

In the most hilarious scene in the movie, Rock visits a funeral parlor operated by Mr. Akien (Paul Lynde), and buys a burial plot.

George enlists Arnold to help him find a suitable spouse to replace him as Judy's husband. On the golf course, her cart malfunctions and runs out of control until Bert Power (Clint Walker) saves the day and rescues her. He was her college beau, and the two have a reunion. Although George (Rock) does not like him personally, he is a rich Texas oil baron, and George thinks he might be suitable as Judy's next spouse.

In the meantime, Judy suspects that George is having an affair with the newly divorced Linda Mullard (Patricia Parry), and that he's pushing her into the arms of Bert as a means of getting rid of her.

However, it all works out in the end as Judy learns that George is not dying. He's also not cheating on her. Expect a happy ending that's equivalent to that of their other two romantic comedies.

Rock told Jewison, "I find the jokes about bad health and death in terrible taste. Making fun of death is dangerous and difficult. In one line he must deliver, he says, "Men of my age are dropping dead like flies. Just read the obituary page. It's enough to scare you to death."

Day liked working with Rock again. "He enjoyed life to a great extent. He called me Doris Mary, and I called him Roy Harold. Those were our original names. Roy Harold was a dear, dear man. He gets such a kick out of little things. He laughs at silly things. It's the most wonderful laugh I've ever heard. I really love him. He has all the qualities I go for—simplicity, honesty, and most of all, a down-to-earth quality that most of us have when we're young, but lose as we grow into our careers. Besides, he's an absolute nut!"

Clint Walker, cast as Rock's smarmy rival, was "the only actor I ever worked with who was bigger than me" (Rock's words). Known for his bare-chested stoicism, the actor stood 6'6" tall with a 48-inch chest and a 32-inch waist. One critic described him as "the biggest, finest-looking Western

In three films, including *Send Me No Flowers* (above), Rock was romantically paired with Doris Day. They were a fun-loving couple both on and off the screen. "We never rolled in the hay," Rock claimed. "We kept it platonic and loving."

hero ever to sag a horse, with a pair of shoulders rivaling King Kong."

Walker was both a singer and an actor from Rock's home state of Illinois. At sixteen, he'd been working on a riverboat before joining the U.S. Marines during the final

months of World War II. Jobs as a sheet-metal worker and a night club bouncer eventually led to Hollywood, where Walker became another of Henry Willson's "pretty boys." The agent wanted to change his name to "Jeff Norman."

Walker is best known for his starring role as cowboy Cheyenne Bodie in the ABC/Warner Brothers hit TV Western series, *Cheyenne* (1955-1963).

Long after working with Rock in May of 1971, Rock heard a bulletin on the radio that Walker had been killed in a skiing accident at Mammoth Mountain in California. The bulletin was later corrected, since Walker had survived. In a fall from a ski lift, a ski pole had pierced his heart, and he'd been pronounced dead. But a doctor detected faint signs of life, and he was

In Henry Willson's Adonis factory, Clint Walker had the broadest shoulders and the best pecs in films of that era.

In the upper photo, he appears in a scene with Doris Day in *Send Me No Flowers*, where he's being set up as a possible beau for her if she should lose Rock to an early death.

rushed into surgery, where the damage was repaired.

As regards *Send Me No Flowers*, In the hip 1960s, many viewers noted the gay contexts surrounding the characters portrayed by Rock and Randall.

In fact, in the film, Randall is more attentive to Rock than Day is. The two men are shown sleeping together in the same bed. Struggling with a cummerbund, Rock utters a command to Randall—"Do me!"

Randall then delivers a nuanced and provocative line: "I need to powder my nose. You need to powder your nose." Audiences who were alert to the lavender context of this interpreted those words as a signal that Randall wanted to stand at the urinal with Rock. Randall also assures Rock that his rival, Walker, doesn't have a physique as good as his.

Outrageous and flamboyantly queer, Paul Lynde, in reference to Tony Randall, said, "Oh, *honey chile*. That queen is so far in the closet she's lost the key. He had to remind me he's married about ten times every hour. To a female, this is. I heard rumors that he sucked off Rock during the making of *Pillow Talk*. But on our picture, Rock kept it zipped up. I knew why. I met this tall blonde guy who came to visit him and spent a lot of time in Rock's dressing room. With a kid like that on the leash, why did Rock need that prissy queen, Tony Randall?"

A self-loathing Hollywood Square: Paul Lynde

Rock spoke privately to his friends about working with Lynde. "At first, he flirted with me, calling me 'Slugger.' I might be hiding in the closet, but he was out front with his campy, snarky TV persona."

Rock was referring to Lynde's long-running gig on *Hollywood Squares,* a chatty game-show series that ran from 1968 to 1981. In many of his appearances, Lynde's gags were thinly veiled allusions to his own homosexuality. Lynde was described as "Liberace without the piano." He was more popular with straight audiences than with gay ones. Homosexuals came to regard him as a symbol of what was perceived as self-loathing in gay culture.

After Rock rejected him, Lynde made a number of nasty remarks. On several occasions, he was known for calling the star "a mentally constipated tight-ass. He lived in fear some reporter would Out him as gay, when his gay life was the worst-kept secret in Tinseltown. He and Doris were always laughing and talking, but he treated the rest of us like we had leprosy. Of course, the big lug knew Tony and me wanted that legendary big cock of his."

When *Send Me No Flowers* opened at Manhattan's Radio City Music Hall, it received mixed reviews. However, some critics maintained that Rock and Day "were the greatest romantic team in movie history. They make sex funny—not tragic."

Time magazine wrote, "Miss Day at age 40 should perhaps stop trying to play Goldilocks. She comes off as cheerful, energetic, and a wildly overdecorated Mama Bear."

Doris Day's biographer, Tom Santopietro, came down hard on the movie's plot. "Who is going to believe that Rock Hudson, the picture of health, would endlessly whine like his loser of a character does? Popping pills with abandon from his seemingly endless supply, this man is interested in nothing but his own health, which makes a very dull character, not one you would want to spend two hours with."

In *The New York Times,* Bosley Crawther wrote: "*Send Me No Flowers* is a beautiful farce situation. Epstein wrote it with a nimble inventiveness and style."

Variety claimed, "It doesn't carry the same voltage or the laughs or originality of the other two films starring Rock Hudson and Doris Day."

However, *Time Out* in London labeled it "the best of all the Day/Hudson vehicles, nicely set in a pastel-colored suburban dreamworld, but the ineradicable blandness gets you down by the end."

***

Rock's next film, *Strange Bedfellows,* was set for a 1964 release by Universal. It would reunite him with the Italian bombshell, Gina Lollobrigida, his leading lady in *Come September.*

The package had been assembled by Melvin Frank, a native, like Rock, of Illinois. He was a screenwriter, producer, and director, having worked on such movies as *Mr. Blandings Builds His Dream House* (1948), with Cary Grant, and *A Touch of Class* (1973), starring George Segal and Glenda Jackson, a performance that would win her a Best Actress Oscar.

On *Strange Bedfellows,* Frank wore many hats: producer, director, and screenwriter. The plot was based on an idea he'd developed with his frequent collaborator, Norman Panama, his partner on numerous pictures crafted

In the publicity poster, Rock and Gina Lollobrigida make love, Italian style.

In the bedroom scene in the lower photo, Rock was asked to wear a heavy-duty jockstrap beneath his boxer shorts. Director Melvin Frank had learned that during the filming of a romantic scene in a previous film, Rock had had a wardrobe malfunction when one of his testicles had popped out during filming.

468

over a quarter of a century.

To support Rock and "La Lollo," Frank rounded up Gig Young, casting him as a P.R. agent, and Terry-Thomas as the Assistant Mortician. Terry-Thomas, an English comedian and character actor, often portrayed disreputable members of the upper class, especially "cads, toffs, and bounders." His trademark was the 1/3-inch gap between his upper front teeth.

On the surface, Young was handsome and debonair, a side of himself that was on display in *That Touch of Mink* (1962) with Doris Day and Cary Grant, who took the role originally slated for Rock.

"There was a deep, dark side to Young," Rock claimed. "I knew he lived deep, deep in the closet, and secretly picked up rough trade hustlers who were hired to punish him."

[It came as no surprise to Rock on October 19, 1978 when Young made front-page news. After three weeks of marriage to Kim Schmidt, a German magazine editor, he shot her before turning the gun on himself. Both of them were found dead in their Manhattan apartment. Young had once been married to the actress (Elizabeth Montgomery) whose fame mostly derived from her involvement in the ABC-TV sitcom Bewitched *(1964-72). She cited his alcoholism as one of the factors in the breakup of their marriage.]*

For the most part, *Strange Bedfellows* was a delightful comedy confection, one quickly forgotten, like that dessert you had last month.

As Carter Harrison, a high-powered business executive, Rock meets an Italian artist (Lollobrigida), who is leading a most unconventional bohemian (as it used to be known) life. They marry on an impulse. Afterward they realize that, except for sex, they have absolutely nothing in common and disagree on everything.

They separate.

Five years later, their divorce is about to become final. Rock's P.R. agent (Young) recommends he try to patch up his marriage and to improve his reputation so he won't be branded a playboy.

Rock and Lollobrigida have a reunion, hoping to rekindle their marriage and stave off the divorce. The question remains: Can he keep her from destroying his career by posing as Lady Godiva in a protest march in London?

Filming of *Strange Bedfellows* was in London, where Rock had maintained his popularity with large groups of gay fans. He didn't go long without a date. Often, he preferred two or three young men visiting his suite at night.

An enraged and deadly ending: Gig Young

469

Perhaps jealous, Young cracked, "I don't know how he has enough energy left to emote in front of the camera in the morning."

Strange Bedfellows was, as *Film Daily* defined it, "a bright and rollicking comedy with slapstick antics and hilarious sight gags."

At the box office, it did not have the impact of the Rock Hudson/Doris Day romantic comedies. "My days as the top box office star are coming to an end," Rock told Frank. "The trouble with rising to the top of the ladder is that you have nowhere to go but down, rung by embarrassing rung."

***

"Oh, God, not another sex comedy," Rock said when he learned of his next film, *A Very Special Favor*, set for release in color in 1965 by Universal. In a nutshell, it was a somewhat forced comedy wherein Charles Boyer asks "ladykiller" Rock to seduce his virginal daughter, Leslie Caron.

A Franco-American actress and dancer, Caron had appeared in 45 films between 1951 and 2003. Before working with Rock, she was known for such acclaimed musicals as *An American in Paris* (1951) and *Gigi* (1958). She'd received an Oscar nomination as Best Actress for her performance in *Lili* (1953), and again for her role in the British drama, *The L-Shaped Room* (1962). She remains one of the few dancers who performed with artists defined as seminal to the art form: Fred Astaire, Gene Kelly, Rudolf Nureyev, and Mikhail Baryshnikov.

At the time she worked with Rock, Caron was divorcing TV producer Christopher John Hall. In the bitter court proceedings, Warren Beatty, with whom she'd had an affair, was named as co-respondent.

Rock met the fading matinee idol, French-born Charles Boyer, during one of the most traumatic times of his life. The year their movie was released, his only child, Michael Charles Boyer, committed suicide at the age of 21. He played Russian roulette with a partially loaded pistol after separating from his girlfriend.

Boyer himself would commit suicide on August 26, 1978, two days after his wife's death from cancer, and two days before his own 79th birthday.

He had thrilled legions of women fans during the 1930s, delivering memorable performances in *Algiers* (1938),

Love Affair (1939), and *Conquest* (1937) with Greta Garbo. For his 1944 performance in *Gaslight,* opposite Ingrid Bergman, he was nominated for a Best Actor Oscar.

By the time Rock worked with him, he was called "the last of cinema's great lovers," because of his enduring record of performances, beginning in silents in 1920, lasting on the screen until 1974.

On the set, Rock had a reunion with the Viennese actor, Walter Slezak, with whom he'd worked in *Come September.*

The fifth lead, Dick Shawn, was an actor and comedian who in the 1960s was known for his small but iconic roles in madcap comedies. Rock remembered him mainly for his performance as the hot-headed Sylvester Marcus, son of the character played by Ethel Merman, in Stanley Kramer's *It's a Mad, Mad, Mad, Mad World* (1963).

He invited Rock to see one of his standup performances as a comedian. At his last such performance, on April 17, 1987 in San Diego, he suffered a fatal heart attack and collapsed face down on the stage. Most of the audience assumed it was part of his *schtick,* and remained seated, some of them giggling, for many minutes.

The men behind the camera of *A Very Special Favor* were familiar figures to Rock. Michael Gordon had helmed Doris Day and him in *Pillow Talk,* for which Stanley Shapiro had penned the screenplay. He not only wrote the screenplay for *A Very Special Favor,* but also spearheaded it as its producer.

The storyline had Rock playing Paul Chadwick as an American *homme fatale* and an oilman who bests French lawyer Charles Boyer as Michel Boullard in a Paris court by sleeping with the judge.

After losing the case, Boullard flies to New York for a reunion with his daughter, Lauren, who he has not seen in a quarter of a century.

On the plane, he encounters Chadwick, who apologizes to the French lawyer for using his fatal charm to entice and influence the judge. In exchange for having taken advantage of him during the court proceedings, he offers to perform a favor for him.

In Manhattan, Boullard

Rock deplored the script of *A Very Special Favor,* in which Leslie Caron's father (Charles Boyer) wants him to take his daughter's virginity. "It was a dirty movie," Rock proclaimed.

learns that Lauren, his daughter, is now a well-known psychologist and very career-minded, dominating her milksop boyfriend, Arnold Plum (Shawn). The Frenchman is utterly shocked to learn that Lauren, a woman in her thirties, is still a virgin.

He has an idea and calls the ladykiller (Chadwick, aka Rock) to deliver to his daughter "the fulfillment of a woman."

In this sex farce, Rock poses as a patient in need of psychiatric counseling, complaining that his problem is that he is irresistible to women and that he is too afraid to turn one down, as, in his past, that has led to some of them committing suicide.

Following through with the favor imposed on him by Boullard, Rock invites Caron to dinner and gives her too much champagne. The next morning, she wakes up in his bed naked and freaks out. Although nothing untoward has happened, he suggests that he has seduced her.

Eventually, she learns the truth and turns the tables on Chadwick. Instead of self-identifying as a virgin, she claims she's a woman of vast experience and that she has played around a lot. Her pseudo-confession makes him feel insecure and impotent.

Expect the usual complications in a romantic comedy before love wins out before the final curtain. Chadwick and Lauren fall in love, marry, and have children.

Rock said he went to Gordon and asked him to remove the most *risqué* of the scenes from the final cut, "but he didn't pay any attention to me. I was really perturbed about them. The things he had me do to Leslie Caron were cruel. They weren't funny for the sake of a joke. And her revenge, that was also too cruel. It completely castrated me, and it didn't work. I was just too strong to be a eunuch."

As Rock admitted to Gordon, "I am insanely bored with playing the lead in romantic comedies. I think the public is growing weary too. The cycle has been pushed about as far as it can go, and I think light comedy is on the wane. The boundaries have been extended almost to the limit in the 60s, and producers are trying to see just how dirty they can get. Our picture is filthy. I thought it was filthy when I read the script, and I still think it's filthy after seeing the final cut."

In a 2006 critique that appeared in *DVD Talk Review*, it was asserted that "The sight of Charles Boyer, begging a Lothario to basically deflower his own child, while trying to convince Hudson it's worth it by describing her like a horse—'excellent teeth'—made 1960s audiences just as queasy as today's."

A critic also noted the "veiled homosexual subplot. I can't imagine Hudson, who was famously close-mouthed about his homosexuality, being comfortable enacting a sequence where he kisses a woman dressed as a man, but that's the level of 'shock value' that's offered in *A Very Special Favor,* and today, as in 1965, it fails to register more than a yawn."

***

As a departure from fluffy romantic comedies, Rock signed with Universal to appear in a spy thriller, *Blindfold,* for a 1966 release by Universal. It was the first movie made by Gibraltar, Rock's new production company. Location sequences were filmed in Silver Springs, Florida.

Weeks before its release, he agreed to a poster advertising the film as BEHIND THE BLINDFOLD IS THE GREATEST SECURITY TRAP EVER DEVISED.

For his leading lady, Rock wanted Sophia Loren, with whom he had never worked, or else Gina Lollobrigida, with whom he'd already made two romantic comedies. Neither of the Italian bombshells was available, so his company contacted yet another sex symbol, this one an Italian-Tunisian beauty, Claudia Cardinale, who signed on as his co-star.

Before ever meeting him, she had appeared in such hits as *Rocco and His Brothers* (1960), and—both in 1963—*The Leopard* with Burt Lancaster, and Fellini's *8½.* Her greatest fame in the U.S. had derived from her appearance in the big hit, *The Pink Panther* (1964) opposite David Niven. In spite of these hits, she never achieved the fame or box office appeal of either Loren or La Lollo.

Blindfold was based on a thriller written by Louise Fletcher, who was known mainly for the plot she devised for what evolved into a *film noir,*

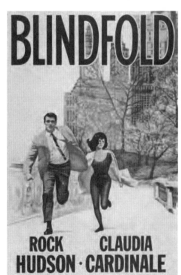

Sorry, Wrong Number (1948), featuring Barbara Stanwyck as a bedridden neurotic who, because of a crossed phone wire, overhears two scary psychopaths plotting a murder.

Fletcher's novel, *Blindfold,* is the story of a psychoanalyst, Dr. Bartholomew Snow (Rock), who is virtually kidnapped by the government to treat a neurotically unhinged nuclear physicist, Arthur Vicenti (Alejandro Rey).

Jack Warden, cast as General Pratt, is a national security chief who has stashed the patient in a remote location ("Base X") in an alligator-infested swamp in Florida.

He forces Dr. Snow to wear a blindfold every time he's in transit to and from the secluded house.

Enemy agents also learn where the patient is concealed. His sister, Vicky Vicenti (Cardinale), becomes convinced that Dr. Snow (Rock) is the villain who has abducted her brother. Although she urges the authorities to arrest him, Dr. Snow convinces them that he and Vicky have had a lovers' quarrel and that they're engaged to be married.

Guy Stockwell, cast as James Fitzpatrick, turns up to assert to Dr. Snow that it is General Pratt himself who is the enemy agent. Consequently, Dr. Snow sets out to rescue his patient. Since he's been blindfolded during his transit to every session with his patient, he tries to recreate the sounds he's heard during his transfers to Base X.

He finally finds the hideaway house. There, he learns that Fitzpatrick is the real enemy, and that he has, by now, captured and imprisoned, both Vicenti and Pratt.

Not to worry: U.S. soldiers arrive in airboats to rescue the captives and to eliminate the spies. That leaves Cardinale to ponder the big question: Should she take Rock as her lover…or not?

A publicist-turned-producer, Marvin Schwartz, had pulled the movie package together, hiring an A-list screenwriter and director, Philip Dunne to craft its script. Dunne was best known for films (including *How Green Was My Valley* (1941) and *The Robe* (1953), starring Richard Burton. The year that Dunne worked with Rock, he was also adapting Irving Stone's novel, *The Agony and the Ecstasy*, into a film with the same name that was released in 1965.

Love á l'Italiano, at least onscreen.

A great champion of the First Amendment, Dunne protested abuse by the House Un-American Activities Committee for destroying careers in the movie industry. Surprisingly, he was never blacklisted himself. As he was quoted as saying, "Had I known I was working in Golden Age Hollywood, I would have enjoyed it more."

In North America, *Blindfold* grossed $2

During the making of *Blindfold* with Claudia Cardinale, Rock secretly leaked "fake news" to the press that he was having an affair with his co-star.

Actually, he was concealing affairs with two other actors appearing in the movie.

474

million, many viewers seeing it as a spoof of Ian Fleming's spy thrillers with James Bond. *Variety* asserted that "Rock Hudson offers one of his customary light portrayals, sometimes cloyingly, and is in for more physical action than usual."

Rock's ego as a box office champion was battered at this point in his film career. In the Motion Picture Buyer's Poll, he had dropped to Number Two, having been Number One for seven years in a row. By 1965, he had dropped to Number Ten and stayed there throughout 1966.

By 1967, however, he had fallen off the list of the *Top Ten Box Office Stars*, and would never again appear on that list, having relinquished his spot to newer luminaries.

"I guess romantic comedies were what the public had come to expect of me," he lamented.

***

During the shooting of *Blindfold*, there were press reports in Rome that Rock and Cardinale were having a fling together in Florida. Although that doesn't appear to be true, Rock was having affairs with two of his co-stars, neither of whom was Cardinale.

During location shooting in Florida, he invited Alejandro Rey and Guy Stockwell to live in the quarters that had been rented to him. It is not known if either of those presumably straight men were aware that Rock was a homosexual.

In his search for a partner, Rock often went for straight guys, as mentioned before. On a few occasions, he was rejected. But since at the time of *Blindfold*, he was among the biggest stars in the world, very few aspiring actors ever turned him down.

As he would later reveal to his friends, he found Rey, an Argentine-American actor, "incredibly handsome and sexy." He'd emigrated from Buenos Aires to the U.S. in 1960, after appearing in several Argentine films. In many ways, his career moves were similar to those of his rival, Fernando Lamas.

In the year of *Blindfold's* release (1966), he would marry Cristina Rudy. The marriage wasn't successful, culminating in divorce a few months later.

Rock later claimed, "I never got around to that other Argentine heartthrob, Fernando Lamas, but I scored big with Alejandro Rey, another import from Buenos Aires."

Rock was first attracted to Rey on-screen when he appeared as a champion diver in *Fun in Acapulco* (1963) with Elvis Presley. He would later become best known for his role as Carlos Ramirez in *The Flying Nun* (1967-70) on TV.

As Rock recalled, "I've had limited experience with Argentine men. But from my few encounters, I'm convinced that no man of the Pampas leaves a person in bed unsatisfied."

Rock was also immensely attracted to the wholesome all-American look of Guy Stockwell, his temporary roommate, an actor/singer from New York City. Although he appeared during the course of his career in 30 films and some 250 TV episodes, he never achieved the acclaim of his younger

Guy Stockwell's manly appeal to Rock was obvious in this scene from *Beau Geste* (1966), where he is being buried alive. He was the brother of the better known actor, Dean Stockwell.

brother, Dean Stockwell, who first achieved fame in movies as a child actor.

Guy was eight years younger than Rock. His greatest exposure to the public resulted from his appearance in the hit ABC TV series, *Adventures in Paradise* (1961-62), starring Gardner McKay as the skipper of a sailing vessel in the South Pacific. According to Rock, "It was that TV series that first turned me on to Guy. The less clothes he wore, the better."

Rock later said, "Guy went through three marriages, all of them disasters. He should have stayed with me."

***

Shot in black and white, *Seconds* (1966) was released by Paramount. It was another film produced by Rock's production company, Gibraltar. Reduced to a nutshell, it asked the question, "Want out of your life? Just pay us $30,000, and we'll fake your death, change your face, and set up a new identity for you."

As one fan noted, "For $30,000—or even a hell of a lot more—I'd be delighted to be transformed into Rock Hudson."

In spite of its many problems in casting and production, Rock always defined *Seconds* as his second most favorite film after *Giant*. It evolved as a pet project for John Frankenheimer, a film and TV director known for his action/suspense films and social dramas. *Seconds* became part of what came to be known as his "paranoid trilogy," an allusion to two other films,

The Manchurian Candidate (1962), starring Frank Sinatra, and *Seven Days in May* (1964), featuring Burt Lancaster, Kirk Douglas, and Ava Gardner.

The director had been so impressed with Kirk Douglas and his repertoire that initially, he had wanted him to star in the movie. Eventually, however, he concluded that Douglas' physical attributes, including his cleft chin, were too distinctive for easy replication into a "before" and "after" version.

At first, it was decided that the same actor would appear in both the "before" role as the unhappy banker, and again after his transformation into Antiochus (Tony) Wilson, a bohemian painter living in Malibu. Frankenheimer flew to London to pitch the role to Laurence Olivier. But Paramount rejected the choice, claiming, "We need a bigger box office star than that! GET ROCK HUDSON!"

But after Rock was cast, it

Salome Jens, appearing with Rock in *Seconds*, heard that he was gay, but recalled their love scenes as "being most authentic. They turned me on. I felt he really loved women. There wasn't an anti-female bone in his body, to judge by his making love to me on camera."

was considered too difficult for the makeup department to transform him into both a "before" and an "after" manifestation of the same man. Consequently, John Randolph, a noted actor who had been blacklisted for 15 years, allegedly as a communist sympathizer, was tapped to play the banker.

Although Randolph's facial structure was similar to Rock's, he was five inches shorter. That problem was solved by fitting him into carefully choreographed camera angles, and by positioning him next to other actors who were also relatively short.

During pre-production, Rock and Randolph spent time together studying each other's mannerisms as a means of synchronizing their movements. The director of photography was the acclaimed cinematographer, James Wong Howe, who pioneered novel techniques in his craft. *Seconds* was his swan song, and for it, he was nominated for an Oscar at the 39th Academy Awards ceremony.

After reading David Ely's novel, *Seconds,* Frankenheimer had acquired the rights and signed Lewis John Carlino to adapt it into a film. In addition to his status as a scriptwriter, Carlino was a director, too. Over the course of his career, he would helm such stars as Sarah Miles, Kris Kristofferson, Jacqueline Bisset, Rob Lowe, and Cliff Robertson. He was also

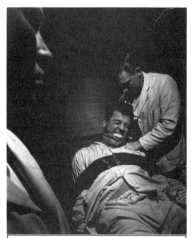

Strapped to a gurney, Rock in *Seconds* desperately struggles to break free from his captors. He knows the fate awaiting him from the psychotic doctors in the next room.

noted for his screen adaptations of works by noted literary authors who included D.H. Lawrence and Yukio Mishima.

Having begun his career at the peak of the Cold War, Frankenheimer was a pioneer of the modern-day political thriller. Rock was both intrigued and intimidated by the idea of working with a director with such a respected pedigree, fearing he would not live up to his expectations.

The producer of *Seconds,* Ed Lewis, became known for his collaborations with Frankenheimer and Kirk Douglas, having produced *Spartacus* (1960) and the adult Western, *The Last Sunset* (1961), starring Rock with Douglas and Dorothy Malone.

In Frankenheimer's view, *Seconds* was "expressionistic, part horror, part thriller, part science fiction, focusing on the obsession with eternal youth and a misplaced faith in the ability of medical science to achieve it."

Seconds tells an improbable story of a middle-aged man, Arthur Hamilton, who leads an unfulfilled life in Scarsdale, an upscale suburb of New York City, with his distant wife.

Through the voice of his dead partner, whom he hears over the telephone, Hamilton learns of a secret coven, known as "The Company," which promises a new life and a second chance.

Through plastic surgery, his physicality changes from that of a middle-aged, rather unattractive banker into the handsome, charismatic artist, Tony Wilson (Rock Hudson). It's only later that Wilson learns that his identity has derived from someone who has recently died in macabre circumstances, and perhaps murdered.

On the beach, in his new, handsome manifestation, Hamilton (as now portrayed by Rock) meets and falls in love with Nora Marcus (Salome Jens), learning later that she, too, is a "reborn."

In the most gruesome scene Rock ever filmed, he appears strapped down in an operating room where doctors prepare to drill into his brain.

The film's most controversial scene depicted nude revelers in an otherwise rather grim melodrama. Frankenheimer ordered the male and female extras, including Jens and Rock, to appear naked at a Bacchanalian wine-crushing ceremony at a local vineyard. Stripped naked by the men, Rock jumps into the large vat of mushy grapes. "I hung out in more ways than one."

The scene was censored and eliminated from the final cut before Paramount released the movie, but it was later restored in the DVD version, as the only (mainstream) nude film Rock ever made.

In time, Arthur Hamilton (*aka* Tony Wilson *aka* Rock Hudson) grows disenchanted with his second life, and at a drunken party attended by other reborns, becomes indiscreet and—in an act rigorously forbidden by The Company—he publicly reveals his former identity.

By doing so, he sets up his own destruction. He's gagged by doctors from The Company, tied to a stretcher, and wheeled into an operating room, where his brain is penetrated with a drill.

Seconds was first shown at the 1966 Cannes Film Festival. Disappointed by the advance criticism, Frankenheimer remained in Monaco and asked Rock to represent him at the question-and-answer session following the screening. Rock agreed, but found the gathering filled with hostile journalists with hostile questions, for many of which he failed to give creditable answers. He later recalled it as "one of the most embarrassing moments of my life."

When *Seconds* opened in the United States, it bombed at the box office, and for years remained one of Rock's most dismal failures, signaling a downfall in his box office desirability. However, over the decades, it found its audience and became a cult classic. Latter-day critics have cited Rock for "giving his most memorable performance."

In 2015, the Library of Congress designated it as a film "culturally, historically, or aesthetically significant."

***

Variety announced that the English actor, Laurence Harvey, would star in a World War II drama, *Tobruk,* for a color release by Universal in 1966. It was a heroic saga of the Allies' attempt to destroy the fuel bunkers of Nazi *Generalfeldmarschall* Erwin Rommel's Panzer Army at Tobruk, in Libya. The events depicted in the film were very loosely based on the actual military strategies of 1942. Five weeks before shooting began, Universal lost Harvey, and immediately signed its still-reigning star, Rock Hudson, as the male lead.

Throughout his career, its director, Arthur Hiller, a Canadian, often collaborated with screenwriters Paddy Chayefsky and Neil Simon, turning out such notable films as *The Americanization of Emily* (1965), starring Julie Andrews, a few years before she worked with Rock. *["Arthur should have warned me about this actress," Rock later said, bitterly, about his unhappy experience working with Andrews as his future co-star in* Darling Lili, *released in 1970.]*

Hiller had a military background, having served with the Royal Canadian Air Force during World War II. He felt at home with this wartime story, since he'd actually bombed Nazi targets himself. Before working with Rock, Hiller had made two films with two of his former co-stars, Leslie Caron in *Promise Her Anything* (1964) and *Penelope* (1966) with Natalie Wood.

Hiller assembled an intriguing cast, including the second lead, George Peppard, as well as actors Robert Wolders, the distinguished star Nigel Green, Jack Watson, and Guy Stockwell.

Rock was delighted to hear that Guy would be in his next film, as they had had a sexual fling during the making of 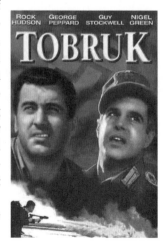 *Blindfold,* and he was looking forward to repeating the affair during the filming of *Tobruk.*

In *Tobruk,* Rock was cast as Major Donald Craig. Unlike Harvey, who had been reared in South Africa, he could not master a British accent, so his character was presented as having been born and reared in Canada. The major had devised a plan to destroy the German fuel bunkers of the Nazi Korps, which were strategically located only 90 miles (144 km) from that vital resource, the Suez Canal.

There's a complication to the British ability

to activate their plan: Vichy French forces based in Algiers had captured Craig and are holding him prisoner, along with other Allied soldiers, in a ship at their port.

His rescue is arranged by Captain Kurt Bergman (George Peppard) of the Special Identification Group, comprised in part of German Jews who had fled from Germany and are now serving under British command.

Rescued from imprisonment aboard the prison ship in Algiers, Major Craig (Rock) applies his skill as a topographer to launch the dangerous mission across scorpion-infested enemy territory. He has to lead his men under the blazing sun of the Sahara, where they face one hazard after another, including weeding out traitors working for the Nazis and air attacks from Italian warplanes overhead.

Guy Stockwell, as Lt. Max Mohnfield, is Bergman's (Peppard's) trusted second-in-command but, as it turns out, he is really a Nazi sympathizer working for the enemy. When Harker discovers his true identity, Stockwell is killed.

Actual filming for *Tobruk* took place amid the arid landscapes near Almería, on the southern coast of Spain, and on the Glamis Sand Dunes in the Imperial Valley of Southern California.

The storyline was complicated, with hard-to-understand diversions from the plotline, a bit of pretentiousness, and much social comment. As reviewed by The Guardian, "With a solid cast, some smart writing and excellent battle scenes, *Tobruk* is nearly a great movie—but it's just too patchy to make the grade."

Cast as Major Donald Craig battling the Nazis in *Tobruk*, Rock formed a lasting, loving relationship with his co-star, George Peppard.

"There was a fire burning inside George's damaged soul that he could never put out."

George Peppard, Rock's co-star in *Tobruk*, was once married to actress Elizabeth Ashley. She wrote: "His decline came as getting whiplash from his dreams."

Rock stood by him in his decline.

481

Since Rock Hudson's inaugural film role at Universal—a bit part in *Undertow* (1949), he had made 45 of his 54 movies at his home studio. His last films had been mostly mediocre, and Universal did not want to renew his contract.

"I've got to be more careful in picking my roles," he said, "or else I'll be a has-been hiding out in the Hollywood Hills, and god knows there are enough of those already."

In reference to his final days at Universal, "I was the one who paid for the wrap party," Rock said. "None of the bigwigs at Universal even came to visit or say goodbye to me. The days when I was worshipped by the chief, Ed Muhl, were over and would never return. As long as you're making the big bucks, the bastards will get down on their knees in front of you...literally."

In August of 1966, he got into his Cadillac convertible and headed for the gates. On his way out, he yelled to the security guards, "I'm never coming back. *Adios!*"

Actually, he did return.

***

In 1971, Richard Burton starred in a film, *Raid on Rommel,* in which director Henry Hathaway cut corners by incorporating a lot of the expensive combat footage from Rock's *Tobruk*. Encountering Burton at a party, the Welsh actor chided him, "My *Tobruk* film was better than yours."

"No argument there," Rock lamented.

***

So far as it is known, Rock's affair with George Peppard, his co-star in *Tobruk,* was his last fling with a "big name" actor, although there would be minor conquests. What had begun as a physical attraction developed over the years into a deep, abiding friendship conducted in secret, away from the gossips of Hollywood. He spoke to George Nader about it, but apparently to no one else.

As the 1970s rolled along, both actors met on the common ground of a mutual understanding. Each of them had faced career disappointments, and each had accepted roles that they needed but did not particularly enjoy. Each found a sympathetic soulmate in each other as their once-promising careers blew south with the southern winds, the fate of nearly all actors if they survive long enough.

Rock's affair with Peppard did not begin during the filming of *Tobruk*, as he was involved then with Guy Stockwell. Peppard and Rock came to know each other and became involved after the movie was wrapped.

Physically, Peppard fitted the mold of what Rock considered "my type of man." His assessment of Peppard's physical attributes matched that of his future wife's appraisal, too. Peppard would marry actress Elizabeth Ashley, whom he'd met when they'd co-starred in *The Carpetbaggers* (1964), a film loosely inspired by the aviator and movie mogul, Howard Hughes. Based on a bestselling novel by Harold Robbins, the movie became one of the biggest box office draws that year.

Ashley wrote, "He (Peppard) looked like some king of Nordic god—six feet tall with beautiful blonde hair, blue eyes, and a body out of every high school cheerleader's teenage lust fantasy."

Rock agreed completely.

Always attracted to straight men, Rock at first hesitated to move in on Peppard, at least until he learned a secret from his past. He heard that Peppard and Paul Newman had had a brief fling when they had co-starred in a teleplay, *Bang the Drum Slowly*, which was aired on *The United States Steel Hour* in September of 1956.

"I decided that George was nine percent gay leaning but 91 percent straight. I went for that nine percent, and I took my time going after him, regarding him as a prize stallion. I first created the bond of friendship, mutual trust, and respect."

"He was a very serious actor with big plans, rather conservative. But I found out behind the façade lurked a man of humor and whimsy. We had a lot of fun together. He often dropped by The Castle where we would listen to music and share our dreams. We liked many of the same things."

"We both smoked too much and drank too much, and one night, we started joking and fooling around, even rolling around on the floor. The inevitable happened…finally. I'd waited long enough, and it was well worth waiting for. I really dug him."

"The sex was one-sided, as I expected it to be, but I loved exploring his beautiful body, which gave me great satisfaction."

Rock shared these memories with Nader, his most trusted friend.

Peppard often spoke of his past. Born to a building contractor in Detroit, he'd had a good life until the Depression deepened and his dad could find almost no work.

Early in his life, he decided he wanted to be an actor, but joined the U.S. Marines in 1946. Leaving the military two years later, he studied civil engineering at Purdue University but also performed with the Purdue

Playmakers theater troupe. He later trained at the Pittsburgh Playhouse, making his stage debut there in 1949.

In Manhattan, he studied acting with Lee Strasberg at the Actors Studio. He landed his first TV role opposite Paul Newman when he was cast as baseball player Piney Woods in *Bang the Drum Slowly*. Before that he'd had a few gay flings in the Marines. He married Helen Davies in 1954. With her, he fathered two children.

Peppard's big breakthrough had come in the 1961 *Breakfast at Tiffany's*, in which he co-starred with Audrey Hepburn. Rock never told him that the first choice of its author, Truman Capote, had been Marilyn Monroe as Holly Golightly, and himself (Rock) as the male hustler, Paul Varjak, supported by a rich older woman (Patricia Neal).

After two big successes, many critics hailed Peppard as "the next best thing." There were predictions that he would become the next Alan Ladd or the next Richard Widmark. But the 1960s had arrived, and there was little demand for another Widmark or Ladd. *Tobruk* had marked the beginning of a long decline in Peppard's career, after which he made a series of B movies that did not advance his status as a star.

"As one disappointment after another mounted," Rock said, "George drank more and more. And smoked and smoked some more. But who am I to talk? I was doing the same damn thing."

Peppard had married Ashley in 1966 and stayed in that troubled, disastrous union until 1972. They produced a son, Christian.

Rock and Peppard saw each other frequently in the 1970s, although secretly and under the radar. He would drop in many a night at The Castle just "to hang out with my soulmate."

ROCK, A DEEPLY ENTRENCHED MEMBER OF "THE ESTABLISHMENT,"

Hosts the Last Great Hollywood Party
But Does Not Invite Mary Poppins

Jack Coates, A Handsome Gas Jockey & College Student, Meets "The Man of My Dreams" & Moves Into The Castle

"Wet or dry, kissing Julie Andrews in *Darling Lili*, a World War I spy drama, was one of the most detestable things I was ever called upon to do," Rock claimed. "I disliked her intensely, and actually hated her husband even more. They were very abusive to me."

In Hollywood during the long, hot summer of 1967, Rock searched for an ideal movie role, "hoping to make up for my recent series of box office flops." He thought he'd found it when George Nader gave him a copy of a Cold War thriller, *Ice Station Zebra*, written by the Scottish author, Alistair MacLean.

He learned that the project was already in pre-production at MGM, and John Sturges had been tapped to direct it. They had also signed the film's three secondary male leads: Ernest Borgnine, Patrick McGoohan, and Jim Brown.

Rock called Sturges to pitch himself as the lead for the role of Commander James Ferraday, USN. Sturges expressed an interest in interviewing him about the role, and arranged a luncheon date in the MGM commissary for the following day.

Like Rock, Sturges was a native of Illinois, and Rock had seen some of his films and been impressed by them, notably *Bad Day at Black Rock* (1955), *Gunfight at the O.K. Corral* (1957), *The Magnificent Seven* (1960), and *The Great Escape* (1963).

Over his breakfast coffee, Rock read an item in *Variety* that alarmed him. It was reported that Gregory Peck had signed with MGM to play the lead in *Ice Station Zebra*. Fortunately for him, that item turned out not to be true. Peck was unavailable, and David Niven was tapped for the role instead. But he, too, had another commitment. It had also been offered to Charlton Heston, who had rejected it because "the role of the commodore lacks characterization."

Sturges thought Rock might be imposing as the naval commander, and by the end of the luncheon, he offered him the part. "You don't have to take a screen test. I've seen many of your movies."

Rock was elated, as he believed that this suspense and espionage movie would restore his status at the box office.

Ice Station Zebra was a British meteorological station constructed on an ice floe in the Arctic Sea. It suffers a catastrophic oil fire, which burns several men alive. The remainder of the crew is holed up in a flimsy shack with almost nothing to eat, facing the cold of an Arctic winter without heat.

As Commander Ferraday, Rock is the captain of a nuclear attack submarine, the *USS Tigerfish* stationed at Holy Loch in Scotland. Here, Admiral Garvy (played by veteran actor Lloyd Nolan) orders him to undertake this dangerous mission to the top of the world to rescue the remaining men trapped in this Arctic wasteland. In time, he learns that his mission, in addition to a rescue, is actually a covert spy assignment that

"ICE STATION ZEBRA"...REMEMBER THE NAME—
YOUR LIFE MAY DEPEND ON IT!
An American nuclear sub...A sky full of Russian paratroopers...
A race for the secret of Ice Station Zebra!

"Ice Station Zebra"
in CINERAMA

Rock   Ernest   Patrick   Jim
Hudson   Borgnine   McGoohan   Brown

will bring his men into conflict with the Soviets.

Ferraday has been ordered to recover a capsule, dropped accidentally by a Soviet satellite, containing film that reveals the site of every nuclear base in the northern hemisphere.

He also has to take a British intelligence agent, David Jones (Patrick McGoohan), with him. USMC Anders (Jim Brown) is also part of the crew in charge of the Marines. Jones trusts another dubious passenger, Boris Vaslov (Ernest Borgnine), a Russian defector.

As is inevitable, the harshness of the Far North threatens the crew. When the submarine finds itself trapped beneath a thick layer of ice, a torpedo is launched to blast an opening, but someone has opened the tube at both of its ends, causing seawater to flood through the submarine. Consequently, it plunges down through the watery depths toward what its designers designated as its "crush depth."

Ferraday fears sabotage, suspecting Vaslov as the guilty one, although Captain Anders is also a suspect.

After much ado, confusion, and perhaps an overabundance of technical jargon, the plot races toward its conclusion. The Soviet double agent is exposed, and Russian paratroopers race to the scene to recover the vital capsule.

Although wintry scenes of the Far North had to be shot on location, the interior footage was filmed on the back lot of MGM. "It was one of the hottest summers I've ever known, and I had to perform the role in Arctic drag," Rock said. "When I got back to my dressing room, I could wring water from my jockey shorts, I sweated so much. One day, when I returned, I found my jockeys had been stolen. For what purpose, I don't dare speculate."

Rock detested working with Borgnine, and the feeling was mutual. "His Machiavellian eyebrows and gap-toothed Cheshire cat grin turned me off," Rock said. "He was the type of bully who could turn a gay man straight."

Rock had no interest in sports and was only vaguely aware that Jim Brown, an African American, had been among the greatest football players of all time during his stint (1957-1965) as a fullback for the Cleveland Browns. "If I had to tackle a man, it would not be be-

Ernest Borgnine in *Ice Station Zebra*.

"This photograph alone reveals why Ethel Merman divorced him after only one night of marriage," Rock said.

cause he was running with some damn ball," Rock said. "I'm sure I'd find a better reason."

For Rock, at least, the premiere of *Ice Station Zebra* was a disaster. As he was walking down the red carpet, smiling and waving at his fans, a heckler loudly screamed, "FAGGOT!"

Rock wanted to jump across the steel barriers and slug the jerk, but his handlers restrained him, hustling him inside the lobby of the theater, trying to calm him down.

Never again would Rock attend a movie premiere.

Regrettably for Rock, *Ice Station Zebra* was to be his last success at the box office, earning $5 million during its showings in the United States and Canada.

[Ice Station Zebra *became the alltime favorite movie of Howard Hughes, the reclusive and very eccentric billionaire. He owned a TV station in Las Vegas, and ordered it to broadcast Rock's film an astonishing one hundred times, saturating the market in ways that local consumers eventually interpreted as "the ultimate re-run."*]

***

During his filming of *Ice Station Zebra*, Rock gave an interview to *Photoplay* magazine.

"I love to smoke, and I keep hoping someone will discover it's a healthy habit, because the smoke kills all the germs in your system. I love to drink, but I hate to exercise. I don't mind going outside on the hill and chopping down a tree, but I detest organized exercise. I built a gym in my house, but I never use it. I don't even like to walk through it."

He did, however, like to play tennis. "More than hitting the ball, I like to socialize with other players."

One afternoon was about to change his life, at least temporarily. He'd become friendly with Frank Shea, who had purchased the home where Joan Blondell had lived with Dick Powell during their marriage, before June Allyson stole him away.

Shea always allowed his friends to use his tennis courts. One afternoon, Rock's new friend, Tom Clark, along with "the old reliables," George Nader and Mark Miller, played a game of tennis in the broiling sun. After the game, Rock's trio of cohorts drove off together as he waved them goodbye. He then returned to the courts to retrieve his racquet.

A new game had been organized with four handsome young men, one of them particularly striking "with great legs in white tennis shorts, showing off a bubble-butt ass."

Rock introduced himself to the man who'd caught his eye.

As he later relayed to Nader, "Jack Coates was twenty-three years old and drop-dead gorgeous. He had blonde hair, blue eyes, and a great tan. There was this twinkle in his eyes and a sort of mischievous grin. The little fucker was flirting with me. He was so vital, so full of life, at the peak of his virility and male beauty. I thought he was ripe for plucking...that's *plucking,* darling, rhymes with...."

Rock left the court, and the men began to play ball. The court was surrounded by an ivy-covered fence. From the other side of the fence, Rock saw an opening through which he could observe the game. Coates recalled, "I knew he was watching me, and I performed like a stallion. I knew where he was standing, because at the bottom of the fence, I could see his feet in those red tennis shoes."

At the age of thirteen in Dallas, Coates had gone to see *Giant* at the local movie house. "Even back then, I knew there was a God in Heaven to have created an incredible man like Bick Benedict. A lot of people raved about Rock. In my wildest dreams, I imagined I would meet him one day. His screen presence mesmerized me. It was like he was sending some direct signal to me, something real personal, a message to a growing pubescent boy with pimples."

After he graduated from high school, Coates began an affair with a real estate developer who took him to live in an apartment in Hollywood. The contractor erected homes for rich residents of Los Angeles.

In the summer of 1967, Coates was attending UCLA, pursuing courses in anthropology. He worked two part-time jobs—one at a gas station, another at a hamburger stand on the beach. With the help of his friend, he purchased a red Corvette convertible, a motorcycle, and a 1947 Mercury station wagon.

On his days off, he went surfing with his friends and became an expert tennis player. "I got so good, I even played a few games with Dinah Shore. She was great, but she wasn't Rock Hudson. The question for me was, 'How to I meet this godlike man?'"

"I came up with this idea. I knew where he lived, a place called The Castle. I rode by his residence very slowly every day on my way to my classes. One morning, my prayers were answered. I saw Rock walking two of his dogs along the side of the road. I stopped near him, got out, and raised the hood of my Corvette, pretending that something was wrong. Rock came up to me."

"Hi!" he said. "Can I be of help?" He recalled his introduction to Coates on the tennis courts at Shea's home.

"Suddenly, I went into a panic," Coates said. "Here I was, alone with

Rock Hudson…at last. My dream had come true. But I was petrified, not knowing what to say beyond a stuttered hello. I slammed down the hood of my car and drove off."

"The next day found me driving by The Castle once again. Coincidentally, Rock was just pulling into the driveway of The Castle in his blue Cadillac convertible. He looked fabulous. He watched as I slowed down in my Corvette and waved to him."

"Hi!" he called out in that masterful voice of his. "Want to come in and stick around for lunch?"

"I can't," Coates answered. "Got to go to work. At Standard Oil, corner of La Cienega and Wilshire. Another time, maybe." Then he smiled again and drove off.

By three o'clock that afternoon, Rock drove his car into the Standard Oil station. "Fill her up, Jack," he called out to Coates. "I've been running on empty."

Coates was flabbergasted that this bigtime movie star remembered his name.

Once his tank was filled, Rock asked, "When do you get off from work?"

"At ten tonight."

"Why not drop by The Castle for a late-night swim?"

"I'd love to. There's nothing in the world I'd like better."

He could hardly wait for quitting time, when he rushed to the men's toilet to freshen up and comb his blonde hair.

Arriving at The Castle, he was greeted by Rock in his bathing trunks. "Ready for a swim? We could go skinny dipping."

"I fucked up royally," Coates said. "I started shaking like a leaf. Here I was in the home of Rock Hudson, Bick Benedict, he was with ME, Jack Coates of Phoenix. A gas station attendant. A nobody. I had a quick beer with him and fled. I was scared out of my wits."

"I feared he'd never invite me again. But apparently, he was used to encountering guys who became nervous meeting him. After all, he was the biggest movie star in the world, and one of the most desirable men on earth, according to some polls. To my surprise, as I was leaving, he invited me to a Sunday afternoon party.

"This time, I arrived promptly at 3PM, and I was still nervous. I brought him the latest *Mamas and the Papas* album. Rock had never heard the group, and he played the recording over and over again. It was a perfect gift."

"I went with him to one of his lime trees and picked the fruit so he could make daiquiris for us. Rock crushed the ice, and we had more than a few, just sitting, talking, listening to music, joking as the smell of jasmine drifted in from his gardens. I began to feel comfortable around him."

"He took my hand and held it as we sat quietly listening to the Mamas and the Papas. He leaned over and gave me a long, passionate kiss. At last, I produced an erection, and so did he. We headed for his bedroom."

"It was the most memorable night of my life," Coates recalled. "He lived up to my fantasy. I think I really satisfied him, too. He made me feel I did."

That was confirmed when Mark Miller flew in from London. Rock told him, "I've found him. He's dynamite. A fun-loving personality. Wonderful sex. A male beauty. I haven't asked a man to move in with me since Jack Navaar. I want this Jack to come and live with me forever."

"You've got it bad," Miller said.

"And how!"

Although he desperately wanted to come and live with Rock as his lover, Coates was leery of breaking off the five-year relationship with the real estate developer. One of Rock's friends had told him, "Rock comes on real strong, passionate sex, but after a while, he gets tired of a guy and boots him out. He them moves on to his next conquest. Thousands upon thousands of guys want him. Don't give up a steady deal you have just for a few weeks of sex with Rock."

Miller and Nader were introduced to Coates at a mixed party with some thirty other guests, including two name stars, Claire Trevor and her husband, along with Nancy Walker. Most of the other guests were aspiring actors.

"I knew at once who Jack was," Miller said, "from Rock's description. He did not exaggerate. The kid was a knockout. So sexy, so mischievous, so alive, with blue eyes that seemed to tap dance."

The more evasive Coates was about moving into The Castle, the more Rock pursued him, urging him to break from the developer. Coates and Rock shared two favorite restaurant venues: Eating juicy cheeseburgers with extra catsup at Bob's Big Boy and sampling the best ice cream in the West at Will Wrights, their favorite being double vanilla ice cream with extra hot fudge sauce.

In early September of 1967, Coates was finally convinced. It began with mint juleps served in silver goblets, which were followed by Rock's promise that his love was genuine. "I want to spend the rest of my life with you," Rock told him.

"We made love that afternoon and then drove to the house of my contractor friend when he was away in Palm Springs. I wrote him a goodbye note. I packed all my possessions into two suitcases and headed out, not forgetting my teddy bear, a koala with a yellow ribbon. There was no turning back now."

For their honeymoon, Rock suggested they head north on a motor trip. "Everything went wrong," Coates said. "It was a disaster. We stopped off for lunch at the Danish town of Solvang. Warm beer and a stale sandwich. In Monterey, Rock was mobbed by fans. It was during the annual jazz festival, and every room in town was booked. We headed for San Jose and stayed at a dreary Holiday Inn that served rubbery steaks."

By the time we reached the Napa Valley and a beautiful inn, our honeymoon really began. We made love..and made more love…and then made some more love. We sat on a terrace drinking wine and taking in the lush vineyards that reminded me of a movie Rock had made with Jean Simmons called *This Earth Is Mine*."

"Our life together had begun," Coates said, "and what a roller-coaster ride it was for me over the next five years."

***

With no other film offers coming in, Rock signed to make a 1968 Italian crime comedy, *A Fine Pair*, for Francesco Maselli. A role had been created for him as an FBI agent who gets involved with the beautiful daughter of an old friend. She turns out to be a jewel thief who gets the G-man involved in a criminal caper in the snow-bound Austrian Alps.

At the time he contracted for the film, Rock had no idea it would get him involved in an intense investigation from the closeted FBI director, J. Edgar Hoover, and his lover and chief aide, Clyde Tolson.

A startling article appeared in *The New York Post* on February 11, 1993, written by Murray Weiss. He exposed an extortion ring in Manhattan that had operated in 1966 and was broken up by the Manhattan district attorney, Frank Hogan, and his "Racquet Squads."

Two blackmailers, Edward Murphy and Sherman Kaminsky, had operated an extortion racket called "The Chicken and the Bulls." They hired well-built, heavily endowed hustlers to prey on older, prosperous-looking men, often movie stars or politicians, even military brass. These hustlers met their prey at airports, bars, or in hotels, soliciting them for sex. Later they

He was a good, law-abiding citizen, but she didn't hold that against him.

Rock Hudson   Claudia Cardinale
A Fine Pair

492

would blackmail them based on photos and videos from cameras installed in shabby hotel rooms into which they took their johns for sex.

One of the ringleaders of this coven of crooks would burst into a hotel room with a photographer, who would shamelessly document the victim having sex with a hustler.

Many prominent men were caught in this trap and paid off to save their reputations. Within a period of one month, a Racquet Squad investigation found that both Rock Hudson and William Church, a naval admiral stationed at Key West, Florida, had been entrapped. Rock never had to pay off, because the hustlers and their ringleaders were arrested. After he was outed, however, the admiral committed suicide.

Rock had met Peter Stark in the bar of the Astor Hotel near Times Square in Manhattan. He was twenty-six and a former sailor once stationed at Pensacola, Florida. He was well built, blonde, and blue-eyed—Rock's ideal type. The hustler and his conquest, in this case Rock himself, went up to his hotel room at the Astor, which Stark had already rented.

In the middle of a sex act (Rock performing fellatio on Stark), a photographer burst into the room and photographed them.

The blackmailers were arrested within a week. Another man named Peter (Peter Frelinghuysen, Jr., a Republican representing his district in New Jersey), had also been entrapped.

In the subsequent investigation, it was learned that Kaminsky also supplied young men to J. Edgar Hoover and to Clyde Tolson. When Hoover heard of Hogan's raid, he dispatched Tolson to New York to meet with the District Attorney. Somehow, Tolson managed to persuade him to turn over to the FBI the data he'd gathered on Rock and on Hoover.

After Tolson flew back to Washington, the matter was hushed up.

Whereas Hoover destroyed the incriminating evidence on himself, he archived the evidence on Rock. Apparently, he was fascinated by the pictures of Rock, considering him a "manly man." He even managed to confiscate, from a different incident, a sex tape that had been secretly filmed, again with Rock as its most visible actor. It had been organized and set up by Johnny Stompanato when he worked for gangster Mickey Cohen. It was reported that Hoover and Tolson repeatedly watched, as part of their private recreation, the sex tape of Rock with Stompanato.

Hoover had begun his compilation on Rock in the late 1950s, when he first became a box office attraction.

In contrast, an overview of the gay life of Hoover and Tolson emerged after their deaths. The most extensive revelations were published in Blood Moon's 2012 biography, *J. Edgar Hoover & Clyde Tolson: Investigating the Sexual Secrets of America's Most Famous Men and Women*.

After his imprisonment, Kaminsky seemingly disappeared, though he was reported to have fled to Denver, where he sold wigs and raised rabbits. Murphy, his associate who was also imprisoned, was known as a "chicken hawk," that is, an adult male who has sex with young boys.

Hoover ordered FBI agents in Los Angeles to keep a close watch over any film that dealt with the FBI. He was enraged when he heard that Rock had been cast as an FBI agent in *A Fine Pair*. Through interviews that agents had conducted with many young men who had "partied" with Rock, it was known

Clyde Tolson, cozy and on holiday with J. Edgar Hoover

to the FBI that he was a homosexual. Hoover's fury at Rock's casting was exposed when Nick Redfern wrote his 1967 tell-all, *Celebrity Secrets: Government Files on the Rich and Famous*.

The author wrote, "FBI agents were clearly in possession of incriminating evidence on Hudson, orgies in which he had partaken, and motels where he conducted his secret affairs."

The casting of Rock as an FBI agent set off a flurry of memos within the FBI. Hoover, through Tolson, brought pressure on the moguls of Universal. Consequently, as a means of deflecting the FBI's pressure, Rock's role was rewritten and reconfigured into that of a detective with the New York Police Department instead of an agent with the FBI.

Universal readily acquiesced, because the professional status of the character Rock played had no effect on the script, and called for no rewrites.

Rock came under FBI scrutiny again after it was announced that he would portray an agent of the Bureau in *The Seven File*, a caper about a kidnapping.

In reference to that film, the FBI in Washington sent a memo to the studio: "Our files indicate that Rock Hudson, a prominent leading man, has been alleged to be a homosexual and/or bisexual. Our Los Angeles office has been instructed to remain alert to all developments regarding this motion picture."

The threat was implied. The film was never made.

Hoover kept his file on Rock locked up in the den of his Washington, D.C. home. Since his death in 1972, the file has never resurfaced, and was presumably destroyed.

Apparently, Rock was not considered "G-manly enough" to play an

FBI agent on screen. Nevertheless, Hoover must have considered him manly enough to be fascinated by his sexual performances on tape.

***

For his leading lady in *A Fine Pair*, set for release by National General in 1969, Rock requested that Sophia Loren be cast. But she had no interest in the role. He then asked for Gina Lollobrigida, with whom he had already made two films. That potential pairing also fell through.

The director and screenwriter of *A Fine Pair*, Francesco Maselli, informed him that Claudia Cardinale would be his leading lady. Rock had already co-starred with her in *Blindfold,* and many critics had pointed out the obvious: There was no sexual chemistry between them. That was worrisome, since a percolating chemistry would be essential for the success this new crime caper.

As Captain Mike Harmon of New York City's Police Department, Rock gets criminally involved with Cardinale in her role as Esmeralda Marini, a jewel thief. She was the daughter of a former police colleague of his from Italy, and he has not seen her since she was a child twelve years ago. She's a child no more, more like an Italian sex bomb. She urgently needs his help, as she's in deep trouble.

In collaboration with a well-known criminal, she has stolen a vast horde of jewelry from the ski lodge of the wealthy Ogden Fairchild family in Kitzbühel, a chic resort in Austria. The Fairchilds are not in residency, and they do not know their cache has been looted.

Esmeralda wants to go straight. Her scheme involves breaking into the villa again and returning the jewelry before it can be discovered as missing and reported to the police. That way, she hopes to avoid prosecution.

The villa has a sophisticated security system, and she needs Rock to help her break in. He foolishly agrees to her wild schemes, and they set out.

Masselli not only wrote the screenplay, but he was the director, too. He'd been making

Claudia Cardinale and Rock are warmly dressed in *A Fine Pair* for their snow-bound scenes in the Austrian Alps.

Some critics pointed out that the frigid temperatures in that setting did not allow for either of them to show off their best assets...their bodies.

movies since 1949, all of them in Italian except two in English, one of which was *A Fine Pair*.

In addition to Rock and Cardinale, he signed two veteran actors into key roles. A Viennese with a triple chin, Leon Askin, was cast as Chief Wellman. His widest popularity would come later, when he played the stern yet comical General Albert Burkhalter in the sitcom, *Hogan's Heroes*, in the late '60s.

The second male lead, Roger, was played by Tomas Milian, born to a Cuban general in Havana who committed suicide. After Milian grew up, he migrated to Manhattan to study at the Actors Studio. By the time he met Rock, he had found success in Italy, starring in a string of spaghetti Westerns.

He and Rock met for drinks on several occasions. He freely admitted that he was bisexual. "I like to fuck beautiful women, but I like to get fucked by handsome men. Want to give me a tumble?"

"Some other time," Rock said. "See that blonde guy over there?" he said, pointing to Massimo, with whom he'd had a reunion. "He keeps me drained."

Most of the scenes in *A Fine Pair* were shot in Rome at the Dino De Laurentiis Cinematografica Studios. With Jack Coates living at The Castle and attending classes at college, Rock had felt free to hook up with Massimo again, flying him in as his bedmate on location in the Austrian Alps.

His passion for Massimo was still intact. The fires of September still burned, albeit with a lower flame.

The reviews of *A Fine Pair* were mostly negative, as critics once again cited "zero chemistry" between Rock and Cardinale. Another reviewer wrote, "*A Fine Pair* will never be on anyone's list of top Rock Hudson films."

Roger Greenspun, a critic who, by the end of his long career, had reviewed almost 400 films, mostly for *The New York Times*, wrote: "Miss Cardinale, whose face is not her greatest asset, is buckled by the rigors of the season (winter in Austria), into far too many shapeless casings for her virtues to appear more than fleetingly. Hudson, in dark-rimmed glasses and a lot of casual dark hair, appears forced, fragile, and strangely listless in his role."

A Fine Pair had so little box office draw that most movie houses put it on a double bill alongside an offbeat Western, *Charro*, starring Elvis Presley as an ex-gunfighter. On screen, in the words of one critic, "Elvis's mouth is hidden behind the mask of a stubble-like beard, his hair is powerfully slicked in place, his walk modest, his manner retiring. Presley is thoroughly tamed."

Charro was obviously not Elvis's finest hour, and neither was Rock's *A Fine Pair.*

After its release, Rock's name appeared on one of the most dubious lists of his entire career: *Variety* designated him as one of the "Top Ten Overpriced Stars of 1968."

***

For more than thirty years, John Cohan had been a celebrity psychic to an all-star cast spearheaded by Rock Hudson, among a coven that included Elizabeth Taylor, Lana Turner, Elvis Presley, LaToya Jackson, Joan Crawford, Natalie Wood, Jayne Mansfield, Vincent Price, and TV host Merv Griffin.

Cohan's colorful life was explored in his tell-all autobiography, *Catch a Falling Star,* published in 2008, in which he wrote about Rock, among other celebrities.

Cohan was aware that Rock and Troy Donahue had been romantically linked, since the handsome, blonde-haired actor had interpreted a minor role in Rock's film, *The Tarnished Angels* (1957), based on *Pylon,* the novel by William Faulkner.

Both Rock and Cohan watched as Donahue's career had skyrocketed in Hollywood during the late 1950s and early 1960s, only to burst into flames and crash.

Cohan was especially close to Sandra Dee, who had co-starred with Rock and her future husband, Singer Bobby Darin, in *Come September.* The young blonde goddess had made a spectacular box office hit when she had also co-starred with Donahue in *A Summer Place* in 1959.

Warner Brothers signed Donahue to a long-term contract at a time when they were firing stars because of the fall-off of revenues based on declining box office receipts during the advent of television.

Cohan and Rock watched as Donahue "was on a roll" (Rock's words), generating more fan mail than he had, an estimated 5,000 to 7,500 letters a week. Yet Donahue complained, telling Cohan, "I always get to play a goody-goody. I need to bite into

Celebrity seer, John Cohan, author of *Catch a Falling Star,* was an eye-witness, friend, and sometimes counselor to the tragic lives of Rock Hudson and Troy Donahue, among other stars.

something stronger."

He got his wish in 1965 when he was cast as a psychopathic killer in *My Blood Runs Cold* opposite Joey Heatherton. It flopped at the box office. "I asked to be released in January of 1966," Donahue told Cohan. "Jack Warner went ballistic, and called every other studio in town and had me blacklisted."

Studio after studio told the young actor that "Henry Willson's pretty boys of the 1950s have come to an end. Get me Dustin Hoffman."

About a year later, in 1967, Donahue walked out on his contract which called for his appearance in a play *Poor Richard*, at the Pheasant Run Playhouse in St. Charles, Illinois, near Chicago. In retaliation, the backers sued him for $200,000, a lawsuit that was later settled out of court.

Cohan was a witness as Donahue's world came tumbling down. Still his friend, Rock used his rapidly declining influence at Universal to get Donahue some TV work. But as he told Cohan, "Troy fucked it up. He's abusing drugs and alcohol...he's loaded all the time. Before breakfast, he's already tanked up on vodka and four lines of coke."

"I would lie, steal, and cheat, all those wonderful things drunks do," Donahue confessed to Cohan.

By 1968, he was forced to declare bankruptcy after his business manager absconded with all his money. Gone was his Cape Cod style house at 1234 Wetherly Drive. It was here he staged midday orgies. A visitor reported, "Troy was zonked out of his mind most of the time. There were usually at least a dozen degenerates hanging out."

Gone were the seven black Cadillac convertibles and the lavish swimming pool.

As his world collapsed around him, the violent streak that Cohan had once noted in Donahue became more pronounced. His explosive side had first been exposed in the press after his girlfriend, Lili Kardell, filed assault-and-battery charges against him. She was a minor actress who had dated James Dean and had a role in the Nazi spy comedy, *Looking for Danger* (1957). She was asking the court for a settlement of $60,000. At the time, Donahue was still under contract to Warner Brothers. Jack Warner made a settlement with her out of court.

One day, Rock contacted Cohan to report on his last encounter with Donahue. According to Rock, "He was living in this shabby apartment when he phoned for me to come and see him. When I got there, he threatened to blackmail me and expose my homosexuality to the scandal rags. As you know, I'm not a violent person like Troy. But I went into a rage. I'd gotten him work at Universal, and now he was turning on me. I beat the shit out of him and fled. The next day, I returned, fearing he might file charges. I settled with him and gave him $10,000 in cash."

That was the money Donahue used to fly out of Los Angeles and relocate to New York City. But that stash of money soon disappeared, and Rock and Cohan learned that Donahue was living for a time in Central Park.

Long after that scandal with Donahue had passed, and as his own career began to falter, Rock continued to confide in Cohan. He'd fallen off the list of the industry's top ten box office stars, but was still working steadily, getting money for a TV series and an occasional movie role.

He spoke to Cohan about his disastrous marriage to Phyllis Gates, the lesbian secretary of Henry Willson.

"If I'd wanted to marry any woman, it would have been Marilyn Maxwell," Rock told Cohan. "But she was hip enough to know that I could never give up the boys."

Elaine Stritch, the entertainer, actress, and singer, had been Rock's nurse in *A Farewell to Arms*. She had also appeared as the lesbian owner of a bar in the cult film, *Who Killed Teddy Bear?* (1965). It had starred Rock's former lover, Sal Mineo.

Stritch was mainly known for her roles on Broadway, appearing in William Inge's *Bus Stop* (1956) and the Noël Coward musical *Sail Away* (1962).

She had told reporters that Rock had once proposed marriage to her. When Cohan asked Rock about that, he said, "Elaine is delusional. She's a notorious lesbian and alcoholic."

In the 1980s, Cohan, along with Mark Miller and George Nader, learned that Rock had full-blown AIDS. He told Cohan that he had developed the disease from a blood transfusion during his open-heart surgery.

The psychic watched with great pain as this giant of a man's weight dropped drastically, his memory growing dimmer and dimmer until his death in 1985.

Cohan later wrote: "It has never been my position to judge people for their sexual beliefs as a human being. To each his own. Rock Hudson was a great human being, and I couldn't have asked for a better friend. The epitome of a macho man, he had a beautiful, sensitive soul. It makes me sad to think that the public has forgotten him, and many times had mocked him for being gay. The man carried himself like a gentleman and never made his sexuality open for public viewing. He was a private man."

***

Troy Donahue was not the only potential blackmailer. Rock's former wife, Phyllis Gates, had never been pleased with her divorce settlement.

In 1968, she contacted Mark Miller to convey a message to her former husband. It was outrageous. She demanded three-fourths of all his future earnings, and if he didn't acquiesce, she would write a tell-all book revealing every "dirty secret" she knew or had ever heard about him. As she told Miller, "Needless to say, he'll be ruined. He'll never work in this town again."

Rock was enraged. He plotted with Miller and Nader to have Phyllis exposed as a lesbian. He needed ammunition.

Rock flew to New York for a meeting with the popular columnist, Liz Smith, who had been his friend.

"He was being threatened with blackmail and wondered what he should do to avoid the destruction of his career. 'The Love that Dare Not Speak its Name' kept Rock afraid for years, and in the closet," she later wrote. "Regrettably, it is still palpable in Hollywood of today, almost as it was yesterday."

Rock knew that Smith had plenty in her files about the lesbian activities of Phyllis, which she was willing to hand over to his lawyers. According to Smith, "I thought Gates was playing dirty pool, and I wanted Rock to know I had extensive incriminating evidence on her. She was not as 'clean as the driven slush,' to borrow a quote from Tallulah Bankhead."

In her autobiography, *Natural Blonde*, released in 2000, Smith, without naming her at the time, wrote about a "would-be blackmailer" of Rock Hudson. In 2006, when Phyllis died at the age of 80, Liz revealed in a newspaper column that the blackmailer was, indeed, Phyllis Gates.

"I helped Rock cover his tracks and save the bacon," Smith claimed. "I did not want to name her when she was alive; that would have been fatal for both her and for Rock. However, Gates did not extract money from her ex. She tried, but we blocked her."

Phyllis was once asked about this by a reporter: "Did you ever threaten to expose Rock in a memoir while he was alive?"

She adamantly denied it. "I had no interest doing that in his lifetime. It would have destroyed him and would have been vicious and vindictive. I faced enough trouble in rebuilding my life after our divorce without coping with that guilt."

Two years after Rock died in 1987, she published *My Husband, Rock Hudson*. She "Outed" him, but went to her grave without Outing herself.

***

Blake Edwards had co-written, with William Peter Blatty, a script for a drama/thriller/romance entitled *Darling Lili*. It was eventually released in

1970 by Paramount.

Edwards had not yet married singer/actress Julie Andrews—that would happen in 1969—but he cast her as its female lead, playing a Mata Hari inspired *femme fatale,* a British music hall performer who is secretly a German spy during World War I.

Her sinister boss is Colonel Kurt von Ruger, played by the English actor Jeremy Kemp, a fellow spy for the Kaiser.

In her efforts to learn military secrets, Lili Smith (Andrews) turns her feminine wiles onto Major William Larrabee (Rock), a top American pilot. Without meaning to, she falls in love with him and can't find the courage to betray him. Likewise, when he discovers that she's a spy, he refuses to turn her in.

In an interview with a reporter for *Films in Review,* Edwards said, "I wanted a tall, handsome man to play opposite Julie. He had to be a dashing type who looks great in a uniform. For my charismatic hero, I interviewed ten leading men. I won't name them because I don't want to embarrass them. But of the bunch, only Rock stood out."

At first, Rock was eager to play the male lead, as he had long wanted to do an A-list musical. He still fancied himself somewhat as a singer.

He had met Andrews on three different occasions at Hollywood premieres or at parties. Ten years younger than him, she'd never been his favorite. Unlike millions of other movie goers, he found her "a bit syrupy" in *Mary Poppins* (1964), her feature film debut, and as Maria von Trapp in *The Sound of Music* (1965).

When Edwards told Andrews that Rock had been cast as her leading man, and she'd have to make love to him on screen, she reportedly complained, "I've worked with Rex Harrison, Richard Burton, and Paul Newman. Now you give me Rock Hudson." *[It was never confirmed that she actually said that.]*

Years before Rock met Edwards, he'd been impressed with his directorial efforts, although lamenting that he did not get cast in Truman Capote's *Breakfast at Tiffany's* in 1961. Rock also found Edwards' *Days of Wine and Roses* (1962) "beautifully acted and very moving," but never became a fan of *The Pink Panther* (1963), starring Peter Sellers.

Rock flew to Europe to shoot

Behind the wheel in his military role in *Darling Lili,* Rock steers Julie Andrews, his leading lady, a Mata Hari type spy, along a rocky road.

Darling Lili, first in France, then in Ireland. There were endless delays, caused by student riots in Paris and later by bad weather in Ireland.

After the first week of shooting, a feud, later denied, developed between Edwards and Rock. He told his companion, Tom Clark, "Blake is a closeted gay. During my third day on the set, he made a pass at me, and I turned him down. Big mistake. By now, I felt I was too big a star to lie on the casting couch."

From the beginning Rock had felt tensions rising between Andrews and himself. Rock also told Clark, "In my first scene with Andrews, she said to me, 'You realize I'm a big movie star now.' I lit a cigarette, looked down at her, and smiled. 'Thanks for joining our ranks,' I told her."

As production costs mounted, Robert Evans, in charge of production at Paramount at the time, was enraged. "*Darling Lili* was the most misappropriation and waste of funds I've seen in my entire career. Edwards was writing a love letter to his lady, and Paramount paid for it."

Dick Morris, Rock's friend who worked for Universal, visited him in his hotel suite in Dublin, where Rock told him, "'The King' (Julie Andrews) is living with 'The Queen' (Blake Edwards) in a castle outside of town. 'The Black Prince' (me) has been exiled to this hotel."

In her gossip column, Joyce Haber was the first to report on the tensions roiling between the film's director, in league with its leading lady, and Rock. From the "warfront," Haber wrote of scandalous interchanges between Edwards and Rock, and between Andrews and Rock.

Rock was required to perform a love scene in which he is supposed to kiss Andrews passionately. Midway through, Edwards called an abrupt halt. "Stand back, faggot!" he shouted at Rock. "I'll show you how to kiss a woman!" He then demonstrated his technique.

In a remark that seemed uncharacteristic of Andrews' cheery image, she was reported to have sarcastically announced, "I'm the only Queen in this movie—and Hudson needs to get that *straight!*"

It is understandable that the star and director wanted to cover up rumors of a

Julie Andrews and Rock Hudson appear distracted from each other in *Darling Lili.*

Their relationship got off to a bad start when she reminded him that she was a bigger box office draw than he was.

feud, and later, both Edwards and Andrews denied that a feud ever existed. "The supposed feud between me and Rock was greatly exaggerated," Andrews claimed. "The remark about me being the only queen on the set was a total fabrication."

Edwards also denied the faggot story. "What the hell!" he said. "Come off it! I wouldn't have insulted him. He's too big. He might have beaten the shit out of me. The story is totally absurd."

After Rock read the Haber column, he was said to have sent off a cable to her which read: "SAW YOUR COLUMN OF YESTERDAY. SUGGEST YOU SEE MY LAWYER. YOU WILL HEAR MORE. ROCK HUDSON."

Tom Clark, one of Rock's closest confidants, denied that his friend ever sent that cable, but he did confirm that tensions were high on the set. According to Clark, "Edwards treated Rock very badly. So did Andrews. Her on-screen image was made up of equal parts of sugar and treacle, but actually, she was more castor oil and cayenne pepper."

On camera, Rock had to tell Andrews, "I think you're the most provocative, exciting, and desirable woman I've ever met." Privately, he claimed, "Andrews is the most detestable bitch I've ever worked with, the least favorite of my leading ladies. I even had to take a shower in a bathtub with this Arctic icicle."

During the shoot, Rock was often confused by the cinematography techniques used by Edwards: long shot zooms, tracking, and focus distortion.

Edwards might have denied allegations of a feud, but he was candid about Rock the actor. "He's not a great actor," he claimed. "Not at all. He has his own style, but it's all on the surface, not deep at all. He has great limitations as an actor. He certainly is good looking, but looks can carry an actor only so far. He gives a surface performance, but then, I wasn't exactly expecting Olivier."

"Darling Lili was a mess," Rock lamented to his lover, Jack Coates. "I was eight months chasing around Europe trying to complete this turkey. My time could have been better spent. The movie should have been played for high camp if it had to be made at all. I had some really great lines. 'I fly at dawn.'" *[Here, he was being sarcastic.]*

"As for Miss Andrews, there's

In this scene from *Darling Lili*, Julie Andrews calls Rock "a bastard," and he punishes her by holding her under a cold shower. He even suggests that she might be virgin.

nothing I couldn't say to her face—both of them!"

"I heard that my *Darling Lili* taskmasters, Blake Edwards and Julie Andrews, were implying to the press that I'm gay. I could hardly believe it! Talk about the kettle calling the pot black!"

"A miserable newspaperwoman wrote something implying that Rock Hudson, Julie, and I were a sexual threesome," Edwards said. "She also implied that Rock and I spent a lot of time together in San Francisco leather bars. I walked up to Rock and repeated the story to him, and I loved his response."

"How in hell did she find out so quickly?" Rock asked.

Budgeted at $12 million, *Darling Lili* ended up costing Paramount $25 million. In 1981, Edwards released *S.O.B.*, a satire in which Andrews bared her breasts. Ironically, the movie he was mocking within the context of *S.O.B.* was his own big flop, *Darling Lili*.

Critic George Morris claimed, "The movie synthesizes every major Edwards' theme: The disappearance of gallantry and honor, the tension between appearances and reality, and the emotional, spiritual, moral, and psychological disorder in such a world."

"*Darling Lili* is an example of the self-indulgent extravagance in filmmaking that is ruining Hollywood," wrote one reporter.

Another critic wrote, "Fans of *Mary Poppins* will be horrified to see this former nanny 'harloting' her way from one man's bed to another."

Darling Lili lives on within the legends of the film industry, frequently compared, because of its cost overruns, to the disastrous *Heaven's Gate* (1980) that almost bankrupted United Artists. As Robert Evans said about *Darling Lili*, "That rotten piece of shit nearly bankrupted us at Paramount, too."

***

Upon his return to L.A. from Europe after his filming of *Darling Lili*, Rock told a story that happened to him when he reported to Paramount. Robert Evans, the chief honcho there, was impressed with the roster of big names at the studio that day. He called the publicity department and asked his agents there to round up a posse of stars for a photo with a banner headline that read, "PARAMOUNT IS WHERE IT'S HAPPENING."

Invitations were sent out for a 2PM photo op that would include Rock himself, John Wayne, Barbra Streisand, Lee Marvin, and, of course, Miss Julie Andrews.

"Barbra is known for being temperamental, but even she showed up on time," Rock said. "Everybody was there waiting and waiting for Miss

Andrews to appear. Finally, after two hours, everyone fled. What happened?"

A maid arrived from Andrews' dressing room. She announced that her boss sends her regrets. "Miss Andrews is resting in her dressing room," the maid said, "and cannot be disturbed."

***

At The Castle, while Rock was away filming *Darling Lili* in Europe, Jack Coates had to remain behind. Rock would send for him as soon as he finished his spring classes in Arizona. With Rock gone, he often flew into Los Angeles from Phoenix to live at The Castle and to play with their dogs.

Rock's two closest friends, George Nader and Mark Miller, were impressed with the handsome young man, realizing why Rock found him so desirable.

In the meanwhile, from his location in Europe, Rock had developed yet another friendship—this one with Tom Clark, a publicist at MGM who was soon involved in the administrative details at The Castle, even during Rock's absences. Clark would remain involved, both at The Castle and in Rock's life, for two decades.

"George, Mark, and Rock were a trio when I arrived on the scene," Clark said. "The trio soon became a quartet."

The arrival of Coates would enlarge that foursome into a quintet.

All four of the older men found Coates "a bundle of energy and a joy to be around." He had invented a machine of perpetual motion," Miller said. Nader chimed in: "Jack smoked pot, always wore jeans or else swimming trunks, and ate no meat. I dubbed him 'Carrot Stick' because he always seemed to have a carrot stick in his mouth. Mark called him Bugs Bunny. God, did that kid like carrots."

"I kept Jack entertained while Rock was on location," Clark said. "I even taught him how to play bridge, although he didn't like sitting for a long time, and was always jumping up and down."

Coates had already completed his freshman and sophomore years at his university in Phoenix. Rock wanted him to transfer to UCLA so that he could live full time at The Castle, but Coates didn't want to lose credits, so he and

Tom Clark was not Rock's handsomest, sexiest, or most exciting lover, but he was the most enduring.

505

Rock devised a plan.

Coates would stay on at Arizona State until he graduated, and commute between Phoenix and Los Angeles, with Rock delivering him to and from the airport. He arranged his schedule so that he never had any classes on Friday. That meant that he could fly to Los Angeles on Thursday evening, not returning until early Monday morning. In essence, Coates became a kept boy, running up a big airfare bill.

When Rock and Coates wanted to attend some event, they never arrived together. "That way, I'll keep my secret that I'm really a dirty old man lusting after a young college kid," he said, jokingly.

On many evenings, Coates and Rock preferred quiet evenings together at The Castle with their dogs, listening to records or screening old movies. Whenever they went in and out of The Castle, the dogs followed them. The animals had such names as "Wee Wee" or "Nick the Dumb."

"Jack became Rock's young husband," Clark said. "He did more than lie around the pool all day. He was a good carpenter and was always remodeling something. On some Saturday mornings, he and Rock shopped for architectural features to add to the mansion. One time, they bought these *faux* Greek columns that had adorned the entrance to a First National Bank. Weekends meant barbecues. All of us, including Jack, tried to keep Rock from the grill. He always cooked steaks until they turned to charcoal."

Clark claimed that he never heard Coates and Rock argue. "The only time Rock bitched was when he criticized Jack for not delivering the load at 5PM that he expected. Jack reminded him that he'd already blasted off at 2PM, and again at 3:30PM, and that he was running a bit low in the sperm department."

"By midnight, I'll be back in operation," he promised. "In the meantime, give me a break. I'm only a man."

In 1968, as soon as Coates finished his spring term, he flew to Paris to join Rock.

It was the first trip to Europe for Coates, and he was so excited that he could not sleep a wink on the plane to France. When he stepped off the plane in Paris, Rock was waiting for him at the airport with a chauffeured limousine parked outside the gates.

After checking into the Crillon, their first stop was at the Café Foch where Rock fed his lover wild raspberries from the lush fields of the Île de France, served with heavy cream from the contented cows of Normandy.

"What's the first thing you want to do in Paris?" Rock asked.

"The Eiffel Tower!"

Off they went to the Eiffel Tower.

Rock had been given a special pass to the private observation deck of the tower, which was reserved for VIPs. Coates recalled the experience as "one of the most memorable of my life. All of Paris was spread before me. I was standing beside the most beautiful, most desirable man on Planet Earth, the likes of which had not been seen since God created Adam. I was in love."

Then it was off to Nôtre Dame, where Coates stood in awe of the majesty of the fabled cathedral. Twilight found them wandering along the Left Bank of the Seine along with other lovers, both foreign and domestic.

"Rock was more open, less guarded in Paris," Coates said. "It seemed a more tolerant city than Los Angeles, where we had to lead a secret life. Rock was more 'himself' here."

"On our last night in Paris, we went to this club where we heard the great Edith Piaf," Coates said. "I loved her unique sound. After the show, we had a drink with her—a virtual monument of Paris in her own right. I was awed by her presence. But Rock on the way back to the Crillon shocked the hell out of me."

"Once in Hollywood, maybe more than once, I fucked Edith Piaf," Rock claimed.

Coates flew to Dublin with Rock. "It was so unlike Paris. It rained every day when Blake Edwards wanted sunshine for his film. On days when he wanted it rainy and cloudy, the sun came out bright over the Emerald Isle."

"Rock was growing more and more impatient," Coates said. "He was irritable, feuding with both his leading lady and his director. He made a point of not letting me meet them. I felt not so much like a lover, but like a secret trick."

"The good news is that I got to spend many loving hours with him, as we set out to explore the countryside of Ireland. Along the way, we came upon this lovely old farmstead with a FOR SALE sign in front. A real estate agent showed us around. It needed a lot of work. Its owners had gone to America. We fell in love with the place."

"In a Dublin pub that night, Rock and I dreamed of our future together. He told me that in a few years, he would no longer be in demand as a leading man, and that we might retire here on a little farm and spend the rest of our lives together. A man can dream, can't he?"

"Rock and I hit the pubs of Dublin at night," Coates said. "Not the fancy ones in the upmarket hotels, but the local taverns, where the working class hung out. If anyone recognized Rock, no one came up to us or asked for an autograph the way they do in America. Rock loved joining in the sing-alongs. His favorite was 'When Irish Eyes Are Smiling.'"

"In Ireland, I want to be plain ol' Roy Fitzgerald again," he said. "You know I never formally changed my name to Rock Hudson. Hudson's not so bad, but I hated the first name, 'Rock.' You and I can grow a garden. Our dogs can roam about freely. We'll raise some livestock, not to eat. We'll make Bessie our pet, and have fun feeding Billy the Goat. We'll gather up stones—stones, that is, not rocks—from the nearby fields and make a wall. I've always wanted to live on a farm with an old stone wall."

Rock was still in Ireland when Coates had to tell him goodbye before his return to Phoenix.

"Every day without you will be a day in hell," Rock said as a farewell at the airport. "I'd kiss you but I'm sure it would appear on the frontpage of some rag. Until we meet again, kid, keep it zipped up."

"Take your own advice," Coates warned him. "Some of these Irish lads are pretty god damn good looking."

***

Weeks after his return from Europe shooting *Darling Lili,* Rock hosted a private party at The Castle for close friends, each of whom was gay. During the course of the evening, and after a few drinks, he described an incident that had happened on the outskirts of Paris while filming.

For a location site, Blake Edwards was granted permission by the Duke of Windsor to film some scenes on the grounds of his château where he lived in exile with his Duchess, the American, Wallis Simpson. The address was 4, route du Champ d'Entraînement, within the Bois de Boulogne, close to the Parisian suburb of Neuilly-sur-Seine.

Having relinquished the throne of England in 1936 "for the woman I love," Edward VIII (his title before his demotion to "Duke of Windsor") had been offered the use of the elegant, 19th-century mansion for a nominal rent by the City of Paris. It was here, in 1952, that he established residency, remaining there until the end of this life. *[The Duke and Duchess both died in the house, in 1972 and 1986 respectively.]* The name of the edifice, at his request, was changed from *Château Le Bois* to *Villa Windsor.]*

Built in the 1860s by members of the Renault dynasty and surrounded by large, tree-filled gardens, the mansion was a graceful building with fifteen rooms. The property had been sequestered by the City of Paris after World War II and for a while had been occupied by Charles de Gaulle.

[After the death of the Duchess, Mohamed Al-Fayed, the London-based Egyptian businessman and the owner of Harrod's, leased the villa, spending 30 million francs on its renovations. Ironically, his son Dodi, with Diana, Princess of Wales, visited the villa for thirty minutes on the day of their deaths in 1997.]

In a memoir, Tom Clark wrote, "Rock told us the Duke doddered out and was friendly with everyone and enjoyed looking through the camera to see what the shoot would look like." After the end of the day's filming, the Duke and Duchess invited the cast in for cocktails.

Clark discreetly omitted the next incident, which Rock relayed to his amused friends.

"Rock needed to take a leak," Clark said. "After putting up with Julie Andrews and Blake Edwards all day, he'd had more than one drink and needed to go to the toilet."

As he rose to his feet and looked around for the loo, the Duke, who had been eyeing him all evening, sensed what was needed.

"I thought he'd summon a servant to direct me, but the Duke himself led the way," Rock said. "I glanced back at the Duchess. I had yet to be presented to her. Her eagle eye was trained on both her husband and me. She was chatting away with Edwards, but seemed to know every move going on around her."

"I thanked the Duke when he showed me the door to the downstairs bathroom," Rock said. "I was surprised—but maybe not that surprised—when he followed me in. I guess even the former rulers of an empire on which the sun never sets had to heed the call of nature on occasion. There was only one toilet. Since he was a royal, and royals have their privileges, I stood aside and beckoned him to go forth. I'd never seen a king take a piss before. He hesitated and went and stood beside a vanity cabinet about four feet to the right of the stool. He reached in and removed a comb, and began running it through his hair. "

"I felt awkward, but couldn't stand there and piss in my pants, so I stood at the toilet and whipped out Jumbo, taking a horse piss, a golden yellow stream."

Later, I heard many stories, some of which were published in books, that he was a closeted gay, and his bitch Duchess a secret lesbian—a lavender marriage of sorts. But I didn't know that at the time of my exhibition."

"Then a strange thing happened," Rock said. "It was obvious to me that the Duke was mesmerized by my dick. I knew he wanted it but didn't dare make the first move. I al-

The Duchess of Windsor cast her hawkeye on her husband, the Duke, as he led Rock to their ground-floor bathroom, where the pair of them were gone "much too long."

most felt sorry for him. He might have been a king, but probably had few chances to satisfy his secret desires."

"Impulsively," as Rock relayed to Clark and others, "I willed myself to have an erection, since I knew the Duke wanted to see it. He stared in amazement at it. I was right proud of it myself. He didn't touch it, but I knew he wanted it. Finally, both of us realized it was time to ring down the curtain and return to the party before the Duchess sent a search party."

"Thank you, Your Royal Highness," Rock said, as the Duke headed for the door.

"Thank you," the Duke answered.

"He seemed nervous," Rock recalled. "I think he feared we'd lingered too long in the can."

Back in the exquisitely decorated, antique-filled parlor, Edwards summoned Rock over to introduce him to the Duchess. She didn't wait to hear his name and eyed him skeptically. "What is it you do for the company, young man?" she asked.

"I'm sorry, Your Majesty, I thought you knew. I'm the chauffeur of Julie Andrews."

As Rock related the incident, he said, "She knew god damn well who I was. Many articles had been written about what an avid movie fan she was. She even had all the fan magazines shipped every month to her from Hollywood. Her pretense in not knowing me was just her way of insulting me. She obviously knew that the Duke enjoyed checking me out instead of dealing with her stale ol' thing."

***

Rock had been introduced to John Wayne at either a party or a premiere in Hollywood, but he had never talked privately with the Duke, as he was called. Rock was therefore surprised when the director, Andrew V. McLaglen, phoned and wanted to cast him immediately in a Western for 20th Century Fox, *The Undefeated* (1969).

Rock later learned why the proceedings were so rushed. James Arness had been offered the role, but dropped out at the last minute. Shooting was to begin the following week in Ciudad de Durango, Mexico, a ten-hour (550 mile) drive northwest of Mexico City.

In 1980, author Michael Munn interviewed Rock about working with Wayne. "I was grateful to the Duke because my movie career was going down the toilet at that time. Then I got this call. Andy McLaglen asked me, 'Are you up to making a Western?' I wanted to fall to the ground and give praise, but I didn't want to appear desperate. I told him I'd be happy to join cast and crew in Durango, but I'd have to get some practice getting on and off a horse. I was more used to getting on and off Doris Day. That sounds terrible, but you know what I mean. I said I'd do it."

Rock later admitted, "*The Undefeated* was crap, but I had a great time doing it. It came out just after Wayne's *True Grit* (also 1969), and that made a lot of people go see it. John Wayne was a legend, and I was on the screen with him. He saved my career back when no other filmmaker wanted me."

The screenplay by James Lee Barrett was rushed to Rock at The Castle, and he studied it carefully over the course of the weekend. He'd have to say goodbye once again to Jack Coates, because he didn't dare take him on location because of Wayne's widely publicized homophobia.

On his first day on the set, Rock talked with McLaglen, finding him, a Londoner, an odd choice to direct an American Western. He was the son of the British actor, Victor McLaglen, the pug-ugly brutish character star, a hell-raising ruffian who had won an Oscar for *The Informer* in 1935.

John Ford had designated McLaglen as the assistant director on the 1952 set of *The Quiet Man*, starring John Wayne and Maureen O'Hara. According to McLaglen, "I'm the best director for Duke. No one admires him more than I do. He respects me, and I respect him. A lot of directors are afraid to say 'boo' to him. Not me. I tell it like it is. I've halted many a shoot and yelled at him. 'Your gut looks too bulky. Go put on your corset, darling.'"

The director told Rock that Wayne was waiting to meet and talk with him before they were needed on the set. Rock was apprehensive *en route* to his dressing room, since it was well known that Wayne detested gay men, referring to them as "fairies." He was also known for his right-wing politics. In 1968, George Wallace, the ultra-conservative former governor of Alabama, had asked him to run on his presidential ticket as his Veep. Wayne turned him down, saying, "I

Upper photo: Two opposing sides in the Civil War in *The Undefeated:* Rock Hudson (left) and John Wayne.

Below: In the Civil War, the characters portrayed by Wayne and Rock were on opposing sides. Later, they were forced to bond against a common enemy in Mexico.

have no interest in going into politics."

Wayne had once said, "With a face like Rock Hudson's, I could have become an even bigger star than I am. Too bad those looks had to be wasted on a queer."

"I was shocked when I came into his dressing room," Rock said. "He was sitting in front of his dressing room mirror applying a natural lipstick. Not only that, but he was wearing a corset to hold in his paunch. We chatted pleasantly, and then he got up and put on his pants and slipped into his high heels." Rock was referring to the lifts that Wayne always wore to make himself look taller on the screen.

Wayne invited Rock to share an early morning "bolt of lightning" before they discussed the script. As the men sipped their bourbon, they discussed their various roles. Rock's part—that of an ex-Confederate colonel, James Langdon—had been loosely based on the escapades of a Confederate general, J.O. Shelby, who escaped to Mexico after the defeat of the South in the Civil War. There, the real-life general (as well as the character portrayed by Rock) planned to join the forces of the Hapsburg emperor, Maximilian, leader of the French invasion of Mexico.

Langdon (Rock) has returned to his family homestead in the South, finding relatives dead and carpetbaggers about to seize his property. Reacting to its reduced circumstances and his new realities, he burns his house to the ground as a means of saving it from larcenous northerners who demand it for almost no money at all. Setting out in hopes of building a new life, Rock, as Langdon, leads a coven of embittered and displaced ex-Confederates south into Mexico.

In contrast, Wayne was cast as an ex-Union officer, Col. John Henry Thomas, who's driving a herd of 3,000 horses across the Rio Grande with the intention of selling them in Durango. Although they begin their relationship as natural enemies of war, Langdon and Thomas eventually bond as they have to battle bandits, double-crosses, and Mexican revolutionaries.

On the first day of the shoot, "The Duke pissed me off," Rock said. Wayne started micro-managing Rock's first scene, telling him that he should have turned his head in a certain direction, that he didn't shoot his gun correctly, and that he didn't make the right moves.

Rock mulled it over that night in his hotel room, deciding he'd pull the same trick on Wayne the next morning. After the Duke's first scene, Rock approached him. "You should have turned your head like this." Then he demonstrated the movement that Duke, in his opinion, should have made.

"After that, Wayne and I became friends," Rock said. "He knew I was on to him and could stand up to him like Monty Clift did during the filming of *Red River* (1948), when Wayne tried to boss him around."

Rock recalled that Wayne was in pain during part of the production, "but he carried bravely on. In one scene, he'd fallen and broken two ribs. In yet another, he tore a ligament in his shoulder and couldn't use one arm."

His wife, Pilar Palette, arrived in Ciudad Durango and told everyone how much she hated the town. She also reported that because of its high elevation, Wayne was forced, on occasion, to breathe through an oxygen mask.

Privately, Wayne confided to Rock that he no longer slept with his wife, and that he was confounded by her conversion to Christian Science. "I don't go in for all this religious cult shit."

Wayne recalled that he came to respect Rock during the shoot. "He was a true professional, always on time, always knowing his lines. Rock is the kind of guy you want to have your back if you get into trouble. Damn, how could a guy like that be queer?"

In 1974, the author, Michael Munn, interviewed Wayne. In reference to Rock Hudson, he said, "Who in hell cares if he's a queer? The man plays a great game of chess, and we had many a game in Durango. And what a good-looking man. I admit, I couldn't understand how a guy with those looks and that build and that manly could be a homosexual, but it never bothered me. Life's too short. He wasn't like some of his type who go around complaining, 'Poor me, I'm discriminated against.' He just got on with his life in private, and I never cared to know about it."

In September of 1974, Rock learned that he was being considered for the title role in *Rooster Cogburn* (1975) a Hal Wallis Western co-starring Katharine Hepburn, aged 67 at the time. (Rock was 49.) That didn't work out, and the role was eventually assigned to Wayne, and well it should, as he was reprising his star performance in the hit movie *True Grit* (1969), and because he was the same age as Hepburn, also born in 1907.

Rock was later asked if he was flattered at even being considered for such a challenging Western.

"I might have been at first," Rock answered. "Then I heard that other actors were considered as well: Clint Eastwood, Paul Newman, Gene Hackman, George C. Scott, Steve McQueen, Marlon Brando, Anthony Quinn, Burt Lancaster, Richard Burton, Charles Bronson, Lee Marvin, Gregory Peck, Kirk Douglas, Charlton Heston, and Robert Mitchum."

***

Rock was back at The Castle in the tumultuous year of 1968, living with Jack Coates and their beloved dogs, whom "we spoiled shamelessly" (Rock's words). Outside their gates, a social and political revolution was raging across America.

"Rock was not politically motivated, and, unlike Jane Fonda and other stars, he preferred to sit out the revolution," Coates said. He watched events unfold on television until he grew bored, calling the revolution "crap."

"What are all these shitheads rioting about?" he angrily asked. He was not sympathetic to the protests over the Vietnam War, any more than he would understand the burgeoning gay rights movement of a decade later. Typical of many men of his generation, he still maintained that "homosexuality was something you did in the dark, never flaunting it in the face of the breeders."

Instead of hearing about the latest demonstration on TV, Rock usually preferred to sneak into his den and watch an old movie on his home screen. One of his alltime favorites was *San Francisco* (1939), starring Clark Gable and Spencer Tracy. He was always amused, time after time, by the clips of Jeanette MacDonald standing in the earthquake-shaken ruins of her beloved city, belting out a rousing rendition of the title song, "San Francisco."

1968 would be defined by assassinations, race riots, anti-war protests, the liberalization of drugs, free love, and the counterculture rise of the hippies.

On April 4 of that year, Martin Luther King, Jr., delivered his most famous speech, proclaiming, "I've been to the Mountain," shortly before he was gunned down. Almost immediately, rioting broke out in some 100 cities.

That seminal year witnessed epic breakthroughs in popular culture, medical advancements, the widespread proliferation of the nuclear bomb, and noteworthy artistic achievements in films, painting, and music.

The first Big Mac went on sale at MacDonald's for 49 cents. In France, 800,000 teachers, workers, and students declared a general strike. In Washington, the Civil Rights Act was passed. In South Africa, Dr. Christiaan Barnard performed the first successful heart transplant.

President Lyndon Johnson announced he would not seek re-election. At the Democratic convention in Chicago, protesters disrupted the city as the Vice President, Hubert Humphrey, was nominated to run for president on the Democratic ticket. That paved the way for Richard Nixon's rise to the presidency, his long-cherished dream.

Also in 1968, a reign of terror enveloped California as "the Zodiac killer" went on a murdering rampage. In Greece, the most famous woman in the world, a presidential widow, Jacqueline Kennedy, married shipping magnate Aristotle Onassis. The Beatles on Apple Records recorded "Hey, Jude," and the musical *Hair*, featuring nudity and recreational drugs, opened in London.

Movie screens in 1968 showed Anne Bancroft seducing Dustin Hoffman in *The Graduate;* Spencer Tracy, Katharine Hepburn, and Sidney Poitier in *Guess Who's Coming to Dinner?;* and *Bonnie and Clyde,* starring Warren Beatty and Faye Dunaway going on a gun-slinging rampage and robbing banks.

What was the highlight of 1968 for Rock?

***

In the late spring of 1968, Rock decided to throw a lavish party for his friend, Carol Burnett. He'd been her close pal ever since he'd appeared with her on *The Carol Burnett Show* in 1966. Both stars had a whimsical sense of fun and immediately bonded together as soulmates.

In was understood that on Burnett's show, as a satire, they'd react against each other in a mock Western, a joint appearance that marked his singing and dancing debut on television. *[Rock had already danced on the big screen. In a feature film,* Has Anybody Seen My Gal? *(1952), he had danced the Charleston with Piper Laurie. In addition, he fancied himself somewhat as a singer. In 1959, he had recorded and released as part of a record album, nationwide, two songs ("Pillow Talk" and "Roly Poly") from his movie with Doris Day.]*

Rock recalled the disaster of what unfolded that night on Burnett's show: "The cameras were rolling in front of a live audience, and the director gave me my cue. I froze. I was disgraced. The director hollered to the crew to hold the tape and start all over again, and the audience burst into hysterical laughter. My friendship with Carol survived that debut in her show," he said.

He and Jack Coates drew up the guest list for Burnett's party. Rock had decided to invite some one hundred VIPs, including some of the biggest names in Hollywood, stars of stage, screen, and television. He never kept a definitive list of the guests who attended, and years later, he couldn't recall everybody who came. A few of the invited stars were out of town, either in New York or else on location shooting a movie.

Because of the shifting romantic liaisons in Hollywood, Rock also could not remember just who showed up with whom.

He and Coates spent a month getting ready for their gala. Coates supervised carpenters as they constructed a platform over the large swimming pool, laying a parquet floor for dancing to the music of a live band.

515

Then, from Tijuana, Rock imported mariachi singers to stroll about the grounds, out of earshot from the other musicians. In the living room, musical instruments were positioned near the grand piano, with the understanding that some of his spectacularly talented guests, especially Judy Garland and Frank Sinatra, might spontaneously perform.

Chains and garlands of fresh flowers were wrapped around the building's Grecian columns, and five valets were hired to park the elegant cars and chauffeured limousines that deposited their passengers at his door. Coates positioned himself near the building's entrance to supervise the arrival of the glitterati, "more stars than there were in heaven," he later said.

Unlike her usual custom of arriving late, Tallulah Bankhead was among the first to barge into the entry hall. Her surprising escort was Sammy Davis, Jr., As she later whispered to Rock, "This Alabama belle crossed the color line when I went down on Hattie McDaniel. Yes, Mammy herself in *Gone With the Wind.*"

On October 8, 1959, Rock and Tallulah had co-hosted the television broadcast of *The Big Party.* Davis, one of the acts for that event, had stolen the show, singing and dancing. Esther Williams, swimming star of many Golden Age movies, had also been a guest on that long-ago program, and she, too, attended Rock's gala.

Jack Benny was invited. Rock had first met him in 1954 when he'd appeared on *The Jack Benny Show.* As Rock remembered it, "Benny was a closeted gay, and at my party, he spent most of the night chasing after poor Jack."

A year later, Rock had appeared with Lucille Ball and Desi Arnaz on *I Love Lucy.* As the evening wore on at Rock's party, Lucille made a confession to him: "I once caught Cesar Romero going down on Desi."

Also invited were Connie Stevens, Michelle Lee, and Bobby Van, who had starred with Rock on *The Kraft Music Hall* in September of 1967.

Many of Rock's co-stars over the years also received invitations. Both George Peppard and Hugh O'Brian arrived, as Rock remembered the good time he'd had in and out of bed with each of them.

His "dear, dear friend," Doris Day, came to Rock's gala on the arm of Tony Randall, who had co-starred with them in a trio of films beginning with *Pillow Talk* (1959).

Of course, not all of his previous co-stars were invited. He went out of his way not to include Blake Edwards and Julie Andrews.

Yvonne De Carlo, who had made movies with Rock in his early days, showed up "with some Mexican stud." A spectacular entrance was made by the overdressed Gabor sisters, Eva and Zsa Zsa.

A parade of his former stars filed in, including James Stewart and his wife; Shelley Winters and Christopher Jones ("looking hotter and better each year," according to Rock's appraisal), and Evelyn Keyes, Scarlett O'Hara's younger sister from *Gone With the Wind.*

John Wayne, Rock's recent co-star in *The Undefeated*, came in with some young woman, not his wife. During a interlude in the garden, he confessed to Rock, "At first when I got your invite, I thought I might not show up. I thought it might be one of those fag parties. But I see you've got some ladies here...well, not ladies, exactly. Let's call them women of dubious repute."

At that point, Joan Crawford walked over to kiss Wayne on the mouth. They'd had an affair in 1942 when they'd co-starred together in *Reunion in France,* Crawford's character helping him escape from the Gestapo. She waxed hot and hot about the Duke, having snubbed him at previous parties.

When Carol Burnett was delivered this copy of *People* magazine, she said, "In Rock's long career, he never appeared with such a beautiful leading lady till I came along. Move over, Liz Taylor!"

Jane Wyman, Rock's co-star in *Magnificent Obsession* and *All That Heaven Allows,* arrived like a dignified matron. She had seemingly forgiven Rock for seducing her husband, bandleader Fred Karger.

All big Hollywood parties brought together stars and players who would rather not encounter each other. Such was the case with Wyman. Rock guided her into another part of The Castle to escape from his friends, Ronald and Nancy Reagan. Rock whispered to Tallulah, "I hope Ronnie has put out the torch he carried for Jane all these years."

Laden with diamonds, Elizabeth Taylor made a regal entrance on the arm of one of her most enduring friends, Roddy McDowall. She grandly kissed Rock, but warned, "We must not get carried away, dear, as I don't want to ruin my makeup." She went on to say, "Let's make another god damn movie together." He promised he would, and he'd eventually keep that vow.

Against his better judgment, he had invited Jennifer Jones, his co-star in the ill-fated *A Farewell to Arms.* He expressed his sympathy for the loss of her husband, producer David O. Selznick, who had died in 1965.

Anthony Perkins, with whom Rock had had a fling, came to the party with a dashingly handsome young man whom he introduced as Kerry X.

Lebre. "That's the first time I ever heard a name like that," Rock said to the young man.

LeBre handed Rock a manila folder, whispering to him, "Please stash these somewhere. They're for your private viewing."

Rock thanked him and immediately went to his den, concealing the envelope in one of the drawers of his desk. As he did, he noticed that XXX was written on its back.

Bea Arthur and Elaine Stritch arrived separately. Tallulah often remained by Rock's side, functioning almost like a co-host. "I see you invited the lesbian contingent," she whispered to him, perhaps a bit too loudly.

Of course, as would be expected, his trio of best friends—Tom Clark, George Nader, and Mark Miller—arrived together. "You'll probably invite us over tomorrow night for the leftovers from Chasen's?" Nader hinted.

In honor of their collaboration together on *The Last Sunset*, Kirk Douglas and Dorothy Malone were among Rock's honored guests.

Rock had previously introduced Coates to Paul Newman and his wife, Joanne Woodward. At the party, Newman came up to him: "You and Rock sure live in grand style, kid," he said.

Rex Harrison was an unexpected guest. Tallulah rushed to kiss the British star. "Why *dah-ling*, do they call you Sexy Rexy? You can't prove it by me...or can you?"

Coates got to meet one of his screen idols, Steve McQueen. Debbie Reynolds came in and later assured Coates, "My dating of Rock was just for the publicity. Nothing happened."

Dean Martin showed up and immediately wanted to know, "Where's the bar?" He and Rock would in the future co-star together in a Western.

Sandra Dee looked like she was already drunk before she arrived at the party. Rock had not seen her since they had co-starred with Bobby Darin in *Come September.*

Arriving next, James Garner talked to Rock about working with Doris in *Move Over, Darling* in 1963. Doris rushed over to kiss Garner and then planted a kiss on Rock's lips, too. "My two favorite leading men," she proclaimed.

A friend of both Carol Burnett and Rock, Jim Nabors, came alone. He and Rock had bonded on many an occasion as friends, never lovers. But in a few months, they would be the victims of a scandal that harmed both of them.

Janet Leigh was there, and was seen talking to Tony Curtis, her former husband and Rock's former lover. TV host Steve Allen, with his wife, Jayne Meadows, chatted with Rock, inviting him onto his show. "Television still scares me to death," Rock confessed.

Jane Fonda ("Hanoi Jane" as she was called at the time), came in accompanied by two famous men—her father, Henry Fonda, and her husband, Roger Vadim, the French director.

Vadim told Rock that he was leaving a copy of a novel by Francis Pollini, called *Pretty Maids All in a Row*. "I'm thinking of making it into a movie. A real offbeat role for you. You'd be great in it."

Hearing a pitch for a movie role was familiar turf to Rock, and he didn't expect anything to come from it.

Robert Mitchum ended up on Rock's guest list, and would also play a role in his future. In Rock's last featured motion picture, made shortly before his death, he and Mitchum would be co-stars.

A drunken Peter Lawford came in with Sal Mineo, his lover. As Lawford later whispered to Rock, "Let's face it. You and I both knew Sal as David knew Bathsheba."

Waiting until nearly all the guests had arrived, Barbra Streisand, the diva, glided in as the other guests flocked around her. But her entrance was upstaged by an even more glittering pair of royals, Grace Kelly and Prince Rainier of Monaco. Virtually all conversations died when they were announced.

Tallulah whispered to Rock, "*Dah-ling,* what a surprise. Surely you can't top the entrances of those two princesses, Grace and Barbra, with that Prince of something-or-other."

"But I can, *dah-ling,*" Rock said.

He led her into the foyer where the singer Andy Williams was followed close behind by Robert F. Kennedy, who was in California campaigning for the presidency of the United States during the 1968 Democratic primary.

Tallulah rushed to his side and kissed him. "*Dah-ling,* I just adored your bother, and you have my entire support."

Rock shook RFK's hand and also pledged his support, even though he'd never voted in an election in his life.

It seemed that everybody at the party wanted to meet Kennedy. The royal couple of Monaco was almost ignored as RFK immediately emerged as the man of the hour. All the guests except John Wayne predicted that he would beat Eugene McCarthy in the Democratic Primary election, and then go on to challenge Republican contender Richard

Robert Kennedy's last visit to a private home was at Rock Hudson's Castle.

Nixon in November.

The saddest part of the evening for Rock involved having to say good-bye to Tallulah. Obviously in poor health, she kissed him rather tenderly. "This will probably be my last public appearance," she lamented. "These tired old bones have been hauled from coast to coast, but now they're giving out on me."

It was farewell. He cried when he heard she'd died on December 12, 1968, and he and Coates that night once again watched her gothic camp horror flick, *Die, Die, My Darling* (1965), her last picture.

Dawn broke over The Castle as the last guest left. Rock, Coates, and Joy, his housekeeper, surveyed the wreckage. "It was one hell of an evening," Joy said. "I'm gonna hit the sack. I'll deal with the ruins of Pompeii *mañana.*"

Rock's gala lives on today in legend. It became known as "The Last Great Hollywood Party."

***

In the wake of Rock's gala, a disaster occurred to one of his guests that would alter the course of American history. Coates and Rock were staying up late watching TV when the program was interrupted by breaking news over NBC.

Their former guest, Andy Williams, had been at the side of Robert F. Kennedy when he delivered his victory speech after the results of the California Democratic Primary were revealed. The night was June 5, 1968, and the setting was the Ambassador Hotel in Los Angeles.

Making his way through the crowd during an exit through the kitchen, he confronted a crazed Jordanian immigrant, Sirhan Sirhan, who shot the senator.

The night that had begun in triumph degenerated into tragedy as hopes for his survival eroded.

At the funeral, Williams sang "Battle Hymn of the Republic."

"It was a sad, sad day for all of us," Rock said. "A horrible end to a horrible decade."

In a few months, he'd face a new decade. The 1970s, that would bring changes to his life that he could hardly have imagined.

Rock Seduces the Former Queen of Iran, Gets Cast as a Serial Killer, & "Marries" Jim Nabors

Dramas at The Castle: Rock Asks His Boyfriend, "Where Has Love Gone?"

Hailed by the underground press as "the gay wedding of the century," Rock Hudson (left) was rumored to have married his friend, comedian Jim Nabors. Invitations were sent out as a practical joke, but hundreds of people believed the union was real. It was even reported in the press.

Rock escaped relatively unscathed, but the career of Jim Nabors was seriously damaged.

After the box office flop, *Darling Lili,* Rock knew he needed a strong action and adventure film to save his faltering movie career. He'd had some success in military roles before, most recently in *Ice Station Zebra.*

A son of Chicago, director Phil Karlson presented Rock with what the actor thought might be an ideal role for him. *Hornets' Nest* was an Italian-American war film to be shot on location in Northern Italy for a 1970 release by United Artists.

In a nutshell, it would cast Rock as Captain Turner, the American leader of a small group of paratroopers ordered into Northern Italy in 1944. He becomes the sole survivor and must recruit a "Baby Brigade" of young Italian boys, ages 7 to 14, to finish his mission of blowing up a strategic Nazi-controlled dam before the American advance into the region.

When he was told that Sophia Loren, the sex bombshell and the leading Italian actress of the day, would be cast opposite him, Rock signed on the dotted line with producer Stanley S. Canter.

Shooting in Italy meant a reunion with his longtime lover, Massimo. At first, when he was told that Massimo would be working outside the country, Rock invited Jack Coates to fly to Italy with him. But later, when Massimo's plans changed, Rock was told that the Italian actor would be in Rome waiting for him. With a certain embarrassment, he made up some excuse and disinvited Coates.

Before filming began, Karlson phoned Rock to tell him that at the last minute, Loren had dropped out. His leading lady would now be Sylva Koscina, a beautiful actress and model born in Dalmatia, in the Kingdom of Yugoslavia (now Croatia).

In the 1950s, Rock had been a devoted fan of all those Steve Reeves muscle movies, a triumph of pecs over talent. Reeves had been Mr. Pacific, Mr. America, Mr. World, and Mr. Universe before becoming a movie star. Before that, he'd been a male hustler servicing such clients as director George Cukor. Rock never missed one of his movies. He had first seen Koscina play the *Bride of Hercules* oppo-site Reeves in 1958.

A decade later, Koscina had de-scended on Hollywood, but didn't quite make it with American audiences, in spite of the fact she'd been cast in 1968 opposite Paul Newman in *The Secret War of Harry Frigg* and with Kirk Douglas in *A Lovely Way to Die*.

Upon Rock's arrival in Rome, Mas-simo, "looking tanned and gorgeous and blonder than ever," was waiting at the airport for a big embrace. A taxi took them to the Grand Hotel, where they were booked into their familiar suite.

As Rock later recalled to friends, "We spent the next two days making love and wandering the Via Veneto. But that old spark just wasn't there like it was when love was new. My heart now centered for the most part around my college student, Jack Coates. Massimo himself seemed to have two or three lovers on the string."

"My time in Italy marked the end of my long love affair with Massimo," Rock claimed. "When I packed to leave and on our last night together, we both knew it was over. We didn't have to speak about it. Both of us just knew. At the airport, I got a final embrace from him. It had been grand, except for a few betrayals, mostly on my part, along the way."

During the filming of *Hornets' Nest*, Rock worked smoothly with Karlson. He is known to Marilyn Monroe biographers for helming her in her first film, *Ladies of the Chorus* (1948), for Columbia. It was at this time that she'd had an affair with the recently divorced Ronald Reagan.

Karlson had directed Elvis Presley in *Kid Galahad* (1962), and the doomed Sharon Tate in *The Wrecking Crew* (1969). Tate was later murdered by members of the crazed Charles Manson gang.

The screenwriter of *Hornets' Nest* was the prolific S.S. Schweitzer, who wrote teleplays for TV series that ranged from *Tarzan* to *The Dirty Dozen*. He had extensive talks with Rock about a possible switchover into a renewed second career performing in a TV series of his own.

When Rock met the sultry beauty, Koscina was in the final months of her marriage to Raimondo Castelli, a small-time producer linked to Minerva Films. Her career was given a boost when she was photographed barebreasted for the Italian edition of *Playboy*. Movie posters always featured her ample bosom.

She said that as a child growing up in Yugoslavia, she could relate to movies and "became emotionally involved very easily. I saw people dying and dead during the war."

A year before signing for her role in *Hornets' Nest*, she had appeared in a state-sponsored film—the most expensive in Yugoslav history— about World War II, *The Battle of Neretva* (1969).

Dino Risi, who had directed Koscina in other films, said, "Sylva had the typical melancholy of the Slavs. I never managed to tie the actress and the woman into a sin-

Rock goes guerrilla, sabotaging Nazis in a *Hornets' Nest* of hand-to-hand fighting during World War II.

gle person. She was always falling in love with the wrong man."

Such was the case with Rock when she became his co-star. She was enthralled by his beauty and physicality. For the first time, he was wearing a mustache, which would become one of his trademarks in films of the 1970s and on television. She confided to Karlson, "I keep sending out the signals, but they are not being received by him."

"That's because you have the wrong equipment," he answered.

She was shocked to learn that he was a homosexual. "I find that so hard to believe. He's so macho!"

She confided to Rock that she'd married Castelli in Mexico, only to create a scandal when she learned, after the wedding, that she'd suddenly became a bigamist. He'd never divorced his former wife.

[Koscina died early, at the age of 61, of breast cancer in Rome.]

Although *Hornets' Nest*—in theory, at least—was set in Northern Italy in 1944, critics noted that it contained "1960s military battle uniforms, attitudes, and hairstyles." The plot centered around a dangerous mission to blow up a dam protected by Nazi soldiers staging their last stand in Italy. The Allies had already taken over the South, including Sicily and Rome, and were moving troops north.

In *Hornets' Nest*, Rock survives a Nazi ambush to lead the "Baby Brigade," a group of ragtail Italian boys, ages 7 to 14, intent on revenge against the Nazis for having killed their parents.

Rock and his U.S. paratroopers slip into Nazi-controlled territory to blow up "the Dam of the North," a strategic outpost they wanted in ruins before the advance of the U.S. Fifth Army. But the *Wehrmacht* learned of their intended sabotage and were waiting for them. All of the American paratroopers are shot and killed. Rock, as Captain Turner, is knocked unconscious and thought to be dead as the Nazis hastily retreat.

He is picked up by a ragtag group of local youths, who

In a torrid scene, Rock rapes his leading lady, Sylva Koscina. Allegedly, during some raunchy dialogue with her director, she complained, "I'm sorry it was only a simulated rape—not the real thing!"

want revenge on the Germans who commandeered their village and killed their parents. The leader of the boys is Aldo (Mark Colleano), who witnessed the execution of his parents. Aldo and his gang rescue Turner by slipping him away from a Nazi ambush. Aware that he desperately needs medical attention, Aldo devises a plan to kidnap a German doctor, Bianca Freedling (Koscina). They keep her captive while she nurses Turner (Rock) back to health.

When he recovers, Turner trains Aldo and his boys in the use of military weapons and tactics, using them to help him destroy the dam and complete his mission.

"I found myself playing the leader of the Italian *Dead End Kids* and training them as saboteurs," Rock said.

When the film was released, Rock's dream of "a big comeback picture" was crushed. The war movie was not well received, either by critics or by the public. *Time* magazine wrote, "It's a weird little war movie full of bizarre energy and merciless violence, a kind of *Dirty Dozen Reach Puberty* story."

Mostly, the depiction of young boys learning violent death techniques, and the portrayal of a sexual assault by the unruly gang on Koscina's German nurse, was interpreted with indignation and horror.

Koscina claimed, "The movie shows how war destroys mentally as well as physically. We are all destroyed, myself, Rock, and the children."

Rock later called *Hornets' Nest* "a dirty picture. I use four-letter words, beat up and rape my co-star, and generally behave like a World War II soldier should not. I'll say this for the picture: Sensationalism isn't just dragged in for the purpose of competing with the flood of stag movies being released to art houses. Given the set of circumstances Captain Turner has to cope with, the man I play is not out of character. And that's no cop-out."

[Rock was not always clear in his articulation.]

After the wrap of *Hornets' Nest,* and a forever farewell to Massimo, Rock departed for a seven-day handshake tour of U.S. combat bases in war-torn Vietnam, cheering up battle-weary G.I.s, most of whom lamented that they didn't have Americans backing them for their sacrifices in war. Many soldiers attacked the protests back home. Rock's jaunt to Southeast Asia had been organized by the USO and the Hollywood Overseas Committee.

After his tour, Rock flew back to Los Angeles, wanting to be back at The Castle in time for Christmas, the most important event of the year for him.

***

525

When Rock returned to The Castle, Jack Coates was still in Phoenix, and would remain there for two more weeks because of complications with his schooling. He assured Rock, however, that he'd be home to celebrate Christmas with him.

Rock experienced a pang of loneliness, although George Nader assured him, "You're just horny."

He confessed that there had been very few opportunities for "sexual expression" during his time in Vietnam. "Over there, some military personnel was with me all the time. You might call me the Virgin Queen."

Facing a long, lonely weekend alone, Rock remembered the strikingly handsome young man, Kerry X. LeBre, who had attended his Hollywood party with his date, Anthony Perkins.

Secretly, Kerry had given him a manila envelope marked XXX, cautioning him that its contents were private, for his eyes only. Rock retrieved the glossy 8" x 10" black and white photos inside, pronouncing them "among the sexiest nudes I've ever seen. Kerry sure knows every provocative sexual position in which to arrange himself. In a sultan's all-male harem, he would have been the favorite."

Who was Kerry X. LeBre? He's referred to in some sources as "a hustler" with an A-list clientele.

In 1969, when director John Schlesinger shot scenes for his controversial *Midnight Cowboy*, he cast Kerry as an extra. In the background, wearing a pair of tight blue jeans, cowboy boots, and a hat, he was portrayed as one of the male prostitutes working Times Square in the 60s. Regrettably for Kerry, except for a brief glimpse, his scene ended up on the cutting room floor. According to Schlesinger, "I didn't want him giving Jon Voight, cast as the hustler Joe Buck, too much competition."

[To the surprise of many, both the public and critics, Midnight Cowboy, *based on a novel by James Leo Herlihy, was voted Best Picture of the Year by the Academy Awards Committee. Both Jon Voight, as well as Dustin Hoffman, playing a street punk, "Ratzo," vied for the Best Actor Oscar, losing to John Wayne for* True Grit.*]*

Around the time *Midnight Cowboy* was shot (1968-69) Kerry was advertising his services in *The Village Voice* under the category MALE MODEL.

Ever since he'd seen Anthony Perkins perform as Norman Bates in Alfred Hitchcock's thriller, *Psycho* (1960), Kerry had harbored a crush on Perkins. Finally, he got to meet him at a party in Greenwich Village. "I told him I was a struggling actor," Kerry claimed. "In fact, during all my time with Tony, I never revealed to him what my profession really was."

Tantalized by Kerry's pictures, Rock phoned him and invited him to The Castle for the weekend.

Although he'd previously arranged to fly to Las Vegas with a john that Saturday morning, the hustler eagerly accepted. Preferring to be with Rock instead, he canceled his earlier gig.

Rock would later gush to Nader that "sex with that stud was great, and I should know. Picasso is a great painter, El Cordobés the world's greatest bullfighter, Nureyev unequaled as a ballet dancer, and Kerry X. LeBre is an artist of the boudoir."

Rock soon learned that Kerry's sexual adventure with him that weekend was very different from his earlier liaisons with Perkins.

Details about his involvement with Perkins were revealed in Charles Winecoff's splendid biography, *Split Image: The Life Anthony Perkins.* LeBre recalled his experiences with Perkins to Winecoff: "Tony was very happy to meet me, very eager to go to bed with me. He was very loving, very touchy, very physical, very affectionate. But he made me nervous as hell. He was very intimidating just because of his size and who he was."

LeBre admitted that he was so awed to be in bed with THE Anthony Perkins that he could not deliver his usual sexual performance. That same thing had happened many times with sexual partners associated with Rock.

Reportedly, Kerry had gone to bed with other movie stars, including such clients as Clifton Webb and Cary Grant. But they were not the object of his hero worship like Perkins. "I'd met many movie stars but not *him,*" Kerry said. "We were naked in bed, he was very eager, but I just couldn't do anything. Neither pot nor poppers were of any help."

Gradually, Kerry got to know Perkins, after talks on the phone and an occasional dinner. More relaxed around him, Kerry finally delivered the performance that Perkins had so eagerly sought.

Kerry learned that Perkins was seeing a psychiatrist two or three times a week, confessing, "I want to go straight."

"I thought how hopeless a quest that was," Kerry said. "He told me this shit as he was kneeling at my feet, massaging my thighs and calves."

Kerry, however, right from the first, had no such problem with Rock. "He was an even bigger star than Tony, but I was not in awe of him like I was of Norman Bates."

"Rock didn't have any of Tony's hangups, and he loved the fun he had being gay," Kerry claimed. "Rock and I had a lot of great times together. Nude swims at midnight. Chases through the garden where I always lost… deliberately. Ten AM romps in bed to take care of our libidos. Rock wanted his pleasure, and he took it. He also gave…he was a great lover. No rough stuff…well, maybe a spanking when I'd been bad."

"Tony was lonely, but I felt that Rock would never lack for a companion, even when he was old and gray. He was that charming."

Kerry found out that neither Rock nor Perkins knew at the time that he was having an affair with the other. Kerry was also entertaining two other clients: Halston and Paul Lynde. "Rock detested Lynde ever since they'd worked together on *Send Me No Flowers* with Doris Day."

Whereas Perkins and Kerry grew closer and closer, his involvement with Rock became "a sometimes thing."

"Tony and I got too close," Kerry claimed. "I learned some of his darkest secrets. He wanted me to wear a mask and slip into his bedroom through a window and viciously rape him. Painfully, I learned that during the sex act, he wanted there to be some form of blood, perhaps from a human bite…Maybe he was Norman Bates of The Bates Hotel after all."

***

Finally, in time for Christmas, Jack Coates flew back to Los Angeles from Phoenix. Rock was waiting at the airport to take him back to The Castle.

"When I get you inside the door, kid, I'm taking you right to my bedroom to make up for lost time. I'm famished for your love."

Coates would remember that Christmas of 1969 with Rock as a joyous time. They went to the L.A. railroad yards, where the workers were unloading Christmas trees, felled in Oregon, from boxcars. Rock wanted the most perfect tree and found it in the form of a fourteen-foot Scottish pine.

"That night Jack and I decorated the pine like a Christmas tree—what else?" Rock said.

The next day at the Flower Market in Los Angeles, "Rock became like a wild man, buying up everything: ruby red poinsettias, pine boughs, mistletoe, lots of flowers, and Yuletide wreaths for the doors."

As was his custom, Rock spent a lot of money that Christmas, buying gifts for friends who dropped in during the holiday season. "To my surprise, Rock liked to give but not to receive," Coates said. "During January, he gave away most of the gifts his friends had presented to him."

Coates had once mentioned that he thought he'd like to learn to ski in Sun Valley if Rock would take him there. Under the Christmas tree that year was everything he'd need to become a skier, including goggles, ski boots, and poles—"even granddaddy red flannel long johns to protect those precious jewels of yours from the cold winter winds," Rock said.

His housekeeper, Joy, prepared plenty of food to have on hand for casual drop-ins, and she always served a feast for Christmas dinner, purchasing four freshly killed turkeys. To please Rock, she bought extra gizzards, his favorite part of the bird. As a turkey vendor told her, "Rock Hudson is the only movie star in Hollywood who eats gizzards."

She lavishly set two or three tables, bringing out the lace tablecloths, crystal ware, and the silver goblets.

"Rock himself insisted on making the eggnog, and he used so much rum it would put four hard-drinking sailors under the table," Joy said.

"Rock's new friend, Jim Nabors, drove up in an apple red Rolls Royce convertible, arriving at Rock's doorstep wearing a Blackglama mink. "Is that you, Jim, underneath all that fur, or is it Zsa Zsa?" Rock asked.

On Christmas Eve, Rock said, "Judy Garland used to be here to sing for us. But not this Christmas."

His dear friend had died in London in June of 1969. She would always ask Rock, "Do I have to sing that god damn 'Over the Rainbow' again?"

Tom Clark recalled that during Garland's final months in Hollywood, she often phoned Rock at 3AM.

"OK, Judy, it's OK," Rock would say. "What's the problem?"

"Oh, nothing," she'd answer in a slurry voice. "No problem. It's just that I don't know who I am, where I am, or what I am."

"Sometimes, if he sensed she was truly desperate and in danger of harming herself, Rock would drive to her home, hold her in his arms, and even sleep with her until she finally drifted off," Clark said.

"I left only after I felt her demons were gone," Rock said.

He always stayed in contact with two of his dearest friends, Doris Day and Elizabeth Taylor. "Doris was usually okay," he said, "but Elizabeth was always in some sort of romantic horror, often with a different man. Her life with Burton had been a rocky road."

That Christmas, Rock broke off his friendship with Ross Hunter, who had produced some of his biggest hits, including *Magnificent Obsession*, *All That Heaven Allows*, and *Pillow Talk*.

Years later, Clark, who had once worked for Hunter, asked him what the feud was about. Hunter answered, "I think we got into an argument about some film I had produced. Things were said, and he got pissed off."

Clark asked Rock, "What things?"

"Damn, I can't remember," Rock said.

Eventually, Clark managed to "mend

Jim Nabors may have appeared on TV in drab military outfits, but he always arrived at The Castle lavishly dressed, including in some cases in a Blackgama mink.

fences" and bring these adversaries together for a reunion dinner. "The feud that had lasted a dozen years was over, and they became friends once again until the end of Rock's life."

Clark wrote that Rock was the kind of person who valued old friends, even if he had time to see them only at Christmastime. Such was the case with Julie Adams, his frequent co-star at Universal during their days together at that studio. "Julie and Rock would get together and reminisce about old times. They laughed a lot, especially about Tony Curtis, their object of mutual derision."

Rock's friendship with Curtis had long ago soured, even though he'd invited him to The Castle for his gala party. At Universal, Curtis and Rock competed for the same roles.

Even though Curtis denied it, "Tony did a lot to sabotage me," Rock told Clark. "He was a born conniver. I was not. When we were up for the same picture, he'd go to the director and tell him that I was a trouble maker on the set and that I often showed up drunk, holding up production. Lies, all lies."

In spite of that, Rock usually won the role anyway, beating out Curtis. "All that backstabbing backfired," Rock said.

Long after both men lost their contracts at Universal, their paths would sometimes cross at a Hollywood party. "I saw them together on a few occasions," Clark said. "They each forced a smile and a handshake, perhaps a few exchanges, before they moved on to the other side of the room."

Rock once told Clark, "There's another reason Tony is jealous of me. I've got the big dick, and he's known as Princess Tiny Meat."

For the first time in his movie career, Rock began showing up at Hollywood parties with Coates as his date. "No more arm candy for me. No more Phyllis Gates. If somebody doesn't like it, he can shove it where the sun don't shine."

***

Rock had long envied the singing career of Tab Hunter, whom he'd once considered as a film rival during the era when the handsome, blonde-haired actor had been big box office at Warners. "Tab Hunter was never the king of the box office," Rock said. "More like a prince. But he sure in hell did better than me as a singer. I was jealous of the fucker."

Hunter's recording of "Young Love" sold more than two million copies. Even though he didn't want to admit it, Rock found Hunter's "Red Sails in the Sunset" one of his favorites, and he played it over and over at The Castle.

When Rock had met Hunter at a party, the actor told him, "I'm making more dough as a pop singer than I am under Jack Warner's damn contract."

In February of 1957, Rock was astounded to read in *Variety* that Hunter's "Young Love" had knocked out Elvis Presley's "Too Much" to top *Billboard's* list of hits.

For three years, Rock had studied singing with a vocal coach. One night, during a rendezvous with his longtime friend, Tallulah Bankhead, she had assured him that, "You are every bit as good as Perry Como."

Rod McKuen had heard Rock sing in several of his films, including *Pillow Talk.* When interviewed by *The Daily Express,* McKuen, the poet, singer, songwriter, and actor, claimed: "I'm impressed with the singing of Rock Hudson, and predict that, like Tab Hunter, he can shoot to the top of *Billboard's* charts. He has a unique sound and an octave-and-a-half vocal range."

Likewise, Rock liked the works of McKuen, the poet-*chansonnier* of Oakland, California, who was eight years younger than he was. McKuen had sold more than 100 million records worldwide, his books of poetry an astounding 60 million copies.

Escaping sexual abuse at home from his stepfather, McKuen had run away when he was only eleven years old, surviving as best he could. In time, he became a railroad worker, ranch hand, lumberjack, rodeo cowboy, radio DJ, and stuntman in Hollywood.

For a time, he worked as a newspaper columnist and a propaganda scriptwriter during the Korean War. In the taverns of San Francisco at the time of the Beat Generation, McKuen had read his poems in appearances with Allen Ginsberg and Jack Kerouac.

Rock had been enchanted with McKuen's adaptations of the songs of Jacques Brel, the Belgian singer and songwriter. Rock's favorite of Brel's output was "If You Go Away," a recording of which he played countless times at The Castle.

When Rock heard that McKuen wanted him to record an album of his songs, he was thrilled and even honored. To do so, he knew he'd be following in the footsteps of other singers who had recorded McKuen songs, no-

Poet and singer Rod McKuen wanted Rock to record an album of his songs. He later said, "Rock and I didn't exactly challenge the success of *The Sound of Music.*"

tably Perry Como, the singer to whom Bankhead had compared him. Other artists recording Brel included Barbra Streisand, Petula Clark, Johnny Cash, Andy Williams, Dusty Springfield, Johnny Mathis, Al Hirt, Frank Sinatra, and the Viennese chanteuse, Greta Keller.

Of them all, Rock favored Sinatra's recording of "Love's Been Good to Me."

Before working with McKuen, Rock assumed he was gay. Publicly, the artist had refused to identify himself as gay, straight, or bisexual. "I can't imagine choosing one sex over the other. That's just too limiting. I can honestly say I have no preference."

McKuen spent Rock's third night in London with him in his suite at the Savoy. As Rock would later tell Tom Clark, a former publicist for McKuen, "Rod is definitely gay, based on my experience with him that night. He does everything, and he's also blonde, which I prefer, although in his case, I think it's bleached."

Rock had never read any poetry until he discovered the poems of McKuen, who remained a popular favorite, although dismissed by the critics. *Newsweek* magazine labeled him "The King of Kitsch." The U.S. Poet Laureate, Karl Shapiro, claimed, "It is irrelevant to speak of McKuen as a poet."

Julia Keller, the Pulitzer Prize-winning culture critic, denounced McKuen as a "gooey schmaltz that wouldn't pass muster in a freshman creative writing class."

Rock and McKuen came together during a low point in Rock's career and a high point in McKuen's. The singer had been nominated for an Oscar for his recording of "Jean," from the 1969 movie, *The Prime of Miss Jean Brodie.*

Through Clark, a meeting was arranged between McKuen and Rock. The singer pitched the idea of Rock recording an album of his songs for his record company, Stanyon, based in London. McKuen promised that the finished product would be distributed across the world, especially in America, by Warner Brothers.

During his first meeting with McKuen, Rock was hesitant, but McKuen assured him that with all the modern recording devices, "We can even make Marjorie Main sound like Maria Callas."

McKuen won him over, and in February of 1970, Rock flew to London to record an entire album of fourteen songs, each written by McKuen. They were lushly orchestrated by Arthur Greenslade, but without vocal background singers like Elvis sometimes included.

"The first thing I learned was how different recording a song was from a movie," Rock said. "In films, you can say something with your eyes. In a record, you've got to convey whatever in hell you're trying to do with your voice."

"It took me three twelve-hour days in the studio to get my throat to loosen up," Rock said. "I spent two weeks in the blasted studio—the British would say bloody—pouring out my heart in song."

His recording of McKuen compositions included "So Long, Stay Well"; "Lonesome Cities"; "Love's Been Good to Me" (competing with Sinatra); "I've Been to Town"; and "As I Love My Own."

Arriving in Los Angeles with the tapes, Rock played them over and over again to George Nader, Tom Clark, Mark Miller, and to Jack Coates when he wasn't in Phoenix.

"I feared Rock wasn't going to go over on records like Tab Hunter," Nader said. "But if I had told him that, it would have ended our friendship. He seemed to be counting on it and wondered if one singer had ever had eight or ten records on the Top Ten of *Billboard's* charts. He was predicting a big singing career for himself."

Clark later said, "Actually, the poor guy couldn't sing. He did have a nice voice—full, rich, resonant—but that's not all a singer needs. Rock had problems with such niceties as pitch and key, things like that. Still, it was an entirely acceptable album, and it might have some sales based on Rock's remaining star power, which seemed to be ebbing every day."

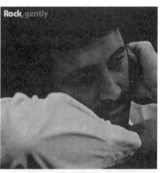

As it turned out, McKuen had misrepresented the Warner distribution deal. There was no deal. Rock's album, entitled *Rock, Gently,* got almost no distribution at all, and was merely listed in the Stanyon catalogue of records available through mail order. In the first month, there were only one hundred albums sold.

"The warehouse was full of them," Clark said. "Most of them were later destroyed. The few that have remained are collectors' items."

After the disappointing release, Rock was furious at McKuen, charging, "The shit betrayed me. Even if it had sold, I would have gotten only a penny or two per album."

He had a favorite record shop in Century City, where he purchased most of his vast collection of music. He went there and or-

Two different album covers were issued for Rock's recordings of Rod McKuen songs. But the album turned into a music publishing disaster.

dered copies of his album, learning that it was being hawked at only a dollar each. He also found out that McKuen and his staff had not sent any albums to any radio disk jockeys, as was the media and PR custom at the time.

Biographer Mark Bego summed up the dire situation. "The album, in a word, was a disaster. The songs are all so maudlin and depressing that Hudson sounds like a hound howling at the moon. If he had attempted some bawdy drinking songs like the one he sang in *All That Heaven Allows* in 1955, he might have pulled it off. But listening to this album is torture, especially Rock's rendition of 'Jean.' He should, however, be saluted for at least trying this project—even if the best thing about it was the album cover!"

There was a footnote to the disastrous Hudson/McKuen collaboration. During a party at Rock's home, where thirty or forty guests came and went, Joy summoned Clark to come to the back door to deal with an uninvited guest.

Dripping wet from a rainstorm, there stood McKuen, asking if he could come in. "I want to wish Rock a Merry Christmas," he said.

Clark thanked him and invited him to remain inside the kitchen while he went to tell Rock he was here.

On hearing the news, Rock headed for the kitchen, where he encountered McKuen. Four minutes later, Rock returned to hear Clark's question: "What happened?"

"He wished me a Merry Christmas, and I opened the back door for him, which was symbolic of what was to happen. 'Don't darken my door ever again,' I told him. 'You're not welcome. At least you had the good sense to use the back door.'"

***

The Paris-born director, Roger Vadim, was married, from 1952 to 1957, to the blonde-haired French goddess, Brigitte Bardot, celebrated for her breasts. Rock had avidly read about their rocky union in the tabloids. "One night with Bardot was worth a lifetime," Vadim confessed to Rock. "The problem is to make a woman know that she wants you."

Bardot gave her own view of her marriage. "If only Vadim had been jealous,

For reasons not known, some of the world's most beautiful women wanted to crawl into bed with French director Roger Vadim.

things might have worked out differently." She was speaking of her many infidelities, which had failed to arouse any emotional response from the director, who was involved in his own adulterous affairs.

Vadim was known for either seducing or marrying some of the world's most beautiful women. In his mid-30s, he had lived with the teenaged Catherine Deneuve, with whom she'd had a child, Christian Vadim, prior to his marriage to Jane Fonda.

Vadim had married Henry Fonda's daughter in January of 1965. At the time Rock worked with the French director, that marriage was falling apart. Vadim made it clear to the press, "There is no part in my new film for Miss Fonda. No part in my life for her, either."

Originally, MGM had acquired the rights to the 1968 novel, *Pretty Maids All in a Row*, written by Francis Pollini. The studio announced a movie would be made of this part comedy, part murder mystery, and that it would star football hero Joe Namath and Jane Fonda. That deal, however, fell through.

MGM then announced that *Pretty Maids All in a Row* would star Brigitte Bardot and Rock. The producer and screenwriter would be Gene Rodden-berry, best remembered for creating the original *Star Trek* TV series.

Pretty Maids All in a Row would join two other Vadim films known for their erotic overtones. His trilogy began with *And God Created Woman* (*Et Dieu... créa la femme*; 1956) with Bardot, followed in 1968 with *Barbarella* with Fonda. She played a 41st Century space adventuress. Barbarella has achieved cult status today largely because of her striptease performed as the credits rolled.

In his first meeting with Vadim, Rock told his friends, "Vadim has sex on the brain. He told me that he'd lost his virginity in a hayloft in Normandy in June of 1944."

"What Hemingway wrote about the sex act—'The earth moved under him'—literally came true for me during my session in that hayloft. I later found out why that barn shook. The Allies had launched their bombard-

Pretty Maids all in a row

Roger Vadim, the director who uncovered Brigitte Bardot, Catherine Deneuve and Jane Fonda, now brings you the American high school girl...and Rock Hudson.

535

ment of the Normandy coast to weaken Nazi positions before the world's greatest armada arrived to liberate France from the Nazis."

Two weeks before filming of *Pretty Maids* was scheduled to begin, Rock received his first disappointment: Bardot was out and would be replaced by Angie Dickinson, another beautiful woman, but this one an American born in the autumnal winds of North Dakota. She later moved with her family to sunny Burbank.

He'd seen Angie in *The Killers* in 1964, starring Ronald Reagan in a remake of the 1946 thriller based on a story by Ernest Hemingway. It was the future president's last motion picture and the only one in which he played a villain, slapping the hell out of Angie Dickinson.

As Vadim told Rock, "Angie has more sex appeal than anyone I've ever directed." It was a statement Rock found astounding in that Vadim had also helmed Bardot. At the time Rock met Angie, she was married to the songwriter and performer, Burt Bacharach.

Her reputation as a sex goddess had preceded her. She was said to have stretched her charms all the way to the White House, when she entertained President John F. Kennedy in one of the upstairs bedrooms while Jacqueline was away from Washington.

Other studs on her star list of seductions reportedly included Eddie Fisher, Richard Burton, Marlon Brando, William Shatner, Johnny Carson (a disaster), David Janssen, Dean Martin, and Frank Sinatra.

In 2017, the press reported that Dickinson, former star of the TV series *Police Woman* (1974-78), at the age of 84, was writing a tell-all memoir.

Vadim had cast Angie as Miss Betty Smith, a sexy substitute teacher at "Oceanfront High School." Her character seduces a sexually inexperienced student, portrayed by John David Carson, who was cast as Ponce de Leon Harper, a nerdy youth who is tormented at being surrounded by such pretty girls in high school. He was suffering from "a chronic priapic condition."

He's susceptible to the influence of his guidance counselor (Rock Hudson), who takes him under his wing. Rock arranges for him to sleep

Vadim's portrayal of lust, yearning, and sexual politics enraged the local school board. Depicted above is a horny student checking out teacher Dickinson's ass.

with the "sexpot teacher.'

Carson admits to the character played by Rock, in his capacity as his guidance counselor, that he's getting frequent "hard-ons" being around such beautiful girls.

Rock's friend and frequent co-star, Roddy McDowall, was cast in the unlikely role of the school principal.

Cast as Michael McGrew, nicknamed "Tiger," Rock played the high school's football coach and guidance counselor. He's also a psycho, seducing pretty maids all in a row and later murdering them to keep them quiet. The film was made at the height of America's sexual revolution, which had reached a crescendo at the time of the movie's release.

Telly Savalas played detective Sam Surcher, who suspects that Tiger is the killer, but cannot get enough evidence to prove it.

After meeting with Savalas, Rock gossiped about him to McDowall: "It seems that all you have to do to be a movie star these days is to have a deep, gravelly voice and a bald head. I found him to be a sexual braggart."

The novel on which the film, *Pretty Maids All in a Row*, was based was one of the few Rock had ever read. "When I put it down, I didn't believe that a shootable script could be made from all that trash. I changed my mind after reading Gene Roddenberry's excellent script."

"I was struck by the sheer brass of Tiger, my character. He is a kind of mastermind, manipulating everyone from students to the police. He's really an intriguing guy, a true schizoid behind a Mr. Nice Guy façade."

For the most part, he worked smoothly with Vadim until a big blow-up occurred one day on the set. Vadim demanded for one scene that Rock appear frontally nude.

"I adamantly refused," Rock claimed. "Not that I have anything to be ashamed of. I told Vadim that if he wanted to see my cock, I'd whip it out for him, or even let him suck it if that was his secret desire. But there was no way in hell that I planned to flash Jumbo to worldwide audiences."

The promise was solved in the scene when Rock appears to be nude, but he's naked only from the waist up.

"Nudity is okay in a movie when it's used in the context of a story," Rock said. "But it becomes offensive when it's exploited. Flashing my dick and big balls on the screen would have obviously been done for mere exploitation and would surely have generated headlines. Fans would flock to *Pretty Maids* just to get a look at what's swinging between my legs."

Vadim's first American film was shot largely at University High School in West Los Angeles. When the school board saw the film, they threatened to fire the school principal for allowing such a "disgraceful, sickening, and vulgar" movie to be made on campus.

In spite of its sexual allure, *Pretty Maids All in a Row* flopped at the box office. Rock admitted, "It was my worst film, and I've made a few."

However, director Quentin Tarantino selected *Pretty Maids* as one of his "Top Ten Greatest Films of All Time" for *Sight & Sound* magazine.

***

There was a footnote to Rock's having starred in Roger Vadim's *Pretty Maids All in a Row*. Perhaps it should be called an interlude.

Rock had agreed to meet Vadim in Paris in the elegant bar of the deluxe Plaza Athénée Hotel, ostensibly to discuss a publicity tour for their just-completed film. But the director had another reason: He was acquiescing to the stated wishes of Princess Soraya (*née* Soraya Esfandiary-Bakhtiari), the exiled former Queen of Iran, the second wife of Mohammad Reza Pahlavi, who sat on the Peacock Throne from 1941 to 1979 as the last Shah of Iran. Their marriage had been in effect from 1951-1958. He had divorced her because of her infertility, the result of an illness whose aftereffects prevented her from having a child.

Living outside of Iran, and against the Shah's wishes, Soraya aggressively pursued a film career. Vadim had had a brief fling with Her Royal Highness in Paris, and had remained friends of hers in its aftermath. She kept hoping that he would cast her in a picture. It was she who requested the rendezvous with Rock, telling Vadim, "This divine creature and I would look fabulous on the screen making love."

When Vadim alerted Rock that he'd be meeting her, he confessed, "I'll go through with it, but I'm intimidated. After all, she was the Queen of

Queen Soraya of Iran was regally photographed on the august occasion of her marriage to the ill-fated Shah of Iran in 1951. After she was dethroned, her scandalous lifestyle made tabloid headlines around the world. Rock played an interlude during her life in Paris.

538

Iran. I've met many a 'queen' in Los Angeles, but nothing like this. But now that she's a mere princess, I guess it's okay. After all, I've already hung out with another princess, Grace Kelly."

As an avid reader of the tabloids, Rock had long read about the exploits of Soraya. Her February 1951 marriage to the Shah had captured the imagination of the world. Gifts from everywhere were flown in, including a Russian mink coat and a desk set with black diamonds from Josef Stalin.

Apparently, the Shah and Soraya had had a genuine love affair, but, as the years went by, the marriage had disintegrated. He was under increased pressure to produce an heir, and she could not come through for him. With deep regret, he felt compelled to divorce her. Having been granted a substantial allowance, she went into exile.

Her exploits as a recently dethroned queen often caused scandals. Although news of many of her exploits was suppressed in Iran, she outraged many devout Muslims by being photographed in a white bikini, waterskiing off the coast of Miami.

From the moment Rock and Vadim walked into the bar of the Plaza Athénée to meet her, he found her warm, gracious, and friendly. She had a knack of putting men at ease in her august presence.

Until his own death, Rock always remembered her as "the princess with the saddest eyes I've ever seen." That did not distract from her almost fabled beauty. The following night, he would be photographed dancing with her in his strong arms.

At the time Rock met her, she was hailed not only as one of the most beautiful women in the world, but one of the most frequently photographed.

She often spoke in melodramatic terms, telling him, "I was named after the constellation of Seven Stars, the *Haft Peykar,* that's visible over the skies of Isfahan, the most beautiful city in Persia, the mecca of 1001 nights."

She even spoke candidly of her former marriage. "I was the Shah's second choice," she claimed. "At first, he seriously considered proposing to our mutual friend, Grace Kelly." Soraya had seen pictures of the Princess of Monaco photographed with Rock on the French Riviera.

Soraya admitted that "I always felt torn between the East and West." She'd been born to a Bakhtiary nobleman, the Iranian ambassador to West Germany, and his German wife, Eva Karl. She'd been educated in London and Switzerland, and "had a very Western outlook" (Rock's words).

Soraya spoke of her dream of a film career, admitting she had not gotten off to a good start. She had been cast in *I Tre Volti* (1965), an Italian film released in English as *Three Faces of a Woman.*

At that time, she'd become the lover of its ambitious young Italian director, Franco Indovina. Their affair was still going on when Rock met her, although he was away from her, in Rome a lot of the time. Indovina was soon to die (in 1972) in a plane crash.

Although Vadim did not want to direct such a movie, Soraya wanted to find another director, perhaps Dino de Laurentiis, to helm her in an epic based on the life of *Catherine the Great,* the Russian empress. She envisioned Rock in the male lead, that of the dashing chief of her imperial palace guardsmen.

"In those glamourous uniforms, with the gold braid, you'd be the most dashing male on the screens of the 1970s, with me as your Queen."

Rock was intrigued, Vadim less so. He soon left for another appointment, leaving Soraya alone with Rock. She had already planned his seduction. If she'd heard rumors of his homosexuality, it didn't matter. Grace Kelly had already informed her that Rock was a great lover.

She had reserved the royal suite for them at the Plaza Athénée, and she invited him upstairs for the weekend, beginning with a lavish dinner served by candlelight on the terrace of her suite.

He didn't check out until Monday morning, when he kissed her goodbye and promised to meet again. He then rushed out to a waiting taxi to take him to Orly Airport for his flight to Los Angeles.

He never saw her again. Nor did she ever star in a movie based on the life of Catherine the Great.

After the death of Indovina, Soraya began a series of affairs, some highly prominent as revealed by the scandal magazines, others under the radar.

She had a fling with the hell-raising Irish star, Richard Harris, the future King Arthur in *Camelot,* and with the Italian comic actor, Alberto Sordi. One of her more serious romances was with the Austrian actor, Maximilian Schell. ("We both had German roots," she explained.) That was followed with flings with the German millionaire playboy Gunter Sachs, the third husband of Brigitte Bardot.

Movie stars also came and went from her boudoir, notably Frank Sinatra. She succumbed to the charms of Kirk Douglas, who introduced her to his best friend, Burt Lancaster. In a surprise affair, she even ended up in the arms of TV's Wyatt Earp, Hugh O'Brian.

As Soraya grew older, when the movie stars faded away, she began a series of notorious one-night stands when she lived in Paris at 46 Avenue Montaigne (Paris 8e), across from the Plaza Athénée. She was frequently seen in the bar of that hotel, where she'd met Rock.

As she confessed, "As I got older, the men got younger until they disappeared from my life altogether, except for the gigolos." She also admitted, "I've seduced more false princes in the Jet Set than the real ones."

At the age of 69, Soraya died and was buried in Munich where her gravesite was desecrated with the letters "MISERABLE PARASITE." There were published reports that she was murdered, but they could not be confirmed.

***

Back installed in The Castle, Rock told his closest friends that he feared his love affair with Jack Coates was winding down. Coates was skipping some weekends and flying in less frequently from Phoenix, choosing to remain in place there. He seemed, to an increasing degree, to define it, not The Castle, as his home.

More and more, he did not want to be drawn into the in-fighting going on at The Castle, as one friend after another jockeyed for position as Rock's favorite. Coates found many of Rock's friends superficial, only hanging out with him because he was a bigtime star.

As their relationship wound down, and because of his status as a long-distance lover with many other commitments, Coates agreed to set Rock free to roam three or four nights a week as a sort of bachelor-at-large.

Tom Clark observed Rock up close whenever Coates was away in Arizona. "Most men, after they live through their salad days, start to turn down the sexual heat. Not so Rock. He could enter the room at a Hollywood party, and the sexual temperature rose. Often, guys crowded around him, hoping he would pick one of them to take home—often two."

"Rock confessed to me he had to have sex at least once a day," Clark claimed. "His exact words were, 'I can't live without it.' On days when he wasn't filming a picture, he often had sex two times a day, even three."

Clark stood by at many a party, watching Rock move in on tall, well-built, blonde-haired guys. He'd approach a possible conquest, ramp up the charm quotient, and say, 'Wanna have some fun tonight?'"

"He was rarely turned down," Clark said, "even if the guy was straight. Rock told me he had three priorities in life: Sex, career, friends, in that order. Where did Jack come in? A distant fourth."

At long last, in the summer of 1971, Coates finished his four undergraduate years, earning his bachelor's degree. He asked Rock to attend his graduation, but he bowed out, claiming he was too busy, even though he wasn't making a film at the time.

After his graduation, Coates moved into The Castle to live there full-time. "At least we'll save on airfares," Rock said. That was not exactly the enthusiastic response that Coates might have expected.

Clark claimed that Rock feared his loss of freedom and the restrictions that Coates' ongoing presence would place on his random sexual flings.

As the days went by, Coates seemed to resent more and more being the Prince Consort to the King of Hollywood. He didn't fit in with the gossipy gay friends Rock surrounded himself with in his living room at night or around the swimming pool. Rock's women friends, like Nancy Walker or Claire Trevor, seemed to regard him more or less like Rock's acolyte, although Elizabeth Taylor always treated him politely. She once told him, "Oh, men! They just come and go from one's life."

As the long hot summer of 1971 dragged on, Coates contemplated returning to Phoenix to study for a master's degree. "I don't want to spend the rest of my life being Rock's wife," he told Clark. "He expects me to be home at his beck and call, while he's free to wander around with his roving eye. Sometimes he comes home very late, making up some dumb excuse."

Rock convinced him not to go back to college, so he sat out the fall semester at The Castle. But by the time the holiday season arrived in December, he made up his mind that he was going to return to the university for a degree in anthropology. This time, Rock made no plea for him to stay.

Years later, Coates was said to have regretted his decision to break up with Rock. "I loved the guy, and I think that in his way he loved me. But I was very young and inexperienced in the ways of the world. At The Castle, I was thrown into the midst of ultra-sophisticated people. Some of Rock's crowd resented me and wanted to break up our relationship. I think they told lies about me to Rock. I did not play around, regardless of what anybody claimed."

"All in all, I found the intrigue and backstabbing at The Castle too brutal for my tender years."

Years later, Coates, in a dialogue with biographer Sara Davidson, compared life at The Castle to a chess game. "Rock was the King. After I left, Tom Clark was the Queen, and he had the most power of anyone else on the chess board. Mark and George were the Bishops. I was the Knight, and I would always do a jump straight for the throne if I needed to."

In November, Coates learned that he had been accepted into graduate school in Arizona for the term beginning in January.

At The Castle, he spent his final hours with Rock. "As Rock later told Clark, "I made love to that kid like I've never done before. I suddenly became aware that I was either losing him or had lost him. But I didn't plead with him to stay this time, realizing he had to write the story of his own life. There was this thing of age, too, creeping in. After all, I was born in 1925, Jack in 1944 when I was in the Navy in the Philippines."

Rock was misty-eyed as he drove Coates to the airport to catch the next plane to Phoenix. But he was told it was not the end of their relationship.

Coates promised he'd visit whenever he could, especially on holidays.

"After Jack left, Rock began a series of one-night stands, but he always booted any trick out when he heard Coates was on his way back from Arizona," Clark said. "When Jack arrived on the doorstep, Rock dropped everything and devoted all his attention to him."

In the great American Southwest, Coates was doing what many young men did in the post-hippie era of the late 60s and early 70s. He was on a quest "to find myself."

Rock had purchased a pickup truck for him. "I virtually lived in that truck, exploring every corner of not just Arizona but Texas and New Mexico, too. I even drove down to the tip of Baja California, in Mexico."

"I visited Indian reservations," Coates said, "and bought artifacts. I also went to centers of meditation."

Once, Rock was talked into joining Coates on a hiking trip. Rock flew to Santa Fe, where he met up with Coates. On their third day, the two of them set out hiking along the trails that riddled the Sangre de Cristo mountain range.

"On our last night, as we camped out," Rock later told Clark, "I was in a nostalgic mood, remembering all the good times Jack and I had had. An idea came that I might ignite the motor of the love machine that had brought us together."

"Was it my fault?" Rock asked Coates one moonlit night. "Could I have loved you more, understood you better? Why did it have to end?"

"You know in your heart that I was not meant for your world in Hollywood," Coates reportedly told him. "It's not my scene. I don't really want that kind of life—or the man I might have become had I stayed on at The Castle. I'm determined to find out what kind of man I really am. I'm on my search right now. When I'm an old man, dying in some trailer camp outside Tucson, I'll look back at my time with you. I'll remember that at one time, there was a Camelot—and he lived in a castle."

***

In September of 1971, *Modern Screen* published an article, in which Rock gave his view of marriage. "Yes, I think I'd like to marry again. Probably not to an actress or a career girl. Two loves pulling in different directions cannot help but put a strain on such bones. Hollywood is crowded with young, beautiful, available girls. I enjoy taking them out. Generally, I'm happy with my life as it is right now. But I could meet somebody today and get married tomorrow."

Debbie Reynolds, who had "dated" Rock, read the article. "He'll get married when pink pigs fly with chartreuse wings, and cockroaches become the preferred food for Texas cattlemen, not T-bone steaks. And I can sell you the Golden Gate Bridge in San Francisco at a real discount. Oh, Rock, talk to me, tell me all about it!"

Within two weeks of that publication, an urban legend was born about Rock's nuptials—not to a girl, but a marriage to Jim Nabors.

The gay actor and singer, Nabors had been friends with Rock for many years. He was always amused by this son of Sylacauga, Alabama. He liked to watch *The Andy Griffith Show*, in which Nabors was cast as Gomer Pyle, the addle-brained gas station attendant. It came as a surprise that Nabors could also sing romantic ballads, even nostalgic songs like "Back Home Again in Indiana."

Rock was especially delighted to watch any appearance of Nabors on *The Carol Burnett Show*. She told Rock, "Jim is my good luck charm."

Two weeks after the publication of the article in *Modern Screen*, a (dubious) legend was born. In Huntington Beach, "two vicious queens" (Rock's words) sent out some 500 invitations to the wedding of Jim Nabors, the bride, to Rock Hudson, the groom. *[Local wits immediately began referring to the "groom" as "Rock Pyle."]*

Some of the invitations were sent to people in the media. Both Rock and Nabors were closeted at the time, and many recipients, amazingly not hip, didn't realize that the invitation was bogus. Previously the two "queens" had sent out bogus invitations to attend the coronation of Queen Elizabeth in Huntington Beach. Hundreds of people across the country thought the Hudson/Nabors nuptials were genuine.

At the time that the rumor spread, Rock's friend was the star of *The Jim Nabors Hour,* a TV variety show broadcast on CBS from 1969 to 1971. After the spread of this fake scandal, Nabors' show was abruptly canceled.

One of the fan magazines accepted the story as a real event. Unaware that it was fake news, they ran an item about it, without ever actually naming either Rock or Nabors for fear of a libel suit. In Chicago, a DJ broadcast news about the wedding, without directly naming Rock and Nabors, but made it rather obvious, calling the newlyweds "a sort of Rock of Hollywood marrying just a plain guy sort of neighbors." It didn't take a genius to translate "neighbors" into "Nabors."

Another reporter commented on the widespread rumor like this: "The fraud proves the adage that no joke is so obvious that some dummies won't get it."

Both Rock and Nabors considered filing libel suits, although their lawyers warned that it might ruin their careers by fanning the rumor to an even wider audience. "The media would have a field day with a lawsuit like that," one attorney warned.

"It was like a bad dream," Nabors said. "No, a nightmare."

Rock told Hy Gardner, the entertainment reporter, "I first heard the rumor from a woman who had heard it from her hairdresser. Then, all of a sudden, I'm getting tons of letters about the stupid invitation. It was absolutely preposterous and ridiculous. The rumor reached titanic proportions even though it was absurd. There's really nothing I can say to refute it, in spite of my denial. From time to time, I heard that a marriage took place in Las Vegas. Others claimed it occurred at The Castle. The marriage actually was confined to the perverted brains of those queens, having a laugh at our expense. After that rumor became widespread, it broke up my friendship with Jim. We didn't dare be seen together again."

Rock stayed in hiding for ten days at The Castle. When he emerged from seclusion, he was besieged by reporters waiting outside his gates. He tried to handle the rumor by being flippant, announcing to the reporters that the wedding had been called off. "I've returned all the diamonds and rubies Nabors showered on me,"

Some people out to make a quick buck tried to peddle their accounts of the wedding to the sex-crazed tabloids, claiming to know what happened at the actual ceremony.

In several accounts, Carol Burnett was said to have been the matron of honor for Nabors, and George Nader was accused of being Rock's best man. The preacher who presided was identified as the minister of a gay church in San Francisco.

The victim of many a fake rumor herself, Elizabeth Taylor advised Rock to treat the rumors like a joke. "Tell the press that Jim as the bride wore virginal white, that Ronald Reagan was your best man, and that the pastor was Zsa Zsa Gabor."

"Hell, no!" Rock said.

There was a postscript—actually two postscripts. Nabors was seen less and less, reported to be living in relative seclusion on his macadamia nut farm on the Hawaiian island of Maui.

In 1982, three years before Rock's death, the *Harvard Lampoon,* in its parody of *Newsweek* magazine, reported that Nabors and Rock had divorced.

On February 15, 2013, when marriage became legal in Washington State, Nabors took Stan Cadawaller, his partner of 38 years, as his lawfully wedded husband during all those years gone by.

The legend of his marriage still lives on in some quarters, and so does

Nabors, at least as of this writing. The retired actor was reported to have said, "Living well is the best revenge. But poor Rock. Look what happened to him."

***

As Rock moved into the 1970s, major changes awaited him in the last complete decade of a life that had been a "wild roller-coaster ride" (his words). Big changes in his personal life and career were on the way.

They began after Jack Coates departed from The Castle, and Rock moved in a new man, a most unlikely choice for him.

As his movie stardom dwindled, and his position as the world's leading box office star was confined to Hollywood history, a career change was in the offing.

The change would make him a multi-millionaire and expose him to a far wider audience than that which had known him as a mere movie star.

Before surrendering to the new medium, he lamented, "That fucking oblong box is a monster that eats everything and everybody. It's called television, and it will become my burial ground."

Although he resisted appearing on it, it was "the little black box" that brought Rock his greatest audience and his biggest paychecks.

Chapter Eighteen

HOW THE LITTLE BLACK BOX (TV) RESCUED ROCK'S CAREER, INTRODUCED HIM TO MILLIONS OF NEW FANS, AND MADE HIM RICH

Musical Chairs:
Tom Clark, Rock's Best Friend and Sometimes Lover, Rules The Castle

The TV series, *McMillan and Wife*, brought Rock his widest audience and "a pot of gold" (his words), although he resented having to appear in the monthly detective episodes. His co-star was Susan St. James, who often appeared in love scenes with him and on the cover of *TV Guide*, wearing what passed for fashion in the 1970s.

At The Castle, Jack Coates was out the door and Tom Clark moved in. Rock had known him casually since 1964, and they had become friends, often playing bridge with two other men. Of all of Rock's lovers, Clark was the least likely choice. "He was not blonde, not muscular, not young (but eight years younger than Rock), and he had a bit of a tire," said George Nader. "He did meet Rock's criterion in that he had blue eyes."

547

Rock had known Clark, a former actor and MGM publicist, for many years before inviting him to move in. There was always some other lover who stood in the way of his getting involved with Rock.

Officially, Clark was introduced as Rock's publicist and personal manager, and that he was to some extent. But one night, Rock extended an invitation to him to share his bed, and that became a frequent occurrence.

According to Miller, "But if Rock met some hot little number that day, and invited him home, Tom was sent off to the guest room, although I suspected there were many three-ways with the trick of the night."

Born in Oklahoma City in 1933, Clark had worked for many years behind the scenes at MGM as a publicist. At the time that he moved in with Rock, he was employed by Rupert Allen, who ran a small PR firm representing Rock.

One night when Clark was away, Nader bluntly confronted Rock, "Tom's no beauty. Spill the beans…Why him?"

"His best asset is hidden," Rock confided. "He's got one of the biggest."

"I guess that makes up for a lot of defects," Nader said.

When Clark first arrived at The Castle to live with Rock, he found the place completely disorganized. "Rock had fan mail from as far back as 1962 in filing boxes in the garage—never answered. He had six or seven cars at one time. He'd run them until they ran out of gas and then he'd abandon a vehicle. "I got to go after the cars with a can of gas to get them running again. What's more, Rock had checks he hadn't cashed in eight months, and he never paid a bill on time."

Clark made a wise move in hiring Mark Miller as Rock's secretary for $100 a week. "Mark began to handle the mail and the phone calls," Nader said. "Rock rushed home every evening. He'd told Mark the only mail he wanted to see was from young men who had sent in nude pictures of themselves."

Nader said, "In time, Rock came to depend almost totally on Tom from the moment he woke up until he went to bed at night. If it were a chilly night in Los Angeles, Tom brought him a sweater, always in baby blue. He fussed over what Rock ate, making sure that chicken gizzards were always in the house. He sent out Rock's laundry, laid out his clothes if he were going out. He babied Rock, competing with Rock's mother, Kay Olsen, as he played the substitute mother role. And yes, lest I forget, when Rock was horny and there wasn't a trick around, Tom hopped into bed with Rock and took it like a man, even though he admitted to me that he found the assaults painful."

Slowly, but not that slowly, Clark took over Rock's life. "He had no trouble at all spending Rock's money, if only to buy things for himself," Miller claimed. "He also set about getting rid of Rock's pals, mostly actors from the 1950s he'd worked with—and seduced—guys who never made it. Many were from Henry Willson's stable who had weird names but no talent."

"These guys were out the door. However, Clark doted on Elizabeth Taylor, his favorite, even though her star had dimmed by the early 1970s. Claire Trevor, Nancy Walker, and her husband, Daniel Craig, were always welcome. Certainly Carol Burnett, too. He adored Carole.

One drunken night, Richard Burton arrived on Rock's doorstep looking for Elizabeth Taylor, but ended up in Rock's bed.

Doris Day was always invited but rarely showed up, if at all."

"One night a drunken Richard Burton arrived on the doorstep looking for Liz," Clark said. "He had risked his life driving to The Castle. He collapsed in our foyer. I helped Rock take him to the bedroom, where we stripped him down. As I was looking at this Welshman's uncut dick, Rock ordered me out of the room."

"As I was leaving, Rock was stripping down to join Burton. I don't know what happened after I shut the door. Burton didn't look like he was good for anything, but perhaps Rock figured on having a little fun. Anyway, Burton and Liz were virtually finished at that time."

"Rock told me that between lovers, Liz surrounded herself with gay men, platonic friends like Roddy McDowall," Clark said. "Women were too jealous of her to be her friend. With gay men, she could have a lot of laughs without some straight guy chomping down on her big breasts or porking her."

According to Nader, "Whereas Clark got rid of the B-list guests, certainly the C-list ones, the A-list crowd was more than welcome. Through their door walked William Holden and Stefanie Powers, Bette Davis, Danny Kaye with Laurence Olivier, George Cukor, Tony Martin and Cyd Charisse, Gene Kelly, Farley Granger, George Stevens dropped in one night, as did Liza Minnelli and Elaine Stritch. Claire Trevor was a regular. So was Nancy Walker and eventually, Martha Raye."

Natalie Wood showed on occasion, telling Clark, "When I worked in a movie with Rock, I was too young. Pass the word to him that I'm grown up and ready, willing, and able, if he wants to try a girl for a change."

"Ok, I'll pass that on," Clark said. "But I think he'd really prefer Robert

Wagner."

Miller noted that cocktail hour at The Castle used to begin at 5PM. "But it soon switched to 10AM at breakfast, when those guys downed three or four Bloody Marys, each. Even Rock's housekeeper, Joy, began to drink heavily. Finally, Tom had to fire her, and it wasn't until 1978 that Rock hired her replacement, a guy named James Wright."

At the age of forty-six, Rock had at least reached middle age. "I was no longer the good-looking mother-fucker I was in *Pillow Talk*," he lamented. "All of the great roles were going to a lot of new guys—not to me."

Every day he looked into the mirror and saw a loss of skin tone. Even though he knew that was from his heavy boozing, he could not give it up.

"Tom and I got wasted every night," he said.

The movie scripts Rock received, as he admitted, were getting worse and worse. "I wasn't exactly viewed as a romantic lead. Offers for TV jobs came in, but I turned them down. They kept coming."

Finally, he agreed to appear in a made-for-TV movie, which, if it went over, might become the basis for a TV series. "With trepidation, I took it."

"The teleplay was called *Once Upon a Dead Man,* and that's exactly what I felt like, going from looking gorgeous on the big screen to looking over the hill on a small box."

"On the big screen, an actor can make the slightest move and it'll register with the audience—the lifting of an eyebrow, the curl of a lip. But on that little box, you have to exaggerate everything—or no one will notice."

"Do you want to know why I turned to television?" he asked Nancy Walker, who would soon be playing his maid in a TV series. "Tom Clark told me that all my former fans were sitting home at night with their families watching TV—and not going to the movies to see Doris and me."

***

In spite of evidence to the contrary, Rock claimed, "I'm still a bigtime movie idol. A big guy, too, too big for a little black box. Besides, appearing on television is against my dignity."

NBC-TV made three offers for Rock to star in a projected series. The first offer of $50,000 per episode was rejected, as was the second offer of $100,000 per episode. When the third offer of $120,000 per episode came in, Rock signed. "I'd be an idiot to turn down money like that. No actor has ever been paid that much per episode."

The series projected was entitled *McMillan and Wife.* It revolved around a 40-ish sophisticated San Francisco police commissioner, Stuart McMillan, and Sally, his attractive, bright, affable, and a bit scatterbrained wife, who is about half his age.

Leonard B. Stern, the executive producer, director, and screenwriter, brought the script for the pilot to Rock at The Castle. He told Rock that it would be a 1970s version of the old Nick and Nora Charles comedy detective series of the 1930s, played by William Powell and Myrna Loy.

Stern had been married to Rock's former co-star, Julie Adams. At the time Rock met him, he was married to actress Gloria Strook who, by 1976, was working with Rock in the series that eventually evolved from *McMillan and Wife* to a series whose name was streamlined to *McMillan*.

"Leonard knew his way around a studio," Rock said. "This New Yorker wrote for such series as *Get Smart*, *The Honeymooners*, *The Phil Silvers Show*, *The Steve Allen Show*, and *The Jackie Gleason Show*. He even wrote *The Jazz Singer* in 1952, starring Danny Thomas and Peggy Lee."

Stern gave an unusual reason for casting Rock: "It was because of his size. In all those Warner Brothers films of the 1930s, all the tough guys— George Raft, Edward G. Robinson, James Cagney, even Humphrey Bogart—were midgets. But they wore hats, making themselves look taller. No man was wearing a hat in the 1970s. Rock was tall and didn't need a hat. To see him stand beside Nancy Walker was like looking at Mutt and Jeff."

After signing with Stern, Rock threw a party for his friends, with Tom Clark making all the arrangements. Instead of announcing his television contract, he said, "I'll soon be starring on illustrated radio."

"Okay, Buster," George Nader said after Rock's revelation. "And you attack me for selling out by doing television in the 1950s. Didn't you think I was terrific in *The Lady Wears a Star* (1953), and in *The Glass Web* (1956)?"

Stern told Rock that *McMillan and Wife* would be a 90-minute teleplay that would alternate monthly with two other hits, *Colombo*, starring Peter Falk, and *McCloud* with Dennis Weaver. Under Rock's contract, he would work three weeks a month with one week off to pursue other endeavors, even vacation or travel. He'd also have the summer off, and could make feature films if one were offered and if he could fit it into his busy schedule.

In an unusual offer, Stern gave Rock permission to select his leading lady. He'd drawn up a list of seven possible actresses for consideration. A dinner was arranged with each of them, and after a few nights, the choices narrowed down to three actresses: Diane Keaton, Jill Clayburgh, and Susan Saint James, the latter unknown to Rock at the time.

Keaton had made her screen debut in 1970, and within two years, she'd won her first major role, that of Kay Adams-Corleone in *The Godfather*. After much consideration and debate between Stern and Rock, she was turned down. Stern speculated that she was too talented as an actress, and Rock feared "she might steal my thunder."

Losing the role was good for Keaton's career. She soon became involved with director and co-star Woody Allen, beginning with *Play It Again Sam* in 1972. By 1977, she'd win a Best Actress Oscar for *Annie Hall.*

A New Yorker, Clayburgh had made her Broadway debut in 1968, but her greatest acclaim would come later in the 1970s, so it was just as well she wasn't tied down with some TV series. She was nominated for the Best Actress Oscar in 1979 for her role in *An Unmarried Woman.* That was followed with *Starting Over* in 1979, which won her another Best Actress Oscar nod.

Rock picked the relatively inexperienced Susan Saint James, who had grown up in Los Angeles. Politically, they were very different, he a conservative Republican, she a liberal Democrat. Stern figured she'd look fabulous dressed in the zany haywire fashions of the 1970s, an aesthetic left over from the "Flower Power" era.

She later was quoted as saying that she found Rock "very attractive and very sexy," even though she was married at the time.

"Rock is the cuddly type," she said. "As a girl, you'd want to sit in his lap. We were together some twelve hours a day. I spent more time with him than I did with my husband. You can't help but fall in love when you're working together so intimately, not only in bed together, but going in for some heavy kissing. We had a certain chemistry that sparked on the screen."

Of course, she hastened to add, "My love for Rock was platonic."

From the beginning, Saint James won over TV audiences who were drawn to her humor, cheerful personality, and good looks, as she played the wife of a police commissioner who fought crime almost as aggressively as he did.

The other regulars on the series included equine-faced John Schuck, cast as Sergeant Enright, the commissioner's loyal but somewhat inept assistant. Schuck's role was that of the overworked, underpaid, and undernourished aide.

Schuck had a footnote in Hollywood history, being the first actor to utter the word "fucking" in a feature film when he appeared in Robert Altman's M*A*S*H* in 1970. He also became known for his appearances on *Star Trek.*

When Rock was introduced to John Schuck, who played his police sidekick in *McMillan*, the actor told him, "I'm not grinning all the time. God made my mouth to look like I am."

As Police Chief Andy Yeakel, Jack Albertson became a regular on the series. He was a show-biz veteran, having performed in vaudeville as a singer and dancer before becoming an actor and comedian. He'd already experienced the highlight of his career before meeting Rock. In 1968, he'd won the Best Supporting Actor Oscar for *The Subject Was Roses*.

Nancy Walker was already a friend of Rock's, and he lobbied to get her cast as Mildred, his sarcastic, wise-cracking, hard-drinking maid. Born Anna Myrtle Swoyer in Philadelphia three years before Rock, Walker was a show business veteran trained by her vaudevillian parents. She was most often seen as a comedian on stage, screen, and television, but was also a film and TV director, notably on *The Mary Tyler Moore Show*.

In *McMillan and Wife*, Nancy Walker brought a comedic relief to the series as his boozing, wise-cracking maid. Between takes, she and Rock shared dirty jokes.

One of the most gay-friendly actresses Rock ever worked with, she became privy to his sexual secrets. He could go to her and discuss his latest crush on one of the blonde-haired extras or members of the crew.

The plot of *Once Upon a Dead Man,* which aired on September 17, 1971, centered on a charity auction whose most valuable artifact was the coffin of Caesarian, son of Julius Caesar and Cleopatra, which was plated in gold and studded with jewels.

Through an elaborate undercover scheme, the crooks, pretending to be workers for the city water department, manage to steal it. Of course, Mac and Sally will solve the crime, as they did in future installments of the series. Sally often got involved in solving a case, sometimes putting herself in harm's way, only to be rescued by Rock.

McMillan and Wife was originally broadcast on Wednesday night, but was later switched to Sunday evenings, where it picked up an even larger audience.

"I liked the idea of combining comedy and mystery," Rock said. "I'm on TV only once a month, and I didn't want to do a weekly show. The god damn pace was rough even for a monthly show. TV is tougher than all those B pictures I made when I was just a kid. As time went by, I grew tired of playing Mac over and over. Also, with the passage of time, the scripts, in my opinion, developed fatigue."

"In spite of my complaints, I had to admit that McMillan extended my film career for another fifteen years," he said.

He was delighted with the initial success of the TV series, although he came to call it "lamentable" after one season. "My character—and the co-stars, too—have the consistency of cigarette paper. A child can finger the suspect. Fools and drunks adore it."

The "drunks and fools" sent in some 3,000 fan letters a week. Rock was impressed, but told Walker, "I remember the day when I got 12,000 fan letters a week."

As a romantic leading man in the movies, Rock had initially attracted an audience mainly comprised of women and gay men. But the strong masculinity of the police commissioner drew thousands upon thousands of straight males who tuned in every month, not wanting to miss a single episode.

***

Inaugurated in 1971, Season One of *McMillan and Wife* included eight episodes, beginning with *Once Upon a Dead Man*. That was followed by *Murder by the Barrel,* the first episode that included Mildred the maid, as played by Nancy Walker.

Sally (Saint James) is directing movers into the new home she'll share with Mac. In one of the barrels they haul in, she discovers a corpse. She calls Mac (Rock) and Enright (Schuck) who arrive at the McMillans' new home.

The body has mysteriously disappeared, but Sally had not been delusional. There really had been a dead man, and Mac eventually "gets to the bottom of the barrel" to solve the mystery.

In Season One's Episode Three, *The Easy Sunday Murder Case,* Mac reluctantly attends Sunday lunch at the home of his mother-in-law (Linda Watkins). There, he gets a phone call from the police station. The beloved pet dog of a wealthy society matron has been kidnapped and is being held for ransom. Incidentally, her husband has also been kidnapped, although the wife seems more concerned about her dog.

The rich matron was played by June Havoc, the ice-cold blonde of those 1940s *films noirs,* and the sister of Gypsy Rose Lee, who at one time was America's most famous stripper.

Wally Cox had a role in the teleplay. Rock

The blonde of many a 1940s film noir, June Havoc (often confused with June Haver) was one of the many fading movie stars who appeared with Rock in his TV series.

554

found him fascinating and tried to uncover aspects of his private life, since the comedian had long been rumored to have been the lover of Marlon Brando.

Rock had watched Cox perform in the hit TV series, *Mister Peepers* (1952-55). When he wasn't filming, he told Rock about working on Marilyn Monroe's unfinished picture, *Something's Got to Give* in 1962. "I think she was murdered," he claimed.

Once, while Brando was high on pot, the writer/editor Beauregard Houston-Montgomery stated that the actor had confessed to him, "Wally was the love of my life."

Brando once told a journalist that, "If Wally Cox had been a woman, I would have married him, and we would have lived happily ever after."

In Season One's Episode Four, *Husbands, Wives, and Killers,* Mac and Sally are entrusted with protection of a valuable necklace until the banks open Monday morning. Its guest star was Tyne Daly. Daly's best work came later on TV when she played Detective Mary Beth Lacey in *Cagney & Lacey* (1982-88), for which she was a four-time Emmy Award winner.

All these episodes were aired in 1971. In January of 1972, *The Face of Murder* was broadcast with guest star Claude Akins. Rock had seen Akins in *From Here to Eternity* (1953) and again as the shipmate of Lee Marvin in *The Caine Mutiny* (1954). He is also remembered as Sheriff Lobo in the 1970s TV series *B.J. and the Bear.*

In *The Face of Murder,* Sally becomes prey to a jewel thief out to dispose of witnesses.

Season One's Episode Seven, *Till Death Do Us Part,* was perhaps the most dramatic of the series so far. Mac investigates a psychotic killer who targets socially prominent people. When he learns that Mac and Sally are on his trail, he targets them, too. After drugging them, he leaves them inside a hermetically sealed tent draped over their house by a pest-exterminating company. As poison gas is pumped in, Mac heroically struggles to save them, and succeeds! Mildred was missing from the episode.

Episode Eight, *An Elementary Case of Murder,* ended the series' first season. Its guest star, Barbara McNair, an old flame of Mac's, has placed a desperate phone call to him, inspiring jealousy in Sally. Her abusive manager and ex-boyfriend has been murdered, and she is the prime suspect. Mac to the rescue.

In what was a bit of unusual casting for the early 1970s, the director,

Robert Michael Lewis, in the person of McNair, configured Mac's ex-girlfriend as an African American. (There had been no mention of race differences in the teleplay.)

Rock had long been a fan of McNair as a singer in addition to her talents as an actress. McNair had recently appeared with Rock's former co-star, Sidney Poitier, in *They Call Me Mister Tibbs* (1970).

She had been described in *The New York Times* as "a gorgeous looking woman with a warm, easy, communicative personality and a voice that can range from softly intense ballads to the edges of gospel."

In one episode of *McMillan*, singer Barbara McNair played Mac's former love interest. For the October 1968 issue of *Playboy*, she'd posed nude.

In 1972, the year McNair worked with Rock, she married Rick Manzie. He was mysteriously murdered four years later.

***

The first episode of the second season of *McMillan and Wife* dealt with the supernatural and included guest star Eileen Brennan. In *The Night of the Wizard*, a man is done in by his wife. He may be dead, but his ghost seemingly lives on. The director was Robert Michael Lewis, who had helmed the final episode of Season One, and would helm Rock in the first three episodes of Season Two.

Having made her feature film debut in *Divorce American Style* (1967), Brennan became one of the most recognizable supporting actresses in film and on TV, appearing on such shows as *Newhart, Taxi,* and *Will & Grace.*

Episode Two, *Blues for Sally M.,* is often cited as one of the best in the entire series. Actors who participated included two "name" stars, both Keir Dullea and Edie Adams. On the set, Rock had a reunion with the very talented singer and actress, Adams, with whom he had worked before in *Lover Come Back* (1961) with Doris Day.

In *Blues for Sally M.,* Dullea played a concert pianist, who is nearly strangled to death in his apartment. The composer/pianist he portrays has dedicated his latest work to Sally, although she claims she doesn't know him. However, in a search of his apartment, Mac discovers evidence that point to a relationship between the musician and his wife.

It's made known to viewers that one of the city's most prominent music critics, in his reviews, has consistently and viciously attacked every concert the musician has ever performed. Mac suspects that something is awry when he discovers that the critic is a dead ringer for the musician's late father.

What's going on here, and just who is this mysterious music critic? Mac, of course, eventually discovers the truth behind the scenes.

In Episode Three of the series' second season, *Cop of the Year*, Sergeant Enright, Mac's trusted aide, moves to the forefront of the action. When he's alone in a room with his abusive ex-wife, she's shot to death, and it appears that the bullet that killed her came from Enright's own gun, which was in his hand at the time of the shooting. Although the evidence is incriminating, Mac believes that his assistant did not do it, and sets out to discover how he was miraculously framed—and why.

Rock had been intrigued by the screen presence of Keir Dullea. He told friends, "He combines physical beauty with talent," ignoring Noël Coward's bitchy assessment, "Keir Dullea, gone tomorrow."

In *Cop of the Year*, Rock, as police commissioner, visits a Hollywood studio. There, he meets a real-life director, George Seaton. *[Ironically Seaton had helmed the real-life Rock in the Western he'd recently completed with Dean Martin,* Showdown *(1973).]* A known authority on guns and ammo, the character played by Seaton provides the unexpected data that will lead to the establishment of Enright's innocence.

As the plot unfolds, it's revealed that Enright's ex-wife had been told by doctors that she's terminally ill and that she'll die soon. Suicidal, embittered, and still raging against Enright for having dumped her in a divorce court, she had faked her "murder" by making it appear as if her ex-had fatally shot her.

As a Hollywood footnote, Rock had a reunion on set with Edmond O'Brien. "He looked like the Wrath of God," Rock confided to his director. As they talked, O'Brien became aware for the first time that Rock had had a bit part in his first film, *Fighter Squadron*, shot way back in 1948 for a release by Warner Brothers. In that film, O'Brien had been the star. "How times have changed" he told Rock.

Season Two, Episode Four, *Terror Times Two*, was the most improbable of all the teleplays. It asked the audience to believe that another man could be surgically altered to the point where he could impersonate the police commissioner, as portrayed by Rock.

In the script, this preposterous notion of two Macs would also be repeated as an artifice in an upcoming episode, *Double & Double Cross*.

Rock, of course, had to play a dual role, interpreting his "usual" portrayal, that of the police commissioner, as well as that of a gangster, Claude

Manton. Manton's deadly assignment is to "liquidate a squealer" who's been secreted away to a tightly guarded hideaway, awaiting his testimony in court.

The real Mac has been kidnapped, but he escapes from his captors, and presents himself to Sergeant Enright, who must decide which of the two competing "Macs" is real.

Andrew Duggan was the guest star of this provocative episode.

Twentieth Century Fox put Sheree North under contract in the late 1950s as a replacement for Betty Grable, its former top box office star during the war years.

Season Two, Episode Five, *No Hearts, No Flowers,* brought on one of the sexiest stars to appear in a *McMillan and Wife* teleplay. Sheree North was cast in the unlikely role of a police psychiatrist.

In *No Hearts, No Flowers,* Sally is the victim of a purse snatcher. Later, her purse is mysteriously returned by some unknown person with a note inside that read, "I love you." She soon learns that the thief has been murdered. She obviously has a secret admirer, a deadly one. Critics cited the teleplay as having been plotted "in almost Hitchcockian style."

Brooklyn-born Albert Salmi had also had a minor role in *No Hearts, No Flowers,* cast as Joe Marley. In 1955, he'd played a dim-witted cowboy, Bo Decker, in *Bus Stop* on Broadway. Despite its success, he refused to reprise his role (a part that Rock had coveted) in the 1956 film starring Marilyn Monroe.

Salmi had once been married to the famous child actress, Peggy Ann Garner.

Rock never lived to see the tragic ending of this actor, but during the short time he knew him, he said, "Salmi was the most depressed actor I've ever known, I mean, deep, deep depression."

[On April 23, 1990, Salmi and his estranged wife, Roberta Pollock Taber, were found dead in their Spokane home. He'd fatally shot her before shooting himself.]

On the set, Rock had a reunion with Scott Brady, who had starred as the lead in his second movie, *Undertow,* shot in 1949 and released by Universal. As Rock privately told his director, Gary Nelson, "Poor Scott has gone to seed. He used to be so handsome, so sexy. Time sure does move on, do it not? It causes me to look in the mirror every morning."

In Season Two, Episode Six, *The Fine Art of Staying Alive,* guest stars were actors Henry Jones and Alan Hale, Jr., the son of an even more famous father, Alan Hale, Sr., who had died in 1950.

In this drama, Sally is kidnapped at an art gallery and held for ransom.

The captors don't want money, but an original Rembrandt. She gives Mac some small clues, which lead back to the setting where they got engaged.

During the course of his career, Hale appeared in some 200 films and teleplays, working with such actors as Ray Milland, Kirk Douglas, Robert Wagner, and James Cagney. He was fated, however, to become best-known for the CBS sitcom, *Gilligan's Island* (1964-1967), in which he played "The Skipper."

William Demarest became best known for playing Uncle Charley O'Casey to Fred MacMurray's *My Three Sons*, which lasted on TV from 1965 to 1972.

Season Two concluded with Episode Seven, *Two Dollars on Trouble to Win,* set mostly at a racetrack. The guest star was veteran actor Willian Demarest, a son of Minnesota and a veteran of World War II, who would go on to appear in some 140 films during his long career. He replaced William Frawley of *I Love Lucy* fame because of his ill health.

Mac and his sleuthing wife investigate strange "accidents" around a thoroughbred stable, suggesting that her old friend (Demarest) is the target. He happens to have a "dodgy ticker." All these horsey goings-on are enlivened by some good bantering dialogue.

Before Rock had to face Season Three, he was offered the starring role in a Technicolor Western for Universal.

***

At last, a break came in the shooting schedule of *McMillan and Wife,* and Rock was able to accept a film role from Universal. He was disappointed when he learned that it was another Western, as he had vowed not to make another Western "as long as I live, even if I'm starving to death, especially one called *Taza, Son of Cochise."*

George Seaton, its director, was one of the best in his field, as well as one of the most talented screenwriters in the history of Hollywood. Breaking into the business in 1933, he'd had a long line of impressive credits, having turned out such classics as *Miracle on 34th Street* in 1947 and *The Country Girl* in 1954, which won Grace Kelly an Oscar for Best Actress.

With a sense of dread equivalent to what he'd suffered working with John Wayne, Rock had some misgivings about Dean Martin, the film's second male lead. As "The King of Cool," Martin had a reputation that preceded him—a glib and charming associate of Frank Sinatra's Rat Pack. Known for his reputation as ultra-cool and unflappable on stage—even when drunk or pretending to be—he was sought-after on the nightclub circuit as a singer, actor, comedian, and former straight man to Jerry Lewis.

"I'll be playing *straight* man to Hudson," Martin had pointedly told Peter Lawford before leaving Beverly Hills.

"You and Rock have only one thing in common," Lawford responded. "Both of you fucked Marilyn Monroe."

"Who hasn't?" Martin quipped.

Lana Turner once told Rock, "Dean was a real bastard. At night, he woos with wine and candlelight. In the morning, you get a quick pat on the ass as he rushes out the door."

On another occasion, Jerry Lewis had said, "The most beautiful broads went crazy for Dean. In truth, I fucked more than he did. But it was always like they wanted to burp me."

The rumor mill had Martin seducing a string of famous women from June Allyson (who fell madly in love with him) to Pier Angeli, from Dorothy Malone to Ann Sheridan.

Rock collected all of Martin's records, his favorites being "Memories Are Made of This," "That's Amore," and "Volare."

Rock knew that both he and Martin had some box office clout, but he worried that his leading lady, Canadian-born Susan Clark, did not. She proved, however, that she was an excellent actress, and an attractive one at that, having posed topless for Hugh Hefner's *Playboy* in the February 1973 issue. Also, she'd previously appeared in other films or teleplays with such A-list actors as Clint Eastwood, Robert Redford, and Burt Lancaster.

Over a weekend at The Castle, Rock sat down with Tom Clark to go over Theodore Taylor's screenplay.

Showdown would be the last Western that either Martin or Rock would ever make. It was also the last movie Seaton would direct. He'd directed Martin in the blockbuster *Airport* three years earlier.

Showdown told a familiar Hollywood story about two boyhood friends who, as they grow older, are on opposite sides of the law. Most of the early friendship of Rock, as Chuck Jarvis, and Billy Massey (Martin) is told in flashback, and rather effectively at that.

After winning a shooting competition, Billy and Chuck pool their money to buy a ranch. A problem arises when both of them fall in love with Kate (Susan Clark), who intends to marry Chuck (Rock).

Realizing that his romantic quest is lost, Billy heads out, destination unknown. He hooks up with a gang of train robbers. Remaining in town, Rock suddenly represents law and order after replacing an old dodger who was the former sheriff.

When a train is robbed, with circumstances revealing that Billy was among the raiders, Chuck is given an unwanted assignment: Tracking down his former friend, for whom he still harbors an affectionate feeling.

In the meantime, and in self-defense, Billy has fatally shot one of the other train robbers, one who was trying to make off with his share of the loot. Billy goes on the run.

In his lonely desperation, while Chuck is away, Billy calls on Kate, who is living happily with Chuck. Unexpectedly, Chuck shows up to confront his friend, urging him to return his share of the stolen money and give himself up. But Billy fears that if he complies, he'll be hanged.

Just before he can become Chuck's prisoner, both men have to battle the gang who originally robbed the train. The picture ends sadly, since Billy does not survive the final shootout at the film's *Showdown*.

Filming it was fraught with disasters.

Shooting was in Chama, New Mexico, a pueblo of some 1,000 hearty souls near the Cumbre Pass Wilderness. Whereas Rock was assigned the best room at a hunting lodge on the outskirts of Chama, Martin preferred to stay some distance away, in an isolated log cabin he rented near the Brazos River. It adjoined a small golf club.

On the first day of shooting, Martin shared his theories about acting with Rock. "Motivation is a lotta crap. Acting is reacting. You jes' gotta be yourself, right baby?"

William Schoell, the biographer who wrote *Martini Man, The Life of Dean Martin*, claimed that the singing actor and Rock did not get along very well. "What bothered him the most was that Rock was even taller and manlier than Dino, and was not the stereotypical 'faggot' he was used to."

Schoell also wrote, "Being in show business and living in L.A., Dean had known and worked with a lot of 'nelly queens'—he'd even had Paul Lynde as a regular on his show—and he could tolerate and even kid around with them, but he didn't know quite what to make of a macho guy like Rock, who was secretly gay. Perhaps he was afraid that Rock was attracted to him, but Dean was not Rock's type."

Still married at the time to Jeanne Biegger, with a divorce pending, Martin was visited on two different occasions by two beautiful women, one rumored to have been designated as Miss Universe three or four years before. The other was a showgirl from Las Vegas who used the professional name "Lola Lollipop."

When the ladies weren't in residence, Martin grew bored and irritable, having arguments on the set with Seaton. He would show up without having memorized his lines. Rock called him "blurred."

During filming, Rock learned why Martin was blurred most of the time. He was drugged, relying heavily on Percodan to relieve his almost constant back pain, a condition that accelerated whenever he had to get on the back of a horse. This drug affected the central nervous system in ways similar to morphine.

One morning, Rock showed up on the set, only to learn from Seaton that Dean had flown back to Beverly Hills. It was not about money, as he was getting $25,000 a week for his involvement in *Showdown*. His departure had been prompted by his difficulties with Seaton.

Universal wasn't going to put up with that kind of temperament, and its lawyers immediately filed a $6 million lawsuit against Martin. Within a week, he was back on the job, and the studio dropped the lawsuit.

Within days, it was Rock who shut down production for a total of six agonizing weeks.

In one scene, he had to drive a 1904 Locomobile, a vintage vehicle that the producer had borrowed from the collection of Laurence Rockefeller. To get used to this antique, Rock decided to practice outside of town, on a football field surrounded by a concrete wall. At one point, as he was speeding along, the brakes failed, and he crashed into that wall.

"I guess you might say I was lucky," he recalled. "You might say that. But I won't. I was lucky only in the sense that I wasn't delivered directly to the Pearly Gates."

Rushed to a local hospital, he was later transferred via ambulance to a hospital near The Castle in Beverly Hills. He had suffered a serious concussion, a broken leg, and three fractured ribs. During the three hours that followed the crash, he'd gone in and out of consciousness.

After two weeks in the hospital, while he was still on crutches, he was allowed to return to The Castle, where Tom Clark attended to his every need.

Rock eventually returned to the movie set in New Mexico, where, in a weakened condition, he resumed filming. Suffering from marital

Susan Clark, Dean Martin (center), and Rock starred together in the Western, *Showdown*.

Writer William Schoell claimed, "*Showdown* is not just another schlocky Rat-Packer type Western, but a fine, well-paged picture."

difficulties and other problems, Martin was resentful of the six-week delay and eager to finish *Showdown*.

"It was a showdown all right," he lamented to Rock. "At least Universal has dropped its lawsuit against me. But now I've got to face my greedy wife's greedy lawyers."

In spite of their difficulties in the past, Rock and Martin apparently harbored no grudges. At the wrap party, hosted and paid for by Martin in the town's only hotel, they were seen laughing and joking with each other.

Dean's final words to Rock were, "Well, baby, let's each of us go our separate ways into our next disaster."

***

Rock found it a grind to churn out an original episode every month for the third season of *McMillan and Wife*. He complained that the directors of the various episodes within the series were always shifting, being replaced by their competitors. At least the "director of the moment," Daniel Petrie, was a familiar face, having previously helmed Rock in *Husbands, Wives, and Killers*.

Season Three, Episode One, was entitled *Death of a Monster...Birth of a Legend*. Rock enjoyed working with his longtime friend, Roddy McDowall. On the second day of the shoot, Elizabeth Taylor welcomed the men to her home for a cozy dinner party—"Just the three of us," she promised.

Over many bottles of champagne, she confessed, "something that the movie mags never discovered: I had an affair with the young naval lieutenant John F. Kennedy. It was arranged through his best friend in Hollywood, Robert Stack."

"Then, when I was competing with that awful Shirley Temple to co-star with Ronald Reagan in *That Hagen Girl* (1947), he seduced me, even though I was jailbait [*i.e., legally underaged*] at the time. He thought he'd popped my cherry, but that honor lay with someone else. His fucking me didn't mean I got the part."

The plot of *Death of a Monster...Birth of a Legend* was so complicated, it might have required mystery writer Agatha Christie to solve it. With Mildred (Nancy Walker) and Sally (Susan Saint James) in tow, vacation-bound police commissioner Mac (Rock) flies to his ancestral home in Scotland for some R&R. That's not what he gets. Perhaps the most understatedly funny line in the teleplay is when Mildred ponders the question, "I wonder if the Scotch is any good here."

There is a lot of mystery awaiting them if they come out alive. Of course, for background relief, expect Highland games, bagpipes (of course), sword dances, and Rock warbling "Just a Wee Jock and Doris."

During the first week of shooting, he was outfitted by wardrobe in formal Highland regalia, woven with the colors and patterns associated with the McMillan clan. It included a kilt that showed off his manly legs.

But as one London critic later lamented, "We got to see his legs, but the movie failed to answer the important question—what was Rock Hudson wearing under his kilt? Was it 'The Garb of the Gods,' like a true Scotsman who never wears panties under his kilt? If Rock played the role authentically, he would be letting his goodies jingle, jangle in the cool breezes of Scotland."

Upon his arrival at the Seat of the McMillans, Rock discovers that his Uncle Michael has been fatally shot. Beside his body was the recently fired rifle. But Rock doesn't buy the charge that it was suicide. He defines it as murder and sets out to investigate.

For centuries, the McMillan family had feuded with the MacCready clan. [*Centuries before, a McMillan soldier had caught a MacCready hiding in a secret passage on the eve of a major battle—and had walled him in alive.*]

In this short teleplay, there's a lot for Mac to untangle: Rumors of a hidden treasure, the spotting of a monster, evocative of the Loch Ness monster. While grouse hunting, bullets fired from a rifle narrowly miss Mac. Adding to his worries, during the Highland Games, Sally is nearly killed by a misguided tree trunk during a Scottish athletic contest known as a caber toss.

After saying goodbye to his friend, McDowall, Rock had another reunion with yet another gay actor, Keenan Wynn, whom he'd known since the days when he was the lover of Van Johnson.

Both of them were cast in Season Three, Episode Two, *The Devil, You Say.* Rock worked with a new director this time, Alex March, who would soon helm him in yet another upcoming episode.

The mystery unfolds during Halloween season, when Mildred the maid thinks she's witnessed a murder at the hospital that employs Sally. Every year at this time, Sally gets strange gifts, including an ancient Egyptian medallion and ring, which she gives to Mildred. When she's mailed a film clip that documents a Satanic ritual, she suspects that the fan who has the hots for her is a devil worshipper. In time, she discovers that her stalker believes that she is the reincarnation of a goddess he loved back in the 1300s.

The highlight of the episode—at least the campiest—is when the killer breaks into the McMillan home and tangles with ferocious Mildred, who is dressed up as a witch for Halloween. (As a witch, Mildred is far more frightening than the one Judy Garland faced in *The Wizard of Oz.*) In the struggle that ensues, Mildred throws everything she's got at the intruder, except her beloved bottle of Scotch.

The Satanic killer escapes from Mildred's fury, but manages to kidnap Sally anyway. She's hauled off to a Satanic coven as a ritual sacrifice on their altar.

Not to worry. At the last minute, just before a dagger pierces Sally's heart, it's Mac to the rescue.

In *The Devil You Say*, Rock enjoyed working with Rita Gam, of Romanian descent. Both of them enjoyed sharing memories of one of their best friends, Grace Kelly. Gam had been a bridesmaid at the wedding of Kelly to Prince Rainier in Monaco. Gam had married the famed director, Sidney Lumet, in 1949, but by 1955, he divorced her to marry the heiress and socialite, Gloria Vanderbilt.

As he bid goodbye to Wynn at the wrap, the older actor said, "Oh Rock, Oh Rock, what have we come to, appearing in shit like this? Even my dear boy Van (Johnson) is working in Europe these days, starring in foreign features just to pay the bills."

In Season Three, Episode Three, *Freefall to Terror*, Mac faces a bizarre incident when his former law partner makes a suicide leap from a skyscraper's window. But his body never reaches the ground. What goes here? Mac sets out to solve the mystery, and the TV viewer knows he will.

On that episode, Rock worked with two talented actors, Barbara Feldon and Tom Bosley, as his guest stars. A former model and stage actress, Feldon was familiar to 1960s TV audiences. She played Agent 99 in the sitcom, *Get Smart* (1965-1970), opposite Don Adams as the ever-so-dumb Maxwell Smart.

Like Rock, a native son of Illinois, Bosley was best known for his TV role as the character of Howard Dunningham in the long-running ABC sitcom, *Happy Days*. Rock remembered him for playing Catholic priests or Protestant ministers with his imperious, gravelly voice.

"I make a good priest, but I'm actually Jewish," he told Rock.

"I'm amazed," Rock said. "You've always portrayed those Christian patriarchs so authentically."

Bosley quipped, "If you don't believe me, come with me to the urinal and I'll prove it."

Season Three, Episode Four, *The Man Without a Face*, was the first installment of *McMillan and Wife* to air in 1974. It took three writers to come up with a plot that involves a double agent, perhaps patterned after James Bond, who is known only as "Venice." Since he is a master of disguises, Mac has never seen his face.

Years before, the killer murdered an old friend of Mac's from his days as a CIA agent. Rock sets out to apprehend the killer—but, first, he's got to find out who he is.

In this episode, Rock was reunited with his co-star, Dana Wynter, from *Something of Value* (1957), which had been shot in Kenya. Both of them shared memories of filming there at the time of the Mau Mau uprisings, wondering how each of them escaped alive.

Rock had long harbored a crush on his other co-star, Steve Forrest, a handsome, tall, blonde-haired Texan, the younger brother of fellow actor Dana Andrews.

Rock appraised Steve Forrest as "my kind of man."

Rock told his friends, "Lana Turner turned me on to Steve. She told me at various times that she seduced both brothers. She gave Dana a six, but Steve a ten."

"Steve is straight," Rock told Tom Clark. "And as you know, that never stopped me. My God, he's been married to the same woman since 1948. Steve and I were born the same year, but he looks much younger than me, a very sexy man."

"From Day One, he sensed what I wanted," Rock said. "It was a tough sell, but I lured him to my dressing room, where I did a 'nose-dive.' He seemed to expect it in advance. As a soldier at eighteen, he'd fought in the Battle of the Bulge. Put the emphasis on *bulge*. He didn't reciprocate, but I saw that he enjoyed himself immensely before I sent him home to his wife. I bet she didn't get any that night."

In Season Three's Episode Five, *Reunion in Terror*, Rock teamed up with comedian Buddy Hackett for a tense drama, centering around a reunion of Mac's college football team.

It was also a chance for him to co-star once again with Salome Jens, his former co-star in the feature film *Seconds* in 1966. He talked over his severe disappointment over the failure of their movie. He told her he thought he'd been too closely associated with romantic comedies or action films and that his fans didn't want to see him in such an offbeat movie with such a bleak outlook on life.

Before the reunion of the football team, a serial killer is murdering the athletes one at a time in sequential order, based on the numbers of their uniforms, working his way up to Mac's number. He desperately tries to uncover the killer's motive in an attempt to apprehend him before he kills again.

Hackett had appeared in one of Rock's alltime favorite musicals, *The Music Man* in 1962. The Brooklyn-born comic was most often seen on *The*

Johnny Carson Show, telling off-color jokes in his brash style and mugging for the TV camera.

In Season Three's Episode Six, the finale of that season, Rock was once again cast in a double role in the teleplay, *Cross & Double Cross.*

Rock was both the police commissioner Mac and the gangster Claudio Manton. The plot revolves around his attempt to intercept a vessel arriving in port with a stolen load of gold which had been originally shipped from France via the port of Lisbon. The plot includes a clever trick about just how the gold was smuggled in.

Rock had long been familiar with the screen image of his co-star, Rhonda Fleming, who was cast as Vera Royal, the empress of an illegal gambling den.

With her ivory skin and flame-colored hair, actress Rhonda Fleming was celebrated in the 1940s and '50s as "The Queen of Technicolor." But so was her rival, Yvonne De Carlo.

After his escape from prison, Claudio Manton looks Vera up again, but it's not Manton at all, but Rock, his lookalike, disguised as the hood, wearing the most awful and flamboyant wardrobe of his career. Her way of welcoming him back, after he'd run out on her, is to have two of her thugs give him a good beating.

This is one of the more thrilling of the McMillan series, and over the years has gained a bit of a cult following. It combines drama with camp humor. In one scene, Nancy Walker, dressed up like a "scarlet woman" ("and even showing off my gams") performs a sexy dance with Rock. What brought screams to the audience is that Walker is so short, she looked like a midget dancing with "The Giant," Rock.

Some of the scenes are thrilling. Vera has devised a unique method of smuggling gold across the border. She has a car made of gold and covered with a veneer of orange paint to disguise it. The vehicle is then dropped from a small plane and parachutes to the ground, as do three accomplices, including Rock. It's one of the most dramatic scenes in any of the episodes of *McMillan and Wife.*

***

Rock had been back at The Castle for only two days when he got a phone call from Mark Miller with some devastating news.

George Nader had been involved in a terrible automobile accident, and had suffered a detached retina, making him permanently blind in his left eye. In the other eye, he had developed glaucoma, causing him to be extremely sensitive to strong lights used during the filming of movies and TV shows. A team of medical experts warned that exposure to such strong lights would lead to the loss of his sight in his remaining eye.

Nader had long supported Miller with his TV and film appearances. In America, he was a frequent guest on *The Loretta Young Show,* a dramatic anthology series aired on NBC.

When he could no longer find steady work in Hollywood, Nader and Miller had migrated to Germany. As unlikely as it seemed, he became one of the most popular American film stars in that country. He starred in a number of movies, one of which cast him as Jerry Cotton, a character clearly based on James Bond. Nader's last two films included *Beyond Atlantis* (1973), and *Nakia* (1974), a TV movie. He would never again appear on the screen.

With Rock back in residence at The Castle, Miller phoned Rock that he wanted to bring Nader over to see him. When Rock came face to face with his longtime best friend, Nader collapsed in his arms and began to cry.

"It was an awful feeling holding him and trying to give him comfort," Rock said. "The thing he lived for, making movies, had been taken away from him in just two minutes in that god damn car accident. I felt sorry for him."

"We talked for hours that night. Mark was my secretary, with a paycheck, and I told George I would help out financially where needed, especially with those mortgage payments."

At the end of the evening, Miller said, "George here has supported me for years. Now it's time for me to work even longer and harder to support him for as long as we both shall live."

***

Rock had first appeared on *The Carol Burnett Show* in 1966, and the two performers had been good friends ever since.

Rock had long believed that Burnett, a daughter of San Antonio, was a far better comedian than Lucille Ball, whose slapstick did not amuse Rock as much as Carol's penchant for satire.

"The first time I met her, I just adored her," he said. "Such a sense of humor, such fun, and she thought I was gorgeous. I'm sure she's had her share of tragedy. But she conceals it well. Both of her parents were alcoholics."

Carol was also a close friend of Jim Nabors, and she was still horrified at all those fake rumors about their same-sex marriage, at which she was supposed to have been the matron of honor. "Such a tragedy. It hurt Jim's career so badly."

"One thing I can say about Carol, she does a better Tarzan yell than all those muscle-bound hunks like Lex Barker," Rock said. "Of course, he had other talents."

During a lull in the scheduling of her TV show, Carol decided that she wanted to take *I Do! I Do!* on the road. She asked Rock to be her co-star.

According to Rock, "After a night of being scared shitless, I phoned Carol and said, 'What the hell! Let's go for it!'"

The previews were held in San Bernardino in June of 1973. Rock worked for weeks preparing to sing and dance onstage.

"Gower Champion coached me well," he said. "He's a living doll. Too bad Marge has gotten him all tied and wrapped up. The guy has a lot of talent, and he kept me from embarrassing myself."

When a reporter asked Carol if Rock could really sing, she shot back, "What does it matter? People will knock down the doors just to watch him breathe."

The same year Rock had appeared on Carol's TV show, he had also attended the Broadway production of *I Do! I Do!* Starring Mary Martin and Robert Preston, the musical with seventeen songs had been based on the

Rock and Carol Burnett toured the country in a summer production of the hit Broadway musical, *I Do! I Do!*

"I've always wanted to be the wife of Rock Hudson," she told the press. "Now I am, at least until the curtain goes down."

Jan de Hartog play, *The Four-Poster*. It was easy to put on, with only two characters. In the center of the stage was an antique four-poster bed, around which a pair of actors portraying Agnes and Michael Snow would relive both the high and low points of theirs live from 1895 to 1925.

Producer David Merrick decided to expand the premises of the original and turn the play into a musical, with book and lyrics by Tom Jones and music by Harvey Schmidt.

Before Rock's opening night, Tony Randall, in a mean-spirited act of sabotage, phoned him with, "You sure have guts, among your other physical assets. Going out there in a musical to perform with a show-stealer like Carol Burnett! Singing and dancing, no less. Who in hell do you think you are? Fred Astaire? You've got to be kidding!"

Its opening night was at the Huntington Hartford Theater in Los Angeles. "*Tout* Hollywood showed up to watch me fall on my ass," Rock said. "When the curtain went up, both Carol and I were on the stage, and I had the opening lyrics. My heart jumped into my throat, and I knew I could not sing a note. But the audience rose to its feet at the sight of us, and the clapping went on and on. Fortunately for me, that gave me time to put my heart back in place—not in my throat. From then on, especially with the support of Carol, I felt I could do it…and I did. There's nothing like performing for a live audience."

The reviews were good for Carol, not so much for Rock in his debut upon the stage. However, one critic delighted him when he wrote, "Rock Hudson in *I Do! I Do!* is having the time of his life on stage. It's catching!"

In the summer of 1974, Rock and Carol teamed up once again to take the show on the road, opening at the Kennedy Center in Washington, D.C. One evening, the stage went black as cast and crew journeyed to the White House to stage the musical there. Carol and Rock were photographed together in the Rose Garden, and were invited for tea by Betty Ford.

That was the summer that Carol, with Rock in tow, returned to her native Texas to perform in Dallas. For Rock, it was his first visit to Texas since the filming of his biggest picture, *Giant* (1956), where he'd played Bick Benedict opposite Elizabeth Taylor.

Then it was off to St. Louis where they were booked into the Municipal Opera House. Here, Rock was overwhelmed meeting members of the Scherer family. "They seem to come out of the woodwork, each of them demanding to meet their famous relative. Kay Olsen showed up, wearing a mink stole in August and laden with jewelry purchased for her by her famous son. She had no good memories of her first husband, Roy Scherer, so she was not enchanted by the idea of an encounter with her former in-laws, since Roy had deserted her and his young son.

During the course of this traumatizing family reunion, Kay, perhaps having had too much to drink, confided a secret to Mark Miller, who had flown to St. Louis with George Nader to see Rock on the stage.

"When I met Roy, I was already two months pregnant," Kay confessed. "So Roy Scherer was not Rock's father."

She did not name the man who had impregnated her.

Back at The Castle, after everyone's return to L.A., Miller confessed to Rock that Scherer had not been his biological father. The next day, Rock phoned his lawyer to draw up his will, designating Tom Clark as his heir.

"I don't want those Scherers in Missouri descending on Hollywood trying to lay claim to my estate," Rock told Clark. "I'm not related to those hayseeds. So, just who is my father?"

***

Rock geared up to appear in Season Four (1974-75) of *McMillan and Wife*. On the set, he met a new director, Lou Antonio, and was given the script for the latest installment, *Downshift to Danger*. An eccentric millionaire, Max, on his deathbed, signs a new will. It stipulates that whomever wins the 20th annual Golden State Rally in Monterey, California, will inherit his entire collection of antique cars, valued at $2 million.

Mac (Rock) and Sally (Susan Saint James) turn out to compete in the Rally, as do an assortment of greedy drivers, some more desperate for the money than others. At the rally, one mishap after another occurs, each a sabotage, Eventually, one entrant is killed.

Antonio asked Rock to appear shirtless in some scenes, even though he was forty-nine years old at the time, Rock agreed, telling his director, "I'm still sexy and hot." In his glory days at Universal, the studio, according to Rock's contract, had demanded that he remove his shirt and appear "topless" in at least one scene in every movie.

Despite his boast to Antonio, Rock secretly feared that he'd faded into a matinee idol of another era. Ironically, during filming, he shared a reunion with one of his first friends in Hollywood, Van Johnson. "Talk about a fading matinee idol," he told Tom Clark. "Van looks like shit."

It seemed like eons since the late 1940s when the handsome blonde actor was hailed as "America's Sweetheart" along with his female counterpart, June Allyson, his sometimes co-star. The role that Johnson played, that of a fading movie star, was certainly type-casted. In the episode, his character was called upon to be obnoxious.

Over lunch with Rock, Johnson discussed the first time he ever heard of Rock Hudson. "It was in the late 1940s. Louis B. Mayer—what a guy!—

called me into his office and alerted me that the 'Van Johnson Boom Years' might be coming to an end. He claimed that new sex symbols, notably John Derek and Rock Hudson, had captured the fantasies of the movie-going public."

He spoke about his own triumphs and tragedies during his tours on the "straw hat circuit," beginning with *The Music Man* in 1962. "I lived mainly on steaks and milk and lost twenty pounds. I played such towns as Tonowanda, New York. Life was just one motel and laundry bag after another. Every time I checked into a motel in the middle of the night, I thought of Janet Leigh in *Psycho*."

The year he teamed with Rock, he was appearing on stage in *6 Rms Riv Vu* in such cities as Tampa and Chicago. "It's standing room only wherever I play," he had boasted at the time.

As he spoke to Rock, who was seated alongside him, he kept patting his leg. "He kept getting closer and closer to my goodies," Rock told Clark. "I wasn't interested. Yesterday was dead and gone. But I didn't want to hurt his feelings. When he sensed I wasn't going to put out, he turned to flirting with the handsome waiter instead. They made a deal to get together between his lunch and dinner shifts."

In what was designated as "Episode 23" of the series, now in its Fourth Season, Henry Falk helmed Rock in *The Game of Survival*. In it, a temperamental tennis star is suspected of murdering a newspaper magnate, who, in a random act of petulance had had him suspended as a professional athlete. Bobby Riggs, one of the world's top tennis players, appeared as himself, and guest stars included Stefanie Powers, a longtime friend of Rock's, and George Maharis, "that sexy Greek" (Rock's appraisal).

When Rock starred with Powers, her greatest fame lay in her immediate future (i.e., in the 1980s) when she was cast in the hit TV series, *Hart to Hart* (1979-84) with Robert Wagner. As a married team, they played a pair of amateur sleuths.

On the set, Rock learned that Powers had divorced her actor husband, Gary Lockwood, and was involved in an affair with William Holden, which led to their joint involvement in wildlife conservation in Kenya.

A Greek American, Maharis, a former U.S. Marine, had first attracted Rock's attention when he had starred as Buz Murdock in the

On the set of McMillan, Stefanie Powers told Rock she was in love with William Holden.

"Who isn't?" he responded.

popular TV series, *Route 66* in 1960 with Martin Milner.

He also confessed to Tom Clark that although he wanted Maharis on the set, he opted not to pursue him. "He's three years younger than me, and still looking good. But I'm lurching near fifty, and I didn't want to embarrass myself and hit on him. I feared he might turn me down."

In Episode 24, *Buried Alive*, a World War II intelligence colleague, long since thought to be dead, turns up and is suddenly murdered. Guest stars were Barry Sullivan and Donna Mills. A veteran actor, Sullivan had worked on *A Gathering of Eagles* (1963) with Rock.

"Barry was one of the tallest stars I ever worked with," Rock said. "Only one inch shorter than me.

Henry Falk, who had recently helmed Rock in *The Art of Survival*, was called back to direct him in Episode 25, *Guilt by Association*, the last of the McMillan series to air in 1974. Mildred (Nancy Walker) is accosted while serving on a sequestered jury, and one of the other jurors is murdered in a locked room.

This was Rock's first appearance with Susan Strasberg, the daughter of Lee Strasberg of the Actors Studio.

The episode's other co-star, David Soul, was both an actor and a recording star. After working with Rock, he starred as Hutch Hutchinson in the ABC-TV series, *Starsky & Hutch* (1975 to 1979).

Episode 26, *A Night Train to L.A.*, was the first of the McMillan series to air in 1975. Mac leaves a very pregnant Sally and heads south to a police convention with fellow officers. Mildred is along for the ride, as is the author of *Cops and Other Crooks*. He is murdered *en route*.

This episode introduced Rock to Linda Evans, who was known mostly for her role as

Rock worked with sexy George Maharis in an episode of *McMillan*. Once, he'd purchased twenty copies of *Playgirl's* 1973 issue in which Maharis had posed nude.

Rock told Tom Clark, "I was most impressed. George's cock is almost as beautiful as my own."

In 1983, long after working with Rock on *McMillan*, David Soul would dare attempt to play the Humphrey Bogart part of Rick Blaine in the five-part NBC-TV remake of *Casablanca*, Bogie's most famous film, released in 1942.

the daughter of Victoria Barkley (Barbara Stanwyck) in the Western TV series, *The Big Valley* (1965-69). Born to professional dancers in Connecticut, Evans later moved to Hollywood, where she was discovered, and went on to pursue an acting career.

Along the way, she married John Derek, who arranged for her to pose for *Playboy* in 1971. She confessed to Rock that she was divorcing Derek because she had discovered that he was having an affair with a starlet who became Bo Derek, 30 years her junior.

During the closing months of Rock's life, Evans would emerge in a stressful and most controversial way.

Episode 27, *Love, Honor, and Swindle,* was aired on February 16, 1975, marking the end of Season Four. Its plot involves Mac's sister, Megan, who seems to be engaged to a confidence man who sets out to swindle a mining company. Not so fast. Mac to the rescue. Guest stars included David Birney and Gretchen Corbett.

Years later, when asked about *Love, Honor, and Swindle,* Rock said, "I really don't remember being in it, but I guess I was if you saw me in it."

***

At The Castle, after *McMillan* was wrapped for another season, Rock got a rare offer for a feature film. He'd been off the big screen for the past three years. The movie would emerge as one of the most controversial of his long career.

Chapter Nineteen

A Middle-Aged Rock at Fifty Looks for Love in All the Wrong Places

On Screen He Creates a Test Tube Woman and Seduces Her. Off Screen, He Spends Cozy Nights with HRH the Princess Margaret Rose, and with her Counterpart in Monaco, Grace Kelly

1976 was a productive, profitable, and regal year for Rock. Taking a break from the *McMillan* series, Rock starred on the London stage in *I Do! I Do!* with singer/dancer Juliet Prowse.

Between performances, he hung out with HRH Princess Margaret Rose (left) in her lavish apartment in Kensington Palace. Then he visited Princess Grace in Monaco, where they resumed their dialogue and their affair. Prince Rainier was in Paris at the time with his mistress.

On November 17, 1975, Rock Hudson reached the half century milestone of his life. He'd arrived in Los Angeles as a truck driver and had morphed over a period of seven years into the top box office movie star in the world. As he put it, "I've come a long way, baby."

For his 50th birthday bash, Tom Clark set out to "throw the greatest birthday celebration in Hollywood." It didn't turn out to be that, but it was a grand party indeed.

Weeks went into its preparation, as Clark ordered all the furniture removed from the Red Room for its conversion into a night club and hired a big band. Six well-muscled bartenders were hired, each naked except for a gold *lamé* G-string. A lavish banquet was catered by Chasen's, and presented in an all-brown palette that included brown dishes, brown table linens, even brown candlesticks and candles, all in honor of Rock's brown eyes.

Ficus trees were hauled in and decorated with twinkling Christmas lights, and enough fresh flowers were ordered to accommodate the funeral of an American president.

Perhaps because they were nervous about the pending onslaught, Rock and Clark fought over the preparations, and after a few "fuck you's," Clark stormed out of the house. He returned two hours later with Rock's birthday present—a T-shirt printed with the slogan, "ROCK HUDSON IS A PRICK!"

Rock was nowhere to be seen when the guests arrived. (He appeared later, as part of a grand entrance, but only after most of them had already gathered.) It was a costume party. For reasons not made clear, most of the guests dressed as Arabs, although George Nader appeared in drag, impersonating Bette Davis and delivering her immortal line: "WHAT A DUMP!"

Clark wore a kilt ("bare-assed underneath") and Roddy McDowall and Nancy Walker came as gauche and screeching fans demanding Rock's autograph. Carol Burnett, a guest of honor, was dressed as a flapper, in honor of Rock's birth in 1925.

Mark Miller and Buddy Hackett starred as "Queens of the Desert," and Michael Miklenda and Juliet Mills roared in on motorcycles like Marlon Brando in *The Wild One*.

Suddenly, the band struck up a number, "You Must Have Been a Beautiful Baby." At the top of the stairs, Rock descended wearing a giant diaper, returning later clad in jeans and the T-shirt from Clark, "ROCK HUDSON IS A PRICK!"

It was a gala night and a raucous time, almost drowning out the fear that nearly all of the guests shared, and that was the dilemma of turning fifty, when many entertainers had to retreat to the Hollywood Hills.

As the evening progressed, Rock kept drinking more and more. Toward midnight, he confronted two old friends, Roddy McDowall and Merv Griffin with: "Let's find out if middle-aged old farts can still cut the mustard. Come up to my bedroom."

About half an hour later, McDowall and Griffin accepted the invitation.

Inside Rock's bedroom, they found him sprawled nude on the bed, fast asleep in a drunken stupor. His two friends quietly departed, leaving him to sleep off his drunk, and to face a hangover as he began a new year as a fifty-year-old.

Rock summed up his feelings the next day: "I welcome my birthdays. Relish them, as a matter of fact. I have confidence now, and look forward to trying new things. I don't think fifty is a crucial age. Forty was, and thirty-nine because I was facing forty. But lately, everything is falling into place for me."

***

After a three-year absence, Rock returned to feature films in the Cine Artists color production of *Embryo* (1976). It was later retitled *Created to Kill*, based on the belief that it would win more viewers, but it did not.

The picture was helmed by the noted director, Ralph Nelson, and cast with a constellation of co-stars, including Diane Ladd, Barbara Carrera, Roddy McDowall, Anne Schedeen, and John Elerick, and included a cameo appearance by Dr. Joyce Brothers, a TV psychologist who at the time was a household name.

"The script by Anita Doohan appealed to me," Rock said. "True, it was sci-fi horror, but not the usual crap. There was a little bit of Frankenstein, though no attempt to create a monster. Throw in some Svengali, some scenes evocative of my movie, *Seconds* (1966), and a dash of God creating Eve, and you've got *Embryo*."

Nelson defined the movie as "a variation of the test-tube theme. Like Pavlov, Dr. Paul Holliston (Rock) is a geneticist who begins on a dog and graduates to creating a living, breathing, terribly bright woman, whom he even fucks."

Rock had several pre-production talks with Nelson about the plot and his character. He'd been impressed with the director's resumé, having helmed such stars as Sidney Poitier, Cary Grant, Steve McQueen, James Garner, and Rita Hayworth in her last film, *Once a Thief* (1972).

During the course of his career, Nelson had directed Cliff Robertson in his Oscar-winning performance in the title role of *Charly* (1968). "I wish you would win of

577

those babies for me," Rock told him.

He was always pleased to work with his close friend and former co-star Roddy McDowall, who had been assigned a rather thankless role in *Embryo* as a champion chess player, Frank Riley.

It was also smooth sailing with Ladd, who'd recently had a far more memorable role in *Alice Doesn't Live Here Anymore* (1974). Ironically, after Rock's death, she would star as his mother, Kay, in the 1989 bio pic, *Rock Hudson*. A Southern belle from Mississippi, Ladd was related to Tennessee Williams.

In second billing as Victoria Spencer, the woman he creates in a lab, Nicaragua-born Barbara Carrera was a former model who in time would play Fatima Blush in the 1983 James Bond thriller, *Never Say Never Again.*

John Elerick was cast as Holliston's son, Gordon, with Anne Schedeen playing his pregnant wife, Helen.

The plot is complicated and strains credulity. As *Embryo* opens, Dr. Holliston (Rock) is living with his sister-in-law, Martha Douglas (Ladd), following the death of his wife in a car crash.

One night he runs over a pregnant Doberman, fatally injuring her, although he rescues one of her unborn puppies. In an artificial uterus in his lab, he uses an experimental growth hormone to create a mature animal within only a few days. But will this lab-created dog turn out to be man's best friend or a predatory killer?

After that creation, Holliston aims for a loftier goal: To create a human being from a fetus rescued from a suicide victim. His complicated experiment works, and out from his lab emerges Victoria Spencer. She is amazingly bright, reading the Bible in one sitting and becoming a master of science, literature, and culture.

She asks Holliston to teach her about sex, and a nude scene follows. "My ass still looks delectable after all these years, but will it make the final cut?" Rock asked.

As the plot unfolds, Victoria discovers that she is aging rapidly. A smart scientist herself, she learns that she can counter her aging process with a pituitary gland removed from a six-month-old fetus. With this as her motive, she murders a pregnant prostitute, only to learn that her unborn child is dead in the womb.

Perhaps *Embryo* co-stars Roddy McDowall (left) and Rock are confused by the film's complicated plot.

When Martha becomes wise to what

Victoria is up to, Victoria administers a lethal injection, claiming afterward that she died of a heart attack.

Holliston learns about Victoria's death and, with Gordon, races back to his lab to confront the monster he has created. There, he discovers Victoria, now in advanced middle age, surgically removing Helen's unborn baby from her womb.

When Holliston and Gordon try to stop Victoria's murderous binge, she kills Gordon by stabbing him with a scalpel. As he collapses, he overturns the experiment's gestation tank.

In a speeding car, Victoria, already pregnant with a fetus artificially transplanted into her womb, drives off. A speed chase follows, with Holliston hot on her trail.

The police join in the chase, and Victoria runs off the road, her car exploding in a fiery crash. Holliston wants her dead, but paramedics arrive on the scene, only to discover Victoria, by now an aging granny, giving birth as she's pulled from the burning wreckage. Holliston wants the child dead too, but his wish isn't granted. The paramedics assist the dying woman in the birth of her newborn child. As the screen goes black, we hear the wailing of a newborn child.

Is it the birth of another *Rosemary's Baby?*

Embryo was a "still born" at the box office.

***

After his travels, his parties, and his "extracurricular filmmaking," Rock returned to Universal to complete Season Five (1975-76) of *McMillan and Wife*. Lou Antonio, by now a familiar face as his director, showed him the script for Episode 28, *The Deadly Inheritance,* written by Peter S. Fischer, who had penned teleplays that included Rock before.

With guest stars Jack Gilford and Lola Albright, the plot involved Mac's eccentric mother, who insists on helping the San Francisco police pursue a killer. Some crazed nut tried to murder her friend, and she fears she'll be next on his hit list.

Rock found actress Mildred Natwick "wickedly amusing," and he praised her supporting role in *Barefoot in the Park* (1969) with Robert Redford and Jane Fonda. Her performance had won Natwick a Best Supporting Oscar nod. Rock feared that their teleplay was a bit of a comedown for her, as she'd already been featured in several John Ford classics, including once as a "Cockney slattern," and had previously worked with such directors as Joshua Logan and Alfred Hitchcock. Her co-stars had ranged from Helen Hayes to Debbie Reynolds.

A New Yorker, "Gilford was such a lovable creature on screen, and such a nasty son of a bitch off screen," Rock claimed. "What a sarcastic fucker. At least he was no longer blacklisted by the McCarthy goons. I'll say this for the shit…The man sure had talent."

In Episode 29, *Requiem for a Bride*, E.W. Swackhamer directed Rock. As Commissioner McMillan, he celebrates an old friend's wedding, but the honeymoon ends abruptly when the bride is murdered. Guest stars included Susan Sullivan, Henry Darrow, Lynn Borden, and Lew Ayres.

Aftershock was the 30th teleplay in the *McMillan and Wife* series. It featured such guest stars as Julie Newmar, Robert Loggia, and Richard Dawson. In the script, unusual interest is shown in McMillan's house when Sally (Susan Saint James) wants to sell it and move on. Then during an earthquake, brickwork collapses, revealing a corpse buried between the walls. Once again, McMillan to the rescue.

Rock was impressed with the talented Newmar, who was an actress, singer, and dancer known for her work on stage, screen, and in television. He'd been amused watching her as *Catwoman* in the campy TV series *Batman* (1966-67). Another camp classic, *To Wong Foo, Thanks for Everything! Julie Newman* (1995), lay in her future.

"She was a woman who could stand up to me," Rock said, "almost six feet tall. She was often cast as a larger-than-life sex symbol, temptress, or Amazonian beauty."

The final installment of *McMillan & Wife* for 1975 was Episode 31, *Secrets for Sale*, with guest stars Meredith Baxter and John Vernon. Bob Finkel directed the teleplay about politicians being blackmailed as San Francisco faces a fiscal crisis. The ever-smiling Sergeant Enright (John Schuck) leaves the police force to marry an heiress and work for a private detective agency.

Finkel later commented on working with Rock, calling him "bored as bloody hell" with playing McMillan. Producers were horrified when Rock attacked the series.

"I only do it for the money," Rock told a reporter in reference to the TV series that had made him rich. "Everything in TV is too rushed. Forget any attempt at artistic endeavor. I'm glad the public buys it, though it's shoddy goods. It could be a hell of a lot better. But it's cut to the chase and flash on a commercial."

Finkel also claimed, "Rock detested Susan Saint James, but he had to make love to her on camera again and again. He was most often drinking heavily and showed up with the bad breath of a guy with a hangover. Perhaps that was his way of punishing Susan in their love scenes. She tried to bring some creativity to her role, but Rock blocked out his action in advance, not wanting any James Dean playing around with the script. He just wanted to perform what he was told to do and then hustle his ass off to his dressing room trailer, where he met with Nancy Walker to tell dirty jokes. Susan was a bit of a hippie in those days, and that also pissed Rock off."

At one point in the series, Saint James announced that she was pregnant, which she was in real life. "Rock was adamant," Finkel said. "No baby scenes."

"I won't do them," Rock said. "Keep the brat in the nursery. We'll just refer to him."

Episode 32, *The Deadly Cure*, was the first installment of the series aired in 1976. Mac, as police commissioner, is wounded in a failed drug raid and sent to the hospital. While confined there, he sees a patient smothered, and, despite his weakened condition, sets out to unravel the mystery.

Guest stars included Lola Albright and Dick Sargent.

As a fellow gay man, Rock bonded with Sargent and was "bewitched" by his sense of humor, a reference to his portrayal of Darrin Stephens during the final years (1969-72) of the hit TV series, *Bewitched*. [*Sargent had replaced the ailing actor Dick York in that famous series. York had played its male lead from 1964-69.*]

Albright had also appeared with Kirk Douglas and Marilyn Maxwell in *Champion* (1949). Rock discussed Maxwell with Albright, saying, "She was the best woman friend I ever had, and not a day goes by that I don't think of her with love."

In Episode 33, Bob Finkel was called in once again to direct Rock in *Greed*, which had an unusual cast. This was the only time Rock would appear in a drama with Tab Hunter, whose star days had come and gone. Both of them recalled their glory years, agreeing that "fame is so very fleeting."

Slim Pickens was also in the cast, well-known for that familiar whiny twang of his. A former clown on the rodeo circuit, he told Rock, "I'm best when cast as a character deep down in the soul of white trash America, living in Hicksville, USA."

Greed cast Nancy Walker in the role of Mildred, playing the sister of Agatha (Martha Raye), both of them good friends of Rock. In the teleplay, they are sisters who are named in a will. But the other heirs start dying mysteriously, and Agatha feels she's next in line. In the 1976-77 season of *McMillan*, Raye would replace Walker in the role of Mac's maid.

Broadcast in March of 1976, *Point of Law*, Episode 34, ended the run of *McMillan and Wife*. It also marked the end of the appearances of Susan Saint James, Nancy Walker, and John Schuck.

Lou Antonio was once again tapped to direct Rock in this story of a naval lieutenant facing a court martial. As a naval reserve officer, Rock, as McMillan, is called back for his annual tour of duty. Since McMillan happens to also be attorney, his naval commander orders him to defend the lieutenant. Mac claims, "I'm too rusty as a lawyer," but he defends him anyway.

He is opposed by the prosecuting attorney, William Daniels, playing a most obnoxious lawyer. Daniels, an actor from Brooklyn, had delivered one of his best performances as Dustin Hoffman's father in *The Graduate* (1967). From 1999 to 2001, he would preside over the Screen Actors Guild.

Antonio noted that Rock was reeling from frequent hangovers and "smoking like it was his last cigarette before facing the gallows. He was bloaty, sweaty, and usually bitter about the Sunday night episode of *McMillan* he'd watched. His breath was like the mustard gas the Germans used in World War I. Chewing gum, gargling with Listerine, and even mints didn't get rid of that dragon breath. My God, that big lug smoked five to six packs of cigarettes a day. He partied till 2AM almost every night, and staggered in to work with only three hours sleep to report to makeup, which he badly needed."

***

Renamed *McMillan,* the TV series would run for only one more season (1976-77). Susan Saint James was said to have left following a contract dispute over money. The other two regulars, Nancy Walker as Mildred, and John Schuck as Rock's aide, also "jumped ship."

In 1976, Schuck was hired to play Gregory "Yo-Yo" Yoyonovitch in the short-lived series, *Holmes & Yo-Yo.* Nancy Walker's new venture also tanked. In 1976 ABC-TV had offered her a contract to headline her own series, *The Nancy Walker Show,* produced by Norman Lear.

As the novelty associated with *McMillan and Wife* diminished, its producers realized that its scripts and its premises had gone stale. In the mid-1970s, they brought in Jon Epstein, who, as *The New York Times* wrote, had a career that read like the history of television in Hollywood. From 1968 to 1970, he had produced numerous series and movies-of-the-week for ABC-TV. Around the same time as *McMillan,* also for ABC, he also produced the widely respected TV mini-series *Rich Man, Poor Man* (1976).

Before he took over *McMillan,* Epstein sat through a screening of each of its previous episodes. "Let's face it," he said at the end. "It's no *Hill Street Blues.* Nor is it *Lou Grant.*"

"Rock continued to dislike the scripts handed to him." Epstein said, "but he acted with a natural instinct that earned him a following among

TV viewers. I knew he wasn't happy, but I promised him I'd beef up the series with better scripts and some well-known names as guest stars."

To get rid of Sally as his wife, the writers had her and her son die in a plane crash. Many viewers and critics commented on how quickly Mac subsequently adjusted to being a widower. "He certainly had no trouble banging a succession of beautiful model-quality women in the final season. There was no *boo-hoo-hoo* over Sally's death or the death of his son," wrote one critic. "Maybe being a playboy/eligible bachelor was Rock's natural state," wrote a fan from Arkansas. "I guess only in the pre-Internet age, or maybe in San Francisco, could a public figure like a police commissioner lead such a scandalous life."

The most wicked conspiracy theory was posted by a viewer from Arizona. "Maybe Mac decided a wife and kid were tying him down, and he killed them. As a homicide investigator, he knew how to cover up a crime. The only two people who suspected him were those closest to him: Mildred and Sgt. Enright. So they were the next two to be killed."

Actually, Rock was relieved to have Saint James out of the series. He told Epstein, "To tell the truth, I wouldn't even stand next to her at a cocktail party. Imagine how I hated crawling into bed with her before TV cameras and making love to her."

When he'd chosen her as his leading lady, he expressed hope that his star power would overwhelm hers. But, as it turned out, she was nominated for four Emmy awards, and he didn't even get a nod.

McMillan stalwartly remained a bachelor throughout the series' final episodes. The woman's role in his life was fulfilled by his secretary, as portrayed by Gloria Strook, who had previously been married to Leonard Stern, the creator of the series.

Rock's dim-witted assistant, Sergeant DiMaggio ("no relation to baseball legend Joe DiMaggio") was played by Richard Gilliland. A Texan, he was 25 years younger than Rock.

Rock had wanted Martha Raye, the veteran comic actress and singer, to replace Walker. But the producers had objections: "She's a has-been," or "she's too old." Rock won out, and Raye was brilliant in the role, many critics claiming that she was even better than Walker.

"Rock just loved Martha Raye and knew how talented she was," said director Bob Finkel. "When she joined the cast, his spirits brightened. Gay men usually adored Raye. Those guys have their favorites: Judy Garland, Bette Davis, Joan Rivers."

As anticipated, *McMillan* generated a lot of feedback. More and more fans were learning about Rock's sexual orientation, and some were rather vocal about it. "Rock is gayer than a tree full of parrots," wrote a New

Hampshire viewer. From Long Island came this comment: "Rock is gayer than a Fire Island pinwheel factory." Yet another viewer from Kentucky expressed it differently: "Rock Hudson is gayer than an explosion in a glitter factory."

Before the beginning of his involvement in the series' concluding season, Rock decided to take *I Do! I Do!* to London.

***

Carol Burnett was not available to co-star with Rock in the London production of *I Do! I Do!*. The show was set to open at the Phoenix Theatre in the West End in February of 1976 for an eight-week run.

Lee Remick was living in London at the time, and Rock phoned her and asked if she'd take over for Carol, but she didn't want to. She would soon be co-starring with Rock in the 1978 mini-series, *Wheels.*

Juliet Prowse, the Anglo-Indian dancer who was reared in South Africa, was approached, and she said she'd be delighted.

Prowse had burst into international fame when she'd performed the Can-Can, the coquettish high-kicking show-stopper, as inspired by the scene that later provided the crescendo in the 1960 film (*Can-Can*) with other dancers in front of Soviet leader Nikita Khrushchev during his 1959 visit to Hollywood. After watching them, he angrily denounced the dancers for showing "their bottoms:" and performing such an immoral dance. After that, Prowse's career shifted into high gear.

On the set of *Can-Can* she began an affair with Frank Sinatra, and followed him to Las Vegas. In 1962, they announced their engagement. When he wanted her to give up her career, she broke off the engagement. She told Rock, "I was flattered by Frank's proposal more than I was in love. He was a very complex person. After a few drinks, he could be very, very difficult, a real bad boy."

After Sinatra, she had a fling with Elvis Presley, with whom she'd performed in *G.I Blues* (1960).

After their nightly performances on the London stage, Prowse often hung out with Tom Clark and Rock "As a dancer, Rock had

When Carol Burnett was not available, actress/dancer Juliet Prowse replaced her in the London stage production of *I Do! I Do!* On the set, she told Rock why she turned down Frank Sinatra's proposal of marriage.

two left feet. But in private, he was one of the most charming men I've ever met. That is, until he and Tom had too much to drink. They downed triple English gin martinis with an orange twist, one after another, whereas one was my limit."

"When it came to young, handsome Englishmen, Rock and I had a roving eye," she said. "He liked variety. So did I. One night, each of us took home a guard from Buckingham Palace. The Queen didn't pay them very much, and they were known for hustling on the side."

Every performance of *I Do! I Do!* was sold out, even though the critics were harsh on Rock, lavishing their praise on Prowse instead. The reviewer for the *London Sun* wrote, "Juliet Prowse is fast enough on her feet to prevent any damage to her toes when Rock is called upon to do an occasional stiff-backed, military two-step."

Another critic claimed, "Hudson isn't as bad as I hoped he would be." That remark particularly angered Rock. "I'd like to punch that jerk in his rotten gut."

At the end of the run, cast and crew flew to Toronto for an even longer run. Once again, the critics came down hard on Rock, but had nothing but praise for Prowse. In spite of the bad reviews, the Canadians filled up every seat at every performance.

When Rock and Clark eventually returned to The Castle in Beverly Hills, George Nader noted that the tensions between them had increased. "They fought...made up...and then fought some more. Rock has a nasty streak in him that is getting worse over the years. He's a guy with two faces—when sober, he was kind, generous, and charming. But when drunk, he was cruel and god damn insulting if you dared cross him. He'd cut your heart out and devour it in bites."

In 1966, when Mark Miller had gone with Nader to see *Who's Afraid of Virginia Wolf?* starring Elizabeth Taylor and Richard Burton, he'd commented that Clark and Rock should have been cast in the leading roles. "I heard that Edward Albee actually wrote the play for two men."

One night, Roddy McDowall escorted Martha Raye to one of Rock's dinner parties. "It was very obvious that Tom had become his whipping boy, but Tom often rebelled,"

That night, to the shock and deep embarrassment of both Raye and McDowall, Clark stood up to Rock. "I hope you die a terrible death. I hope you go to bed and never wake up. We'll all be better off, and I'll be rich when your will is read. Thank God. Then I can do what I god damn please, spending your fucking money."

The producer, Jon Epstein, said, "Tom protected Rock, but sometimes our star resented his smothering presence. He wanted to hit the gay bars and go wild. Tom had the thankless role of being Mrs. Rock Hudson. I had no respect for Tom. How could I respect a man who sacrifices his own dignity to please another man? He was like a slave in bondage."

***

While Rock was appearing in London in the West End production of *I Do! I Do!*, Roddy McDowall introduced him to Princess Margaret at an exclusive party in Mayfair, right off Grosvenor Square. As Tom Clark would later write, "Roddy knew everybody in the world except Muammar Qaddafi."

Rock had already been formally introduced to Queen Elizabeth in a "line-up" backstage following a gala. That had been back in 1954, when Rock said, "That was the most nervous I ever was!"

"Princess Margaret was a lot of fun," Rock said. "She wasn't like her sister at all. Frankly, I heard Queen Elizabeth was a bit of a bore. I didn't know what to call Margaret at first. 'Your Royal Highness' sounded a bit stiff. I finally decided to call her 'Ma'am,' but I later switched to 'P.M.,' meaning Princess Margaret, of course."

"After meeting her, I began to hang out with her," he said. "The following afternoon she invited me to tea at her residence in Kensington Palace. The folks back home won't believe this, but the aristocratic English make a sandwich out of cucumber slices. I swear, I'm not making that up."

"P.M. knew every lyric to every song ever written. To her, a grand evening was to line up her pals around a grand piano for a royal event. She could imitate any dialect, going from Stepin Fetchit to Bette Davis (*'what a dump!'*). She could even do a Chinese coolie, and she did a better Scarlett O'Hara than Vivien Leigh. One minute it would be Marilyn Monroe's baby voice, the next minute, she'd be belting out an Ethel Merman number. You know, I once sang on TV with Merman. She's a dyke, you know."

Before Rock met Margaret Rose, the black sheep of the Windsor family, her reputation had preceded her. In reference to their affair, Peter O'Toole once said, "From the souks of Marrakech to the sands of the Grenadines, the Princess fell for Lawrence of Arabia—and got me."

Peter Sellers, her ex-lover, said, "Beautiful, vivacious, and violet-eyed, Margaret Rose was the Diana of her day—and not above a little canoodling from time to time."

Sellers was not surprised by Margaret's interest in Rock. "She was always drawn to men of dubious sexuality."

In his apartment in Rome, after Gore Vidal had entertained Margaret

586

at his villa in Ravello, he told Rock, "From Danny Kaye on, Margaret is imbued with a zest for life. She inherited it from her great-grandfather, Edward VII, and his 7,000 sexual conquests."

With Rock, Margaret laughed about tales of her exploits. "I don't have to behave like the future Queen of England, because I know I'll never inherit the throne. Too many others in the brood before me."

Before meeting Rock, Margaret had been an integral fixture in the Swinging London of the 1960s. She was devoted to the music of Louis Armstrong, and the musician referred to her as "a hip chick." She also adored the Beatles. John Lennon nicknamed her "Priceless Margarine."

She took frequent trips to Paris and was seen dancing the night away at fashionable nightspots before returning to London to patronize its chic clubs. On two occasions, Rock was her escort. "I towered over her. She fitted right in and followed all my awkward dance steps."

"She objected to being trailed around by security guards from British Intelligence," Rock said.

She told him, "I like to pull the Scottish wool over their eyes, slipping around doing things I should not do."

"She was known for her late night parties at Kensington Palace, where I often headed after curtain call," Rock said. "She defied royal protocol and smoked cigarettes in public and sniffed coke in private."

According to Clark, "Sometimes, if the event involved a party, I was invited to go along," Clark said. "But if Rock and Margaret wanted to be alone in her apartments, he told me to hit the gay pubs and go on the prowl that night. I never inquired about what Rock and Margaret did when they were alone. Before leaving London, he saw her several times, and they became friends,"

"Once, when Rock and I were in San Francisco, and he was shooting an episode of *McMillan,* Her Highness invited Rock to a dinner in her honor. It was at the lavish home of the multi-millionaire, J. Paul Getty."

***

"Margaret Rose was not the only Princess Rock saw that summer," Clark claimed. "After the show in London closed, he put me on a plane back to Los Angeles, and he flew to Nice. From there, he traveled by palace limousine to join Princess Grace in Monaco. Fortunately, Rainier was in Paris, once again, visiting his mistress."

"Rock and Grace were pals for a long time," Clark said. "they were on the same wave length and, although Her Serene Highness exuded ultrasophistication and pompy circumstances, she was actually a pretty down-home gal. she liked nothing better than to kick off her shoes, tell jokes, and roar with very unregal laughter."

On one of Grace's visits to Hollywood, Clark recalled that his former boss, PR man Rupert Allen, hosted a party in her honor. She was visiting without her prince. At the time, the Princess was staying with director Mervyn LeRoy and his wife, Kitty."

"When the LeRoys stood up to leave, since it was growing late, Grace was having so much fun with Rock, she wanted to stay. She informed the LeRoys that Rock would drive her home, although both of them were too drunk to hit the road without a driver."

They left the party together an hour later, and Grace asserted that she was hungry. Los Angeles in those days wasn't like New York. Not many eateries were open at that hour of the morning. Rock drove her to a diner, Ollie Hammond's, on La Cienega Boulevard.

At the end of a chicken-fried steak dinner, Grace and Rock each realized that neither had brought any money with them. He approached the cashier, who was most forgiving: "I know who you are, and I know who Grace Kelly is. I saw her in *The Country Girl*. You can skip out on the check early this morning, but I want you to show up before noon and bring $7.59 with you."

During her visit, Rock tossed a party at The Castle in honor of the Princess. She loved it. The columnist, Joyce Haber, was invited. Later, she wrote that only A-list people received invitations. That was the beginning of dividing the denizens of Hollywood into upper-tier movers and shakers (i.e., members of the "A-List") and folk who were less than top-drawer (i.e., members of the "B-List").

References to those hierarchies are still widely in use today.

***

Rock had seen his close friend, Tyrone Power, perform on stage in *John Brown's Body*, admitting "I don't really dig it." But when he was offered one of the lead roles for a 20-city American tour in the summer of 1975, he said, "I'll do it." His co-stars were his close friend, Claire Trevor, and Leif Ericson, his former co-star in *Twilight for the Gods*.

In celebration of America's Bicentennial, *John Brown's Body* had been tapped as a patriotic

Rock's trusted friend, Claire Trevor, shared in Rock's triumphs and tragedies.

presentation. Rock always saw himself as a loyal American, deeply disturbed by the anti-war protests of the Vietnam era.

Even though the show was sparsely attended, Rock was delighted to receive some of the finest reviews of his career. *Variety* claimed, "Rock Hudson shows what a fine actor he is, revealing a strong side to his dramatic talent that has seldom been explored in his movies. He is able to take his place in the ranks of exceptional stage actors."

I Do! I Do! had been a big hit. Not so *John Brown's Body*. It often was booked into university theaters when the student body was away on holidays. In Rock's final summation, he said, "Ty Power was a hell of a lot better in the role than I was."

Two years after their road tour, Rock became one of Trevor's strongest emotional supports. In 1978, she lost her son, Charles, in an airplane crash. That was followed, the same year, by the death of her husband, Milton Bren, from a brain tumor.

***

After one of *John Brown's Body's* performances at the San Bernardino Playhouse, Jack Coates, a surprise visitor, knocked on Rock's dressing room door. The former lovers embraced warmly and kissed each other on the cheek. The passion they'd known for each other had long ago subsided. As it turned out, Coates had a new lover, Steven Del Re, a handsome young champion diver.

Coates introduced Rock to one of his friends, Armistead Maupin, who would in time become a temporary fixture in Rock's life. Maupin had recently become famous as the author of a series of nine novels, *Tales of the City*, set in San Francisco during its explosion of promiscuity and recreational drug use in the late 60s, 70s and 80s.

Maupin was about twenty years younger than Rock, and really wasn't his type, but, even so, Rock flirted with him. Their introduction was immediately followed by a power failure, plunging the theater into darkness. Maupin reached for Rock's big hand. "The chance of a lifetime," he said, half in jest, half seriously.

Maupin's second encounter with Rock oc-

The San Francisco writer, Armistead Maupin, claimed that his time with Rock "wasn't a real romance. Rock and I became friends, and sex was his way of expressing intimacy."

589

curred in May of 1976 when Rock and Tom Clark passed through San Francisco. Rock was there with Steven Del Re, Coates' lover, along with five other young men. Coates was not present on this occasion.

Rock whispered to Maupin, "I'm not going to put the make on Steven because he's just too young, and I'm a ripe ol' fifty."

Maupin joined Rock and Clark, along with the young men for a nightcap in Rock's suite at the Fairmont. The first serialized episode of Maupin's book, *Tales of the City,* had just appeared in an early edition of the *San Francisco Chronicle.* Rock had bought a copy on the newsstand, and, even though he was a bit drunk, insisted on reading it out loud to his guests.

There was no orgy that night. After the reading, the young men headed out to the bars. Before retreating to bed, Rock asked Maupin to join Clark and himself the following night for dinner.

It was a Saturday night when Maupin dined with Rock and Clark at Le Bourgogne, a stylish French restaurant at the end of an alley in the Tenderloin district. It was said to have the best stuffed escargots and French onion soup in San Francisco. Maupin might have preferred marijuana, but Clark and Rock were heavy connoisseurs of Bullshots.

During their meal, Maupin pitched the idea that he'd like to ghostwrite Rock's tell-all autobiography, in which he'd out himself as a homosexual. "Not until my mother dies," protested Clark. As they'd traveled and partied together, Clark and Rock had often discussed incidents from their lives that would one day go into "The Book," a tome never written, at least not in the way they had originally envisioned.

After dinner, the drunken trio staggered up Nob Hill. Impulsively Rock summoned a cab for Clark, who climbed in and zoomed away, and then continued his uphill walk with Maupin. With Clark gone, Rock decided to play a little game. He'd stick out his thumb to any passing car. Several stopped, its passengers screaming, "It's Rock Hudson!" Then he and Maupin would race off, giggling.

Back at the Fairmont, in Rock's suite, the two men found Clark passed out in bed. What happened next is chronicled in Patrick Gale's *Armistead Maupin,* published by Absolute Press.

Seated across from the writer, Rock said, "Well, I should be over there, or you should be over here."

"I thought that was about the sexiest thing I've ever heard," Maupin later said. "We were rolling around on the floor, a sort of making out session. Then Rock told me to 'hang on,' and he went to produce a little black leather case that had his initials embossed in gold. He unzipped it and pulled out poppers."

"Regrettably, I completely lost my hard-on," Maupin recalled. "I was so overwhelmed at the notion that I was about to go to bed with Rock Hudson, not to mention the fact that I'd seen the baby's arm hanging between his legs."

The two men sat on his sofa. Rock put his arm around Maupin and said, "You know, I'm just another guy. You know that, don't you?"

All Maupin could say was, "No, you're not. And I'm Doris Day."

The pair didn't make out that night, but later attempts at sexual intimacy would go more smoothly.

***

Back in Los Angeles, Rock began shooting Season Six (1976-77) of *McMillan.* It was no more *"and Wife,"* since Susan Saint James had bolted.

Episode 35, *All Bets Off,* launched the final season. Mac is now a widower, a bachelor-at-large. As such, he would be cast with a rotating series of girlfriends, one of whom would highlight each episode. In this one, the lucky girl is Jessica Walter, a Brooklyn-born actress who grew up in a Jewish family. Her most notable feature film had been opposite Clint Eastwood in the 1971 thriller, *Play Misty for Me.*

In the plot, Mac is on vacation in Las Vegas. He falls for a tennis pro whose stepson is being held for ransom, his kidnappers demanding a super expensive diamond necklace.

Rock was shocked when he was introduced to his director, Jackie Cooper, the former child star. As a boy, Rock had grown up watching Cooper on the screen. At age nine, he'd been the youngest star ever nominated for a Best Actor Oscar, this one for his role in *Skippy* (1931).

Cooper had also had a longtime on-screen relationship with crusty old Wallace Beery, beginning with *The Champ* in 1931. As Cooper told Rock, "I detested the son of a bitch."

As director of this latest episode of *McMillan,* Cooper had selected a strong supporting cast. It included Charles Drake, with whom Rock had appeared in one of his first movies, *I Was a Shoplifter* (1950).

As a boy himself, Rock had gone to see child actor Jackie Cooper starring in the films of the 1930s. Now, as a grown man, Cooper was directing him in *McMillan.*

Rock also met another co-star, Dane Clark, who was known as "The Poor Man's John Garfield." He had only a small role in the teleplay, although in his heyday (1945), he'd been voted the 16th most popular star in America. Despite of his label as "Joe Average," his co-stars had included Bette Davis, John Garfield, Cary Grant, and Humphrey Bogart.

In a surprise appearance in *All Bets Off*, Dick Haymes, the Argentine singer, was cast. In the 1940s and early 50s, he'd been one of the most popular vocalists in America, and from 1953 to 1955, he'd been married to screen goddess Rita Hayworth. Life had gone badly for him, and in the 1960s, he'd been forced to declare bankruptcy.

All Bets Off marked the first appearance of a character new to the series, Sergeant Steve DiMaggio (Richard Gilliland), who had replaced John Schuck as Mac's trusted aide.

Bob Finkel, a frequent *McMillan* director, was called back to help with Episode 36, *Dark Sunrise*. Martha Raye appeared in this episode as Mac's maid, replacing Nancy Walker.

Rock's assistant on *McMillan*, Richard Gilliland, later became known for his recurring role in *Designing Women* (1986-93), on the set of which he met his wife-to-be, Jean Smart, who had starred as Charlene in the series.

Rock was delighted to be working with his longtime friend, Julie Adams, who had co-starred with him in a number of movies, including *Bend in the River* (1952) and *Horizons West* (also 1952), in the seemingly distant past, when both of them had been contract players at Universal.

In this episode, Mac is on vacation when he learns, through inaccurate news and police reports, that he has been murdered. His apartment had been blown up, and a body was discovered amid its wreckage. Although it was burned beyond recognition, the police assumed it was Mac's body.

Since Mack is presumed to be dead, he sets out in disguise to locate the killer.

Kim Basinger, then a relatively unknown singer and model on the dawn of launching her film career, played a key role. A native of Athens, Georgia, she would marry actor Alec Baldwin in 1993.

Another guest star was Karen Valentine, best known for playing a school teacher in the ABC comedy / drama series *Room 222*, which ran from 1969 to 1974.

The first of the McMillan series to be aired in 1977, *Philip's Law* was Episode 37. In this teleplay, Mac is wined and dined by an elegant man (Tony Roberts), who commits murder in most imaginative ways. Roberts is best known for being Woody Allen's screen pal in such films as *Annie Hall* (1977), which he made after co-starring with Rock in *McMillan*.

Mac gets involved with an old flame, played by Shirley Jones, the star of such musicals as *Carousel* (1956). Although she'd won a Best Supporting Actress Oscar when she co-starred with Burt Lancaster in *Elmer Gantry* (1960), she became best known for starring in the hit TV series, *The Partridge Family*, from 1970 to 1974.

James Sheldon, who had last helmed Rock in *The Deadly Game*, was tagged to guide him once again through the mystery drama, *Coffee, Tea, or Cyanide* (Episode 38). Aboard a flight to Hawaii, a passenger is poisoned—and then the poisoner himself is stabbed to death.

Kim Basinger appeared with Rock in an episode of *McMillan* at the dawn of her movie career.

Julie Sommars played a nosey reporter who helps Mac finger the murderer. This daughter of Nebraska had won a golden Globe as Best Actress in a musical or comedy for her part in *The Governor & J.J.* in 1970.

In a supporting role, Marisa Pavan, the Italian-born actress, was a twin of Pier Angeli and was married to the French heartthrob, Jean-Pierre Aumont.

In a surprise appearance, the crooner, Jack Jones, was also cast. He'd been a popular vocalist in the 1960s, and Rock had a number of his records, his favorite singles being "Wives and Lovers" and "Where Love Has Gone."

As the series neared its end, Jackie Cooper came back to direct Rock in Episode 39, *Affair of the Heart*. One of his best friends, Stefanie Powers, co-starred as his love interest, playing a deputy district attorney.

As the plot unfolds, Mac's dentist discovers his wife's illicit lover, a local TV news anchorman, dead from a heart attack. Jumping to conclusions, he immediately assumes that he has been murdered, and that he will be automatically blamed for it. Terrified, and acting irrationally, the dentist loads the corpse into the anchorman's car and drives it to the edge of a cliff, where he allows the vehicle to crash down into the ravine, hoping that it will appear that his death resulted from a car accident. But as it's later revealed during an autopsy, the victim had been poisoned.

Key roles in the episode were assigned to Larry Hagman and John Kerr. Hagman was the son of Mary Martin, and he would become a household word when he interpreted the role of the ruthless oil baron, J.R. Ewing, in the primetime TV soap opera, *Dallas* (1978-1991).

Rock had been enchanted with Kerr when he had co-starred with Deborah Kerr (no relation) in the 1956 *Tea and Sympathy*. "Deborah seduced him onscreen as part of the plot, but he didn't fool me. The character Kerr played in that movie was gay."

He'd also seen Kerr as Joe Cable, a marine, in the Rodgers and Hammerstein musical, *South Pacific* (1958).

The *McMillan* series ended forever on April 24, 1977, with the broadcasting of Episode 40, *Have You Heard About Vanessa?*.

In the plot, as directed by James Sheldon, Vanessa Vale, a glamorous model, apparently jumps from the balcony of her 15th-floor apartment. But, as it turns out, the body that fell to its death was a mere lookalike. The real Vanessa pushed the victim to her death in retaliation for the theft of her lover. Mac is on the case. Vanessa was played by Joan Van Ark, who became better known for her role as Valnee Ewing, a character who first appeared on the CBS TV series *Dallas,* and then for thirteen seasons on *Dallas's* spin-off, *Knots Landing* (1979-92).

After he completed his final scene, Rock told his director, "It's over! It's all over! I can't believe it. All that the role of Mac ever did for me was to make me rich!"

After the end of his *McMillan* gig, Rock sold his rights to the producers "for several million dollars," instead of waiting to collect residuals he'd otherwise have received for syndication.

***

PLAYBILL

Oakdale MUSICAL THEATRE

ROCK HUDSON
in
CAMELOT

Tom Clark had been ordered by Rock to find a suitable road show, even a musical, in which Rock could star for a multiple city tour of America during the summer of 1977. With that in mind, he met with producer Bill Ross, who often set up road show adaptations of musicals that had been successful on Broadway.

At first, Ross favored Rock for the role of Nathan Detroit in *Guys and Dolls.* But according to Clark, "Rock had seen that show and didn't like it. It was a flashy part, but not for Rock."

Then Ross tossed off the idea of casting Rock as King Arthur in *Camelot.* "That was it!" Clark said. "Rock loved that show."

On the Road Again: King Rock plays King Arthur in *Camelot*

594

In 1960, during one of his sojourns in New York, Rock had seen the original production of *Camelot*, a musical with book and lyrics by Alan Jay Lerner and music by Frederick Loewe. King Arthur was played by Richard Burton, the other roles going to Julie Andrews, Roddy McDowall, and—as his first role on Broadway—Robert Goulet. The original cast recording had become the country's top-selling LP for 60 weeks, and at the White House, John F. Kennedy made it his favorite bedtime listening album. Lerner had been his classmate at Harvard.

Rock met with the director, Sheldon Briggle, and he guided him through the show and even became a good friend of his. "Every night, when Rock sang the haunting refrain, 'Let it never be forgot that once was a place called Camelot,' he cried real tears. But he had a problem: Snot. I advised him not to bother wiping it off because the audience couldn't see it. 'Blow your nose once you go off the stage,' I told him. One night he forgot to turn off his wireless microphone. The audience was treated to a lot of honking as Rock blew out a blast of snot."

He was overheard saying, "Hot damn, that was good!"

Rock was allowed to sit in on casting with Briggle, and the two men selected Sherry Mathis as Guinevere and Jerry Lanning as Lancelot.

The show opened in Dallas, breaking all records. It played across the country, including at the Westbury Music Fair in New York. But its alltime record for ticket sales was set in Atlanta.

"During that summer, I think Rock was the happiest he'd ever been in his life," said Clark. "He sold the marvelous songs magnificently, and he looked regal. He was no singer, but neither was Richard Burton, and he pulled it off."

Because of Jacqueline Kennedy, *Camelot* was forever linked to JFK. Rock was aware of this when the musical played Hyannisport. Right before the show opened there, Clark spotted three late arrivals at the box office, each a Kennedy: Teddy, Rose, and Ethel.

After the show, Teddy came backstage to congratulate Rock. "Had I known you guys were sitting out front, watching me, I would have pissed my armor," Rock said.

***

In 1977, Rock had sent his mother, Kay Wood Scherer Fitzgerald Olsen, on an around-the-world cruise after her husband, Joe Olsen, had died.

Since 1963, she'd lived in Rock's former house in Newport Beach, decorating it in her own style. But during the world cruise, she suffered a stroke and was so greatly impaired that he had to hire a full-time housekeeper for her.

Through a link with Claire Trevor, Rock hired a young girl named Benzelia. She had fled from Honduras to escape the brutality of her husband, a guerilla warrior. She tended to Kay night and day, cooking for her, doing her laundry, whatever.

For the last six months of Kay's life, Rock refused to see her. "I can't bear to look at her in her present condition," he told Mark Miller. "She was always a pillar of strength for me. I want to remember her behind the wheel of her car when she was queen of the road."

He dispatched Miller to visit her in Newport Beach three times a week. As part of his duties, he hauled in groceries, supplies, and prescription drugs. Every time he came back, he reported to Rock. "She keeps asking me, 'Why doesn't Rock come and see me?'"

Claire Trevor visited her frequently, too.

It was late one October night when a call from Newport Beach came in for Rock at The Castle. He and Clark had been drinking heavily, as was their custom. "It's Kay," said Trevor from the other end of the line. "She's had another stroke. I summoned her doctor."

Although he was intoxicated, Clark got behind the wheel of Rock's Cadillac and sped south, avoiding getting caught speeding or arrested for drunk driving. When they reached Kay's home, Trevor was waiting for them at the door. "Kay has passed on."

After the doctor left, Rock went into his mother's bedroom to pay his final visit. "Tom and I could hear him talking through the door," Trevor said. "Perhaps he was saying all those things to her he had wanted to tell her in life. It was too late. He came out of her room, completely devastated."

Although Christmas had always been a time of celebration at The Castle, that year (1977) Rock opted to travel. Without telling any of his friends exactly where he was going (in this case, to New Mexico) or what he was doing.

"He kept it a secret," Miller said. "Rock began to drink more heavily after Kay's death. He complained of headaches. I drove him to his doctor for a checkup. He told Rock that his blood pressure was dangerously high."

When a lot of his film work dried up, he decided to live part of every year in New York. "I'm tired of Hollywood," he announced. "Or, more to the point, Hollywood is tired of me."

***

The British-Canadian author, Arthur Hailey, was one of the hit novelists of the 20th Century, selling 170 million copies in 38 languages. His meticulously researched novels included *Hotel* (1965), and *Airport* (1968). Doubleday published *Wheels,* an exposé of the automobile industry, in 1971, and it became the best-selling novel of the year. Film producers wanted to adapt it into a five-part TV series for release in 1978.

Rock was assigned the lead role of Adam Trenton, cast opposite Lee Remick as Erica Trenton, his wife. "She was one of the most talented actresses I ever appeared with," he recalled. He'd lauded her work ever since he'd seen *Days of Wine and Roses* (1962), her role in which won her a Best Actress Oscar nomination.

Lee Remick with Rock in a promotional photo for NBC's five-part TV miniseries, *Wheels* (1978)

Other key roles were played by Blair Brown (as Barbara Lipton); Ralph Bellamy (as Lowell Baxter); Anthony (Tony) Franciosa (as Smokey Stevenson); and Scott Brady (as Matt Zaleski). Once again, Rock shared a reunion with Brady, his lover of long ago.

Rock had long been fascinated by Franciosa, finding him "very sexy." He'd first been enthralled with his dynamic personality when he'd seen him in the 1957 film, *A Face in the Crowd.*

Over lunch with drinks, Franciosa told Rock tales of his life, notably details of his marriage (1957-60) to Shelley Winters, with whom Rock had once co-starred. Both actors shared stories of stars with whom they had worked. Franciosa could drop names with gusto, citing friendships—or at least extended interchanges—with Ava Gardner, Patricia Neal, Paul Newman, Orson Welles, Dean Martin, Shirley MacLaine, Jane Fonda, Frank Sinatra, and two of Rock's former lovers, Robert Stack and Hugh O'Brian.

In *Wheels,* all the topical issues of Detroit in the 1960s were explored: Corporate politics, race relations, business ethics (or the lack thereof), family feuds, greed, backstabbing, power plays, and plenty of romantic intrigue.

Rock is married to the daughter of the President of National Motors (read that "American Motors"). Wanting to capture the youth market, he proposes a new sports car, the Hawk. (It evokes the AMC Javelin.)

The script called for Rock to slap Remick, and she told him to do it hard. "I didn't want to put her in the hospital, so Lee and I rehearsed the scene carefully. But when the director called for action, my hand became paralyzed. It was as if some invisible force froze my hand in midair. I finally got through the scene, but my slap wasn't very convincing."

Rock enjoyed working with Bellamy, who had been a leading man of the 1930s, although he usually didn't get the girl before his final scenes. He told Tom Clark, "When I get older, I want to do character parts like Ralph, playing fathers, whatever. By doing so, I can extend my career by twenty years. I think my future is going to be just great!"

***

Rock and Clark decided it was time to buy an apartment in Manhattan. The decision was made after they spent $3,500 for a three-day sojourn at The Plaza—"and we didn't even order room service," Clark said.

While Rock was busy with rehearsals, Clark went on an apartment-buying hunt. The real estate agent showed him an apartment recently vacated by Barbra Streisand, but Clark decided, "It's not for Rock and me."

The search seemed hopeless, as he was in and out of 37 apartments, finding something wrong—"sometimes awfully wrong"—with each of them.

Then one day a friend on Broadway alerted Clark that an apartment had become available in the Beresford Building, one of the grand old apartment buildings of New York, at the corner of 81st Street and Central Park West.

When he was ushered into the apartment on the building's 19th floor, he told the agent, "The physical layout is ideal, but some queen must have decorated it." The parquet floors were painted pink, the elaborate moldings jet black. "We'll have to completely redo the décor." Special features inside included a fireplace and two panoramic terraces.

Fearing other offers would be forthcoming, Rock quickly made up his mind and shelled out $375,000 for it, a good investment, incidentally. At the time of his death, it sold for two million dollars. Of course, it cost $200,000 to redecorate, getting rid of the pinks and blacks that covered the floors and mouldings.

In 1978, they moved in, learning that their neighbors included the opera star, Beverly Sills, and Angela Lansbury and her husband, Peter Shaw.

[Around the same time, Claire Trevor also decided to relocate to New York, taking an apartment on Fifth Avenue.]

Although he had vowed never to host another Christmas party, that vow applied only to The Castle. To celebrate Christmas of 1978, he invited Betty Comden and Adolph Greene, Phyllis Newman, Joan Bennett, Lauren Bacall, and Dina Merrill, who arrived with her husband, Cliff Robertson. Even Marilyn Horne and Myrna Loy showed up, as did Hal Prince. Ethel Merman and Hermione Gingold arrived too, "to put some life into the party" (Rock's words).

"Merman wanted to fuck me," Rock said, half-jokingly, "and Hermione proposed a night of glorious passion."

As the New Year approached, Rock turned to Clark: "You and I have become bicoastal."

"You were always a secret bi-," Clark answered.

***

In New York, Rock began to take his acting more seriously, as he still hoped to make it to Broadway and not confine his stage work to road shows in summer.

Since 1962, he'd been fascinated by the German actress, Uta Hagen, ever since he'd gone to see her in the role of Martha that she'd brilliantly originated in the Broadway premiere of Edward Albee's *Who's Afraid of Virginia Wolff?*

He phoned her and asked if she'd consent to giving him private acting lessons. She declined, but invited him to join her acting classes at the Herbert Berghof Studio in Greenwich Village.

Rock showed up for only three classes, but did not participate in any of the exercises. "I think he was shy," Hagen said. "Here was this bigtime movie star, a former Oscar nominee, sitting in a classroom filled with young people trying to break into the theater."

Rock was going through a difficult period in his life at the time. Sara Davidson, who wrote *Rock Hudson, His Story*, claimed that the late 1970s, in the wake of his mother's death, was the most promiscuous period of his life. "In the early years, when Rock had single-mindedly pursued an acting career, sex had taken second place," she wrote. "But as his career waned, sex became predominant. Rock thrived on intrigue and conquest."

"The minute the prey fell into the lair, the chase was over and a new one had begun," said a friend who knew him at the time.

"Rock liked multiple partners," Davidson said, "and he had trysts with airline stewards in San Diego or carpenters in Manhattan. He gave all-male parties where he would not know most of his guests."

As evening fell over Manhattan, Rock plotted his nighttime wanderings through the city, and he kept abreast of what was the hottest new club, often in remote and dangerous neighborhoods.

His favorite club was the notorious, members-only Mineshaft, which was tucked away behind a steel door on Little West 12th Street in the meat-packing district of Greenwich Village.

Once inside, a visitor on the prowl confronted a maze of small rooms that was action-packed with guys having sex with each other. Below, in the dungeon, was a network of jail cells where gay men would act through their fantasies, often sadistic. In one room was a bathtub where a willing victim would strip down and sit in the tub as men, filled with beer and often high on recreational drugs, gathered around to urinate on him, some-times directly in his face.

Many celebrities joined the scene. One memorable night, Rock arrived with filmmaker Rainer Werner Fassbinder, along with Vincente Minnelli, whom Rock had known since his marriage to Judy Garland. On another occasion, the noted photographer, Robert Mapplethorpe, kept pursuing Rock, pleading with him to pose nude for "figure studies."

During his first full year in New York (1980), Rock was introduced and became friends with Freddie Mercury at the Mineshaft. The rock star of the supergroup Queen bonded with Rock. Rumors persist that they had an affair, but that doesn't appear to be true. Mercury was not Rock's type, and vice versa.

Rock had long been drawn to Mercury's music, one of his favorite songs being "Killer Queen." At the time of their meeting, Mer-cury was about twenty years younger than Rock, having been born in the British pro-tectorate of the Sultanate of Zanzibar in East Africa, now part of Tanzania.

Like Rock, Mercury would die of AIDS, in Mercury's case, at the age of 45 in Novem-ber of 1991. A lot of rumors arose at the time of his death, including a fake report pub-lished in one underground newspaper that Rock had infected the singer with the virus.

Pippa Lang's obit for Mercury, "A Very Private Man," could almost have been writ-ten for Rock:

Perhaps it was because he had 'tried every-thing' to the fullest, with both men and

Freddie Mercury—best known as the lead singer of the British rock band Queen— and Rock bonded and became friends, not lovers.

Both were fated to die of AIDS.

600

women, that Freddie could no longer tell whether a relationship was genuine or not. It is true that he must have had more lovers than Elizabeth Taylor, and he may have hoped that each one would turn out to be 'the one.' But his desperate search for love was impossible because of two overriding weaknesses: His almost intangible need to be loved on a personal level, and his overwhelming personality and fame.

*****

Rock's aggressive sexual behavior was not confined just to Manhattan. In the summer of 1978, Tom Clark, George Nader, Mark Miller, and Rock flew to San Francisco.

The men from Hollywood dined at the home of author Armistead Maupin, one of Rock's newer friends. In his home on Telegraph Hill, he lived with a handsome young man, Jim Gagner, who struck up a friendship with Rock. As a prospective screenwriter, he was invited by Rock to visit The Castle during his next visit to Los Angeles.

After dinner, the men headed for Club Fugazi to enjoy a revue that Maupin had written entitled *Beach Blanket Babylon*. "It is beyond camp," was Rock's review.

After the show, Gagner wandered off and Miller and Nader returned to the Fairmont to go to bed.

Maupin invited Rock for a late-night cruise of the gay clubs of San Francisco, starting with the relatively tame I-Beam, a gay disco. It was filled with the cream of the crop of the young men of San Francisco, each dancing on the floor to a disco beat and, if not shirtless, wearing tank tops. "Rock stood observing the scene," Maupin said. "He was dressed in a red alpaca sweater that made him look like he'd just gotten off the boat from Kansas. Once he'd been viewed as the most desirable male on the planet, but now, he was a wallflower at the Hell Ball."

At this point, Clark, too, went back to the Fairmont, and Rock and Maupin headed for the notorious dive, The Black and the Blue, the most heavily patronized leather bar in the city. Most of the patrons looked like they had ridden with Marlon Brando in *The Wild One* (1953).

Motorcycles were suspended from the ceiling, and, for most of the men, the outfit of choice was a black leather jacket and black leather boots. In the rear was a backroom where a full-blown orgy was unfolding. "I smell semen in the air," Rock told Maupin.

The final stopover of the night was at the even raunchier South of Market Club. You had to be a member to get in. Rock signed his own name and paid the membership fee.

601

The club might more aptly have been called "The Glory Hole," as it consisted of a series of plywood petitions separating the cubicles. Into each had been carved one or more glory holes, through which a man could insert his cock and balls to be fellated, anonymously, on the other side by some unknown person.

On the balcony above, where Rock retreated, one could voyeuristically oversee, from above, the action in the cubicles of the fellator and the fellated.

By 3AM, Rock staggered back to the Fairmont after his night on the town.

All these clubs, both in New York and in San Francisco, would, within months, be shut down by the police as the scourge of AIDS swept the land, killing thousands.

***

Jim Gagner, Maupin's roommate in San Francisco, did show up at The Castle in Beverly Hills, having accepted Rock's invitation. He was trying to break into screenwriting, finding it a difficult endeavor.

Rock invited him to come and live with him, and even offered him a job of transferring his 35-mm movie collection to videotape.

Unlike Maupin, Gagner was Rock's ideal type—well-built, blonde, and blue-eyed. In time, he would become a yoga instructor.

Sara Davidson quoted Gagner's appraisal of Rock's libido: "His sexual energy was so extreme, you could feel the heat. It made my ears burn. He sucked people in like a black hole. If he could get you, he did. He could have sex once or twice a day with several different people."

As Rock's latest infatuation, Gagner may have felt that he was in an ideal situation, bonding with the former matinee idol as the new "Prince of the Castle."

But within weeks, he learned about the dark side of Camelot. "His heavy drinking was out of control. You could at times just smell the poison oozing from him. He had an astronomical ego, which didn't make for easy physical intimacy. Living with him was like a roller-coaster ride."

On a good day, he could be the most charming man on the planet, but he could suddenly denounce Gagner, objecting to how he was conducting the videotape transfers, even order him out of the den.

It soon became obvious that the Gagner/Hudson liaison would be short-lived. "At the end, I felt sorry for him. Here was this man, once the biggest box office attraction in the world and voted the handsomest man on the planet. Now he was 53 years old, a bit overweight, and driven to following his dick around."

***

Rock faced the summer of 1979 with no offers of work. In New York, he'd seen *On the Twentieth Century,* a screwball musical comedy, part farce, part operetta, with book and lyrics by Betty Comden and Adolph Green, both of whom were friends of his.

Originally, in 1932, Charles MacArthur and Ben Hecht, two of the best-known playwrights of their day, had conceived the story. It revolved around Lily Garland, a temperamental actresss, and Oscar, a bankrupt theater producer whose last plays have flopped. Now, a glamourous Hollywood star, Lily, is being cajoled to play the lead in Oscar's new drama. Privately, he wishes to rekindle their former romance.

The musical opened on Broadway in 1978, winning five Tony Awards. Madeline Kahn in the role of Lily Garland had left the show and had been replaced by Judy Kaye. As *The New York Times* wrote, "Judy Kaye replaced Madeline Kahn...and, *bang, boom,* overnight she is a star."

Kaye wanted to take the Broadway show on the road, with performances in such cities as Detroit, Chicago, and Los Angeles.

Imogene Coca had also been part of the original Broadway cast, and this talented actress wanted to tour it with Rock. He had first seen her when she appeared on TV opposite Sid Caesar in *Your Show of Shows* from 1950 to 1954. She was known for her rubbery face, which *Life* magazine had compared to a combination of Charlie Chaplin and Beatrice Lillie. Coca, in the arch humor with which she delivered some of her lines, was also said to be capable of "beating a tiger to death with a feather."

She told Rock that she'd been blinded in one eye in 1971 in a car accident in Florida and that she wore a cosmetic lens to conceal that fact.

Rock took a ride *On the Twentieth Century* with the talented actress, Judy Kaye, depicted above. Imogene Coca, famous for her TV appearances with Sid Caesar, also went along for the ride.

"The show was not right for Rock, and he certainly was not right for the show," said his faithful friend, Tom Clark.

603

Up until the last minute before going on the road with *On the Twentieth Century*, Tom Clark had urged Rock not to sign for it. "The show is lousy, and the part isn't right for you."

But Rock had made a friend of the director, Hal Prince, and enjoyed working with him, along with Kaye and Coca.

"Rock soon became part of the giddy hoopla," Clark said. "He was top banana in a big cast. He would sing, or at least his version of singing, with a big orchestra backing him up. Coca and Kaye got rave notices, but Rock's reviews were bad. Unlike *Camelot*, audiences were sparse, and Rock ended up feeling dejected."

Coincidentally, Rock might have been blinded or seriously injured after the premiere in Los Angeles. After having a few drinks, he drove his Cadillac in the direction of The Castle, but ran off the road and smashed his car into a palm tree. He was bruised but not badly injured.

Rather ominously, for weeks after the crash, he complained of chest pains. The pain persisted, and he began to wonder if something more serious might be looming for his health.

***

Rock was still eager for a breakthrough feature film hit, envying his box office grosses of yesteryear. Over Tom Clark's objection, he met with producer Roger Corman and agreed to play the lead in a disaster film, *Avalanche*, scheduled for a 1978 release by New World Pictures.

His decision quickly turned sour: The *Official Razzie Movie Guide* would list it as "One of the 100 Most Enjoyable Bad Movies Ever Made."

Corman had helped launch the careers of actors Peter Fonda and Jack Nicholson, and the directing careers of Francis Ford Coppola, Ron Howard, Martin Scorsese, and James Cameron. A trailblazer in the world of independent films, he was called "the Pope of

Rock (left) and Mia Farrow in *Avalanche*.

"It wasn't an *Avalanche* for my career, but I felt caught in a disaster after making this movie with Mia Farrow. I'm sure she'd rather forget she worked on it. Roger Corman and I had high hopes for it, but those melted with the heavy snows of yesteryear. I think I'll not mention it in my memoirs."

Pop Cinema."

"With Corman, I'll be in good hands," Rock predicted. "The movie is about an avalanche at a resort in a dangerous spot at the foot of a snow-covered mountain. Mia Farrow will play my divorced wife whom I invite to the opening of the resort."

Clark warned, "Corman is known for his low budgets. I bet that avalanche will look like it was shot in his kitchen sink."

"The hell it will," Rock said. "He's budgeted the movie at $6.5 million."

After seeing the completed film a few months later, Clark said, "I was right. As it turned out, Corman used some new French electronics system that created special effects by computer. The avalanche looked like it was shot through tapioca pudding."

Avalanche was filmed in eight weeks at Durango, Colorado. There, he met Mia Farrow, who played a magazine reporter, Caroline Shelby. Shelby was said to have divorced her husband, David Shelby, because he was "a control freak." It seems he wants her back.

The daughter of director John Farrow and screen actress Maureen O'-Sullivan, Mia had divorced Rock's friend, Frank Sinatra, back in 1968, and now her second marriage to the respected conductor and composer, André Previn, was also coming to an end. Soon, after her appearance with Rock, she would launch a disastrous relationship with Woody Allen.

The competition for Mia's onscreen affections derived from Robert Forster, who played Nick Thorne, an environmental photographer, who insists that the resort is unsafe and could be buried under an avalanche. Caroline seems to be attracted to him.

Rock had found Forster's appearance as Private Williams stunning in John Huston's *Reflections in a Golden Eye* (1967), co-starring Elizabeth Taylor and Marlon Brando.

Avalanche was a disappointment at the box office, crashing Rock's hopes for a "comeback" in a big movie. After counting the box office receipts, Corman said: "The film did not create an avalanche at the box office—not even a light snowfall."

***

Ray Bradbury was an author and screenwriter at home in several genres, not just science fiction, but fantasies, horror stories, and mysteries. *The New York Times* called him "the writer most responsible for bringing modern science fiction into the literary mainstream."

Way back in 1950, he had published a novel, *The Martian Chronicles,* which most booksellers defined as science fiction. He objected to that label. "It's not that, it's a fantasy, meaning it couldn't happen. That's the reason it's going to be around for a long time, because it's a Greek myth, and myths have staying power." That said, he became even better known for his sci-fi dystopian novel, *Fahrenheit 451,* published in 1953.

It wasn't until 1979 that Charles Fries Productions launched a three-part TV series, *The Martian Chronicles,* based on Bradbury's novel. It was divided into three episodes: "The Expeditions," "The New Settlers," and "The Martians."

Hired as their director, a Londoner, Michael Anderson, was best known for having helmed Mike Todd's grandiose, hype-saturated epic, *Around the World in 80 Days* (1956). Anderson cast Rock as the male lead, the role of Colonel John Wilder. His supporting players included a number of "name" actors, including his friend and frequent co-star, Roddy McDowall, cast as Father Stone. Other key roles went to Darren McGavin, Bernadette Peters, and Maria Schell.

The biggest surprise of the series centered on the second mission to Mars when a crew from Earth arrive in 2000. Astronauts were astonished to discover that they had landed in a town that looks exactly like Green Bluff, Illinois, circa 1979. Long-departed loved ones, each of whom had died, are there to greet them. Martians have used the memories of the astronauts to lure them into convincing replicas of their former homes, where they are killed in the middle of the night.

At the end of the series, after convoluted dramas and incredible events, Wilder (Rock) remains on Mars with his wife, Ruth Wilder (played by Gayle Hunnicutt), and his two children. He pushes a button on his remote control to blow up the last remaining rocket ship that could return them to Earth.

Then he guides his family to a pool of water in which their faces are reflected. "*Those* are the Mar-

The Martian Chronicles: "Hello, I'm Rock Hudson from Planet Earth. And who might you be?"

tians," he tells these former Earthlings who now must set out to inhabit a strange new world.

Rock worked smoothly with the director and the cast, and he was particularly fascinated by Darren McGavin, who had run away from home at the age of eleven, living in abandoned warehouses in Tacoma, Washington, during his teen years. Over the course of his career, McGavin would star in seven different TV series. Cast as Sam Parkhill in *The Martian Chronicles*, he opens a hamburger stand on Mars, and is prepared to feed hungry settlers from Earth. They never arrive, and he sadly learns that his former planet has been destroyed in a nuclear war.

Rock wondered why such an acclaimed singer and actress as Bernadette Peters had accepted such a minor role in this TV series. A much-honored performer, she was the foremost interpreter of the works of Stephen Sondheim, and Rock owned many of her albums.

[Perhaps in memory of Rock, Peters, in later years, served on the Board of Trustees of Broadway Cares/Equity Fights AIDS.]

Also in the series was the older sister of actor Maximilian Schell, Maria Schell, an Austrian/Swiss actress, one of the leading stars of German cinema in the 1950s and 1960s. After appearing in *The Martian Chronicles*, she could add Rock's name to her roster of leading men: Gary Cooper, Yul Brynner, Glenn Ford, Marcella Mastroianni, and Marlon Brando.

Like Rock, her life would end tragically in 2005 after she suffered several strokes and had attempted suicide in 1991.

The Martian Chronicles was filmed for the most part on the tiny Mediterranean island of Malta. Before flying there with Tom Clark, Rock vacationed in Sicily.

The script by Richard Matheson departed in significant ways from the original Bradbury novel with the same name. At home in his living room, the author watched all three episodes, later lamenting to the press, "The mini-series is just boring."

***

It was 1980 as Rock entered the last decade in which he would be alive. It started out promising when Ross Hunter approached him with a script for *Pillow Talk II*, hoping to restore Rock's glory days of 1959. Hunter planned to ask Doris Day to co-star with Rock in what would have been their fourth romantic comedy together.

Hunter pitched the sequel idea to Delbert Mann, who had helmed Rock in *Lover Come Back*, co-starring Day and Tony Randall. Bruce Kane, a screenwriter, was brought in to create the plot.

In his scenario, Rock and Doris are divorced. Their daughter (to be played by Kristie McNichol) is planning to get married to Gregory Harrison (known on TV for performing in *Trapper John*).

Randall, who for years has longed to marry Day, now thinks it's possible to become her second husband.

Rock arrives early for his daughter's wedding, and he and Randall go for a game of golf. However, Rock crashes his golf cart into a tree and is thrown onto a hard surface, hitting it hard enough to cause a case of amnesia.

His doctors approach Day and ask her to help restore her former husband's memory by taking him to all the romantic places they'd shared when they were falling in love. At this point the story follows a predictable line: Does Rock really have amnesia, or was he just pretending as part of an attempt to get Day back? Or was Day hip to his scheme all along, hoping to remarry him? Once again, Randall loses Day.

Much to Rock's disappointment, *Pillow Talk II* fell through, possible producers considered the re-teaming of Day with Rock as "too evocative of those old 1950s romantic comedies."

***

Instead of that, he was offered a feature film role, *The Mirror Crack'd*, based on a mystery by Agatha Christie. His leading lady would be Natalie Wood, cast as an actress, Marina Gregg-Rudd, who's making a comeback picture. But a dispute between her and the producers led to Wood's being dropped from the cast.

The role went instead to Elizabeth Taylor, Rock's friend "for eternity," who had last appeared on the screen with him in *Giant*. In preparation for the role, she went on a rigid diet, dropping down to 125 pounds. For her involvement, she didn't receive one of the astronomical

Trapped between two battling divas, Rock was the man in the middle with arms around Kim Novak (left) and his longtime friend, Elizabeth Taylor, who played his doomed wife in *The Mirror Crack'd*.

608

salaries of her heyday, but accepted $125,000 from EMI Films, which planned to release the movie in 1980.

Its director was Guy Hamilton, who had made a name for himself helming Agent 007 in such pictures as *Goldfinger* (1964) and *Diamonds Are Forever* (1971). "In my latest picture, I wanted to create a feel for the Golden Age of Hollywood, a glimpse into the glamour of that era. What better way to accomplish that than casting the movie with actual stars of that time—and not just Rock Hudson or Elizabeth Taylor."

In the pursuit of that goal, Hamilton also signed Angela Lansbury, Tony Curtis, Kim Novak, and Geraldine Chaplin.

In *The Mirror Crack'd*, Angela Lansbury insisted on portraying master sleuth Miss Jane Marple in her own way and in her own style.

And so she did, coming out as the best player in an all-star cast that included Tony Curtis and Geraldine Chaplin.

A future move star and a future Agent 007, Pierce Brosnan would make his film debut in the bit part of Jamie.

As for the casting, Tom Clark said, "Let's face it: Those stars may have been big at one time, but by 1980, all of them had seen better days. That was especially true of my dear buddy Rock, who looked ill…and was."

Lansbury later commented, "All those movie stars did was turn out a film that was unwatchable." Born in 1925, Lansbury was the same age as Rock, but was made up to look older, her true age hidden behind a white wig and "old" makeup.

Before accepting her role as the sleuth in *The Mirror Crack'd*, Lansbury made it clear to Hamilton that she wanted to break free of Margaret Rutherford's "English sheepdog interpretation of Miss Marple in previous pictures. I don't want to be a fat galumph of a creature in gumboots falling into duckponds." Lansbury's Miss Marple was a dapper, tweedy, English lady, with just a touch of the risqué, a character who might even smoke a Turkish cigarette after dinner.

For the most part, Rock felt comfortable working with such a stellar cast. He'd been aware of Lansbury's career since he first saw her in *Gaslight* in 1944, followed by *The Picture of Dorian Gray* in 1945. Both films earned her an Oscar nod. Rock had also seen her in the Broadway musical *Mame* (1966), a role that had made her a gay icon.

In her new role, Lansbury played a forerunner of the Jessica Fletcher character she developed in her long-running hit TV series, *Murder, She Wrote* (1984-96).

On the set, she had a reunion with Elizabeth Taylor, with whom she'd appeared when the little British girl was a child star in *National Velvet* (1944) with Mickey Rooney.

"Elizabeth was such an innocent little thing back then," Lansbury said. "Now she's playing a pill-addicted movie queen trying for a comeback."

Lansbury was adored by the rest of the cast, with one exception. Curtis found her "most disagreeable and arrogant."

The setting for the movie was a small English village, St. Mary Mead, in 1953, the home of Miss Jane Marple, the amateur crime detective. A movie crew had descended on the town to film an elaborate costume drama starring Kim Novak (as Lola Brewster playing Mary, Queen of Scots) and Elizabeth (as Marina Rudd playing Queen Elizabeth I). Marina is working again after a prolonged retirement sparked by her son being born with severe brain damage and her subsequent nervous breakdown. Her husband, Jason Rudd (Rock), is directing the film, and Novak's husband, Marty Fenn (Curtis), is the producer of the historical British drama that unfolds as a subplot within the murder mystery.

In the film, Novak and Elizabeth are rivals, exchanging bitchy insults. When Novak encounters Elizabeth, she says, "I'm glad to see you've kept your figure—and added so much to it!"

The producer hosts a reception for the people of the village, since he needs their cooperation during filming. At the party, Marina meets Heather Babcock (Maureen Bennett), who describes their first encounter during World War II. Despite the fact that she was stricken at the time with a severe and highly contagious case of the German measles, she relays to Marina details about how she rose from her sickbed, determined to greet her favorite movie star—"up close and personal." Marina was pregnant with her son at the time, and the virus was passed on to her. As a result, Marina's child, it's revealed, was born with a debilitating disability.

Agatha Christie was said to have based her story on an actual event that had tragically occurred in the life of Gene Tierney. In June of 1943, she'd contracted German measles from an infected fan, and her

Even this trio of talented supporting players (left to right)—Tony Curtis, Geraldine Chaplin, and Edward Fox—couldn't save *The Mirror Crack'd*.

daughter was born deaf, disabled, and partially blind.

At the producer's reception for residents of St. Mary Mead, gossipy, dim-witted Heather is served a cocktail ostensibly
meant for Marina. The drink was poisoned, and she dies. The apparent attempt
to murder her is repeated when Marina is
also served a cup of coffee that contains
poison. On what appears to be a whim, she
avoids drinking it.

These apparent attempts on Marina's
life bring in Inspector Craddock (Edward
Fox), a detective from Scotland Yard. To assist with his investigation, he turns to his

Looking gritty, as life catches up,
Rock in *The Mirror Crack'd.*

savvy aunt, Jane Marple. A prime suspect becomes Ella Zielinsky (Chaplin), who is in love with Jason. Miss Marple, however, does not want to
rush to judgment.

The murder mystery has some camp humor thrown in. Before her vanity mirror, Elizabeth, as Marina, looks into her reflection and says, "Bags,
bags, go away, Come right back on Doris Day." The camera zooms in a
Rock's face as he appears shocked at this dig on his friend and former co-
star.

Of course, Miss Marple will solve the mystery, as she always does. It
turns out that Marina has artfully positioned herself to appear as the victim. To retaliate against Heather for giving her the measles, which cat-
alyzed the disabilities of her child, she is the one who dispensed the poison
that killed her crazed fan.

But in the end, Marina is not brought to justice. She is found dead, having poisoned herself.

In another moment of camp, Rock reviews the lavishly costumed
palace guards who appeared in the historical saga within the context of the
otherwise modern-day film. "They're supposed to be the queen's soldiers—not ballerinas!" he says.

When a policeman asks Curtis if he knows anyone who might want to
harm Marina (i.e., Elizabeth), Curtis snaps, "Yeah, Hedda Hopper!"

Although rivals and for a very brief period, lovers, Curtis and Rock
had each mellowed into middle age. "Between takes, I did my sketches,
and Rock sat beside me knitting a sweater. We were like two senior citizens
in some retirement home talking about the good old days."

Elizabeth and Curtis worked smoothly together. "We'd had many good times together," he said, "but our relationship never went from friendship to romance."

Before working with Rock, Kim Novak had appeared with some of the biggest stars in Hollywood: Frank Sinatra, Tyrone Power, Kirk Douglas, Laurence Olivier, Laurence Harvey, William Holden, James Stewart, and Fred MacMurray.

Another Londoner, like Lansbury, Edward Fox had just portrayed King Edward VIII in the TV drama, *Edward and Mrs. Simpson* (1978).

Geraldine Chaplin was the daughter of Charlie Chaplin and Oona O'Neill. She'd made her film debut in David Lean's *Doctor Zhivago* in 1965.

When Rock met her, she was going through a personal crisis. The Chaplin family was facing a failed extortion attempt by kidnappers who had dug up the body of the Little Tramp from his burial plot in Switzerland. She was personally negotiating with the kidnappers, who were also threatening to abduct her infant son.

Shooting of *The Mirror Crack'd* was in Kent in the southeast of England, where Elizabeth had lived as a little girl. When not needed for the movie, Rock and Elizabeth were driven around by a chauffeur, as she showed him scenes from her girlhood. She was worried about his condition, and his persistent chest pains. "I kept urging him to go to a specialist. I feared there was something dreadfully wrong—and I was right."

As one vicious London critic wrote, "*The Mirror Crack'd* has an all-star cast of has-beens. The film has fizzled at the box office, trapped in a hoary plot and the mediocre writing of Jonathan Hales and Barry Sandler."

Film writer Alan Hunter wrote, "The makers of this gaudy galaxy of stars encouraged the stars to do their own thing to the point of self-parody. Rock Hudson, as the movie director, and Tony Curtis as producer, dispense broad brands of Hollywood machismo. Hudson is strong-jawed and immovable as Mount Rushmore, Curtis mercurial and Brooklynite."

***

In 1981, it was back to the television screen when Rock signed to star in the mini-series, *The Star Maker*. His director was Lou Antonio, who had helmed him in episodes of *McMillan and Wife*.

After reading the script by William Bast (a roommate of James Dean during that troubled actor's relatively unknown early years), Rock told Tom Clark, "This is trash...pure junk. I'll do it!"

Antonio himself called it "tits-and-tinsel, total sleaze, but Rock and I will have fun with it."

"I'll base my character on Roger Vadim, who directed me in *Pretty*

Maids All in a Row," said Rock. "Like the character I'm playing, Danny Youngblood, Vadim knows all about falling in love with his leading ladies from Bardot to Jane Fonda."

What Antonio didn't tell Rock was that he'd been fourth choice for the role. He'd made previous offers to Peter Lawford, James Garner, and Michael Caine. Rock's leading ladies would be Suzanne Pleshette, Melanie Griffith, and Brenda Vaccaro. Ed McMahon also signed on, taking time off from playing Johnny Carson's sidekick and second banana on *The Tonight Show,* a gig he'd had since 1962.

The girl from Brooklyn, Pleshette had made such films as Alfred Hitchcock's *The Birds* (1963) and had played Emily Hartley on *The Bob Newhart Show* from 1972 to 1978.

She had married Troy Donahue, Rock's former lover, in 1964, divorcing him after a few months. "Why did a smart gal like Suzanne ever marry Troy?" Rock asked. "Why, oh why?"

Also born in Brooklyn, Vaccaro was an Italian American at home on the stage, on TV, and in the movies. She had appeared with Dustin Hoffman and Jon Voight in the 1969 film, *Midnight Cowboy,* which had been named Best Picture of the Year.

When Rock met Griffith, she had already divorced actor Don Johnson after being married to him for six months in 1976. She was later romantically linked to Jack Nicholson, Ryan O'Neal, and Warren Beatty.

During filming, Rock complained to Antonio, "I detest the role of Youngblood. I'm just a big, stupid marshmallow, grinning all the time, something out of a comic book."

In the plot, Youngblood is a film director notorious for morphing sexy models into superstars on the screen. Sometimes, his discoveries become one of his serial wives. However, he meets his match when his radar zeros in on his latest conquest, Margot Murray (Pleshette), who turns the tables on him.

The cast member who intrigued Rock the most was not any of the women, but Jack Scalia, cast as Vince Martino. "With the physique that kid has, he could take over my title of 'Baron of Beefcake,' Rock told Antonio. "I'd really like to get to know him…somehow, some way. It'll just be my

Rock with Suzanne Pleshette in *The Star Maker.*

He later said, "She and I had one thing in common: Both of us had been fucked by Troy Donahue."

luck if I discover he's straight as a ruler."

The Star Maker didn't do anything for any of its actors' careers. In fact, one reviewer was unkind enough to mention "the extended gut of Rock Hudson."

One of the most amusing reviews was posted on the Internet by "Twister":

> *"Not even a hormone-raging 13-year-old could sit through this gem. The acting, except for Pleshette, is rote and uninspired, and poor Rock's attempts at virile heterosexuality fall away limp. I can enjoy movies for their train-wreck fascination, but this one is just too gory. The other characters range from a brainless blonde to a scheming backstage mother to a bimbo stripper."*

***

Rock told his director, Lou Antonio, that in his selection as Danny Youngblood in *The Star Maker*, he'd been type cast. "Like Danny, I'm a heavy smoker and an all-night boozer."

Facing the final curtain, Youngblood collapses with a stroke and dies. Rock wanted the scene to be realistic, so he met with a heart specialist in Los Angeles, asking him about what a stroke victim goes through, and how he should act during his portrayal of such a victim.

What he opted to conceal from the doctor was that he, too, had frequent chest pains. While consulting with the specialist, he could have had his own heart examined, but he chose not to.

"I didn't want to face the music," he told Clark.

"I do find myself dragging my ass around the set all day. I haven't really felt well in a long time."

"You've got to see a doctor," Clark urged, "beginning with you own man, Rex Kennamer, 'the doctor to the stars.'"

"I'll think about it tomorrow," he said, "because tomorrow is another day."

"Wasn't that Scarlett O'Hara's line from *Gone With the Wind?*" Clark asked.

Chapter Twenty

ROCK ENDURES A QUINTUPLE BYPASS, BRAVELY CONFRONTING THE LAST SUNSET OF A FABLED CAREER

Doctors Deliver a Death Sentence: "You Have AIDS. There Is No Cure."

Rock Hudson met Ronald and Nancy Reagan at the twilight of their film careers, just as he was on the dawn of becoming the biggest box office star in America. Over the years, always at the invitation of Nancy (never Ronald), he attended parties at their home.

She was always gracious to him and invited him to the White House for a gala. But when he showed up, she was shocked by his appearance and his weight loss. She noted an ominous blotch on his neck. When it was announced that he had become infected with AIDS, this picture of him greeting the Reagans was flashed around the world on the wire services.

In spite of his continued heavy drinking and

smoking, Rock had always been very healthy. In times of tension, he smoked five packages of cigarettes a day. He'd been hospitalized before, but that was because of an automobile accident.

When he did manage to come down with a cold, he recovered quickly. He watched Mark Miller, Tom Clark, and George Nader go through both large and small ailments, especially Nader's eye condition that caused him to make no more movies. Rock boasted to his buddies, "I'm gonna live to be one hundred, and I'll bury all of you."

Trouble began on the last Sunday morning of October 1981. Rock had been working the previous week on his latest TV series, *The Devlin Connection*. He'd spent Saturday night in his bedroom with Tom Clark. It was 5AM when Clark, who usually slept until around noon on a Sunday, was awakened by a stirring in the room. He sat up in bed and was startled to see Rock in an armchair nearby, fully dressed.

"Going somewhere, big guy?" Clark asked. "At this hour of the morning?"

"Yeah, maybe," Rock said. "To the fucking hospital. I'm having severe chest pains, the worst ever."

Clark bolted from the bed and told Rock he was taking him to the emergency room of the Cedars-Sinai Hospital. Before heading out the door, he placed a call to Rock's doctor, Rex Kennamer, who agreed to meet them there.

En route, Rock, resting in the back seat of his Cadillac as Clark drove, expressed concern that he might not be able to report to work Monday to the set of *The Devlin Connection*.

At the hospital, Kennamer speeded up the check-in process and immediately got Rock a room. He pointed the way to the waiting room for Clark, after warning him, "the tests may take several hours."

"When I saw Rock the following day, he was morbidly depressed, telling me that he had an ominous feeling that this was his final 24 hours," Clark said.

"I think I'm going to pass on by noon tomorrow," Rock said. He spent the rest of the day making farewell calls to his best friends, George Nader and Mark Miller. He also phoned Nancy Walker, Doris Day, Carol Burnett, Claire Trevor, Roddy McDowall, and Elizabeth Taylor.

By that afternoon, reporters began to arrive at the hospital. Cedars-Sinai often hospitalized stars in emergencies, including for attempting suicide. It was believed that the hospital had "spies" tipping off the press.

There was even a death threat for Rock from a gruff voice who told the operator, "I'm gonna kill the faggot slime."

On hearing this, Clark hired a 24-hour security force to guard Rock's private room.

The switchboard was swamped with calls coming in from around the world, from Egypt to Chile. During Rock's stay at the hospital, some 50,000 cards and letters arrived, wishing him a speedy recovery. A few of Jerry Falwell's followers wrote in that "God is punishing you."

The operation that Tuesday, a quintuple-bypass, was delicate, lasting six hours because surgeons found extensive arterial damage, more than the initial tests revealed.

Clark admitted, "While waiting, I smoked enough cigarettes myself. I could have gotten either cancer or had a stroke."

Kennamer emerged, telling him that the operation had gone well, but had required several blood transfusions. Rock later claimed, "It gave me a second chance at life."

The surgeon warned Clark that previous patients who went through such surgery often experienced a personality change. "It could last for a few weeks, maybe months, but rarely much longer."

"I understand that with all the new blood you pumped into him," Clark said. "Maybe the new blood once flowed through a serial killer."

"Let's not make jokes," Kennamer said. "This is serious. Just be alert that the Rock Hudson you drove to the hospital may not be the Rock Hudson you take back to The Castle."

After meeting with Kennamer, Clark addressed the press outside. "We're lucky Rock caught his trouble early. The doctors claimed he might have had a fatal heart attack. But now he is in recovery, and his heart is performing satisfactorily. There are no bad signs, no complication. It's not known when he can return to work on *The Devlin Connection,* but he thinks it'll be the first working day in January of 1982."

Clark visited every day, and Kennamer told him that "Rock's bouncing back faster than any patient I ever had."

When Clark came into his room, Rock showed him the letter that Nancy Reagan had written from the White House. On his last day in the hospital, Rock allowed three members of the press to enter his room.

"I've been told I've got to become a health nut—watching my diet, denying myself even one gin martini. No more cigarettes. What's the fun in all that? Well, now that I'm fifty-six, my days as a sex symbol are gone with the summer winds. Perhaps directors will now give me roles that call for some serious acting—you know, the parts that Fredric March played as he got older."

On the day of Rock's release, Clark pulled up in his Cadillac. There was only one reporter. "I feel great, just great," Rock told the newsman. "I'll soon be back to work. I've got to face the future—not look back. I once had this dear friend, Tallulah Bankhead, who had her share of troubles. I still remember her advice in times of stress. 'Press on, *dah-ling*,' she always said. 'Press on.' Indeed, I will."

***

In spite of his dislike of playing police commissioner Stewart McMillan for years on TV, Rock surprised his friends when he agreed to star as Brian Devlin in a TV series, *The Devlin Connection*, set to air in October of 1982.

His character would have been a former military intelligence officer and the ex-owner of a detective agency before he became the director of the Performing Arts Center of Los Angeles.

Fred Silverman had assumed the presidency of NBC, and he wanted to give his major competitors, CBS and ABC, stiff competition by launching some block buster series on the tube with bigname movie stars such as Rock and James Garner.

Never in the history of television had an actor been offered such a sweetheart deal as Silverman dangled before Rock. He would be able to select the cast, approve the scripts, and was even given the choice of director. Not only that, but after NBC aired the series for two seasons, all rights would revert to Mammoth Pictures, the production company owned by Rock. "That could mean millions in reruns," said Tom Clark.

Silverman even offered Rock more money than he'd been paid for *McMillan*. Not only that, but he was granted a

television ST. LOUIS POST-DISPATCH FEBRUARY 7-13

JACK SCALIA, left, and ROCK HUDSON "The Devlin Connection"

Rock appeared with the handsome actor, Jack Scalia, in the TV drama, *The Devlin Connection*.

"Jack was like a son to me. I had a genuine love for him, and he brought joy to my life in spite of the difference in our age. I thought he had all the elements needed—the looks, the talent—to make it big as a movie star. Of course, becoming a movie star is such a gamble."

four-day work week, lasting ten hours per day. "My 100 percent control was virtually unheard of in the industry," Rock said.

John Wilder was signed as the producer and director. A much awarded writer/producer, he started off acting in such productions as TV's *Wagon Train*. While attending UCLA, he wrote *The Rifleman,* a Western TV series starring Chuck Connors. He later adapted James Michener's *Centennial* into a 26-hour mini-series for NBC.

Instead of husband-and-wife sleuthers on *McMillan* , the new series would feature father-and-son amateur detectives. For the role of his son, Nick Corsello, a racquetball pro and private detective just getting launched, Jack Scalia was cast. He had impressed Rock so very much when they had co-starred in *The Star Maker*. In the new series, he meets his son, Nick (Scalia), the result of a brief affair he had 28 years earlier.

The "dynamic duo" set out to solve the mystery of the week.

Rock also had a hand in selecting the supporting players: Leigh Taylor-Young as Lauren Dane; Brian's assistant; Louis Giambalvo as Lt. Earl Borden, Nick's friend and former colleague from New York; and Takayo, as Mrs. Watanbe, Brian's housekeeper.

Jack Scalia "was a good-looking mother fucker" (Rock's words) standing 6'1", with black curly hair. Born in Brooklyn of Italian and Irish parents, he was the son of Rocky Tedesco, a former player for the Brooklyn Dodgers. In 1971, Jack himself had been drafted by the Montreal Expos as a pitcher, but an arm injury ended his career as a baseball star.

Before becoming an actor, he had been a model for a series of ads for Eminence Briefs and Jordache jeans, both of which showed off his muscled body. To publicize *The Devlin Connection,* publicists asked him to pose shirtless with cigarette in hand. The poster adorned many a bedroom, especially those of gay men, who idolized him for his body and his looks.

Before the series began, Rock wanted to develop a rapport with Jack. In Manhattan , he occupied an apartment on Central Park West, a few blocks from Rock's apartment on West 81st Street. The two actors often went on long walks through Central Park and to other places in the city, as a warm friendship developed between them.

Clark believed that Rock was falling in love with Jack, who, unfortunately for him, was "hopelessly straight." Although Rock had a long history when he was younger of seducing straight men, that does not appear to be the case with Jack.

In his private life, Jack was separating from his first wife, a model, Joan Rankin. In 1982, he would marry a former Miss Universe, Karen Baldwin, with whom he would have two daughters.

Rather quickly, Jack became like a son to Rock, and he related to him as if he were his own father, hugging him and kissing his cheek whenever they met. Rock hoped the chemistry between them would show up in their onscreen relationship as father and son.

When Jack moved to California, Rock practically adopted him, introducing him to Clark.

"I felt I had two dads," Jack said. "They helped me relocate, and Rock even took me to his dentist, Dr. Phillip Tennis, to get my teeth fixed. I wanted Rock to open up more to me, but he didn't. There was a whole side of him that he kept hidden."

During the filming of the series' second episode, *The Lady on the Billboard*, Mark Rowland of *Playgirl* magazine approached Rock and Jack with a proposition: He wanted them to pose frontally nude for a father-and-son centerfold. He reminded them that Fabian, George Maharis, and Sam Jones (the movies' Flash Gordon) had already posed frontally nude. He was very persuasive, but Rock turned down the offer.

Episode 3, *Love, Sin, and Death at Point Dune,* when aired on October 16, faced diminishing numbers of viewers.

After only three days of shooting, *The Corpse in the Corniche* (Episode Four), Rock complained of chest pains and went home early. That was the weekend he was rushed to Cedars-Sinai for his bypass surgery, which was life-threatening.

Only four episodes had been filmed before Rock had his bypass surgery. He was missing in action during November and December, not returning until January to finish the final episodes with such less than dazzling titles as *Of Nuns and Other Blackbirds; Ring of Kings, Ring of Thieves;* and *Arsenic and Old Caviar.*

While Rock was in the hospital, Jack had visited him daily, holding his hand to comfort him. At one point, Rock broke down and cried.

Back at work, Rock learned that Silverman had left NBC as part of an executive shakeup, to be replaced by Brandon Tartikoff, the new head of the entertainment division. He was shocked when he read Rock's "sweetheart contract."

"Everything is in his corner, nothing for NBC," he complained. He called Rock's agent, Flo Allen, and tried to renegotiate it, but she refused.

Rock faced a new producer, Jerry Thorpe, to whom he said, "The scripts are worse than ever."

Tartikoff and Thorpe agreed, discarding them and ordering new ones written.

Even with the new scripts, *The Devlin Connection* didn't seem to click, and Rock became morbidly depressed at its failure, lashing out at Clark, blaming him for luring him into the series. He told Jack that he felt sorry, having hoped that *Devlin* would be a career breakthrough for him. However, the younger actor went on to shine in other roles. "I ended up feeling as mediocre as the series," Rock said.

The projected eleven episodes for the autumn of 1983 were never shot. Rock left the studio, never to return.

***

An early morning call came in from Elizabeth Taylor on November 29, 1981. Tom Clark picked up the receiver to hear her request that he wake Rock up and put him on the phone.

"Morning, Elizabeth," came Rock's sleepy voice over the wire. "What's wrong?"

"Natalie's dead," she said. "She was found drowned this morning off the coast of Catalina."

He knew at once she was referring to Natalie Wood, their mutual friend, who had gone sailing with her husband, Robert Wagner, aboard his 55-foot cabin cruiser, *Splendour.*

By drowning, Natalie had fulfilled a long-ago prophecy of an old Russian gypsy fortune teller, who had warned her, "Beware of dark waters."

On board *Splendour* that fateful night was another guest, actor Christopher Walken, who was co-starring with Natalie in a sci-fi flick, *Brainstorm.* Some of the cast had reported rumors that Natalie had fallen for the charismatic Walken, the son of a lion tamer. She was said to have

The yacht, *Splendour (above),* was supposed to bring joy to the "fairy-tale" marriage of Natalie Wood and Robert Wagner.

But reporters over the years have filed stories that the "idyllic" couple were "jealous, possessive, and distrustful" of each other. That was certainly true when R.J. sailed the *Splendour* to Catalina with Natalie and Christopher Walken aboard.

Simultaneously, Hollywood gossips were spreading stories that Natalie had fallen for Walken while co-starring with him in *Brainstorm* (1983).

Natalie in a rare photograph aboard the *Splendour's* dingy, a small vessel that would forever be linked to her death. To travel ashore in this dingy, Natalie would have had to overcome her life-long fear of the water. The star was filled with a dread of darkness and a belief that she would die by drowning.

The lonely dingy was found floating in the waters offshore Blue Cavern Point, with scratch marks on its side, as though a doomed Natalie had desperately tried to climb aboard.

621

been entranced by his differently colored eyes—one blue, the other hazel.

Speculation centered around a possible lovers' quarrel between a jealous husband and an errant wife. Reporters, as well as the public, were asking, "Did she accidentally fall overboard, and her husband was too drunk to save her? Or else was she pushed after a violent argument, perhaps over infidelity?"

The mystery lingers to this day.

Rock made his first public appearance after his bypass surgery when he escorted Elizabeth to Natalie's funeral at the Westwood Memorial Park where Marilyn Monroe—or what was left of her—was entombed.

Even in his weakened condition, Rock served as one of the pallbearers of the white-and-gold trimmed coffin covered with a blanket of 450 white gardenias worked into candlelight lace set off with a green ribbon.

Rock greeted Laurence Olivier, who had flown in from London for the service. He was joined by Frank Sinatra, Fred Astaire, David Niven, Gene Kelly, Gregory Peck, and director Elia Kazan. Walken was seen chatting with Stefanie Powers, Rock's friend.

At the peak of their beauty, Natalie Wood and Robert ("R.J.") Wagner were two stars who flourished on the Hollywood scene during the closing days of the studio system. As a child star she delivered a legendary performance in *Miracle on 34th Street* (1947).

Natalie's mother, a superstitious Russian immigrant laying her claims to royalty, told her daughter, "You will become a star, the biggest in Hollywood."

R.J., as a teenager, had grown up with such mentors as Gary Cooper and Clark Gable. Gable reportedly told R.J., "You're too handsome not to become a matinee idol. Just keep it zipped for the hundreds of faggots you'll meet in this damn business."

Eulogies were delivered by some of her closest friends, especially Roddy McDowall, as well as Tommy Thompson and Hope Lange. Mourners formed a semi-circle around the coffin, as they listened to a balalaika player, symbolic of Natalie's Russian heritage.

After the service, Rock escorted Elizabeth to the Wagner home in Beverly Hills, where mourners indulged in some heavy drinking, including Rock, who had promised his doctors that he'd give it up.

Friends assembled in the living room to say a few words of remembrance. Rock spoke, "Natalie was just a wide-eyed little kid when I worked with her on our picture, *One Desire*, back in 1955. God those were the days, my friends. Over the years, I watched as she grew into an international symbol of grace and beauty, enchanting not only us, but the world. Our hearts go out to Robert in his hour of grief…and ours."

Driving Elizabeth back to her home, he said in a low voice, slightly slurred by alcohol, "I think Natalie was murdered."

***

Dr. Rex Kennamer had warned Tom Clark that Rock might experience a personality change in the weeks after his bypass surgery. For some mysterious reason, patients often went through rapid mood shifts, including deep depressions, even periods of hostility, after such surgery and blood transfusions.

Clark said, "The doctor told me that such changes often lasted no more than a few weeks, not for the rest of one's life., which was the case with Rock. I'm not saying Dr. Jekyll became Mr. Hyde, but gone was the joking, fun-loving, good-natured big guy who had been my companion for seven years."

Two days after returning to The Castle, Rock demanded that Clark move out of his bedroom and into a guest room on the far side of the building. "I've got the night sweats, and I'm sleepless most of the time. I don't want to be disturbed."

Even close friends like Claire Trevor, who usually came for Sunday dinner, noted the change in him. She was worried that he had not only resumed his heavy drinking, but his heavy smoking. Even though Kennamer warned that might cause complications to his health, even leading to an early death. "If you're gonna die, you die," Rock said.

After dinner, Rock started his boozing and at one point seemed annoyed with Trevor, even though she'd always been very supportive of him. "What does it feel like to be a has-been?" he asked her. Her feelings seemed seriously wounded, and she made a gracious exit a few minutes later. He usually hugged and kissed her goodbye, but not this time. He walked out into his garden, not inviting company.

He took a number of pills during his recovery. George Nader noted, "He'd enter deep periods of depression and retreat to his bedroom for two or three days without coming out. His butler, James Wright, served him meals, but often, he hardly touched his food. He left word that he didn't want to see anybody, nor did he want to accept any phone calls even from such friends as Roddy McDowall."

Kennamer had also warned Clark that he could expect renewed sexual energy from Rock. "I thought it would be the opposite of that. That he would give that raging libido of his a rest. That didn't happen. He no longer had sex with me, and had not for quite a while. But he began to see a parade of young men, often hustlers. Sometimes, he'd have two a night, giving each of them a hundred-dollar bill and sending them on their way. He didn't like 'repeats.'"

In the midst of all this, Rock received word that his so-called father, Roy Scherer, had died at the age of 83 at the Motion Picture Home. He had never been an actor, but Rock had been a heavy contributor to the home, and used his influence to get him installed there. In his final years, Scherer had suffered from dementia following the death of his third wife, Edith. For thirty years, Rock had been sending him $200 a month, even though he'd deserted Kay and himself when Rock was just a boy.

Rock sent flowers to the funeral, but didn't show up himself. He called the funeral home and agreed to pay for the burial expenses. "Just bury him and be done with it. He wasn't my real father anyway." Then he slammed down the phone.

For weeks after *The Devlin Connection* had aired on TV, Rock blamed Clark for its failure. "I occasionally brought him scripts he'd been offered, especially if I thought they were good, but he'd turn them down without reading them. Once, he told Clark, "A joke like you wouldn't know a good script if you were handed one. You would have turned down the Burt Lancaster role for me in *From Here to Eternity.*"

"Rock ordered no more parties, no more dinners for friends. He also said no more feature films, no more TV series," Clark said.

"Sometimes he joined me for dinner, but had little to say," Clark said. "His mind was far, far away. He often left the house late at night and didn't return until dawn. He never mentioned where he'd been or what he had done. When asked, he'd say, 'Oh, I just went for a walk by the beach.'"

The first-ever fight between Clark and Rock occurred on October 7, 1982 in the kitchen of The Castle. Wright had retired for the evening, but his bedroom adjoined the kitchen and Rock's trusted servant heard it, telling Mark Miller what had happened when Miller reported to work the next day.

"Mr. Hudson and Tom were shouting at each other louder than I have ever heard," Wright said. "Mr. Hudson, in fact, ordered him out of his house."

"I should have kicked you out eight years ago!" Rock shouted. "It was finished then. I let you linger around like a fucking parasite. You've been nothing but a burden to me. It's over between us. Get the hell out of here!"

"You can't do this to me," Clark shouted back, with Wright hearing every word. "I've done everything for you: Managed your career, your life. Taken care of you. Everything."

"You've done nothing but enrich your fat ass at my expense!" Rock charged.

"Suddenly, I heard what sounded like Mr. Hudson knocking Tom down," Wright claimed. "There was this crash and some breaking dishes. I think Tom hit the floor. I heard him say, 'You punched me in the eye.'"

"It serves you right, you fucker," Rock yelled. "If you keep this up, I'll black your other eye, too. Blind it like George Nader's."

"Go ahead!" Clark yelled. "I dare you!"

Retreating to the guest room, Clark began to clean up his business affairs in Hollywood. In the meantime, Rock avoided him, staying in a different part of The Castle. By the end of October, Clark left. Rock did not come out to tell him goodbye.

When Trevor told Clark that she was leaving California and going to live permanently in her Fifth Avenue apartment in New York, he decided to fly east with her. He packed his bags and prepared to go, since he still had the keys to Rock's apartment at The Beresford, which he had helped to restore and redecorate.

"I felt empty in Manhattan living by myself after having been Rock's faithful companion all these years. A part of my life was missing, and that part was 'The Rock.' Every day I expected him to call, knowing we would make up and he'd invite me back."

"Very rarely, he phoned, but it was always about some unfinished business about our dealings together," Clark said. "Once he called and told me he was sending over a contract for *The Ambassador*, a picture deal he'd made with Cannon Films to be shot in Israel with Bob Mitchum. He wanted me to look over the contract, which I did. But I also read the script, and advised him not to do it. He didn't take my advice."

Finally, it dawned on Clark that he had to start a new life, a life on his own…without Rock Hudson.

In the TV teleplay, *World War III*, in his role as President of the United States, Rock orders a nuclear strike on the Soviet Union.

***

Rock's next acting job was an appearance as the (fictional) President of the United States, Thomas McKenna. In a mini-series in two parts, *World War III* (1982). This production of Telepictures ran for 200 minutes.

Its original director was Boris Segal, but he'd died in a helicopter accident in Oregon. At the last minute, David Greene was called in. This British director had helmed Carol Burnett in *Friendly Fire* (1979), for which he'd won an Emmy.

The lead in *World War III* was David Soul, who starred as Col Jacob Caffey. The actor and Rock had previously co-starred in another teleplay, *Guilt by Association.*

A well-established actor, Brian Keith, who usually played on-screen tough guys, was cast as the Soviet premier, Secretary Gorny. More than a dozen years before, in *Reflections in a Golden Eye* 1967), Keith had played the stern military husband of Julie Harris in this Southern Gothic tale that had co-starred Elizabeth Taylor and Marlon Brando cast as her homosexual husband.

In *World War III*, Cathy Lee Crosby (no relation to Bing) played the female lead, Kate Breckenridge. She invited Rock for a game of tennis, to which he responded, "No way!" He'd heard that she'd been a professional player at Wimbledon. From 1980 to 1984 on ABC, she'd co-hosted the TV series, *That's Incredible,* and had also starred as *Wonder Woman* (1974) in that made-for-TV movie.

The plot of *World War III* focused on Cold War themes of brinkmanship, political loyalty, and the mutual distrust of the Americans and the Soviets.

The mini-series begins in 1987, which was a projection into the future since the movie was made in 1982. The Soviets make a secret incursion into Alaska. The tension mounts, as the two nations move toward nuclear war.

As President, Rock is last seen horrified and nearly in tears, as he concludes that an atomic confrontation with the Soviets is inevitable. He orders a full nuclear counterstrike upon the Soviet Union.

The series ends with a photo montage of people across the globe awaiting their annihilation, looking up to the sky at their last sunset before the screen fades to black.

If the ratings had been high enough, the producers wanted to spin *World War III* into a mini-series with Rock. But when it aired, the teleplay "bombed," so to speak.

***

La Cage aux Folles, a farcical gay musical, opened on Broadway in 1983, and became an enormous hit, followed by a series of international revivals. *[In French,* Folles *translates either as "mad women" or as a slang term for effem-*

inate gay men.] The book was by Harvey Fierstein, with lyrics and music by Jerry Herman of *Hello, Dolly* fame.

The plot centers around a French nightclub in St. Tropez, run by Georges and his lover, Albin, the club's star attraction whenever he performs in drag. The action heats up when Georges' son, Jean-Michel, makes an announcement. *[In Paris years ago, Georges had a brief heterosexual fling, during which he fathered a son.]* Now Jean-Michel is in love and wants to marry, and he's invited his fiancée's ultra-conservative parents to meet his family.

Claire Trevor thought that the role of Georges "would be a lot of fun" for Rock, and she purchased tickets and invited him to go and see it with her.

He found it hilarious but asked, "Do I dare?" Backstage, they were introduced to the stars, Gene Barry, as Georges, and George Hearn as Albin.

The musical was set for an opening in London's West End for the New Year, and the producers offered Rock the lead.

While negotiating with the producers of the show, Rock was sent an item that appeared in *Him Monthly,* the leading gay magazine of Britain. It read, *"La Cage aux Folles,* the musical, is whispered to be opening in London. Normally, you could count me out but ROCK HUDSON is playing a faggot. This is a must see!"

Fearing many such stories and unwilling to expose himself to ridicule, Rock phoned the producers. "After careful consideration, I've decided the role is not right for me."

***

The TV drama, *The Vegas Strip War* (aka *The Vegas Casino War*), was another teleplay that soured for Rock.

For a 1984 production for television, Rock signed with ITC Entertainment to play the lead in *The Vegas Strip War* with James Earl Jones and Sharon Stone, for which

He had two strong supporting players, sexy Sharon Stone and very talented James Earl Jones, but even they could not keep this gambling drama from going broke.

he was paid $260,000.

It was his last major acting gig on television before *Dynasty*. In it, he was cast *as* Neil Chaine, the owner of a Las Vegas casino, trying to become the top attraction along the Strip. He's aided by Sarah Shipman (Stone), a young casino hostess who tried to help him get a gaming license from the Nevada authorities. Jack Madrid (Jones) is a flamboyant sports promoter, surely based on Don King. Rock wants him to stage a major boxing match at his hotel.

The producer was George Englund, who was Marlon Brando's best friend. The actor had starred in Englund's 1963 movie, *The Ugly American*, and he later wrote a memoir about their friendship. At one time, Englund was married to the actress, Cloris Leachman.

Jones, an African American son of Mississippi, has been hailed as "one of the greatest actors in American history," but even such an august presence could not save this teleplay. His stirring *basso profundo* led to producers using it as the voice of Darth Vader in the *Star Wars* series.

A beauty and a former fashion model, Stone would increasingly become an international sex symbol, noted for her roles in erotic and adult-themed feature films such as the notorious *Basic Instinct* (1992). She would also pose nude for *Playboy*. She had a good reason to remember her forgettable role in the Vegas movie: On the set, she met the producer, Michael Greenberg, and married him that same year.

If Stone looked gorgeous, Rock did not, many of his fans finding that he appeared "haggard." When Rock heard complaints of his diminishing good looks, he said, "In a few years, I'll be drawing Social Security. Let's face it: The dew is off the Morning Glory."

The Vegas Strip War was aired on NBC on November 25, 1984. One critic wrote: "George Englund wrote and directed it and cast Rock Hudson in the lead, a series of three big mistakes. The less said about Hudson, the better. Talk about a bad performance. Even sexy Sharon Stone can't save this dud."

What was Rock's reaction? "The title tells you the whole story, doesn't it? In the teleplay, I own a casino—doesn't everybody?"

***

Flo Allen of the William Morris Agency had long represented Rock. But in the declining months of his career, "she was shooting blanks" (his words), and he was getting no acceptable offers.

In his search to replace her, he'd been hearing good reports about Martin ("Marty") Baum, who was known for his work at Creative Artists

628

Agency (CAA), including the first head of that agency's motion picture department. He represented such artists as Bette Davis, Richard Attenborough, Red Buttons, Carroll O'Connor, Dyan Cannon, Gene Wilder, Julie Andrews, Richard Harris, Harry Belafonte, Stockard Channing, Joanne Woodward, John Cassavetes, Gena Rowlands, Rod Steiger, Cliff Robertson, and Maggie Smith. He'd also overseen the production of such films as *They Shoot Horses, Don't They?* (1969) and *Cabaret* (1972). Baum was also instrumental in putting together a package deal that included Sidney Poitier, Rock's former co-star, in the 1963 *Lilies of the Field,* which brought the star a Best Actor Oscar.

The Ambassador, filmed in Israel, would be the last featured film in which Rock would appear. Shot months before his death, it would co-star Robert Mitchum.

As movie-goers noted, these once handsome, macho, and charismatic stars of Hollywood's Golden Age had seen better days.

Baum quickly learned that Rock had millions in the bank and didn't need to work to survive. "He wanted jobs because he loved making movies—he knew nothing else," Baum said. "It had been his entire life, and he wasn't ready to retire." Rock signed with Creative Artists on September 19, 1983.

Baum immediately got Rock cast as the second lead in *The Ambassador,* a political thriller about Middle East intrigue, for which he was paid $500,000. Released by Cannon Films in 1984, it would be Rock's final feature film. For the first time in thirty years, he accepted "second banana billing" (his words) to another actor, in this case, Robert Mitchum. Its plot was inspired by a decades-old crime novel, *53 Pick-Up,* by Elmore Leonard.

Rock flew to Israel to play the minor role of Frank Stevenson, a CIA agent in what was really a subplot. The overall focus of the movie was on Mitchum, cast as Peter Hacker, the U.S. Ambassador to Israel. Both men were *en route* to a secret location in the Judean desert to meet with agents of the PLO (Palestinian Liberation Organization).

Ellen Burstyn was cast as Mitchum's lonely wife, Alex Hacker, who, while in Jerusalem, secretly conducts an affair with a radical PLO leader. Regrettably for her, this tryst was videotaped.

Rock's director was the British-born J. Lee Thompson, whose glory days were over. Once, he'd turned out such international hits as *The Guns of Navarone* (1961), starring Gregory Peck. He'd also helmed Peck again, in league with Mitchum, in the psychological thriller, *Cape Fear* (1962). Now, he was turning out low-budget exploitation movies, but in his heyday, he'd directed an array of British and American stars who had included John Mills, Anthony Quayle, Dirk Bogarde, Yul Brynner, Shirley MacLaine, and Dinah Dors, the sexy British blonde bombshell with whom Rock had once shared a lover.

The Ambassador was shot in both Israel and on the West Bank. Cast and crew were threatened with terrorist attacks, and the production hired armed patrols to guard them.

"Rock had not recovered from heart surgery," Thompson later said. "He was losing weight, and he blamed it on 'night sweats,' but I suspected that there was something more seriously wrong with him. I was surprised he'd accepted such a minor role. I know he didn't need the money. I tried to improve his part a bit. He was smoking a lot, and Bob was boozing a lot. The two actors didn't like each other. Let's face it: Both of them as stars had seen better days."

When his work on the film ended, back in Hollywood, Rock told a reporter, "In *The Ambassador*, I played a sort of CIA-security enigma, and I keep calling in to somebody. I don't know who. While we were shooting the film, soldiers with machine guns were all over the streets. We were constantly reminded of war and how people get used to it as a way of life. When I was much younger, I foolishly thought of war as a glamourous, exciting thing, as it had been depicted in all those old movies I went to. Today, I'm more aware of just how really stupid it is. "

After playing in just a few cities, *The Ambassador*, by now defined as a commercial failure, was put in mothballs. After Rock died, it was released on home video to take advantage of the publicity surrounding his well-publicized death.

Then Cannon did an amazing thing, almost unheard of in the movie industry. In just two years, the studio remade the film under its original title, *52 Pick-Up*, this time directed by John Frankenheimer.

***

To Rock's most devoted friends and his fans, the name of Marc Christian will live in infamy. There are various versions of how the pair met, and Christian told three different stories, depending on what month it was. The most reliable report came from George Nader, who quoted Rock directly.

Rock patronized the Brooks Baths, across from the CBS Studio. By the autumn of 1982, Rock went there two or three times a week, seeking a massage, a steambath, a sauna, and a possible conquest. He had a private room, where he took his trick of the afternoon. On the road to sixty, he was not in good shape at the time, but he was still THE ROCK HUDSON. Many handsome young men, often wannabe actors, were willing to do his bidding. Sometimes, money was exchanged. Rock started carrying around at least five hundred dollars in one-hundred dollar denominations.

Tom Clark was still living at The Castle when Rock first met Christian. Like the other men there, Rock was sitting nude on a wooden bench when Christian, equally nude, made his entrance into the sauna.

As Rock told Nader "on the first look, he was my ideal type: blonde hair, blue eyes, good physique, weighing in at about 170 pounds, a beard and mustache—that would have to go—broad chest, wide shoulders, sculpted pectorals, and muscular legs, and he stood 6'2"."

The other men in the sauna soon left, leaving Christian and Rock alone. As he confided to Nader, "The kid kept waving his dick at me until I finally took the bait."

The men left the sauna and stood under cold showers before retreating to Rock's private room. "He was a hot little number," Rock told Nader. "Great sex. I took his phone number and soon would be calling him."

At this point, he knew nothing about Christian, but wanted to see him again. As the young man handed him his phone number, he warned, "Don't be surprised if a woman answers. I'm bisexual."

The woman referenced, as Rock was soon to learn, was Liberty Martin, with whom he lived in her small apartment in West Hollywood.

The attorney for Rock's estate, Robert Parker Mills, later likened her to the silent screen vamp and has-been, Norma Desmond, that Gloria Swanson played in *Sunset Blvd* (1950). Flamboyant in dress and mannerisms, she wore wide-brimmed hats to conceal her age. Christian admitted that he and this former publicist had been lovers for four years until 1979.

In the final months of his life, Rock entered into a disastrous union with a Hollywood hustler, Marc Christian.

The young man would do more than any other person to tarnish Rock's already tarnished reputation, his macho image destroyed when the world learned he had AIDS.

631

"I no longer sleep in her bedroom. I'm confined to the sofa."

"Do you think I'm still attractive?" Rock asked. "Or should I ask that?"

Christian said he didn't necessarily go for young lovers, and that Liberty was actually some thirty years older than him. He was 29 at the time.

Over dinner two nights later at a gay restaurant, Christian said he'd worked at a series of odd jobs since leaving his family in conservative Orange County and striking out on his own. "I've told them I'm gay, or bisexual, I mean. That's not a problem for them."

He said that he was creating a music anthology based on his love of jazz and other forms of music. Rock talked to him about remastering his extensive archive of 78 rpm records, and getting his film collection in order.

As their relationship developed, Rock also offered to send him to his dentist, Dr. Philipp Tennis, to have his teeth fixed. He offered him the use of a car. There was talk of moving him into The Castle, which Rock claimed would be possible as soon as he got rid of Tom Clark, his personal manager who had been his sometimes lover.

Rock held out the possibility that Christian come to work for him at the salary of $400 a week. [*At the time, he was paying $100 a week, respectively, to Mark Miller, to James Wright (his butler), and to his elderly longtime gardener, Clarence Morimoto.*] Christian eagerly accepted Rock's generous offer.

At one point, when they'd spent the night together in a West Hollywood motel, Christian confessed that he actually came to Hollywood to be an actor. The next day, Rock drove him to meet the still glamorous Nina Foch, with whom he'd appeared in a *McMillan* teleplay, *Philip's Game*. With the falloff of film roles, Foch had opened a small drama school. She and Christian got along surprisingly well, and she enrolled him in her classes that late afternoon.

At one point, Christian expressed anxiety to Rock that he was worried about his father, who was suffering from lung cancer. Rock volunteered to help with his medical expenses. It is not known if the money Rock gave with that intention, amounting over months to thousands of dollars, ever actually paid any hospital bills. Clark thought Christian put the money into his own bank account.

One night at a restaurant in Hollywood, Rock met his long-ago acquaintance, the author, Gore Vidal. When he started to introduce him to Christian, Vidal said, "Marc and I are very well acquainted." He said that in a suggestive way.

When Vidal departed, Christian admitted that he'd driven Vidal around in 1982, during the author's failed attempt to win a Senate seat in California.

Christian would later maintain that he met Rock at a political rally for

Vidal. But his campaign had ended in June of 1982, and Christian didn't meet Rock until that October.

The next day, Vidal phoned Rock with some details about Christian's past: "Watch the little shit. Don't trust him even in your sight. He's also a potential blackmailer."

Christian never confessed to having been a hustler, claiming instead that he had worked for the Institute of American Musicals. A check later revealed that there was no such organization.

Rock was disheartened to hear Vidal's gossipy assessment, but nonetheless, he continued in his relationship with the young man, even behaving indiscreetly.

Before flying to Israel to make *The Ambassador* with Robert Mitchum, Rock invited Christian to move into The Castle, alerting his staff.

Rock was already on location in the Middle East when Christian arrived with all of his possessions, which he transferred from the apartment of Liberty Martin. The date was November 5, 1983.

Depressed and lonely in his hotel room in Israel, Rock wrote Christian a series of letters, which he later described as "affectionate in nature." When Christian introduced them as evidence of their intimacy in a court case, the young man labeled them as "love letters." He used these letters to blackmail Rock during the final months of his life.

Rock arrived back at The Castle just in time to celebrate Christmas with Christian. Both Nader and Miller enjoyed the holiday season with the two lovers. "They looked like honeymooners," Nader said. "Rock couldn't keep his hands off Christian."

The highlight of Christmas was when Christian presented Rock with his gift. It was a tape of himself (Christian) dressed as Doris Day, wearing a blonde wig and lipsynching "Sentimental Journey." Rock thought it was hilarious.

James Wright, Rock's butler, kept a sharp eye on the comings and goings at The Castle. Right before the New Year, he approached his employer and told him that during Rock's sojourn in Israel, Christian had entertained several male lovers in The Castle's master bedroom. Rock was furious but didn't confront Christian. However, he ordered Wright to move all of Christian's clothing and possessions out of his bedroom and into the guest room formerly occupied by Clark.

After that episode, the relationship between Christian and Rock began to erode. Christian always slept late, and Rock had, somewhat sarcastically, dubbed him, "My Sleeping Prince."

But Wright, and even Nader, noted that as 1984 deepened, Rock referred to him as "The Asshole," "The Jerk," "The Ditz," or more commonly,

"Dickhead." Wright estimated that Christian and Rock never had sexual relations after February of 1984. "They were leading separate lives under one roof."

Rock was not faithful to Christian either. In March of 1984, he was asked to present Shirley MacLaine with the Best Actress Oscar for her performance as Aurora Greenway in *Terms of Endearment* (1983).

On the night of the Oscars, he did not return home to The Castle. He was later reported to having booked a bungalow on the grounds of the Beverly Hills Hotel, where he had stayed before. His companion was Julian Français, who had formerly been a member of the Royal Mounties in Canada before he was kicked out "for immoral behavior."

Rock was so pleased with the performance of this "hunk from the north" that the following day, he paid for a budget apartment for the 28-year-old in West Hollywood, and would visit him frequently. When Rock didn't need his services, Français saw a number of older women, who paid for his charms.

Back at The Castle, a wall of indifference was growing between Christian and Rock. Wright noticed that on some late mornings when Rock was having coffee in the kitchen, Christian would enter and Rock would not even look up from his newspaper. "Those guys didn't have anything to say to each other."

Miller urged Rock to give Christian the boot, but he did not. "If I kick him out, he's threatening blackmail. He said he'd splash me all over the tabloids."

Christian often complained to Miller that Rock never introduced him to his straight friends such as Carol Burnett or Elizabeth Taylor. He "bitched" to Miller that Rock was doing absolutely nothing to help launch his own career.

Miller told him, "Rock right now isn't doing all that great with his own career."

Wright became alarmed when he noted a number of valuable objects disappearing from The Castle. Christian was the prime suspect. Clark confirmed that when he returned to arrange the shipment of the remainder of his possessions to New York, "Several things were stolen, including some gold-and-lapis studs and cufflinks Rock had given me one Christmas. I think Christian was stealing the items and stashing them somewhere."

"He seemed to have some power over Rock," Clark said. "I think Rock was afraid of exposure."

As Rock told Clark goodbye, he said, "The guy scares me. He may be psycho. I definitely feel he's nuts."

"Maybe you can pay him off and get rid of him," Clark advised. "I see nothing but trouble ahead for you and 'Asshole,' as you call him. Don't say I didn't warn you."

On that ominous note, Clark departed in a taxi for the airport.

Rock's life at this point was growing more complicated. A new man had entered into his world.

***

He was a good-looking, 28-year-old man from Tampa, Florida. His name was Ron Channell.

After his bypass operation, Rock wanted to get into shape and went to a local health club, Sports Connection. Ron was a trainer there, and he showed Rock around the gym, explaining the workout equipment to him. Rock told him he didn't like a lot of people staring at him while he worked out, and he asked Ron if he'd sign on as his personal trainer.

Ron agreed and began arriving at The Castle at 10AM, using the gym equipment that Rock had installed at The Castle but always avoided.

Robert Parker Mills, the attorney for Rock's estate after his death, said that Ron "reminded me a lot of the 'Bluto' character in Popeye. He was very tall, muscular, a young man with a day's grown of beard and a mustache."

As Sara Davidson wrote, "Ron was a new physical type for Rock: He had dark skin, brown eyes, and very dark hair. Ron knew that Rock was infatuated with him and that he hoped that the relationship would grow to something more than friendship, but Ron kept things on the buddy level. He indicated that he was straight, and didn't feel as Rock did, and yet there was an element of flirtation and pursuit. They fell in love as two men friends do, excited about discovering each other."

A friendship was rapidly developing. After the workout, Rock started inviting Ron for lunch, followed by a shopping expedition or some other jaunt in the afternoon. Back at The Castle, Rock would ask, "Why don't you stick around for dinner?" The meal was often followed with a screening of movies from Rock's extensive vault, many of them Rock's own movies which Ron had never seen.

After Ron saw *Iron Man* (1951), which Rock had made with his off-screen lover, Jeff Chandler, he started calling Rock "Speed," based on the name of the boxer he'd played in the film.

Rock was fascinated by Channell and, according to Nader, hoped that the relationship would become sexual, but Channell really meant it when he told Rock he was straight. "In the past, Rock would probably have come on to him, but in late middle age, he'd mellowed and viewed his friendship with Ron as too important to ruin by making passes at him."

Most of his friends, however, just assumed they were lovers. "Ron brought laughter back to Rock, something that had gone out of his life," Nader said. "They were always laughing, joking, giggling, telling fart jokes, their favorite. Rock would sometimes sit in Ron's lap, pretending they were comedian Edgar Bergen and his puppet, Charlie McCarthy.

James Wright noted that "Every morning when Ron arrived, Mr. Hudson's spirits brightened. I think they were as close as two guys can get without sexual intimacy. In locker room talk, they might be called 'asshole buddies.'"

On some nights "Rock and Ron" as they came to be called, visited friends. Without prying into their privacy, Elizabeth Taylor assumed they were lovers.

They also went to restaurants, mostly in West Hollywood or Malibu. But Rock seemed to prefer nights at home, if not watching movies, then playing songs at his piano. Ron soon learned that Rock "just loved Boogie-Woogie." Rock also urged Ron to pursue his acting ambition, and even arranged a screen test for him.

Even though Marc Christian and Rock had ended their affair, Christian steadfastly refused to move out of The Castle. He detested Ron and never spoke to him except one time. He asked Ron, "Why does a straight guy hang out all the time in a gay household?"

"I open the mail," was Ron's replay.

At one point, Christian threatened to sell an *exposé* about Ron and Rock to the *Enquirer*, alleging that they were having a torrid affair.

Soon, it was Ron, not Christian, going everywhere with Rock, including trips to New York, where they stayed in his apartment at the Beresford, or to Honolulu, even flights to London and Paris.

Ron would later testify in court that at no time did he ever see any relationship, much less a friendship, that Rock had with Marc Christian. "They were not friendly—in fact, they weren't speaking—Christian seemed to be the guy who came to dinner—and never left. I think Rock detested him."

"Rock's deepest desire was to have Ron fall in love with him, even though he was straight," said Nader. "But that didn't happen. I think Ron came to love Rock, but, of course, that was different from being *in love* with him."

What did Rock say about all those reports that he'd fallen in love with Ron Channel?

"Love? It's overexaggerated. Being in love with someone has been too romanticized. People expect just too much from it, more than it can be."

***

Rock's longtime friends, ex-actors Ronald and Nancy Reagan, now President of the United States and First Lady, invited him to fly to Washington to attend a presidential dinner at the White House on May 15, 1984. In the 1950s and 60s, Rock often attended their parties in Hollywood, and he was eager to accept the invitation.

When he arrived at the White House, he was delighted that the First Lady had chosen him, among others, to be among the honored guests at her table. The President also greeted him warmly, although the two actors had never been particularly close.

As Rock later told Mark Miller, "I was bowled over by the 'New Nancy.' She was funny, she was charming, and she sure knew how to work the room. She told me I should fatten up, as my weight had dropped to 195 pounds. I told her she could also put on a few pounds herself, since a heavy wind gust might lift her off the ground and blow her all the way back to California."

He explained his weight loss to her by telling her he'd contracted the flu while making a movie with Robert Mitchum in Israel. With her eagle eye, the First Lady also noticed a large, discolored blemish on his neck, which he told her was a mole. She recommended a dermatologist in Beverly Hills, who had "done some special work for me one time." She gave Rock his name and phone number.

In phone calls, Nancy later told gossipy Hollywood friends that, "I've never seen Rock look so bad. He was once so handsome. I suspect he might be ill. If not that, he's aging rapidly, the curse of all of us, the former stars of yesterday. Thank God I married Ronnie, found a second act in Sacramento and Washington, and didn't end up in some motion picture retirement home, the curse of too many of us."

When Rock returned to Beverly Hills, he phoned his own doctor, Rex Kennamer, and set up an appointment. The doctor seemed somewhat confused by the large red sore on Rock's neck just below his hairline. "That doesn't look like any mole to me," he said.

He set up an appointment for a consultation with a noted dermatologist, Dr. Letantia Bussell. She examined Rock and advised him that the growth was too large for her to remove. She recommended that he set up an appointment with Dr. Frank Kamer, a noted plastic surgeon, who, in 1981, had performed eyelid surgery on Rock.

Kamer ordered a biopsy on a tissue sample from the sore.

Back home, Rock "became a smoke stack," in the words of Wright. "He

637

paced up and down the floor waiting for the results of some sort of test. I feared he might have the clap."

The call he dreaded came in from Dr. Kamer: "It's Kaposi's sarcoma all right," he said. "Since 1982, the disease, which often infects homosexual men, has been referred to as Acquired Immune Deficiency Syndrome, or AIDS for short."

"I'm gonna lick it," Rock told Kamer. "I've overcome a lot of shit in my life, and I think I can beat this, somehow, some way. It's been a good life for me, and I'm not too eager to exit from Planet Earth."

At this point, Rock had not told Miller he had AIDS. "He looked okay," Miller said, "although he didn't say much on the way back to The Castle. Wright had prepared one of his favorite meals, hot dogs and Boston baked beans. Rock ate it and retired to his bedroom for about two hours. Finally, he met me in the garden."

Sitting facing him on a bench, Rock admitted, "Two doctors told me I have AIDS."

"Oh god, Oh, shit!" said Miller.

After confessing to the disease, Rock got up and left. "I want to be by myself."

"I went into a panic," Miller said. "My first fear was that I might get it, or else George would be infected. In those days, we didn't know how AIDS was transmitted. George and I live close to Rock, who has this annoying habit of eating off my plate."

"The only thing I knew about AIDS at the time was what I read in *Newsweek* the year before. The magazine editors called it "The Health Threat of the Century."

"At first, I thought only 'bottoms' selling their asses along Santa Monica Boulevard got infected," Miller said. "Rock and I often used the same toilet. Could it be passed by urine? George and I kiss Rock on the mouth whenever we greeted him. He often sampled something cooking on the stove, then put the spoon back into the pot. Could that cause someone to get AIDS? I didn't know, and I was afraid. I had to tell George everything."

Rock also wanted Nader to know, but he warned Miller, "Don't tell Asshole," referring to Marc Christian. "That fucker might sell the story to the tabloids."

Nader went out and purchased a paperback entitled *AIDS*. In it, he learned that the disease was most often contracted through an exchange of semen and blood. A tear in the anal canal could cause a sexual partner to become infected.

Millions of people, especially if they were straight, lived without fear of getting the virus, seemingly unaware that any human being with a bloodstream was vulnerable. As late as July of 1984, the president of American Airlines opened a breakfast at the Republican National Convention with "Know what GAY stands for?" he asked. "Got AIDS yet?"

Authorities knew that half the people identified with the syndrome were not homosexuals. The virus also infected hemophiliacs, users of intravenous drugs like heroin, and Haitian immigrants—in fact, some researchers called it "the 4H disease."

AIDS was known at first as "the gay plague," before it swept across the planet, killing millions of people every year, including children.

Even at the White House, the subject of AIDS was taboo. However, the Surgeon General, C. Everett Koop, brought AIDS into a policy discussion on the national level with his groundbreaking reports on the rapid spread of the disease. Only the very ignorant felt the disease could not strike them. But it wasn't until the waning months of his presidency that Reagan even mentioned the subject.

On June 7, 1984, Dr. Kennamer canceled all afternoon appointments to clear his office for the arrival of Dr. Michael Gottlieb from UCLA to examine Rock. At the age of 67, the distinguished doctor, an immunologist, was the first to identify AIDS as a new disease.

[He would later serve on the board of the Elizabeth Taylor AIDS Foundation.]

"When I arrived at Dr. Kennamer's office, I had not been told who my patient was," Gottlieb said. "I just knew it was some movie star, because he treated quite a few of them. I walked into his back office, and there sat a shirtless Rock Hudson on the examination table. We made eye contact. The first thing I said to him was, 'How tall are you?'"

"Six feet four," he said in a shy, almost boyish voice."

The extensive examination lasted for three hours, at the end of which Gottlieb told Rock, "You definitely have AIDS."

"Am I going to die?" he asked.

"There is no cure," Gottlieb answered. "I suggest you get your affairs in order."

"What about sex?"

"You should refrain," Gottlieb said. "If you're driven, then use a condom and be extra careful. Do you have a sexual partner at the moment?"

"I did, but that's over," Rock said. "He still lives in my house. I've had three recent partners. Unprotected sex. I know how to reach only one of them. The other two were ships that passed in the night."

"That's up to you, but it might be wise to alert him," Gottlieb said.

On the way back to The Castle, with Miller at the wheel, Rock poured out his anguish, often sobbing. "It's all over for me. My career, my love life. No one will ever go to bed with me again. I'll be shunned like a leper.

I feel so ashamed. If word gets out, I'll never work again: No actor will want to appear with me. You know I hug and kiss my friends on the cheek when I greet them. They'll be afraid of me. The doctor told me I have only months to live, perhaps a year at the very most."

"Don't tell Christian," Rock ordered. "We stopped having sex months ago."

"What about Ron Channel?" Miller asked.

"No way," Rock said. "We're just good buddies, and that's the way it's going to be."

The next day, Rock had Nader write a letter to a Secret Service agent at the White House. Rock had made eye contact with him at the presidential dinner and had set up a rendezvous at midnight when he got off from work. The letter was mailed from San Diego and anonymously, signed "A Friend."

Rock had claimed that the Secret Service agent had come on to him. "He was a dead ringer for Chuck Connors in *The Rifleman*. Really hot. I slipped him into my hotel suite, and he spent the night. After sex, he told me delicious stories about some of the wild sex parties members of the Secret Service had. I gathered he was promiscuous, so he would not know the letter warning him about AIDS came from me. He'll think it was from one of his other sexual partners."

For the next few months, Rock put up a brave front, telling anyone who asked, "I feel just great. I've been dieting and I have this personal trainer to keep me in shape. I'm ready and willing to go to work if the right role comes along."

After Rock's death, in an interview, Gottlieb described their first encounter: "When I met him, I never could have imagined that he would be the pivotal person in the history of the AIDS epidemic, the single most influential patient ever."

Chapter Twenty-One

ROCK'S AIDS SHOCKS THE WORLD
WIDELY BROADCAST, THE SYNDROME AND ITS STIGMA DESTROYS HIS CAREFULLY CULTIVATED SCREEN IMAGE

Experimental Treatments in Paris Fail
As Rock Suffers a Slow, Agonizing Death.
Friends Flock to His Bedside.

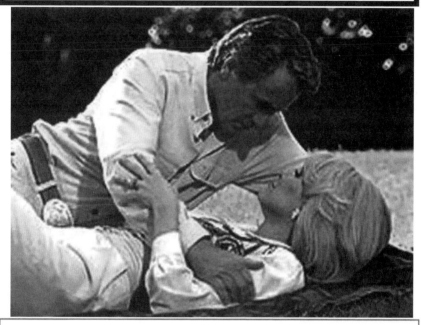

In a romantic scene from the hit TV series, *Dynasty,* Rock is about to kiss Linda Evans. It was to become one of the most notorious onscreen kisses of the 20th Century.

At a time when thousands of people thought one could get AIDS by merely shaking hands, the kiss caused panic. The press speculated that kissing Rock might have infected Evans with the virus. The most outrageous comment appeared in the *Sunday Express* in London, when John Junor accused Rock of making a calculated attempt to sicken the TV actress.

Rock wanted as few of his friends as possible to know he had AIDS, a condition he referred to as "a deadly secret." He made an exception for Dean Dittman. He had met the Kansas-born actor during their five-month tour with the musical *On the Twentieth Century.* The heavyset actor had played Daddy Warbucks in the Off-Broadway production of *Little Orphan Annie* starring Rock's dear friend, Martha Raye.

One night at a drunken dinner at Dittman's all-green apartment in Los Angeles, Rock broke down and confessed to his friend that he had contracted AIDS. As he did, he pulled some condoms from his pocket. "I've never worn one of these damn things in my life. I don't even know how to put one on."

That evening, he broke down and cried, pouring out his frustration to Dittman. "Why me?" he asked. "Why do I have to die? I wanted to settle into old age like such mature actors as Spencer Tracy, Henry Fonda, and Jimmy Stewart. Now it seems that wish will be denied me, like life itself."

Dittman tried to be as supportive as he could, suggesting that scientists were working overtime to find a cure. "There is hope," he said to Rock, although he didn't really believe that.

The next day, Dittman went to work, trying to find a ray of hope that might save his friend. He read some of the latest medical research about AIDS, especially what was happening in Paris, where doctors seemed to be desperately working to find a cure before the syndrome evolved from a "gay plague" into a worldwide humanitarian disaster.

As Rock confessed to Dittman that night, "I hope I die of a heart attack before the world finds out I have AIDS."

In the days ahead, he seemed in denial. He drank more, smoked more, and avoided the advice of his doctors. Against their orders, he attended a performance of the musical *Evita*. [*Dr. Gottlieb had told him to avoid crowds because his immune system was weakened, and germs might be passed on to him if any person he encountered was sick with some virus such as the flu.*]

As George Nader noticed, "He almost defied death." As is typical in most cases, at least in the beginning, Rock began to deny he had AIDS in spite of overwhelming evidence that he did. Mark Miller was horrified at how reckless he became with his health.

Rock continued his visits to Dittman's apartment for dinners, and many friends there asked if Rock were sick. Dittman dismissed their queries. "He may have cancer, but I think it's anorexia."

Rock continued to see Elizabeth Taylor, who was alarmed at his weight loss. She told their mutual friend, Roddy McDowall, "I think he has cancer. But until he admits it to me, I don't want to invade his privacy and bluntly ask him. Maybe he can't face it."

Dittman learned through a friend who had AIDS that in Paris, a new drug was being tested. Called HPA-23, it was rumored not to cure AIDS, but to retard the virus.

As soon as Rock heard about it, he phoned Dr. Gottlieb, who was already aware of its reputation as a miracle drug. He made a transatlantic call to Dr. Dominique Dormont at the Percy Hospital on the outskirts of Paris and set up an appointment for Rock.

Before he departed, Gottlieb warned Rock, "There is no guarantee, certainly no guarantee that this HPA-23 can cure AIDS. But if you take the drug, it may prolong your life. At any rate, it's worth taking a chance."

He still had not told his new best friend, Ron Channell, whom he invited to fly to Paris with him, ostensibly to accept an invitation to the Deauville Film Festival on the northern coast of France. The French had organized a retrospective honoring director George Stevens, who had helmed Rock and Elizabeth Taylor in their major motion picture, *Giant* (1956). *Giant* was scheduled for a screening at the festival on August 31, 1984.

Before flying to France, Rock and Ron stopped in New York, where Rock had scheduled a meeting with Wallace Sheft, his business manager, and with the two lawyers who had previously drawn up earlier versions of his Last Will and Testament. In his new will, Rock disinherited Tom Clark and named George Nader in first place as the beneficiary of his trust, with Mark Miller second.

With the document signed, Ron and Rock taxied to one of the NYC airports to take the Concorde to Paris, where they were booked into a suite at the Ritz Hotel on the Place Vendôme. Their first night in Paris was festive, as Rock was still pretending it was a holiday, disguising the grim mission that had prompted his trip to France.

The next day, while Ron went shopping, Rock took a taxi to Percy Hospital, finding that Dormont's office was in a building that had been constructed for American soldiers wounded on the battlefields of France during World War I.

After examining him, Dormont suggested that he remain in Paris for three months for treatments. Rock wanted the process speeded up, because he'd been offered film work back in Hollywood.

Dormont later told his assistant, "I just can't believe some of these movie stars. Making some silly soap opera on TV, as he suggested, seemed more important to him than saving his life. *C'est incroyable!*"

It was then decided that Rock would visit Percy Hospital every day, including weekends, enduring a gruesome three-hour session in which he was injected with the (then-experimental) drug. He kept telling Ron that he was meeting with French film officials to discuss a big upcoming movie.

There were downsides to ingestion of the drug. They included vomiting, extreme fatigue, vertigo, and an almost complete loss of appetite. Amazingly, de-

AIDS specialist Dr. Dominque Dormont helped Rock retard the virus.

643

spite these side effects, Rock continued to keep Ron in the dark, suggesting he'd come down with some bug. Rock's compulsive need for rest allowed the young man to explore Paris, including its night life, at his leisure and on his own.

In Paris, he and Ron were joined by his publicist, Dale Olson. During a respite from the debilitating treatments, when Rock felt better, the three of them drove north to Deauville for the festival honoring George Stevens.

For the most part, Rock avoided the press and the paparazzi. However, one photographer snapped a picture of him, and Rock was horrified when it was widely distributed in a Paris newspaper. "I looked like something that had been dug up from a graveyard," he told Olson. "Those large bags under my eyes looked like they could contain my entire wardrobe."

Back in Los Angeles, Tom Clark had yet to learn that he had been completely cut out of Rock's will. For a while, despite his alienation from Rock, Marc Christian continued to believe that he was one of the heirs to Rock's fortune.

Eventually, however, sometime during Rock's sojourn in Paris, Christian learned that Rock had signed a new will. Immediately, he suspected that his name had been removed. *[Actually, at no point, even in the old will, had he been named as an heir.]*

Christian began to plot how to get cut in on Rock's millions. He went to Dittman's apartment, arriving unannounced. Over drinks, he confessed, "I'm going to sue the hell out of Rock when he dies."

"On what grounds?" Dittman asked.

"I don't know yet, but I'm working on it," Christian replied. "I'm seeing this lawyer in a few days, a guy who specializes in palimony cases."

Then he pitched an offer to Dittman: "If you'll back up my testimony in my case, I'll cut you in for ten percent of my settlement."

Enraged, Dittman ordered him out of his apartment, denouncing him as "a fucking whore."

Exactly one week later, Dittman's apartment was fire-bombed, and the actor was heartbroken to have lost all of his possessions. He went to the Los Angeles police and named Christian as a suspect, but no concrete evidence could be found.

A month in Paris had passed before Rock submitted to his final session with Dormont. He learned that the latest culture of his blood had found no sign of the AIDS virus. Rock was elated, at first erroneously thinking he had been cured. "That's not the case," Dormont warned. "The virus has merely been inhibited. Even though the culture tested negative, you can still have AIDS. The virus can come back, and it's vital that you return to Paris just as soon as you finish your TV work."

Rock said he could not possibly return until February. Dormont warned him, "That may be too late."

Amazingly, in spite of such a dire warning, Rock did not return to Paris that winter. Nor did he visit in the spring. It was during the heat of July, as Parisians prepared for their August vacations, that Rock returned to Paris.

They remained in the French capital until October 7, 1984, when the two of them flew back to Los Angeles. At the airport, Mark Miller was waiting in one of Rock's Cadillacs to drive them back to The Castle.

Rock told Miller and later, Nader, that Dr. Dormont had found no more signs of the virus in his bloodstream. "I've licked AIDS. I can accept Esther Shapiro's offer to star on *Dynasty.*" *[Shapiro was one of the creators of that hit series.]*

***

Rock's euphoria was short-lived. By October 5, following an examination in the office of Dr. Gottlieb, he learned that he'd lost another twelve pounds. He complained that he never got enough sleep and that he was tired all the time. "Every time I look in the mirror, my face, once voted as that of the most beautiful male animal in the world, seems to be collapsing."

James Wright, the butler, had learned from Miller that Rock had AIDS, and he urged him to eat a big breakfast every day, replete with bacon and eggs. But Rock only picked at his food.

He started parading around the house in his jockey shorts. Ron thought his bones looked like they were protruding. Miller questioned him about whether he'd made the right decision to commit himself to a role in *Dynasty.*

"I'm determined to go through with it," Rock said.

***

Dynasty was a primetime soap opera created by Richard and Esther Shapiro and produced by Aaron Spelling. It was first aired on January 12, 1981 to great success as ABC's answer to CBS's prime time hit series, *Dallas.*

By the spring of 1985, *Dynasty* was the number one television show in America. The story spun around the Carringtons, a mega-rich family in Denver. John Forsythe was cast as the oil magnate, Blake Carrington, with Linda Evans playing his new wife, Krystle. Later, Joan Collins was added to the show, appearing as Blake's former wife, "the bitch Alexis." Collins appeared in super-glam wardrobes, her lavish hats setting new styles in upscale fashion.

645

Esther had flow to Paris to meet with Rock at the Ritz Hotel to urge him to join the cast of *Dynasty*, playing the role of Daniel Reece, a wealthy rancher.

In Hollywood, she'd heard rumors that Rock was sick. But, as she later reported back to Spelling, "Rock has lost some weight. Of course, he doesn't look like he did in *Pillow Talk*. But he had a personal trainer with him. He looks in fairly good shape. After all, he's almost sixty, and none of us look as good as we did in 1959."

Tea in the elegant lobby of the Ritz was followed by dinner at a little Italian restaurant near the Eiffel Tower. Rock was frank in admitting, "I don't like doing television. After *McMillan and Wife*, I vowed never to appear in a series again: But I've read some of the scripts you submitted, and I like the character I would play."

One of the alltime biggest TV producers, Aaron Spelling had great faith in Rock's power to attract a wide TV audience.

Behind closed doors, he even pitched to him the idea of playing the lead role on *The Colbys*, a spinoff of the hit TV series, *Dynasty.*

The next morning, he met with her over ten o'clock coffee. "What the hell," he told her. "I'll be your Daniel Reece." He kissed her on both cheeks and saw her into a Ritz limousine headed for Charles de Gaulle Airport.

During the last week of October, Rock reported to work on the set of *Dynasty* in L.A. The first person he met was the Texan producer, Aaron Spelling, the most prolific writer and producer in the history of television. Among his achievements had been the hit TV series, *Charlie's Angels* (1976-81). Rock had committed himself to appear in six episodes of *Dynasty*, with four more to follow, perhaps even a spinoff in 1986.

Rock got along with cast and crew, bonding with Forsythe. Spelling didn't need to introduce him to his leading lady, Linda Evans. She had been playing the role of Krystle Carrington since 1981. Rock had first met her when she'd appeared in an episode of *McMillan and Wife*, and he'd also been on intimate terms with her former husband, John Derek.

For the most part, however, he didn't hang out with cast and crew, preferring instead to retreat to his trailer to relax or sleep when his scenes were finished. One afternoon, an assistant director had a hard time arousing him, at first fearing he'd had a heart attack. On that day, Rock seemed to have drifted into some unconscious state. The director brought him around again with a cup of strong black coffee.

Rock's appearance did not match Esther's description of him when she'd met with him at the Ritz in Paris. Many of his most ardent fans were shocked by his first appearance on *Dynasty* when the first episode was aired on December 19, 1984.

The writer, Mark Bego, stated it well: "His once-sparkling eyes were eerie sunken orbs, there were deep pits in his once full cheeks, and any glance at his wrists or ankles revealed skeletal bones."

One line uttered by Forsythe in *Dynasty* was ironic. "I don't know about you," he says to Rock's character, "but I'm not ready to die yet!"

In spite of the reaction of certain fans, Rock sat in his living room, watching the episode with Miller and Nader. "I think I look great for a man of my age," he claimed.

Miller and Nader did not think so, but politely refused to voice their opinions.

Rock went into a panic when he got the script for an episode in which he had to kiss Evans. He meets her in her role of Krystle when he is the owner of Delta Rho Stables. She is estranged from her husband, Blake, and is fascinated by horses and horse breeding. She spends a lot of time at his stables and seems to be contemplating having an affair with Daniel, the character he plays.

He met with Nader and Miller. "What in the fuck am I going to do? I've got to give Linda a passionate kiss, and I just can't tell her I have AIDS. Some doctors claim you can't get AIDS by kissing, but others are not so sure. There seems to be no agreement, with some saying AIDS can be transmitted by saliva through a sore in the mouth. Dr. Gottlieb told me I should avoid kissing anyone on the mouth, either on or off the screen."

Rock decided to go ahead with the kissing scene without alerting Spelling, Esther Shapiro, or Evans that he was infected with the AIDS virus. Rock later started referring to *Dynasty* as "Die Nasty."

Early in the morning of the day he had to kiss Evans, he began gargling with Listerine. "He must have gone through a large bottle before he left for the studio," Miller said.

Rock later claimed that the kissing scene with Evans "was the most miserable day of my life before a movie camera."

Weeks later, he sat with Miller watching the scene with Evans. Rock claimed, "it was the least passionate kiss in the history of the movies."

"It was very close-mouthed," Miller claimed. "Not even the slightest hint of saliva."

Esther admitted, "It wasn't any great kiss. Rock wasn't a great kisser. We knew he was gay, and perhaps he didn't like kissing a woman all that much. It was okay, though. Linda's character was still in love with her husband, Blake. So maybe it was better that the kiss not be too hot."

"I sensed that something was wrong with Rock," Evans later said. "I sat with Spelling and watched the dailies. At first, he thought he might order it to be reshot, telling Rock to put more passion into it. I was the one just lying on the ground. The passion had to come from Rock."

Although Spelling decided not to reshoot, he was beginning to have his doubts. "Rock could not remember his lines and needed cue cards. That was a sign he was in deep shit. His speech had begun to deteriorate."

[Marty Baum, Rock's agent, in the months ahead, called Rock's smooch of Linda Evans "the kiss heard around the world. When it was revealed that Rock had AIDS, there was a vast uproar. It was initially reported that Rock may have given the beautiful star AIDS by kissing her."

"I got tested, and I was free of the virus," Evans said. "But friends and co-workers started shying away from me."

The columnist, Liz Smith, told The Advocate, *"You go to parties and people had this really negative view. They seemed afraid to shake hands, fearing they might get AIDS from somebody. I mean, people were just so ignorant."*

Panic seemed to sweep across Hollywood. The homophobic Charlton Heston told The New York Times, *"I think a member of that lovely euphemism, that 'high risk group' (an obvious reference to gays), has an obligation to refuse to do kissing scenes."*

In contrast, Elizabeth Taylor said, "I don't think it is anybody's business who is sick. It's like McCarthyism. Who is sick is not public property whether they are in or out of show business. Actors have a right to some privacy."

The Screen Actors Guild debated requiring actors' contracts to notify performers in advance of possible scenes requiring an open-mouth kiss.

In August of 1985, KABC-TV (Channel 7 in Los Angeles) caused undue alarm by broadcasting, "It is possible that Rock Hudson transmitted AIDS to the actress Linda Evans during a love scene in Dynasty."

Spelling said that he wished the media would not transform Rock Hudson's illness into a carnival. "We're not part of the witch hunt in Hollywood. It's taken all this time for gays to come out of the closet, and now we seem to be driving them back in."

Right wing radio blasted Rock and homosexuals in general. One announcer said, "Hudson kissed he beautiful, innocent Linda Evans without telling her he had AIDS. I care about her. As for queers like Rock Hudson, after all, those bastards deserved it for leading a perverted lifestyle."]

When his involvement with that episode of *Dynasty* was finished, Rock flew to Hawaii with Ron Channell for a seven-day vacation at the Mauna Kea Beach Hotel. There, he got some sun, hoping it would bring some relief from his constant urge to scratch his rashes, which were infecting his groin, his chest, and his back. His weight dropped to 110 pounds. He tried to eat, but often vomited his meals.

***

Unaware that Rock was sick, much less that he had AIDS, Doris Day, in early July of 1985, contacted him and asked him to be a guest star on her new cable TV program, *Doris Day's Best Friends,* to be aired on the Christian Broadcast Network. Her best friends were not people, but her beloved animals co-habiting with her in her home at Carmel. Rock looked gaunt and skeletal.

Miller and Dale Olson, the publicist, urged him not to go, but Rock stubbornly ignored their pleas. "I'm going and to hell with you guys," he said. "Doris has been a good friend, and she needs me to help launch this show. We'll be united on the screen after all these years."

A press conference was called for July 15 at Carmel for reporters and photographers, especially those from *Life* magazine, which wanted to shoot a cover picture of Rock and Doris together again "after all these years." Rock, however, appeared almost two hours late, and many members of the press departed in anger before he arrived.

Day had not seen Rock in years, and when he walked into her garden to hug and kiss her, she was shocked, but she was good enough as an actress to mask her horror. Her son, Terry Melcher, who was the producer of the show, later said, "Rock looks like a zombie. Real cadaverous."

Robert Osborne, columnist for the *Hollywood Reporter,* wrote: "Eunice and Ernie are dead."

It was billed as "the biggest show business reunion of the decade," and there was speculation that both Rock and Doris Day might team up for another movie about an older couple, still vibrant and still in love.

All of that was dashed when Rock was photographed on July 16, 1985. He had traveled to his co-star's home in Carmel for an appearance on her new television program, *Doris Day's Best Friends,* a reference to her beloved animals.

He never told her that he had AIDS, but when the world press published photos of the two of them, there was widespread speculation in the media.

649

Those were the nicknames the two stars had used when they'd made movies together.

That night when Olson visited Rock at his hotel suite in Carmel, the star admitted to his publicist for the first time that he had AIDS.

The shoot would take two days, and Melcher urged his mother to cancel her former co-star's appearance. "Rock should not have come," Day said. "Had I known he was in such bad shape, I would never had invited him. But since he's insisting on doing the show with me, I can't turn him away. That would be too cruel to a sick and dying man."

After *U.S.A. Today* ran a picture of the reunion of Doris with Rock, it was flashed around the world, causing shock in all quarters.

Rock managed to get through the shoot with great difficulty. Day was kind and patient with him. She even urged him to stay with her in her home at Carmel so she could look after him, but he turned down her kind offer, telling her he was flying to Paris for medical treatments. He did not mention AIDS, but left the suggestion that he had liver cancer.

The day he left, critic James Wolcott wrote, "Doris Day and Rock Hudson are not making *Pillow Talk* but *Send Me No Flowers*," the latter a reference to the film they'd made in which Rock, playing a shtick as a hypochondriac, was convinced that he was dying. "History has repeated itself, the first time as farce, the second as tragedy."

In a stirring finale, the episode of *Doris Day's Best Friends* ended with her singing "My Buddy" over a progression of stills from their three films together.

On the day Rock left Carmel for his flight back to L.A., he hugged and kissed Day goodbye for the final time. It would be his last public appearance.

Tom Santopietro, author of *Considering Doris Day*, wrote: "The contrast between the frail Hudson and the beautiful and vibrant Day is poignant, as is the contrast between the dying Hudson and the pictures of his younger, strapping self."

Many fans of Rock weighed in with their opinions. Most of their questions echoed a similar refrain. "Could that bag of bones that used to be Rock Hudson, the Baron of Beefcake, really be him? Say it isn't so!"

During their short flight, Rock collapsed on the plane, but revived in time to be driven back to The Castle. When Miller saw him, he later said, "His last time on TV seemed to have sapped most of the life—or what was left of it—out of him."

[The episode Rock filmed for Doris Day's Best Friends *was broadcast on CBN eleven days after his death. Day addressed his passing: "All his friends, and there were so many, could always count on Rock Hudson. We had a ball making those romantic comedies together. I feel that without my deep faith, I would be a*

lot sadder than I am today. I know that life is eternal, and that something good is going to come from this experience."

In spite of the worldwide publicity it had generated because of Rock, the network canceled Day's show after 26 episodes

David Kaufman, author of Doris Day, The Untold Story of the Girl Next Door, *wrote: "In the end, Doris was right. Some good did come from Hudson's startling death. AIDS now had a famous face, which helped erode the hypocrisy and prejudice against its earliest casualties. Hollywood, which had, in effect, created him, began to respond to the epidemic with increased awareness."]*

***

Rock flew to Paris on July 20 with Ron Channell at his side. At first the Air France crew did not want to take him aboard, fearing he was too sick and perhaps contagious. After much persuasion, and some threats, they agreed. Miller booked four seats for him in first class, so he and Ron would have more privacy.

Air France Flight Four left Los Angeles International Airport at 10 that evening, flying nonstop to Charles de Gaulle, taking 10½ hours.

Rock was nauseated several times and frequently visited the toilet. At one point, he said to Ron, "I know what hell is like. It's enduring an Air France flight to Paris."

When he phoned Dr. Dormont, he received devastating news: "You should have come in February, Mr. Hudson. It's useless to resume HPS-23 treatments at this point. I can't stop this devastating disease. I never could cure it. I only could slow it down. Why didn't you come in February?"

Rock didn't answer.

Accompanied by Ron, Rock staggered into the lobby of the Ritz at the Place Vendôme in Paris, familiar territory to him. He collapsed near the reception desk, and three bellhops escorted him to his suite in a wheelchair.

The hotel's doctor rushed to his suite and performed a superficial examination, noting the scar on Rock's chest from his bypass surgery. The doctor told the hotel manager, "I think his heart condition has returned. He should be rushed to the American Hospital at once."

At The Castle in Beverly Hills, Miller was alerted and flew that afternoon to Paris to attend to any duties involving Rock.

At the hospital, Rock was examined by two cardiologists, who began a series of tests.

But by July 23, the information that Rock had tried to suppress for months leaked to the world. The breakout came in *Daily Variety* and was written by columnist Army Archerd. In part, the veteran columnist claimed: "Rock Hudson is hospitalized in Paris, where the Institute Pasteur has been very active in research of AIDS. His illness with this disease was no secret to close Hollywood friends, but its true nature was divulged to very, very few. He left for France. Doctors warn that the dread disease, AIDS, is going to reach catastrophic proportions in all communities if a cure is not found soon."

Somehow, the columnist had gotten his hands on Rock's lab reports, which contained the words "Kaposi's sarcoma." Within hours, the news was broadcast on virtually every TV and radio station in the United States.

Later, during a TV interview with Larry King, Archerd claimed, "I took a lot of heat for breaking the news. Press agents such as Dale Olson and others had worked with Rock and was very fond of him and thought I should not have done it. Many of them never spoke to me again. I got the cold shoulder. I'd been invited to a book party for Carol Bayer Sager, hosted by Elizabeth Taylor. I got a call from a publicist, telling me that if I showed up, Miss Taylor would refuse to go."

Almost immediately, Prudential Life Insurance killed its longtime commercial slogan—*GET A PIECE OF THE ROCK.*

By now, Rock's once-secret disease had become fodder for the tabloids, but he was largely unaware of that. One newspaper in Paris ran fake news: "Rock Hudson's longtime lover, Mark Miller, has flown in from Los Angeles to be at the deathbed of his beloved. The two men have been lovers since the 1950s."

Jerry Falwell, the right-wing extremist of the so-called Moral Majority, led the attack, not only against Rock but against homosexuals in general. Mockingly, he broadcast descriptions and innuendoes about Rock's long-ago all-male parties.

To handle the press frenzy in Paris, Yanou Collart, a local publicist, was asked to work as Rock's spokeswoman. She met with Miller at the Ritz, plotting a scenario to handle the massive public interest in Rock's condition.

She had not been made aware that he had AIDS.

Collart had handled publicity for Rock during his first visit to Paris, although she wasn't told that he was there to receive HPA-23 treatments. She thought he was in France to attend the Deauville Film Festival.

A battalion of reporters and paparazzi gathered daily at the entrance to the American Hospital, demanding some statement on Rock's condition. The task of making this announcement, which would be heard around the world, fell on Collart.

She had gone to several people, not only Dr. Dormont, but to the spokesperson for the American Hospital, as well as to Miller, and had typed an English-language draft which was immediately translated into French. She went to Rock's room, where she was shocked to see how much he'd deteriorated physically since his previous visit to Paris in 1984.

She wished him well and held out hope for a cure. She then read him the English-language version of her press statement. "I felt I was destroying him, but decided we must tell the truth."

After he heard it, he looked blank for a moment, then said, "Go and give it to the dogs. It's what they want. I'm destroyed now anyway. What does it matter at this point?" He then seemed to drift off into unconsciousness.

Doubt was later expressed that Rock might not have been conscious enough to approve or disapprove a statement that would shake and shock the world.

Collart faced the press and spoke in a voice in which she tried not to show emotion. She said, "Mr. Rock Hudson has Acquired Immune Deficiency Syndrome, which was first diagnosed in the United States. He came to Paris to consult with specialists in this disease." After some additional comments, she announced, "Mr. Hudson does not have any idea how he contracted the disease."

In Carmel, Doris Day finally learned what was ailing Rock. She addressed reporters, asserting, "I am praying for him."

Echoing her sentiments, his other friend, Elizabeth Taylor, said, "All my love and prayers go out to my beloved friend."

Dale Olson was asked if he knew Rock was a homosexual. "Our relationship was on a purely professional basis. Mr. Hudson is a very private person, and I prefer to respect his privacy."

Several people, including Tom Clark, maintained that Rock possibly contracted AIDS during his heart bypass surgery when he received a number of untested blood transfusions, mainly from contributors in West Hollywood, known for its large gay population.

If he is to be believed, Marc Christian later claimed he was alone at The Castle when news of Collart's press conference was broadcast throughout California. "Rock had not told me. Miller hadn't told me. I felt I had been lied to. I was a total wreck, thinking I was gonna die, too."

Dr. Dormont urged Rock to remain in Paris, claiming he was too weak for a transatlantic flight. But in a conversation with Miller, Rock told him he wanted to return home to die in The Castle. Actually, it was doubtful if any major airline would take him in his condition.

Looking for a remedy, Collart called Pierre Salinger, who had been press secretary to John F. Kennedy. He was now ABC's chief foreign correspondent in London. He called a high-placed official at Air France and received permission from the president to charter a private 747 to fly Rock back to Los Angeles for $250,000.

Wallace Sheft, Rock's business manager, claimed that he got a last-minute call from Air France while the 747 was on the tarmac, waiting to take off. Rock had already been taken aboard. "They wanted to make sure funds had been wired before that plane was airborne."

***

On July 30, 1985, the Air France 747 carrying the dying body of Rock Hudson set down at the Los Angeles International Airport, where a helicopter was waiting to whisk him to the UCLA Medical Center.

Pictures of Rock's arrival, emerging on a stretcher from the jetliner, though blurry, were aired on ABC, CBS, NBC, and CNN.

Dr. Gottlieb later claimed that he examined Rock on the roof of the hospital, near its helipad, at 2:30AM, reporting that "he was weak and barely responsive."

Later, he told associates, "He will probably die within the month, as he's hanging onto life by just a thread. He's dreadfully debilitated, and there is no hope for recovery. His condition will grow worse day by day. He is merely clinging to life."

On Rock's first day at the hospital, he had a surprise visitor. Elizabeth Taylor had arranged with Dr. Gottlieb to be escorted to his private room. To keep her visit a secret, she arrived at the hospital's rear entrance, where the doctor waited to take her up in a freight elevator.

"She was dressed to the nines," he said. "On the way up, I heard this loud bang, and I jumped. 'What was that?' I asked her."

"Just my jewels," she said. "I was jolted against the wall of the elevator and my Krupp diamond hit it."

Before she exited from the elevator, she asked Gottlieb if she could hug and kiss Rock, as was her custom. "She wasn't worried about him infecting her, but in her possible harming his weakened immune system by bringing in germs from the outside. What a woman!"

At his bedside, Elizabeth offered what love and comfort she could. After she left, Rock drifted in and out of consciousness. For every day that remained for him in the hospital, the faithful Elizabeth called on him, sadly watching as his condition worsened. At one point, she recalled that he referred to her as Leslie, the name of the character she'd played (his wife) in *Giant*.

Slowly, Rock became aware of the publicity his illness was generating. According to Gottlieb, "He was glad it had an impact on making the public aware of AIDS. He knew the curse of AIDS had stigmatized so many unfortunate people. They were looking for some glimmer of hope as they faced death, and that came when Rock went public. Maybe it would speed

654

up research money to help find a cure for AIDS. His going public showed tremendous deathbed courage and allowed his diagnosis to change the face of AIDS."

Rock was discharged from UCLA Medical Center on August 24 with the understanding that he would return to The Castle to live out his final days. Tom Clark came back into his life, promising, "I will be there for you doing whatever I can. Know that I'm here."

Back at The Castle, he found that Mark Miller had hired around-the-clock nurses for him, as he was not able to take care of himself, and not able to go to the toilet alone.

For the next few weeks, a parade of visitors came and went. Heavily medicated, Rock drifted in and out of consciousness. Two of his closest friends, Carol Burnett and Elizabeth Taylor, visited frequently, as did Claire Trevor. Even Anthony Perkins, his long-ago lover, showed up. *[The dreaded disease awaited Perkins in his own future.]* When Roddy McDowall was ushered into Rock's bedroom and gazed upon his longtime friend, he became hysterical and had to be ushered out. Ross Hunter came about three times a week.

Even though visitors were arriving daily, Rock on some days, said, "I want to be left alone to die in peace."

Rock had long talked to George Nader about writing "The Book" one day. As he told Nader, "The time has come for that."

In advance of anyone actually writing it, Rock's business manager, Wallace Sheft, shopped the proposed autobiography to various publishing houses in New York. Alert to its potential commercial appeal, William Morrow offered a six-figure advance.

To produce it, Miller hired Sara Davidson, the author of the best-selling *Loose Change,* as its ghost writer, with the understanding that she'd pen it based on conversations and revelations that would be revealed to her by Rock, even though he wasn't in much of a condition to recall the details of many previous episodes of his life. He asked that all earnings from the book, except for Davidson's fee, should be donated to the Rock Hudson Research Foundation.

***

The first major AIDS benefit was staged in Los Angeles on September 19, 1985, at the West Bonaventure Hotel. It raised one million dollars for AIDS research. Co-hosts Elizabeth Taylor and Shirley MacLaine headed a committee that included everyone from Brooke Shields to Yoko Ono, from Richard Pryor to Roddy McDowall.

Frank Sinatra turned down an invitation to appear, not wanting to link himself to the growing disease. In visible contrast, Burt Lancaster showed a great deal of courage and lent his full support.

Linda Evans also showed a certain kind of courage by appearing after all that angry publicity Rock had generated when he'd kissed her on camera in *Dynasty*. She showed not the least bit of bitterness toward Rock and even introduced Lancaster, who read a statement, allegedly by Rock.

In addition to thanking all his supporters, the statement in part read: "I am not happy I have AIDS. But if that is helping others, I can, at least, know that my own misfortune had had some positive worth."

A blonde Elizabeth Taylor became the most famous advocate of raising money for AIDS research, hoping to find a cure.

Here, she is seen addressing a gathering of AMFAR, the Foundation for AIDS Research, an international organization devoted to combating the virus and lessening its stigma.

Elizabeth introduced Burt Reynolds, who read a message from Ronald Reagan at the White House. The President called on all Americans to do whatever was in their power "to ensure that this pernicious syndrome is halted in its tracks and ultimately cured."

An array of stars performed at Rock's AIDS benefit, none of them more entertaining than Sammy Davis, Jr. He was followed with appearances by Carol Burnett and singer Diahann Carroll. Rod Stewart and Cyndi Lauper sang "Time After Time."

On the week of the benefit, the tabloids were in a frenzy, publishing one outrageous story after another, most of them of dubious origin, such as a hustler who falsely claimed, "I GAVE ROCK HUDSON AIDS." *People* magazine published three cover stories about Rock's life, the issues becoming the largest selling ones in that publication's history.

Seemingly, everyone who knew Rock weighed in with some opinion, including author and gay activist Armistead Maupin. He wrote: "Rock learned his lessons well in Hollywood. He played by the rules which demanded that you keep quiet about being gay, and everyone will lie about it for you. The gossip columnists will make up girlfriends for you, and everyone in Hollywood will know you are gay except the public."

What was going on at The Castle during all this hoopla?

Growing weaker every day, Rock occasionally wanted to see a movie. The last two films he requested were Tyrone Power in *Blood and Sand* (1941) and Lana Turner in *The Postman Always Rings Twice* (1946). As he told Nader, "I made love to both Ty and Lana back in my heyday. I was desired then."

One night as a full moon was out and the winds were blowing in from Santa Ana, Rock asked Tom Clark to assist him in transiting himself downstairs and out into his garden.

"I want to sit here one final time, enjoying the garden I worked so hard to help create."

In total silence, he sat there for an hour, looking up at the sky and the distant mountains, which seemed to have a purplish glow to them. Then he turned to Clark: "Help me back up the steps."

In his bedroom, Clark undressed him and lifted him up to his bed. " He later said, "Rock's weight had fallen to just 140 pounds. As I took him into my arms, I actually felt his bones protruding as if trying to break free of his skin. Oh, God, what was happening to my long, dear friend?"

***

In the final days of Rock's life, the postman made special trips to The Castle to deliver cards and letters from all over the world, from Greenland to Patagonia. Most of them were supportive, although hate mail flowed in, too, predicting Rock would burn in hell's fire for eternity.

In an irony-filled attempt to comfort him, Nader told him, "You're a dozen times more popular today than you were in the late 1950s and early 60s, when you were the world's number one box office attraction."

Rock had spent decades signing autographs, but his last signature was on a check for $250,000 to the National AIDS Research Foundation.

Although not a religious man, he was visited on September 25 by a Catholic priest, Terry Sweeney, a Jesuit who lived at Loyola at Marymount University in Los Angeles. He performed the last rites, although telling Clark, "It is no longer called that."

The priest was a fan of Rock's movies, especially *Magnificent Obsession* (1954). He'd visited the bedside of many men and women during their last hours of life. But nothing shocked him more than the "skeleton" in Rock's bed. The contrast between him on the screen and the nude man under the sheet was startling. It is not known what the priest said to Rock, or even if the patient comprehended what was going on.

For reasons known only to himself, Tom Clark allowed a number of Born Again Christians into Rock's "death chamber," including one strange woman who claimed she had the power to save his life.

Miller called them "religious nuts."

None of these Born Agains were more notable than Pat and Shirley

Boone. Rock had known the singer since he'd recorded romantic ballads in the 1950s. "Shirley and I believed that even though there was no medical help for him, we still had the miracle of prayer," Boone said.

It is most likely that Rock no longer recognized Boone. The singer could hardly recognize this emaciated, rapidly fading figure with breathing tubes in his nose. Since Rock was unconscious at the time, all that the singer could do was stand at the foot of his bed and pray for God to save him.

At 5AM on October 2, 1985, a harsh, ill wind rattled the shutters of The Castle. Clark had remained beside Rock's bed all night in case he needed him. He did not seem to be breathing very well, and every now and then a sound would originate from his throat that was more like a gurgle.

Clark left the night nurse, who was still on duty at that early hour, to attend to Rock while he went down to the kitchen to make a pot of coffee. He was just pouring his first cup of the day when the nurse rushed down the steps and roared into the kitchen. "He's gone!" she shouted.

Still clad in his pajamas, Clark raced up the steps to become the second person to gaze upon the corpse of the late Rock Hudson.

The time, if he remembered it correctly, was 9:02AM. By 9:15, news of his death was broadcast around the world, many TV or radio stations interrupting their broadcasts with his death bulletin.

Clark was stunned at how fast this news escaped from The Castle. Obviously, someone in the household leaked it pre-emptively. It wasn't until Rock's phone bill came in at the end of the month that Mark Miller knew how the news got out.

The moment Marc Christian heard that Rock had died, he placed a call to Marvin Michelson, his attorney in New York, to tell him to begin filing the palimony suit.

Elizabeth Taylor was asleep when the news came over the radio. Her maid woke her up. By 9:30AM, she was on the phone, speaking to Clark. She told him she was sending over some of her own security guards to protect the gate to The Castle. "I predict hordes of people will be gathering there—and not just those vultures from the press."

Ever hip to the ways of Hollywood, this legendary star was right. At 11AM, a van from Pierre-Hamrock-Reed Mortuary had a hard time driving through the open but guarded gate. By then, some 300 people had gathered, members of the press and photographers mingling with the idle curious.

The once-celebrated physique was placed in a body bag and hauled out from the house on a gurney. Clark and Rock had traveled the world together. Now, with Clark riding in the van with Rock's corpse, this was to be their last journey together. At the crematorium, he watched as two men from the staff placed the body, still within its bag, into a large cardboard box marked in foreboding black letters, ROCK HUDSON.

"My last vision of my beloved friend was watching his body rolled into the blazing ovens. I stood there for only a minute as the box burst into flames. I could take it no more. I said to myself, 'That's the end of Rock Hudson, but the beginning of the legend.'"

By noon, Roddy McDowall had arrived at Elizabeth's house to share in their mutual grief over the loss of a friend. "All of a sudden," she told him, "Hollywood is in a spin. It's 'Oh, oh, oh, one of us got it.' Rock's death showed them that AIDS is not just for homeless bums in the gutter."

In the New York office of *Time* magazine, reporters were gathering data for a cover story, referring to Rock as "THE MOST FAMOUS HOMOSEX-UAL IN THE WORLD."

On hearing of his death, writer Gar Williams wrote: "Can you just imagine the last days of Rock Hudson, a 140-pound skeleton with lesions and bedsores in that big mansion? Could you honestly imagine Rock dying? Maybe your Cousin Joe, or even your Uncle Mike—but never Rock Hudson! He's strong. He beat the Indians. He fought off John Wayne. Well, anyway, it challenges our own mortality."

"We know that Rock isn't really dead," Williams continued. "Not so long as we can see him cure Jane Wyman's blindness in *Magnificent Obsession*, solve all those murders on *McMillan and Wife*, play a bigger-than life character in *Giant*, making love to Elizabeth Taylor or Doris Day in *Pillow Talk*. We know he isn't really dead. His films will last forever after his mere mortal being is gone. We can still see him in the prime of his male beauty at the peak of his artistry. His films will keep him alive."

***

On October 19, 1985, some 150 of Rock's friends and associates gathered by invitation at The Castle for a memorial service led by Father Sweeney.

The VIP guests arrived in an array of limousines, Cadillacs, Rolls-Royces, and Mercedes-Benzes. Beverly Crest Drive had been closed off to the general public, its surfaces reconfigured into parking spaces for this armada of super-expensive cars, many of them custom-made. Security guards carefully screened the guests, turning away a total of 38 people who pretended to have been invited but weren't on the master list.

When the guests had assembled, Father Sweeney was the first speaker, leading Rock's friends in prayer. Elizabeth Taylor was the first celebrity to speak, talking of the early days when she'd first met Rock. He had become her friend when they were shooting *Giant* in Marfa, Texas. "The chances are I will never meet the likes of this wonderful man again. I still remember that hot, sticky night in Texas when Rock and I invented the chocolate martini."

Yanou Collart, the publicist from Paris, said, "Rock would not want his guests to be sad, but to be happy in the fact that he led the good life."

Standing before the crowd, Carol Burnett claimed, "The most fun I ever had was working on the stage with Rock in *I Do! I Do!*"

Linda Evans spoke. "Rock's death is a great loss to all of us, but his legacy will be our continued fight to find a cure for AIDS."

Doris Day made a rare appearance. "At a time like this, our faith is tested. His death is terrible. I can't believe it. I always saw him as so big, so healthy, that I came to think he was indestructible. Life is Eternal, and I hope Rock and I meet again on some distant shore."

Jane Wyman, who had once fallen in love with Rock, spoke softly, seemingly not remembering the friction between them. "He was a dear friend and a great talent, and all of us who worked with him will miss him terribly."

Burt Reynolds addressed the gathering. "It's the end of an era when a movie star really looked like Rock Hudson. He was six feet four, incredibly handsome, and with *Giant* and *Pillow Talk*, he showed us his unbelievable versatility. I never knew anyone who didn't like him."

Guests drank champagne, ate caviar, mingled with the other guests, and listened to the sounds of Mexican mariachi bands. The crowd was widely diversified, and Roddy McDowall, in tears, worked the room, trying to greet everybody, since he knew most of them. He embraced such people as Glenn Ford, Tab Hunter, Jessica Walter, Lee Remick, Richard Montalban, Robert Wagner, Stefanie Powers, Susan Saint James, Jane Withers, Dale Olson, and Esther Williams.

A statement from Ronald Reagan at the White House was read: "Nancy and I are saddened by the news of Rock Hudson's death. He will always be remembered for his dynamic impact on the film industry, and fans all over the world will certainly mourn his loss. He will be remembered for his humanity, his sympathetic and well-deserved reputation for kindness. May God rest his soul."

At the end of the service, Elizabeth spoke again. "Let's raise a glass to our dear friend, Mr. Rock Hudson. He graced all of our lives in some small or large way. I loved that man, and he is tragically gone. Please, God, let him not die in vain."

At the end of the evening, as the guests were filing out, Miller turned to Nader: "Oh, my God, I forgot to invite Ron Channell. He was Rock's dearest friend at the end."

Under an overcast sky the following foggy morning, thirty invited guests gathered in Marina Del Ray. There, they boarded a motor yacht, *Tasia II,* whose grim duty it was to head out into the Catalina Channel. There, Tom Clark would dump the ashes of Rock Hudson, in accordance with his final request.

The party was kept that small because thirty passengers was all that the yacht could accommodate. While holding the jar that contained the ashes, Clark addressed Rock's closest friends. "He gave me the greatest gift one person can give another—an exciting and happy life."

After he tossed the ashes into the sea, the guests threw flowers onto the water. *Tasia II* then encircled the ashes and flowers two times before heading back to Marina Del Rey.

Before he left the vessel, Nader said, "Some day, I bet, those ashes of Rock's will wash up on the shores of the Philippines, where, as a young man, Rock fought in the Navy in World War II."

At that moment, a seagull flew overhead, dropping his load on Miller. "Oh, my God," he shouted. "That damn bird has crapped." Then he looked up at the sky. "Well, Rock, the dear departed, you've had the last laugh… and it's all over me!"

***

On November 12, 1985, just five days before what would have been Rock's 60th birthday, Christian filed his long-threatened lawsuit against the Rock Hudson Estate and Mark Miller.

He was represented by "palimony attorney," Marvin Mitchelson. Christian made charges that would tarnish his own reputation, and that of Rock, forever. Charges and counter-charges at the trial would leave no one's reputation intact.

The gay press in particular came down hard on Christian. Jim Schrodder, writing in the *Advocate,* said, "There is the Christian portrayed by Hudson's lawyers—the greed-head starfucker party boy, the plastic Hollywood slut whose meter was always running. Hudson's lawyers maintain that the actor saw through Christian's act so fast he stopped having sex with him long before the AIDS diagnosis. They say they'll show how Christian was a blackmailing little hustler who wanted drugs and money. They note that Christian is not the surname that the plaintiff was born with."

[Christian's legal surname was MacGinnis.]

He sued Rock's estate for $10 million, alleging that he had suffered severe emotional distress after hearing a news broadcast from Paris that Rock had AIDS.

It was revealed that he had tested negative several times for AIDS after he knew Rock's diagnosis, but nevertheless, he maintained in court that the former matinee idol put him at risk by concealing his disease while continuing to have unprotected anal intercourse with him.

Miller was included in the suit, because Christian claimed he concealed the fact that his boss had AIDS.

Christian spoke to the print media and appeared on television, talking about his former lover. He told *People* magazine, "My purpose was not to sleaze Rock. It was to say that if you have AIDS, you ought to tell your partner, whether you're a movie star or a postman."

"When I learned that Rock had AIDS, the first thought that flashed through my mind was that Rock had sent me to the electric chair to die the death he'd just suffered. It's amazing that he could be so cruel and thoughtless to me, recklessly jeopardizing my life."

In 1989, a Los Angeles Superior Court jury asserted that Rock had "displayed outrageous conduct" and awarded Christian $21.75 million in damages, twice what he'd asked for. That was later reduced to $5 million by the California Court of Appeal, which called it "just compensation for the ultimate in personal horror, the fear of a slow, agonizing death."

The California Supreme Court decided not to hear the case, thereby allowing the judgment of the lower court to stand.

Celebrity journalist David Hartnell, who lives in New Zealand, got to know Christian when he conducted an interview with him on a breakfast TV show, *Good Morning, Australia,* in 1985. *[Deeply respected for his charity work and his services to the entertainment industry, Hartnell is a recipient of The New Zealand Order of Merit, (MNZM) an order of chivalry in New Zealand's honors system established by royal warrant in 1996 by Queen Elizabeth II.]*

"Knowing Marc Christian was like relaxing in a warm bubble bath, but always being conscious that there's a cold shower overhead that could be turned on at any time," said the savvy columnist.

"He was a very likable person," Hartnell continued. "There is no doubt he had

Celebrity journalist David Hartnell was photographed with Marc Christian, who wore a shirt that had once belonged to Rock.

Perhaps it was symbolic that the esteemed columnist was in bright sunlight, with Christian emerging as a shadowy figure.

charisma and good looks that could charm the birds out of the trees. He also had a wicked sense of humor; he never really took himself seriously."

Christian told the journalist that he was contemplating writing a very personal tell-all entitled *Between Rock and a Hard Place.* He never did, however.

"Marc and I shared the same star sign," Hartnell said, "so we were very similar in thought and mind, and we immediately understood each other and bonded as friends. He was a great one for working the Hollywood system—in fact, he was a master at it."

Hartnell was shown clothing and possessions which had once belonged to Rock, including an antique foot stool, with needlework by Elizabeth Taylor which she'd crafted while co-starring with Rock in *Giant.* Christian also had some of Rock's clothing, including a lumberjack-style plaid shirt that he wore during his interview on *Good Morning, Australia.*

During Christian's residency at The Castle, the butler, James Wright, Tom Clark, and Mark Miller accused the young man of stealing items from the residence and storing them elsewhere. Christian showed Hartnell his most valuable possession, a 1959 Chevy Nomad, which had cost Rock $30,000 in repairs and restoration, and which had, one way or another, ended up as Christian's. Although Miller, during his tenure as Rock's financial secretary, used his influence to stop this kind of flagrant excess, Hartnell was impressed with the retro style and pizzazz of the vintage vehicle.

In April of 1990, after the publication of Tom Clark's autobiography, *Rock Hudson, My Friend,* Christian filed a $23 million libel suit against both its author and its publisher.

[In the manuscript, Clark defined

A spontaneous, unrehearsed, late-in-life portrait of Rock at his Castle, courtesy of David Hartnell.

Christian as "a criminal, a thief, an unclean person, a blackmailer, a psychotic, an extortionist, a forger, a perjurer, a liar, a whore, an arsonist, and a squatter." The case never went to court.]

Christian and Hartnell were out of touch for many years. But on a trip from New Zealand to Hollywood, the "Celebrity Kiwi Journalist" encountered Christian at Tower Records on Sunset Strip.

"His life had changed, but not necessarily for the better," Hartnell said. "Sure, he had money and an extremely good-looking lover by his side. I couldn't help thinking he'd essentially turned himself, unknowingly, into a mirror image of Rock. And his young blonde lover was Marc."

[Tom Clark died in 1995; George Nader in 2002, and Mark Miller in 2015.

In December, 2009, Marc Christian died at the age of 56—not from AIDS, which he never contracted, but from a pulmonary infection.]

ROCK HUDSON
A Great American Movie Star
(1925-1985)

DARWIN PORTER

As an intense nine-year-old, **Darwin Porter** began meeting movie stars, TV personalities, politicians, and singers through his vivacious and attractive mother, Hazel, an eccentric but charismatic Southern girl who had lost her husband in World War II. Migrating from the Depression-ravaged valleys of western North Carolina to Miami Beach during its most ebullient heyday, Hazel became a stylist, wardrobe mistress, and personal assistant to the vaudeville *comedienne* **Sophie Tucker**, the bawdy and irrepressible "Last of the Red Hot Mamas."

Virtually every show-biz celebrity who visited Miami Beach paid a call on "Miss Sophie," and Darwin as a pre-teen loosely and indulgently supervised by his mother, was regularly dazzled by the likes of **Judy Garland, Dinah Shore,** and **Frank Sinatra.**

It was at Miss Sophie's that he met his first political figure, who was actually an actor at the time. Between marriages, **Ronald Reagan** came to call on Ms. Sophie, who was his favorite singer. He was accompanied by a young blonde starlet, **Marilyn Monroe.**

At the University of Miami, Darwin edited the school newspaper.

He first met and interviewed **Eleanor Roosevelt** at the Fontainebleau Hotel on Miami Beach and invited her to spend a day at the university. She accepted, much to his delight.

After graduation, he became the Bureau Chief of *The Miami Herald* in Key West, Florida, where he got to take early morning walks with the former U.S. president **Harry S Truman**, discussing his presidency and the events that had shaped it.

Through Truman, Darwin was introduced and later joined the staff of **Senator George Smathers** of Florida. His best friend was a young senator, **John F. Kennedy.** Through "Gorgeous George," as Smathers was known in the Senate, Darwin got to meet Jack and Jacqueline in Palm Beach. He later wrote two books about them—*The Kennedys, All the Gossip Unfit to Print,* and one of his all-time bestsellers, *Jacqueline Kennedy Onassis—A Life Beyond Her Wildest Dreams.*

For about a decade in New York, Darwin worked in television journalism and advertising with his long-time partner, the journalist, art director, and distinguished arts-industry socialite **Stanley Mills Haggart.**

Stanley (as an art director) and Darwin (as a writer and assistant), worked as freelance agents in television. Jointly, they helped produce TV commercials that included testimonials from **Joan Crawford** (then feverishly promoting Pepsi-Cola); **Ronald Reagan** (General Electric); and **Debbie Reynolds** (Singer sewing machines). Other personalities appearing and delivering televised sales pitches included **Louis Armstrong, Lena Horne,** and **Arlene Dahl,** each of them hawking a commercial product.

Beginning in the early 1960s, Darwin joined forces with the then-fledgling **Arthur Frommer** organization, playing a key role in researching and writing more than 50 titles and defining the style and values that later emerged as the world's leading travel guidebooks, *The Frommer Guides,* with particular emphasis on Europe, California, New England, and the Caribbean. Between the creation and updating of hundreds of editions of detailed travel guides to England, France, Italy, Spain, Portugal, Austria, Hungary, Germany, Switzerland, the Caribbean, and California, he continued to interview and discuss the triumphs, feuds, and frustrations of celebrities, many by then reclusive, whom he either sought out or encountered randomly as part of his extensive travels. **Ava Gardner** and **Lana Turner** were particularly insightful.

It was while living in New York that Darwin became fascinated by the career of a rising real estate mogul changing the skyline of Manhattan. He later, of course, became the "gambling czar" of Atlantic City and a star of reality TV.

Darwin began collecting an astonishing amount of data on Donald Trump, squirreling it away in boxes, hoping one day to write a biography of this charismatic, controversial figure.

Before doing that, he penned more than thirty-five uncensored, unvarnished, and unauthorized biographies on subjects that included **Donald Trump, Bill and Hillary Clinton, Ronald Reagan and Nancy Davis, Jane Wyman, Jacqueline Kennedy, Jack Kennedy, Lana Turner, Peter O'Toole, James Dean, Marlon Brando, Merv Griffin, Katharine Hepburn, Howard Hughes, Humphrey Bogart, Michael Jackson, Paul Newman, Steve McQueen, Marilyn Monroe, Elizabeth Taylor, Frank Sinatra, Vivien Leigh, Laurence Olivier, the notorious porn star Linda Lovelace, Zsa Zsa Gabor and her sisters, Tennessee Williams, Gore Vidal,** and **Truman Capote.**

As a departure from his usual repertoire, Darwin also wrote the controversial *J. Edgar Hoover & Clyde Tolson: Investigating the Sexual Secrets of America's Most Famous Men and Women,* a book about celebrity, voyeurism, political and sexual repression, and blackmail within the highest circles of the U.S. government.

Porter's biographies, over the years, have won twenty-five first prize or "runner-up to first prize" awards at literary festivals in cities or states which include New England, New York, Los Angeles, Hollywood, San Francisco,

Florida, California, and Paris.

Darwin can be heard at regular intervals as a radio and television commentator, "dishing" celebrities, pop culture, politics, and scandal.

A resident of New York City, Darwin is currently at work on the first comprehensive biography of Debbie Reynolds and Carrie Fisher.

DANFORTH PRINCE

The co-author of this book, **Danforth Prince** is president and founder of Blood Moon Productions, a firm devoted to salvaging, compiling, and marketing the oral histories of America's entertainment industry.

Prince launched his career in journalism in the 1970s at the Paris Bureau of *The New York Times*. In the early '80s, he joined Darwin Porter in developing first editions of many of the titles within *The Frommer Guides*. Together, they reviewed and articulated the travel scenes of more than 50 nations, most of them within Europe and The Caribbean. Authoritative and comprehensive, they became best-selling "travel bibles" for millions of readers.

Prince, in collaboration with Porter, is also the co-author of several award-winning celebrity biographies, each configured as a title within Blood Moon's Babylon series. These have included *Hollywood Babylon—It's Back!*; *Hollywood Babylon Strikes Again*; *The Kennedys: All the Gossip Unfit to Print*; *Frank Sinatra, The Boudoir Singer*, *Elizabeth Taylor: There Is Nothing Like a Dame*; *Pink Triangle: The Feuds and Private Lives of Tennessee Williams, Gore Vidal, Truman Capote, and Members of their Entourages*; and *Jacqueline Kennedy Onassis: A Life Beyond Her Wildest Dreams*. More recent efforts include *Lana Turner, Hearts and Diamonds Take All*; *Peter O'Toole—Hellraiser, Sexual Outlaw, Irish Rebel*; *Bill & Hillary—So This Is That Thing Called Love*; and *James Dean, Tomorrow Never Comes*.

One of his recent projects, co-authored with Darwin Porter, is *Donald Trump, The Man Who Would Be King*. Configured for release directly into the frenzy of the 2016 presidential elections, and winner of at least three literary awards, it's a celebrity overview of the decades of pre-presidential scandals—personal, political, and dynastic—associated with The Donald during the rambunctious decades when no one ever thought he'd actually get elected.

Prince is also the co-author of four books on film criticism, three of which won honors at regional bookfests in Los Angeles and San Francisco.

Prince, a graduate of Hamilton College and a native of Easton and Bethlehem, Pennsylvania, is the president and founder of the Georgia Literary Association (1996), and of the Porter and Prince Corporation (1983) which has produced dozens of titles for Simon & Schuster, Prentice Hall, and John Wiley & Sons. In 2011, he was named "Publisher of the Year" by a consortium of literary critics and marketers spearheaded by the J.M. Northern Media Group.

Publishing in collaboration with the National Book Network *(www.NBN-Books.com)*, he has electronically documented some of the controversies associated with his stewardship of Blood Moon in at least 50 documentaries, book trailers, public speeches, and TV or radio interviews. Most of these are available on **YouTube.com** and **Facebook** *(keywords: "Danforth Prince" or "Blood Moon Productions")*; on **Twitter** *(#BloodyandLunar)*; or by clicking on **BloodMoonProductions.com**.

He is currently at work writing and researching an upcoming biography that focuses on the mother-daughter saga of Carrie Fisher and Debbie Reynolds.

Prince is also an innkeeper, running a historic bed-and-breakfast in a New York City **AirBnb** known as **Magnolia House** and dating from 1827. It lies in the rapidly gentrifying old Saint George neighborhood of Staten Island, the retreat of novelists Henry James and Theodore Dreiser, and the 90-room summer home of the Vanderbilts.

Set in a leafy garden, the inn is a ten-minute walk to the ferries sailing at frequent intervals to the Financial District of Lower Manhattan. (Transit time is about 27 minutes.) A celebrity-centric retreat, it is loaded with memorabilia Prince collected from his years as a globe-trotting travel journalist for the Frommer Guides. The venerated old house has sheltered everyone from Gloria Swanson to Tennessee Williams.

For more information, click on **www.MagnoliaHouseSaintGeorge.com**.

DONALD TRUMP IS THE MAN WHO WOULD BE KING

This is the most famous book about our President you've probably never heard of.

Winner of three respected literary awards, this is an entertainingly packaged, artfully sala-cious bombshell of a book, a world-class first, a post-recession overview of America during its 2016 election cycle, a portrait unlike anything ever published on America's President-Elect and the climate in which he thrived.

Its release during the heat and venom of the Presidential campaign has already been her-alded by the *Midwestern Book Review, California Book Watch, the Seattle Gay News,* the staunchly right-wing *WILS-AM* **radio**, and also by the editors at the most popular Seniors' magazine in Florida, *BOOMER TIMES*, which designated it as their September choice for **BOOK OF THE MONTH.**

TRUMPOCALYPSE: *"Donald Trump: The Man Who Would Be King* is recommended reading for all sides, no matter what political stance is being adopted: Republican, Democrat, or other.

"One of its driving forces is its ability to synthesize an unbelievable amount of information into a for-mat and presentation which blends lively irony with outrageous observations, entertaining even as it presents eye-opening information in a format accessible to all.

"Politics dovetail with American obsessions and fascinations with trends, figureheads, drama, and sizzling news stories, but blend well with the ob-servations of sociologists, psychologists, politi-cians, and others in a wide range of fields who lend their expertise and insights to create a much broader review of the Trump phenomena than a more casual book could provide.

"The result is a 'must read' for any American inter-ested in issues of race, freedom, equality, and jus-tice—and for any non-American who wonders just what is going on behind the scenes in this coun-try's latest election debacle."

Diane Donovan
Senior Editor, California Bookwatch

DONALD TRUMP, THE MAN WHO WOULD BE KING
WINNER OF "BEST BIOGRAPHY" AWARDS FROM BOOK FESTIVALS IN
NEW YORK, CALIFORNIA, AND FLORIDA
by Darwin Porter and Danforth Prince
Softcover, with 822 pages and hundreds of photos. ISBN 978-1-936003-51-8.
Available now from Amazon.com, B&N.com, and other internet purveyors, worldwide.
Biography/Presidential & Rich & Famous.

LOVE TRIANGLE

RONALD REAGAN, JANE WYMAN, & NANCY DAVIS

Unique in the history of publishing, this scandalous triple biography focuses on the Hollywood indiscretions of former U.S. president Ronald Reagan and his two wives. A proud and Presidential addition to Blood Moon's Babylon series, it digs deep into what these three young and attractive movie stars were doing decades before two of them took over the Free World.

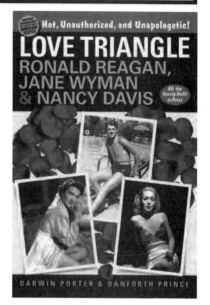

As reviewed by Diane Donovan, Senior Reviewer at the California Bookwatch section of the Midwest Book Review: *"Love Triangle: Ronald Reagan, Jane Wyman & Nancy Davis may find its way onto many a Republican Reagan fan's reading shelf; but those who expect another Reagan celebration will be surprised: this is lurid Hollywood exposé writing at its best, and outlines the truths surrounding one of the most provocative industry scandals in the world.*

"There are already so many biographies of the Reagans on the market that one might expect similar mile-markers from this: be prepared for shock and awe; because Love Triangle doesn't take your ordinary approach to biography and describes a love triangle that eventually bumped a major Hollywood movie star from the possibility of being First Lady and replaced her with a lesser-known Grade B actress (Nancy Davis).

"From politics and betrayal to romance, infidelity, and sordid affairs, Love Triangle is a steamy, eye-opening story that blows the lid off of the Reagan illusion to raise eyebrows on both sides of the big screen.

"Black and white photos liberally pepper an account of the careers of all three and the lasting shock of their stormy relationships in a delightful pursuit especially recommended for any who relish Hollywood gossip."

In 2015, LOVE TRIANGLE, Blood Moon Productions' overview of the early dramas associated with Ronald Reagan's scandal-soaked career in Hollywood, was designated by the Awards Committee of the **HOLLYWOOD BOOK FESTIVAL** as Runner-Up to Best Biography of the Year.

PINK TRIANGLE: The Feuds and Private Lives of Tennessee Williams, Gore Vidal, Truman Capote, and Famous Members of their Entourages
Darwin Porter & Danforth Prince

This book, the only one of its kind, reveals the backlot intrigues associated with the literary and script-writing *enfants terribles* of America's entertainment community during the mid-20th century.

It exposes their bitchfests, their slugfests, and their relationships with the *glitterati*—Marilyn Monroe, Brando, the Oliviers, the Paleys, U.S. Presidents, a gaggle of other movie stars, millionaires, and international *débauchés*.

This is for anyone who's interested in the formerly concealed scandals of Hollywood and Broadway, and the values and pretentions of both the literary community and the entertainment industry.

"A banquet... If PINK TRIANGLE had not been written for us, we would have had to research and type it all up for ourselves...Pink Triangle is nearly seven hundred pages of the most entertaining histrionics ever sliced, spiced, heated, and serviced up to the reading public. Everything that Blood Moon has done before pales in comparison.
Given the fact that the subjects of the book themselves were nearly delusional on the subject of themselves (to say nothing of each other) it is hard to find fault. Add to this the intertwined jungle that was the relationship among Williams, Capote, and Vidal, of the times they vied for things they loved most—especially attention—and the times they enthralled each other and the world, [Pink Triangle is] the perfect antidote to the Polar Vortex."
—Vinton McCabe in the NY JOURNAL OF BOOKS

"Full disclosure: I have been a friend and follower of Blood Moon Productions' tomes for years, and always marveled at the amount of information in their books—it's staggering. The index alone to Pink Triangle runs to 21 pages—and the scale of names in it runs like a Who's Who of American social, cultural and political life through much of the 20th century."
—Perry Brass in THE HUFFINGTON POST

"We Brits are not spared the Porter/Prince silken lash either. PINK TRIANGLE's research is, quite frankly, breathtaking. PINK TRIANGLE will fascinate you for many weeks to come. Once you have made the initial titillating dip, the day will seem dull without it."
—Jeffery Tayor in THE SUNDAY EXPRESS (UK)

PINK TRIANGLE—The Feuds and Private Lives of Tennessee Williams, Gore Vidal, Truman Capote, and Famous Members of their Entourages
Darwin Porter & Danforth Prince
Softcover, 700 pages, with photos   ISBN 978-1-936003-37-2   Also Available for E-Readers

THOSE GLAMOROUS GABORS
Bombshells from Budapest, by Darwin Porter

Zsa Zsa, Eva, and Magda Gabor transferred their glittery dreams and gold-digging ambitions from the twilight of the Austro-Hungarian Empire to Hollywood. There, more effectively than any army, these Bombshells from Budapest broke hearts, amassed fortunes, lovers, and A-list husbands, and amused millions of *voyeurs* through the medium of television, movies, and the social registers. In this astonishing "triple-play" biography, designated "Best Biography of the Year" by the Hollywood Book Festival, Blood Moon lifts the "mink-and-diamond" curtain on this amazing trio of blood-related sisters, whose complicated intrigues have never been fully explored before.

"You will never be Ga-bored…this book gives new meaning to the term compelling. Be warned, *Those Glamorous Gabors* is both an epic and a pip. Not since *Gone With the Wind* have so many characters on the printed page been forced to run for their lives for one reason or another. And Scarlett making a dress out of the curtains is nothing compared to what a Gabor will do when she needs to scrap together an outfit for a movie premiere or late-night outing.

"For those not up to speed, Jolie Tilleman came from a family of jewelers and therefore came by her love for the shiny stones honestly, perhaps genetically. She married Vilmos Gabor somewhere around World War 1 (exact dates, especially birth dates, are always somewhat vague in order to establish plausible deniability later on) and they were soon blessed with three daughters: **Magda**, the oldest, whose hair, sadly, was naturally brown, although it would turn quite red in America; **Zsa Zsa** (born 'Sari') a natural blond who at a very young age exhibited the desire for fame with none of the talents usually associated with achievement, excepting beauty and a natural wit; and **Eva**, the youngest and blondest of the girls, who after seeing Grace Moore perform at the National Theater, decided that she wanted to be an actress and that she would one day move to Hollywood to become a star.

"Given that the Gabor family at that time lived in Budapest, Hungary, at the period of time between the World Wars, that Hollywood dream seemed a distant one indeed. The story—the riches to rags to riches to rags to riches again myth of survival against all odds as the four women, because of their Jewish heritage, flee Europe with only the minks on their backs and what jewels they could smuggle along with them in their *decolletage*, only to have to battle afresh for their places in the vicious Hollywood pecking order—gives new meaning to the term 'compelling.' The reader, as if he were witnessing a particularly gore-drenched traffic accident, is incapable of looking away."

—New York Review of Books

Those Glamorous Gabors, Bombshells from Budapest, by Darwin Porter.
Softcover, 730 pages, with hundreds of photos   ISBN 978-1-936003-35-8

PETER O'TOOLE
Hellraiser, Sexual Outlaw, Irish Rebel

At the time of its publication early in 2015, this book was widely publicized in the *Daily Mail*, the *New York Daily News*, the *New York Post*, the *Midwest Book Review*, *The Express (London)*, *The Globe*, the *National Enquirer*, and in equivalent publications worldwide

One of the world's most admired (and brilliant) actors, Peter O'Toole wined and wenched his way through a labyrinth of sexual and interpersonal betrayals, sometimes with disastrous results. Away from the stage and screen, where such films as *Becket* and *Lawrence of Arabia*, made film history, his life was filled with drunken, debauched nights and edgy sexual experimentations, most of which were never openly examined in the press. A hellraiser, he shared wild times with his "best blokes" Richard Burton and Richard Harris. Peter Finch, also his close friend, once invited him to join him in sharing the pleasures of his mistress, Vivien Leigh.

Peter O'Toole
HELLRAISER | SEXUAL OUTLAW | IRISH REBEL

DARWIN PORTER & DANFORTH PRINCE

"My father, a bookie, moved us to the Mick community of Leeds," O'Toole once told a reporter. "We were very poor, but I was born an Irishman, which accounts for my gift of gab, my unruly behavior, my passionate devotion to women and the bottle, and my loathing of any authority figure."

Author Robert Sellers described O'Toole's boyhood neighborhood. "Three of his playmates went on to be hanged for murder; one strangled a girl in a lovers' quarrel; one killed a man during a robbery; another cut up a warden in South Africa with a pair of shears. It was a heavy bunch."

Peter O'Toole's hell-raising life story has never been told, until now. Hot and uncensored, from a writing team which, even prior to O'Toole's death in 2013, had been collecting under-the-radar info about him for years, this book has everything you ever wanted to know about how THE LION navigated his way through the boudoirs of the Entertainment Industry IN WINTER, Spring, Summer, and a dissipated Autumn as well.

Blood Moon has ripped away the imperial robe, scepter, and crown usually associated with this quixotic problem child of the British Midlands. Provocatively uncensored, this illusion-shattering overview of Peter O'Toole's hellraising (or at least very naughty) and demented life is unique in the history of publishing.

PETER O'TOOLE: Hellraiser, Sexual Outlaw, Irish Rebel
Softcover, with photos. ISBN 978-1-936003-45-7.
Also available for e-readers

James Dean, *Tomorrow Never Comes*

Honoring the 60th anniversary of his violent and early death

America's most enduring and legendary symbol of young, enraged rebellion, James Dean continues into the 21st Century to capture the imagination of the world.

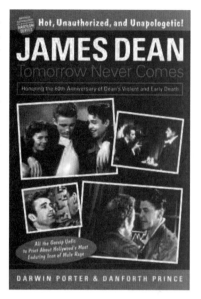

After one of his many flirtations with Death, which caught up with him when he was a celebrity-soaked 24-year-old, he said, "If a man can live after he dies, then maybe he's a great man." Today, bars from Nigeria to Patagonia are named in honor of this international, spectacularly self-destructive movie star icon.

Migrating from the dusty backroads of Indiana to center stage in the most formidable boudoirs of Hollywood, his saga is electrifying.

A strikingly handsome heart-throb, Dean is a study in contrasts: Tough but tender, brutal but remarkably sensitive; he was a reckless hellraiser badass who could revert to a little boy in bed.

A rampant bisexual, he claimed that he didn't want to go through life "with one hand tied behind my back." He demonstrated that during bedroom trysts with Marilyn Monroe, Rock Hudson, Elizabeth Taylor, Paul Newman, Natalie Wood, Shelley Winters, Marlon Brando, Steve McQueen, Ursula Andress, Montgomery Clift, Pier Angeli, Tennessee Williams, Susan Strasberg, Tallulah Bankhead, and FBI director J. Edgar Hoover.

Woolworth heiress Barbara Hutton, one of the richest and most dissipated women of her era, wanted to make him her toy boy.

Tomorrow Never Comes is the most penetrating look at James Dean to have   emerged from the wreckage of his Porsche Spyder in 1955.

Before setting out on his last ride, he said, "I feel life too intensely to bear living it."

Tomorrow Never Comes presents a damaged but beautiful soul.

JAMES DEAN—TOMORROW NEVER COMES
DARWIN PORTER & DANFORTH PRINCE
Softcover, with photos. ISBN 978-1-936003-49-5

Scarlett O'Hara,

Desperately in Love with Heathcliff,

Together on the Road to Hell

Damn You, Scarlett O'Hara
The Private Lives of **Vivien Leigh** and **Laurence Olivier**

by Darwin Porter and Roy Moseley

Here, for the first time, is a biography that raises the curtain on the secret lives of **Lord Laurence Olivier,** often cited as the finest actor in the history of England, and **Vivien Leigh,** who immortalized herself with her Oscar-winning portrayals of Scarlett O'Hara in *Gone With the Wind,* and as Blanche DuBois in Tennessee Williams' *A Streetcar Named Desire.*

Dashing and "impossibly handsome," Laurence Olivier was pursued by the most dazzling luminaries, male and female, of the movie and theater worlds.

Lord Olivier's beautiful and brilliant but emotionally disturbed wife (Viv to her lovers) led a tumultuous off-the-record life whose paramours ranged from the A-list celebrities to men she selected randomly off the street. But none of the brilliant roles depicted by Lord and Lady Olivier, on stage or on screen, ever matched the power and drama of personal dramas which wavered between Wagnerian opera and Greek tragedy. *Damn You, Scarlett O'Hara* is the definitive and most revelatory portrait ever published of the most talented and tormented actor and actress of the 20th century.

Darwin Porter is the principal author of this seminal work.

Roy Moseley, this book's co-author, was an intimate friend of both Lord and Lady Olivier, maintaining a decades-long association with the famous couple, nurturing them through triumphs, emotional breakdowns, and streams of suppressed scandal. A resident of California who spent most of his life in England, Moseley has authored or co-authored biographies of Queen Elizabeth and Prince Philip, Rex Harrison, Cary Grant, Merle Oberon, Roger Moore, and Bette Davis.

*"**Damn You, Scarlett O'Hara** can be a dazzling read, the prose unmannered and instantly digestible. The authors' ability to pile scandal atop scandal, seduction after seduction, can be impossible to resist."*
—THE WASHINGTON TIMES

DAMN YOU, SCARLETT O'HARA
THE PRIVATE LIFES OF LAURENCE OLIVIER AND VIVIEN LEIGH

Darwin Porter and Roy Moseley

Winner of four distinguished literary awards, this is the best biography of Vivien Leigh and Laurence Olivier ever published, with hundreds of insights into the London Theatre, the role of the Oliviers in the politics of World War II, and the passion, fury, and frustration of their lives together as actors in the West End, on Broadway, and in Hollywood.

ISBN 978-1-936003-15-0   Hardcover, 708 pages, with about a hundred photos.
Also available for E-Readers